Libraries in American
Periodicals Before 1876

Libraries in American Periodicals Before 1876

A Bibliography with Abstracts and an Index

compiled by
Larry J. Barr
Haynes McMullen
Steven G. Leach

edited by Haynes McMullen

McFarland & Company, Inc., Publishers   1983
Jefferson, North Carolina, and London

Library of Congress Cataloguing-in-Publication Data

Barr, Larry J., 1938–
 Libraries in American periodicals before 1876.

  "This bibliography extends Cannons' Bibliography of library economy from 1876 to 1920 (Chicago: American Library Association, 1927) back to the beginning, as far as periodicals in the United States are concerned" — Introd.
  Includes index.
  1. Library science — Bibliography. 2. Library science — Abstracts. 3. Libraries — Bibliography. 4. Libraries — Abstracts. I. McMullen, Haynes, 1915–   . II. Leach, Steven G. III. Title.
Z666.B33 1983   016.02   83-780

ISBN 0-89950-066-8

© 1983 by Larry J. Barr, Haynes McMullen and Steven G. Leach
All rights reserved.

Manufactured in the United States of America

Acknowledgments

The compilers are grateful to many persons at the library schools at Indiana University, where this bibliography had its beginning, and at the University of North Carolina at Chapel Hill, where most of the work has been done.

The main part of our gratitude goes to all the graduate assistants who have helped us very patiently, efficiently, and cheerfully over the years. We wish to thank Barry, Carolyn, Cheryl, David, Deborah, Donna, Edie, Janice, Joan, Julie, Kris, Libby, Linda, Margaret, Mary, Mary Ann, Paul, Sally, Susan, Walter, and several others whose names we have forgotten.

We are also grateful to those who authorized expenditures to pay these graduate assistants. Dean Edward G. Holley at UNC–Chapel Hill has been particularly helpful, not only in finding funds but in his very friendly and encouraging attitude toward the project as a whole. The members of the staff of the Institute for Research in Social Science and of the Library School at Chapel Hill have done the typing, carefully and with good humor.

We have a special kind of gratitude for reference librarians and interlibrary loan staff members in several libraries across the United States who helped us find articles about whose existence we had only the flimsiest of evidence. One author-librarian, Harry R. Skallerup, generously supplied us with photocopies of some of the more difficult-to-locate articles that he used in writing *Books Afloat and Ashore*, published by Archon in 1974.

Table of Contents

Acknowledgments   v
Periodicals Indexed   xi
Introduction   xv
Symbols for Libraries   xix

The Abstracts

World   2
    Classical Libraries   5
    England and the United States   6
    Europe and the United States   8
    Ships at Sea   17

United States   21
    Types of Libraries
        Agricultural Libraries   40
        Agricultural Library Associations   41
        Agricultural Society Libraries   41
        College and University Libraries   43
        Commercial Circulating Libraries   44
        Historical Society Libraries   45
        Law Libraries   45
        Lyceums   45
        Mechanics' Libraries   46
        Mercantile Libraries   46
        Military Post Libraries   47
        Music Libraries   48
        Public Libraries   48
        Religious Society Libraries   53
        School District Libraries   54
        School Libraries   59
        Social Libraries   63
        State Libraries   64
        Sunday School Libraries   65

Table of Contents   viii

          Teachers' Libraries   66
          Temperance Libraries   67
          Theological Seminary Libraries   67
     New England   68
     *States and Territories**
        California   70
        Connecticut   82
        District of Columbia   90
        Georgia   103
        Illinois   104
        Indiana   112
        Kentucky   113
        Louisiana   115
        Maine   118
        Maryland   120
        Massachusetts   121
        Michigan   185
        Missouri   186
        New Hampshire   190
        New Jersey   192
        New York   193
        North Carolina   252
        Ohio   253
        Pennsylvania   258
        Rhode Island   286
        South Carolina   293
        Vermont   295
        Virginia   296
        Washington Territory   298
        Wisconsin   299
Europe   303
     Middle Ages   309
     *Individual Countries**
        Austria   310
        Belgium   310
        Bohemia   312
        Denmark   312
        England   313
        France   344
        Germany   357
        Great Britain   367
        Iceland   368

*Following articles statewide (countrywide), these listings are subarranged by city or town, within which they are alphabetical by name of library.

    Ireland   369
    Italy   369
    The Netherlands   376
    Poland   376
    Portugal   377
    Russia   377
    Scotland   379
    Spain   381
    Sweden   382
    Switzerland   383
    Turkey   384

Other Countries
    Australia   385
    Brazil   386
    Canada   386
    China   388
    Egypt   388
    India   390
    Israel   391
    Mesopotamia   391
    Mexico   391
    Turkey in Asia   392
    Venezuela   392

Illustrations Accompanying the Articles   393
Index   395

Periodicals Indexed

This list contains 187 titles that were associated with the 153 periodicals containing articles in the bibliography. The list includes both the actual titles that appeared on the indexed issues and the titles used for the periodicals in the *Union List of Serials*. The compilers were not able to examine all issues of all the periodicals listed.

Albany Law Journal
American Agriculturalist
American Agriculturist
American and Foreign Christian Union
American Annals of Education
American Bibliopolist
American Eclectic; or Selections from the Periodical Literature of All Foreign Countries
American Farmer
American Journal of Education, Boston
American Journal of Education, Hartford, Conn. (Barnard)
American Journal of Education, St. Louis
American Journal of Science
American Ladies' Magazine; Containing Original Tales, Essays, Literary and Historical Sketches, Poetry, Criticism, Music, and a Great Variety of Matter Connected with Many Subjects of Importance and Interest
American Literary Magazine
American Magazine of Useful and Entertaining Knowledge
American Monthly Review
American Penny Magazine
American Publisher and Bookseller
American Quarterly Register
American Quarterly Register and Magazine (Stryker's)
American Register or Summary Review of History, Politics, and Literature
American Repertory of Arts, Sciences, and Manufactures
American Unitarian Association. Monthly Journal
American Unitarian Association. Quarterly Journal
Appleton's Journal; a Magazine of General Literature
Ariel
Army and Navy Chronicle
Association Monthly (YMCA)
Atlantic
Ballou's Pictorial Drawing-Room Companion
Bankers Magazine
Baptist Banner and Western Pioneer
Baptist Record
Biblical Reporter and Princeton Review

Biblical Repository and Classical Review
Biblical Repository and Quarterly Observer
Bibliotheca Sacra
Bibliotheca Sacra and Theological Review
Boston Magazine
Boston Public Library. Bulletin
Boston Quarterly Review
Boston Weekly Magazine
California Teacher
Catholic World
Century, a Popular Quarterly
Chicago Librarian
Christian Chronicle
Christian Examiner
Christian Herald and Seaman's Magazine
Christian Inquirer
Christian Review
Christian Union
Christian World
Commercial Review
Common School Journal
Congregational Education Society. Quarterly Journal
Congregational Quarterly
Connecticut Common School Journal and Annals of Education
Cornell Era
Cornell Review
Daguerreotype; a Magazine of Foreign Literature and Science
De Bow's Review
De Bow's Southern and Western Review
Dial; a Magazine for Literature, Philosophy and Religion
Dollar Magazine
Dwight's American Magazine, and Family Newspaper...for the Diffusion of Useful and Moral and Religious Principles
Dwight's Journal of Music; a Paper of Art and Literature
Eclectic Magazine of Foreign Literature
Eclectic Museum of Foreign Literature, Science and Art
Emerson's Magazine and Putnam's Monthly
Escritoir; or Masonic and Miscellaneous Album
Every Saturday; a Journal of Choice Reading
Federal American Monthly
Firelands Pioneer
Franklin Institute, Philadelphia. Journal
Galaxy
Genesee Farmer
Genius of Universal Emancipation
Harbinger, Devoted to Social and Political Progress
Harper's Magazine
Harper's Weekly
Harvard Advocate
Hazard's Register of Pennsylvania
Hazard's United States Commercial and Statistical Register
Historical Magazine, and Notes and Queries Concerning the Antiquities, History, and Biography of America
Holden's Dollar Magazine
Home Journal, N.Y.
Hours at Home; a Popular Monthly of Instruction and Recreation
Hunt's Merchants' Magazine
Hutchings' California Magazine
Hutchings' Illustrated California Magazine
Iconoclast
Index, a Weekly Paper (Free Religious Association)
Inquirer

International Monthly Magazine of Literature, Science and Art
Jeffersonian
Journal of Education, St. Louis
Journal of Social Science, Containing the Proceedings of the American Association
Journal of Speculative Philosophy
Knickerbocker
Ladies' Magazine
Ladies Repository; a Monthly Periodical, Devoted to Literature, Art, and Religion
Ladies Weekly Museum, or Polite Repository of Amusement and Instruction...
Lakeside Monthly
Legal Gazette
Life Boat; Children's Work for Seamen
Lippincott's Magazine of Literature, Science, and Education
Lippincott's Magazine of Popular Literature
Lippincott's Magazine of Popular Literature and Science
Literary World, Boston
Literary World, N.Y.
Lowell Offering
McBride's Magazine
Magazine of Useful and Entertaining Knowledge
Massachusetts Historical Society, Boston. Collections
Massachusetts Teacher; a Journal of School and Home Education
Merchants' Magazine and Commercial Review
Merry's Museum and Parley's Magazine
Methodist Quarterly Review
Monthly Anthology and Boston Review
Monthly Literary Miscellany
Monthly Magazine, and American Review
Museum of Foreign Literature, Science, and Art
Nation
National Advocate
National Era
National Magazine; Devoted to Literature, Art, and Religion, N.Y.
National Recorder
National Temperance Advocate
New Age
New England Farmer; a Monthly Journal
New England Farmer and Horticultural Register
New Englander and Yale Review
New Hampshire Historical Society, Concord. Collections
New Hampshire Journal of Education
New Jerusalem Magazine
New Outlook
New World; a Weekly Family Journal of Popular Literature, Science, Art and News
New York Chronicle
New York Literary Gazette
New York Mirror; a Weekly Gazette of Literature and the Fine Arts
New York Mirror and Ladies Literary Gazette
New York Weekly Museum
Niles' National Register
North American Miscellany and Dollar Magazine
North American Review
Norton's Literary Advertiser
Norton's Literary Gazette and Publishers' Circular
Old and New
Pacific; a Weekly Journal De-

voted to Religion, Education & Useful Intelligence
Parley's Magazine
Pennsylvania School Journal
Philadelphia Album and Ladies' Literary Port Folio
Port Folio by Oliver Oldschool
Portfolio, and Companion to the Select Circulating Library
Poughkeepsie Casket
Princeton Review
Publisher' and Stationers' Weekly Trade Circular
Publishers' Weekly
Putnam's Magazine
Rhode Island Institute of Instruction Journal
Sailors' Magazine and Seamen's Friend
Saturday Magazine; Being in Great Part a Compilation from the British Reviews, Magazines, and Scientific Journals
Scribner's Monthly
Select Circulating Library
Southern and Western Review
Southern Literary Messenger
Southern Quarterly Review
Southern Repertory and College Review
Stryker's American Register and Magazine
Sunday-School Times
Today; a Boston Literary Journal
Town and Country, N.Y.
Transylvania Journal of Medicine and the Associate Sciences
Union College Magazine
Unitarian Review
Unitarian Review and Religious Magazine
United States Literary Gazette
United States Magazine
University Quarterly; Conducted by an Association of Collegiate and Professional Students, in the United States and Europe
Waldie's Select Circulating Library
Wellman's Miscellany
Western: a Journal of Literature, Education, and Art
Western Recorder
Western Review and Miscellaneous Magazine, a Monthly Publication, Devoted to Literature and Science
Yale Literary Magazine
Young Men's Christian Journal

Introduction

This bibliography extends Cannons' *Bibliography of Library Economy from 1876 to 1920* (Chicago: American Library Association, 1927) back to the beginning, as far as periodicals published in the United States are concerned. The term "periodical" means here any magazine or journal issued at least twice a year; newspapers and annual publications are not included. The term "libraries" refers to collections used by more than one person; collections used only by their owners are excluded.

Arrangement of the bibliography. Articles about libraries on more than one continent come first, followed by those about the United States as a whole or about more than one state; then come those about libraries in the various states, arranged alphabetically by state and subarranged by city or town. Within each city or town, articles are arranged alphabetically by name of library.

Articles on each topic — a particular library, most often — are arranged chronologically by date of publication.

A somewhat similar arrangement is followed for foreign libraries: Articles about European libraries come first, then the articles about libraries in other parts of the world. Within each country, articles are first arranged by city and then subarranged by name of library. Two groups of articles did not fit very neatly into this scheme: those about shipboard libraries (placed at the end of the section for more than one continent) and those about the Librarians' Conference of 1853 in New York City (placed just before the articles on individual libraries in that city).

The individual bibliographic entries also require explanation.

Titles for periodical articles have been devised and supplied in brackets for those articles that do not have titles. The compilers have tried to make these titles descriptive yet written in the style of their period (e.g., with the spelling "cataloguing").

Titles of periodicals are those used in the *Union List of Serials*. If the actual title of the periodical varies considerably from the *ULS* title, the actual title is given in brackets, following the *ULS* one.

Length of articles. The approximate number of words has been recorded for any article that appears on a single page and has not been presented verbatim.

Introduction   xvi

Location of periodicals is indicated by the *ULS* symbol for the library where the article or a microfilm copy was examined or for the library from which a photocopy was obtained. Two locations are noted for some entries because after each abstract was written it was checked and edited by a second person who may have examined a copy of the periodical in a different library.

An *abstract* has been written for every article of more than 150 words. An article of 150 words or fewer has been presented verbatim if it consists of at least two sentences or contains at least 50 words; it is preceded by a note that reads "The entire article follows" or words to that effect. The inclusion of these short articles seems justified because they sometimes contain information not available elsewhere; library historians have occasionally cited articles of this length. A small number of very short and insignificant notices were found, each consisting of a single sentence of fewer than 50 words; these notices have not been included in this work.

Parts of articles have been abstracted or copied if they meet the criteria mentioned above for subject matter and length. For example, if an article is about the need for schools and libraries, the part about libraries has been abstracted or copied.

Reprinted articles. When an article has been reprinted from another periodical, a reasonable, albeit frequently unsuccessful, effort has been made to determine the date, volume, and page of the original.

Illustrations are not common in these articles, but when present, they have been noted in the abstracts and in the separate list of illustrations on pages 393-94.

Sources. All available periodical indexes have been used, including the manuscript "Index to Early American Periodical Literature, 1728-1850," compiled on cards at New York University and reproduced on microprint in 1964 with the title *Early American Periodicals Index to 1850*. References in many theses, books, and articles about the history of early American libraries have been used as well. Several hundred articles have been found while following up citations; often, when a volume contains one or two references to libraries, more have been found by scanning its pages or using its index.

A few articles have been included that are not about libraries or librarians. These are the texts or summaries of lectures given before members of library associations. Each such article has been placed with articles about the library owned by the association.

The *index* includes six kinds of entries in a single alphabet: authors, types of libraries (e.g., mercantile libraries or agricultural libraries), cities or other places, names of individual libraries, librarians, donors, and other persons prominently mentioned in the articles, and a few ideas (e.g., the educational value of libraries) or events (e.g., fires in libraries). Further explanation about the index is given in a note at its beginning, on page 395.

A future supplement or new edition. The compilers cannot have found all periodical articles about libraries published in the United States before 1876, and there is no chance they have eliminated all errors in the bibliography. Therefore, any of the three compilers will be delighted to learn about additions or needed corrections.

> Larry J. Barr
> *Appalachian State University, Boone, N.C.*
>
> Haynes McMullen
> *University of North Carolina at Chapel Hill*
>
> Steven G. Leach
> *United States Department of State*

Symbols for Libraries

(From *Union List of Serials*, 3d ed., 1965)

C	California State Library, Sacramento
CoGrS	University of Northern Colorado, Greeley
CSaT	Graduate Theological Union Library, San Anselmo, Calif.
CtHi	Connecticut Historical Society, Hartford
CU	University of California, Berkeley
CU-B	Bancroft Library, University of California, Berkeley
DeU	University of Delaware, Newark
DLC	Library of Congress, Washington, D.C.
IaAS	Iowa State College, Ames
IaU	University of Iowa Libraries, Iowa City
IC	Chicago Public Library
ICM	Meadville-Lombard Theological School Library, Chicago
ICN	Newberry Library, Chicago
ICU	University of Chicago
IEG	Garrett-Evangelical Theological Seminary Library, Evanston, Ill.
IEN	Northwestern University Library, Evanston, Ill.
InU	Indiana University at Bloomington
IU	University of Illinois Library at Urbana-Champaign
KyL	Louisville Free Public Library, Louisville, Ky.
KyLoS	Southern Baptist Theological Seminary, Louisville, Ky.
KyU	University of Kentucky, Lexington
MB	Boston Public Library
MBC	Congregational Library, Boston
MdAN	United States Naval Academy, Annapolis, Md.
MdBE	Enoch Pratt Free Library, Baltimore
MeB	Bowdoin College Library, Brunswick, Me.
MH-AH	Andover-Harvard Theological Library, Harvard University Library, Cambridge, Mass.
MiU	University of Michigan Libraries, Ann Arbor
MnU	University of Minnesota, Minneapolis
MoS	St. Louis Public Library

MWelC	Wellesley College, Wellesley, Mass.
MWiW	Williams College, Williamstown, Mass.
N	New York State Library, Albany
NbO	Omaha Public Library
NcD	Duke University, Durham, N.C.
NcD-L	Duke University Law School, Durham, N.C.
NcU	University of North Carolina at Chapel Hill
NcU-H	Health Sciences Library, University of North Carolina at Chapel Hill
NhD	Dartmouth College, Hanover, N.H.
NHi	New-York Historical Society, New York
NIC	Cornell University Libraries, Ithaca, N.Y.
NjR	Rutgers University, New Brunswick, N.J.
NN	New York Public Library
NNCorM	Cornell University Medical College Library, New York
NRAB	American Baptist Historical Society, Rochester, N.Y.
NSchU	Union College, Schenectady, N.Y.
OC	Public Library of Cincinnati & Hamilton County
OCl	Cleveland Public Library
OCU	University of Cincinnati
OO	Oberlin College, Oberlin, Ohio
OOxM	Miami University, Oxford, Ohio
PSC	Swarthmore College, Swarthmore, Pa.
TU	University of Tennessee, Knoxville
TxU	University of Texas, Austin
WHi	State Historical Society of Wisconsin Library, Madison

The Abstracts

World

1 "Public Libraries." *Congregational Education Society. Quarterly Journal* [American Quarterly Register], 10 (August 1837), p72–74 (NcU).
The author mainly summarizes part of an article about libraries by George W. Greene *(see 26)*.
Greene uses Adrien Balbi's *Statistical Essay*, describing the libraries of Vienna. He examines the principal libraries of ancient and modern times and describes the basis for the calculations made. None of the present major libraries dates from before the 15th century; 10 were formed between 1430 and 1500. Most grew with private donations, some by legal requirements to deposit books in them. (A table from Balbi is given, showing the annual appropriations of some major European libraries. Other tables give the salaries of officers of the Vienna library; a comparison of the sizes of ancient and modern European, African, and Asian libraries; and the growth of the Royal Library in Paris. The sizes of other libraries are discussed, including some in America.)

2 "Ancient and Modern Libraries." *American Eclectic: or Selections from the Periodical Literature of All Foreign Countries*, 1 (March 1841), p351–67 (NcU).
The article summarized below was translated and condensed from the *Journal des Travaux de la Société Française de Statistique Universelle*.
An introductory note describes the French Society of Universal Statistics, in whose journal M. Bailly's paper on this topic was originally published in April and May 1833. Ancient libraries of Phoenicia, Egypt, Greece, Rome, and the Roman Empire are described. Modern libraries discussed are those of Asia, Africa, and Europe (Turkey, Great Britain, Denmark, Sweden, Russia, Poland, Holland and Belgium, Germany, Switzerland, Italy, Spain, Portugal, and France). The histories of a number of individual libraries in these areas are discussed, and statistics are given for some.

3 X. "Public Libraries." *Dwight's American Magazine and Family Newspaper...for the Diffusion of Useful and Moral and Religious Principles* [American Penny Magazine], 2 (July 1846), p341–43 (NcD).
The article is taken from the *New York Observer*. The original article has not been seen by the compilers of this bibliography.
Ancient historians mention an Egyptian library at Thebes; the early Greeks did not have libraries and we must return to Alexandria to find a great and famous library. In Rome, libraries were not of importance until Cicero's time and in medieval times the ignorant monks did not preserve earlier writing. The Reformation gave an impetus to intellectual activity; the Vatican has valuable manuscripts but the most interesting are not available to the public. The royal library in France was small until the time of Louis XIV, who really created it.

The Revolution brought it more than 100,000 volumes but Napoleon and recent rulers have done little for it. The public libraries of France are little used because they mainly contain material from suppressed monasteries. France needs popular libraries; Guizot planned for them when he was minister of public instruction but the plan has not been executed.

4 [Review of 3 items.] *"Report from the Select Committee on Public Libraries, together with the Proceedings of the Committee, Minutes of Evidence, &c. ordered by the House of Commons to be printed. July 23d, 1849. Folio. p317; Evening Schools and District Libraries. An Appeal to Philadelphians in behalf of improved means of Education and Self-Culture, for Apprentices and Young Workmen. p27. Philadelphia: King & Baird, 1850; Free Reading Room of Spring Garden, for Young Men and Apprentices. p12. Philadelphia: Collins and Co., 1850."* Princeton Review [Biblical Reporter and Princeton Review], 23 (January 1851), p1–50 (InU).

The distribution of libraries around the world is shown. Libraries for deposit and research are distinguished from those for popular use. Itinerating libraries are advocated. Advice on catalogs is given. The testimonial of several House of Commons committee witnesses is included. The benefits of libraries are summarized using the examples of Peebles (Scotland) and libraries for English workingmen such as mechanics' libraries. The library of St. Martin in the Fields (London) is described to show that one must recognize the personal benefits derived from libraries before supporting them. The library at Salford, near Manchester, is compared to those contemplated in the Philadelphia pamphlet. The difficulties of influencing the gangs of criminal young men in Philadelphia are considered. The elements of a popular library are outlined and the places of fiction and newspapers are discussed but no rules for selection are given.

5 "On Bibliothecology. No. 2.—Bibliography." *Norton's Literary Gazette and Publishers' Circular* [Norton's Literary Advertiser], 1 (August 15, 1851), p30, 1740 wds (NcU).

The term "general history of literature" includes biography, history and bibliography. "Bibliography," or the science of books, may be pure (scientific) or material (practical). "Scientific bibliography" concerns the critical review of the contents of books and their classification. "Material" or "practical bibliography" relates to the value or cost of books and to their physical description. Bibliography originated in France and owes much to Germany. A bibliographer must study literature continuously. Literature encompasses all times and all nations. Manuscripts may be classified as autographs or copies. Incunabula are printed books issued before 1500; the Royal Library of Munich has 3500 examples. Rare books include incunabula and other books of distinction. The size of books is designated by the terms folio, quarto, etc. A knowledge of bindings is useful. Bibliographers are rarely appreciated fully, but their services are indispensable to a good library.

6 "Management of Libraries." *American Journal of Education* (Barnard), 2 (July 1856), p210–12 (NcU).

The article consists only of the table of contents of Edward Edwards' book, *Memoirs of Libraries* (1859). Among the main topics discussed by Edwards are library history, statistics, architecture, catalogs, management and administration.

7 "Memoirs of Libraries, Ancient and Modern." *Eclectic Magazine of Foreign Literature*, 49 (February 1860), p180–94 (IEN, InU, NcU).

The article summarized below was taken from the *North British Review*; it is a review of Edward Edwards' *Memoirs of Libraries* (1859) and *A List of the Books of Reference in the Reading Room of the British Museum* (1859).

Since "librarian" has almost become the title of a new profession, Mr. Edwards' book should appeal to a sizable audience of general readers "of the higher and more studious class." Fewer readers will be interested in the second part of the two-volume work dealing with library economy. About one-fifth of the book could have been omitted without loss to most readers, but it is a worthy effort that should prove useful to a select group. Mr. Edwards has not given as much attention to British libraries as he should have, perhaps having overrated the literary resources of other countries. (Summaries of the material concerning the histories of several libraries, such as the Alexandrian, the British Museum, the Imperial Library of France, and Harvard are given in the review.) The list of reference books compiled by Mr. Rye and edited by Mr. Winter Jones, both of the British Museum, is a step toward a model reference library for the new libraries being formed under the Libraries' Act of 1855.

8 [Petzholdt's Bibliography of Bibliographies.] *Nation*, 2 (June 1, 1866), p691, 190 wds (NcU).

A catalog of catalogs will be very welcome to booksellers and librarians. Mr. Julius Petzholdt, the Librarian of the Royal Library at Dresden, has prepared one, with the title *Bibliotheca Bibliographica; Kritisches Verzeichniss der Gesammtgebiet der Bibliographie betreffenden Litteratur des In- und Auslandes in systematischer Ordnung*. The first part includes lists of books on bibliography and libraries; the second part presents materials for general literature, anonymous, pseudonymous, and other types of literature; and the third contains lists of works on national literatures. It is an invaluable manual for every librarian.

9 [Photobibliography.] *American Bibliopolist*, 5 (January 1873), p3. 350 wds (NcD).

The article summarized below is reprinted from *Publisher's Circular*.

Henry Stevens has issued an essay called "Photobibliography: a Word on Catalogues and How to Make Them." In it, he attacks the present system of cataloging and proposes to photograph all valuable title-pages of rare books, certain editions of which need to be identified. Stevens reduces these pages to the ninth part of the original, producing miniature title-pages to insert in any catalog to identify the edition. Stevens claims that to do this would make bibliography an exact science. We agree with the idea if it is used only by those who can afford the luxury of a perfect catalog; the only problem is the expense of doing it. Stevens' collection of photograms already includes many early or rare editions, examples of which are listed.

10 "Libraries; History of Libraries, Ancient and Modern."*Chicago Librarian*, 1 (June 1873), p25–28 (IC).

The article very briefly outlines the history of libraries in the Mediterranean region and Europe to the Middle Ages, and then, for each of ten European countries, names the important present-day libraries, sometimes giving a little history and always giving the number of volumes. For the United States, it lists 24 major libraries, with dates of founding for most and number of volumes for all of them.

11 "Edwards' Library Manuals." *Publishers' Weekly*, 5 (April 4, 1874), p360 (NcU).
The entire article follows.
"To meet the wishes of several valued correspondents, engaged in the formation of public Libraries in India, in America, and in the Colonies, to whom the publications of Mr. Edwards on the subject furnish the most valuable aid, Messrs. Trübner & Co. will, for a short time only, supply complete sets of the six volumes at the reduced price of £3-3^S, instead of £5-15^S, at which they were published. The set comprises: I. 'Memoirs of Libraries,' including a Practical Handbook of Library Economy,' 2 vols, II. 'Libraries and Founders of Libraries,' 1 vol, III. 'Free Town Libraries, their Formation, Working, and Results in Britain, France, Germany, and America,' 1 vol, and, IV., 'Lives of the Founders and other Benefactors of the British Museum.'"

Classical Libraries

12 [Classical World.] *Norton's Literary Gazette and Publishers' Circular*, 2 (August 15, 1852), p148, 780 wds (ICN, NcU).
The earliest library of which there is any record was that of Osymandyas, who reigned in Egypt around 1754 B.C. There were ancient libraries at Susa, residence of the Persian kings, and at the temple of Vulcan in Memphis. The most important ancient library was the Alexandrian Library, founded by Ptolemy Soter in 290 B.C. At one time the library held 700,000 items, but in 47 B.C. a fire consumed 400,000 items in the collection. Despite that fire and frequent plunderings, the collection continued to grow. Then, in A.D. 640 the library was destroyed by the Saracens, who distributed its collection among the city's baths for use as kindling. Ironically, the Saracens later established a number of libraries in North Africa and Spain.

13 "Notices of Ancient Libraries." *Norton's Literary Gazette and Publishers' Circular*, n.s. 2 (June 15, 1855), p253-55 (MWW).
Page 255 is incorrectly numbered as 265. The article is taken from *Notes and Queries*, on three separate pages in volume 11 for 1855: p258, April 7; p337, May 5; and p361, May 12.
The article is made up of a series of notes about individual libraries, public and private. It begins with libraries of the Greeks, then considers pagan libraries in ancient Rome and libraries owned by the early Jews and the Egyptians. Libraries in early Christian Rome, the Middle Ages in Europe, and the Renaissance are mentioned and the article ends with references to some monastery libraries in several regions.

14 "Ancient Libraries." *American Bibliopolist*, 1 (October 1869), p299-301 (NcD, OC).
The Alexandrian Library was founded by Ptolemy Soter in the third century B.C. At the death of Ptolemy Philadelphus, the founder's son, the library contained 200,000 volumes. The number of volumes later increased to 700,000 in the Brucheion and Serapeum collections. Cleopatra repaired the library after the fire during Caesar's campaign against the city, and added the 200,000 volume collection from Pergamum, presented by Anthony. The library was destroyed by

the Saracens in 642. The library at Pergamum was founded by Eumenes, and it was here that parchment was invented to replace papyrus; Alexander had forbidden Pergamum to import papyrus from Egypt in order to prevent the establishment of a library great enough to rival the Alexandrian. The loss of most Roman libraries is attributed to Constantine's order to destroy heathen temples, and to the barbarian invasions. The first of the Roman public libraries was founded by Asinius Pollio. Others were founded by Augustus and Trajan.

England and the United States

15 [Circulating Libraries.] *Port Folio* by Oliver Oldschool, 2 (February 27, 1802), p63 (InU, NcU).
The entire article follows.
"Circulating Libraries, now so general and useful, says an English writer, are of no greater standing than fifty or sixty years. The first in London was commenced in the Strand, by a bookseller of the name of Wright, about the year 1740; he was succeeded by Batho, who was succeeded by Mr. John Bell: his library has lately been sold at auction. The number of circulating libraries in Great Britain in 1800 was one thousand. In the Capital of the United States there are two, and Boston in New England boasts of one."

16 Edwards, B. B. "Importance of a Puritan Library in New England." *Bibliotheca Sacra* [and Theological Review], 4 (August 1847), p582–98 (NcU).
The Red Cross library in Cripplegate, founded by Dr. Daniel Williams, was opened in 1729; its annual income for books is £100; there are 30,000 volumes. The librarian, Dr. Cogan, prepared a catalog of the portraits of the nonconformist fathers in the library, which is reprinted here. It is desirable to establish a Puritan library and museum in New England. It should include a department of books, pamphlets and periodicals published by Puritans in England and America; manuscripts; portraits, prints, etc.; and miscellaneous memorials of and articles about distinguished men. The reasons for establishing such a library and museum include forming a center of patriotic and religious reminiscence for New England, forming a memorial to the theological and literary labors of the Puritans, perpetuating the religious principles and usages of the Puritans, helping future historians, uniting the descendants of the Puritans, aiding literature, and preserving valuable documents and curiosities.

17 Cogswell, J. G. "Letter from Dr. Cogswell." *Literary World*, N.Y., 4 (February 24, 1849), p169–71 (IEN, NcU).
The part of the letter about libraries (p170, 900 wds) is summarized below.
The Stowe Library, which was auctioned at Sotheby's, disappointed me; its books neither were carefully selected nor are they in good condition. The library has many incomplete sets of serials, and its collection seemed to have been acquired without reference to any selection criteria. I must admit, however, that the library did have a few valuable books, some of which I acquired for the Astor Library. In my selection of books, I follow the principle that the Astor Library collection should be learned and useful. I am pleased to state that the library is growing rapidly and that there already are more than 10,000 volumes, some of them very expensive, in its catalog.

18 [Livermore, George.] "Public Libraries." *North American Review*, 71 (July 1850), p185-220 (NcU).

American scholars often are forced either to purchase books or to travel to Europe and use its libraries to find the books necessary to their studies. There is at present no large, well-selected public library collection in the United States, and surely this fact has been detrimental to the advancement of American scholarship. (The article then summarizes the contents of the following two reports and comments upon certain points considered in the reports which are relevant to American libraries: *Report* of the Committee on Public Libraries appointed in March 1849 by the House of Commons and *Report* of the Commissioners appointed in June 1847 to inquire into the administration of the British Museum. Note is taken of the *Annual Report* of the Trustees of the Astor Library, submitted in January 1850, and more briefly of the third *Annual Report* of the Smithsonian Institution.)

19 Bailey, J. J. "Hints on Library Economy." *American Journal of Education*, St. Louis [Journal of Education], 1 (May 1869), p150-51 (MoS).

The librarian is supposed to pass his time in easy indulgence, to lead in all but a pecuniary respect, an enviable life. Actually, the librarian of a flourishing library is frequently perplexed because the books awaken a thirst for knowledge which cannot be satisfied because of his multifarious duties. The Trustees of the Boston Public Library have discussed duties of a librarian that require a man of thorough culture, who is resourceful and of a conciliating character. Edwards' *Memoirs of Libraries* shows that salaries in the British Museum are low and hard-earned; mental disease has been more prevalent among that staff than among literary or scientific men in general. The librarian educates and elevates generations to come. I do not advocate high salaries but there should be enough assistants to allow the chief librarian to do what he alone can do.

20 Wellman, J. W. "Free Public Libraries." *Bibliotheca Sacra* [and Theological Review], 28 (April 1871), p[209]-34 (NcU).

The substance of the article was delivered as an address at the opening of the Free Public Library at Newton, Mass. on June 17, 1870.

The ancient Egyptians, Greeks, and Hebrews had libraries. The free public library is a Christian institution begun during the Reformation, but not meeting the public need until 1847. The issue as to which community began the first free public library in America is in dispute. Free libraries appeared in Britain after 1849. The free public library is an educational institution as well as a storehouse. Its value depends on how it is used. Libraries have always influenced our country's history; Daniel Webster's use of books is an example. Libraries will enrich young minds, and will be invaluable to the community in many ways — culturally, socially, practically, morally and otherwise. Private donations have often been instrumental in the founding of libraries. It is now possible to fund free libraries with taxes in the same manner as free schools.

21 [Exchange of Books and Photographs between Libraries in Leicester, Massachusetts, and Leicester, England.] *Nation*, 14 (April 25, 1872), p274, 300 wds (NcU).

The article summarized below is reprinted in *American Bibliopolist (see 22)*.

Abraham Firth, now a resident of Boston, was born in Leicester, England, and grew up in Leicester, Massachusetts. While on a trip to England, he collected books, photographs, and other materials about Leicester, England, and upon his return to this country he donated these materials to the public library of Leicester, Massachusetts. He then sent a gift of similar materials about that city to the Literary and Philosophical Society's library in Leicester, England. In turn, the Society sent more materials about Leicester, England, to the library in Leicester, Massachusetts, and that library reciprocated with a gift in kind.

22 [Exchange of Books and Photographs between Libraries in Leicester, Massachusetts, and Leicester, England.] *American Bibliopolist*, 4 (June 1872), p298, 300 wds (IEN,OC).
The article was reprinted from *Nation (see 21)*.

Europe and the United States

23 "Of Libraries." *American Register; or Summary Review of History, Politics, and Literature*, 1 (1817), p319–27 (InU, NcU).
The article summarized below is taken from the *European Magazine* of March 1816.
The British Museum library is a poor one because the collection has not been carefully selected. The Royal Library is better in the areas of geography and history. Britain's college libraries are poorly supported except for Bodley's Library. The Advocates' Library is the largest in Scotland. On the whole British libraries are inadequate. Every society and governmental department should collect extensively in its area of interest. The best and most used libraries in Germany are those of the universities. France's libraries are carefully selected. The Royal Library catalog, begun in 1739, is not yet completed. The largest collection in the U.S. is owned by the Philadelphia Library Company. Other good libraries are in the Boston Athenaeum, the Historical Society of New York and Harvard. Jefferson's library has been purchased to replace the recently burned Congressional Library, to form a basis for a national library. (Some private libraries are also discussed.)

24 [Willard, Sidney.] "On the Means of Education, and the State of Learning in the United States of America. On the State of Learning in the United States of America, 1819." *North American Review*, 9 (September 1819), p240–59 (InU, NcU).
The article is an answer to two articles in *Blackwood's Edinburgh Magazine*, both in vol. 4. The first appeared in February 1819, p546–53, and the second in March 1819, p641–49. The titles given above are correct except that the second one omits "1819." The part about libraries in the *North American Review* article (p246–48), is summarized below. It is based on p552–53 in the first *Blackwood's* article.
A paragraph from the *Blackwood's* article tells the number of volumes in several of the larger libraries of the United States and estimates that, excluding social libraries in small towns, the country possesses about 150,000 volumes, which represent only 30,000 distinct works. The largest library in Europe contains about 400,000 volumes; America has about 1/13th the means of extending learning that the city of Paris has; these figures are probably correct. However, the Harvard library is growing and the Boston Athenaeum collection has increased rapidly. Collections, generally, may be scanty but we are not indifferent

to learning. It is fallacious to relate learning to the number of volumes available to scholars; many authors of the books in European libraries merely repeat what other authors have written.

25 U. "Libraries." *Western Review and Miscellaneous Magazine, a Monthly Publication, Devoted to Literature and Science*, 1 (November 1819), p249–52 (NcD).

The attack on the article in *Blackwood's* mentioned in this article, is evidently the September 1819 one in *North American Review (see 24).*

We may have good and wise citizens without having large libraries. However, our country is now ready to take aim at higher degrees of learning and refinement; these and other pursuits are not necessarily anti-republican. (A list of the larger libraries in Europe is given, with the number of volumes in each.) A recent article in *Blackwood's* about the condition of literature in the United States has been justly attacked in this country but its author is probably right in one conjecture. He estimates that only 30,000 learned works are in the United States out of the world's total of 500,000. Each of our state capitals and each college or university should have a library of 10,000 volumes as a nucleus for building a larger collection in the future.

26 [Greene, George Washington. Review of 3 books.] *Essai statistique sur les Bibliothèques de Vienne*, par Adrien Balbi, Vienne. 1835. 8 vo.; *Catalogue de la Bibliothèque de son Excellence, M. le Comte Boutourlin.* Florence. 1831. 8 vo.; *Manuel de Libraire et de l'Amateur de Libres*, par J. C. Brunet. 3me ed. Paris. 1820. 4 tom. 8 vo. *North American Review*, 45 (July 1837), p116–49 (InU, NcU).

Part of this article is summarized in another one in the August 1837 *American Quarterly Register (see 1).*

(Several tables are translated from Balbi which give comparative statistics of European and other libraries; some of the difficulties involved in arriving at comparable figures are discussed.) The Imperial Library in Vienna, like other great European libraries, has managed to acquire whole collections previously privately owned; thus these libraries have developed strong collections in certain subjects and have become great reference libraries. The United States is comparatively much poorer in library resources than the European countries. The Boston Athenaeum and Harvard are developing strong collections; the Library of Congress should become the greatest library of this country. Congress should acquire the papers of our national leaders and begin to buy private collections as they become available. The library of Count Boutourlin (described in the article) has been offered for purchase to the Library of Congress. There are indications that Americans are interested in developing a first-rate body of literature.

27 Patton, Robert B. "Public Libraries." *Biblical Repository and Classical Review* [American Biblical Repository], (January 1838), p174–87 (NcU, OC).

The library resources of the United States are inadequate to support professors and students in serious research, although Americans are a reading people. Great libraries have not developed in this country because they are not compatible with our system of government. Only what is in the general interest of all deserves government support; thus, private money must be used to create large libraries. About $800,000 would be needed to secure a generally adequate library for the University of New York City. Library statistics (which are provided) show how inadequate this country is in books in comparison to Europe. It cannot be said that the larger collections of European libraries result from their longer history. Harvard is 200 years old and has only 42,000 volumes, while Göttingen, founded a century later, has 300,000 volumes, and the University of Berlin, founded in 1809, already has 200,000 volumes in its library.

28 Tyson, Job R. "National Library." *Hazard's United States Commercial and Statistical Register*, 1 (September 25, 1839), p221–22 (InU, NcU).

The article is an extract from Tyson's address to the Athenian Institute and Mercantile Library Company in Philadelphia on April 13, 1838.

America should develop its own national literature; the necessary materials are at hand. The Library Company of Philadelphia is the nation's largest but its 46,000 volumes constitute a small collection compared with the 700,000 of the Royal Library in Paris or the 240,000 volumes of the British Museum. Congress should require the deposit of a copy of every book printed in the country, following the examples of France, Austria, and Russia. Congress should also encourage private citizens to make available their libraries in which are deposited those documents that are so necessary to illustrate our national history. Although American scholars are beginning to produce significant works, such as Irving's *Columbus*, they must do their research in Europe.

29 Robinson, E. "The Aspect of Literature and Science in the United States, As Compared With Europe." *Bibliotheca Sacra* [and Theological Review], 1 (February 1844), p1–39 (NcU).

The part of the article about libraries (p24–27) is summarized below.

European governments aid libraries and universities. The great public libraries there are often old, but some have grown recently. Small countries have expended great effort on their libraries. Had it the will, America could do likewise. Agents should be sent to Europe to purchase libraries now. While we can never be rich in ancient or medieval manuscripts at so late a date, we can acquire vast and strong libraries. Of what importance is such a library? That depends on its nature. A universal library should have products from all countries in all ages on all subjects. The scholar needs to survey his field before he can progress.

30 "National Exchanges." *Literary World*, N.Y., 3 (June 17, 1848), p389–91 (NcU).

M. Vattemare's memorial to Congress proposing international exchange of science and literature explains that American hospitality has created in him an enthusiasm for the American people and has led to his plan for conducting scientific and literary exchanges between Europe and the U.S. He says there should be central exchange offices in each country, regular communications, and full reports of exchanges. Those gaining patents and copyrights should deposit them with national offices. There should be duty-free exchanges, and the Librarian of Congress should exchange duplicate books and documents. The report of the House Committee on the Library of Congress contains reservations about patents and copyrights. Vattemare has summarized French gifts; he has expressed concern over American neglect of them. We agree; the works given America are stored in Washington, and America has sent few in exchange.

31 "Mons. Vattemare." *Dollar Magazine* [Holden's Dollar Magazine] 3 (February 1849), p125–26 (InU, NcD).

Vattemare was originally a surgeon but became famous and wealthy as a ventriloquist. (A poem in praise of Vattemare's talent by Walter Scott is reproduced.) Vattemare proposed a scheme for international exchanges in New York in 1839 and returned to France in 1841 with 1800 books, 500 engravings, 250 drawings, and a collection of museum items. These he distributed among French public institutions, receiving rich exchanges with which he returned to the United States. Vattemare hopes that each nation will establish an institution for receiving these exchanges, consisting of a museum and a patent office. Paris has taken the first step by setting aside an alcove in the Hotel de Ville for books received from the United States.

32 "Books and the People." *National Era*, 3 (March 1, 1849), p36, 380 wds (NcU).
The four public libraries in London have a combined collection of 397,000 volumes while the five public libraries of Paris contain 1.3 million volumes. Paris, with one-half the population of London, has four times as many books in its libraries. (A table for the United States is included which shows, state by state, the number of public libraries and the total number of volumes held.) We have provided a table that gives the proportion of books to population, based upon the 1840 census, for each state. Private libraries are not included. A total of 1,209,800 volumes are held by all public libraries in the United States. The higher proportion of books per person in Paris than in this country can be attributed to royalty's pride in book collecting and to the fact that European libraries have been growing for centuries.

33 "Libraries." *Stryker's American Register and Magazine* [American Quarterly Register and Magazine], 2 (June 1849), p422, 170 wds (NcU).
In London there are four public libraries containing 397,000 volumes. In Paris there are five, containing 1.3 million volumes; there are also other libraries to which the public has access with satisfactory recommendations. London, with twice the population of Paris, has one-fourth as many books. (A table follows, compiled by Hermann Ludewig of New York, showing, for each state in the United States, the number of public libraries and the total number of volumes held by all public libraries in that state.)

34 "Public Libraries." *Inquirer* [Christian Inquirer], 4 (August 3, 1850), p4, 630 wds (MB).
The article summarized below was taken from an abridgment made by the *Boston Evening Transcript* from an article that appeared in the July 1850 issue of *North American Review*; for the original article *see 18*.
The number of volumes in ten European and ten American libraries is given, and, for ten countries, the number of library books per 100 population. Brief reference is made to the Smithsonian and Astor libraries. British Museum collections are described and the status of the work on the Museum's catalog is briefly mentioned.

35 "Public Libraries." *International Monthly Magazine of Literature, Science and Art*, 2 (February 1, 1851), p359-77 (NcU).
The article summarized below is reprinted from *Chambers's Papers for the People*.
Several ancient libraries are described and reasons for the greater size of modern libraries are cited. Five major present-day British libraries are discussed; minor ones are listed. Seventeen other foreign libraries are discussed. The 1849 report of the House of Commons Select Committee on extending free public

libraries in the major towns of Britain is discussed; more public libraries are advised as popular libraries are insufficient. Tables are given showing holdings of public libraries in each European country and capital city, of public and university libraries, and of large British and American libraries. The testimonies of committee witnesses are discussed. Advice is given as to the nature of the books to be bought for new libraries.

36 "Hints upon Library Buildings." *Norton's Literary Gazette and Publishers' Circular*, 3 (January 15, 1853), p1–2 (ICN, NcU).

Architects too frequently attach more importance to the design of impressive façades for public buildings than to the design of their interiors. While a librarian may know little about architecture, he should know how to arrange rooms and books. When planning a new library, he must consider how the books can be best protected against fire and water, the choice of a building site, and the interior arrangement. Heating rooms with warmed air and lighting them with gas are recommended. In European libraries, skylights have been used successfully to admit light. The most suitable room is one that is long and wide and has an adequate number of windows for lighting. In a public library the users should be separated from the books and employees by a railing; a separate reading room is advisable. (A suggested floor plan is illustrated.) Perhaps the best arranged library to be built recently in Europe is the Bibliothèque St. Geneviève in Paris. (Its floor plan is illustrated.)

37 "International Exchanges." *Norton's Literary Gazette and Publishers' Circular*, 3 (May 15, 1853), p84, 500 wds (ICN, NcU).

The article summarized below was translated from *L'Athenaeum Française*.

Everyone knows that for the last twenty years M. Vattemare, a worthy man, has devoted his energies to the great work of literary and scientific extension. His plan is to establish a system whereby governments exchange their publications and libraries exchange their duplicates. Germany, England, Russia, Italy, Holland, Belgium, and the United States have entered into a literary confederation of which France is the center. From the United States alone, at least 17,000 volumes have been received, many of which are of great historical and scientific importance. The American books will be placed in a hall, to be called La Salle Américaine, containing at least 10,000 volumes, and open to the public. The plans of M. Vattemare extend further; we hope that this first practical application will hasten their realization.

38 T., A. W. "More about Musical Libraries." *Dwight's Journal of Music, a Paper of Art and Literature*, 6 (February 17, 1855), p156–57 (NcU).

There are many places in Europe where one can buy a complete musical library for a university. Had we but a nucleus, it would of itself grow. Having no school of their own, Americans appreciate all music, and will have a great part in the future development of music. No science or art can prosper without due means of instruction. Harvard's astronomy collection and the American history branch at Cambridge are examples. Germans say we are superficial, having no depth of knowledge in any subject. One must go 3,000 miles to find music books. Five hundred volumes is considered a good music collection in America. Professor Dehn, Librarian of the music department of the Royal Library in Berlin, is selling his collection of the complete works of the leading music theorists. Some American should buy it. (The collection is described; it might be bought for 200–215 thalers.)

39 "The Educational Interest of the United States." *American Journal of Education* (Barnard), 1 (August 1855), p364-70 (NcU).

Among the tables prepared for this article is a statistical table of the libraries in the United States (p369), which lists by state the number of volumes held by libraries and the number of the different types of libraries, e.g., state, social, college, or public. On the following page is found a statistical table, reproduced from *Burritt's Year Book of the Nations*, of the principal university and public libraries in Europe.

40 "Notes on Libraries and Literature." *Pennsylvania School Journal*, 12 (January 1864), p214-15 (IU).

More than 30 European libraries have reached 150,000 volumes; no American library has. The Imperial Library in Paris is the world's largest. (Libraries with over 300,000 volumes are listed in a table based on Edwards' *Memoirs of Libraries* and the *Annuaire du Bibliophile* for 1862.) The Royal Library in Munich seems to claim more volumes than it actually has. (A second table, extracted from the *Parliamentary Report on Public Libraries* in 1850, gives the average annual increase of the libraries already enumerated.) European libraries had an enormous start on American libraries; progress here has been slow, but America must remember that quality is more important than quantity. Several American libraries have received donations of private libraries and money. One such library, the Boston Public, has grown rapidly to a high rank, and the Library Company of Philadelphia can also be justly proud of its collection.

41 Benjamin, Samuel Greene Wheeler. "Libraries." *Harper's Magazine*, 29 (September 1864), p482-88 (NcU).

In the dark ages the monastic libraries preserved the classics of Greece and Rome. Today the attention given to collecting books indicates the prosperity and intelligence of the age. Some of the world's grandest collections are found in England and Europe. In this country, libraries have prospered since the founding of the Harvard College library; in America, collections claim quality rather than quantity of volumes. There are also numerous public libraries. In 1856, the number of libraries in Great Britain exceeding 10,000 volumes was 43, in France 28, and in the United States 104. Many people misjudge the job of a librarian; his is an industrious employment and not suitable for the old or the inexperienced. For the librarian who has time, the library's patrons provide a continuous study of human nature. One of the most perplexing aspects of libraries is the design of the buildings; this can only be accomplished well by a librarian who is also conversant with architecture.

42 [Publications about Times of Civil Commotion.] *Nation*, 1 (September 7, 1865), p312, 460 wds (NcU).

We hope that the announcement of the intention of Mr. John R. Bartlett, Secretary of State for Rhode Island, to publish a bibliography of all items relating to the late rebellion will induce possessors of tracts, etc. to inform him of the titles and other particulars; he already knows of four thousand items. (A discussion of bibliographies about other civil commotions follows.) The collection which the bookseller Thomason made about the Great Rebellion and Commonwealth in England is now in the British Museum, as are three large collections about the French Revolution. The most conspicuous collection on this latter subject is that belonging to the Duc de la Bédoyère, acquired last year for the Imperial Library [Bibliothèque Nationale] for 100,000 francs.

43 [Printed Catalogues of Libraries.] *Nation*, 1 (October 26, 1865), p532, 560 wds (NcU).

The contemplated retirement of Mr. Antonio Panizzi from the chief librarianship of the British Museum will probably revive discussion of the expediency of a printed catalog for that institution; Mr. Panizzi had objected because its preparation would have meant sacrificing other desirable ends. A few years ago Louis Napoleon ordered the publication of a catalog of the Imperial Library [Bibliothèque Nationale] but only two sections, "History of France" and "Medicine" are to be completed. In this country, because of a vicious desire for brevity, we have scarcely a single good catalog. The catalog that Franklin printed for the Library Company of Philadelphia in 1764 is excellent; every word from the title of each book is given, producing, in effect a synopsis. We hope that Franklin will find imitators.

44 [Steps Toward a Free Public Library for New York] *Nation*, 3 (August 9, 1866), p104, 260 wds (NcU).

Steps have been taken by the New York City government toward the establishment of a large free public library. London papers, agitating for a similar institution, (erroneously) cite New York as a city abounding in free libraries. People busy during the day cannot use the Astor Library and have to pay a small fee to use the imperfect Mercantile Library. Since Mr. Ewart's act of 1850, smaller English towns have taxed themselves to establish free libraries, but all of London's libraries have restrictions. Paris has seven perfectly free libraries, Berlin two, and Vienna three. If the city government of New York would only start one, rich men could be found to fill it with books.

45 "Libraries, Old and New." *Hours at Home: a Popular Monthly of Instruction and Recreation*, 4 (January 1867), p22–27 (NcU).

Dr. [Richard] Hildreth, a historian, has lamented the fact that in the past, private papers and documents were destroyed because individuals were unaware of their potential historical value. He has proposed that tracts, pamphlets, sermons, and similar items be deposited in "savings libraries" where their value would increase with age. At present, Paris has many fine libraries; their contents have for the most part managed to escape destruction. The Vatican library contains a very valuable collection of manuscripts, as does the collection of Cosimo de Medici in Florence. In England, the British Museum's collection is composed of formerly private libraries and contains many rare volumes. The Free Library of Manchester possesses a collection widely used and appreciated by the common people. In the United States, only the Boston Public Library is the equal of Manchester's. Although New York has a number of excellent libraries, the city needs a free library similar to the ones in Boston and Manchester.

46 Felsenthal, B. "A Valuable Library to Be Sold." *Nation*, 6 (June 18, 1868), p492, 330 wds (NcU).

The article summarized below is a letter from Felsenthal to the editor of the *Nation*. The collection was later acquired by Temple Emanuel in New York City.

I have received a letter from Mr. M. Roest, of Amsterdam, an eminent Hebrew bibliographer; I should not withhold from the American public what he says about a Jewish library for sale by an Amsterdam bookseller, Frederik Muller. Mr. Roest writes that some American public library, institution of learning, or Jewish congregation ought to buy it. The collection contains more than 3,000 printed *Hebraica*, more than 2,000 *Judaica*, about 100 manuscripts and

Europe and U.S.

many engravings. Is there no American library, no rich Jewish congregation in New York, to buy this literary treasure?

47 [Sale of the Emperor Maximilian's Library.] *Nation*, 8 (March 4, 1869), p174 (NcU).
The part of the article about libraries is quoted below.
"As announced, the sale of the Emperor Maximilian's (or, as it is called from the collector, the Andrade) library took place at Leipzig, Jan. 18-27, at the establishment of Messrs. List & Francke. Agents were present from the leading houses of England and the Continent; the United States was being represented by Mr. Sabin, of this city, who purchased about one seventh of the collection, partly on account of the Library of Congress. The highest interest of the sale centred in six volumes published in Mexico, 1544-47, one of which (Çummaraga's 'Doctrina Breve') was the first book printed in America with date affixed. It should be cause of lasting regret that this book, at least, was not ordered to be secured at any price for the Library of Congress, but that it has instead fallen to the British Museum, which bought it for 805 thalers."

48 [Cutter, Charles A.] "A Librarian on Free Libraries: *Free Town Libraries: Their Formation, Management, and History in Britain, France, Germany, and America. Together With Brief Notices of Book-Collectors and of the Respective Places of Deposit of Their Surviving Collections*. By Edward Edwards. New York: John Wiley and Son. London: Trübner and Co. 1869. *Nation* 9 (September 16, 1869), p233-34 (IEN, InU).
A review of Edwards' book. Sidney H. Ditzion, in *Arsenals of a Democratic Culture* (1947), p108, says the review was written by Charles A. Cutter.
Though it exhibits much research, the book will give librarians little practical assistance. It is primarily devoted to the history of town libraries and lessons to be drawn from that history. Edwards recounts the difficulties of promoters of free libraries, and the success of the libraries themselves. Thirty-four towns in the United Kingdom have accumulated 420,000 volumes since the first Library Act was passed; 2,938,000 volumes are issued annually there. Edwards does not discuss the good effect of these many circulations; such statistics would be hard to compile. The account of American libraries is unsatisfactory; the next census should yield more information. In 1850, there were nearly 4 million volumes in 10,000 libraries available to the American public; in 1860, 8½ million in 20,000 libraries; and by 1870 perhaps 12-15 million in 25,000 libraries. The last third of the book contains a list of 1,120 book collectors.

49 "Free Town Libraries, their Formation, Management, and History in Britain, France, Germany, and America, together with Brief Notices of Book Collectors, and of Respective Places of Deposit of their Surviving Collections. By Edward Edwards. (Trubner and Co.)." *American Bibliopolist*, 1 (November 1869), p349, 170 wds (ICN, ICU, OC).
The article summarized below is a review of Edwards' book.
The public library is an older institution than most people realize. For example, Richard Whittington founded the Common Library at Guildhall in 1420, and shortly afterwards John Carpenter made a gift of books to that library. Today, there is scarcely a town that does not have some kind of library. Edwards' book is intended to serve as a handbook for managing public libraries; additionally, it compares the success of the public library movement in Britain to other countries—particularly the United States.

50 [Hebrew and Jewish Books for Sale in Amsterdam.] *Nation*, 12 (January 5, 1871, p7, 310 wds (NcU).

Mr. Frederick Muller, bookseller of Amsterdam, has a collection of 2,800 volumes of Hebrew and Jewish books which he intends to sell *en bloc*. So far as we know, there is no public or private library in the United States with a respectable collection of post-Biblical Hebrew literature. The great Hebrew libraries of London, Oxford, Leyden, Paris, Berlin, Munich, Vienna, and Parma have no parallel in America. Is this not an opportunity to lay the foundation of a decent Hebrew library? (A listing of the number of volumes in each of fifteen divisions of the collection follows.)

51 [Hebrew Library for Temple Emanuel.] *Nation*, 12 (May 18, 1871), p338 (NcU).

The entire article follows.

"We are glad to observe that the Hebrew Library which we announced in January as about to be sold by Mr. Frederick Muller, in Amsterdam, and whose rare value made it a highly desirable acquisition for this country, has in fact been purchased by a committee of members of the Temple Emanuel, in this city. This must be considered one of the most important of the recent transfers of fine collections from Europe to America. It is stated that Cornell University has offered to take charge of this library, and in return to establish a Hebrew professorship and ten scholarships at Ithaca; but without success, as the new owners naturally prefer that the library should remain in this city. Columbia College would stand a better chance of getting it; or why should it not go to swell the Lenox free library?"

52 Howland, Edward. "Public Libraries, and Their Management." *McBride's Magazine* [Lippincott's Magazine of Popular Literature and Science], 8 (July 1871), p76–87 (NcU, OC).

Libraries must acquire insignificant material. The Bodleian now has to pay high prices for Elizabethan ephemera; the British Museum is wisely acquiring much material on the recent history of America. No library in the United States is making much effort in this area. The *Report of the Commissioners Appointed to Inquire into the Constitution and Government of the British Museum* (1850) shows the difficulties in printing a library catalog. Panizzi favored a manuscript catalog with full titles; Payne Collier, a member of the Commission, favored short titles. The Reading Room of the British Museum is convenient for the user. The Boston Public Library provides a good pattern for American libraries to follow; it is an active agent in public education. The French insist on reclaiming any book in a sale if the item formerly belonged to a French public institution; the British do not do this.

53 [Rosenthal Hebrew Library.] *Nation*, 19 (October 22, 1874), p268, 220 wds (NcU).

Some years ago the *Nation* called attention to the great Hebrew library in Amsterdam that later became the library of Temple Emanuel in New York City. Another Hebrew library, still larger, is to be sold *en bloc*, the one owned originally by L. Rosenthal of Hanover and now owned by his son, G. Rosenthal of Amsterdam. We hope that some institution or some Jewish congregation in this country will buy it. The collection numbers between 8,000 and 9,000 volumes; we believe it is richer in Hebrew books than the famous Oppenheimer Library in the Bodleian or the Heimann Michael Library in the British Museum.

54 [European and American Library Statistics.] *Publishers' Weekly*, 7 (January 30, 1875), p114 (NcU).
The entire article follows.
"The National Library of Paris shows an increase of 824,000 to 2,000,000 volumes in twenty-five years; that of the British Museum from 435,000 to 1,100,000; the Bodleian and that of the University of Cambridge respectively, from 220,000 to 310,000, and from 166,700 to 250,000. The National Library at Paris alone now contains above half a million more volumes than were in the former period contained in all the seven public libraries of Paris put together. In 1848 all the public libraries in the United States together held only 980,000 volumes; now they contain very nearly twenty millions. On the other hand, the great German libraries of München, Berlin, and Vienna appear to have not increased 50 per cent in this period. These facts we glean from an interesting report to the American Social Science Association."

Ships at Sea

55 "The American Navy &c." *Niles' National Register* [Niles' Register], 23 (November 30, 1822), p194–98 (NcU).
The part about libraries (p197, 240 wds) is summarized below. This portion of the article was reprinted from *The Liverpool Mercury*.
The 74 gun ship Franklin is presently cruising off the coast of Chile. The 700 men on board have a library of about 1,000 volumes for their use. The captain has 700 volumes in his cabin. A library of books for the men on board a ship has never been seen or heard of before. It is only possible on a ship manned by *freemen*.

56 "The President's Address" (Third Anniversary of the New York Bethel Union). *Christian Herald and Seaman's Magazine*, 11 (January 3, 1824), p28–29 (NcU).
The parts of the article about libraries are given in their entirety.
[On p28] "Every Christian heart must have beat high with joy, on reading even a newspaper account that Commodore [Isaac] Hull had ordered a library of one thousand volumes for the use of his crew, preparatory to a long and distant voyage."
[On p29] "I delight to present to my own mind the appearance of this ship of war, lately ordered by our government to visit the Sandwich Islands, during her cruize [*sic*] in the Pacific. 'Who,' say the wondering Islanders, 'are these, carrying, as on eagle's wings, their stripes and stars into far distant seas? What gallant ship is this?' 'She is the United States, Commodore Hull, displaying her broad pennant in the Pacific Ocean, armed with fifty guns, for her Seamen to fight; and with her thousand volumes for her Seamen to read.'"

57 "The United States Frigate Brandywine." *The Sailors' Magazine and Seamen's Friend*, 2 (April 1830), p229–31 (MdAN).
The part of the article about the ship's library (p229) follows.
"Attached to the cabin is an elegant library, comprising several hundred volumes of choice books, of science, history, religion, general literature, &c. It belongs to the ship."

58 "Want of Books at Sea." *Sailors' Magazine and Seamen's Friend*, 6 (July 1834), p352, 160 wds (MdAN).

The article is an extract from a letter written by a seaman on board the U.S.S. Potomac, and dated, Cape of Good Hope, December 6, 1831.

"Our time would be very pleasant if we had a library on board for us sailors; I have not found a book worth reading among the crew. Libraries are common on board every sloop of war, supplied by subscription among the crew and selected by the chaplain. A library was proposed by our crew some weeks before our departure but we sailed without it. Conceive for yourself the evil of being confined for three years on a ship without having a single book to read."

59 Harris, John. "On the Moral Claims of Seamen." *Sailors' Magazine and Seamen's Friend*, 11 (September 1838), p15–19 (MdAN).

Above the title, a line reads "From Harris's Prize Essay"; the year before, Harris had won a prize given by the British and Foreign Sailors' Society for the best essay on the claims of seamen to the regard of the Christian world. Other parts of the essay had appeared in earlier 1838 issues of the periodical; the concluding section, in the September issue, contains three references to libraries; they are quoted below.

[On p16, advocating the establishment of a Sailor's Institute where instruction should be given in the way it is given in mechanics' institutes, and referring to a seaman's time in port.] "During these weeks he has necessarily much leisure, and were he comfortably lodged, and his money at rest in a savings' bank, he might find instruction and profitable amusement at his Institute, and from a lending library that might be attached to it. He would, consequently, be less exposed to drunkenness and disease, and the knowledge gained would make him neither less useful nor less happy. Assuredly he would not feel less attached to the country which had shown so much interest in his comfort and welfare."

[On the same page, referring to efforts already being made.] "Libraries containing approved religious works, are lent to the ships about to sail."

[On p17, advocating normal schools to train sailors to promote the religious improvement of their shipmates, and referring to the sailor's time at sea.] "And why should his improvement be left during this long period to the uncertainty of his taking a book from the loan library on board?"

60 "Economy of Ships of War." *Army and Navy Chronicle*, 11 (September 10, 1840), p161–64 (NcU).

The article summarized below is taken from Dr. John Wilson's "Statistical Reports on the Health of the Navy (1840)." The part about libraries (p162–63) is summarized.

Until recently, little was done for sailors in the way of providing moral and intellectual culture. Sailors can generally read, and enjoy doing so. Only religious materials were provided until, in August of 1838, an admiralty order directed that libraries be established on each ship in the Royal Navy. For large ships, 270 volumes were provided, and 100 for smaller ships. The books will put idle time to good use in improving the men. When better understood, the service will become more popular.

61 "All Ready." *Sailors' Magazine and Seamen's Friend*, 15 (May 1843), p281–82 (MdAN).

The part of the article (p281) containing the catalog of the library is reproduced on p99 of *Books Afloat & Ashore* by Harry R. Skallerup, Archon, 1974.

We are happy to announce that the Sailor's Library is now ready for orders. In selecting the volumes, the committee has considered variety, interest, simplicity in style and moral effect. (The titles, and sometimes authors, are given for the 50 works in 60 volumes.) The committee has arranged with Mark H. Newman to publish the library; it will be furnished in a sturdy case at the low price of $25.00. Twenty dollars has been received from the Ladies' Seamen's Friend Society of Saxonville, Massachusetts; if someone will add $5.00 the bread will soon be cast upon the waters.

62 Hunt, T. Dwight. "Wants of Seamen." *Sailors' Magazine and Seamen's Friend*, 22 (March 1850) p193–96 (MdAN).

The article summarized below was taken from the *Honolulu Friend*. It also appeared in the appendix in Henry T. Cheever's *The Whale and His Captors*, new ed., 1855, p347–56.

Seamen need a good library on shipboard. They have the same capacity for mental elevation and enjoyment as other men, and the sphere of their influence is much greater than that of many men because they are thought of in foreign ports as the representatives of their native country. A library is the best method of bringing godliness and knowledge to seamen. Comical, tragic, and fictitious writing should, as a rule, not be included. Of course infidel and licentious works should be excluded. Books of history, especially of countries to be visited on the voyage, should be included, and so should books of travels. Books of religion are the most important and are available in great variety. While libraries are being established on land, the "broad and peopled" ocean should not be forgotten.

63 Taylor, T. E. "Lahaina Chaplaincy, Report of Rev. T. E. Taylor, Lahaina, Dec. 25, 1849." *Sailors' Magazine and Seamen's Friend*, 22 (April 1850), p249–52 (MdAN).

The "Forecastle Literature" (p250–52) part of the article is about libraries.

I believe that intemperance and licentiousness are the two whirlpools into which many seamen are drawn. Apparently, forecastles always have books but often the books chiefly tell of the feats of pirates and robbers and lead the reader through dens of infamy. At sea the imagination is active because of the comparative solitude; the seaman's soul may become steeped in licentiousness. This is why, on shore, seamen are often found in the house of her "whose feet take hold on death." The only way to remove the evil influence of these books is to supply libraries of better books for ships. There should be interesting biographies, histories and travels, not just religious books. Even books that disappear from libraries may do good when they are read by others. Officers, seamen, and good people on shore would be willing to contribute to this cause.

64 "Seamen's Libraries." *Life Boat; Children's Work for Seamen*, 2 (October 1859), p1–2 (MdAN).

The article refers to the work of the American Seamen's Friend Society. Because *Life Boat* was also issued as part of *Sailors' Magazine and Seamen's Friend*, the article also appears in that periodical on p61–62 of vol. 32 for October 1859.

About fifty libraries, containing from forty to fifty volumes each, have been sent to sea, principally from Boston and New Bedford; the collections have been put in the hands of Christian seamen. On board one ship, five conversions have occurred; on another, twelve. Often, the libraries are read by the whole ship's company. Two letters from custodians of the libraries are quoted.

65 B., J. K. "The Best Medicine Chest." *Life Boat; Children's Work for Seamen*, 4 (September 1861), p2 (MdAN).

The entire article follows; it refers to a library given by the American Seamen's Friend Society. Because *Life Boat* was also issued as part of *Sailors' Magazine and Seamen's Friend*, the article also appears in that periodical in vol. 34, p30 for September 1861.

"The Seaman who had Library No. 28, says, in a letter dated at sea, Jan. 5th, 1861. Lat. 24.10, Long. 72. 'Today, I have been 45 years at sea, and these *Libraries* are the best *Medicine Chest* I have ever seen — a cure for all the diseases of sin. I have a colored crew, and only two can read. Could the donors see them read, and the others listen, they would feel well paid; and especially to hear them say when they return the book, and take another, "Dat bery good book." May God bless you and your Society.' "

66 "Sea Missions." *Sailors' Magazine and Seamen's Friend*, 34 (June 1862), p290–91 (MdAN).

The article summarized below refers to the work of the American Seamen's Friend Society.

This work was begun four years ago. In the first year ten libraries were put on ships in the care of pious sailors; in the second year, 94 were added; in the third, 113; and in the present year, 108; a total of 325 are now afloat, in the care of religious sailors and officers. Eighty of these libraries are on men-of-war and the rest on merchant ships; a total of about 16,000 volumes are accessible to more than 15,000 seamen. The men in charge of the libraries often act as missionaries, conducting prayer meetings. The work is supported mainly by gifts of money from Sabbath school children; we bespeak their prayers and efforts until each of the 30,000 American vessels has a library and a converted sailor to take care of it.

United States

67 M. "On the State of American Literature." *Monthly Magazine, and American Review*, 1 (April 1799), p15–19 (NcU).
The part about libraries (p19, 180 wds) is summarized below.
There is hardly a library in the United States, public or private, which would enable a man to be thoroughly learned in any one language. The public library of Philadelphia [the Library Company of Philadelphia] and the University of Cambridge [Harvard] are respectable, considering their youth, but are both very defective. The student should not have to spend as much time locating a book as it would take him to read it ten times and should not have the mortification of giving up after a long search. Nor do private libraries or booksellers make up for the deficiencies of the public libraries.

68 [Kirkland, John Thornton.] "Literary Institutions. — University. — Library." *North American Review*, 8 (December 1818), p191–200 (InU, NcU).
One way to develop universities in different sections of this country is first to increase the number of professorships and to add to the literary and scientific equipment of older and larger universities. Harvard's resources give it advantages in providing more advanced instruction. In this country, the lack of large libraries is a serious disadvantage; our two best libraries, that at Harvard and that of the Library Company of Philadelphia, are far apart, whereas in Europe there are many large libraries. (The strengths and weaknesses of the Harvard collection are considered in detail. Then principles of book selection for a scholarly library are discussed.) If we decide to do without large libraries we will either despise literature or have to invent over again the arts and sciences and will have to rewrite the books of all other countries and ages.

69 [Number of Volumes in Libraries in Major U.S. Cities.] *Philadelphia Album and Ladies' Literary Port Folio*, 1 (September 27, 1826), p7 (InU, WHi).
The entire article follows.
"New York, with a population of 170,000, possesses ten libraries, containing 44,000 volumes; Baltimore, with a population of 70,000, has four public libraries, containing 30,000 volumes; Philadelphia, with a population of 160,000, possesses nineteen public libraries, containing 70,000 volumes; Boston, with a population of 60,000, possesses thirteen public libraries, containing 55,000 volumes."

70 "Inhabitants and Libraries." *New England Farmer and Horticultural Register*, 5 (October 13, 1826), p96 (MdBE).

United States

The entire article follows.

"Boston, with a population of 60,000, possesses 13 public libraries containing 50,000 vols; Baltimore, 70,000 inhabitants, 4 public libraries, 30,000 volumes; Philadelphia, 150,000 inhabitants, 19 public libraries, 70,000 vols; New York, 180,000 inhabitants, 10 public libra[sic] 44,000 vols; Harvard University, at Cambridge, contains 30,000 volumes."

71 "Improved Hinge for Library Doors." *Franklin Institute, Philadelphia: Journal*, 5 (April 1828), p264, 270 wds (OCU, NcU).

The ordinary method of hanging doors on library shelves makes it necessary to move some of the adjoining books before removing the book next to the partition upon which the door is mounted. A newly designed hinge (shown in a drawing) relieves this problem. The two adjoining doors of adjoining sections of shelving are mounted on the same hinge. The hinge is attached to the outside edge of the upright partition that separates the sections of shelving. Thus there is nothing attached to the inside of the partition and any book can be withdrawn without interference.

72 "Public Libraries." *Hazard's Register of Pennsylvania*, 12 (August 10, 1833), p86–87 (InU, NcU).

The article summarized below quotes from the *Boston Mercantile Journal* and is reprinted from the *Commercial Herald*.

Citizens of Boston have provided 45,000 volumes for the public libraries in Boston, and there are 20,000 in circulating libraries. The largest collections on the continent are at the Athenaeum (28,000) and at Cambridge (36,000). There are thus about 100,000 volumes constantly accessible. We believe Philadelphia has a 25,000 volume library, and Charleston one of 16,000. We of Philadelphia think the Boston paper is wrong in its above claim to the best libraries in America. The Philadelphia library alone has over 42,000 volumes; 10,000 are rare and valuable works in foreign languages. (Other Philadelphia area libraries are briefly described; circulating libraries belonging to individuals are not discussed.) Philadelphia is second to none as to the number, usefulness and size of her libraries.

73 Bartlett, Richard. "Remarks and Documents Relating to the Preservation and Keeping of the Public Archives." *New Hampshire Historical Society, Concord: Collections*, 5 (1837), p7–76 (NcD).

The parts about libraries (p10–11, 21, 57–58, and 65–67) are summarized below:

Several state libraries have been destroyed by fire. The Library of Congress, already destroyed once by fire, is probably in danger of being destroyed again. (The sizes of several American libraries are given.) Are any or all of these collections protected in fire-proof rooms? The library of the town of Portsmouth [NH] was burnt in 1813. (An appendix includes official reports about the burning of the building and library of the War Department in 1800 and of the fire in the Library of Congress in 1825.)

74 [American Libraries.] *Biblical Repository and Classical Review* [American Biblical Repository], 9 (January 1837), p251, 180 wds (NcU).

There are about 300,000 volumes in college libraries in the United States, 120,000 in students' libraries, 80,000 in theological libraries, and 300,000 in other public libraries. There are 800,000 volumes in all. The Philadelphia library has 44,000 volumes; Harvard has 42,000; the Boston Athenaeum, almost 30,000; and New York City, 25,000. The best theological library, at the Andover Theological Seminary, contains 13,000 volumes. Professor Stowe has just purchased a library in Europe for Lane Thelogical Seminary. Some libraries contain numerous pamphlets, maps, etc. Harvard has a collection of 10,000 maps, charts, and views. American libraries lack systematic and scientific catalogs of books. This deficiency is supplied at Cambridge, and soon will be at Andover, and the library of the American Antiquarian Society at Worcester. The Andover catalog, prepared by Mr. O. A. Taylor, is very elaborate.

75 Doughty, Charles I. "Report of the Missionary and Tract Board." *New Jerusalem Magazine*, 10 (July 1837), p367–68 (NIC).
  The proceedings of the Board for last year consisted entirely of distributing books. (A list is given of public institutions and libraries supplied with various books.) The Board has received $200 from the Convention's Finance Committee, has paid a debt of $100, and had a balance of $6 at the beginning of the year, so the present balance is $106.

76 Tyson, Job R. "A Lecture, Delivered at Philadelphia, on the 13th April, 1838, Before the Athenian Institute and Mercantile Library Company, on the Moral and Social Influences of the American Revolution." *Select Circulating Library* [Waldie's Select Circulating Library], 12 (July 3, 1838), p225–28 (NcD, OC).
  The first colonists brought with them the seeds of revolution; that war was a contest of doctrine, resulting in the triumph of the principle of the sovereignty of the people at large. Library collections in this country are not sufficient to meet the needs of learned students. The libraries of England and France far outstrip ours in size and quality. Congress should enact a deposit law similar to those in England, France, and Austria.

77 [Review of 3 catalogues.] "Catalogue of Editions of the Holy Scriptures in Various Languages, and Other Biblical Works, in the Library of the American Bible Society. 1837, p31; Catalogue of the Library of the Theological Seminary in Andover, Ms by Oliver A. Taylor, M.A. 1838, p531; Catalogue of the Books Belonging to the Library of the University of Vermont. 1836, p93." *Congregational Education Society. Quarterly Journal* [American Quarterly Register], 11 (August 1838), p91–92 (NcU).
  (The subject headings in the library of the Bible Society Catalog are listed.) One reason for publishing it is to request donations for the library. Rare books, books related to Biblical learning and books of travels and topography relating to the progress of Christianity are all acceptable. The first catalog of the Andover Library was published in 1819. Since then, the library has grown through donations and a trip by Dr. Robinson to Germany in 1826. The Andover library now has more than 12,000 volumes, and is strong in the department of theology and sacred literature, but weak in English literature. Much of the library of the University of Vermont was selected by Professor Torrey in Germany. Though smaller than that of many colleges, the library is one of the best in proportion to its size.

78 Smith, Robert L., William Roberts, Joseph L. Smith, and Otis Clapp. "Report of the Book Committee." *New Jerusalem Magazine*, 13 (July 1840), p415–16 (NIC).

(Libraries receiving a supply of Swedenborg's writings from the committee are listed.) A circular was sent to the presidents of various colleges asking whether their libraries possessed any of the writings of Swedenborg, and if not, whether they would accept them as a donation from the convention. (College libraries furnished with sets of the writings are then listed.) The total cost of all the works thus distributed is $333.36. (Next, colleges not responding to the circulars are listed.) The Committee has 77 colleges and 31 theological seminaries not yet supplied with the books; the work of supplying colleges and other public institutions has only begun. Circulars have not yet been sent to all the colleges because of insufficient funds. Since the Missionary and Tract Board began supplying works in 1834, books have been furnished to 24 colleges, 8 theological seminaries, 8 athenaeums, 25 library associations, 19 packet ships, 12 steamboats and 1 naval lyceum.

79 L., F. W. "Agricultural Books and Papers in District Schools." *Genesee Farmer*, 5 (October 1844), p86, 350 wds (InU, NcU).

(A letter to the editors.) There is an increasing interest in agriculture as a subject in the common schools. Among various libraries in predominantly agricultural districts, few works on agriculture have been found. Perhaps the introduction of agricultural papers into the libraries would help relieve this shortage and prove beneficial to the neighborhoods. If the school authorities cannot afford to subscribe to the papers, perhaps individuals already receiving them could deposit their copies in the libraries. Those in charge of the libraries should purchase bound volumes of back issues. (At the end of the letter, the editors note that they would make bound copies available for little more than the cost of binding.)

80 "Libraries in the United States." *Dwight's American Magazine and Family Newspaper...for the Diffusion of Useful and Moral and Religious Principles*, 3 (April 1847), p263, 650 wds (NcD).

The New York Historical Society presented Mr. Herman Ludwig [Hermann Ludewig] of Germany at its April meeting. Mr. Ludwig has published in the *Serapeum*, a magazine of Leipsig, an article about American libraries. The essay includes a bibliography of bibliographies of American history and biography published between 1629 and 1846; a list of 258 libraries in the United States and descriptions of 115 catalogs from 62 of these institutions; a discussion and description of the bibliography of the American book trade between 1804 and 1846; and a section on the "Curiosities of American Literature," describing the bibliophily of Mr. Force of Washington, D.C., the Cambridge Bay Psalm-Book, and books of Ana published in the United States.

81 "Libraries in the United States." *De Bow's Review* [Commercial Review of the South and West], 4 (December 1847), p560 (InU, NcU).

The entire article follows; it probably refers to Hermann Ludewig.

"According to a table compiled from the researches of a literary gentleman of New York, there are in the United States no less than 235 public libraries. The aggregate number of volumes is set down at 2,351,260. It appears that the State of New York has 33 libraries, with 174,000 volumes; Pennsylvania, 32 libraries, with 176,100 volumes; Massachusetts, 30 libraries, with 203,000 volumes; Ohio, 23 libraries, with 68,000 volumes; Maryland, 11 libraries, with 54,200 volumes; the District of Columbia, 9 libraries, with 75,600 volumes; and the other States smaller numbers. Rhode Island, in proportion to her population, has the largest number of volumes of any State in the Union."

82 [Plea for Libraries.] *New Englander and Yale Review*, 6 (April 1848), p311 (InU, NcU).
The entire article follows; it refers to Noah Porter.
"We find by us a number of pamphlets, some of which deserve a more extended notice than we are able to bestow on them collectively. Prof. Porter's 'Plea for Libraries,' has been republished in this form by 'the Society for the promotion of Collegiate and Theological Education at the West;' and it is sent forth 'in the hope that it may arrest the attention of many an individual who has the ability and heart to do a noble work for the West,' by contributing to furnish its infant colleges with ample libraries — a hope which it is of the first importance should be realized."

83 "Hints on Reading." *Rhode Island Institute of Instruction Journal* [Reports and Documents Relating to the Public Schools of Rhode Island for 1848], (1849), p441–54 (NcU).
The article summarized below refers to the remarks on the catalogs of the Pawcatuck library, which were in the same journal on p437–40 (*see 1110*).
Since the remarks on the catalogs were written, it has been thought advisable to collect more distinctly some suggestions on the subject of reading. The opinions of writers and guides are here arranged, under the headings: definition of reading; objects of reading; general advantages of reading; importance of reading to the business man, the mechanic, and the manufacturer; choice of books; systematic reading or reading in courses or by subjects; reading conjoined with thinking; social or class reading; re-reading or reviewing; reading connected with writing; method of reading — general hints and directions; effects of books — influence of authors; early reading — first studies; and the plan of reading recommended by Thomas S. Grimké.

84 [Jewett, Charles Coffin.] "Public Libraries." *Common School Journal*, o.s. 11, n.s. 1, (February 15, 1849), p55–57 (NcU).
The article is an abstract of the Report of the Acting Librarian to the Regents of the Smithsonian Institution.
A study undertaken by the Library during the preceding year shows that there are 182 public libraries in the United States, which together hold 1,294,000 volumes; of these libraries only 43 have collections surpassing 10,000 volumes. In comparison to European countries, the United States ranks last in this and other related statistical categories. We have a great number of small libraries, widely scattered throughout the country; thus we possess the means to improve the general level of culture. However, we have no large libraries, which means that our scholars are compelled to go to Europe in order to conduct their research. The relationship between large library collections and learning is not well understood in this country. The number of books in a collection is an inadequate criterion for assessing the value of a library because judicious selection of books can do much to compensate for numerical inferiority; therefore it is entirely possible that our libraries could be made more useful for learning than Europe's large libraries.

85 Stevens, Henry. "The Public Libraries of America." *Literary World*, N.Y., 6 (March 2, 1850), p195–97 (NcU).
The article is an abstract of Stevens' testimony before the Committee of the House of Commons on Public Libraries.
The public libraries of the United States are small but numerous. There are

1,294,000 volumes held by 182 of the largest libraries in the United States. One deficiency of our library system is felt by those students who wish to conduct extensive research; however, this deficiency is partially corrected by the existence of many fine private libraries, which are opened to the serious student. Certain outstanding institutions are: the Smithsonian Institution, soon to be completed; the Astor Library in New York, under construction; the New York State Library; and the Library of Congress with its 45,000 volumes. Schools, academies, societies, and other corporate bodies commonly have libraries.

86 "Duties of a Librarian." *Norton's Literary Gazette and Publishers' Circular*, 1 (June 1851), p6, 1010 wds (DLC, ICN).

As the number of libraries increases, so does the need for well qualified librarians. The ideal librarian will be familiar with all branches of knowledge, will be a skillful and dedicated manager, and will possess endurance and a good memory. While everyday we cannot expect to meet a librarian who displays the learning and intelligence of a Johnson or a Kant, there are in this country many outstanding librarians, e.g., Cogswell, Folsom, and Jewett. A well qualified librarian will be knowledgeable in the history of literature and bibliography and in ancient and modern languages. Additionally, he will keep abreast of scientific developments and of the history of literature in other countries. We shall continue this discussion in a future issue.

87 "Libraries in the United States." *Norton's Literary Gazette and Publishers' Circular*, 1 (June 1851), p7 (DLC, ICN).

For each of the thirty states, a table lists the number of public libraries, the number of school libraries, and the number of books held by these two categories of libraries. The national totals for the two types of libraries and their holdings also are given. Not included are church, college, and private school libraries.

88 [Bradford, Gamaliel. Extract of a Lecture by Daniel Webster and 1793 Statistics of American Libraries.] *North American Miscellany and Dollar Magazine*, 2 (July 19, 1851), p575, 450 wds (NcU).

Daniel Webster delivered an address at the laying of the cornerstone of the new Capitol building on July 4. We copy some of his statistics about libraries. We also copy from the *Express* a more definite mention of the old libraries of the country. There were only 35 public libraries in the whole country in 1793; their aggregate number of volumes was less than 74,000. In 1851, there were 694 public libraries, excluding those in schools, with an aggregate of 2,201,632 volumes in the United States. If the libraries of district schools are added, there are over 10,000 libraries, with nearly 4 million books. In a number of institutions, we already are ahead of all other nations. (A list of the libraries in 1793 follows; estimates of the number of volumes in each are given.) The libraries of Harvard University and of Philadelphia were the largest.

89 "The Jarvis Library Sale." *Norton's Literary Gazette and Publishers' Circular*, 1 (November 15, 1851), p70, 390 wds (NcU).

Jarvis lived in Middletown, Connecticut; the sale took place in New York City.

The sale of the Jarvis library is the largest sale of a private library in this country. Agents from the most prominent libraries in the United States attended. Institutions represented included the Smithsonian Institution, Harvard College,

Yale College, General Theological Seminary of New York, College of New Jersey, Brown University, Rochester University, Andover Theological Seminary, New York State Library, New York Society Library, and the Historical Society of New York. Rochester University purchased the Complutensian Polyglot Bible for $130, and Cranmer's Bible for $26; Harvard College bought a *Vetus Testamentum Graecum* for $40; New York Theological Seminary acquired the Muratori, 37 volumes folio for $207; and Brown University was sold Duchesne's *Historical Collections* for $24.50.

90 [Announcement of Librarian's and Book-Buyer's Manual.] *Norton's Literary Gazette and Publishers' Circular*, 1 (December 15, 1851), p90 (NcU).

The entire article follows. The last sentence refers to an article that was printed in the *Gazette* for January 15, 1852 (*see* 92).

"We are able to announce that there is a work now in preparation which cannot but be looked for with great interest. It will be a LIBRARIAN'S and BOOK-BUYER'S MANUAL, intended as a complete guide for the Formation, Arrangement, Preservation, and Proper Management, of Libraries, both Public and Private, forming a volume of about 500 pages 8vo., embracing the Principles of Bibliography, 'Libraryography,' Typography, &c., &c. Such a book is very much needed, as none now exists which is sufficiently explicit and modern. Horne's *Introduction to the Study of Bibliography*, an excellent work of its kind, has become antiquated, (Published in 1814), and does not enter into those minute details which are so absolutely essential to a thorough knowledge of Books, Catalogues, Libraries, &c., &c. We shall speak more particularly of this matter in our next."

91 "Important to Librarians and Book Buyers." *Norton's Literary Gazette and Publishers' Circular*, 2 (January 15, 1852), p19, 320 wds (NcU).

This advertisement also appeared in several later issues of this periodical during 1852; the part of most interest to librarians (160 wds) is summarized below.

We have in press *The Librarian's Manual, or a Complete Guide for the Formation, Arrangement, Preservation, and Administration or Management of Public and Private Libraries*, by R. A. Guild, Librarian of Brown University, including principles of bibliography and typography, classifications for books, and statistics of libraries. Also in press, *Poole's Index to Periodical Literature*, a complete index to prominent subjects in reviews and periodicals with the names of writers when it has been possible to obtain them; one of the most valuable aids for the scholar, politician, or literary man. Charles B. Norton, Irving Book Agency, N.Y.

92 "A Permanent Book-Buyer's Manual." *Norton's Literary Gazette and Publishers' Circular*, 2 (January 15, 1852), p4, 250 wds (NcU).

We announced this book last month; we can now give further particulars. Mr. Reuben A. Guild, Librarian of Brown University, is its author. It will contain a history of printing, a history of libraries, statistics of modern libraries here and abroad, a complete list of bibliographical works and a select list for smaller libraries, a plan for the classification of books together with an abridged plan, information about rare and curious books, and principles of book selection. The proprietor of this paper will publish it and it will be a valuable and permanent work of reference.

United States

93 "Poole's Index to Periodical Literature." *Norton's Literary Gazette and Publishers' Circular*, 2 (January 15, 1852), p4, 220 wds (NcU).

Mr. William F. Poole, now connected with the Boston Athenaeum, has been engaged for some time past in compiling an index to the standard reviews of England and America. He is able to give several references to each article by examining the articles themselves rather than depending on tables of contents of volumes. He is able to give the names of all the writers in the *North American Review* and has procured some for certain other reviews. Mr. Poole published a similar but less extensive index a few years ago; the present work will contain about five times as many references. It will be brought down to the close of 1851 and will go to press immediately.

94 "Literary Correspondence [Libraries in Rochester, Buffalo, and Cleveland]." *Norton's Literary Gazette and Publishers' Circular*, 2 (February 15, 1852), p24-25 (ICN, NcU).

The parts of the article about libraries (p24-25) are summarized below.

The Rochester University Library deservedly is attracting attention due to its recent purchase of the valuable Neander Library. The Rochester Athenaeum has a collection with more than 5,000 volumes that are very satisfactorily arranged and classed; its reading room is spacious; and it subscribes to about 50 newspapers. The 3,500 volume library of the Court of Appeals shares the building with the Athenaeum. There are no public libraries in Buffalo except for the 5,500 volume library owned by the Young Men's Association. The Cleveland Library Association has 125 members and a collection of approximately 1,700 volumes; the Mercantile Library Association recently was established; and the Western Reserve Medical College has a library with about 1,000 volumes.

95 "Important to Librarians and Book Buyers." *Norton's Literary Gazette and Publishers' Circular*, 2 (November 15, 1852), p231, 150 wds (NcU).

Part of the advertisement, for publications of Charles B. Norton, is of particular interest for librarians; it is reproduced below:

"THE SUBSCRIBER HAS IN PRESS / THE LIBRARIANS' MANUAL; / OR, / A COMPLETE GUIDE FOR THE FORMATION, ARRANGEMENT, PRESERVATION, AND ADMINISTRATION OR MANAGEMENT / OF / PUBLIC AND PRIVATE LIBRARIES. / EMBRACING / THE PRINCIPLES OF BIBLIOGRAPHY AND TYPOGRAPHY: LIST OF BIBLIOGRAPHICAL WORKS; PLANS FOR THE CLASSIFICATION / OF BOOKS; STATISTICS OF LIBRARIES BOTH AT HOME AND ABROAD; &C., &C. / BY R. A. GUILD, A. M., / LIBRARIAN OF BROWN UNIVERSITY."

96 "Prof. Jewett's Cataloguing." *Norton's Literary Gazette and Publishers' Circular*, 2 (December 15, 1852), p237 (ICN, NcU).

The entire article follows.

"The London Athenaeum for October 30th, p1179, examines Prof. Jewett's plan for publishing Catalogues of Libraries, to which we have often alluded, commending its adoption, but claiming some portions of the ideas as English in their origin. We trust that the plan will before long be made public, that on this and on other points connected with it, we may express more fully our views than we have as yet been able to do."

97 "Poole's Index." *Norton's Literary Gazette and Publishers' Circular*, 3 (March 15, 1853), p39 (ICN, NcU).

The entire article follows.

"In answer to frequent inquiries concerning the appearance of this work, we are happy to say that at length the printing has commenced. The delays and difficulties incident to the publication of such a work, are almost innumerable; but they are now almost wholly overcome, and the work may be soon expected."

98 "Poole's Index." *Norton's Literary Gazette and Publishers' Circular*, 3 (March 15, 1853), p40, 240 wds (ICN).
The article summarized below is reprinted from the London *Athenaeum*.

Mr. Poole, an American librarian, is about to publish an index to recent periodical literature. The work will be, perhaps, curious rather than useful but may help to show how much can be done by a single person earnestly engaged in his work. Fourteen English periodicals and forty-two American ones will be indexed by subjects. However defective its plan, an index to 1500 volumes must be the result of long reading, classification, and correspondence. It will help to prove that indexing and cataloging are not so difficult as the officers of some of our London libraries would have people believe.

99 "Protection against Fire." *Norton's Literary Gazette and Publishers' Circular*, 3 (March 15, 1853), p38 (ICN, NcU).
The entire article follows.

"The recent injury by fire, amounting almost to the entire destruction, of the Library of Illinois College at Jacksonville, as well as the great loss sustained by the Congressional Library, should serve as warnings to those who have charge of important collections of books. We have so often seen in Libraries great carelessness in regard to the exposure to fire, that we cannot forebear to throw out one or two hints. 1. Let the Library Room if possible be fire proof. 2. Let it be remote from extra hazardous neighborhoods, from theaters, drug stores, billiard rooms, &c. 3. Let constant watchfulness be exercised over stoves and lights. 4. Let trays with handles or large baskets be always on hand for the speedy removal of books. 5. Let the Library BE FULLY INSURED."

100 [The American Congregational Union Library in New York and the Congregational Library Association in Boston.] *Norton's Literary Gazette and Publishers' Circular*, 3 (July 15, 1853), p115 (ICN, NcU).
The entire article follows.

"*The American Congregational Union* have taken rooms at No. 15 and 16 Clinton Hall, New York, and are about to commence a Library and Reading Room, for the accumulation and diffusion of religious information. In order to advance these objects, an act of incorporation has been secured. A similar organization has been formed at Boston, under the title of the Congregational Library Association, the aim of which will be to collect books, manuscripts, and other memorials illustrative of the Fathers of New England, and the congregational order of church government.

101 Osgood, Samuel. "Prospects of Popular Libraries." *Inquirer* [Christian Inquirer], 7 (September 24, 1853), p1, 2070 wds (MB, MH-AH).
Osgood's remarks were made at the opening of the Librarians' Convention, held recently in New York City; he was a delegate from the Boston Athenaeum.

Libraries are to be praised for their work in providing good reading. Rather than striving to build great centralized collections, we should develop many smaller libraries for the nation's towns. Three resolutions are offered: the first praises the few great collections but maintains that the establishment and improvement of popular libraries is a more important objective. The second calls for the development of a popular library manual that would consider methods for organizing a library society, problems of library architecture, methods of making catalogs, and methods of selecting and purchasing books. Lists of desirable books should be included. The third resolution calls upon the Business Committee to petition Congress to have the manual prepared at the Smithsonian Institution.

102 [The Need for a National Library.] *Norton's Literary Gazette and Publishers' Circular*, 3 (November 15, 1853), p195, 1130 wds (NcU).

American libraries are deficient; none meets the scholar's needs. Even the largest libraries are restrained in their purchases because of a lack of funds. We have none too many popular libraries, but in these we are rich compared to our libraries for scholars; scholars abroad are much better cared for. We are proud of the donations made to libraries in America, but donations cannot form the foundation of a great library. The country needs a library so rich that American scholars need not go to other countries. The government should create such a library. Eventually every state will need one; for now, a national library in Washington is needed, and Congress should provide it. The Congressional Library, if expanded, could serve this purpose. Some suggest that the Smithsonian Institution can serve this purpose, but its funds are too small, its purpose different, and it should remain distinct from a national library.

103 [Notes on Several American Libraries.] *National Magazine: Devoted to Literature, Art, and Religion*, 6 (March 1855), p286 (InU, NcU).

The entire article follows.

"The Newark Library Association has at present about 5,000 volumes on its shelves. — The Printers' Free Library, located at No. 3 Chambers-street, New-York, has nearly 3,000 vols. — The munificent donation of $5,000 by the Hon. Josiah Little to the city of Newburyport, for the founding of a Public Library, has been accepted, and a spacious room of the City Hall building has been set apart for this purpose. — Hon. D. S. Gregory has presented the Young Men's Christian Association of Jersey City with 2,000 volumes of literary, religious, scientific and miscellaneous works. — The new Public Hall at Lawrence, Mass., connected with the Pacific Mills, has about 1,500 carefully selected volumes. — The catalogue of the library of Rochester Athenaeum and Mechanics' Association has now between seven and eight thousand volumes, and embraces a large number of standard works."

104 [Public Libraries in the U.S.] *National Magazine: Devoted to Literature, Art, and Religion*, 6 (March 1855), p286 (InU, NcU).

The entire article follows.

"According to the census, there are 15,615 *public libraries* in the United States, and 4,636,411 volumes, of which 1,760,820 are in this state. Comparing the free with the slave states, the former have by far the most libraries. For instance, Virginia has 54, and New-York 11,013; Alabama 56, and Massachusetts 1,462; South Carolina 26, and Connecticut 164; Georgia 7; and Rhode Island 96. Of the slave states, in proportion to population, Mississippi has the most public libraries, and Virginia the fewest, although those of the latter contain a greater number of volumes than those of any slave state, excepting Louisiana, South Carolina, and Virginia.

United States

105 "Libraries in the United States." *National Magazine: Devoted to Literature, Art, and Religion,* 6 (May 1855), p479 (InU, NcU).

The entire article follows.

"Professor Jewett, of the Smithsonian Institute [*sic*], at Washington, gives the following table of the public libraries in the United States: — State libraries, 39 — 288,937 volumes; college libraries, 126 — 586,912 volumes; social libraries, 126 — 611,334 volumes; students' libraries, 142 — 254,639 volumes; seminaries and professional libraries, 227 — 320,909 volumes; scientific and historical societies' libraries, 34 — 138,901 volumes."

106 "Public Libraries." *Ladies' Repository: A Monthly Periodical, Devoted to Literature, Art, and Religion,* 16 (April 1856), p247 (InU, NcU).

The entire article follows.

"Of public libraries in the United States, there were, in 1850, more than 1,200, containing 1,446,015 volumes. There were 213 college libraries, containing 942,321 volumes. If we add those of the common schools, of Sunday schools, and of churches, the whole number of volumes could not have been less than four millions and a half. Several of the public libraries are large and well-selected. That of Harvard College has more than 85,000 volumes; the Astor Library — at New York — has nearly, if not quite as many; the Philadelphia Library has more than 60,000 volumes. The Library of Congress has at least as many."

107 Horton, R. G. "The Public Libraries of New-York." *National Magazine: Devoted to Literature, Art, and Religion,* 9 (July 1856), p95, 480 wds (InU, NcU).

The article summarized below is quoted verbatim from an unidentified source.

There are 11,718 public school libraries in the state of New York containing 1,505,370 volumes. The United States is ahead of other countries in the number of small libraries that generally diffuse books within the country. The public libraries of Paris contained 1,474,000 volumes in 1848. Only 350,000 are currently held in New York City's libraries. The 1854 *Norton's Literary Register* estimated that New York had 295,000 volumes, while Boston had 150,000; Philadelphia, 238,000; Providence, 69,300; and Albany, 87,000. Many of the prominent libraries of New York have been handicapped by financial troubles, partly caused by the costs of building new quarters. However, the future looks brighter.

108 Thomson, E. "Literary Associations." *Ladies' Repository: A Monthly Periodical, Devoted to Literature, Art, and Religion,* 17 (May 1857), p257–62 (NcU).

The article summarized below is taken from *Select London Lectures,* ed. by D. W. Clark, published by the Western Book Concern, Cincinnati.

A series of lectures may cost much more than a sizable library without providing really useful information. Good lectures are worth while because they provide stimulus to thought and bring young people together for worth-while purposes, but reading rooms can have the same effect. Newspaper reading leads to more serious reading. Periodical reading rooms lead to the formation of public libraries. Public libraries purchase only the rare and standard works rather than the common books found in homes. These libraries supply lawyers, clerics, and physicians with books they need but cannot afford to buy. Literary associations might band together after the fashion of the literary and scientific societies of Great Britain; these associations might provide examinations for advancement in commercial or government positions. Intellectual pursuits help prevent crime and other social disgraces such as drunkenness.

109 "The Late William Wood, Esq." *Ballou's Pictorial Drawing-Room Companion*, 13 (September 19, 1857), p188, 1110 wds (NcD, NcU).

Wood was born in Charlestown in 1777 and died on August 5, 1857. He is mourned because of his many humanitarian enterprises. The first library he founded was the Apprentices' Library in Boston; at about the same time he helped found what is now the Mercantile Library in Boston. Later he was responsible for founding other mechanics' and mercantile libraries in this country and England; he also worked to establish libraries in prisons, in churches, and on ships. Wood was not wealthy; he mainly persuaded others to act. Mr. F. W. Lincoln, Jr. has supplied these facts. (A portrait of Wood, painted for the Apprentices' Library Association of Canandaigua, accompanies the article.)

110 "The Library." *Harvard Advocate*, 4 (January 28, 1868), p145–46 (InU, NcD).

The Harvard Library was formerly the largest collection of books in the country; the Library of Congress is now the largest, as it should be. The Harvard Library has not been growing as rapidly as have the Astor, Boston Public, and Boston Athenaeum libraries. The 1866 Astor report notes $3,375.83 spent for books and binding. During the year 587 volumes and 63 pamphlets were purchased; 198 volumes and 112 pamphlets were donated. In 1867, the Boston Athenaeum spent $8,895.63 for materials and binding, purchasing 1,723 volumes and 2,122 pamphlets; 395 volumes and 592 pamphlets were donated. The Boston Public in 1866–67 added by purchase 7,395 volumes and 104 pamphlets, received donations of 1,465 volumes and 7,769 pamphlets, and acquired 337 volumes and 4 pamphlets by exchange. That library spent $16,879.59 for materials and binding. In 1866–67, Harvard expended for books and binding, only $4,285.97 for about 3,000 volumes. The library's condition needs improvement. Are not the alumni able to provide needed funds?

111 [Reports and Catalogues of Libraries.] *Nation*, 8 (June 3, 1869), p435, 520 wds (NcU).

Several recent reports and catalogs have reached us from libraries that are public but not free. A joint stock library in Skowhegan, Maine is scarcely a year and a half old. At Portland, Oregon, the Public Library Association, in its sixth year, has 144 subscribers. As on the Atlantic coast, light literature is heavily read there; romances constitute 73 percent of the circulation. The catalog of the Young Men's Library Association of Milwaukee is bulky and well printed. The Mercantile Library Association of St. Louis has 29,810 volumes and a fine property worth over $200,000. A catalog from the Skowhegan Library is wretchedly printed and poorly arranged; the Milwaukee catalog is much better. The St. Louis report is bound with a lecture by Captain Silas Bent about ocean currents and climate. The practice of binding substantial lectures with library publications is good; people will preserve them.

112 Perkins, F. B. "Library Catalogues. First Paper—Introductory." *American Publisher and Bookseller*, 2 (July 1869), p4–5 (MB).

Each of the libraries in the United States should have a new catalog every 10 years and a supplement in the intermediate 5 years. Fast-growing libraries need catalogs every 6 years, supplements every 3. Much labor and thought must be expended to achieve this goal, and many problems arise in making catalogs. Professor Jewett's pamphlet on cataloging is the only treatise on the subject printed in this country that I know of. Jewett gives full titles, which make for bulky catalogs. My cataloging doctrine calls for short titles, an alphabetical listing of authors and titles with a secondary classification by subjects, a card catalog in the library itself, and an octavo printed format. Librarians and customers do not use catalogs in the same way. Customers usually remember titles or subjects. Persons interested in cataloging should write to the author of this paper.

113 Perkins, F. B. "Library Catalogues. Second Paper: the Catalogue Title." *American Publisher and Bookseller*, 2 (August 1869), p6–8 (MB).
The article refers to an article in the issue of the *American Publisher and Bookseller* (see *112*).
The matter of using short titles instead of long titles in library catalogs has been controversial. I began with a belief in the long title principle, but now favor short titles for circulating libraries and for practical purposes, as they are much cheaper to make. The parts of a title, for a short title printed catalog, are: heading, title proper, size, imprint, and shelf-mark. Rules for headings follow under the classes of author's name, prefixes, compound surnames, translations, corporate authors, United States, pseudonyms and anonyms, women's names, the Bible, joint publications, collective titles, first or Christian names as headings, and titles of honor. The catalog of the Library of the Young Men's Association of Milwaukee has been received.

114 "George Peabody's Gifts to Libraries and Institutes." *American Bibliopolist*, 1 (December 1869), p373 (NcD, OC).
The entire article follows.
"For Institutes in Danvers and Peabody, $250,000; Peabody Museum in Salem, $150,000; Newburyport, for a library $30,000; Free Public Library in Georgetown, Mass., $100,000; Philipps [sic] Academy, Andover, $30,000; Massachusetts Historical Society, $20,000; Harvard College, for Museum and Professorship of American Archaeology and Ethnology, $150,000; Yale College, for Museum and Natural History, $150,000; Peabody Institute in Baltimore, $1,000,000; Maryland Historical Society, $20,000; Kenyon College, $25,000; Public Library in Post Mills, Thetford, Vermont, $10,000; Southern Educational Fund, $3,000,000. These figures speak more than volumes."

115 Spofford, A. R. "Public Libraries of the United States." *American Bibliopolist*, 1 (December 1869), p356–58 (ICU, OC).
From an article in the October 27, 1869, *New York Tribune*.
No American library contains 200,000 volumes; more than twenty in Europe are larger than that. (The size of the ten largest libraries in the United States is given.) In order to serve the legislators and other people, the Library of Congress should complete its subject catalog and should be open in the evenings. Astor's gift for a library was the largest in the United States; the Astor Library, also, should be open in the evenings. The bequest of James Rush to the Philadelphia Library Company of over $1,000,200 has recently been accepted by the stockholders despite its senseless barring of periodicals and newspapers. Eleven states authorize the use of taxes for libraries. Great libraries should collect broadly; weeding should be carefully done because what one man judges to be trash may be of importance to another. (A number of instances are cited from literature and history in which the weeding of collections caused problems.)

116 [Boston as the Intellectual Center of the United States.] *Nation*, 9 (Dec. 9, 1869), p506–08 (NcU).
The part of the article about libraries summarized below (p506) is partially reprinted in *American Bibliopolist* 2 (February 1870) (*see 172*).

A representation of half the globe, including all civilized portions, has been issued on which Boston appears as the geographical as well as intellectual and moral center. Measured by private libraries, we presume Boston could not now pretend to be the intellectual center of the United States, even if competing with Philadelphia alone. Its Public Library does not even approach Joseph Drexel's musical library in Philadelphia, of which a catalog of the nearly 3,000 volumes has just been printed. This collection is said to be surpassed only by the British Museum and the Leipzig libraries. In Philadelphia itself, the centers are changing as the Academy of Natural Sciences, the Historical Society, and the Academy of Fine Arts move into locations further west in the city.

117/8 Spofford, Ainsworth R. "The Public Libraries in the United States." *Journal of Social Science, Containing the Proceedings of the American Association*, no. 2 (1870), p92–114 (NcU).
The article is the paper read by Spofford before the general meeting of the American Social Science Association on October 26, 1869 in New York City.

The first record of books dedicated to a public purpose is an entry found in the 1620 records of the Virginia Company. Harvard College founded its library in 1638; New York opened its first public library in 1700; and the Philadelphia Library was founded in 1731 through the efforts of Benjamin Franklin. The Library of Congress came into existence in 1800, was destroyed in 1814 by the British, and resumed operation after Jefferson's collection was purchased. It now possesses 183,000 volumes and 50,000 pamphlets. The Boston Athenaeum opened in 1806 and now has a library of 100,000 volumes. New York's Astor Library was opened in 1854 as a result of the generosity of John Jacob Astor. The earliest statistics on libraries were gathered in 1831; I have compiled a table showing the ten largest libraries in the United States for 1869. There exist many different types of libraries, and for each type the problem of book selection is a difficult, albeit an important, consideration.

119 [New Titles on Reprinted Books.] *Nation*, 10 (April 21, 1870), p256 (NcU).
After complaining about the issuing of "new editions" without revising the contents of the books, the author turns to the habit of issuing old books under new titles. The part about libraries is copied below.

"There is still another practice which is especially irritating to librarians, and that is the revival of old and forgotten books under a new title, without any warning to the public...Librarians do their best to exclude these new titles from their shelves, but they cannot escape the annoyance of constant enquiries for them, and of repeated explanations; and the wrath they bring down upon themselves from the publishers whose sales they thus injure, it is easy to conceive of."

120 [The Spread of Public Libraries.] *Nation*, 10 (May 26, 1870), p337, 250 wds (NcU).
We offer no apologies for returning often to the subject of the spread of public libraries. Newport, R.I. is receiving, from an eminent citizen, Mr. Christopher Townsend, a "People's Library" on condition that it not be named for him and on condition that he selects the 7,000 volumes; it will be combined with the Free Library, already started, making in all 10,000 volumes. The town also

has a mechanics' library and the Redwood Library, plundered by the British. In Philadelphia, British officers in contrast, scrupulously respected libraries. In that city, the Apprentices' Library celebrates its fiftieth anniversary by raising an endowment fund and offering its services to adults. It has served some fifty thousand persons, many of whom are now feeling in their pockets to make proper acknowledgement of services received.

121 "Our Two Great Libraries." *Appletons' Journal: a Magazine of General Literature*, 5 (March 17, 1871), p299, 280 wds (NcU).
The latest annual report from the Library of Congress notes a total collection of 197,668 volumes; the latest report from the Astor Library claims 145,558 volumes. Figures from the Astor Library also indicate that the most popular books are those of British literature, excluding novels, which claimed only seven per cent of the readers. The special utility of this library is illuminated by the fact that of the more than five thousand readers who visited the alcoves, almost half selected works on inventions, theology, and the fine arts.

122 [Largest American Libraries.] *The American Bibliopolist*, 4 (February 1872), p66 (IEN, OC).
Entire article follows. Item 580 corrects information about the Boston Public.
"The ten largest libraries in the United States, with the number of books in each, are as follows: Library of Congress, 236,846; Boston Public Library, 153,000; Astor Library, New York, 138,000; Harvard Library, Cambridge, 118,000; Mercantile Library, New York, 104,500; Athenaeum Library, Boston, 100,000; Philadelphia Library, 85,000; New York State Library, Albany, 76,000; New York Society Library, 57,000; Yale College Library, 50,000."

123 Beecher, Henry Ward. "Should the Public Libraries Be Open on Sunday?" *New Outlook* [Christian Union], 5 (May 1, 1872), p379-81 (InU, IEG).
The address summarized below was delivered at Cooper Union, April 22.
On the basis of the teaching of Jesus that the Sabbath was made for man, not man for the Sabbath, libraries and reading rooms ought to be opened on Sundays in the afternoon and evening for the benefit of man. Instead of taking young men away from church services the Sunday use of libraries will lead them into the services. If Sunday opening would deprive library staffs of their day of rest, YMCA volunteers could be used. The Mercantile Library in Philadelphia has tried Sunday opening for two years and found it successful, no evil results being apparent. The traditional Sabbath has been of real benefit only to the prosperous; the poorer classes have very little opportunity to observe a Sabbath that provides leisure or moral betterment.

124 Homans, I. S. "A Library Number of the 'Weekly'." *Publishers' Weekly*, 4 (July 26, 1873), p119, 170 wds (NcU).
The article summarized below is a letter from Mr. Homans to the *Weekly*, followed by a short note by the editor.
I suggest that you publish an issue of your paper once or twice a year to be sent to every public library in the United States and Canada. If such an issue contained a list of libraries, with the number of volumes in each, and the date of its establishment, you would probably have orders for several hundred copies and could procure ten or twenty additional pages of advertisements from publishers. My firm would be willing to have one page at $25.00 For each publisher to send out his own trade list to libraries is quite expensive; in the proposed publication,

United States

numerous publishers could advertise; librarians would preserve it. (The editor comments that the suggestion should be considered; the "Library Number" published last October has given much satisfaction.)

125 "The Library Corner." *Publishers' Weekly*, 5 (January 10, 1874), p33–34, 190 wds (NcU).

Under this heading we propose, at the suggestion of an active librarian, to gather information of interest to managers of libraries and those interested in libraries. Items will include practical suggestions, descriptions of new methods, summaries of library reports, items about personnel, and news as to benefactions. Libraries have at present no organ of communication; they need the same information as booksellers and are to some extent already subscribers to the *Weekly*. The frequency and extent of this department will depend upon the supply of material for it and upon the increase in subscriptions from libraries.

126 Fentress, George W. "The 'Library Corner'." *Publishers' Weekly*, 5 (February 7, 1874), p136–37, 170 wds (NcU).

The article summarized below is a letter to the editor of the *Weekly* from Fentress, who was Librarian of the San Jose, California, Library Association.

I was glad to see the "Library Corner" in the *Publishers' Weekly*; I enclose our pamphlet (not described). A list of real names of authors of pseudonymous and anonymous works would be helpful; could you prepare one? Please let us know, in the "Library Corner," when the next edition of the *Encyclopaedia Britannica* will be published. I suggest that you secure a librarian correspondent for the "Library Corner" from each state and from each foreign country; if so, instead of a "corner" you could have a regular department; I shall send you California items soon. We need men educated for library work; it is a distinct profession, that should have special training.

127 "The Library Corner." *Publishers' Weekly*, 5 (February 7, 1874), p141, 190 wds (NcU).

This article is the same, except for slight changes in wording, as the one with the same title in the January 10, 1874 issue of the *Weekly* (see 125).

128 [Lists of Authors Using Pseudonyms.] *Publishers' Weekly*, 5 (February 7, 1874), p141 (NcU).

The entire article follows.

"In reply to an inquiry regarding the preparation of a key to anonyms and pseudonyms we would say that it would hardly pay us to undertake such work. We would suggest to librarians the plan of having a copy of Hamst's 'Hand-Book for Fictitious Names,' interleaved, and to complete the list from recent catalogues and daily experience. A careful examination of the recent Boston Public Library Catalogues will at once supply ample material. 'A Key to some *noms de plume*' (and anonyms), published by us in the 'Trade Circular Annual for 1871,' might also be used as a basis for preparing such a list."

129 [Annual Reports of Libraries.] *Nation*, 18 (March 5, 1874), p157, 1,000 wds (NcU).

Part of the text of this article was quoted in another article in *Publishers' Weekly* for March 14, 1874 (see 185). The table at the end of the *Nation* article was reproduced, slightly changed, in a second article in the same issue of *Publishers' Weekly* (see 249).

About this time of year the annual reports of the great public libraries begin to appear in print. The General Theological Library of Boston was founded in 1860 and now owns 11,000 volumes. Its books circulated this year to borrowers in fifty-four New England towns and villages. Bucknell Library of the Crozer Theological Seminary is at Chester, Pennsylvania. A pamphlet about it quotes opinions of experts as to its high quality; it is especially rich in Baptist history. The twentieth annual report of the Wisconsin Historical Society shows the usual steady and solid increase of its library. In the Public Library of Lawrence, Massachusetts, about one-fourth of the books are fiction; these provide about three-fourths of the circulation. (A table shows the relative popularity of twelve novelists in the Lawrence and Quincy Public Libraries and the Bangor Mercantile Association Library.)

130 Fletcher, William J. [sic]. "Statistics of Public Library Reading." *Nation*, 18 (March 26, 1874), p201-02 (NcU).

A letter to the editor is summarized below; Fletcher was librarian of the Free Library of Lawrence, Massachusetts; his middle initial was "I."

Some wrong inferences are drawn from library statistics. Many families buy and read historical, religious and other standard literature and send to the library for fiction. Again, it cannot be inferred that a taste for frivolous reading is fostered and increased by public libraries. Rather, the taste for sensational literature is *discovered* by the library. Here are the facts: (1) The demand already exists; sales of this literature prove this; (2) The establishment of a public library lessens these sales; (3) No published library statistics show any increase over the years in the proportionate demand for the lightest reading. Finally, I hope that the increasing interest in these matters will result in some such measure as the formation of a national association of librarians which would promote uniformity in library administration and give us humbler members of the profession contact with its greater lights.

131 "The Minor Librarian." *Every Saturday; a Journal of Choice Reading*, 4th ser., 1 (March 28, 1874), p363, 1050 wds (KyL).

The Census reports that there are 56,015 libraries other than private ones in the United States and only 213 librarians. We may infer that thousands of libraries are managed by persons who are not professional librarians. The readers of books and magazines in this country are mostly between the ages of 10 and 25. They devour the contents of libraries of all kinds; much of our later education is obtained through independent study. The minor librarians, those who manage small libraries, should be selected with care. They should be intelligent, quick-witted, and sympathetic, and should know where to find facts for girls and boys. The librarian should be a friend to the borrower; the librarian's experience, knowledge, and taste will turn the scales in favor of sound, honest literature.

132 [Libraries in Southbridge and Hyde Park, Mass., and in San Francisco.] *Literary World*, Boston, 4 (May 1874), p190 (NcU).

The entire article follows.

"The annual report of the Southbridge (Mass.) Public Library shows that of the 8,547 books taken out from that institution in the last year, 5,409, or 64 per cent, belong to the department of fiction. From the annual report of the San Francisco Mercantile Library we learn that the total number of volumes in the library, Jan. 1, 1874, was 36,356, — an increase of 3,023 in 1873. The total number of volumes taken out during that year was 88,751, of which 66,985, or more than 74 per cent, were fiction. The catalogue of the Public Library recently opened at Hyde Park is very creditable to the skill and industry of the Librarian, Mr. W. E. Foster."

133 [*Poole's Index.*] *Publishers' Weekly*, 5 (May 2, 1874), p428 (NcU).
The entire article follows.
"A communication in 'The Library Corner' notes the desire of many librarians for a continuation of 'Poole's Index.' We wish this valuable work could be b[r]ought up to date, and shall be glad to have subscriptions offered to Mr. Poole through that department of *The Weekly*; but from our own success with the Finding List subscriptions, we are not hopeful of the result."

134 B., M. [*Poole's Index.*] *Publishers' Weekly*, 5 (May 2, 1874), p430, 280 wds (NcU).
This article appeared in the "Library Corner" section of the *Weekly*.
" 'The Library Corner' seems *the* place to agitate for a new edition of *Poole's Index to Periodical Literature*. Librarians on all sides express a great desire for one and many are making their own manuscript supplements, expensive to provide and unsatisfactory in use. Now, in an age of cheap printing, it could be done if those who feel the need will subscribe enough to justify publication. We might look to the Library of Congress to produce the work but just now that library cannot handle much extra labor. Both American and English libraries need, at once, an index with annual supplements, to be cumulated at ten-year intervals. Mr. Poole has the work in an advanced stage; the 'corner' should have a subscription list. Prof. [William L.] Montague, librarian at Amherst College, will subscribe $100 for six copies; who will follow the lead of Amherst?"

135 "Libraries." *Appletons' Journal: a Magazine of General Literature*, 11 (May 9, 1874), p606, 1240 wds (NcU).
Our nation is too young to have accumulated libraries as large as those of Europe, but no other country has as many public libraries in relation to its population. In the last twenty years, while the United States' population has grown 67%, the number of libraries has increased 267%. There are fifteen libraries that hold more than 50,000 volumes; the largest of these is the Congressional Library. Most of the larger collections of valuable books are associated with colleges and universities. The most impressive aspect of American library growth is the number of free public libraries; there are now 1,101 of them with an accumulated total of 1,237,430 volumes. New England, New York, and Michigan claim four-fifths of these institutions. Circulation records show that 75% of the books selected for general reading are fiction.

136 [Registers of the Company of Stationers Transcript.] *Publishers' Weekly*, 6 (July 11, 1874), p39 (NcU).
The entire article follows; it is corrected in the August 15, 1874 issue of *Publishers' Weekly (see 1068)*.
"It is stated that not one of the libraries or historical societies of the United States have yet subscribed for Mr. Edward Arber's proposed literal transcript of the Registers of the Company of Stationers of London, between 1554 and 1640, which, he says, 'are to the entire Saxon race in respect to the books of our Golden Age what Domesday Book is to the inhabitants of England as to our Iron Age.' We trust this deficiency will be immediately remedied. Mr. Arber may be

addressed at 87 Augustine Road, Camden Square, N.W., London. The edition will not exceed 460 copies, the price being 20 guineas, large paper, 50 guineas, and all copies not subscribed for by publication day will then be destroyed."

137 ["Uniform Trade List Annual."] *Publishers' Weekly*, 7 (January 30, 1875), p110, 310 wds (NcU).

This being our Library Number, we wish to call the attention of librarians to the *Uniform Trade List Annual*, both for their shelves as a matter of literary need and for their offices as a volume for daily use. (A quotation from the London *Bookseller* is given, praising the *List*.) We cannot supply the 1873 volume, even to libraries, but the 1874 volume is still available at $1.50. The *Annual Reference Lists* are also essential to progressive libraries.

138 "What and How to Read." *Literary World*, Boston, 6 (August 1875), p34–35 (NcU).

This is a letter reviewing *What and How to Read* by G. A. F. Van Rhyn, published by Appleton in 1875. The letter is signed "A Librarian," with the place and date "Hyde Park, Mass., July 16, 1875;" it was possibly written by W. E. Foster, head of he public library in that town.

Every work on bibliography is welcomed by those in charge of libraries, whether it furnished information needed by the librarian in cataloging or contains classified lists for the public. This book promises to include "noteworthy" books published in the last five years; however, it includes many older books. Many novels in it are not worthy of being included, and several fine ones are omitted. (Examples are given.) Several books are misclassified; one on American Indians is put under India, and a book on Cuba is put under Africa. (Many other errors are mentioned.) As a guide to users of libraries it is untrustworthy; with some omissions it could be called *A Classified List of the Publications of D. Appleton & Co.*

139 B., M. "From a Clergyman and a Librarian." *Publishers' Weekly*, 8 (December 11, 1875), p909, 260 wds (NcU).

A librarian in New Jersey who is also a clergyman speaks of the *Weekly* as "the most valuable and useful publication of the kind for our purposes of any we receive." He advocates that the *New York Evening Post*'s series of articles on the "Bookmakers" be published in a volume. He recommends cutting off all discounts to professional men, confining discounts to the regular trade and libraries. As a librarian, he would cheerfully sustain the 20 percent rule. As to the *Post* articles, the paper decided to leave the matter of publication in book form to the author; usually the demand for such articles is not large enough to justify their collection in book form.

140 "Library Statistics." *Publishers' Weekly*, 8 (December 11, 1875), p911, 330 wds (NcU).

It should certainly be a subject of very deep regret that the only general annual library statistics are the ones in the annual report of the Commissioner of Education. However, the Department deserves credit for the care with which these very limited statistics are compiled. The number of libraries reported in 1870 was 152; in 1871, 180; in 1872, 251; in 1873, 351, and in 1874, 340. (The numbers of volumes in 1874 are given for several kinds of libraries.) The Commissioner mentions a work soon to be issued on the history and management of libraries in the United States which will contain statistics from as many libraries as possible. The Centennial Commission has recognized library work as a separate class within the field of education, for purposes of representation in the Centennial Exhibition.

Types of Libraries

Agricultural Libraries

141 "Catalogue of an Agricultural Library." *American Farmer*, 2 (June 16, 1820), p93–94 (InU, NcU).

The article, summarized below, reprinted the three letters received by George W. Jeffreys in reply to his request for a list of books for an agricultural library. The letter from John Taylor is dated August 1816; the one from Thomas Jefferson, March 1817, and the one from John Adams, July 1817.

Taylor suggests the writings of Arthur Young, the volumes published by the Agricultural Society of Philadelphia, the books by Tull and Davy, and the proceedings of the Board of Agriculture in England. Jefferson appends a list of about fifty-four titles to his letter, and answers a query about horizontal ploughing. Several of the books are in French, Italian, or Latin. Adams refers Jeffreys' letter to the corresponding secretary of the Massachusetts Agricultural Society. Adams says his knowledge is superficial but suggests Tull and Duhammel whom he had read fifty or sixty years ago.

142 Peters, Richard. [Letter to George W. Jeffreys.] *American Farmer*, 2 (December 29, 1820), p318–19 (InU, NcU).

This is a reply, sent from Belmont, near Philadelphia, to Jeffreys' request for a list of books suitable for an agricultural library. The part about libraries (200 wds) is summarized below.

An agricultural library should have works that will amuse as well as those that will instruct. The effort at establishing a library is commendable; a library that I founded has improved the minds and the agricultural practices of my neighbors. You should order immediately Dickson's work on agriculture, Lord Dundonald's *Connexion between Chemistry and Agriculture*, and others. In Philadelphia you can purchase Sir Humphrey Davy's *Agricultural Chemistry*.

143 "Town and County Libraries." *Genesee Farmer*, 11 (December 1850), p289 (InU, NcU).

The entire article follows.

"The opportunity afforded to establish town and county agricultural libraries, we hope, will not be forgotten. Although *fifty dollars* is but a small sum for a library, yet it will furnish most of the good agricultural works published in this country, and form a nucleus, to which additions can be made as found necessary."

144 "Farmers' Libraries." *American Agriculturist*, 13 (January 10, 1855), p282, 600 wds (InU, IaAS).

Every farmer should acquire and use a library of periodicals and books, which are now so readily available at low cost. the excuse that the farmer's money is gone for other needs and investments before he comes to books is not the real reason why more farmers do not collect libraries. Too many lack any real desire to read and study about their vocation. In addition to home libraries, every farming community needs to have a farmers' library. This collection would provide the more costly reference books, and should acquire the annual transactions of the various state and county agricultural societies. Such a library could be the basis for organizing a local farmers' club; if such a club already exists, a library can give it new energy.

145 Sawtell, Rowland, W. "Circulating Library." *Genesee Farmer*, 19, 2nd ser. (April 1858), p131, 430 wds (InU, NcU).
(A letter to the editor. Sawtell has placed fifth in the competition for the January premiums. The prize is $12 worth of agricultural books.) I intend to use these books, along with others I already own, to form a farmer's circulating library. Those who think that agricultural literature is too dry are of an abnormal state of mind from reading too much fiction. Agriculture is a subject of nature that offers a wide range of study, both pleasurable and profitable. Other agents who have won premiums should consider forming circulating libraries for the benefit of the farmers in their localties.

Agricultural Library Associations

146 "Farmers' Libraries." *American Agriculturist*, 20 (November 1861), p335, 300 wds (InU, NcU).
The only way for individual farmers to have all the books they might find useful is to form agricultural subscription libraries. A membership fee of one or two dollars per year would be a sound investment, as the books of such a library could help provide improvements in agricultural yields and equipment.

Agricultural Society Libraries

147 "Premiums for 1851!" *Genesee Farmer*, 11 (December 1850), p290, 1050 wds (InU, NcU).
The article summarized below also appeared in the same periodical in vol. 12 (January 1851), on p31.
As an aid to establishing agricultural libraries a premium of a library valued at $50 will be given to the county in which the greatest number of subscriptions to the *Genesee Farmer* is taken by April 16. The books are to be kept as a county agricultural library and cared for by the agricultural society. A library of $30 in value, to serve as a town agricultural library, will be given to the town in which the greatest number of subscriptions is sold. Since these premiums are likely to be won in the state of New York, libraries of the same values as those for New York will be given to the county and town outside New York State in which the greatest number of subscriptions is taken.

United States

148 "Premiums for 1851!" *Genesee Farmer*, 12 (January 1851), p31, 1050 wds (InU, NcU).
This article is identical to item 147.

149 "Premiums." *Genesee Farmer*, 12 (June 1851), p147, 530 wds (InU, NcU).
The article summarized below refers to the contest announced in the same periodical, vol. 11 (December 1850) *(see 147)*.
(An announcement of premium winners for securing the greatest number of subscriptions to *The Genesee Farmer*). Noted is that fifty dollars worth of books for use as a county agricultural library was won by Ontario County, New York and Calhoun County, Michigan. Marshall, Michigan appears to be the town receiving the greatest number of copies and is apparently the winner of $30 worth of books to be used as a town agricultural library. (Individuals who won premiums are also listed.)

150 "Premiums for 1852!" *Genesee Farmer*, 12 (November 1851), p269, 260 wds (InU, NcU).
The article summarized below was also in vol. 12 (December 1851), p292.
As an aid in establishing county agricultural libraries, $40 worth of books to be used as a county agricultural library will be sent to the New York county from which the greatest number of subscriptions to the *Genesee Farmer* are received by April 15, 1852. A premium of the same value will be given to the county outside New York that provides the greatest number of subscriptions. Books worth $25 will be given to the New York county and to the county outside New York that have the second highest numbers of subscribers. These books are also to be used as county agricultural libraries. Duplicate prizes for New York and the other states are offered because it is expected that New York counties will win both premiums if only two are offered.

151 "Premiums." *Genesee Farmer*, 13 (July 1852), p223, 340 wds (InU, NcU).
The article gives the results of the contest announced in the same periodical, vol. 12 (November 1851) *(see item 150)*. The part of the article about libraries follows.
"COUNTY PREMIUMS. 1st Chautaque [sic] County, N.Y., *Forty Dollars* in agricultural books, for the greatest number of copies of the *Genesee Farmer* taken in any county, being 490. This Library, according to the offer, is 'to be kept as a County Agricultural Library, under the care of the Agricultural Society.' 2d. Steuben County, N.Y., *Twenty-five Dollars* in agricultural books, for the next greatest number, (473) on the same conditions as above.
"COUNTY PREMIUMS OUT OF NEW YORK. 1st. Erie County, Pa., an Agricultural Library worth *Forty Dollars*, for the greatest number of copies of the *Farmer* taken in any county out of the State of New York, (333). 2d. Calhoun County, Mich., *Twenty-five Dollars* as above, for the next greatest number taken in any county out of the State of New York, (216). Selections of books can be made by those entitled to them, or the choice left to us. Those entitled to premiums will please order."

152 "Premiums for 1853." *Genesee Farmer*, 13 (November 1852), p357, 860 wds (InU, NcU).
As an aid in establishing county agricultural libraries, $40 worth of agricultural books will be sent to the New York county and to the county outside New York state from which the greatest number of subscriptions to the *Genesee*

Farmer are received. Books valued at $25 will be sent to the New York county and the county outside the state of New York from which the second greatest number of subscriptions are received. The books are to be used as county agricultural libraries, and will be managed by an appropriate agricultural society.

153 "Premiums for 1853." *Genesee Farmer*, 13 (December 1852), p387, 860 wds (InU, NcU).
This article is identical to item 152.

College and University Libraries

154 "View of the American Colleges, 1831." *Congregational Education Society. Quarterly Journal* [American Education Society. Quarterly Register], 3 (May 1831), p294–97 (ICN).
This is a set of three tables that contain various kinds of information about a number of colleges. In the first table (p294–95), figures for volumes in the college libraries and for volumes in the student society libraries are given for most of the 49 colleges listed.

155 "Education and Literary Institutions." *Congregational Education Society. Quarterly Journal* [American Quarterly Register], 5 (May 1833), p273–333 (NcU).
The article reviews the educational institutions in each state, including elementary schools, private academies, public schools, and colleges. For many institutions there is some information concerning the library, such as the size of the collection, the existence of special library rooms or buildings, and the name of the librarian if he is a faculty member. The article concludes with a table of information about the colleges, including information about the number of volumes in each college's library. The 62 colleges listed have 207,990 volumes in their combined libraries, and 88,382 volumes in their student libraries.

156 "Foreign Donations for Libraries." *American Annals of Education*, 3d ser., 4 (December 1834), p579 (NcU).
The entire article follows.
"The British Government have recently made the liberal donation of 80 folio volmes to each of the fifteen principal college libraries in the United States, and also to six other important city libraries, including the Atheneum, [sic] of Boston. These volumes contain a collection of ancient documents and state papers, recently printed by order of Parliament."

157 [Incorporated Colleges and Universities in the United States.] *Biblical Repository and Classical Review* [Biblical Repository and Quarterly Observer], 5 (April 1835), p481 (NcU).
The part of the article about libraries follows.
"The volumes of books, possessed by these 79 colleges, including the social libraries of the students, is 350,000. Subtracting the 40,000 of the Harvard

library, the remainder, 310,000, would give, on an average, about 4,000 volumes to each of the colleges."

158 Porter, N., Jr. "A Plea for Libraries, With Especial Reference to the Wants of Western Institutions." *Biblical Repository and Classical Review*, 3rd ser., 4 (January 1848), p166–86 (NcU).

Buildings are often thought more important to American colleges, such as Yale, than libraries. (The reasons for having good libraries are discussed.) Instructors call in vain for libraries to aid teaching and scholarship. Education means learning how to use books wisely; the educated man needs better libraries to keep his scholarship fresh and current. As a stronghold of truth and power, a good library is especially needed in a new country to protect from those whose slight knowledge gained from reading leads them to error. A good library reminds a student of his task as a scholar, and stimulates him to pursue questions. Libraries are essential to combat systems of error such as infidelity and Romanism; great Protestant leaders recognized the need for reading and learning.

159 [Sumner, W. G.] "The 'Ways and Means' for Our Colleges." *Nation*, 11 (September 8, 1870), p152–54 (NcU).

Sumner is identified as the author of this article in Daniel C. Haskell's *The Nation, Volumes 1-105, New York, 1865–1917, Indexes of Titles and Contributors*, 1953, v. 2, p472. The part about libraries (on p152) is copied below.

"The library stands among the most important of the instrumentalities of education. A good library belongs to the definition of a college or university. An institution which cannot buy new books which are being continually produced in every department of science, is doomed to become a fossil. Weakness in this particular does not strike the popular mind, in its judgment of a college, so distinctly as weakness in many others, but there is no defect more fatal, or more important in the view of those who hold a high theory of what a college ought to be and do. The purchase of books, however, involves money and resources, and we are thrown back again upon the same vulgar necessity."

Commercial Circulating Libraries

160 "A Needed Reform." *Literary World*, Boston, 2 (May 1872), p184, 250 wds (NcU).

Social science has an opportunity to reform the literary taste of the masses in our cities and large towns. The proprietor of a circulating library recently said that it was impossible to get books trashy enough for his customers. He said that they neglect Scott, Cooper and Dickens; Mrs. Southworth has been their standard, but they are beginning to have a belief that there are still lower depths and are beginning to long to fathom them. A person passing along our streets, as well, can see dozens of boys reading vicious weekly papers and can see half-grown girls reading exciting dime novels. Police reports mention frequent crimes that are the direct result of vicious literature. Some dealers have refused to sell it; if the news companies would follow their example, the evil might be partly repressed. However, we supposed that their profits are too great.

Historical Society Libraries

161 "Historical Societies in the United States." *Norton's Literary Gazette and Publishers' Circular*, n.s. 2 (February 15, 1855), p70–72 (MnU).
The article was to be continued but its continuation has not been found.
The article mainly consists of information about the history and present condition of twelve American historical societies, part of which is presented in this issue. For eleven of the societies, information about their libraries is given: typically, the number of volumes, the nature of the manuscript collection, the space available, and a reference to a catalog if one has been published.

Law Libraries

162 Hackett, F. W. "A Word or Two About Law Libraries." *Albany Law Journal*, 2 (October 29, 1870), p332–33 (NcU).
The article also was printed in *Legal Gazette*, 2 (November 4, 1870) (*see 163*).
It is true that a lawyer can become learned without reading many books. Only recently have we had large and well-arranged law libraries in this country. The Dane Hall library at Harvard is more nearly complete than British law libraries. In several American cities there are good collections. Libraries are not as large in the West, but when I was in Dubuque, Iowa, recently, I found that lawyers there had contributed from their private collections to form a law library. Still, a young lawyer should not depend too heavily on cases; he should learn to establish points by means of his general knowledge.

163 Hackett, F. W. "A Word about Law Libraries." *Legal Gazette*, 2 (November 4, 1870), p348, 1500 wds (NcD-L).
This article is the same as the one appearing in the *Albany Law Journal*, 2 (October 29, 1870) (*see 162*).

Lyceums

164 "American Lyceum." *American Annals of Education* [American Journal of Education], 3 (December 1828), p715–21 (NcU).
Following is a summary of the fifth statement concerning libraries submitted to a meeting in Boston on the subject of the American Lyceum (p719–20).
It is regrettable that such a benevolent institution as the library has not fulfilled the highest expectations of its founders and friends. In order to cultivate inquiry and to induce a lasting taste for reading among farmers, mechanics, youths, and children, who are the hope and strength of our country, weekly meetings or exercises on diverse subjects should be arranged in conjunction with the library.

165 "Results of Lyceums." *American Annals of Education*, 3d ser., 1 (November 1831), p526–29 (NcU).

The Committee of the American Lyceum presented a series of statements which attest to the practical value of lyceums; the statement about libraries (p528) follows.

A deep and general regret has been expressed that town and village libraries are but little read, or that they are entirely neglected and scattered. The cause for this regret is removed by the meetings of Lyceums. The moment that young people come together for mutual instruction, in subjects of useful knowledge, they call for books. The old library is looked up, or a new one formed, and when the members are not conversing with each other, they are perhaps conversing with their books.

Mechanics' Libraries

166 "Libraries for the People." *Norton's Literary Gazette and Publishers' Circular*, n.s. 2 (May 15, 1855), p207, 270 wds (MnU).

A means of instruction and profitable amusement is now offered to organized bodies of workingmen in the United States. Mr. William Maclure left a considerable estate for the diffusion of knowledge among institutions, libraries, or clubs for manual laborers. The Supreme Court of Indiana has just upheld the will. The executors are authorized to give up to $500 to any club with a reading and lecture room and a library of at least 100 volumes. Mr. Charles B. Norton, proprietor of this paper, has already helped several organizations apply and is willing to help others. Mr. Maclure was a remarkable man. Besides his business labors, he found time for scientific studies; he was a geologist, he wrote on political economy, and he was the patron of Thomas Say, the naturalist.

Mercantile Libraries

167 "Mercantile Libraries in the United States." *American Annals of Education* [American Journal of Education], 1 (March 1826), p188, 360 wds (InU, NcU).

(The article consists of several brief news items on the mercantile libraries of Philadelphia, New York and Boston.) The Philadelphia library has 1,500 volumes and charges an annual subscription of $2.00. The New York Library contains 2,200 volumes. Both the Philadelphia and New York libraries are five years old. The Boston library was first proposed in 1820. It is open every evening except Sunday between September 1 and May 1. During the summer it is open three evenings each week. The books in the 1,100 volume collection may circulate or may be used in the reading room. The library has not recently purchased any new books. Because of this, many old subscribers have withdrawn and there is some difficulty in finding new ones.

168 "Mercantile Library Associations." *Merchants' Magazine and Commercial Review* [Hunt's Merchants' Magazine], 29 (October 1853), p437–48 (IEN, NcU).

The sources for the article summarized below were the annual reports of the New York, Boston, Cincinnati, and St. Louis Mercantile Library Associations.

Mercantile library associations have done much to improve the education and moral character of many young men, who are at an age most susceptible to evil influences. The Boston Association, incorporated in March 1820, is the oldest one in this country. New York's was founded in November 1820, Cincinnati's in 1835, and St. Louis' in 1846. These associations primarily were established for the benefit of the young men who in the future will become the merchants of these cities and are centered around libraries. It has been the experience of the New York Association that as its library users became better educated the demand for better quality books also increased. For our readers who are not familiar with these associations, a brief account of their activities and management is provided.

Military Post Libraries

169 [The U.S. Military Post Library Association.] *Nation*, 14 (April 25, 1872), p273–74 (NcU).

Books and papers too good to throw away may usefully be sent to the U.S. Military Post Library Association, at no. 58 Broadway [New York City]. When one considers that there are 279 army posts spread over our great territory, most of them isolated and without diversion except card-playing, one sees how important it is to provide plenty of wholesome reading, if merely to keep out the flood of nasty literature. The association seems sufficiently regardful of religious needs; money and good secular works, not tracts, would seem to be proper gifts. We presume that the corresponding secretary will send the association's last annual report to anyone desiring information.

170 [United States Military Post Library Association.] *Publishers' Weekly* [Publishers' and Stationers' Weekly Trade Circular], 2 (September 5, 1872), p231 (NcU).

The entire article follows.

"The United States Military Post Library Association, whose object is 'to improve the social, moral, and religious condition of the enlisted men of the United States Army,' by seeking to influence legislation in Congress to that end, and by aiding in the establishment of libraries and reading-rooms at the various posts, and distributing books and reading matter among them, has issued its annual report. The success of the association during the past year has been considerable. Eighty thousand copies of news, religious, and literary papers have been sent to the army, besides magazines and miscellaneous periodicals, and thirty thousand copies of the association's 18mo publications, gratuitously distributed, while thirty-six posts and nine companies have been aided in procuring permanent libraries. Among the contributions for the year we notice the names of Appleton, Osgood, Peterson, Routledge, and the other publishers for sums from $25 to $100."

Music Libraries

171 [Icarian Musical Library.] *Norton's Literary Gazette and Publishers' Circular*, n.s. 1 (October 2, 1854), p493, 220 wds (NcU).
The article summarized below is taken from the *Newport (R.I.) News*.
The most extensive musical library in the United States will be presented to the Icarian Community at Nauvoo, Illinois, by Mr. H. Albrecht of the Germania Musical Society. This collection contains 478 works in 665 volumes exclusively devoted to musical matters, such as history of music, biographies of composers, theories of music, musical dictionaries and journals. Libraries of this kind are very rare. Among the 80,000 to 100,000 volumes in the public libraries of this country, scarcely 50 books can be found on the subject of musical literature. Besides Albrecht's collection, we know only of those of Dr. LaRoche of Philadelphia, the musical library of the Harvard Musical Association of Boston, and Lowell Mason of Boston, each of which has 300 to 400 volumes. Most collections of music consist mainly of choral books, hymns, psalms, and other music, which are out of place in a collection of musical writings.

172 [Joseph Drexel's Music Library.] *American Bibliopolist*, 2 (February 1870), p76–77 (ICU, NcD).
The entire article follows; it is reprinted from part of an article in *Nation* 9 (December 9, 1869) *(see 116)*.
The increase of the Boston Public Library during the year has been 8,689 volumes, and the whole number is now 153,000 volumes. Perhaps its Public Library does not approach in richness one, at least, of Philadelphia collections, the musical library of Mr. Joseph Drexel, of Philadelphia, of which a catalogue has just been printed, containing fifteen hundred numbers, which represent almost twice as many volumes. This is said to be surpassed only by the British Museum and the Leipzig libraries."

Public Libraries

173 [Plans for Establishing Free Public Libraries in Boston and Elsewhere; St. Louis Mercantile Library's New Building.] *National Magazine: Devoted to Literature, Art, and Religion*, 1 (November 1852), p476 (InU, NcU).
The entire article follows.
"A decided movement is making in Boston for the establishment of a free public library, open to all classes, for reference and circulation. Libraries are also being formed at Stamford, Conn.; Alexandria, Va.; and at Scranton, Luzerne County, Pa. The St. Louis Mercantile Library having collected eight thousand volumes, are about removing to their new building, the cost of which we learn is nearly $100,000, the whole amount of which, and greatly to their honor, has been subscribed by the merchants of that city."

174 "Free Fiction." *Nation*, 2 (February 1, 1866), p138–39 (NcU).
We have spoken, lately, of our high appreciation for the value of the Boston Public Library. However, we recently borrowed a catalog of the popular depart-

ment in this library from a young woman who had marked, for her own reading, every book of prose fiction. What would our grandmother, who secretly read fiction, have thought if municipal authorities had sanctioned this kind of reading? However innocent novel-reading may be, it is hardly worth while to take it under public patronage. (The respective merits of various authors are discussed.) Perhaps even the poorest works of fiction have their uses; an extremely bad novel can be as entertaining as a good one. (Famous men who have enjoyed fiction are mentioned.) However, collectors of even small private libraries tend to acquire good standard volumes. Franklin did this; what would he have thought of supplying the rising generation with an unlimited supply of romances?

175 Drake, Samuel G. "Libraries and How to Manage Them." *Historical Magazine and Notes and Queries Concerning the Antiquities, History, and Biography of America*, o.s. 13, n.s. 3 (January 1868), p11–13 (IEN).
The part of the article about libraries (p13) follows.
"Respecting the management of public libraries and those of institutions, it is not proposed to enlarge; for they have living examples, by which if they have profited, they are already under a system so nearly perfect, that there seems not much room for improvement. As regards the interior arrangement of buildings, there is no excuse for defects; yet, in some of the most modern and costly edifices, quackery has been allowed to a most culpable extent, by which taxpayers have been swindled out of thousands of dollars."

176 [Brochure on the Founding and Administration of Free Public Libraries.] *Nation*, 12 (March 23, 1871), p198, 310 wds (NcU).
The American Social Science Association has just issued a brochure, *Free Public Libraries: Suggestions on their Foundation and Administration, with a Selected List of Books*. This handbook is only secondarily for the kind of American who desires to bestow a library on a town; it is primarily for the townspeople who establish a library, stock it, and operate it. The practical suggestions on management are the results of the experience of the Library of Congress and the Boston Public Library. The list of books contains a few thousand titles; it has been prepared with great care. Such a collection would be superior to many a larger collection; the Astor Library, as now conducted for the public disadvantage, is less useful than this proposed library is likely to be.

177 Winser, F. "The Boston Public Library." *Century, a Popular Quarterly* [Scribner's Monthly], 3 (December 1871), p150–56 (InU, NcU).
Cogswell and George Ticknor, both students of the University of Göttingen in their youth, were to influence the formation of two of America's greatest libraries. Cogswell modeled the Astor after the great European libraries, but the Boston Public freely circulates its materials with very little loss. At his own expense Cogswell gave the Astor an excellent bibliographical collection; Ticknor gave the Boston library his collection of Spanish and Portuguese books and manuscripts. The Boston Public's registration system provides security against thefts. After a fortnight a fine of two cents per day is charged for any overdue book. When a book becomes a week overdue, a messenger is sent to collect it; out of a circulation of 300,000 only 40 borrowers never returned their books. The Upper Hall, or Bates Hall, is selected with great care as to what is the best, while the Lower Hall buys almost anything requested because the library is intended to be both a popular and a scholarly institution. (A portrait of Ticknor,

a picture of a bust of Joshua Bates, and exterior and interior views of the Boston Public Library accompany the article.)

178 "The Binding of Books." *Literary World*, Boston, 2 (April, 1872), p168, 390 wds (NcU).
The letter-writer mentioned in this article wrote again; *see 179.*
   A correspondent "representing the Public Library Committee in a neighboring town" writes to us as follows (the letter is summarized here:) Should not one or more booksellers begin to supply well-bound books for town libraries? The fancy cloth covers are extravagant, and they last only a short time. Alternatively, publishers might have some copies of each book bound substantially for libraries. (The editor comments:) Publishers say that cloth binding is the most durable except for leather, which is expensive. It may be that our correspondent does not ask for a substitute for cloth. We heartily agree that books should be furnished to libraries in plain cloth. Sheep is next to cloth in cost, but sheep-bound books have never been popular.

179 "The Binding of Books." *Literary World*, Boston, 2 (May 1872), p184, 270 wds (NcU).
   Most of this article consists of a letter from the same person whose letter was quoted and commented upon in item 178.
   The correspondent whose letter formed the basis for our article in our April issue makes his complaint clearer in a second letter, which we commend to publishers. (The letter is quoted; a summary of its follows here.) I wish to illustrate my earlier letter. Most of the books received in our public library are bound in cloth with gilt ornamentation. We cover the backs with strong paper, so the gilding is useless and the backs soon come off; we then have them rebound. We wish to purchase books bound strongly and plainly in cloth or sheepskin. Would it not pay for someone to provide such books? (The letter is signed "A Library Committee.")

180 F. "Novel Readers and Our Public Libraries." *Nation*, 15 (July 18, 1872), p42, 600 wds (NcU).
   The article, a letter to the editor of the *Nation* from Waterbury, Conn., was quite possibly written by William I. Fletcher, who was public librarian there from 1869 to 1872. The article refers to another in the *Nation* (see 174).
   The recently published report of [William F. Poole] the accomplished librarian of the Cincinnati Public Library, takes the same view as does the author of a recent *Nation* article, that the heavy demand for light and sensational reading is justified. However, in the public library with which I am familiar, it is not just workingmen and persons with little education who prefer these books; those who can be expected to have refined tastes also prefer Mrs. Southworth. The public library must be manipulated in order to lead people from lower to higher levels. A library should not have a separate fiction catalog, and its catalog should indicate the contents of books. Furthermore, it should advertise its good books in a bulletin or in a newspaper.

181 Quincy, J. P. "The Functions of Town Libraries." *Old and New*, 6 (September 1872), p358–61 (InU, NcU).
   It is questionable whether town libraries should provide large numbers of novels at public expense. There are some good novels, and these should be available, but a popular library ought to provide a greater number of books that

treat serious subjects. The presentation of these subjects should be in a style that the graduates of the public schools can read with understanding; popular in the best sense of the word. Excessive novel reading has been shown by Dr. Isaac Ray to be the cause of many of the mental abnormalities that are more prevalent now than in the past.

182 [Library Buildings.] *Nation*, 15 (October 3, 1872), p216, 440 wds (NcU).

The twentieth *Annual Report* of the Boston Public Library includes three plans for a branch library in Roxbury. (Details are given.) All books are close to the delivery counter. This is a much better plan for town libraries where the public is not admitted to the shelves than is the plan involving a large central hall with alcoves. Architects like the vista down the hall, but no library committee should listen to them. If a hall is desired, do not have alcoves; parallel stacks will store more books. In libraries where the books are accessible to readers, space between the tiers of stacks should be wider. It should never be necessary to climb to reach a book; it is time for ladders to be banished from libraries.

183 [A Call for Public Library Statistics.] *Literary World*, Boston, 4 (December 1873), p104, 180 wds (NcU).

The results of the request made in this article were reported in the March 1874 issue of the *Literary World* (*see 184*).

We have heard fears expressed that the establishment of public libraries would not prove an unmixed good, that they promote a taste for fiction which is not always wholesome, and that novels of the baser sort constitute the bulk of the books read by patrons. We think that this is true only of a few of the largest libraries; that others, obliged to make a selection, choose standard books. The *Literary World* goes to nearly every public library in the country; we make it the vehicle of a request that librarians send us statistics that will show the direction of American literary taste. Let them state the number of volumes, the average circulation, the proportion of demand for novels to more solid matter and, if possible, the names of the most popular authors. From these materials we can make an exhibit which will be valuable and interesting.

184 "What the People Read." *Literary World*, Boston, 4 (March 1874), p153–54 (NcU).

This article refers to one published in the *Literary World* in December 1873 (*see 183*).

We have received only a few responses to our request for statistics concerning the demand for the various kinds of books in public libraries. (A few figures from the Wakefield, Mass. Public Library are given.) In this library, 67 percent of the circulation is adult or juvenile fiction. (More detailed figures are quoted from the report of W. I. Fletcher, Librarian of the Lawrence, Mass. Public Library.) It appears that the patrons of the Lawrence Library consume 25 percent solid literary food and 75 percent sensational food. The latest report of the Boston Public Library shows 74 percent fiction, and the latest Cincinnati Public Library report, 73.8 percent. Much of this fiction may be "wholesome," but how many persons read fiction to improve their minds? Perhaps if people had to buy their novels, they would fall back on the more substantial books in their public libraries.

185 [U.S. Public Libraries.] *Publishers' Weekly*, 5 (March 14, 1874), p273 (NcU).

The entire article follows; it is quoted from the article about annual reports of libraries that appeared in the *Nation* for March 5, 1874 *(see 129)*.

"In speaking of the Lawrence Librarian's report, the *Nation* says: 'His statistics confirm the well-established law that in any public library three-fourths of the circulation is of works of fiction. Thus, in Lawrence the proportion is 77 per cent. in summer, 74 per cent. in winter, and for the year about 75 per cent. In Boston, we may remark for purposes of comparison, the proportion has been in successive years 76, 78, and 77 per cent.; in Cincinnati, 74 per cent.; in Quincy, Mass., with a population not unlike that of Lawrence, 80 per cent.'"

186 [Scudder, Horace E.] "City and Country Libraries." *Every Saturday; a Journal of Choice Reading*, 4th ser., (March 21, 1874), p335, 1000 wds (KyL).
In *Publishers' Weekly* for April 4, 1874 *(see 188)*, this article is attributed to "Mr. Scudder," presumably Horace E. Scudder.

We are suffering from preconceived notions about public libraries. We are thankful that large, well organized collections in fine buildings are available to students and men of letters in large cities. But country people cannot get to them and need small circulating public libraries that are joined in a great network so that there could be economical use of the same material.

187 "Public Libraries and Fiction." *Literary World*, Boston, 4 (April 1874), p169, 900 wds (NcU).

Public libraries are for the benefit of the least cultivated classes, who do not possess private collections of books; the influence of these institutions should be wholesome and elevating. Public libraries should aid in the intellectual improvement of the unlettered immigrants. Libraries should stop supplying trashy novels; the public appetite must not be gratified at the risk of the public health. Those managers of our public libraries who deem Mrs. Southworth's novels injurious should throw them out. We have no hostility to fiction as such; some of it is well worth reading. Perhaps Superintendent Winsor will make a beginning by reducing the Boston Public Library stock of 409 copies of Mrs. Southworth's novels, 359 of which were in circulation on the 24th of last February.

188 [Public Libraries.] *Publishers' Weekly*, 5 (April 4, 1874), p360, 210 wds (NcU).
This is a summary of an article in the March 21, 1874 issue of *Every Saturday (see 186)*.

189 ["Superintendent of the American Public Libraries."] *Publishers' Weekly*, 5 (May 9, 1874), p458 (NcU).
The entire article follows.
"A London literary weekly speaks of 'the Superintendent of the American Public Libraries.' Here is a new opening for those wanting situations."

190 Greenough, William W. "Some Conclusions Relative to Public Libraries." *Journal of Social Science Containing the Proceedings of the American Association*, 7 (September 1874), p323–32 (IEN, NcU).
I shall discuss in my paper this country's public libraries, their functions, and their relation to taxpayers. Although the growth rate of our libraries has been astounding, the number of books per capita indicates that much more needs to be done to support our libraries. I discern eight principles central to the

support of any public library: initially a library must obtain, according to its resources, the largest number of books useful to its public; one-third of the collection should be fiction and two-thirds nonfiction; a library should purchase the books wanted by its public; tastes in literature differ between communities; a library should have books for specialists as well as for students; a good catalog is necessary; libraries do elevate the education and cultural levels of the public; and experience indicates that libraries are a necessity in any civilized society.

191 [The Boston Public Library and the Chicago Public Library.] *Nation*, 19 (September 3, 1874), p153 (NcU).

The portion of this article that is about the Chicago Public Library was quoted in *Publishers' Weekly* for January 30, 1875 *(see 409)*. The entire *Nation* article is reproduced below.

"The Boston Public Library has, by annexation of suburban libraries erected into branches, and by the usual means of purchases and donations, been increased by nearly 25 per cent. during the past year. The total number of volumes is now 260,550. No less than 103 persons are employed in the library and its branches. The new Chicago Public Library reports about 26,000 volumes, of which 21,000 are adapted for circulation. In the sixteenth week after opening (on the 1st of May) the average daily circulation had reached the surprising figure of 1,118 volumes, or one in twenty of the entire collection; a striking evidence of the deprivation caused by the great fire."

Religious Society Libraries

192 P[eabody], E[phraim]. "Pastoral Library Magazine. No. 1, November 1840." *Christian Examiner*, 30 (March 1841), p49–56 (NcU).

The article summarized below is a review of a plan for the establishment of ministerial libraries, proposed in the *Pastoral Library Magazine*.

Young ministers with families to support cannot afford to purchase books out of their small salaries. Even if a man can afford to buy books every year, he will not, for when he dies his family will be left with a library that will fetch little when auctioned off. For the minister who has bought a library and who leaves the ministry, the books will have little value; and for the man who does not have a library, the habit of study and enquiry is lost. According to the proposal, a local religious society would provide a yearly sum for a library to be used by each successive pastor. The money could be subtracted from the yearly salary or could come out of the parish taxes, or subscriptions and donations could be solicited. Subscribers could be given the privilege of using the library.

193 "Library." *Christian World* [American and Foreign Christian Union], 5 (June 1854), p279, 170 wds (NcU).

The periodical was published by the American and Foreign Christian Union; the board referred to in the article summarized below is presumably that of the Union.

The importance of a full and well-selected library of standard papal and Protestant works becomes increasingly apparent with the progress of time and the increase of the Romish population. The need has been especially great within the past year, but the board has had only small means at their control for this object. A few volumes have been added, however, and they hope soon to receive some valuable works from Europe, which were unobtainable in this country. A friend was engaged to procure them. Donations of books or of funds to purchase them will be thankfully received, and may be addressed to the secretaries or the general agent.

194 "Library." *Christian World* [American and Foreign Christian Union], 6 (June 1855), p265, 200 wds (NcU).

The periodical was published by the American and Foreign Christian Union; the board referred to in the article summarized below is presumably that of the Union.

As Romanists multiply in the country, develop their policy, and set to work, the need for a well-selected library of standard Roman Catholic authorities, and also of Protestant writers on the subject of Romanism, becomes more and more felt. This need was mentioned in our last report. At no time was it needed more than within the past year, which saw a general inquiry in our land in regard to the Papacy. Works should be collected from which the public may obtain reliable information about the Papal organization, its teachings and practices. The rooms of the American and Foreign Christian Union are the natural place for this information to be found. The board commends the subject to consideration, and assures that donation of books or funds will be accepted for this purpose. Some contributions have been received within the year; many more are desired.

School District Libraries

195 "Common School Libraries." *Connecticut Common School Journal and Annals of Education*, 1 (March 1, 1839), p119 (NcU).

The entire article follows.

"This subject commends itself to the judgment of all, and is of too much importance to be any longer neglected. It is spoken of with deep interest throughout the State, and the public appears to expect some action on the part of the Legislature. New York has appropriated a sum of money to each of the districts, on condition that they will raise in the district an equal amount for the purchase of district libraries."

196 "Common School Libraries." *Common School Journal*, 1 (April 15, 1839), p126-28 (NcU).

The article summarized below is reprinted from *The Cultivator*.

The need for suitable books in our district school libraries is generally acknowledged; however, those collections of books recommended by the American Society for the Diffusion of Knowledge and the American Sunday School Union are wholly inadequate to meet the peculiar needs of the mechanic and the farmer. Certainly, many of our farmers would benefit if books on agriculture were to be made available at state expense in our school libraries. New York has appropriated $55,000 to be divided up among district libraries for the purchase of books. Unfortunately, this scheme's effectiveness has been compromised because the responsibility for book selection has been delegated to the local school boards. Alternatively, Massachusetts has adopted a more feasible plan whereby the Board of Education has undertaken the sponsorship of a Common School Library which can be purchased by the district schools.

197 Barnard, Henry. "[First] Annual Report of the Secretary of the Board to the Board of Commissioners of Common Schools." *Connecticut Common School Journal and Annals of Education*, 1 (June 1839), p155–76 (NcU).

The part of the article about libraries, "School Apparatus and Libraries" (p170–71), is summarized below.

There are six school libraries in Connecticut; four are the contributions of friends of schools. Teachers and committees testify to their usefulness. Well-selected libraries, also embracing works on agriculture, manufactures and other employments, aid older children and adults of both sexes. New York has consecrated her share of the surplus revenue to her schools. When matched by taxes, $15,000 are annually appropriated to her colleges, $40,000 to her academies, and $275,000 to her common schools. Fifty-five thousand dollars are devoted annually for three years to purchase district school libraries, with an equal sum to be raised by taxation in each district. This $330,000 total will buy 600,000 to 700,000 volumes to be scattered throughout New York. Massachusetts has also provided for school libraries. Their libraries will have separate collections for children and adults. Ohio and Pennsylvania have also set up school libraries.

198 "The School Library." *Common School Journal*, 1 (June 15, 1839), p177–81 (NcU).

The part of the article about libraries (p178–81) is summarized below.

A few years ago James Wadsworth of Geneseo, New York, made a donation to the State for the purpose of providing several district schools with libraries; subsequently sponsorship of this idea has been assumed by the New York and Massachusetts state governments. New York annually distributes $275,000 to the common schools; in April 1838, a law was passed authorizing that, for three years, $110,000 a year be disbursed for the purchase of school district libraries. In April 1837 the Massachusetts Legislature enacted a law that authorized the establishment of district schools and the procurement of libraries for these schools. As a means to ensure school libraries of good quality, the Massachusetts State Board of Education has been empowered to select and arrange for the publication of a series of books, called the Common School Library, which can be purchased at the local schools' discretion for the school libraries. In this way, the questions, "What shall our children read?" can be best answered.

199 "The School Library." *American Repertory of Arts, Sciences, and Manufactures*, 1 (February 1840) p66, 430 wds (NcU, TU).

It is a responsibility of all journals to call attention to the means by which people may gain information. To this end, school libraries are deemed essential as a means to disseminate practical knowledge. First New York and later Massachusetts have adopted legislation that supports the establishment of such libraries. Under the auspices of the [Massachusetts?] Board of Education numerous books have been recommended for inclusion in school libraries; hopefully the local schools will choose to purchase these books, which are now for sale.

200 "District School Libraries." *Connecticut Common School Journal and Annals of Education*, 2 (May 1, 1840), p186–87 (NcU).

The article summarized below was taken from part of an article in *Common School Journal* for March 2, 1840 *(see 454)*.

We are little educated in comparison to what we might know. Much of our mental alertness is squandered. Youth should have available some allurements to usefulness and virtue. Common school libraries are destined to make schools more valuable. New York first adopted the plan in 1838, appropriating $165,000 from the school fund to purchase district school libraries. In 1839, the same sum was appropriated; individual towns and districts were to raise an equal amount. In 1837, the Massachusetts legislature authorized districts to raise, by tax, a sum not greater than $30 the first year and $10 in each succeeding year, to be expended for a school library. Only about 50 of 3,000 districts now have libraries, and few of these came out of the 1837 act. Most are indebted to private subscription or individual generosity.

201 Shunk, Frs. R. "Pennsylvania. Sixth Annual Report of the Superintendent of Common Schools." *Connecticut Common School Journal and Annals of Education*, 2 (May 1, 1840), p192–95 (NcU).

The part of the article about libraries, "Common School Libraries" (p194, 700 wds), is summarized below.

The establishment of common school libraries in every school district is a cheap, simple, and effective way of placing valuable knowledge within the reach of the whole people. It should embrace every department of science and literature, and especially American history, institutions, manners and customs. New York has appropriated $55,000 annually for 5 years to buy books for district libraries, to be distributed as public school money is distributed. Massachusetts is publishing 100 volumes in "The School Library Series," ten of which have already been published. The establishment of school libraries is a powerful means of extending the diffusion of knowledge devised by free men to perpetuate freedom. Washington, Jefferson, and Madison all write about the value of knowledge in preserving freedom. A well-instructed people alone can be a permanently free people.

202 "District School Libraries." *Connecticut Common School Journal and Annals of Education*, 3 (February 1, 1841), p87, 720 wds (NcU).

This subject is beginning to receive attention in New England. New York already has a large program. By appropriating five cents per scholar, Connecticut can purchase 24,000 volumes a year. Massachusetts has already provided for such libraries. The subject receives the notice of the committees in their reports. Excerpts are reprinted, indicating a desire for district school libraries. South Reading emphasizes the usefulness of libraries in training the young; Lenox their inexpensiveness and varied uses; Goshen their ability to ward off idleness and bad company; and Randolph their help in attaining political equality.

203 "Christian Library." *Connecticut Common School Journal and Annals of Education*, 3 (March 15, 1841), p123–24 (NcU).

The article summarized below is part of a section describing catalogs of books prepared for school districts and families.

This series is for library associations, schools, and families. It contains 45 volumes of 430 pages each. The price is $20 with a case, $19 without. The set embraces 19,530 pages, with 24 steel plates and numerous other engravings. The first 33 volumes contain 63 distinct works; 20 of these were written especially for the young. (The 45 volumes are then listed. Titles are given for all; some include the author, some note features such as engravings and portraits.)

204 Pradt, J. B. "District Libraries." *Pennsylvania School Journal*, 5 (October 1856), p116–18 (IU).
The article summarized below refers to "Libraries," *Pennsylvania School Journal*, 4 (May 1856) *(see 989)*.
A previous editorial in the *Journal* gave four arguments against school and district libraries created at public expense. This article takes the opposite viewpoint. More than one-half of the people do not have access to good book collections, and libraries can furnish reading matter for both children and adults. Like the need for schools, the need for libraries justifies taxing all for a service used by some. Books are perishable, but their decay and disappearance indicates that they are being used. In no other way can more good be done for so little money. New York, for example, spends $55,000, or seven cents per child, for books. If school libraries interfere with the rights of parents, it is only to meet future needs, and any dangers to the children are minimized by using approved lists of books as guides.

205 Griscom, Rachel D. "Report on District Libraries to the Berks County Institute." *Pennsylvania School Journal*, 6 (January 1858), p219–20 (IU).
Libraries help to achieve the object of education — cultivating that seed or talent of the mind which awaits culture. The best way to establish libraries is by public authority and with public funds, so everyone will feel that he has a right to such a library. School libraries can be secured by a steady appropriation or private contributions. Books should contain facts. Reference books, dictionaries, and encyclopedias should be abundant. The other books should be useful to their particular readers. Books are best arranged by subject. Advice should be given a pupil on his reading, but individuality should also be encouraged. Books should be labeled, a catalog and accurate records kept, and a slight fine charged to ensure punctual return of books. Libraries are useful in keeping old and young out of mischief and as aids to work and to opening the mind to its full capacity.

206 Z., X. Y. "Libraries in District Schools." *New Hampshire Journal of Education*, 3 (November 1859) p327–28 (NhD).
Reading is too much neglected by those who are in a process of education. More will be accomplished by those who, in connection with their studies, carry forward a systematic and carefully selected course of reading. Pupils who read would also find their studies more pleasant. A wise course of reading would obviate the necessity of studying geography, arithmetic, and grammar year after year. Parents could furnish a choice library in every school district, but such libraries are still in the future. In their absence, each student should buy a book and lend it to his schoolmates, the process continuing until each book is read by every pupil in the class.

207 "District Libraries." *Pennsylvania School Journal*, 12 (January 1864), p198–99 (CoGrS).
The author of the article summarized below recommends the reading of "Books and Libraries," *Pennsylvania School Journal*, 12 (January 1864) *(see 1157)*.
We do not think that the government should be responsible for establishing school libraries. If government is permitted to select books and control people's reading, a large step has been taken toward influencing religious and political beliefs. If every government established libraries, many would fail

because no one wanted them or desired to use them; a love of reading cannot be forced on anyone. A popular library must be wanted by the community, procured by community means and selected by the community. When a district desires a library, it should be part of the school system, and the board of directors should initiate and control it. The board should designate the library's location and should select books. The secretary of the board should be the chief librarian. Funds should come from voluntary contributions and entrance fees. Money, not books, should be donated. Every citizen should be permitted to take out books.

208 "Common Schools in Connecticut." *American Journal of Education* (Barnard), 14 (June 1864), p244–75 (NcU).

The part of the article about libraries (p248–49) is summarized below. The first sentence probably refers to the Bingham Library for Youth, founded in 1803.

Perhaps the first juvenile library in the world was begun in Salisbury, Connecticut, but that is about the extent of that State's effort in providing libraries for children. In 1839 New York appropriated $53,000 for its district school libraries on the condition that an equal amount of money be raised by each district for the purchase of books. Six years later, a cumulative total of 1.5 million books was held by these libraries. Massachusetts also supports its district school libraries. In contrast, Connecticut has given little financial support either for district schools or for school libraries.

209 "Libraries for Public Schools." *American Journal of Education*, St. Louis [Journal of Education], 1 (January 1869), p80, 830 wds (MoS).

We have repeatedly been asked to give the features of a successful library. It is of no use to depend on irregular stipends from a board of education; the best form of revenue is that derived from subscription. The cost of membership in the St. Louis Public Library is $3.00 per year; gifts of money or books add substantially to resources. When people pay for a privilege they are far more interested in the management of the institution. The board of management of a library should be independent, free of pressures that might weaken the library's resources. The printed word is more important to Americans than to others; books contain the most mature and well-digested arrangement of thoughts and, unlike lectures, adapt themselves to our speed of apprehension; soon the library will become recognized as the great feature of our educational system.

210 Divoll, Ira. "Popular Libraries." *American Journal of Education*, St. Louis, 2 (July 1870), p203–204 (MoS).

The article summarized below is in the form of a letter written to a school trustee.

The benefit that you derived, twenty-odd years ago, from one of the district school libraries of New York has led you to form a too favorable opinion of those libraries. I favor state aid for libraries but not on the basis adopted by other states; nearly all have failed. The books were generally well-chosen and, at first, well-read, but no money was provided to pay continuing costs. You must get people to subscribe money to secure rooms, bookcases, a librarian, etc. and a small amount for books. The St. Louis Public School Library was founded on the basis of life-membership fees, but it is connected with the schools; there is a children's department, and women are equal with men in all rights and privileges. Professor R. R. Calkins can tell you about the library at St. Joseph; on the basis of population, that library is a greater success than ours in St. Louis.

211 Divoll, Ira. "Popular Libraries." *Appletons' Journal: a Magazine of General Literature*, Educational Supplement, 4 (October 29, 1870), p1–5 (IEN).

It was formerly widely claimed that school district libraries would provide the public with many benefits, and consequently a number of states passed laws that supported their establishment. However, an examination of school district libraries in New York, Ohio, Wisconsin, Michigan, Indiana, Massachusetts, Connecticut, and Pennsylvania reveals that for various reasons the erstwhile efforts to establish those libraries have failed and that much of the money expended has been wasted. Yet the establishment of libraries in the educational system remains a worthwhile goal, one that only can be realized by a systematic plan such as the one that herein is outlined. The effectiveness of that plan is demonstrated by the St. Louis Public School Library, which is based on it; I helped found that library and now manage it.

212 "School Libraries." *American Journal of Education*, St. Louis [Journal of Education], 3 (November 1870), p9, 300 wds (MoS).

The article summarized below refers to an article in the Educational Supplement of *Appleton's Journal*, vol. 4 (October 29, 1870) *(see 211)*.

Mr. Ira Divoll of this city has written a valuable article in a recent number of *Appleton's Journal*. Since the New York legislature first took action on the subject of school libraries in 1835, eleven other states (named in the article) have passed laws on this subject. Mr. Divoll examines the causes of failure in these plans and suggests remedies. Becuase of his participation in the formation of libraries in New Orleans and St. Louis, he has had peculiar opportunities for the study of this subject; his article will be of especial value to educators throughout the South and West.

School Libraries

213 "Discussion on School Libraries." *American Annals of Education*, 3d ser., 6 (December 1836), p549–54 (NcU).

During the final day of the meeting of the American Institute of Instruction, there occurred a discussion on the use of libraries in schools; it is recounted from memory. One gentleman questioned the wisdom of providing books for children. Another gentleman disagreed by declaring that a well-selected juvenile library was beneficial. Other participants in the discussion concurred with the latter gentleman. The first gentleman qualified his opening remarks by insisting that he merely was opposed to reading when it filled children's minds with trivia. He thought that the matter of book selection and reading guidance was critically important in school libraries. The remainder of the discussion centered around the origin of the taste for reading, the kinds of books to be selected, and the need for reflection before forming a school library. Some of the participants in the discussion cited personal experiences to support their observations.

214 Abbott, Gorham D. "The American Library of Useful Knowledge." *American Annals of Education*, 3d ser., 8 (January 1838), p62–66 (NcU).

The article summarized below was submitted by the American Society for the Diffusion of Useful Knowledge to explain the advantages of the society's proposed system of school libraries.

The society has proposed the publication of a series of books suitable to the purpose of the school library; these books would be circulated among the country's public schools. The following considerations influenced the society's proposal: 1) the circulating library is the best means of making knowledge available to students; 2) students between ten and twenty years old would make good use of the libraries because during these years the desire for learning is most intense; and 3) the libraries would improve the system of education. Each library would have books on various subjects, e.g., history, travel, biography, and natural science. Other considerations are that 4) the libraries would contribute to the preservation of morals; 5) parents' reading would be influenced; and 6) the plan is economical. Each collection initially would contain fifty books and could be shipped in a case (illustrated).

215 "The American Society for the Diffusion of Useful Knowledge." *Connecticut Common School Journal and Annals of Education*, 1 (May 1, 1839), p148–50 (NcU).

The article consists of extracts from an account taken from an unidentified article in *The Christian Statesman* about a Washington meeting of the society. The *Union List of Serials* gives no location for the issues of *The Christian Statesman* that appeared in the months of February through April 1839, so the original article cannot be included in this bibliography. The parts of the *Connecticut Common School Journal* article that are about libraries (1530 wds) are summarized below.

The great objective of the society is the publication and introduction of a national school library. The society proposes publishing a series of popular works for that purpose. The benefits of such a library are discussed. It would cost $1,000,000 to place such a library in each of the 50,000 schools in the United States. It was resolved that, as the goal of elevating the character and extending the influence of public instruction is worthy, the plan for the American school library should be encouraged in state legislatures and should receive the patronage of all schools. The 50-volume set published by Harper is discussed; it is a good beginning. Each legislature should make provisions for buying books for libraries. The society will advise in the selection of books, but the schools will make the specific selections. The society's guideline is: What does the book teach people to do?

216 "The School District Library." *Connecticut Common School Journal and Annals of Education*, 3 (March 15, 1841), p122–23 (NcU).

The article summarized below is part of a section describing catalogs of books prepared for school districts and families.

The *School District Library*, published by Harper and Brothers, embraces history, voyages and travels, biography, natural history, the physical sciences, agriculture, manufactures, arts, commerce, belles-lettres, the history and philosophy of education, and other subjects. (The volumes are listed in order; title and author information is given.) The first series has 50 volumes; the second has 45, including 26 in a series of American biographies edited by Jared Sparks; and the third series has 50 volumes. Most of the volumes cost 38 cents each if purchased separately. A fourth series is in preparation.

217 "The School Library." *Connecticut Common School Journal and Annals of Education*, 3 (March 15, 1841), p121, 1380 wds (NcU).

The article summarized below is a part of a section describing catalogs of collections of books prepared for school districts and families. In an introduction, editors recommend *The School Library* of Marsh, Capen, Lyon, and Webb.

Marsh, Capen, Lyon, and Webb of Boston are publishing a collection of works entitled *The School Library* under the sanction of the Massachusetts Board of Education. There are two series of 50 volumes each. Each will contain a glossary and illustrations. All subjects, particularly American ones, will be included. The set is to be used for the whole community, not just one group or class. The larger series, for adults and advanced scholars, will cost 75 cents per volume; the smaller one, for juveniles, 40 cents per volume. A list of writers is given, and a list of the members of the Board of Education. The Silver Medal of the American Institute of New York was awarded to this library. (A list is given of the books already published.)

218 "School Library of the American Sunday School Union." *Connecticut Common School Journal and Annals of Education*, 3 (March 15, 1841), p123, 710 wds (NcU).

The article summarized below is part of a section describing catalogs of books prepared for school districts and families.

This series of books can be purchased and delivered anywhere in New York, Boston, or Philadelphia for $33. (Four addresses are given for the orders. The 121 titles in the series are listed.)

219 "School and District Libraries." *Pennsylvania School Journal*, 3 (November 1854), p131, 670 wds (IU).

There are many aspects of the problem of providing school libraries: we hope that readers will send us their opinions on the topic. Though friends have asked us to support the cause in the past, we have not felt the time was right nor that there was enough desire for books to justify their purchase. Now we feel that there is a change in the general attitude of the people and a greater interest in matters of education. While this change has not yet brought about the general establishment of libraries and other learning facilities, it does mark the time for serious discussion of these matters.

220 Challens, James C. "School and District Libraries." *Pennsylvania School Journal*, 3 (January 1855), p208-11 (IU).

The time is now ripe for the establishment of school and district libraries. It is our duty to provide good material for the book-hungry populace. Surely we cannot be faulted by God for seeking to circulate knowledge. He has not commanded it, but neither has he forbidden it. In fact, the promotion of reading and study will only make men more Christian. History gives examples of the power of books. The establishment of libraries upgrades the morality, manners and ambitions of the citizenry. Although books are no longer scarce, we do not feel their full influence. The books published are an accurate index to the civilization of an era. We are inspired by the example of such leaders as Ben Franklin, a practical man rather than a scholar, who labored all his life for free libraries. (Examples of laws for the support of libraries in Ohio and New York are given. A resolution is offered by the Pennsylvania State Teachers' Association, supporting the passage of a law to incorporate free libraries in the district schools.)

221 Hammond, Charles. "Libraries for Academies and High Schools." *Massachusetts Teacher: a Journal of School and Home Education*, 10 (June 1857), p241-54 (NcU).

One of the first acts of the founders of Yale College was to form a library, but today, when an institution is founded, the library is one of the last things considered. The point of our article is to show the importance of libraries to elementary and secondary education. Schools have special needs, and the library should be organized to fulfill these needs as far as possible. Consider these points: 1) the school library must meet specific needs; 2) the school library is one of the instructors' tools; 3) the teachers should attempt judiciously to select books for the library on a wide variety of subjects; 4) the library should be formed to meet the needs of the students; and 5) all books which merely provide amusement or entertainment should be excluded from the library. (The article also briefly discusses the efforts of certain Massachusetts schools to acquire libraries.)

222 Barker, John. "Establishment of School Libraries. A Lecture Delivered before the Crawford County Teachers' Institute." *Pennsylvania School Journal*, 6 (June 1858), p380–84 (IU).

Libraries are designed to contain all of human knowledge and experience; however, libraries for public school students should be limited to those works that do not exceed the student's intellectual capabilities and that fire the imagination. School studies are so wearisome that books provided by the library should be entertaining and refreshing. Because the schools are designed to benefit all the people, care must be taken that none of the books oppose the teachings of any of the Christian denominations. It is also necessary that the books convey the precepts and spirit of democracy, as well as the dignity and value of labor. Books promoting social prejudice should be avoided. The narrative form teaches morality and virtue easily, and stories and works of great men form strong impressions in young minds. As a depository of great literature, especially English poetry, the library preserves the genius of our people and enobles all who read its books.

223 "School Libraries." *Pennsylvania School Journal*, 13 (August 1864), p31–33 (IU).

A lady has written requesting advice about the selection of books for her school library. We believe that the library should promote a desire to read and should also guide that desire in the right directions. The first works a child reads should be of an interesting, narrative kind, but aimed to elevate and lead to right thought, manly action, and scientific truth. A child with a love of reading so created will eventually read for the purpose of knowing and not just as a pastime. There should also be a full set of reference works which the children should be taught to use properly. We offer no list of books to be procured, but we suggest that booksellers, catalogs, and trade lists of publishers be consulted. We do advise against buying a few expensive books at the cost of the entire fund.

224 S., D. C. "School Libraries." *California Teacher*, 2 (December 1864), p141–43 (C).

The article summarized below is reprinted in *Pennsylvania School Journal*, 13 (April 1865) *(see 225)*.

School libraries are valuable auxiliaries to the classroom, but they are few and far between. A habit to be avoided in schools is the routine pouring of knowledge into the minds of students. The aim of education is to cultivate and draw forth the powers of the mind. Books aid in this purpose, increasing the knowledge of youth. Establishing libraries for schools is thought difficult, but it can be done if each of 10 to 20 children gives money to buy a single book to be shared among all classmates. A dozen books will awaken a taste for reading and cause more to be purchased. The books must be carefully selected and interesting if they are to be read. Money could be raised by subscriptions, but the union of resources is a better method. Every well-established school in the state should have a school library.

225 S., D. C. "School Libraries." *Pennsylvania School Journal*, 13 (April 1865), p238–39 (IU).
   The article is reprinted from the *California Teacher*, 2 (December 1864), p141–43 *(see 224)*.

226 [The Uselessness of School Libraries.] *Nation*, 10 (May 19, 1870), p321, 360 wds (NcU).
   If there is anything which experience in education has settled, it is that school libraries for the pupils' use are altogether unprofitable. The money spent on them, if applied to the repair of buildings or the furnishing of apparatus or the purchase of books of reference for the teachers, would have an appreciable effect on the standard of instruction. In larger towns, school libraries cannot compete with public libraries. The fifteenth annual report of the St. Louis School Board tells about the Public School Library, which has 20,000 volumes. Members of the School Board, teachers, students in the Normal School and a few others may use it without charge; other persons may use it three months for one dollar, or for their entire lives for twelve dollars.

Social Libraries

227 [Inadequacies in the Basic Plans of Library Companies.] *Boston Magazine* [Boston Weekly Magazine], 2 (January 28, 1804), p53–54 (NcU).
   The article summarized below is no. 18 in a series, each called "The Passenger." No. 19, in the February 11 issue of the same periodical *(see 228)* is a sequel to it.
   Many people who would use libraries cannot afford the cost of a share in a library. Also, many who can afford the shares hold them as patrimonies without really using them. Therefore, many people are unnecessarily deprived of an opportunity to develop their intellectual abilities.

228 [Needed Reforms in the Basic Plans of Library Companies.] *Boston Magazine* [Boston Weekly Magazine], 2 (February 11, 1804), p61, 700 wds (NcU).
   The article summarized below is no. 19 in a series, each called "The Passenger." It is a sequel to no. 18, in the January issue of the same volume, *(see 227)*.
   The present article suggests solutions for problems mentioned in the earlier article. Shares for a library company should be valid for only a few years, not in perpetuity as at present. The shares should cost $3.00 each and in no year should a shareholder have to pay as much as $1.00. One book at a time could be taken on each share. Temporary memberships at $1.00 per year should be available. Poor widows with children should be given free use of the library, as should children who demonstrate aptitude for any particular art or science.

United States

229 "Review of Plans for Libraries." *American Annals of Education*, 3d ser., 4 (February 1834), p81–85 (NcU).
The virtues of public education are widely acknowledged. The diffusion of knowledge has a beneficial influence on the public character and serves the progress of society. In light of this, one author has proposed that well-selected libraries be established in every community throughout the United States. In his pamphlet the author recognizes three important considerations for any of these libraries: the selection, the expense, and the circulation of the books. The author proposes that for each library a committee should be appointed to select the books; subscriptions for the library should be sold; and a local agent should be hired to manage library affairs. He then contrasts his scheme to the itinerative library system in Scotland. If undertaken, the author's plan would further the increase of knowledge, as well as the desire for it, particularly among our youths. Therefore, we strongly recommend its adoption.

230 [Plan for a Circulating Library for the South.] *DeBow's Review*, 15 (October 1853), p432 (InU, NcU).
The entire article follows.
"A gentleman in Tennessee has sent us a plan for a grand circulating library for the South, as a means of distributing information where the population is proportionately sparse. He proposes that central depots be established from which books will be distributed to the county towns of counties in the proportion of their subscription, which books, at the end of twelve months, will be returned, and new ones obtained. Every county subscribing 1,000 dollars would receive, perhaps, 1,000 new books each year, etc. We wish our people were as ready to take up county subscriptions, and as ready to tax themselves for the purchase of books and libraries, as they are for subscribing to railroads, etc. Something certainly may be done, but who will take the lead?"

State Libraries

231 [Sparks, Jared.] "Materials for American History: Memoirs of the Historical Society of Pennsylvania. 8 vo. p228, Philadelphia, McCarty & Davis." *North American Review*, 23 (October 1826), p275–94 (InU, NcU).
The part of the review about libraries (p286–91) is summarized below.
Historical societies should collect and preserve documents relating to American history, publishing the more important and making those of minor value available to scholars. Very few libraries in this country have sizable collections of works in American history; even the Library of Congress has purchased only current books since the acquisition of Thomas Jefferson's library. The state libraries can be helpful in acquiring and preserving materials relating to the history of the states. Particularly, they should seek out colonial documents. North Carolina's library recently paid $60.00 for Lawson's *History of Carolina* printed in 1718; Pennsylvania's library has preserved the volumes given by William Penn. All the states should follow the examples of North Carolina, Pennsylvania, and New Jersey in establishing state libraries. Those in charge of historical collections should also seek to acquire complete sets of statutes.

Sunday School Libraries

232 Lunt, H. E., C. H. Dall, and S. C. Beane. "Literature for the Young." *American Unitarian Association. Monthly Journal*, 10 (October 1869), p374–82 (NcD).

Report of the [Association's?] Committee on Juvenile Literature. Several books that have been taken from a Unitarian Sunday school library teach doctrines that are contrary to the denomination's beliefs. Perhaps such books have been in the library because parents are not fully convinced of the truth of their own avowed beliefs. Books in Sunday school libraries should be well-written and should have believable characters whose actions and words teach sound doctrine. There are too few books with these qualities. In addition, dealers practice several kinds of fraud on book purchasers so that they buy unwanted books.

233 [Prizes for Stories Suitable for Sunday-School Libraries.] *Publishers' Weekly* [Publishers' and Stationers' Weekly Trade Circular], 1 (January 18, 1872), p12 (NcU).

The entire article follows. It refers to a commission established by the Unitarian Church.

"A friend of Unitarian Sunday-schools offers, through the Ladies' Commission on Sunday-school Books, a prize of $150 for the best manuscript story, suitable for Unitarian Sunday-school libraries, and adapted to children from ten to fifteen years of age. Another prize of $100 is offered for the second best story. Each story must fill about three hundred and fifty 16mo pages. The copyright will be the property of the author, and the Commission will take charge of the publication, or leave that arrangement with the author, if preferred. In the latter case, the proof-sheets must be submitted to the Commission. A sealed envelope containing the name and address of the author should accompany each manuscript. The stories offered for competition must be clearly written, upon alternate pages, and sent to the Ladies' Commission on Sunday-school Books, 42 Chauncy Street, Boston, before June 1, 1872."

234 "Sunday-School Books—The Ladies' Commission." *Publishers' Weekly*, 4 (November 22, 1873), p584 (NcU).

The part of the article about libraries is reproduced below; it is a direct quotation from a "recent report" of the Ladies' Commission on Sunday School Books, established by the Unitarian Church. After stating that "sensational" books were excluded, the report continues:

"We have met more than once both approval and objection on this score, but the arguments used against such exclusion, such as the popularity of such books, and their use in cultivating a taste for reading, have seemed to us applicable to circulating and public libraries, rather than to Sunday-school libraries, for which alone we attempt to provide in our regular work.

"Two years ago we prepared a list of books for the use of young persons, and intended also as a guide in the formation of small libraries. We have had pleasant testimony that this has proved useful, and are glad to supply it to any one who cares to see it."

235 "The Catalogue of the Ladies' Commission on Sunday-School Books."
Unitarian Review [Unitarian Review and Religious Magazine], 1 (July 1874), p467-70 (NcU).

The commission was organized to prepare a catalog of books suitable for the libraries of Unitarian Sunday schools. There was much debate over what kinds of works should be considered. Three different lists were finally prepared. The first contains titles that could be recommended without qualification to Unitarian parents and superintendents of Sunday schools. The second list contains books we could not spare, even though they contain some material of which Unitarians do not approve. The third list contains valuable and profitable books not fully adapted for a Sunday school library. Final assignment was by majority vote. Distinction should be made in libraries concerning the first two lists. The second list contains works that have merit despite their doctrinal defects. Libraries should mark them as such. It is important that children know and discuss these objectionable doctrines with their teachers.

236 Crane, J. T. "The Library Question." *Sunday-School Times* 16 (October 24, 1874), unpaged, 1000 wds (MBC).

Reference is made to this article in the *Publishers' Weekly* for January 30, 1875 *(see 237)*.

Several million children obtain reading matter from Sunday school libraries; if they do not find what they want in one they migrate to another. They like the poorly written narratives with wild adventures and startling surprises; these books convey no information and teach no moral. Our libraries are not entirely made up of such works but we need more books that inform, cultivate taste, and lift the being toward God and virtue. Children read the petty romances by sunset on Sunday; they should also have more substantial books to read through the week. The addition of better books to a collection could be gradual; it would help if someone would address the Sunday school on the evils of poor books and the value of good ones.

237 [Sunday-school Libraries.] *Publishers' Weekly*, 7 (January 30, 1875), p114 (NcU).

The entire article follows. It refers to an article in the October 24 issue of the *Sunday-School Times (see 236)*.

"A noticeable suggestion as to Sunday-school libraries, especially in places where no other libraries exist, has been made by Rev. Dr. J. T. Crane, in the *Sunday-School Times*. He proposes to have two departments to the libraries — one from which the children can take books for their week-day reading, and of which their parents can have the benefit, and the other the Sunday library proper. Such a secular library might in many places prove the foundation of public libraries hereafter."

Teachers' Libraries

238 "A Teachers' 'Library." *Pennsylvania School Journal*, 12 (March 1864), p290-91 (CoGrS).

A teachers' library should include professional treatises, at least one standard work on every science and department of knowledge, and a literature collection. We present a list of Messrs. Barnes and Burr's books named the "Teachers' Library," which to our knowledge is the only published set of books for the profession. It should, therefore, be prominent in every teachers' and district library. The list is neither complete nor are the books necessarily the best ones. (Twelve books are listed; for each work, the author's name is given and a summary of the contents is provided.)

Temperance Libraries

239 "Free Reading-Rooms." *National Advocate* [National Temperance Advocate], 2 (January 1867), p8–9 (TxU).
   Large numbers of young men between the ages of fifteen and thirty who live in New York and elsewhere lack places of diversion other than saloons and similar resorts. Recently an answer to this deplorable situation has been suggested in the form of reading and coffee-rooms. In Cincinnati such an establishment has been opened by the Committee on Temperance of the Young Men's Christian Association. The place has proved a success. A similar effort is being undertaken in Chicago. Why not follow suit in New York, Philadelphia, and all our large cities?

240 "Temperance Libraries." *National Advocate* [National Temperance Advocate], 2 (May 1867), p89, 200 wds (TxU).
   Temperance societies are increasing in number and are well organized; they should become more efficient by disseminating literature. In order for members to inform themselves about temperance, libraries should be established in Divisions, Lodges, and Temples. Such libraries may now be obtained from the National Society; all publications of this country and all standard English works on the subject may be ordered.

Theological Seminary Libraries

241 "View of the Theological Seminaries in the United States, 1831." *Congregational Education Society. Quarterly Journal* [American Education Society. Quarterly Register], 3 (May 1831), p303, 700 wds (ICN).
   This is a table that gives several kinds of information about 22 theological seminaries. For each of 14 seminaries, the number of volumes in the library is shown and for 5, the number in the student society libraries is indicated.

242 A Society of Clergymen. "Thoughts on the State of Theological Science and Education in Our Country." *Bibliotheca Sacra* [and Theological Review], 1 (November 1844), p735–67 (NcU).
   The part of the article about libraries (p763–64) is summarized below.
   Theological education would be improved by more extensive and valuable seminary libraries. It would be better to have fewer seminaries, but with strong libraries, than to have many seminaries with mediocre libraries, as we have now. There are about 130,000 volumes in the libraries of all the American theological

seminaries collectively. If located in fewer libraries, these could be better chosen and better arranged. There is some access to larger libraries, but none like the royal libraries at Berlin and Paris and the libraries at Göttingen and Munich. The theological department in each of these is well supplied with books for students and faculty. The lack of extensive libraries in America hampers efforts of scholars who must use European libraries for their researches. Our free and independent country should not be so beholden to foreign lands.

New England

243 "American Lyceum." *American Annals of Education* [American Journal of Education], 3 (November 1828), p701–04 (NcU).
The article considers the advantages of the lyceum in stimulating library use (p701–03 — summarized below).
Although the benefits of libraries are so evident and although almost every New England town has attempted to establish a library at some point in its history, it is thought that nine-tenths of the public libraries established in New England have for one reason or another ceased to exist. Merely having books within reach does not necessarily introduce the habit of reading to the public. Why do libraries fall into disuse? The most obvious reason is the want of interest in and taste for reading on the part of the public. When exercises or weekly courses are offered in connection with the library and on subjects treated by the books in the library, the public's desire for reading will be stimulated, and the library will be used. This connection between instruction and libraries is one object of the Lyceum.

244 "Massachusetts Associations of the New Jerusalem." *New Jerusalem Magazine*, 13 (February 1840), p239–40 (NIC).
The part of the article about libraries follows.
"From the report of the "Book Board," made at the late meeting in January, it appears that they have collected the sum of $146, of which $126.08 has been expended for books. The object of the board is to supply the social libraries of Massachusetts and Rhode Island with the writings of Swedenborg and other New Church publications. The plan adopted for the present is to supply to each library one copy each of the *True Christian Religion*, *Heaven and Hell*, and *The Four Leading Doctrines*. These have been furnished to thirty-seven libraries; and from the manner in which they have been received, and other facts which have come to the knowledge of the board, the highest confidence is expressed, that they will become a means of much use."

245 "Public Libraries." *New Englander and Yale Review*, 1 (July 1843), p307–11 (InU, NcU).
William Bartlet of Newburyport deserves to be honored because he supported the library of the Andover Theological Seminary while he was still living. He asked a professor there why the library needed more books since no one could read all it had already. The professor compared the library to a dictionary; one referred to its various sections when the need arose. In this country only public libraries have the potential to become great libraries; a tax of $1,000 annually would support a town library that would attract the best sort of citizens,

and benefit the townspeople greatly. Yale, unlike many colleges, began its existence with a library collection. A new library building is being erected there; it will cost something less than $30,000. The trustees have begun the building with only $13,000; they will complete it when additional money is obtained. (A picture of the exterior and a floor plan accompany this article.)

246 "Public Libraries in New England." *Bibliotheca Sacra* [and Theological Review], 7 (April 1850), p402–407 (NcU, OC).

(Individual libraries in New England, outside the Boston area, are described; for each, the total number of volumes and other information is given.) Most of the libraries mentioned are college libraries. There are 452,567 volumes in the libraries of New England; 233,334 in Massachusetts, 94,166 in Connecticut, 46,000 in Rhode Island, 23,167 in Vermont, 21,400 in New Hampshire, and 34,500 in Maine.

247 [Additions and Corrections to "Public Libraries in New England."] *Bibliotheca Sacra* [and Theological Review], 7 (July 1850), p607, 250 wds (NcD, OC).

The article consists of corrections and additions to two previous articles (p173–91 and 402–407) in this same volume *(see 477 and 246)*.

The Redwood Library was founded at Newport, R.I. in 1730. Abraham Redwood gave £500 for books in 1747. The collection numbers 5,500 volumes. The library has 100 members who subscribe $2.00 annually. The American Board of Commissioners for Foreign Missions has a 4,000 volume library in Boston. Salem, Mass., also has a library. Three errors in the statistics of the previous article are corrected.

248 "Books As Educators." *Literary World*, Boston, 2 (May 1872), p184, 550 wds (NcU).

It is safe to say that in every town in New England there are at least three or four persons who thirst for whatever is new and good in literature. But most of these cannot afford to buy books and, in rural areas, cannot borrow them. Country women need the exhilaration and stimulation of literature. We hope to see the day when public libraries are reckoned among the indispensable auxiliaries of public schools. The lack of access to good books has prevented men from educating themselves. Town libraries are found only in places of considerable size; small villages are no better off than they were twenty years ago. Until this deficiency is supplied, the three or four persons in each town with literary tastes will have to form a club to purchase books; these people will attract associates and see their library increase.

249 [Fiction in Three New England Libraries.] *Publishers' Weekly*, 5 (March 14, 1874), p273 (NcU).

The entire article follows; its information is identical with that in the table in an article in the *Nation* for March 5, 1874 *(see 29)*. The three libraries were the Bangor (Maine) Mercantile Library Association, the Quincy (Massachusetts) Public Library and the Lawrence (Massachusetts) Free Public Library.

"Here are the ranks in three Yankee libraries, of popular fictionists, in respect to call for their books:

[*See table on next page.*]

United States 70

	Bangor	Quincy	Lawrence
Mrs. M. J. Holmes	1	11	4
Mrs. Southworth	2	—*	1
Charles Reade	3	4	22
Wilkie Collins	4	10	17
Dickens	6	5	3
Hawthorne	8	19	43
Mrs. Whitney	9	2	13
A. S. Roe	11	8	64
Mrs. Muloch Craik	15	19	6
Lever	22	17	10
Bulwer	23	20	20
Scott	25	25	8

*Works excluded."

States and Territories

California

250 "California Academy of Natural Sciences." *Pacific. A Weekly Journal Devoted to Religion, Education & Useful Intelligence*, 2 (May 27, 1853), p344, 360 wds (CSaT, DLC).
At the society's meeting on May 23 a slate of officers was elected, and Dr. Henry Gibbons was appointed to deliver an address on the natural sciences. A regular series of lectures is being considered. Arrangements have been made to collect a library dealing with the natural sciences. A system of exchanges with scientific associations in the other states and in Europe will be undertaken. Anyone who may be able to make contributions of natural history specimens from California or the Pacific Islands is requested to send them to the society.

251 "Library Intelligence." *Norton's Literary Gazette and Publishers' Circular*, n.s. 2 (January 15, 1855), p33, 280 wds (MnU).
Libraries are springing up on the Pacific coast with a rapidity that marks the development of all things in that progressive region. The public library in Monterey is said to be the first established in California; its constitution and rules have just been published. In Sacramento there is a movement to establish a public library. In San Francisco the Law Library has capital of $30,000 and a library of 5,000 volumes. The Mercantile Library Association there has nearly 600 members and a library of more than 3,200 volumes; the Young Men's Christian Association has a collection of some 500 religious books, and two German societies combine reading rooms or libraries and gymnasiums. In Stockton there is a young organization, the Stockton Library Association; in Sacramento there is no public library, but the state has a respectable collection in the capitol.

ALVARADO — ODD FELLOWS LIBRARY

252 "The History of Odd Fellowship in California. Crusade Lodge, no. 93." *New Age*, 2 (December 1, 1866), p4 (CU).

Crusade Lodge was located in Alvarado, Alameda County. The part of the article about its library follows:

"The Lodge has commenced the purchase of a library for the exclusive use of the members, which already numbers over a thousand volumes. P. G., C. G. Eigenbrodt, Captain of Co. E, California Battalion, attached to the 2d Cavalry Regiment, Massachusetts Volunteers, and who was killed in battle August 25th, 1864, bequeathed to this Lodge one thousand dollars, which will form the nucleus of the library."

COLD SPRINGS

253 "Cold Springs, El Dorado Co." *Pacific. A Weekly Journal Devoted to Religion, Education & Useful Intelligence*, 3 (May 26, 1854), p114 (CSaT).

The article includes this paragraph:

"This enterprising mining town situated between Coloma and Placerville, in El Dorado county, is one of the most flourishing places in that region. A public Library of well selected literary and scientific works has been established, connected with which is a Lyceum, before which interesting lectures and debates have taken place during the past few months. This evidence of mental cultivation is highly credible [sic] to the citizens of that place and the parties engaged in the praiseworthy work."

254 V., S. "Early Public Library." *Pacific. A Weekly Journal Devoted to Religion, Education & Useful Intelligence*, 5 (March 20, 1856), p2, 200 wds (CSaT).

We were told that the library at Cold Springs, California is the oldest in the state except for the library in Los Angeles, so honor is due the residents of this mountain community. Money spent here is much better utilized than the larger amounts spent for theatres, circuses, balls, drinking parties, saloon recreations, and other such amusements. It is much better to obtain a permanent library and a series of lectures. May the good example of Cold Springs be followed by neighboring towns so all will have libraries.

COLUMBIA — PRESBYTERIAN CHURCH SABBATH SCHOOL LIBRARY

255 "S. S. Books." *Pacific. A Weekly Journal Devoted to Religion, Education & Useful Intelligence*, 6 (December 4, 1856), p2 (CSaT).

The entire article follows.

"In a visit to the Sabbath school of the Presbyterian Church at Columbia a few days since, we were struck with the selection of S.S. books, as very remarkably appropriate. We learn upon inquiry, that they were sent to the sabbath school by Mr. A. D. F. Randolph, of Broadway, New York. The Librarian sent the list of books on hand, to Mr. R., and the library was forthcoming. In looking over the books, we came to the conclusion that there was not a questionable book in the whole—nor yet one the children would leave lying on the shelves. Two great desiderata in a S.S. Library."

U.S. — California

COPPEROPOLIS

256 [Reading Room in Copperopolis, California.] *Pacific. A Weekly Journal Devoted to Religion, Education & Useful Intelligence*, 15 (May 17, 1866), p1 (CSaT).
The entire paragraph on the reading room follows.
"The social education and religious interests of Copperopolis have also been most encouragingly progressing. The curse of the thirty-six liquor-selling places in the town is less than the usual proportion for villages of the same size, while there is in the place the rare fact of an open resort where no liquors are sold and no cards played, but where all varieties of good papers, pamphlets and books can be read or bought, and an hour or an evening be spent in a good warm, comfortable apartment. This excellent establishment is kept by Westley & Williams, and is most worthy of imitation in all other towns."

JACKSON — ODD FELLOWS LIBRARY

257 "Odd Fellows' Library." *New Age*, 1 (December 30, 1865), p413 (C).
The entire article follows.
"The Amador DISPATCH of Dec. 23d, says the library of Jackson Lodge, No. 36, I.O.O.F., is a reality. It consists of two of the best encyclopedias in the world—Appleton's New American and the Iconographic. The latter is bound in morocco antique, and consists of six volumes, two of plates, the finest that art can produce, embracing every department of science, and four volumes of text. The former consists of sixteen volumes. They also have a full set of physiological and anatomical plates, acknowledged to be the best published, and they contemplate making additions to the library as fast as funds will permit.

NEVADA CITY — YOUNG MEN'S CHRISTIAN ASSOCIATION

258 "Religious Intelligence. The West." [Young Men's Christian Association of Nevada. *Pacific. A Weekly Journal Devoted to Religion, Education & Useful Intelligence*, 18 (September 23, 1869), p4 (CSaT).
The entire article follows. It apparently refers to Nevada City, California.
"The reading and lecture rooms of the Young Men's Christian Association of Nevada were dedicated with interesting exercises on the tenth instant. Rev. C. V. Anthony, of Grass Valley, delivered an address; and Rev. Alexander Parker, of Nevada, the Secretary, read the by-laws and regulations and made a short speech, setting forth the objects of the association."

OAKLAND — PACIFIC THEOLOGICAL SEMINARY LIBRARY

259 "Additions to the Library." *Pacific. A Weekly Journal Devoted to Religion, Education & Useful Intelligence*, 20 (March 9, 1871), p4, 220 wds (CSaT).
The Pacific Theological Seminary has been given $250 worth of books for $150. Edward Taylor and William G. Means, of Andover, Massachusetts supplied the money. The collection thus acquired includes complete runs of *Bibliotheca Sacra*, *Christian Spectator*, and *Congregational Quarterly*, along with such books as Parks' life of Emmons and Hunt's history of rationalism. Other small donations have been received and further gifts will be welcome.

PETALUMA — ODD FELLOWS LIBRARY

260 "Petaluma Lodge, No. 30, I. O. O. F." *New Age*, 3 (January 19, 1867), p8, 450 wds (CU-B).

We have received an interesting letter about progress of the order in Petaluma. The number of members diminished during the recent depression but now, with general prosperity, the lodge is flourishing. The members hope to erect their own building and have already taken an important step: The Petaluma Odd Fellows' Library Association was incorporated December 22; officers have been elected. The library will be beneficial for the entire community. The ladies connected with the order have held a fair, realizing the handsome sum of $200.

SAN FRANCISCO

261 "Anniversary of the San Francisco Sunday School Union." *Pacific. A Weekly Journal Devoted to Religion, Education & Useful Intelligence*, 3 (May 19, 1854), p110, 1730 wds (CSaT, DLC).

The following statistics of Sunday school libraries are provided: First Baptist Church, 500 volumes; Pine Street Baptist Church, 1,000; First Congregational Church, 450; Howard Street Presbyterian Church, 1,000; Folsom Street Methodist Episcopal Church, 250; First Presbyterian Church, 735; Powell Street Methodist Episcopal Church, 250; Trinity Church, 300; Bethel Church, 175; Market Street Church, 125.

262 "San Francisco Sunday School Union Anniversary." *Pacific. A Weekly Journal Devoted to Religion, Education & Useful Intelligence*, 16 (July 11, 1867), p2, 1100 wds (CSaT).

The secretary's report notes that four Sunday schools have been added to the union during the past year. Of these four, the South Park Congregational Sabbath School has a library of 200 volumes, and the Union Square Baptist Church Sabbath School also has a 200 volume library. The African Union has a small library. The Secretary has donated libraries to five locations. (A table presents the condition of the Sunday Schools. For most, the number of volumes in the library is noted.) There are 15,616 volumes in all combined.

— BANCROFT PACIFIC LIBRARY

263 Johnston, Henry P. "A Noteworthy Library." *New Outlook* [Christian Union], 10 (December 16, 1874), p478, 1740 wds (NcU).

Much of the article summarized below was abridged in *Publishers' Weekly* for January 30, 1875 *(see 264)*; some of it was printed verbatim in *American Bibliopolist* for February 1875 *(see 265)*.

Many libraries on the subject of American history owe their existence to private individuals and their collections. The new library of Pacific coast history is one example. Peter Force of Washington, D.C., and James Lenox of New York are examples of private collectors. Hubert Bancoft, a San Francisco publisher, has collected the library about which we speak. It consists of more than 16,000 works on the history of the Pacific coast from the Bering Strait to the Isthmus of Darien. Others have donated their collections on the subject to Bancroft; he purchased 3,000 volumes from the sale of what was to have been Emperor Maximilian's library in Mexico City. Anyone studying the original sources about Pacific coast history must hereafter go to Bancroft's library.

U.S. — California

264 "Americana Libraries." *Publishers' Weekly*, 7 (January 30, 1875), p109–10 (NcU).
This article is a summary of much of an article that appeared in *The Christian Union* (later *New Outlook*) for December 16, 1874 *(see 263)*.

265 Johnston, Henry P. "A Noteworthy Library." *American Bibliopolist*, 7 (February 1875), p44–46 (NcD, OC).
The article summarized below is reprinted from part of an article in *The Christian Union* (later *New Outlook*) for December 16, 1874 *(see 263)*.
For the preservation of our history, we are indebted to a few private book collectors. The library of Hubert Bancroft, a San Francisco publisher, contains more than 16,000 volumes, pamphlets, and documents, in several languages, dealing with the history of the Pacific coast from the Bering Straits to the Isthmus of Darien. Bancroft has acquired several other smaller collections and 3,000 volumes of what was to have been the Imperial Library ordered by Maximilian to be established in Mexico City.

— LAW LIBRARY

266 "Law Library at San Francisco." *Norton's Literary Gazette and Publishers' Circular*, 3 (January 15, 1853), p3 (ICN, NcU).
The entire article follows.
"W. B. Olds, Esq., Clerk of the Superior Court at San Francisco, has at the request of the Bar of that city, commenced the formation of a complete Law Library, which, it is intended, shall be second to none in the United States. One shipment of fifteen hundred volumes has already been made, to be followed soon by others."

267 "San Francisco (Cal.) Law Library." *Norton's Literary Gazette and Publishers' Circular*, 3 (March 15, 1853), p40 (NcU).
The entire article follows.
"We learn from the San Francisco Whig, in regard to this library, that 'William B. Olds, Esq., the Clerk of the Superior Court, has taken the necessary steps to procure a well-selected assortment of law books, as well as miscellaneous standard and classical works, for the commencement of an extensive public library for the reference of all the profession. The money has been remitted for the purchase, and a portion of the books are now on their way. He will expend some $12,000 in the commencement of this enterprise, with the determination to prosecute the work till he has secured for San Francisco, a library which shall compare favorably with those of older cities, and be well worthy of our city and its bar. Mr. Olds has petitioned the Common Council for convenient and commodious rooms in the City Hall for the accommodation of this library.'"

— MECHANICS' INSTITUTE LIBRARY

268 [Mechanics' Institute Library and Reading Room]. *Pacific. A Weekly Journal Devoted to Religion, Education & Useful Intelligence*, 21 (September 19, 1872), p5 (CSaT).
The following article refers to the Mechanics' Institute in San Francisco.
The reading room of the Mechanics Institute will be open on Sunday as heretofore. The library only will be closed. The reading room is a place of resort for a large number of members on Sundays, and the closing of its doors that day has not been contemplated.

San Francisco

— MERCANTILE LIBRARY

269 "San Francisco, Cal." *Norton's Literary Gazette and Publishers' Circular*, p19 (ICN, NcU).
The entire article follows.
"Some enterprising men of this flourishing place are about to establish a Mercantile Library. We wish them the best success. A public meeting has already been held, and committees chosen for the preparation of Constitution, By-Laws, etc."

270 "Mercantile Library at San Francisco." *Norton's Literary Gazette and Publishers' Circular*, 3 (May 15, 1853), p84 (ICN, NcU).
The entire article follows.
"This new association, to which we have before alluded, solicits donations of books from individuals and societies at the East. Booksellers, publishers, merchants, and all who, from motives of benevolence, patriotism, or business, are willing to forward this praiseworthy undertaking are requested to send their contributions to Messrs. Adams & Co., whose express offices are located all over the country. By the courtesy of these gentlemen, any parcels of books for the San Francisco Mercantile Library will be brought by their expresses to New York *without charge*, and will there be packed and shipped to Chas. E. Bowers, jr., Esq., Treasurer of the Association. Donors are requested to place their autographs in the volumes which they send."

271 "Mercantile Library Association." *Pacific. A Weekly Journal Devoted to Religion, Education & Useful Intelligence*, 3 (January 27, 1854), p54, 220 wds (CSaT).
The Mercantile Library Association [of San Francisco] elected officers on Tuesday evening for the coming year. David S. Turner will serve as president. The association has 276 members and 3,000 volumes in the library. The cash receipts for the last year were about $11,000, but there is a current indebtedness of $1,500. A subscription was taken at the meeting and about $1,000 was raised.

272 [Mercantile Library Association of San Francisco — Annual Meeting.] *Norton's Literary Gazette and Publishers' Circular*, n.s. 1 (March 15, 1854), p144 (NcU).
The entire article follows.
"The annual meeting of the Mercantile Library Association of San Francisco, was held on the 25th of January. From the Reports presented on that occasion, we learn that the Association has now 3,000 volumes in its library, and 276 regular members connected with it. The receipts for the past year were about $11,000 leaving a debt for rent, which is the heaviest item of their expenditure, of $1,500. About $1,000 of this were raised at once. At the election for officers, Mr. David S. Turner was unanimously reelected President."

273 [San Francisco Mercantile Library.] *Norton's Literary Gazette and Publishers' Circular*, n.s. 1 (October 16, 1854), p532, 290 wds (NcU).
A copy of the recent valuable catalog of the San Francisco Mercantile Library has been sent to us. Although the library has been established only about one year, there are over 3,000 volumes. (The number of works held in each of nine categories is given.) There is a valuable general reference collection, including maps, charts, encyclopedias, and dictionaries. The catalog has an alpha-

U.S. — California 76

betical arrangement of titles and a full analytical index in which titles are arranged by subjects. The catalog speaks well for the direction of this young state. Since its inception, this library has needed an agency on the Atlantic coast where donations might be left with a certainty of their reaching their destination; the publisher of this journal has now been appointed as the representative. Next spring, the library will make a vigorous effort to secure a building.

274 [Lecture Series of the Mercantile Library Association of San Francisco Published.] *National Magazine: Devoted to Literature, Art, and Religion*, 9 (December 1856), p570 (InU, NcU).
The entire article follows.
"*Carter & Brothers* have published, in a neat little volume, three lectures, entitled *Trade and Letters: their Journeyings Round the World*. They were delivered by the Rev. Dr. W. A. Scott, before the Mercantile Library Association of San Francisco, and are published at the request of those who heard them. It is gratifying to know that away off there, among the gold-hunters, appreciative audiences find time to listen to lectures, and that mental improvement is not altogether neglected. The lectures are fully equal to the average of those heard on this side of the Rocky Mountains."

275 [Lectures at the Mercantile Library, San Francisco.] *Pacific. A Weekly Journal Devoted to Religion, Education & Useful Intelligence*, 18 (April 8, 1869), p5 (CSaT).
The entire article follows.
"Rev. Mr. Ames (Unitarian), delivers three lectures at the Mercantile Library Hall on three successive Thursday evenings, the first being Thursday the 8th. The subject is — 'Men and Women, Marriage and Domestic Life.' "

276 [Mercantile Library, San Francisco.] *Pacific. A Weekly Journal Devoted to Religion, Education & Useful Intelligence*, 20 (March 9, 1871), p4, 200 wds (CSaT).
The annual report of the Mercantile Library Association of this city indicates that the circulation for 1870 was 82,564. Of this total, 62,850 were classed as "Romance," 3,303 as "Travel," and 560 as "Religion." The library's collection numbered 30,000 volumes. The much heavier circulation of romances than religious books was a not altogether pleasing indication of the reading tastes of the city.

277 "San Francisco Mercantile Library Association." *Publishers' Weekly* [Publishers' and Stationers' Weekly Trade Circular], 2 (October 24, 1872), p416 (NcU).
The entire article follows.
"According [to] the 19th annual report of this institution, being that for the past year, 1871, the Association has now 2,062 members, and has added 4,741 volumes to its Library since January, 1871, making a total of 30,006 volumes on the shelves and in circulation. The authorities of this library make it a special point to collect all the printed matter relative to California and the Pacific coast. The Librarian, in his report says, 'We are building up on this coast a civilization peculiar, isolated. The libraries and educational institutions of the Eastern States are far removed. We must have all these resources within ourselves; the implements out of which to fashion thought, stimulate and promote culture.' "

278 [San Francisco Mercantile Library.] *Publishers' Weekly*, 5 (May 9, 1874), p458 (NcU).
The entire article follows.
"According to the annual report of the San Francisco Mercantile Library, the number of books taken from the library during 1873 was 88,751, against 88,916 drawn out in 1872, and 84,710 in 1871. The membership remains about the same (2,000) as it was a year ago, but the number of books has increased (36,000–33,000 [sic]). As to the kind of books or authors patronized, the librarian gives no statistics."

279 [The Catalogue of the Mercantile Library of San Francisco.] *Nation*, 19 (September 24, 1874), p203, 550 wds (NcU).
The catalog of the Mercantile Library of San Francisco is now before us, the third which the association has issued in twenty years; this catalog lists more than 36,000 volumes. It is on the general plan of the Boston Public Library catalog, but it is an improvement on the model; the titles are very full and the topical arrangement very detailed. The reader's time is saved by listing parts of collections and of contents of works alphabetically; for example, all dramas in the collection are arranged alphabetically by title. The work deserves to be kept in all libraries as a guide for readers and students.

280 [Mercantile Library of San Francisco.] *Literary World*, Boston, 5 (April 1875), p174, 160 wds (NcU).
The report of Alfred E. Whitaker, Librarian in 1874 at the Mercantile Library of San Francisco, makes clear the condition of the institution and contains some well-considered observations on the management of libraries. During the past year a catalog, skillfully compiled by Mr. Whitaker, has been published. The total number of volumes on January 1, 1875 was 39,148, and circulation was 84,763; of this circulation, 69.8 percent belonged to the department of romance. Only 4,227 juvenile volumes circulated; evidently, San Francisco children do not begin to read as early as do those in New England. The number of foreign books circulating—2,516 in French, 1,932 in German, and 87 in Spanish—indicates the mixed character of the population.

281 [Catalogue of the Mercantile Library of San Francisco.] *Nation*, 21 (December 2, 1875), p356 (NcU).
The entire article follows.
"Quite recently we had occasion to notice the supplement to the catalogue of the Wisconsin Historical Society's library, and now we receive from the Pacific Coast a supplement to that of the Mercantile Library of San Francisco. The main work is, as our readers are aware, one of the very best of the recent improved catalogues on the dictionary plan. The supplement fills 168 pages, and represents an accession of about 5,000 volumes to the 36,000 reported up to February 1, 1874—certainly a very healthy growth. It merits the same praise as its predecessor for attractive typography, judicious subdivisions, and full analyses of contents. The only new feature is a numbering with reference to position on the shelves."

— MILITARY LIBRARY

282 [Military Library of San Francisco.] *Literary World*, Boston, 5 (April 1875), p175 (NcU).

U.S. — California

The entire article follows.

"We have received a copy of the catalogue of the Military Library of San Francisco, of which David Wilder is Secretary and Treasurer. This Library was organized two years ago, and has been sustained by officers of the National Guard of California. It comprises six hundred volumes, which seem to have been selected with exceptionally good judgment."

— ODD FELLOWS LIBRARY

283 "Library Bust." *New Age*, 2 (June 30, 1866), p1 (CU).
The following article refers to the library of the Odd Fellows in San Francisco.
Brother P. G., John Q. Piper, has purchased the first Copy of the Bust of P. G. M. Parker, and presented it to the Library, where it is installed, the inanimate figure, presiding at an institution over which the spirit exercised its fostering influence, during the life time of the original.

284 "Lithograph." *New Age*, 2 (June 30, 1866), p1 (CU-B).
The entire article is reproduced below. It refers to the Odd Fellows Library in San Francisco.
"An elegant lithograph of the bust of P. G. M. Parker, may be seen in the O. F. Library rooms in this city. If there were any doubts as to the truthfulness of the bust, this lithograph would at once dispel them, for it is a striking likeness of Brother Parker when in this life, and pays a high compliment to the artist who sculptured the bust, of which it is the shadow."

285 [Picnic at Sausalito for Benefit of the Odd Fellows' Library Fund.] *Pacific. A Weekly Journal Devoted to Religion, Education & Useful Intelligence*, 19 (July 7, 1870), p5 (CSaT).
The following article apparently refers to the Odd Fellows' Library at San Francisco.
"The Odd Fellows' picnic at Saucelito [*sic*] some weeks ago, netted $1,935 for the benefit of the Order, clear of all expenses. This sum will be put to the credit of the Library Fund."

— WHAT CHEER HOUSE LIBRARY

286 "The Museum at the What Cheer House." *Hutchings' Illustrated California Magazine*, 5 (November 1860), p206–08 (C).
The part of the article about libraries (170 wds) is summarized below.
R. B. Woodward, proprietor of the What Cheer House in San Francisco, established a large library for the use of his patrons. We think it must be the most heavily used library in the state. The large reading room, with books arranged on two sides, frequently is entirely filled with readers. The more sober and better classes waiting for conveyance find amusement and instruction in the library. Mr. Woodward should be named a public benefactor for establishing his reading room.

287 "Library of the What Cheer House, San Francisco." *Hutchings' Illustrated California Magazine*, 5 (January 1861), p294–95 (C).
The library in this public hotel is the only one of its kind as far as the author knows. The inauguration of such a book collection is judicious, as travelers

frequently experience days in which they would like to read in the comfort and familiarity of their accommodations. The reading room has files of newspapers from all over California and from many places in the eastern states and Europe. The book collection of between 2,000 and 3,000 volumes includes works on agriculture, biographies, novels, and works of history. There are also volumes of poetry and drama, and books about voyages and travels. The excellent selection reflects the taste of the purchaser. The service is free to patrons of the hotel. (A view of the library room is shown.)

288 "A California Caravansary." *Harper's Magazine*, 34 (April 1867), p603-06 (NcU).
The article concerns the hotel, What Cheer House, in San Francisco. The part about libraries (p605-06), is summarized below.
The library of What Cheer House was begun by R. B. Woodward, the present proprietor. All hotels feed the body, but there were none serving the mind, so Woodward decided in 1856 to found a library. He went east, consulted with Harper & Brothers, and purchased 1,500 books. The library now has 3,000-4,000 volumes, selected to suit the tastes of travelers. There are works on gardening, ranching, etc., biography and history, fiction, English translations of the classics, and current journals. The annual newspaper bill is $1,200. This reading room is full all day. Were it not for the library, a bar would have been needed to occupy the guests' spare time. All large hotels should consider having a library. At present, few even have decent reading rooms.

— YOUNG MEN'S CHRISTIAN ASSOCIATION LIBRARY

289 "The Y. M. C. A. Building, San Francisco." *Harper's Weekly*, 13 (February 6, 1869), p81 (InU, NcU).
The entire article follows. The picture is an exterior view.
"This elegant and commodious building, of which we give an illustration on this page, has been recently erected for the use of the Young Men's Christian Association in San Francisco. It is located on Suttee Street, and has a frontage of 54 feet with 120 feet depth. It consists of a basement and two stories with a Mansard roof overlooked by a tower, and contains a reading-room, lecture-hall, a library, and lodging and bath rooms. There is also a gymnasium connected with the building. The front is built of blue sandstone wrought after the Venetian style. The building and lot cost $75,000."

290 [Young Men's Christian Association of San Francisco.] *Pacific. A Weekly Journal Devoted to Religion, Education & Useful Intelligence*, 18 (April 29, 1869), p1, 260 wds (CSaT).
The association has just published the fifteenth annual report since its organization in July 1853. Since its beginning the association has had 1,441 members, 115 admitted last year. The library contains about 2,000 volumes. There are 22 newspapers and 11 periodicals in the reading room. A new building was erected (an engraving of the façade is provided) during the last year, at a cost of $80,375. The funded indebtedness is $57,000. The various YMCAs of California will hold a convention here on May 14.

U.S. — California

SAN JOSE — PRESBYTERIAN CHURCH LIBRARY

291 [Library of the Presbyterian Church in San Jose.] *Pacific. A Weekly Journal Devoted to Religion, Education & Useful Intelligence*, 21 (September 5, 1872), p4 (CSaT).

The entire reference to the library, in the column: "Religious Intelligence; the West" is reproduced below.

"There are 857 volumes in the library, which is kept fresh by the constant addition of new books and the as constant removal of obsolete ones. The new books are ordered directly from the east, placed in the hands of teachers, and only after careful scrutiny admitted to the library."

SHASTA — ODD FELLOWS LIBRARY

292 "Traveling Correspondence. Shasta." *New Age*, 4 (December 12, 1868), p791 (CU).

The author tells of visiting the I. O. O. F. lodge no. 57, at Shasta, California. The part about the library follows:

"This Lodge has just started a library, which will be an attraction, and add to the influence and interest of the Order in that vicinity. The collection of libraries should command more of the consideration of Lodges. The result must necessarily be beneficial."

— SHASTA LIBRARY ASSOCIATION

293 "Shasta a Good Example." *Pacific. A Weekly Journal Devoted to Religion, Education & Useful Intelligence*, 8 (January 6, 1859), p4 (CSaT).

The part of the article about a library follows.

"The young men have formed a Library Association, whose growing bookcases and well stocked reading room, make many a pleasant evening for those who would otherwise be left to the loneliness and perils of California leisure.

"Here is an example for some other towns. Communities, like individuals, have their times of reflection. Why should they not lead to such *action* as is here recorded?"

SPANISH FLAT — FRANKLIN LIBRARY ASSOCIATION

294 "Lyceums and Libraries in the Mines." *Pacific. A Weekly Journal Devoted to Religion, Education & Useful Intelligence*, 4 (December 8, 1854), p6, 380 wds (CSaT, DLC).

As mining towns become more permanent, more young men are turning from the saloons and gaming tables to public libraries, lyceums, and debating societies. These men seek to raise the level of public morals in their communities. Spanish Flat in Sierra County is one town where this is happening. There, the Franklin Library Association has been formed, and a library has been purchased. Most of the books are histories and biographies, but there are also some poetry and science books. The Association holds weekly meetings; its members are especially interested in the history and natural history of California.

STOCKTON — LITERARY ASSOCIATION LIBRARY

295 [Literary Association of Stockton, California.] *Pacific. A Weekly Journal Devoted to Religion, Education & Useful Intelligence*, 3 (January 27, 1854, p55 (CSaT).
The entire article follows.
"A Literary Association is sustained in Stockton, before which some free lectures are to be delivered this season. Provision also is to be made for a library."

— YOUNG MEN'S CHRISTIAN ASSOCIATION LIBRARY

296 "Stockton." *Pacific. A Weekly Journal Devoted to Religion, Education & Useful Intelligence*, 20 (December 21, 1871), p5 (CSaT).
The entire article follows.
"The Young Men's Christian Association held its anniversary in the Presbyterian church on the evening of the 12th inst. Rev. Dr. Scott, of San Francisco, delivered the address. The President, Treasurer and Secretary made their annual reports of last year's operations and of the present condition of the association. The value of assets, including library, is $885.25; the number of members is: active, 95; associate, 25; auxiliary, 10—total, 130; receipts, $615.71; expenditures, $601.30. A reading-room is kept open, and a room for conversation and meetings, and a Young Men's Literary Society is maintained, for debates, essays, orations, etc."

— YOUNG MEN'S LIBRARY ASSOCIATION

297 "Young Men's Library Association." *Pacific. A Weekly Journal Devoted to Religion, Education & Useful Intelligence*, 3 (March 10, 1854), p78, 110 wds (CSaT).
The entire article follows; it was reprinted from the Stockton *Journal* of March 2, 1854.
"Last evening the lecture of Judge Baine upon the subject of 'True Greatness' before The Association, drew a large audience. It was one of the ablest of the course now in progress of delivery before The Society, and one that proved deeply interesting to all who were present. The affairs of The Association are in a flourishing condition. Books are open at the office of Judge Baine, soliciting the membership of all who are disposed to aid in the permanent establishment of a library in this city. The lecture on next Thursday evening will be delivered by Rev. Dr. Stevenson on the subject of 'Truth.'"

VALLEJO — LIBRARY ASSOCIATION

298 [Vallejo, California Library Association.] *Pacific. A Weekly Journal Devoted to Religion, Education & Useful Intelligence*, 18 (January 28, 1869), p4 (CSaT).
The entire reference to the library under the heading "Miscellaneous" is reproduced below.
"The Vallejo Library Association has just reorganized, and received an acquisition of forty new members. The library contains over 600 volumes."

Connecticut

299 "Benevolent Expectations for Libraries in Schools." *American Annals of Education*, 3d ser., 1 (April 1831), p177-78 (NcU).
In a Cheshire, Connecticut school district, an instructor has spent, during the past two years, more than $100 of his salary on books for the school library. In the same region another instructor purchases a small collection at the beginning of the school term, and then at the end of the term he divides the books among his students. To these men, libraries are indispensable.

300 "Common School Libraries." *Connecticut Common School Journal and Annals of Education*, 2 (August 1839), p11-12 (NcU).
The law of the last session gives every school district in the state the power to establish and maintain a common school library. We urge that this be done. Connecticut is behind other states in this matter. Each district may gain a valuable collection of books by spending the amount authorized for the first year. The Board of Commissioners of Common Schools have just appointed a committee to devise the best plan to execute the law. (A quotation from "Means and Ends, or Self Training," by Miss Sedgwick, is given. It is intended for girls from 10 to 16 years of age, and concerns what and how to read.)

301 Paddock, S. B. and Perkins, F. A. "Reports of School Visitors and Local Intelligence. Norwich Second School Society." *Connecticut Common School Journal and Annals of Education*, 3 (November 15, 1840), p25-26 (NcU).
The part of the article about libraries (p26) follows.
"We earnestly recommend that libraries of useful books be introduced into all the districts. It may now be done at a small expense, and the result, in creating a taste for reading, and an increased desire to treasure up knowledge, cannot be too highly estimated."

302 Barnard, Henry. "Third Annual Report of the Board of Commissioners of Common Schools in Connecticut: Together with the Third Annual Report of the Secretary of the Board, May, 1841." *Connecticut Common School Journal and Annals of Education*, 3 (September 1, 1841), p241-56 (NcU).
The parts of the Secretary's report that are about libraries (p253-56) are summarized below.
"School District or Society Libraries," p253-54: There are not more than twenty school district libraries in the state; in New York, by the end of 1843, $530,000 had been spent for more than two million volumes. Connecticut should hold out inducements to school societies and districts to purchase libraries; perhaps books should be bought and passed from one district to another, thus keeping readers interested through access to more books. On p255-56 is a list of the contents of the library in a new schoolhouse for district no. 6, in Windsor. "History and Progress of School District Libraries," on p256 (800 wds) traces the movement with emphasis on developments in New York State and brief mention of Michigan, Massachusetts, New Jersey, and Connecticut.

EAST BERLIN — SCHOOL DISTRICT LIBRARY

303 "East Berlin Library." *Connecticut Common School Journal and Annals of Education*, n.s. 6 (December 1852), p369–72 (CtHi).

The article summarized below was reprinted in the *Pennsylvania School Journal* 1 (February 1853), p338–39 *(see 304)*.

The friends of educational improvement in the East Berlin School District have replaced a dilapidated building in a poor location with a spacious and attractive edifice in a good location and have hired a well-qualified teacher at a salary on which he can support himself and family. Mr. Charles F. Dowd, the teacher, has been instrumental in the establishment of an excellent library to serve the school and all citizens of the district. The necessary money was obtained in three ways: Mr. Dowd taught an evening class, charging tuition: the ladies of the district held a "fair"; and a subscription paper was circulated. Using the funds thus collected, Dowd purchased 620 volumes, which he presented to the town on behalf of the subscribers. (The bylaws and regulations of the library follow the article.)

304 "East Berlin Library—Connecticut." *Pennsylvania School Journal*, 1 (February 1853), p338–39 (IU).

The article was reprinted from the *Connecticut Common School Journal*, n.s. 6 (December 1852) *(see 303)*.

HARTFORD

305 "Wadsworth Athenaeum and Libraries in Hartford." *Norton's Literary Gazette and Publishers' Circular*, n.s. 2 (February 15, 1855), p69–70 (MnU).

In 1841 Mr. Wadsworth offered to give the citizens of Hartford whatever money was needed if they would erect a building to house an art gallery, the Connecticut Historical Society and the Hartford Young Men's Institute. A subscription was taken and the Hartford Athenaeum was incorporated in 1842. The Athenaeum building is 100 x 70 feet, divided into three sections: the northern part is occupied by the Young Men's Institute and its library of more than 11,000 volumes; the central part, by the Wadsworth gallery of art, containing about 140 paintings; and the third part by the Connecticut Historical Society. (Other Hartford libraries are described; a table gives the number of volumes in each of the larger ones, and in groups of smaller ones, a total of 51,000 volumes.)

— STATE LIBRARY

306 "The Connecticut State Library." *Albany Law Journal*, 7 (January 25, 1873), p63, 160 wds (NcU).

The information is taken from the *Hartford (CT) Post*.

The collection of American law reports in this library is now complete, comprising the reports of all states and territories. Not more than one or two other libraries in the country have complete sets. It has been very difficult to obtain some of the volumes; the last one was procured last week. The purchases have been carefully and economically made by Mr. Charles J. Hoadly, the state Librarian. The library also has a complete collection of English and Irish law reports.

U.S. — Connecticut 84

307 "The Connecticut State Library." *Publishers' Weekly*, 3 (January 30, 1873), p114, 160 wds (NcU).

The collection of American law reports at Hartford is now complete, comprising the reports from every state and territory in the Union. Only one or two other libraries in the country have all of these; the State Library at Albany probably does. The difficult job of collecting the reports has been accomplished carefully and economically by Mr. [Charles J.] Hoadly, the Connecticut State Librarian, whose faithful and efficient services deserve this public acknowledgement. The library also has the English and Irish law reports, beginning with the Year Books, first written in 1292, and recently published from the manuscript.

— YOUNG MEN'S INSTITUTE LIBRARY

308 "Hartford, Conn., Young Men's Institute." *Norton's Literary Gazette and Publishers' Circular*, 3 (September 15, 1853), p150 (N).
The entire article follows.
"The 15th report of this Association, has just been published. The present number of volumes in the library, is not stated; but 324 have been added by purchase, and 63 by donation, making the additions for the year, 387. The Institute numbers about 725 members. The Constitution of the society, together with a list of the members, is printed with the report. Mr. H. M. Bailey continues to discharge the duties of Librarian."

309 [The Hartford Young Men's Institute.] *Nation*, 21 (August 12, 1875), p102, 260 wds (NcU).

The city of Hartford has a cultivated society and is the seat of a great deal of solid learning. We regret that the Young Men's Institute there, according to its thirty-seventh annual report, is in danger of having to close its doors. Its collection is large and up-to-date, and its catalog of 1873 is creditable; nothing seems wanting but public spirit. If the city authorities are unwilling to make it a free library, there is wealth enough in Hartford to make the transformation easy. The worthy citizens who plan to leave money for a new college in New England should put their money where it will do more good.

NEW HAVEN — YALE COLLEGE — LAW SCHOOL LIBRARY

310 "The Yale Law School Library." *Albany Law Journal*, 7 (February 22, 1873), p128, 200 wds (NcU).

The library of the Yale Law School has been arranged in the new library room in the county courthouse in New Haven; the books have been classified by subject. The reports of the various states have the names of the states on cards placed above them; considerable additions are needed for this part of the collection. Bindings have been repaired or replaced. There are many old and rare books, including a set of the session laws of Connecticut back to colonial times. Ex-Governor English and others have given a total of $30,000, the income of which is to be used for book purchases.

— YALE COLLEGE LIBRARY

311 "Munificent Donation to Yale College Library." *American Journal of Science*, 27 (January 1835), p184–85 (InU, NcU).

About 30 titles in 74 volumes have been presented to the Yale College Library by the Record Commission in England through the efforts of Mr. O. Rich, of London. The titles include: *Domesday Book*, 2 volumes; *Statutes of the Realm*, 9 volumes; *Inquisitionum Retornatarum Scotiae Abbreviatio*, 3 volumes; *Acts of Parliament of Scotland*, volumes II to XI; and *Catalogue of the MSS in the Cottonian Library*. Resolutions of acknowledgment and thanks have been made by the Corporation of the College to the Record Commission and to Mr. Rich.

312 Kingsley. "A Sketch of the History of Yale College, in Connecticut." *Congregational Education Society. Quarterly Journal* [American Quarterly Register], 8 (August 1835), p13–40 (NcU).

The article is concluded in the February 1836 issue, p201–18, *(see 313)*. The part of the article about libraries is summarized below.

The college was actually begun in 1700 when the trustees all brought books for a library to a meeting in Branford. In the move from Saybrook to New Haven in 1716, many books and papers were lost, and the library was about a week on the road. A wooden building for the students was built in 1718; it contained the library also. After the first public commencement in 1718, the men dined in the college hall; the ladies were entertained in the library. The library was enriched with many valuable books, principally by donation from England. The library books were rearranged and a catalog printed in 1743. In 1763, the library was moved to the new chapel, begun in 1761.

313 Kingsley. "A Sketch of the History of Yale College, in Connecticut." *Congregational Education Society. Quarterly Journal* [American Quarterly Register], 8 (February 1836), p201–218 (NcU).

This article is a continuation of the one in the August 1835 issue of the *American Quarterly Register (see 312)*. The parts of the article about libraries are summarized below.

The Connecticut Lyceum, a building containing a library and other rooms, was finished in 1803. The library was increased through an appropriation in 1804, and a trip was made to Europe to purchase books. When the new chapel was built in 1824, the old one was devoted to the literary society libraries and recitations; the library of the college was moved to the new chapel. (Gifts of money and books to the library are discussed, including those of George Berkeley and Eli Whitney.) The library grew slowly. The original trustees gave 40 folio volumes, almost all about theology. The deficiencies of the library have always been strongly felt. There are now over 10,000 volumes. The departments of law and medicine have few books. The library is weak in classical and general literature, strongest in theology and science. The literary society libraries, strong in general literature, contain 15,000 volumes combined.

314 "College Edifices and their Relation to Education." *American Literary Magazine*, 1 (November 1847), p269–74 (NcU).

The part of the article about the Yale Library (p269–70) is summarized below.

(The dimensions of the library, now under construction, are given in the article.) The fireproof building will house the college library, the libraries of the Brothers in Unity and the Linonian and Calliopean Societies, the librarian's office and a reading room. It is estimated that the room for the college library may be able to contain from 60,000 to 70,000 books. The building is intended to meet future as well as present needs. When the building is occupied, it will house the college library's 20,000 volumes, and the 26,000 to 27,000 volumes held in the society libraries; including the departmental libraries, which will be gathered together, there will be a total of 50,000 volumes in the library. The collection comprises books on the several branches of science and literature which are part of the curriculum. Thus far, construction costs have totaled $34,000; $6,000 more is needed for completion. (An exterior view of the building accompanies the article.)

315 "Yale College Library." *Norton's Literary Gazette and Publishers' Circular*, 2 (October 15, 1852), p187, 2000 wds (ICN, NcU).

In 1700 ten clergymen met in New Haven for the purpose of founding a college. At their meeting, each one donated some of his own books to the new college. In October 1701, the college was established; in 1717-18 it was moved to New Haven and was named Yale College. The library's growth was slow until 1733 when the Rev. George Berkeley gave his 1,000 volume collection to the library. Although it did suffer some losses during the Revolutionary War, since then it has received a number of bequests of books and money. The library along with the literary society libraries occupied a new building in 1846. The library has a good, albeit small, collection of 24,000 volumes that gradually is being enlarged. Anyone may use the library, but only the faculty, professional men, and upperclassmen may borrow books. There are about 53,500 books in the college and literary society libraries. (An exterior view of the building accompanies the article.)

316 Gilman, Daniel Coit. "The Library of Yale College." *University Quarterly: Conducted by an Association of Collegiate and Professional Students, in the U.S. and Europe*, 2 (October 1860), p244-61 (InU).

(The significant events in the library's history are briefly mentioned, beginning with the formation of the college in 1700. The list compiled by President Stiles in 1784 of works given by four of the founders is reprinted. Several of the more important eighteenth and nineteenth century donations are described.) The first catalog was printed in 1743. Since the last printed catalog, in 1823, a manuscript catalog on cards has been developed, but there are no plans to print it. The library currently has 38,000 volumes and the library building also houses the libraries of the Linonian Society and the society of the Brothers in Unity, each with about 12,000 volumes. The Medical and Law Libraries and the Library of the American Oriental Society are also kept in the College Library. The College Library building was commenced in 1842, and when the stone pinnacles are added the total cost will be about $40,000. There are eleven library funds worth $26,021.62. The annual income from these funds is about $1,500. (The laws governing the use of the library are reprinted.)

317 "Archaeological Collection in the Library of Yale College." *University Quarterly: Conducted by an Association of Collegiate and Professional Students, in the U.S. and Europe*, 4 (October 1861), p277-86 (InU).

The library of Yale College now contains what is believed to be the most valuable collection of ancient inscriptions on this side of the Atlantic. Some are owned by the college, and others are deposited in the Library as a part of the Cabinet of the American Oriental Society. Individual items are described, and some are translated. The collection contains four Assyrian inscriptions from Nineveh; a Greek inscription from near Antioch; a Greek inscription from

Beirut; two sepulchral inscriptions from Kula, in Asia Minor; three Sanskrit inscriptions from Central India; a facsimile of the Rosetta Stone; and a facsimile of the Potidaean Inscription. Two scrolls are displayed near this archaeological collection; one of them, a eulogy in Chinese of George Washington, is translated.

318 Skinner, Richard. "An Hour or Two in the College Library." *Yale Literary Magazine*, 27 (November 1861), 41–52 (IaU).

Most Yalensians are aware of the Library but few know much of its character or value. We have recently spent some time there, examining its curiosities and rarities; we present a guide to them: I. *Bibliographical curiosities*. (Several manuscripts and significant examples of printing are described, including Eliot's Indian Bible and the manuscript "Laws of Yale College," 1726; excerpts from the latter are given.) II. *Coins*. (Some of the coins from the United States, Great Britain, other European countries, and elsewhere are described.) III. *Works of Art*. (Busts of famous men, portraits, important photographs and engravings and a few pieces of historically significant furniture are described.) IV. *Archaeological*. (Ancient inscriptions and various artifacts are described.) Mr. Daniel C. Gilman, the librarian, and Mr. Edward C. Herrick, his predecessor, have aided us in the preparation of this article.

319 Beach, Harlan P. "Consolidation of the Libraries." *Yale Literary Magazine*, 29 (March 1864), p193–98 (DLC).

A plan to form a united reading room of the Linonian Society and the Brothers of Unity became a plan to consolidate the libraries and to expand the scope of the reading room. Practically, the libraries are already consolidated; both societies use both libraries. It is inconvenient, however, to consult different ones. The librarians support a reorganization. Only one librarian and one catalog would be needed for the consolidated library. The characters of the college and society libraries are uncertain. The college library should be one of reference; society libraries should be circulating libraries. The room made vacant by the reorganization can house a reading and reference room. Some say the plan will decrease society rivalries, but the libraries have been cooperating for many years with no abatement of society feeling. Other objections deal with the details of the plan rather than the plan itself.

320 "A Catalogue of Official Reports upon Geological Surveys of the United States and British Provinces." *American Journal of Science*, 2nd ser. 43 (January, May 1867), p116–21 and p399–404 (InU, NcU).

The catalog of a set of American geological reports in the Yale College Library to aid geologists and to permit any inaccuracies or deficiencies to be noted. Reports for states east of the Mississippi River are listed in the January issue (p116–21); reports for western states and Canadian provinces, as well as corrections for the January list, are in the May issue (p399–404).

321 "The Library." *Yale Literary Magazine*, 34 (March 1869), p215–19 (IaU).

A gift of, perhaps, $100,000 to the Yale University Library would be hailed with a universal shout of approbation. The faculty of a university is expected to add to knowledge as well as to teach, so its members must be aware of progress made elsewhere through information obtained in a library. The library needs not only standard works but also pamphlets and ephemeral material. (Statistics of several of the larger American libraries and of a few European university

U.S. — Connecticut

libraries are given; all of them are larger than Yale's. The annual income of several American libraries is given, in every one, an amount greater than Yale's.) The library needs the income from a gift of $100,000. It has received relatively few gifts; alumni should send it books, newspapers and pamphlets.

322 [Needs of the Yale College Libraries.] *Nation*, 8 (March 11, 1869), p190, 450 wds (NcU).
This article refers to another in the March 1869 issue of the *Yale Literary Magazine (see 321)*.
The example of the graduates of Harvard in attempting to raise a fund for that library has moved some Yale undergraduates to call the attention of their alumni to the condition of the Yale libraries in the *Yale Literary Magazine*. (Some of the arguments in the earlier article are given.) As an encouragement to the alumni we may mention that one of their number has given a sum of money for acquiring, arranging, and binding handbills, pamphlets, and papers illustrative of the recent war. The authorities desire even seemingly useless material for this collection; duplicates can be exchanged for needed items.

323 [The Rau Collection.] *Nation*, 11 (September 15, 1870), p175, 190 wds (NcU).
Yale did not acquire the library mentioned in this article; the collection went to the University of Michigan.
Yale College, has, we trust, made a very valuable acquisition in the purchase, for the extraordinarily low price of $1,200 in gold, of the library of the late Professor [C. H.] Rau of Heidelberg. It contains 4,400 volumes and 2,000 pamphlets on political economy; there is nothing like it in America. Yale has telegraphed its acceptance of the offer; it is to be hoped that no other purchaser will anticipate the telegram. The coming year is likely to be favorable for acquisitions from Germany; deaths in the army and the impoverishment of families are likely to cause libraries to be thrown on the market.

324 [Mohl Collection for Yale.] *Nation*, 12 (February 23, 1871), p126, 310 wds (NcU).
Yale College will have no reason to regret that the Rau library of political economy went to Ann Arbor because the loss is more than replaced by the larger library of Robert von Mohl, the distinguished German writer on political science; the library contains some 6,000 volumes. (The number of volumes in each of six divisions of the library is given.) The college is largely indebted to Mr. William Walter Phelps of New Haven for the means of purchasing this collection.

325 Dana, James D. "What Yale College Needs." *Nation*, 12 (June 1, 1871), p379–80 (NcU).
The part about the Yale Library (on p380) is copied verbatim below.
"2. *An adequate Library Fund*. The fund for the purchase of books for the University library yields annually, at the present time, only $1,800, while it should afford at least $10,000 a year, if the professors of the College are to keep up with the progress of science in their several departments. To make the income even $10,000 would require an addition to the fund of $135,000."

— YOUNG MEN'S INSTITUTE LIBRARY

326 "Young Men's Institute, New Haven." *Norton's Literary Gazette and Publishers' Circular*, 3 (February 15, 1853), p18 (ICN, NcU).
The entire article follows.
"An effort is making to procure sufficient funds for the erection of a handsome and commodious building for the uses of the Institute, with accommodations for Library, Classes, Lectures, etc. The Library is represented as containing about five thousand volumes. The evening schools, or classes, of this Association, are remarkably large, numbering three hundred young men. We know of no place of corresponding size and character, where such valuable means of instruction are so widely made use of."

SALISBURY — BINGHAM LIBRARY FOR YOUTH

327 Fowle, William B. "Memoir of Caleb Bingham." *American Journal of Education* (Barnard), 5 (September 1858), p325–49 (NcU).
The par+ of the article about libraries (p342–44) is summarized below. It undoubtedly refers to the Bingham Library for Youth in Salisbury, Connecticut and to the Boston Library Society.
Caleb Bingham was especially interested in the establishment of town libraries. In January 1803 he selected a library of 150 volumes and presented it to his home town of Salisbury, Massachusetts [sic] for the use of all children between the ages of nine and sixteen. The library soon became a valued addition to the community. One citizen observed that Bingham's memory remained very dear to all of the town's citizens. In 1793, before he became a bookseller, Bingham played a principal role in the founding of the Boston library, and later served for two years as its librarian. The library now contains approximately 18,000 volumes.

STAMFORD — LIBRARY ASSOCIATION

328 "Stamford, Connecticut Public Library." *Norton's Literary Gazette and Publishers' Circular*, 2 (September 15, 1852), p169 (ICN, NcU).
The entire article follows. It apparently refers to the Stamford Library Association, incorporated in 1853.
"A Public Library is about to be established in the town of *Stamford, Conn.* The place is rapidly growing under the influence of the New York and New Haven Railroad, and a wiser plan for attracting still more of our city residents could not be devised than this of a Public Library."

WINDSOR — SCHOOL DISTRICT LIBRARY

329 "New District Schoolhouse, Windsor." *Connecticut Common School Journal and Annals of Education*, 3 (March 1, 1841), p105–108 (NcU).
The article is about the new building for District no. 6, Windsor, Connecticut. The part about the library (p107–108) is summarized below.
The library is now or soon will be supplied with the following books for the use of the teacher. (Several reference books and books and journals on education

are listed.) The following sets constitute the reading for the scholars and their parents: *The School Library*, 26 vols. to date, published by Marsh, Capen, Lyon & Webb; *The District School Library*, 3 series, 145 vols., published by Harper & Brothers; *The School Library*, 121 vols., published by the Sunday School Union; and *The Christian Library*, 45 vols., published by the American Tract Society. There are also 30 or 40 miscellaneous volumes. (The rules for the management of the library are given.) Any person in the district may borrow books if he or she complies with the rules for circulation, which are given.

WOLCOTT

330 "Tract School Library." *American Annals of Education*, 3d ser., 1 (April 1831), p177 (NcU).
The entire article follows.
"Several individuals in a district in Wolcott, Conn. perceiving the value of libraries in common schools, and encouraged by the cheapness of tracts, have established a library of this description for their school. These publications are drawn every Saturday, and read with much interest, both by parents and children."

331 "Juvenile Libraries. A True Story." *Parley's Magazine*, 4 (February 1836), p46–47 (InU, NcU).
The article is in the form of a letter to the editor and is signed "A Friend of Children."
In Wolcott, Connecticut, about forty years ago, two 12 to 14 year old boys who were both great readers resolved to form a library. There were few books in the town; the remnant of an old library had books that few people cared about. The boys formed a society, drew up a constitution and laws and appointed officers, all without help from any adults. About seven boys joined the association, each agreeing to pay 17 cents a year; only three paid. A book was bought with the 50 cents and was read by the paying members. Later, one boy bought out the others. The two surviving members contanued to read and became teachers; they have since formed libraries for their students and themselves, and now have more books than the whole town had when they were children. One has helped form a town library and a Sabbath school library.

District of Columbia — Washington

332 "Libraries at Washington." *National Magazine: Devoted to Literature, Art, and Religion*, 1 (August 1852), p178, 350 wds (InU, NcU).
A correspondent of the *Tribune* says that the Congressional Library is being filled with useless books that booksellers have been unable to sell elsewhere. The War Department Library is small but is systematically arranged. The Smithsonian collection has been thrown together without any regard to the rules of bibliography. The collection assembled by Mr. Peter Force is an exception in that it is well selected and arranged.

— LIBRARY OF CONGRESS

333 Watterston, George. "Library of the United States. Card." *Ladies' Weekly*

Museum, or Polite Repository of Amusement and Instruction; Being an Assemblage of Whatever Can Interest the Mind, or Exalt the Character of the American Fair [New York Weekly Museum], 2 (September 23, 1815), p336, 160 wds (NjR).

(Watterston, the Librarian of Congress, requests that American authors, engravers, and painters forward copies of their work to the Library in order that the taste of the times may be displayed and preserved.) Congress has purchased a library, perhaps equal in value, as far as it extends, to any in Europe; this replaces the one burnt by our late enemy.

334 Watterston, George. "Library of the United States." *Niles' National Register*, 9 (September 30, 1815), p76, 180 wds (NcU).

Congress has purchased a library, perhaps equal in value to any in Europe, to replace the collection destroyed by the British. It is the intent of Congress that the library shall become a great national repository; the librarian [the author] will do everything within his power to carry out the instructions of Congress.

335 "The New Library at the Capital." *Niles' National Register*, 27 (January 8, 1825), p204, 360 wds (NcU).

The article summarized below was reprinted from the *National Intelligencer*.

The new permanent accommodations for the Library of Congress have been completed. The room, 90 x 30 feet, occupies the west front of the center of the Capitol building. The architecture, a blend of classical styles, and the appointments are exceedingly handsome.

336 [Library of Congress.] *North American Miscellany and Dollar Magazine*, 4 (1852), p329, 160 wds (NcU).

The information summarized below is taken from *Norton's Literary Gazette*, probably the article, "The Congress Library," in the issue for July 15, 1852 *(see 338)*.

The interior of the new library will be made of iron in order to avoid another fire. The library's quarters will occupy five rooms with two stories of alcoves. The shelves will be made of porcelain, and it is expected that there will be space for 50,000 volumes. The cost of the new quarters will be $72,000. Books have been purchased with $10,000 already appropriated.

337 "The Congressional Library." *Literary World*, N.Y., 10 (January 3, 1852), p8, 370 wds (NcU).

(An account of the Congressional Library, 35,000 volumes of which were lost in a recent fire.) The fire was blamed on a faulty flue. Among the losses were Jefferson's books, some of the collections received from Vattemare, art works, medals, and presentation copies from foreign governments. About 20,000 volumes were saved. The library appropriation has recently been about $6,000: $1,000 for law books, the remainder for miscellaneous books. The yearly increase has been about 1,800 volumes. The library uses the classification system Jefferson adapted from Lord Bacon, dividing the collection into sections of memory, imagination, judgment.

338 "The Congress Library." *Norton's Literary Gazette and Publishers' Circular*, 2 (July 15, 1852), p129, 1100 wds (ICN, NcU).

Having recently visited the library, we can state that the allegations made by the *Tribune*'s correspondent are incorrect. The books were wisely selected, are good editions, and were purchased at fair prices. We were pleased to learn that a large portion of the collection was not damaged in the recent fire, and we found the arrangements for the iron shelving to be entirely satisfactory. We were dismayed to learn that some publishers refuse to send depository copies to the library, for it would be in their best interest to do so. We examined the architect's plans for the addition to the library; his description of it is reprinted for our readers. The addition will cost $72,000 and will accommodate 50,000 volumes.

339 [Library of Congress.] *National Magazine: Devoted to Literature, Art and Religion*, 1 (August 1852), p179 (InU, NcU).

This article refers to one appearing in *Norton's Literary Gazette* for July 15, 1852 *(see 338)*. The entire article as given in the *National Magazine* follows.

"*Norton's Literary Gazette* contradicts the statements of the Tribune's correspondent respecting the Congressional Library. It says: — 'Having recently had the pleasure of visiting this Library, we are enabled to state, from personal observation, that the attack made through the columns of the *Tribune*, and by its regular correspondent, upon the selection of books lately added, is entirely undeserved; the books are well selected, of good editions, and, as we were enabled to learn from information afforded us by the gentlemanly Librarian, Mr. Meehan, they have been bought at fair prices, and are not 'the old stock of some bookseller, foisted on Government at a high price.'"

340 "The New Library of Congress." *Wellman's Miscellany* [Monthly Literary Miscellany], 7 (September 1852), p431 (ICN).

The entire article follows.

"*Norton's Literary Gazette* gives a description of the proposed arrangement of the new library. There will be a suite of five rooms, in all, three hundred and ten feet. — There will be two stories of alcoves, the second one receding three feet from the first, so as to admit of a gallery with but little projection; and above the second story of alcoves will be a third story, with book cases against the walls. The whole interior is to be of iron, and fire-proof, so as to avoid the possibility of another calamitous fire and is to be finished in a style of great architectural beauty. The shelves will be of porcelain. The expense will amount to $72,000, and the library is calculated, when finished, to accommodate 50,000 volumes. — Ten thousand dollars have been appropriated, and the books purchased to take their place in the new library; and valuable additions will be made to the library from time to time."

341 "Congressional Library." *Norton's Literary Gazette and Publishers' Circular*, 2 (October 15, 1852), p188, 220 wds (ICN, NcU).

We have learned from the *Boston Literary Journal* that the building for the Congressional Library will be ready for occupancy by December. Workmen now are putting copper on the roof, and the interior iron fixtures have been delivered. The alcoves will be two stories high; the skylights will be made out of ornamental glass; and all interior iron work will be bronzed. All in all, the new building should prove to be quite handsome.

342 Hunt, E. B. "Project of a Geographical Department of the Library of Congress; Presented at the Scientific Convention." *Norton's Literary Gazette and Publishers' Circular*, 3 (August 15, 1853), p129–30 (NcU).

A library of geographical materials relating to the coasts and interiors of the entire world is needed; the Library of Congress is the best place for this collection to be housed. Ten points outlining a definite plan include provisions for a distinct geographical department of the Library; special appropriations specifically for that department, to be spent for the collection, arrangement, indexing and administration of materials; the purchase of various types of materials; the preparation of catalogs; a room for copying the materials; an executive officer; an annual report; and recommendations for future exploration. No American collection meets these needs. Congress has great need for such a collection. A resolution is given, proposing that the American Association for the Advancement of Science endorse the creation of a geographical department in the Library of Congress.

343 "Congressional Library, Washington." *Norton's Literary Gazette and Publishers' Circular*, 3 (September 15, 1853), p150, 420 wds (N).

Since our last number, the rooms of this library, so much damaged by fire a few months ago, have been re-opened. They have been fitted up in an elegant and substantial manner and new purchases of books have been made. A recent issue of the *Washington Union* describes the new hall: It is completely of iron but so elaborately painted and gilded that you can scarcely believe it is iron; the skylight is decorated with hundreds of stars. The two long galleries are handsomely decorated and the velvet carpets are brilliant. The library now comprises 25,000 volumes and will be much increased; for the present it is open Tuesdays, Thursdays, and Saturdays.

344 "The Library of Congress." *Norton's Literary Gazette and Publishers' Circular*, n.s. 1 (February 1, 1854), p60–61 (NcU).

Restoration is rapidly progressing. About 20,000 volumes were saved from the fire, including those on law, and Jefferson's collection on American history, politics, etc. With the new purchases, the library now has 40,000 volumes. (Several additions are listed.) Congress made two special appropriations of $10,000 and $75,000 to supply the library. Half of the money has been spent, and orders have been prepared to expend the remainder. The average cost of the new purchases is only $1.95 per volume. The Library of Congress is expected to be fully restored within a few months. A catalog on the design of the Smithsonian plan is to be completed this year.

345 [*London Gazette* Acquired by the Library of Congress.] *Norton's Literary Gazette and Publishers' Circular*, n.s. 1 (May 15, 1854), p253 (NcU).

The entire article follows.

"A complete file of the London Gazette, from 1656 to the present time, has been secured to the Library of Congress by their English agent. It is said to be the only complete file in existence, of this journal, which has contained, for nearly two hundred years, the official records of the British Government."

346 [*London Gazette* Acquired by the Library of Congress.] *National Magazine: Devoted to Literature, Art, and Religion*, 5 (September 1854), p286 (InU, NcU).

This article is almost identical with one in *Norton's Literary Gazette* for May 15, 1854 *(see 345).*

U.S. — District of Columbia

347 [The Improvement of the Library of Congress.] *Nation*, 2 (April 5, 1866), p436, 420 wds (NcU).

The United States possesses no great national library; the niggardly appropriations for the Library of Congress have not indicated that its deficiencies will ever be supplied. This library should not continue to be poor in all that relates to the discovery, settlement, and political history of our country. The Congress needs a library of reference on the diversity of subjects upon which it is called to legislate, and men of letters and science need a good library, also. Ultimately, it should have a complete representation of the books the country has produced. A good step is the bill that has passed the Senate to transfer the Smithsonian books to the Library of Congress, thus adding 40,000 volumes on science and the arts, subjects in which the library is deficient. Soon it may become the largest library in the country; it is now one of the most select.

348 [The Library of Congress.] *Nation*, 4 (January 31, 1867), p84, 200 wds (NcU).

Mr. A. R. Spofford reports on the state of the National Library on December 1, 1866. One wing of the library extension has been completed; the library now has nearly five miles of shelving, and is considered fire-proof. During the past year 7,251 volumes and about 600 pamphlets were received; the library now contains 99,650 volumes exclusive of the Smithsonian collection of 40,000 volumes to be deposited in it. The librarian recommends a more stringent copyright law because few except the leading publishers send copies of their works without being notified.

349 [The Peter Force Collection.] *Nation*, 4 (February 14, 1867), p124 (NcU).

Mr. Spofford, the Librarian of Congress, has presented a report on the library of Mr. Peter Force, by far the most valuable collection of books and manuscripts relating to American history that has ever been brought together by one person. There are ten times as many early American books as in the Congressional Library, a far greater number of early American newspapers, a unique collection of maps and atlases, many volumes of the letters and papers of Revolutionary generals and statesmen, and about 310 manuscript volumes prepared as a basis for Mr. Force's *American Archives* series. He is willing to sell this superb collection for $100,000; he has refused this amount from private individuals. The most complete collection of books on America is in the British Museum; the addition of the Force library to the Library of Congress will go far toward remedying this situation.

350 [The Peter Force Collection.] *Nation*, 4 (March 7, 1867), p184 (NcU).

The entire article follows.

"The untiring efforts of Mr. A. R. Spofford to secure for the library of Congress, which is under his charge, the extensive historical collection of Col. Peter Force, have been completely successful. We presume since the national library was founded there has been no addition to it at all approaching this in value, and it ought to be the cause of general gratulation that the views of the owner and the librarian as to its proper destination have been adopted by Congress, and the liberal offer accepted without higgling."

351 [Mr. Spofford's Report on the Library of Congress.] *Nation*, 6 (January 2, 1868), p10, 250 wds (NcU).

Mr. Spofford, in his report to the Joint Committee on the Library of

Congress, says that the collection was never more prosperous. Excluding unbound pamphlets, periodicals, etc. there are 165,467 volumes on the shelves. The library has doubled in size during the last two years; the Peter Force collection has been moved to the Capitol and will, we suppose, make the library the richest in the country in political and historical material about the U.S. The Smithsonian Library has been added and a stricter enforcement of the copyright law has caused a very decided increase in the number of books received. (Statistics are given.)

352 [The Library of Congress.] *Nation*, 8 (January 21, 1869), p50, 430 wds (NcU).

Mr. A. R. Spofford, the Librarian of Congress, has recently issued his annual report. (Statistics of acquisitions by purchases, by gift, and by operation of the copyright law are given.) If we were to suppose that every publisher in the United States complied with the law, we would conclude that 5,091 publications of all kinds were issued from December 1, 1867 to December 1, 1868. But it is unlikely that more than three-fourths of our publications find their way to Mr. Spofford. Many works are copyrighted by persons other than publishers; some persons may be either ignorant of the law or dishonest; and some works copyrighted from title-pages in clerks' offices are never published. Mr. Spofford reports on the progress of the catalogs.

353 K., W. T. "Thomas Jefferson's Library." *American Bibliopolist*, 1 (November 1869), p343 (NcD).

The entire article, which is a letter, follows.

"I have a copy of the 'Catalogue of the Library of the United States, Washington, 1815. 4to. Upon a blank page is written, 'This is the Library which Congress purchased of Mr. Jefferson in 1815 for $23,000.' Is it possible so much was paid for this library?"

354 Richardson, A. D. "The Private Libraries of Chicago." *American Bibliopolist*, 1 (November 1869), p329–31 (NcD).

On pages 329–30 there is a reference to the Library of Congress; that part of the article is summarized below.

A. R. Spofford is better acquainted with books than any other librarian in the country. Under his inspiration the Congress last year paid $100,000 for the library of Peter Force. This rich library of Americana, added to the materials already in the Congressional Library, which is strong in this subject, creates an excellent collection for the future historian who will write for us a worthy history of the United States.

355 [The Library of Congress Acquisitions for 1869.] *The American Bibliopolist*, 2 (February 1870), p76 (ICN, ICU).

The entire article follows.

"The Librarian of Congress reports that on December 1 there were 185,227 volumes on hand, exclusive of pamphlets and periodicals unbound; 26,936 volumes belong to the law department; 11,262 volumes were added during the year, as follows: From purchases, 6,180 volumes; from copyright, 1,831; from deposit by the Smithsonian Institute, 1,879; from presentation, 724; from exchanges, 648."

U.S. — District of Columbia

356 "Congress Library." *American Bibliopolist*, 4 (February 1872), p78, 430 wds (NcD).

In his annual report, Librarian of Congress Spofford counts 236,846 books and 40,000 pamphlets in the library against 197,668 books and 30,000 pamphlets last year. The law department has 28,302 volumes. Books purchased numbered 8,851; 5,640 were received under the copyright law; the rest came from the Smithsonian Institution, the Patent Office, or by exchange or presentation. Total materials received through the copyright law numbered 19,826, plus $10,187 in fees. Showing the need for more room for the library, 7,000 linear feet of shelving was erected in the Capitol basement. The requirements for a periodical reading room are described. Spofford believes a new fireproof building is needed for the main library, copyright business, duplicates, archives, records of Congress, and original papers of Congress. Space now used by the library could house a library for reference and jurisprudence. He suggests extending the Capitol's west front 60 or 100 feet.

357 "The Library of Congress." *Appletons' Journal: a Magazine of General Literature*, 7 (February 10, 1872), p166, 300 wds (NcU).

The librarian's yearly report shows that as of December 1, 1871 the Library of Congress held 236,846 volumes and 40,000 pamphlets. The year's additions included 39,178 volumes and 9,000 pamphlets and came to the library by means of purchase, copyright regulation, deposit by the Smithsonian Institution, donation, and exchange. Copyrights recorded for the same year numbered 12,688 and resulted in fees paid to the amount of $10,187. Both authors and publishers are satisfied with the new copyright system. The librarian urges Congress to authorize extensions of the building which would double the library's capacity and provide enough room to accommodate the expansion of the collection over the next 25 years.

358 Poore, Ben[jamin] Perley. "The Library of Congress." *Harper's Magazine*, 46 (December 1872), p41–50 (InU, NcU).

The Library of Congress was created in 1800 when $5,000 was appropriated for purchasing books and furnishing suitable quarters in the Capitol. The annual appropriation in the early days of the library was $1,000. In 1814 the library was burned by the British; subsequently, Congress purchased 6,700 volumes of Jefferson's library for $23,950. The library suffered other fires in 1825 and 1851. The new quarters completed in 1853 were made of cast iron. Spofford, who became the librarian in 1864, made the library more useful to Congress. Appropriations were considerably increased; 40,000 volumes were transferred from the Smithsonian; $100,000 was appropriated to acquire the Peter Force Collection, and the quarters were expanded. The copyright law assures for the library a record of American writings that could not otherwise be had. The library is beginning to assume a national character. (An illustration depicts Justice John Marshall falling down in the stacks.)

359 [Spofford, Ainsworth Rand.] "The Progress of the Library of Congress." *Publishers' Weekly*, 3 (January 16, 1873), p48–49 (NcU).

The article is taken from the Librarian's *Annual Report*.

On December 1, 1872, the library contained 246,345 volumes. The operations of the copyright law continue highly satisfactory, but the law should be changed so that labels for commercial products are registered with the Patent Office, and are not copyrighted. As soon as labels are no longer subject to copyright, the librarian should be required to print a weekly list of copyright entries. The library badly needs more space, and the situation is growing worse; books and periodicals have to be piled on the floor. The work of the Copyright Office and the work of cataloging has to be conducted in areas that should be kept free for readers.

360 [Report of the Librarian of Congress.] *American Bibliopolist,* 6 (January–February 1874), p1 (ICU).
The entire article follows.
"In his Annual Report the Librarian of Congress mentions that 12,407 volumes have been added to the collection during the year closing December 1st. The aggregate number of books now in the library is 258,752 volumes, besides about 50,000 pamphlets. In the copyright department there have been 15,352 entries made during the year, and the Librarian has paid into the treasury the sum of $13,404 as the receipts from copyright fees. This exceeds the entries of the year preceding by about ten per cent. The rapid growth of the library and of the copyright business of the country renders a new building to accommodate the overflowing collections an imperative necessity. While retaining in the Capitol a sufficiently large library for legislative and judicial use, Congress has already authorized the preparation of plans for a separate building, and the Commission appointed to select a plan will shortly make the award of premiums. The site of the building, however, is not yet selected."

361 [Library of Congress.] *Publishers' Weekly,* 5 (January 10, 1874), p34 (NcU).
The entire article follows.
"The annual report of the librarian of Congress for the year ending December 1, 1873, shows that at that date the library contained 258,752 volumes (of which 31,190 were in the law department), an increase during the year of 12,407, and 48,000 pamphlets. Mr. Spofford estimates that in twenty years the library will outnumber half a million. Its collection of English county and local histories is approaching completeness, and is a feature of great interest."

362 [Library of Congress.] *Publishers' Weekly,* 5 (January 10, 1874), p34 (NcU).
The entire article follows.
"The Library of Congress has again quite outgrown its present accommodations, notwithstanding the hundred supplementary cases of shelving introduced two years ago, and Mr. Spofford has to work with a small staff in hinderingly close quarters. Twenty-eight designs for a new building were submitted by architects under the offer of the late Congress, but we believe none were found satisfactory. A larger *bonus* is needed to tempt our best designers."

363 [Copyright Law.] *Publishers' Weekly,* 6 (July 11, 1874), p39, 190 wds (NcU).
We give elsewhere a summary from the *Tribune's* Washington correspondence about the changes in the copyright law. Besides the use of the shorter copyright notice, the chief improvement is having the trade marks and labels sent to the Patent Office; they have cluttered up the Copyright Office, much to Mr. Spofford's embarrassment and disgust. We trust that, under the new arrangement, we shall be able to publish a bulletin of copyright entries for use by libraries and the booktrade. Our thanks are due to librarian Spofford and

Mr. Howe [Senator Timothy O. Howe], chairman of the Library Committee, for courtesies received during planning for the bulletin.

364 "The National Library." *Publishers' Weekly*, 6 (December 26, 1874), p695, 650 wds (NcU).

The interests of the National Library should be felt as the interests of all people in the country who are concerned about books, especially since the library has become the registering office for the entire book production industry. Mr. Spofford's statement of the harm that is coming to this library because of the lack of space should, therefore, meet an immediate response. (Statistics of its recent growth are given.) There have been annual catalogs; it is now proposed to issue a short-title catalog of the entire library. Mr. Spofford reports progress on a complete index to the documents and debates of Congress. However, the great question is the future of the library; already, 50,000 volumes are piled on the floor. We heartily agree with Spofford that a separate building is needed for the library; it is only a question of how soon the government will act.

365 [Library of Congress.] *Literary World*, Boston, 5 (January 1875), p127 (NcU).

The entire article follows.

"At the date of the Librarian's last report, Dec. 1, 1874, the National Library, at Washington, contained 274,157 volumes and 53,000 pamphlets. The receipts under the Copyright Law, which requires that two copies of every American publication shall be deposited in the Library, were 6,810 copies of books and 6,436 periodicals. The total number of single copies of books received was 3,424, which is the number of American books published during the year. Mr. Spofford, the librarian, predicts that in twenty years the library will comprise half a million volumes."

366 [The Library of Congress.] *Nation*, 20 (January 21, 1875), p40, 600 wds (NcU).

The part of this article that is about the Ohio Historical and Philosophical Society is identical with an article in *Publishers' Weekly* for January 30, 1875 *(see 969).*

The *Annual Report* of the Librarian of Congress shows a total of 274,157 volumes including duplicates. Mr. Spofford makes it clear, we think, that a separate building is needed; fifty thousand volumes are piled on the floor. A condensed catalog is being prepared for printing, as well as an index to the debates and documents of Congress. The pamphlets in the library are estimated at 53,000. The method of cataloging them and caring for them is not described. Because the handling of pamphlets is of some importance, we append here and extract from a report by Mr. Julius Dexter, Librarian of the Ohio Historical and Philosophical Society, of Cincinnati. (The rest of the article is identical with the *Publishers' Weekly* article mentioned above.)

367 [The Cataloging of Copyright Books in the Library of Congress.] *Nation*, 20 (June 10, 1875), p396, 430 wds (NcU).

The [New York] *Tribune* proposes that the Library of Congress should prepare a title card, with necessary cross references, for every book received for copyright, distributing the cards to libraries that pay a small annual fee. The libraries would use these cards in selecting books and would have the catalog cards ready when the books arrive. The fact is that this system would be of little help to libraries beyond what they get from the publishing trade now. And why restrict the service to native literature? Book catalogs from other libraries are helpful, but card catalogs are bulky. Writing cards by hand is vastly more expeditious than printing; a polygraph could produce duplicates. It is doubtful whether the *Tribune's* scheme for saving clerical labor should be the concern of the government and whether the scheme would foster intelligent cataloging.

— SMITHSONIAN INSTITUTION LIBRARY

368 "The Smithsonian Institute and the Astor Library." *Dollar Magazine* [Holden's Dollar Magazine], 3 (February 1849), p126, 200 wds (InU, NcD).

It is reported that $242,129 in interest has accrued on the Smithson bequest and that $30,000 has been spent. The building must be completed within three years, and if the present financial policy is pursued, $150,000 of additional interest will be added to the original bequest in that period. The librarian of the Astor Library is in Europe purchasing books, while the trustees are in the process of selecting a building site.

369 [Henry, Joseph.] "Smithsonian Institution." *Stryker's American Register and Magazine* [American Quarterly Register and Magazine], 3 (September 1849), p99–108 (NcU, OC).

Pages 102–03 and 105–07 — summarized below — are concerned with libraries.

Section II of the "Plan of Organization" requires the library to obtain learned societies' transactions and proceedings, and other books and periodicals that will be needed in preparing reports. The library is also to collect the catalogs of other libraries in order that first choice in book purchases can be given to works not already owned by an American library. Catalogs of foreign libraries will also be collected. (A statistical comparison of the number of libraries and their holdings in ten countries, made by Jewett, is then summarized. He is quoted on the inadequacy of America's book collections and on the need for developing large libraries.) Jewett could find no record in the catalogs of American libraries about 75 of the 251 works mentioned in J. C. F. Hoefer's *History of Chemistry*.

370 King, Horatio. "The Smithsonian Institution." *Southern Repertory and College Review*, 1 (October 1851), p82–105 (NcD).

The parts about the library, on pages 86, 92, 93, and 101–03 are summarized below.

The plan of organization for the Smithsonian Institution calls for the establishment of a library that is to make a complete collection of the transactions and proceedings of all the learned societies in the world, and to acquire the most important current periodical publications and other works. The library is also to collect library catalogs and to develop a means to produce a universal bibliography. The librarian is to be the only permanent assistant to the secretary. In addition to his duties as collector and keeper of books, the librarian is to collect information and statistics about other libraries and to make the Institution an international bibliographic center.

371 "Smithsonian Institution." *Norton's Literary Gazette and Publishers' Circular*, 2 (February 15, 1852), p23, 1650 wds (NcU).

U.S. — District of Columbia

The parts of the article about the library are scattered through it and are summarized below.

The act establishing the Smithsonian Institution provides for the establishment of a library, museum, chemical laboratory, etc. There are two great ways in which the institution will increase and diffuse knowledge: 1) by publications, researches, and lectures, and 2) by collections in literature, science, and art. The library has been commenced; although funds are not available for its rapid growth, we hope it is destined to serve as a national library for reference and research. The library is on the first floor of the central part of the building; it is 134 x 50 feet and is divided into alcoves. The western wing will contain the reading room; beneath are rooms for unpacking books. Charles C. Jewett is the assistant secretary of the institution, and is in charge of the library. (An exterior view of the institution's new building is included.)

372 "Report of the Smithsonian Institution." *Norton's Literary Gazette and Publishers' Circular*, 2 (May 15, 1852), p84, 960 wds (NcU).

The part about the library (170 wds) is summarized below. The article refers to the fifth *Annual Report* (1850).

Professor Jewett's report on the library is concerned principally with cataloging. He has proposed a plan to stereotype the titles of books, each on a separate plate, so that any library that owns the book may print the title for its own catalog. The report discusses the present means of printing library catalogs and the advantages and disadvantages of his method. A report of the Commissioners appointed to examine Professor Jewett's proposal is appended to the Annual Report. The Commissioners, Edward Everett, Charles Folsom, George Livermore, Joseph G. Cogswell, S. F. Haven, and Edward E. Hale, favor the plan for stereotyping catalog entries.

373 "Washington Libraries." *Norton's Literary Gazette and Publishers' Circular*, 2 (June 15, 1852), p108, 630 wds (ICN, NcU).

A *Tribune* correspondent, reporting on libraries in Washington, D.C., has called attention to all of the "useless editions" and "bibliographical trash" that is being purchased while valuable books are overlooked. In regard to the Smithsonian Institution we must take exception to this allegation, for that institution purchases only those bibliographical and scientific works that otherwise would not be available. The miscellaneous character of the collection is due to the requirement that copies of all copyrighted books are to be deposited in the library; in this way the Smithsonian will become a national library. Certainly, we do not understand the correspondent's charge that the Smithsonian administration is utterly ignorant about the rules of bibliography; Prof. Jewett, Director, is preeminent in his profession and is widely respected by his fellow librarians and bibliographers.

374 "Smithsonian System of Cataloguing." *Norton's Literary Gazette and Publishers' Circular*, 2 (September 15, 1852), p169 (ICN, NcU).

The entire article follows.

"It has been understood for some time past, that Prof. Jewett was engaged in maturing a plan for the preparation of Library Catalogues, and also for stereotyping the titles of Books. So soon as any thing further is actually published upon the subject, we shall take pleasure in laying before our readers the prominent features of his plan. Meanwhile, we are assured from what we have privately learned, that his rules for the construction of Catalogues will be, in the main, much superior to any which have before been printed, and by their simplicity and comprehensiveness, will do much towards producing uniformity and completeness in this difficult department of the Science of Bibliography."

375 "The Smithsonian Institution." *Norton's Literary Gazette and Publishers' Circular*, 2 (October 15, 1852), p188 (ICN, NcU).
The entire article follows.
"As a single instance of what is accomplished by this institution, we would mention, that, on the 21st of June there were sent off to three hundred different literary societies at home and abroad, and sixty-two individuals, 572 parcels and 46 boxes, weighing 9,885 pounds, and measuring 263 cubic feet. The Transactions of all American scientific societies are forwarded by them, as also one hundred and fifty sets of Schoolcraft's new work on the Indians, besides large quantities of the Patent Office and Coast Survey reports, &c. &c. The Smithsonian Institution receive [sic] donations for *all* foreign societies, and forward them free of expense."

376 "Smithsonian Report." *Norton's Literary Gazette and Publishers' Circular*, 2 (December 15, 1852), p236, 360 wds (ICN, NcU).
The 1851 report of the Smithsonian Institution has been presented to Congress and has gone to press. We quote from that document: "The idea never should be entertained that our funds ever can be sufficient to purchase all of the books desired by our scholars. On the contrary, it is the duty of the Institution to increase their needs by stimulating research, and it is a part of that duty to see that the value of libraries becomes more widely appreciated. This country's libraries ought to be supported by all levels of our government and by our wealthier citizens."

377 [Hale, Charles.] *Report of the Special Committee of the Board of Regents of the Smithsonian Institution, on the Distribution of the Income of the Smithsonian Fund, &c (Signed by Hon. James A. Pearce.). Washington. 1854. 8vo. pp. 25. Report of Hon. James Meacham, of the Special Committee of the Board of Regents of the Smithsonian Institution, on the Distribution of the Income of the Smithsonian Fund, &c. Washington. 1854. 8vo. pp. 63. North American Review*, 79 (October 1854), p441-64 (NcU).
The article is a criticism of the policies of the Board of Regents, based partly on the documents listed above. The library is discussed mainly on p453-57 and p460-63; the sections about the library are summarized below.
Congress appropriated a sum not exceeding $25,000 per year for the Smithsonian library but the Regents have expended less than $2,000 per year for it; the Regents have spent half of the income for purposes not authorized in the act. (The history of the passage of the original law is given; the viewpoints of various Congressional leaders are discussed.) We feel it is the duty of the Regents to carry out the plan of Congress, not the one they themselves have contrived. Congress did not mention "active operations," "researches," or "publications" and it plainly intended that the Institution should have a large library; its intentions have been most impudently disregarded.

378 "The Smithsonian Institution and a National Library." *Norton's Literary Gazette and Publishers' Circular*, n.s. 2 (February 15, 1855), p67-68 (MnU).
Everyone will rejoice that the question of the Smithsonian's future direction

will soon be settled. At the last meeting of the Regents it was decided that the library and museum should not receive a regular part of the income, rather, special appropriations when needed. A Senate committee of inquiry has approved of the present management but a House committee has not yet reported. What is needed is a separate national library; the Smithson bequest is insufficient to support one properly. The Astor Library is the only library in the country in which most departments of knowledge are fairly well represented. A national library should include maps and government archives; Congress would support it and we look forward to one that would compare with the Bibliothèque Impériale, the Royal Library of Berlin, and the British Museum.

379 [Rules for Distribution of Smithsonian Institution Publications]. *National Magazine: Devoted to Literature, Art, and Religion*, 8 (January 1856), p95, 170 wds (InU, NcU).

Smithsonian publications will be presented to all learned societies that publish transactions, to larger foreign libraries, and to the federal, state, and territorial governments. The receiving organizations must send their publications in exchange. The Smithsonian will also send its publications to incorporated U.S. public libraries of more than 7,000 volumes, and to smaller libraries if a whole state or large area would otherwise not have access to the publications.

380 [Smithsonian Institution Acquisition of Book about Paper.] *National Magazine: Devoted to Literature, Art, and Religion*, 8 (March 1856), p286 (InU, NcU).

The entire article follows.

"The *Smithsonian Institute* has succeeded in obtaining for its library, a rare and valuable book, printed in Low Dutch, and published in Regensberg in 1772. It contains specimens of paper from almost every species of fibrous material, and even animal substances, and has accounts of the experiments made in their manufacture. The following materials were employed, and specimens are given in the book: — Wasps' nests, saw-dust, shavings, moss, sea-weed, hop and grape vines, hemp, mulberries, aloe leaves, nettles, seeds, ground moss, straw, cabbage-stems, asbestos, wool, grass, thistle stems, seed wool of thistles, turf or peat, silk plant, fir wood, Indian corn, pine-apples, potatoes, shingles, beans, poplar-wood, beech-wood, willow, sugar-cane, &c."

— SURGEON-GENERAL'S LIBRARY

381 [Surgeon General's Library.] *Publishers' Weekly*, 7 (January 30, 1875), p114 (NcU).

The entire article follows; it refers to *Trübner's American and Oriental Literary Record*, London.

"Trübner's *Record* speaks of the list of medical periodicals printed by the Surgeon-General's Department, as a portion of the Catalogue of the Library of the Medical Department of the U.S. Army, as probably the most complete ever compiled. This list has been struck off and issued separately in pamphlet form, and contains 99 pages. Classed under the various countries in which they are published, each country's periodicals are arranged in alphabetical order."

382 [A British Comment on the Surgeon-General's Library.] *American Bibliopolist*, 7 (February 1875), p9 (ICN, ICU, NcD).

The entire article follows; it was reprinted from the London *Athenaeum*.

"They multiply libraries in America much more than we do in England. Since the war, for instance, a handsome library has sprung up at Washington, at the office of the Surgeon-General of the United States Army. It consists of no less than 25,000 volumes and 15,000 single pamphlets. The subjects of these works are, of course, for the most part, medicine and surgery, with the sciences akin to the same. A complete catalogue of the collection, in three large octavo volumes, has been published. The first two volumes contain the books arranged according to authors' names; the third gives a list of the anonymous works and periodicals. A fourth volume is in progress, intended to contain an index of subjects."

— WASHINGTON LIBRARY COMPANY

383 "Libraries at Washington." *National Magazine: Devoted to Literature, Art, and Religion*, 8 (February 1856), p191 (InU, NcU).

The article apparently refers to the Peabody Institute at Peabody (formerly South Danvers), Massachusetts and the Washington (D.C.) Library Company. The entire article follows.

"A correspondent of the *National Intelligencer*, noticing the fact that the Peabody Institute in Danvers, with a library of only five thousand volumes, has over one thousand four hundred regular subscribers, says: —

'The Washington Library has been in existence probably thirty years, and contains over ten thousand volumes, many of them standard historical and scientific works, with all the publications made by the Government and the Smithsonian Institution presented to the library, yet, with a population of near sixty thousand inhabitants, this valuable library has *near fifty subscribers!*'"

Georgia

ATHENS — UNIVERSITY OF GEORGIA LIBRARY

384 Church, Alonzo. "University of Georgia." *Congregational Education Society. Quarterly Journal* [American Education Society. Quarterly Register], 3 (May 1831), p301 (ICN, NcU).

The entire article follows. The author was president of the University of Georgia.

"One of our college buildings, containing the library and mathematical apparatus, was consumed by fire last October. The building was 100 feet by 40, and four stories, of brick. Library burnt, about 2,500 volumes of very valuable books. Mathematical and astronomical apparatus burnt was not valuable. Our philosophical apparatus, which is very valuable and complete, was not injured, being in another house. Our Legislature have made provision for rebuilding the house burnt down, which is expected to be completed during the summer. The Legislature, also, at their last session, increased the permanent fund of the institution, so as to make the annual income $14,000, besides tuition. It was before, only $8,000 and tuition. The object of this increase is to establish two or three new professorships, and have an annual surplus also for library, apparatus, and buildings."

SAVANNAH — GEORGIA HISTORICAL SOCIETY LIBRARY

385 Stevens, William B. "Account of the Georgia Historical Society." *Congregational Education Society Quarterly Journal* [American Quarterly Register], 12 (May 1840), p344–51 (NcU).

The parts of the article about libraries (p345–47 and p349–50) are summarized below.

The society was organized in 1839 in a meeting at the Savannah Library Society's room. The constitution provides for a librarian as an officer of the society. The bylaws define the duties of the librarian—preserving, arranging, and maintaining materials, preparing a catalog, ensuring that nothing is removed from the room, and recording donations. The committee on the library shall supervise all the materials, provide shelves, cases and fixtures, and propose purchases for the library. Committee members must visit the library at least once a week, and provide a book in which the librarian will record their proceedings. (The librarian and the members of the committee on the library are listed.) The library already contains many rare and choice works and manuscripts. The cabinet contains some interesting curiosities and a few coins and medals. A circular issued by the library committee requesting materials for the archives is reprinted; the types of materials wanted are described.

Illinois

386 [Illinois Bill for Free Public Libraries.] *Nation*, 12 (June 1, 1871), p382, 210 wds (NcU).

We shall be glad to see the Illinois Legislature, when it meets in November, pass House Bill No. 563 authorizing cities to establish and maintain free public libraries and reading rooms; its passage is not likely to have opposition. The law is carefully drawn, agreeing in scope with the Free Public Libraries Act of England. If a city council wishes a library, it must appoint a board of nine members, three of whom go out of office each year. It seems to us that the Hare system of election of members should be used; the system should first be tried in elections with which politics have or should have nothing to do.

CHICAGO

387 "Chicago." *American Bibliopolist*, 3 (November 1871), p424–26 (ICU).

Most of the article is about destruction of bookstores and private libraries in the Chicago Fire. The part about other libraries, p424–25, is summarized below.

Chicago had few public libraries although a library worthy of a wealthy city had been talked of before the fire. The Chicago Historical Society's elegant building was lost along with the collection of more than 70,000 pamphlets. The book collection was not an important one and the loss is not especially serious, but some good portraits were lost. The most lamentable loss is the original draft of Lincoln's Emancipation Proclamation. The Young Men's Association, also, has lost its library and building.

388 Upton, G. P. "Institutions of Art, Science, Literature." *Lakeside Monthly*, 7 (January 1872), p75–82 (IEN, InU).

(Some of the losses in the recent Chicago fire are described.) Among the libraries lost were the Metropolitan Hall, sometimes called Library Hall, used for the lectures and meetings of the Young Men's Library Association (p77), and the library of conchology at the Academy of Sciences (p79). Several public libraries were lost (p79–80). These included the 20,000 volumes of general works owned by the Young Men's Library; the Historical Society's collection of 17,500 bound volumes, 145,000 pamphlets, and manuscripts and newspapers; the Academy of Science Library of 5,000 volumes; the Young Men's Christian Association's collection of 10,000 volumes; the Union Catholic Library containing 5,000 volumes; the Franklin Library of 3,000 volumes; and the 5,000 volumes in Cobb's Library, a circulating library on Washington Street. In all, over 100,000 volumes were lost in Chicago's public libraries.

389 "Other Libraries." *Chicago Librarian*, 1 (November 1872), p22–23 (IC).

Of the Chicago libraries other than the Chicago Public Library, the more prominent ones will be mentioned here. The Young Men's Christian Association lost a library of more than 8,000 volumes in the Great Fire; it has already made a creditable beginning, in temporary rooms, now having some 2,400 new and valuable books. The collection is miscellaneous and popular in nature. The Young Men's Christian Union Library was begun ten days after the fire; it has about 2,000 volumes, and may be used on the payment of $1.00 per year. The Chicago Law Institute lost most of its books in the fire; already, 3,830 books have been obtained. By means of its yearly assessment of $25.00 per member, and with gifts from friends, its shelves soon will be replenished. (Ten other libraries are named, with a promise to give them attention in future issues of the *Chicago Librarian*.)

390 "General City Libraries." *Chicago Librarian*, 1 (June 1873), p21–24 (IC).

The article contains three sections that are almost identical with the sections on the same subjects in the November 1872 issue of this periodical: those on the libraries of the Young Men's Christian Association, the Young Men's Christian Union, and the Chicago Law Institute *(see 389)*. A summary of the rest of the article follows.

Next to the Chicago Public Library in importance is the Hengstenberg Library, acquired for the purpose of establishing a Free Theological Library, but now housed in the University of Chicago. The 10,000 volume private library of the theologian, E. W. Hengstenberg, of Berlin, was purchased for $8,000 and shipped to Chicago in 1869. (The library is described in some detail.) The library of the Chicago Theological Seminary was established in 1858 and now numbers about 5,000 volumes. This library is in a somewhat chaotic condition; the Congregationalists, to whom the seminary and library belong, intend to organize the collection and erect a building for it. (Several other libraries are named but not described.)

— CHICAGO LIBRARY ASSOCIATION

391 "The Robson Case for Magazines, Pamphlets, Etc. in Library Reading Rooms." *Publishers' Weekly*, 4 (October 25, 1873), p453–54 (NcU).

The article is taken from *Trübner's American and Oriental Literary Record*, London.

U.S. — Illinois

In a public reading room, periodical issues and pamphlets easily get out of place. This case provides a place for everything as soon as a reader lays it down. It is a frame to be set on a reading table, with separate numbered compartments for octavos and quartos. (Details of construction are given.) A printed list must be provided to show the readers which magazines belong in each compartment. If a periodical ceases to be received, the list can be changed in ink. These cases were introduced by Mr. [John] Robson of the Chicago Library [Association] and were used until the library burned down in October, 1871.

— FRANKLIN SOCIETY LIBRARY

392 [Franklin Society.] *American Bibliopolist*, 4 (May 1872), p250 (NcD).
The entire article follows.
"Prominent among the sufferers by the Chicago fire is the Franklin society, established for the collection and preservation of the historical records of Journalism and the Printing Art. At the time of the fire it had a splendid collection, which had been formed at great expense and trouble, besides a very handsome library. All that remains now is one single volume. Fortunately, the endowment is still intact, and, with this and the help of brother societies in other countries, the loss can be somewhat ameliorated."

— HENGSTENBERG THEOLOGICAL LIBRARY

393 [Hengstenberg Theological Library.] *Nation*, 12 (February 16, 1871), p107, 160 wds (NcU).
This library may never have had a separate existence in Chicago. The collection remained at the (old) University of Chicago for a while; it was acquired by the (new) University of Chicago in 1891.
Chicago has spent $8,000 on the acquisition of the theological library of the late [E. W.] Hengstenberg of Berlin. The collection has been deposited at the University of Chicago; it is intended to be the "nucleus of a Universal or General Theological Library, to be managed and controlled without any sectarian prejudices against, or special advantages to, any religious body, persons, or denomination." The library will confer benefit on the entire country so the association which has undertaken this enterprise feels justified in asking for subscriptions to pay for the library and for additions to it. A circular describing the over 12,000 volumes, as yet uncataloged, may be had from Mr. J. Young Scammon, President, of Mr. W. W. Everts, Jr., Secretary of the Free Theological Library of Chicago, to whom also subscriptions may be sent.

— MICHIGAN AVENUE FREE LIBRARY AND READING ROOM

394 [The Michigan Avenue Free Library and Reading Room, Chicago.] *Nation*, 13 (November 16, 1871), p321 (NcU).
The entire article follows.
"The Michigan Avenue Free Library and Reading Room in Chicago was the only one which escaped the flames, but it was also the newest, and its store of reading-matter is but small. The Association which opens it to the public is now soliciting contributions of books, periodicals, and money, to enable it to meet the demand on it for more extensive reading than it can now afford; and they may be sent either direct to the Library by the American Merchants' Union Express, or to the agent in this city, Rev. J. B. Thomas, 677 Broadway."

— PUBLIC LIBRARY

395 [Anglo-American Association to Send Books to Chicago.] *American Bibliopolist*, 4 (January 1872), p2 (ICU, NcD).
The entire article follows.
"The Anglo-American Association of London is about to give Chicago a free library. 'Tom Brown, of Rugby' (Mr. Hughes), is the chief manager of the undertaking. It will have one very interesting feature—presentation copies, with autographs, of the works of all the leading living authors, are to be sent by themselves. The Anglo-American Association was formed for the promotion of good feeling between the two countries, and this generous testimonial will not fail to promote good-will. The German contributions for the restoration of the Strasburg Library were a grand success. This effort in England may, we hope, have a similar result. Even Carlyle, notwithstanding his anti-American eccentricities, has consented to present his voluminous works."

396 "Chicago Public Library." *Publishers' Weekly* [Publishers' and Stationers' Weekly Trade Circular], 1 (January 18, 1872), p3 (NcU).
The entire article follows.
"At a meeting at Plymouth Church, Jan. 8, Mayor Medill was authorized to appoint a committee 'to prepare, without delay, such legislation as may be needful for the purpose of establishing a free public library in Chicago, and report such a bill at the earliest moment to a public meeting, to be called by them for that purpose, and also to take charge of any books that may be contributed for the establishment of such a library.' The committee was yesterday announced to consist of the following gentlemen: Thomas Hoyne, Chairman; Judge Henry Booth, W. E. Doggett, E. C. Larned, S. S. Hayes, James Warrack, D. L. Shorey, J. M. Walker, W. B. Ogden, Henry Greenebaum, Geo. S. Bowen, Levi Z. Leiter, Geo. Schneider, Edwin Lee Brown, Wm. Bross, John V. Farwell, C. H. McCormick, Julius Rosenthal, J. Y. Scammon, Carter H. Harrison."

397 "Correspondence on the Question of a Free Library for Chicago." *American Bibliopolist*, 4 (February 1872), p68–69 (ICN, IEN, NcD).
The four letters summarized below originally were printed in the London *Daily News*.
According to A. H. Burgess, donations of books and money in behalf of the Chicago Library now are being accepted. Although this undertaking is not directed by the Anglo-American Association, that organization is providing valuable assistance. In reply, George W. Smalley gives notice of his resignation from the Association because, although the gifts have been appreciated, the Association's participation implies that its American members have asked England to supply Chicago with a library. Edward Jenkins, in reply, chides Smalley for his ungracious comments as well as the Association for its role in the project. Jenkins believes that the Association was founded for more important purposes than for collecting books for American libraries. In rebuttal, Smalley reiterates the reasons for his resignation and points out the inconsistency of Jenkins' criticisms.

398 "The Chicago Library." *Publishers' Weekly* [Publishers' and Stationers' Weekly Trade Circular], 1 (May 30, 1872), p494 (NcU).
The entire article follows.
"Some important contributions, says the London *Athenaeum*, May 11,

have been made this week to the Chicago Library, Crystal Palace. The proprietor of the *Times* promises a series of volumes of that journal; and sets of the *Art Journal* and *Public Opinion* have been sent in. Mr. John Murray's donation is accompanied by gifts of Dr. William Smith's Dictionaries (11 vols.) and works by Mr. Layard, Dr. A. P. Stanley, and Mr. Smiles from the authors. Messrs. James Parker & Co. have forwarded a large donation of both theological and classical reprints. Among the more considerable gifts by societies are the publications of the Philological Society, the Royal Geographical Society, the Statistical Society, the Society for Promoting Christianity among the Jews, and the Highland and Agricultural Society of Scotland, — the latter offering to continue their contributions."

399 [Contributions to the Chicago Public Library.] *American Bibliopolist*, 4 (June 1872), p296, 215 wds (IEN, OC).
Several important contributions to the Chicago Public Library have been made in London. The *Times* is sending a series of volumes of that journal. The Philological Society, the Royal Geographical Society, the Statistical Society, the Society for Promoting Christianity among the Jews, and the Highland and Agricultural Society of Scotland are all sending gifts. The Duke of Wellington intends to send a 23 volume set of his dispatches. Sets of *Art Journal* and *Public Opinion* have also been given. The library's growth has not been seriously affected by recent political complications.

400 [English Gifts to the Chicago Public Library.] *American Bibliopolist*, 4 (July-August 1872), p378 (ICN, OC).
The entire article follows.
"Among numerous additions just made in London to the Chicago Library, are large donations from Messrs. Trübner & Co., Messrs. Boosey & Co., the Royal Historical Association of Ireland, the Irish Ossianic Society, the Moravian Mission Society, the St. Albans Archaeological Society, the Institution of Engineers of Scotland, the Manchester Geological Society, the Lord's Day Observance Society, the Scripture Reader's Society, St. Bartholomew's Hospital, &c."

401 [Chicago Free Library.] *Publishers' Weekly* [Publishers' and Stationers' Weekly Trade Circular], 2 (October 24, 1872), p417 (NcU).
The entire article follows.
"The Chicago Free Library and Reading Committee have resorted to a novel expedient in securing and fitting up the old city water-tank as a temporary library and reading room. The reading room is 51 feet square on the third story of the building and heated by steam. The library is reached by a flight of narrow stairs and a double fire-proof door and is lighted from above with a skylight. The shelf capacity thus obtained will accommodate about 25,000 volumes. Some of the books contributed by English publishers have already arrived and others are on the way. The reading room will probably not be opened to the public for six months yet."

402 *Chicago Librarian*. 1 (November 1872-August 1873) (IC).
Only five numbers of this periodical were issued, all in vol. 1: no. 1, for November 1872; no. 2 for January 1873; no. 3 for May 1873; no. 4 for June 1873; and no. 5 for August 1873; each number was paged separately. Nine-tenths of the contents (other than advertisements) were about the Chicago Public Library. The few articles on other subjects (descriptions of several other Chicago libraries

and a general history of libraries of the world) are abstracted separately in this bibliography; the material from all five issues that was about the Chicago Public Library is summarized in the following note.

The November 1873 issue contains a long article, "The Chicago Public Library; History of Its Origin and Formation" (p5–10) that covers the period from the Chicago Fire in October 1871 to the date of publication of the issue. The next issue, for January 1873 contains an article with the same title (p3–17) that is a reprint of the earlier article with the addition of the texts of speeches by Thomas Hoyne, President of the Board of Directors, and Joseph Medill, the mayor of the city, at the opening of the reading room on January 1. In the issue for May of that year, an article with the same title (p3–8) repeats the first part of the other two articles but gives a greatly abridged account of the opening and adds information on negotiations about obtaining a site for the library, as well as a statistical report for the first quarter of 1873.

The issue for June 1873 contains a brief version of the first annual report of the Board of Directors (p3) and the issue for August contains a longer section consisting of extracts from the "President's Report" in which some numbers are slightly different from those in the June issue.

Each of the first four issues has a section "Catalogue of the Books Now in the Chicago Public Library" but the content of each list is different. The first list, in the November 1872 issue (p13–20) is arranged alphabetically by title and includes "the more prominent books." The second, in the January 1873 issue (p19–27) is a list of "books, periodicals, and papers," still alphabetical by title, including those in the first issue, with additions. In the issue for May 1873, (p9–22) the list of "a considerable number of the books" is arranged by subject; and in the issue for June 1873 (p10–16) a similarly arranged list is a supplement to the one in the May issue. The August 1873 issue does not contain a general list but devotes p6 through 21 to a list of the volumes in the library's set of the Tauchnitz edition of English authors.

A separate list of periodicals and newspapers in the reading room appears in each of the five issues. In the November 1872 issue it is on p21; in the January 1873 issue, on p28–29; in the May 1873 issue, on p23–24; in the June 1873 issue, on p17–18; and in the August 1873 issue, on p23–24.

Lists of donors, with the number of volumes or pamphlets given by each, appear in two issues: The first list, a brief one, appears on p29 of the January 1873 issue; the second, longer, is on p4–9 of the issue for June of that year. A single gift, a set of the *Gentleman's Magazine*, from Thomas Hoyne, is described in detail on p22 of the August issue.

The by-laws of the library appear in all but the first issue. They are regulations about meetings of the Board of Directors, the employment of staff, and the use of the library by the public. For January 1873, they are on p30; for May 1873, a slightly longer list is on p25–26; for June 1873, a still longer list is on p19–20; and for August 1873, this longer list is on p25–26.

403 "Record of Progress in Chicago." *The Lakeside Monthly*, 9 (February 1873), p171–74 (MdBE).

The part of the article summarized below (on p173–74) is about the Chicago Public Library. It was copied verbatim by *Publishers' Weekly* in its March 1, 1873 issue *(see 404)*.

On New Year's Day, the Chicago Public Library was dedicated, an institution modeled after the free libraries of Boston, Cincinnati, and numerous English cities. It is mainly supported by a tax of one-fifth of a mill on the dollar,

U.S. — Illinois

yielding between $50,000 and $60,000 per year. The library occupies a building erected around an unused water tank; 18,000 books can be shelved in the tank itself. Of gifts received, the English contributions are by far the greatest; the British government has given valuable documents and famous British authors have given autographed copies of their works. The reading room is constantly full, and well-to-do citizens allow the president, Mr. Thomas Hoyne, to select items from their book collections.

404 "The Chicago Free Library." *Publishers' Weekly*, 3 (March 1, 1873), p229, 680 wds (NcU).

This article is copied verbatim from part of an article in the *Lakeside Monthly* for February 1873 *(see 403)*.

405 [Chicago Public Library.] *Publishers' Weekly*, 3 (March 15, 1873), p264 (NcU).

The entire article follows.

"The ratification of the exchange of the City Bridewell lot for the old post-office building here gives the Public Library enterprise the prospect of a local habitation soon, and no mean one either. The walls of the building are in a state of good preservation, and the whole can be fitted up at a comparatively trifling outlay, giving commodious and elegant quarters for library, museum, etc., centrally located and easy of access. With the auspicious beginning it has had we see no reason why the Public Library of Chicago has not a glorious and influential future before it."

406 [Chicago Public Library.] *Publishers' Weekly*, 5 (March 14, 1874), p273 (NcU).

The entire article follows.

"John Hadden, John Turner, and F. Kiss have been engaged on a trial as assistants in cataloguing at the Chicago Public Library, at a salary of $1,000 per year each. The award for supplying the books of current American literature, consisting of about 12,000 volumes, was made to W. B. Keen, Cooke & Co., their bid being the lowest. A similar contract for foreign literature is yet to be awarded."

407 [Chicago Public Library.] *Publishers' Weekly*, 6 (September 19, 1874), p313 (NcU).

The entire article follows.

"The Chicago Public Library dates from the fire of 1871. Its foundation was laid in the gifts made it at that time from home and abroad, and now, with the additions made by purchase, the second annual report shows it to number some forty thousand volumes. Mr. W. F. Poole, formerly of the Boston Athenaeum and later of the Cincinnati Public Library, took charge in January, and in May the library was opened for the distribution of books. Its resources are derived from one-fifth of a mill tax, which now affords an annual income of about $65,000, with a certainty of increasing with the city's growth. The serial publications in the reading-room represent twenty-three nationalities besides the United States and Great Britain. There is no library in the city to compete with it, and its success is sure and immediate."

408 [Chicago Public Library.] *Publishers' Weekly*, 6 (November 14, 1874), p551 (NcU).

The entire article follows.

"We learn from the Chicago *Tribune* that there are now in the new Public Library 30,809 volumes, of which 5000 are for reference and other books which are not circulated, leaving for the circulating department 25,000 volumes. The number of registered book-borrowers is, males, 8116; females, 5197; total, 13,313. And this number is increasing at the rate of 100 per day. The total circulation during the week ending Oct. 17, was 8471, or a daily average of 1412. The number of books given out on Saturday, the 17th, was 2194."

409 [Chicago Public Library.] *Publishers' Weekly*, 7 (January 30, 1875), p113 (NcU).

The article is a quotation (60 wds) of the portion about the Chicago Public Library from an article about the Boston Public Library and the Chicago Public Library that appeared in the *Nation* for September 3, 1874 *(see 191)*.

— YOUNG MEN'S CHRISTIAN UNION

410 [The Young Men's Christian Union in Chicago.] *Nation*, 13 (December 7, 1871), p368, 160 wds (NcU).

The article refers to Hale's popular inspirational book, published the year before.

The Rev. Edward Everett Hale's *Ten Times One is Ten* appears to have taken root in Chicago, where the new Young Men's Christian Union, having hearty non-sectarian support, is to build, next spring, a large hall for lectures and music in connection with a library, gymnasium, etc. The library's central location will make it the most useful, and, indeed, the only easily accessible library for the north and west sides. We believe that donations of books and papers will be welcome.

EVANSTON — NORTHWESTERN UNIVERSITY LIBRARY

411 [Northwestern University Acquires Library of Johann Schulze.] *American Bibliopolist*, 2 (February 1870), p77 (ICN, ICU).

The entire article follows. It refers to Johann Schulze, a member of the Prussian Ministry of Public Instruction — in Berlin, not Russia.

"The large and excellent library of the late John Schultze [sic], Minister of Public Instruction in Russia [sic], comprising 20,000 volumes, has been secured to the Northwestern University, Evanston, Ill., through the munificence of Luther L. Greenleaf, Esq., of that place. The library was purchased at a cost of $40,000, and is to be known as the Greenleaf Library."

JACKSONVILLE — ILLINOIS COLLEGE LIBRARY

412 "Illinois College, Jacksonville." *Norton's Literary Gazette and Publishers' Circular*, 3 (February 15, 1853), p19 (ICN, NcU).

The entire article follows.

"A large portion of the books belonging to the Libraries of Illinois College were recently destroyed by fire. There was very little, if any, insurance."

NAUVOO — ICARIAN COMMUNITY LIBRARY

413 "The Germania Musical Society." *Dwight's Journal of Music, a Paper of Art and Literature*, 5 (September 16, 1854), p189, 1190 wds (NcU).
The part of the article about libraries (530 wds) is summarized below.
The Germanians have disbanded. Second clarinetist Mr. Albrecht is going to M. Cabet's Icarian Community at Nauvoo, Illinois. His library of music and music books is remarkable for one so young. The Newport *Daily News* reports that he has given the collection to the Icarian community. We quote from the article, giving the number of works in each of twelve classes. There are 478 works in 665 volumes. Libraries of this kind are very rare. Scarcely 50 books can be found about musical literature among the 80,000 to 100,000 volumes in the public libraries of this country. The only other musical collections we know of are those of Dr. LaRoche, Lowell Mason, and the Harvard Musical Association.

PEORIA — MERCANTILE LIBRARY

414 [Mercantile Library of Peoria, Ill.] *Literary World*, Boston, 6 (July 1875), p23 (NcU).
The entire article follows.
"The Mercantile Library of Peoria, Ill., was established in 1866, with 4,200 volumes. It now has 8,534 volumes. Annual subscriptions of four dollars are paid by 256 persons. Among the recent additions to the library is a complete set of the Tauchnitz edition of British authors, 1,203 volumes bound in 751. The library seems to be managed with good judgment and energy, and the people of Peoria have reason to feel proud of it. Mr. E. S. Wilcox is Presiding Director."

Indiana

415 "Indiana. Fourth Annual Report of the Superintendent of Public Instruction (Caleb Mills) for the State of Indiana. February 11, 1856. 126 pages."
American Journal of Education (Barnard), 2 (September 1856), p480-87 (NcU).
Extracts from the report are reprinted; the part about libraries (p483, 460 wds) is summarized below.
The operation of the system of township libraries has been quite successful. The township library is patronized by parents, teachers, men of science, artisans, and many others, all of whom feel that the library is a center of culture, learning, and friendship. These libraries are a valuable component of our public education system.

INDIANAPOLIS — PUBLIC LIBRARY

416 [Public Library at Indianapolis.] *Publishers' Weekly*, 5 (March 7, 1874), p257, 180 wds (NcU).
We are indebted to Mr. Charles Evans, Librarian of the Public Library of Indianapolis, for a copy of the catalog of that library, just issued. The complete-

ness and accuracy of the work are quite remarkable, considering the short time for collecting the books and cataloging them; the work of collecting was begun in January, 1873. The committee was fortunate in having the assistance of Mr. William F. Poole, Librarian of the Public Library of Cincinnati; the judiciousness of selection must be credited to his long experience and well-known judgment. The catalog includes nearly 13,000 volumes, and, like most catalogs in public libraries, has each book entered under author, title, and subject in a single alphabet. The typographical excellence of the work is noticeable.

Kentucky

FRANKFORT — PUBLIC (I.E. STATE) LIBRARY

417 [Public Library of Kentucky.] *The American Bibliopolist*, 4 (November 1872), p578 (ICU, OC).
The entire article follows.
"Mr. Harvey Yeaman, a member of the Louisville, Ky., Bar, has presented to the Public Library of Kentucky a file of the Winchester, Va., *Gazette*, covering a period from the 2d of January, 1799, to the 29th of September, 1802. The numbers dated December 25, 1799, and January 1, 8, and 15, 1800, contain a full account of the death, funeral ceremonies, and burial of General Washington. The number of February 2, 1800, gives an account of the placing of Bonaparte in command at Paris, and in that of May 18, 1800, are mentioned the surrender of the French troops in Egypt, and the appointment of General William Henry Harrison as Governor of the Northwestern Territory of the United States."

GEORGETOWN — GEORGETOWN COLLEGE LIBRARY

418 Malcom, Howard. "To the Baptist Ministers of Kentucky. The Collection of a Library." *Baptist Banner and Western Pioneer*, 8 (April 15, 1841), p2 (KyLoS).
The entire article follows.
"This always forms one of the great attractions of a College; and is a most important means of its usefulness. The students require various authors, every day, to consnlt [sic] in regard not only to their studies, but their compositions, debates, &c. Scarcely any work would be useless on our shelves. Old text books in Greek, Latin or Mathematics, would save our buying them for the beneficiaries. Pamphlets, old and new, would be very acceptable. We are forming a collection, which in a hundred years, will be one of the most valuable parts of the Library. There is scarcely a family in the State, that might not furnish some book which now lies idle on an unfrequented shelf. If you will gather us some of these, and send them either to Lexington, Frankfort, or Louisville, you will render a valuable service."

419 "Georgetown College. Donations of Books to the Library." *Baptist Banner and Western Pioneer*, 8 (October 7, 1841), p2, 330 wds (KyLoS).
In his recent travels, the President of Georgetown College has received a

U.S. — Kentucky 114

number of presents of books for the library. (Twenty-five donors are named, their counties of residence are given, and the size of their donations noted.) In all, 304 volumes have been given by those persons. Most are valuable books and important additions to the library. No volume has been received except upon the personal application of the president. Other friends and ministers should interest themselves in this project. (Several Kentucky ministers are named as being willing to receive and forward books.)

420 Malcom, Howard. "Extracts from the Semi-Annual Report of the President of Georgetown College, Ky." *Baptist Banner and Western Pioneer*, 11 (January 18, 1844), p3 (KyLoS).

The part of the article about the library follows.

"Handsome donations have been made, during the past session, to the LIBRARY, by ROBERT M. SCOTT, of Franklin co., Ky., and Rev. Dr. BABCOCK, of Poughkeepsie, New York: each of whom has given more than fifty volumes; and CHANDLER HOLBROOK, ESQ., MATTHEW VASSAR, ESQ., &c., of Poughkeepsie, N.Y., have given ninety-five volumes. Various persons have given valuable works, the names of which, and of the donors, are recorded in a book kept for the purpose, which is herewith submitted to your inspection. The Library now contains about 2000 volumes, which however, I regard as a mere beginning."

421 M, T. S. "Georgetown College, Ky." *Baptist Record*, 9 (July 17, 1844), p114 (ICU).

The part of the article about libraries follows.

"During the year, 470 volumes have been added to the library. Five hundred dollars worth of philosophical instruments have been purchased, and are daily expected to arrive. The workmen are completing, for use next session, three large rooms in the college edifice, one for the library, 40 feet by 30, one for the philosophical apparatus and cabinet, of the same size, and another for the chapel, 60 feet by 40. The other six rooms in the building, have been in use for recitation rooms, for two years."

422 Malcom, Howard. "Extracts from the Semi-Annual Report of the President of Georgetown College, to the Board of Trustees: Rendered June 29, 1848." *Baptist Banner and Western Pioneer*, 15 (July 12, 1848), p1 (InU, KyLoS).

The part of the report about the library (410 wds) is summarized below.

About 500 volumes have been added in the last six months along with some paintings and engravings. These last include portraits of Washington and Daniel Boone. New quarters are needed for the library and the paintings; it is hoped that someone will soon come forth with the necessary donation. A seventy-eight page catalog of the library's 5,000 volumes has been printed as ordered by the Board. The books are classed under 22 headings. With the president's collection of 1,700 volumes and the 500 volumes belonging to the voluntary societies, the students have more than 7,000 volumes available to them. The reading room regularly receives several of the best American periodicals.

423 Dejalma. "A Suggestion." *Western Recorder*, 18 (October 8, 1851), p186, 170 wds (KyLoS).

All churches and associations having record books should deposit them in the library of Georgetown College, where future historians may have access to them; there are many such valuable materials that will otherwise be lost. The records would be almost indispensable in furnishing a complete history of Baptists in Kentucky. If deposited in the library of the college, the records will be safely kept, and much time and labor saved in collecting materials for biographies and histories. A valuable service would be rendered to the college and to the denomination.

LEXINGTON — LEXINGTON MEDICAL SOCIETY LIBRARY (PROPOSED)

424 [Medical Library of the Lexington, Ky. Medical Society.] *Transylvania Journal of Medicine and the Associate Sciences*, 7 (April, May, June 1834), p291, 170 wds (KyU, NcU-H).

The article consists of the text of a resolution to form a library; no evidence of the existence of the library has been found.

W. K. Stone moved that a medical library be formed, and the society resolved to do so. A book is to be kept for recording the names of contributors and the amounts donated. Books will also be accepted. All contributions, books or money, will be received by the treasurer, who will in turn pass them on to the president or vice-president of the society. William K. Stone, William H. Inge, and W. D. Dorris were appointed a committee to solicit donations of books from the honorary members.

Louisiana

NEW ORLEANS

425 "Libraries in New Orleans." *De Bow's Review* [Commercial Review], 1 (April 1846), p381–82 (InU, NcU).

There are four libraries accessible to the public: the private library of B. F. French, the library in the State House on Baconne street, the Public School Library of the Second Municipality and the Young Men's Free Library Association. The French library is available free for reference and contains about 7,500 volumes. The books are in Greek, Latin, French, Spanish, and English, and include some printed books from the fifteenth century. The State House library has about 3,000 volumes. The school library is a subscription library, open from 2:00 until 9:00 daily, with a collection of about 3,000 volumes. The young men's library is also a subscription library, with about 2,000 volumes. It is open from 9:00 until 9:00 every day.

426 De Bow, J. D. B. "The Moral Advance of New Orleans." *De Bow's Review* [The Commercial Review], 2 (November 1846), p348–51 (NcU).

The part about libraries, on p350–51, is condensed below.

Booksellers receive few of the new publications from the North or from Europe; these books are unproductive capital because of lack of demand. The city needs public libraries that would acquire these works. The state has a collection of public documents for the use of the legislature. The Second Municipality has collected about 5,000 volumes, half for the use of children. Mr. French's library of 3,000 volumes is available to subscribers to the reading room at the Merchants' Exchange. This library includes the old Commercial Library which had been sold to French. The New Exchange Reading Room receives American and European journals. The Young Men's Society has a small collection which the legislature has been inclined to encourage. The society has also offered some public lectures. The city needs mercantile associations such as those that exist in New York, Boston, and Philadelphia.

427 De Bow, J. D. B. "Commerce and Agriculture Subjects of University Instruction." *De Bow's Review* [The Commercial Review], 3 (June 1847), p502–516 (NcU).

The part of the article about libraries ("Library of the Chair of Public Economy, Commerce and Statistics," p514-16) is summarized below.

The library to support the Chair will require all the standard periodicals and selected world journals relating to commerce, agriculture, manufacturing, etc. The list of books appended is made from the author's own library and from a catalog published by Mr. McCulloch. Most of the titles listed are not available in New Orleans, nor are many, it is supposed, to be found in the United States. Numerous maps and charts would also be appropriate. We hope some wealthy merchants will take action to provide this important service. (The list is divided into three parts: Economics; Commerce (the largest section); and Agriculture, Manufactures, Internal Improvements, Statistics, etc. The author and title of each book is given.)

428 "Professorship of Public Economy, Commerce and Statistics." *De Bow's Review* [The Commercial Review], 5 (March 1848), p241–43 (NcU).

The part about libraries is summarized below. A similar article on the same subject appeared in *De Bow's Review* 3 (June 1847) *(see 427)*.

The immediate purchase of a library is necessary to support the Chair. A catalog of the most important works on the subject is included. A public library, centrally located, open at all times and free to all persons, is needed in New Orleans. No city in the nation is so lacking in regard to a library as is New Orleans. What is being done with the Fisk donation of books and building? What would be more appropriate than to construct a building for this library on university property? A letter from Alvarez Fisk to B. F. French, printed here, describes the gift.

— FISK FREE LIBRARY

429 "The Fisk Public Library." *De Bow's Review* [De Bow's Southern and Western Review], 10 (February 1851), p235, 300 wds (NcU).

The city of New Orleans has shamefully neglected the donation to the city by the Fisk brothers of 6,000 volumes and a building on Customhouse Street for a public library. Several years have passed without provision for permanent establishment of the library. The building on Customhouse Street is not suitable for the purpose. It should be sold and the proceeds used to buy more books. The University of Louisiana would no doubt provide perpetual quarters for the collection and a professor or a student could be hired at little expense as a librarian. The Municipalities of the City should carry out this plan at once.

430 "New Orleans Free Library." *De Bow's Review*, 17 (August 1854), p218, 200 wds (NcU).

New Orleans

The library was founded by Mr. Fisk and many books have been donated by B. F. French or through his efforts. The Councils of New Orleans have not carried out all of Fisk's intentions. If there were a free library it would provide people with an opportunity for intellectual pursuits after leaving public school. The townspeople and City Councils should make a determined effort to provide a public library for the continuation of public education.

— LOUISIANA STATE LIBRARY

431 "Louisiana State Library." *Norton's Literary Gazette and Publishers' Circular*, 3 (February 15, 1853), p19, 210 wds (ICN, NcU).

A friend has handed us the following information: The report of the Louisiana State Library, submitted by Henry Droz, shows that during the year 1852, 224 volumes were purchased, 192 volumes were acquired by exchange, 333 volumes were received from other states, and 20 volumes were given to the state. Other statistics are given, leading to the conclusion that the library is becoming every day more worthy of the patronage of the state. The Hon. Charles Gayarre prefaces the report with a brief statement in which he advises the publication of the valuable and important French and Spanish documents owned by the state.

432 [Report of the Louisiana State Library for 1853.] *Norton's Literary Gazette and Publishers' Circular*, n.s. 1 (May 1, 1854), p226, 230 wds (NcU).

Secretary of State Andrew S. Herron has presented the Report of the Louisiana State Library for 1853 to the legislature. The library receives $1,000 annually; this year $350 has been added to procure *Audubon's Quadrupeds of America*. In all, 189 volumes were added by purchase; seven are listed. Publications of the state are also exchanged with other institutions and governments, and 874 additional volumes were added in this way; eight are listed. More than 500 volumes of public documents and state reports were obtained. The facilities for exchange enjoyed by the State Library were especially presented to the Librarians' Convention by J. L. Sheafe of New Orleans. Mr. Henry Droz is the librarian.

— MERCANTILE LIBRARY ASSOCIATION

433 [Mercantile Library Association of New Orleans.] *De Bow's Review*, 26 (March 1859), p352 (NcU).

The entire article follows.

"Thanks to the Board of Directors for the first annual report of the Mercantile Library Association of New Orleans. The number of volumes in the library at present is 3,485. The number of newspapers and periodicals taken is, foreign 35, domestic 50 — total, 85. This Association, which is of recent date among us, and appeals most loudly for the encouragement and support of the mercantile community of New-Orleans, gives evidence of great vitality. Shall New-Orleans be the only large city in America which does not liberally support an association of this kind, and will the appeal be made in vain to her citizens? In New-York, in Boston, Cincinnati, St. Louis and Charleston, the mercantile associations have long existed and prospered. It will be so among us, too, when we perform our whole duty. During the last year lectures were delivered before the Association by Dr. Brownlow, John Mitchel, Dr. Mackay, the Rev. Dr. Bolles, and Dr. Palmer."

— PUBLIC SCHOOL LYCEUM AND LIBRARY SOCIETY
(SECOND MUNICIPALITY)

434 "Second Municipality Library." *De Bow's Review* [The Commercial Review], 5 (June 1848), p539, 300 wds (InU, NcU).

A catalog of the library, 150 pages in length, has been printed. It includes an alphabetical list of authors and a classed list under such subjects as "Religion and History." The library is supported by a tax, not to exceed 25¢ per month on each of the children attending the public school in the municipality. After three years of these payments the child becomes a life member. Any other citizen may use the library by paying an annual fee of $5.00. The library has 7,516 volumes, many in French and other European languages, along with the standard works in English. Income over a certain amount is used to purchase apparatus needed for the lecture series.

Maine

435 Davis, John. "Address Delivered by *John Davis*, Esq. of Augusta, before the Members of the *Agricultural Society of Maine*, at their Annual Meeting, on October 31, 1821; beginning the day of their Shew of Cattle, &c. then held at *Hallowell*." *American Farmer*, 3 (January 25, 1822), p345–47 (InU, NcU).

The article is a reprint of Davis' address on October 31, 1821 before the Agricultural Society of Maine. The part of the address about libraries (p345) is given below.

"Again, an agricultural *Library* is required both for readers and for writers on husbandry. — The directors of the *social libraries* throughout the country should also be invited, (where this is not done already) to make their purchases of Agricultural books, as extensive as their readers will permit."

436 "Free Town Libraries." *Common School Journal*, o.s. 13, n.s. 3 (October 1, 1851), p302–04 (NcU).

The article summarized below is a reprint of the report by the Secretary of the Maine Board of Education.

In Maine, only nine communities have school district libraries. A small population, lack of money, and poor physical facilities combine to discourage the establishment of school libraries; therefore, it appears that the only feasible way for a system of public libraries to be established in Maine is to apply the system to towns rather than to schools. A law could be enacted that would provide towns with the legal authority to establish and maintain public libraries. The one drawback to this plan is that when such matters are left to the discretion of towns, the decision usually is on the side of inaction. Recent experience in Massachusetts has confirmed this generalization; there, school districts have not taken advantage of the law authorizing the establishment of school libraries. If Maine chooses to enact legislation to support public libraries, we trust that the Massachusetts laws will not be used as models.

BANGOR — BANGOR THEOLOGICAL SEMINARY LIBRARY

437   Pond, Enoch. "Historical Sketch of the Theological Seminary at Bangor."
Congregational Education Society. Quarterly Journal [American Quarterly Register], 14 (August 1841), p27–33 (NcU).
The part of the article about libraries (p32–33) is summarized below.
One-third of the general subscription to the college in 1835 will be used to erect and furnish buildings, make additions to the library, and meet the expenses of the institution for the past five years. The libraries connected with the institution have 7,000–8,000 carefully selected volumes, chosen with special reference to the wants of theology students. A chapel is needed, and should contain a room for the library. There needs to be a means of making gradual but continued accessions to the library. The Seminary needs an endowment.

— MERCANTILE LIBRARY

438   [Popular Authors in the Bangor, Me. Mercantile Library.] *Nation*, 15 (July 25, 1872), p60, 250 wds (NcU).
The article refers to an earlier one in the *Nation, (see 677);* "Library X" was probably at Quincy, Mass.
A writer in the Bangor, Me. *Commercial* compares the popular authors in the Mercantile Library of that city with those mentioned in our recent article on Library X. (The ranking of eleven novelists is given for both libraries.) The rankings cannot be used to determine the relative culture of the two towns; nevertheless, it is worthwhile to remark that several authors have almost the same rank on both lists. If the Bangor library has a paying membership it should have a better class of readers than that of X., but we doubt that its books have been more judiciously selected.

BRUNSWICK — BOWDOIN COLLEGE AND MEDICAL SCHOOL LIBRARY

439   "Catalogue of the Officers and Students of Bowdoin College and Medical School of Maine, 1871. Brunswick: Nelson Dingley, Jr. & Co., Lewiston, College Printers. 1871. 8 vo., pp. 48." *American Bibliopolist*, 4 (March 1872), p127 (ICU).
The article, given below, is misleading. The cited catalog merely gives the number of volumes in the library, along with other information about the college. The third sentence probably refers to a catalog of the library, in two volumes, published in 1863. The entire article follows.
"There is nothing unusual about this catalogue, except that it is elegantly printed. It is gratifying to know that the combined libraries of the college comprise over 34,000 volumes. The Catalogue of the Library is one of the best we have ever seen."

PORTLAND — INSTITUTE AND PUBLIC LIBRARY

440   "Public Library Catalogues." *American Bibliopolist*, 1 (November 1869), p348 (ICU, OC).
The entire article follows.
"The Portland Institute and Public Library send their first printed cata-

logue. The library was opened to the public in June 1868, and contains at present about 10,000 volumes. The catalogue is purely alphabetical in its arrangement. The catalogue of the Library of the Young Men's Association of the City of Milwaukee is arranged on the classifying plan. The number of volumes in this collection is nearly 23,000 — a goodly number for Milwaukee, and all accumulated within the last twenty years."

Maryland

BALTIMORE

441 "Baltimore Library Project." *Niles' National Register*, 68 (April 12, 1845), p85 (NcU).
The entire article follows.
"Maryland. The 'Historical Society of Maryland' and 'the Baltimore Library company,' have a project for erecting an appropriate edifice for the accommodation of their libraries and collections and to embrace also a gallery for the fine arts, and a reading room. Their prospectus limits the expenditure to $25,000. The scheme is announced over the signatures of gentlemen that will hardly allow it to falter. It is a worthy object."

— MARYLAND HISTORICAL SOCIETY LIBRARY

442 "Maryland Historical Society." *Norton's Literary Gazette and Publishers' Circular*, 2 (November 15, 1852), p211–12 (ICN).
The parts of the article about libraries (p211–12) are summarized below.
The ground floor of the Society's building is assigned to the Mercantile Library Association, the main floor is assigned to the Baltimore Library Association, and the second floor is devoted to the Maryland Historical Society. The Society's library has grown slowly but steadily over the years to the point where it has 2,000 volumes. It has a collection of documents about the State's early history and recently has been presented with a series of abstracts for documents in Her Majesty's State Paper Office. The library also has a collection of medals and coins and is attempting to procure portraits of some of Maryland's past prominent citizens.

— MERCANTILE LIBRARY

443 "Baltimore (Md.) Mercantile Library." *Norton's Literary Gazette and Publishers' Circular*, 3 (February 15, 1853), p19 (ICN, NcU).
The entire article follows.
"The report of this association was presented November 17, and has just been printed. The number of volumes is 9,700; of active members, 634, of which 158 are accessions of the past year. There are fifty lady subscribers. The income of the year was somewhat over $4,000, of which $1,872 was expended upon the Library. A supplementary catalogue has been prepared during the year, and printed for the members. There is every indication in the report that the Institution is in a flourishing condition. Two points are forcibly urged upon the members, which are equally applicable to kindred associations: an increase

in the number of members, and consequent increase in the number of books, and the prompt return of works which are taken out of the Library."

444 [Baltimore Mercantile Library Catalogue.] *Nation*, 19 (November 19, 1874), p331 (NcU).
The entire article follows.
"This is certainly a year of catalogues. The last one we have received is that of the English prose fiction in the Baltimore Mercantile Library, which is brought down to October, 1874. Peculiar features are: referring the several anonymous works by one author to the title on which the writer's reputation chiefly depends, and then grouping all his works under that title; and certain somewhat arbitrary classifications — e.g., translations from the French, German, Swedish, Danish, and Norwegian; fairy tales; and musical stories. Typographically, this catalogue is less attractive than the excellent one published a year ago by Mr. Noyes, of the Mercantile Library, Brooklyn, and it is difficult to estimate the comparative number of volumes in the two collections. They are by no means identical, however, and will be found complementary to each other by fiction-hunters."

— PEABODY INSTITUTE LIBRARY

445 "Baltimore Public Library, Lectures, and Gallery of Fine Arts." *American Journal of Education* (Barnard), 3 (March 1857), p226–30 (NcU).
The article originally appeared in the *National Intelligencer;* and it included George Peabody's letter wherein he set forth his proposal to donate $300,000 to establish an institute in Baltimore. The part of the letter about libraries (p226–27) is summarized below.
I want the Institute to be provided with an extensive library that will contain books in every category of knowledge; it must be maintained for the use of the public. The collection should contain materials useful to scholars. Regulations should be adopted to protect and preserve the collection; therefore it is recommended that the collection be non-circulating.

Massachusetts

446 "Libraries." *North American Review*, 5 (September 1817), p430–32 (INU, NcU).
The article summarized below apparently refers to Robert Walsh's *American Register*, Philadelphia, 1817.
We make the following extract from Mr. Walsh's *Register*, both because of the information it gives and also in order to add more information about libraries around Boston. The *Register* refers briefly to the Harvard collection, the Boston Athenaeum and the Historical Society of New York; it describes the Philadelphia Library in more detail. We add the following information: the library at Harvard has about 18,000 volumes, its chief benefactor being the Englishman, Hollis. The library of the Athenaeum contains 11,600 volumes; two other libraries in its building bring the total there to 18,000. Other libraries are more briefly described: those of the American Academy, the Historical Society, the Medical College, a church library, the Social Law Library, and the

Boston Library. The 7,000 volumes in the larger commercial circulating libraries bring the total available to the public to not less than 60,000 volumes.

447 [Rantoul, Robert, Jr.] "Education in New England." *North American Review*, 47 (October 1838), p273–318 (InU, NcU).

The article reviews eleven different documents about education. A summary of the remarks concerning the act authorizing district school libraries (270 wds on p302) follows.

Every Massachusetts school district should take advantage of the act of April 12, 1837. Expenditures of $30 the first year and $10 in each subsequent year can be made by each district for the purchase of library books. A publisher is to prepare a fifty-volume set that has been approved by the Board of Education as suitable for a school library.

448 "Common School Library." *Common School Journal*, 1 (January 1839), p29–30 (NcU).

The Massachusetts Board of Education will prepare two series of books to be entitled the *Common School Library*. Each series will comprise fifty individual titles; publication of the series has been undertaken by Marsh, Capen, and Lyon. Each book in the series will have been approved by the Board. A law passed in April 1837 by the Massachusetts Legislature authorized expenditures by each school district to start a district school library. The *North American Review* praised the project in an article, portions of which are quoted. The above information was taken from the publisher's announcement of the series. We think that this series will prove a valuable tool for educators.

449 "Massachusetts School Library." *Connecticut Common School Journal and Annals of Education*, 1 (March 1, 1839), p116, 800 wds (NcU).

The article summarized below consists of extracts from Horace Mann's "Second Annual Report of the Board of Education, Together With the Second Annual Report of the Secretary of the Board."

The 1837 school library law will add much to education in Massachusetts. Books are not so readily available as they could be. Social libraries depend on annual subscriptions, and are often in a declining condition. The Board will try to facilitate the new law authorizing the establishment of school libraries. The Board will arrange for Marsh, Capen, and Lyon, of Boston, to publish books for children and older readers. Books selected for their series must have the unanimous recommendation of the Board. School districts will have the option in deciding whether to buy the series; the individual districts will also decide what kinds of regulations to adopt concerning the libraries. The Board will only act to assist and encourage the production of the books to be offered by the publisher.

450 "Chapter 147. (1837). An Act Authorizing School Districts to Establish Libraries for the Use of Common Schools." *Common School Journal*, 1 (April 1, 1839), p107–108 (NcU).

The text of this law is printed verbatim in the journal and is summarized below.

Section I: Each legally constituted school district in Massachusetts is authorized to raise money for the purpose of procuring and maintaining a school library for use of the students; such libraries will be used in accordance with the regulations adopted by the school district. Expenditures for such libraries may not exceed $30 the first year or $10 during any subsequent year. Section II: Funds raised for these libraries are to be assessed, collected, and expended as are other school district taxes.

451 "First Annual Report of the Board of Education [Massachusetts]." *Common School Journal*, 1 (August 15, 1839), p241–46 (NcU).
The part of the report about libraries (p244–45) is summarized below.
The Board deems the subject of school libraries to be of great importance. Under the 1837 Massachusetts law, provisions were made for the establishment of district school libraries. To encourage the development of such libraries, it is hoped that publishers soon will make available inexpensive editions of good books suitable for school libraries. At present, members of the Board do not think that it would be advisable for the Board to recommend or to prepare a series of books specifically selected for school libraries.

452 Mann, Horace. "First Annual Report of the Secretary of the Board of Education." *Common School Journal*, 1 (September 2, 1839), p257–68 (NcU).
The article concludes the secretary's report, begun in an article in *Common School Journal*, 1 (August 15, 1839), p246–56, which contained nothing about libraries. The part of this article about libraries (p267, 180 wds) is summarized below.
The lack of teaching apparatus, in schools, except for occasional globes or Holbrook's common school apparatus, is likely to be rectified by the law of April 12, 1837, which authorizes school districts to raise money by taxation for apparatus and common school libraries.

453 "Second Annual Report of the Board of Education [Massachusetts]." *Common School Journal*, 1 (October 15, 1839), p305–313 (NcU).
The part of the report about libraries (p310–12) is summarized below.
Members of the Board have learned that, to date, very few district schools have availed themselves of the authority granted by the Act of 1837 to use local tax revenues for the purpose of establishing school libraries. Hopefully, as suitable books become available and as public awareness of this subject grows, more district school libraries will be founded. It is speculated that one cause of this delay has been the difficulty inherent in book selection; therefore Board members have decided to recommend to a publisher the production of a series of books, entitled the *Common School Library*, that will meet the special needs of district school libraries. A Boston publishing house, Marsh, Capen, Lyon, and Webb, has agreed to carry out this proposal. Purchase of this library by the district school will be optional; regulation and maintenance of the libraries is left entirely in the hands of the district schools. The Board has no inclination to encroach upon the authority granted to the local school boards.

454 "District School Libraries." *Common School Journal*, 2 (March 2, 1840), p65–72 (NcU).
The State of New York took the first step in establishing common school libraries in 1833; the first Massachusetts law was passed in 1837. Suppose several friends of public schools in a district want to obtain a library and call a meeting. Someone would point out the great advantages of intelligent reading; then someone might ask who was qualified to select the books, and another might ask about expense and the difficulty of finding the books in stores. All the arguments

against the library can now be answered. The Massachusetts Board of Education has arranged with Marsh, Capen, and Lyon to publish two inexpensive sets of books, one for children and one for young people; the selection has been made by Board members of varying religious and political backgrounds. Let us suppose that the result of the meeting is a unanimous vote to procure a library.

455 [Brownson, Orestes Augustus.] "The School Library. Published under the Sanction of the Board of Education of the State of Massachusetts. Boston: Marsh, Capen, Lyon, & Webb." *Boston Quarterly Review*, 3 (April 1840), p225-37 (InU, NcU).

Brownson, the editor of the *Boston Quarterly Review*, is the author of the review summarized below.

If books are available, anyone who can read can acquire any knowledge he desires. The common schools do not advance learning; libraries might solve some of the problems of the common schools. However, the books should not be selected by the Board of Education. Rather, the people in each school district should take part in selecting the libraries. If libraries are selected by the Board, they will be uniform for every district; publishers will print only books sanctioned by the Board; and authors will limit their thoughts. Other objections are advanced. Books should be included that treat both sides of a question. Duncan's *Sacred Philosophy of the Seasons* and Paley's *Natural Theology*, for instance, are poor choices that need the counterweight of sectarian selections. The management and selection of school libraries should be the responsibility of the inhabitants of each town.

456 [Peabody, Andrew Preston.] "The District School Library." *North American Review*, 50 (April 1840), p505-515 (NcU).

The article reviews *The School Library*, a series of books specially selected and published for inclusion in school district libraries. The part of the article about libraries (p509-512) is summarized below.

The typical New England village library cannot adequately provide books for a population that is scattered, not concentrated. However, if a library were to be established in each school district, books would be within easy reach of all citizens. An 1837 Massachusetts law authorizes a tax that can be levied by school districts to finance district libraries. To aid these libraries in book selection, the Board of Education has undertaken a plan whereby it will recommend books for acquisition. Of course local selection committees are not obligated to follow the Board's recommendations. The books selected are to be published in a series, and it can be safely assumed that the Board's plan will be judiciously executed.

457 Mann, Horace. "Third Annual Report of the Secretary of the Board of Education [Massachusetts]." *Common School Journal*, 2 (April 15, 1840), p113-28 (NcU).

The part of the report about libraries (p121-27) is summarized below.

Town, social, and district school libraries are educational resources; therefore it would be especially useful to know the answers to these questions: 1) Does your community have any libraries? 2) If so, how many volumes are held and what is the monetary value of these collections? 3) How many individuals have the right of access to these libraries? To answer these and related questions, an account of libraries by county with relevant data is provided (p123-25). Omitting the circulating libraries, it appears that the aggregate number of volumes held by this state's public libraries totals approximately 300,000, but out of 700,000 people only 100,000 individuals have access to these books. Unfortunately, most of the state's libraries are located in one area, hence to many citizens the benefits of reading are unknown. It is generally agreed that the libraries do not adequately meet the special needs of our children.

458 "Public Libraries." *Hazard's United States Commercial and Statistical Register*, 3 (August 12, 1840), p98–99 (InU, NcU).

The article summarized below is reprinted from the *New York Observer*, dated June 29, 1840. That article has not been seen by the compilers of this bibliography.

The Boston Athenaeum has 32,000 volumes, including 1,500 volumes of bound pamphlets and is located on Pearl Street; the annual fee for its use is $10. The Massachusetts Historical Society has a small collection, but books do not circulate except by vote of the society. Isaiah Thomas founded the American Antiquarian Society in Worcester; the catalog of 1837 included 700 bound and 1,000 unbound volumes of newspapers as well as 1,200 bound volumes of pamphlets and several hundred unbound ones. The manuscript collection includes the papers of Richard, Increase, Cotton, and Samuel Mather. The library of the Old South Church was given by Thomas Prince; that collection suffered damage during the Revolution and in 1814 about 200 volumes were removed to the Massachusetts Historical Society. The library at Harvard is available to local ministers; there is a catalog in three volumes.

459 [Reviews of the following books:] "Second Annual Report of the Board of Education, Together With the Second Annual Report of the Secretary of the Board. Boston: Dutton and Wentworth. 8 vo. pp 79; Third Annual Report of the Board of Education, Together With the Third Annual Report of the Secretary of the Board...." *North American Review*, 52 (January 1841), p148–91 (InU).

The article reviews five books about the Massachusetts Common School System; the parts about libraries (p159, 162, 163–65) are contained in the sections reviewing the two books listed above. These are summarized below.

In 1837, the legislature authorized school districts to expend money for district libraries. The Board projected two series of books for the libraries; districts are not required to buy them. The third annual report of the Board discusses the preparation of books for the common school library. The third annual report of the secretary shows that he elicited information about the number, value, and character of books in the public libraries, and the number of people having access to them. In those that replied, there are 299 social libraries containing 180,028 volumes, worth about $191,538, and accessible to 25,705 persons. There are also 10 to 15 town libraries, about 50 district school libraries, and 8 mechanics' institutes, lyceums, and sabbath-school libraries. About one-seventh of the population has access to the 300,000 volumes in all the public libraries in the state. Many of the books are the merest trash.

460 "Normal Schools." *Common School Journal*, 3 (November 1, 1841), p328–33 (NcU).

Reprinted from the Salem *Gazette*; the part of the article about libraries (p330–32) is summarized below.

During a discussion about normal schools that occurred at the meeting of the American Institute of Education, one member observed that the Massachusetts Board of Education has not overstepped its authority by recommending

U.S. — Massachusetts

books for school libraries which local schools are not obligated to purchase. He referred to the law as binding on the Board to recommend to district schools books suitable for school libraries; however, under the law, the district schools are not required to purchase these books. The Board fulfilled its legal obligation by recommending books for use in school libraries; in this and related matters, the Board acted in an advisory capacity.

461 "Common School Library Recommended and Provided for." *Connecticut Common School Journal and Annals of Education*, 4 (June 1, 1842), p136, 170 wds (NcU).

The article is part of a series on Massachusetts education (p136–39) which draws upon the Massachusetts school returns for 1840–41, the fifth annual report of the Board of Education, and the fifth annual report of the Secretary of the Board. The part of the article about libraries is summarized below.

Earlier reports have referred to school libraries. The report of the Secretary of the Board of Education says that more than 100 towns in the state have not a single town, social, or district school library. It seems that many of the state's children thus have inadequate means of self-improvement. The Board respectfully suggests furnishing assistance to the districts, to aid and encourage them in procuring school libraries. Funds might be taken from the state school fund, either once, or in two or more successive years, without impairing the usefulness of the fund. (The article notes parenthetically that the legislature acted upon the recommendation and appropriated $15 from the school fund for each district that would raise that same sum.)

462 [Libraries of Harvard, Boston Athenaeum and Andover Theological Seminary], *Bibliotheca Sacra* [and Theological Review], 4 (August 1847), p598–604 (NcU).

The part of the article about libraries (p604, 230 wds) is summarized below.

The Harvard University Library grows each year; 1,000 volumes were added last year. Previous subscriptions and a stated fund finance the additions. The new building of the Boston Athenaeum will be completed within a year. Charles Folsom is the librarian. About $2,000 was spent last year to increase the library of the Andover Theological Seminary. Most was spent to purchase works in English. (Several of the important multi-volume purchases are listed.)

463 B., W. "Farmers' Libraries." *New England Farmer; A Monthly Journal*, 5 (April 1853), p167–68 (NcU).

Libraries should be important features of farmers' lyceums; agricultural libraries in lyceums would encourage all to read, and would not cost anyone very much money. One could learn the principles and progress of science, and the results of those principles in practice. How many Massachusetts farmers will pledge to join such an association? The lyceums would check the discontent which some young men have with farming. The editor notes that not one town in ten has a farmer's club or lyceum. A few agricultural books are supplied in some town libraries. Other farmers can only form a club and purchase a few books, merging them into the town library when it is formed.

464 P., B. K. "Boston Newsletter." *National Magazine: Devoted to Literature, Art, and Religion*, 4 (April 1854), p380–81 (InU, NcU).

Harvard's library is lacking a fund to provide an annual income for the purchase of current books. A committee of the Board of Overseers has recommended that an attempt be made to acquire $100,000 for the library from the friends of the University. The Mercantile Library Association has added about $2,000 worth of books, and during the winter, lecturers for two courses were secured. After expenses, $1,700 was realized and this sum has been added to the $20,000 building fund. The reading public is indebted to Librarian Poole for his *Index*, the first edition of which is almost sold out.

465 "Musical Libraries." *Dwight's Journal of Music, a Paper of Art and Literature*, 6 (October 21, 1854), p21–22 (NcU).

The article summarized below refers to an article in the September 16, 1854 issue of *Dwight's Journal (see 413)*.

A library is usually a good index of the culture of a community. However, libraries contain little about music. Many wish to know about the subject, but Boston has done little compared to what may be done. The Newport paper's account of Mr. Albrecht's musical library, presented to the Icarian Community at Nauvoo, was copied here recently. That collection includes books and periodicals relating to music, but not works of music. The Boston Public Library may some day become a valuable depository of music. Lowell Mason's collection is much larger than the Newport account indicated. The Harvard Musical Association has a nucleus for a fine library, with 455 bound volumes and much other material. The library is managed by a committee that increases it systematically. Many people collect books of music and works about it; they should bequeath their collections to the library of the Harvard Musical Association.

466 "Donations for Public Libraries and to Publication Societies." *Norton's Literary Gazette and Publishers' Circular*, n.s. 2 (January 15, 1855), p33 (MnU).

The entire article follows. It apparently refers to the region around Boston.

"In this section, there seems to be a growing disposition to found libraries for the use of the common people. Some time since, George Peabody, Esq., a wealthy London Banker, gave to the town of Danvers, his native place, some $10,000 for the establishment of the 'Peabody Institute,' which, it is said, has already a fine collection of books. A gentleman of Newburyport has also recently put $5,000 at the disposal of the city authorities, for the commencement of a public library. In this connection, the munificent donation of the late Samuel Appleton, of Boston, deserves mention. Mr. Appleton left bequests, amounting, in all, to $210,000; of which $10,000 were for the Academy of Arts and Sciences for publishing their Transactions, and $10,000 as a publishing fund for the Massachusetts Historical Society. He also bequeathed $25,000 to the Boston Athenaeum."

467 "Libraries." *The Massachusetts Teacher: A Journal of School and Home Education*, 18 (March 1865), p85–87 (NcU).

The part of the article about town libraries (p85–86) is summarized below.

During the past year, public libraries have opened in several towns. In another year I hope to have gathered such library statistics [for Massachusetts] as the number of libraries, volumes held, and the sources of support. The practical value of libraries cannot be denied. I am told that since the Goodnow Library here at Sudbury has opened, the quality of reading materials has improved and the quantity of reading has quadrupled. The library has become the pride of the community. Town libraries encourage social reading and the establishment of "reading circles" for our young people; moreover they bring together people in the community who otherwise might not associate socially.

U.S. — Massachusetts

468 [William F. Poole Resignation.] *American Publisher and Bookseller*, 2 (March 1869), p11 (DLC).
The entire article follows.
"Mr. William F. Poole, for thirteen years the librarian of the Boston Athenaeum, has resigned, and Mr. Charles A. Cutter, assistant librarian at the Harvard College Library, is to be his successor. The Boston *Advertiser* says: Mr. Poole proposes to give his attention hereafter to more exclusively literary employments. His 'Index to Periodical Literature' — long out of print — for which a vast amount of material has accumulated since the edition of 1853 was published, will probably soon be revised and brought down to the present time."

469 [Popular Reading in Boston and Southbridge, Massachusetts.] *Literary World*, 4 (April 1874), p176, 360 wds (NcU).
Mr. Winsor's Boston Public Library report for last February has some interesting statistics as to the popular demand for reading matter. (Figures are given for books returned on a single day: 971 volumes of English fiction and far fewer of several other kinds. The circulation for the more popular novelists is given.) Cooper and Dickens are relatively high on the list because the library does not stock enough copies of Mrs. Southworth to meet the demand. (A table is given, showing that of 409 copies of her novels, only 52 were on the shelves that day.) We give the following statistics of the Public Library at Southbridge, a representative Massachusetts town. (Statistics are given for ten kinds of books.) Fiction and juveniles account for 67.5 percent of the circulation.

AMHERST — AMHERST COLLEGE LIBRARY

470 "Amherst." *Congregational Education Society. Quarterly Journal* [American Education Society. Quarterly Register], 3 (May 1831), p300 (ICN).
The part of the article about the library follows.
"Efforts are making to increase the library and the philosophical apparatus in this College. Several thousand dollars will soon be expended for this object."

471 "New Library Building of Amherst College." *Norton's Literary Gazette and Publishers' Circular*, 3 (December 15, 1853), p217, 570 wds (NcU).
The opening ceremony of the new library building of Amherst College has taken place recently. An alumnus of the college has written to the *New York Times* concerning the new building and the college cabinet. There is a philosophical cabinet, a zoological museum, a geological cabinet, and a mineralogical collection. The new library is built of Pelham granite in the Italian style of the fifteenth century. The first floor includes a packing room, reading room, pamphlet room, and librarian's room. The library proper is on the second floor. The existing shelves, all on the walls, will hold 25,000 volumes. The building blends the substantial with the elegant. The architect was Mr. Sikes of Springfield.

— PUBLIC LIBRARY

472 [Amherst, Mass. Free Library.] *Publishers' Weekly*, 5 (May 2, 1874), p430, 350 wds (NcU).
Amherst, Mass. has a new free library whose history may help some other town desirous of a like institution. In January, 1873, a few persons organized a book club, agreeing to give their books to a free library when it should be

established. On three days, during the summer, the club served dinner and supper, clearing $700. Then a library association was formed, each member contributing $5 for the future library. Subscriptions of $700 were obtained, and many books donated. A thousand dollars was spent for books, two very pleasant rooms were rented for $75, and other sums were spent for shelves, furniture, supplies, and a printed catalog. Miss Beaman acts as librarian for $50 per year, and a young man who is a volunteer keeps the library open each evening. Dr. Cate visited several of the best-managed free libraries and has wisely applied their methods.

473 [Free Public Library, Amherst, Mass.] *Publishers' Weekly*, 7 (January 30, 1875), p114 (NcU).
The entire article follows.
"Amherst, Mass., has a free public library which has published a twenty-eight page fine catalogue. It owes its origin to a local book-club, gradually expanding into the present promising proportions."

ANDOVER — ANDOVER THEOLOGICAL SEMINARY LIBRARY

474 [Catalog of the Library of the Andover Theological Seminary.] *Biblical Repository and Classical Review* [American Biblical Repository], 11 (April 1838), p522–23 (NcU).
The article summarized below refers to an article in *Biblical Repository and Classical Review*, 9 (January 1837) *(see 74)*.
Mr. O. A. Taylor's 531 page catalog of the library of the Andover Theological Seminary is now complete. It was begun by Mr. Robinson, the late librarian; Mr. Taylor worked on it for two years. It is alphabetical; the author's name is given first, followed by each of his works, whole works first. A short biographical notice is given. A foundation is given for an index at some future time. Mr. Taylor gives all the titles of books, pamphlets, etc., and all the important articles in the largest and most valuable works and periodicals. There are almost 12,000 volumes. Many are in Latin and German and are connected with biblical and theological studies; the library is deficient in English literature. Industry, perseverance, and accurate and extensive bibliographical learning have been lavishly expended.

BOSTON

475 Quincy, Josiah. [Massachusetts Institution.] *North American Review*, 2 (March 1816), p309–19 (NcU).
Quincy's report accompanied the bill providing for a building to contain the libraries of the American Academy of Arts and Sciences, the Historical Society, the Agricultural Society, the Massachusetts Medical Society, the Boston Athenaeum and the Linnaean Society. The union of those institutions would be called the Massachusetts Institution; the state would authorize a loan of $50,000 at 5 percent interest to erect the building. The bill was voted down by the legislature because of the financial burdens created by the War of 1812; the bill will be passed after these debts are settled. A committee was authorized to study the institutions in question. (Quincy's report, included in the article, gives information about their creation, financial state, library holdings, and public usefulness.

Precedents are cited for granting state aid to private institutions of public usefulness.) The institutions need such a building if they are to be fully utilized.

476 "Library for Blacks." *Genius of Universal Emancipation*, 1 (September 1821), p46 (InU, NcU).
The entire article follows.
"The New York Journal states, that 'a library is about to be established at Boston, for the exclusive use of people of color.' This is praise-worthy, and we hope will be imitated.'"

477 "Libraries in Boston and Its Vicinity." *Bibliotheca Sacra* [and Theological Review], 7 (January 1850), p173–91 (NcU, OC).
With the aim of encouraging the development of a common catalog of the rare and valuable books available in the libraries in or near Boston, several libraries are discussed: Harvard, Boston Athenaeum, Massachusetts State library, Historical Society library, Natural History library, Prince Library, Andover Theological Seminary library, American Antiquarian Society library at Worcester, and Brown University. For each, this information is usually included: history, the size and composition of the collections, the names of the rare and important items in the collections, some information on finances, and the name of the librarian. The quarters of the Harvard and Boston Athenaeum libraries are described; the contents of some private collections are mentioned. Statistics about holdings of large European libraries are given, extracted from the *Report on Public Libraries* of the Select Committee on Public Libraries of the House of Commons.

478 Everett, Edward. "A Public Library." *The Massachusetts Teacher: A Journal of School and Home Education*, 4 (August 1851), p255–56 (NcU).
The article summarized below is an extract from a letter from Edward Everett to the Mayor of Boston, dated June 7, 1851.
The city of Boston liberally supports its public school system. Although through our schools we instill in our citizens the desire for learning, we make no provisions for supplying them with books wherein useful knowledge is contained. Books are the record of original thought and inquiry. Where are the young men of Boston to get access to books that will help them in their respective professions? Presently, there exists no public library in Boston. I think that a public library is essential to make our system of education complete; also, it soon would become an object of pride to Boston citizens.

479 "Our Common School System, No. XV. Public Libraries." *Common School Journal*, o.s. 13, n.s. 3 (September 1, 1851), p257–64 (NcU).
The article summarized below is a verbatim transcription of Mr. Wight's remarks before the Massachusetts House in support of a bill that would give municipalities the authority to establish public libraries.
Through our public schools, we provide the advantages of education to our children. Through public libraries, we could extend these advantages to adults; that is a principal objective of the bill now before us. Consider these points: if enacted, the bill will not obligate municipalities to support public libraries; to prevent public extravagance, the bill imposes a limit on the amount of money that can be used for the establishment of a public library; and, the bill has provisions for the receipt and utilization of privately donated funds. Public libraries will provide the adults with the means to supplement their education; these

libraries will be used by the people as important sources for information; public libraries will contribute to the economic, intellectual, and moral well-being of the people; and these libraries will become depositories for valuable public documents. In view of the many benefits which will accrue from public libraries, this bill should be passed into law.

480 "Boston Free Library." *Norton's Literary Gazette and Publishers' Circular*, 2 (October 15, 1852), p188, 450 wds (ICN, NcU).

A room in one of the local public schools has been secured for the use of a public library, and some citizens already have pledged money and books for its establishment. Members of the Athenaeum and the Mercantile Library favor this project, which will expand this city's system of public education. The new library is intended to provide books for our educated poor. All resident graduates of our public schools will have borrowing privileges. We hope that the project will succeed, but its prospects for success would be improved if the library were to be supported by a small annual tax or by user fees.

481 P., W. F. "Library Matters in Boston." *Norton's Literary Gazette and Publishers' Circular*, 3 (April 15, 1853), p64, 1000 wds (ICN, NcU).

The controversial proposal to transfer the Athenaeum's library to the Free City Library was laid to rest at a recent meeting of the Athenaeum's proprietors, who overwhelmingly defeated a motion to appoint a committee to study the feasibility of that proposal. Subsequently, the proprietors unanimously adopted resolutions reaffirming their desire not to dispose of the Athenaeum's property and their confidence that the Athenaeum's needs would be met by Boston's citizens. All the city's libraries should benefit from this discussion, which served to make the public more aware of the importance and needs of libraries. Meanwhile, the city is considering the purchase of a lot for the future site of the Free City Library. The Mercantile Library Association has never been more prosperous than at present. An increasing interest in libraries is apparent not only in Boston but also in neighboring cities and towns.

482 "Boston Athenaeum." *Norton's Literary Gazette and Publishers' Circular*, 3 (May 15, 1853), p83–84, 500 wds (ICN, NcU).

Our readers are already aware of the discussion about the possible merger of the Boston Athenaeum with the Boston City Library. It has been decided that such a merger would not be wise because the purposes of the two institutions are so dissimilar. Whereas the City Library must supply the people, generally, with new and popular works, the Athenaeum must supply scholars with books in a variety of sciences and arts. The trustees of the Athenaeum propose to raise, by the sale of 400 shares, $120,000, to be invested as a fund, the interest of which will secure the constant growth of the library. James Brown of Little & Brown has recently given the Athenaeum a number of costly illustrated works, worth about $1,000. Such a gift is an honor to the booktrade.

483 P., B. K. "Literary Letter." *National Magazine: Devoted to Literature, Art, and Religion*, 4 (January 1854), p92–93 (NcU).

The part about libraries (p92–93) is summarized below.

The Boston City Library is now one year old and about 10,000 volumes have been received through purchase and donations. The library is endowed with $60,000, the income of which is for the enlargement of the collection. A building site has been purchased and preliminary planning is in progress. The

U.S. — Massachusetts

Mercantile Library of Boston is conducting a double series of lectures. The series opened with a discourse on the effect of the material upon the spiritual progress of the age by Judge Thomas of Worcester at the Monday evening session. The Wednesday evening series began with an address on physical, mental and moral "implements" by Rev. Mr. Chapin of New York. The poets for these two meetings were James T. Fields and John G. Saxe.

484 [Libraries of Boston.] *Norton's Literary Gazette and Publishers' Circular*, n.s. 1 (October 16, 1854), p532, 200 wds (NcU).
The article summarized below is from a Boston correspondent.
The 50 public libraries in Boston and vicinity contain 350,000 volumes. Cambridge College [Harvard?], including the students' libraries, has nearly 100,000 of these; the Boston Athenaeum, including the library of the American Academy of Arts and Sciences, has 70,000 more. The private libraries of the area have as many volumes as the public libraries or perhaps more. Ten private libraries probably contain 100,000 volumes; the largest has 15,000 volumes. Libraries with 5,000 volumes are quite common. There are 200,000 more books in the public libraries of Massachusetts than in any other state: including school, Sunday school, college, and church libraries, there are 1,462 public libraries, containing 684,015 volumes.

— AMERICAN UNITARIAN ASSOCIATION LIBRARY

485 "Library of the American Unitarian Association." *American Unitarian Association. Quarterly Journal*, 2 (January 1, 1855), p186–89 (NcD, OCl).
The Executive Committee wishes to collect a library of all Unitarian publications, and has set aside space in the rooms at 21 Bromfield Street for the collection. This library should include: 1) works that relate to the history of Unitarian Christianity; 2) works that show the earliest tendencies toward Unitarian thought in this country; 3) reports of literary, philanthropic, missionary, and reformatory societies; 4) copies of the books published by Unitarian authors; and 5) complete sets of the periodicals devoted to the interests of the denomination. Several sets of periodicals and some books are already in the library. These include the *Western Messenger, Unitarian Miscellany, Liberal Preacher*, and some of the works of Norton, Channing, Dewey, Palfrey, Ware, Greenwood, Follen, and Livermore. Contributions will be gratefully acknowledged, and a few exchanges can be arranged.

— ATHENAEUM

486 "Boston Athenaeum." *Monthly Anthology and Boston Review*, 4 (May 1807), p225–34 (NcU).
A society of gentlemen who publish the *Monthly Anthology* proposed last year the establishment of a reading room. The idea succeeded and a library soon developed. The founders transferred their rights to a group of trustees who incorporated the institution under the title of the Boston Athenaeum. The object of the Athenaeum is to provide a reading room with all the current gazettes published in the United States, magazines and journals, memoirs of learned societies, newspapers, and documents of various governments; a library; a museum cabinet; a repository of art; and a laboratory with apparatus for experiments and observations. The organization now has 160 subscribers who pay $10 per year. The Athenaeum proposes to raise capital for a building by

selling 150 shares for $300 each to persons who would become proprietors of the institution. Other individuals may be admitted by purchasing life shares for $100.

487 "Boston Athenaeum." *Monthly Anthology and Boston Review*, 4 (November 1807), p599-601 (NcU).
For the article mentioned in the summary below, *see 486*.
The public is congratulated for its support and advancement of the Athenaeum. A memoir of its history and purpose published in the May 1807 *Monthly Anthology* resulted in the sale of 150 shares, at a cost of $300 per share. A few $100 life-shares and numerous $10 annual subscriptions were also sold. The liberal generosity of the public for so worthy a purpose brings honor to the citizens of Boston and its vicinity. (Recent gifts of books and periodicals are listed.)

488 "Boston Athenaeum." *Monthly Anthology and Boston Review*, 5 (July 1808), p400 (NcU).
The entire article follows.
"The following order passed the House of Representatives of this State. Commonwealth of Massachusetts. In the House of Representatives, June 2, 1808.
Whereas the Boston Athenaeum is an institution of great publick benefit in promoting a taste for the arts and sciences, and for polite literature, and as such is worthy of legislative patronage:
Ordered, That the Clerk of this House be and hereby is required to deposite with the Secretary of said Athenaeum a copy of all the papers, which, during the present year are printed for the use of the House, and also a copy of the Journals of this House which now are, or which during the year ensuing may be printed by order of this House.
Attest, N. Tillinghast, *Clerk*."

489 "Boston Athenaeum." *United States Literary Gazette*, 4 (July 1826), p310, 400 wds (InU, NcU).
The Boston Athenaeum has merged with the Medical Library and the Scientific Association. The Medical Library has spent over $4,500 in the last ten years acquiring a collection of more than 2,000 volumes. Most of the Medical Library proprietors have become shareholders in the Athenaeum by paying $150 each. The Scientific Association had been formed only a short time previously, but raised $3,700 by subscription, which will be used to purchase books for the Athenaeum's scientific department. Thomas H. and James Perkins have each pledged $8,000 for the completion of the lecture rooms. Over $10,000 in subscriptions have been received from local citizens, and $4,500 have been received from the sale of fifteen new shares. Altogether, property amounting to $44,500 has been received since January.

490 "De Kay's Address; Anniversary Address on the Progress of the Natural Sciences in the United States; delivered before the Lyceum of Natural History of New York, February, 1826. By James E. De Kay. New York. G. & C. Carvill. 8 vo. pp. 78 and Report of a committee of the Trustees of the Boston Athenaeum, made to the Proprietors, May 25, 1826." *North American Review*, 23 (July 1826), p204-10 (InU, NcU).
The part of the review about libraries (p206-10) is summarized below.
A great obstacle to scientific advancement is the lack of books, specimens, and apparatus. The Boston Athenaeum is helping to supply the deficiency and

U.S. — Massachusetts

has effected a union with the Medical Library of Boston and the Scientific Association. The Medical Library has more than 2,000 volumes, all purchased in the last decade for $4,500. The thirty-one Medical Library Proprietors have become life members of the Athenaeum. The Scientific Association has collected more than $3,000 which will be used by the Athenaeum to purchase scientific books. Since January 1826, $40,000 have been added to the Athenaeum through sizeable donations from Thomas H. Perkins and James Perkins, which were matched by the sale of shares, the funds of the Scientific Association, and other donations. Of this, $16,500 was added to the permanent fund; $23,500 will be used to complete the lecture rooms and to purchase, bind, and repair books.

491 [Hale, Nathan.] "Catalogue of Books in the Boston Athenaeum, to Which Are Added the By Laws of the Institution, and a List of Its Proprietors and Subscribers. 8 vo. pp. 360. William L. Lewis." *North American Review*, 24 (April 1827), p477–80 (InU).

The article summarized below refers to an article in the July 1826 issue of the same journal *(see 490)*.

Suggestions we made last July for improving the library have been completed in the last year; between thirteen and fourteen thousand dollars have been spent for books in Europe; 460 volumes were purchased here; 3,552 volumes were bound or repaired; 673 volumes and 155 pamphlets were donated. Books may now be checked out to certain individuals. The printed catalog is an alphabetical index of books, with descriptions of editions. The catalog of tracts is unfinished. When it is, a subject catalog will probably be made of the 23,000 volumes at the Athenaeum. A new arrangement of the books has been made. The collection of medals and coins is extensive. The exhibition and lecture rooms are in a new building (which is described in the article). Nearly all the objectives proposed by the founders can now be achieved. The committee of the trustees writes concerning the bequest of former Athenaeum librarian, William S. Shaw.

492 [Eliot, Samuel Atkins.] "Catalogue of Pictures in the Athenaeum Gallery. Boston. 1829." *North American Review*, 29 (July 1829), p258–64 (InU).

The review of the catalog is summarized below.

The exhibition, open the last two months, has been successful. Collections have been presented for three years now without repeating a picture. Seven-eighths of the paintings shown this year belong to residents of Boston and the vicinity. The best works in the collection are those of Americans. Artists have benefitted and improved themselves by the series of exhibitions. (Some of the works in the collection are discussed.)

493 [Everett, Alexander Hill.] "Catalogue of the Pictures Exhibited at the Fourth Exhibition in the Gallery of the Boston Athenaeum. Boston. 1830." *North American Review*, 31 (October 1830), p309–37 (InU).

The article summarized below reviews the catalog and the exhibition itself.

The Athenaeum offers an annual exhibition of paintings that both entertain and refine character. The exhibition this year was not quite equal to earlier ones. It contained several works of old masters, several copies of originals in Europe, and several native productions. (Individual paintings and painters are discussed.) One Titian painting is in the Escorial, which contains two libraries, one having the richest collection of Arabic manuscripts in Europe.

494 Wigglesworth, Edward. "Sketch of the Boston Athenaeum." *Congregational Education Society. Quarterly Journal* [American Quarterly Journal], 12 (November 1839), p149–53 (NcU).

A reading room was proposed in 1806; a library was soon added. When the periodicals arrived, 1,000 books were also present. A board of trustees was formed and the institution incorporated. Donations were very important. Several libraries have been deposited or merged into the collection. In 1823, the library was classified and arranged like those in Europe. A new building was erected and the circulation of books permitted in 1826. An annual exhibition of paintings was begun in 1827. The Athenaeum now contains 30,000 volumes, of which 1,400 contain 27,000 pamphlets. There is a printed catalog and two manuscript catalogs of pamphlets. The permanent fund is $30,000; annual income is $2,800, expenses $1,600, and the surplus is expended for books. (Regulations are given covering officers, membership, fees, and privileges. Each officer is listed and his time of service noted; there have been two librarians.)

495 "Boston Atheneum [sic]." *Christian Examiner*, 36 (May 1844), p440–41. (IEG, NcU).

The purchase of property on Tremont St. for the Athenaeum's new building has been delayed due to the property's high selling price. The need for a new building becomes increasingly apparent as the Athenaeum's present neighborhood becomes more commercialized. The Athenaeum's assets consist of its Pearl St. property, $38,441; stocks, $26,553; paintings and objets d'art, $20,196; and the library, $57,671; total assets are $142,862. The library has 32,775 volumes. The Athenaeum is owned by 263 shareholders. To avoid indebtedness, 237 new shares valued at $300 each have been issued. By this means $71,000 will be raised, and the value of each of the 500 outstanding shares will be $430. All of the new shares have been sold.

496 [The Boston Athenaeum and Other Libraries.] *Stryker's American Register and Magazine* [American Quarterly Register and Magazine], 2 (March 1849), p232, 270 wds (NcU).

The Boston Athenaeum added 3,342 volumes and 18,393 pamphlets in the preceding year, increasing its collection to about 50,000 bound volumes and 100,000 pamphlets. Among the pamphlets acquired the preceding year, 6,000 had belonged to John Quincy Adams. The Smithsonian reports that there are 1,249,000 volumes in 182 American libraries. There are four European countries with library collections which are larger than those of the United States: Germany, 5,500,000 volumes; France, 5,000,000; Great Britain, 2,500,000; and Russia, 1,500,000.

497 [Boston Athenaeum Building.] *Literary World*, N.Y., 5 (August 11, 1849), p111–12 (NcU).

The first floor has two large reading rooms, a room for the trustees and a sculpture gallery. The second floor has three rooms for the library collection, the largest being 109 by 40 feet with a gallery. This large room houses about 40,000 volumes. The two smaller rooms, when completed, will accommodate 25,000 volumes. The third floor will have six rooms when completed, and will be a picture gallery. The basement contains workrooms, the heating system, janitors' quarters, and a bindery.

U.S. — Massachusetts

498 [Ellis, George Edward.] "The Boston Athenaeum." *Christian Examiner*, o.s. 47, 4th ser. 12 (September 1849), p322-23 (IEG, NcU).
The new $100,000 building for the Athenaeum soon will open to the public. It has a Palladian front that is 114 feet long. The basement contains rooms for storage, binding, and the heating equipment. The first floor, not yet completed, is divided into an exhibition hall and two reading rooms; the second floor is devoted to the library; and the third floor will be used as a gallery. The interior furnishings and other adornments will cost $25,000, a sum which we trust soon will be subscribed by the public. Access to the library's 40,000 volumes will be extended to visitors to the city as well as to many of its citizens who are not shareholders.

499 [Ticknor, George.] "Memoirs of the Buckminsters; Memoirs of the Rev. Joseph Buckminster, D.D. and of His Son, Rev. Joseph Stevens Buckminster. By Eliza Buckminster Lee. Boston: William Crosby and H. P. Nichols, 1849." *Christian Examiner*, 47 (September 1849), p169-203 (NcU).
The article reviews Mrs. Lee's book; part of a footnote is about a library. After a reference to an event that took place in 1808, this sections follows (p186).
"And when, somewhat earlier, — in May, 1805, and at subsequent meetings, — under the leading of Mr. William Smith Shaw, one of the members of the club, arrangements were made for establishing the 'Anthology Reading Room,' which two years afterwards became the 'Boston Athenaeum,' no one gave more active assistance which, as we see from Mrs. Lee's life, was very important while he was in Europe, and which, as we know, was continued in other ways to the moment of his death."

500 "The Memories of the Boston Athenaeum." *Literary World*, N.Y., 6 (April 20, 1850), p397-98 (NcU).
The new Athenaeum Library in Boston probably will be completed within the year. The old building on Pearl Street, now demolished and formerly the home of the library, was well known to me. The old building, its furnishings and peculiar odors, seemed immutable and oblivious to change. As a child I frequently went to the old library, and those visits have become the source of many pleasant memories.

501 [Ellis, George Edward.] "The History of the Boston Athenaeum, With Biographical Notices of Its Deceased Founders. By Josiah Quincy. Cambridge: Metcalf and Co. 1851." *Christian Examiner*, 50 (March 1851), p355, 200 wds (NcU).
The article summarized below is a review of Quincy's work.
Those who read the memoir of Rev. J. S. Buckminster by his sister will remember many references to the Boston Athenaeum. The history of that institution is told by Josiah Quincy, always the friend of the institution and its founders, and for many years its president. He gives a careful statement of all statistical and financial matters. He combines a literary history and a series of personal memoirs. The Athenaeum originated in the Anthology Club. Boston merchants became shareholders and gave large gifts.

502 "The Boston Athenaeum." *Norton's Literary Gazette and Publishers' Circular*, 2 (May 15, 1852), p83, 1220 wds (ICN, NcU).
The Anthology Club, the Athenaeum's predecessor, was founded early in this century. In 1807 the club was incorporated as the Boston Athenaeum, whose

150 shares of stock sold at $300 each. Starting with a total capital of $46,800, the Athenaeum now has capital assets worth more than $327,000. One of the library's most valuable possessions is George Washington's private library. The reading room receives American and European journals and has state, federal, and British government documents. The Athenaeum is located in a large three-story building. The combined value of the building and lot is $191,000. Mr. Charles Folsom is librarian. A lifetime membership costs $100; an annual membership costs $10 but does not carry the privilege of charging out books. (A picture of the exterior of the building accompanies the article.)

503 "Boston Athenaeum." *Norton's Literary Gazette and Publishers' Circular*, 3 (July 15, 1853), p115, 420 wds (ICN).
The source of the article condensed below is given in one place as the *Boston Advertiser* and in another as "Chn. Register," apparently the *Christian Register*. Neither of those articles has been seen by the compilers of this bibliography.
The library now has, by actual count, 55,567 volumes exclusive of the collection of the American Oriental Society and of the American Academy of Arts and Sciences, located in the building. The Hon. Francis C. Gray has recently given the library a copy of Lord [E. K.] Kingsborough's celebrated work on the antiquities of Mexico. We quote a description of it from the *Boston Advertiser*. It comprises facsimiles of ancient Mexican paintings and hieroglyphics from European collections together with monuments of New Spain by Mr. Dupaix. His lordship spent more than $150,000 upon the work. Because of difficulties with his paper maker, whose charges he believed to be exorbitant, he was thrown into prison; he died there.

504 "The Athenaeum Library." *Literary World*, N.Y., 12 (July 16, 1853), p564, 750 wds (NcU, OC).
Francis C. Gray has recently given the Boston Athenaeum a copy of [E. K.] Kingsborough's nine-volume work on Mexico. The production of this work cost over £30,000. The Athenaeum is in the process of selling new shares which will provide a fund of $150,000. The collection currently numbers 55,767, not counting pamphlets. The collections of the American Academy and the American Oriental Society are housed in the same building. The bound volumes of the three collections exceed 70,000.

505 [New Shares of the Boston Athenaeum.] *Norton's Literary Gazette and Publishers' Circular*, n.s. 1 (January 1, 1854), p9 (NcU).
The entire article follows.
"A recent effort in behalf of the Boston Athenaeum has resulted in the subscription of four hundred new shares, at $300 each. This institution has now a permanent fund of $150,000."

506 "The Boston Athenaeum." *Norton's Literary Gazette and Publishers' Circular*, n.s. 1 (January 15, 1854), p34, 800 wds (NcU).
The annual meeting was held recently at the Boston Athenaeum; the institution is flourishing, according to the annual report of the treasurer. With subscriptions for 339 shares, the amount drawing interest is $114,496, which is $8,896 more than the proposed goal. The Committee on the Library reports that $873 were spent for books and periodicals last year, with $1,597.50 received from subscribers. Over 200 donors gave 777 volumes and 3,179 pamphlets. In all, 1,185 volumes and 3,179 pamphlets were added. The library now has 56,593 bound

volumes, excluding pamphlets. The libraries of the American Academy of Arts and Sciences and the American Oriental Society, also in the building, increase the number of volumes available to 70,000, which is thought to be the most of any library building in the country. (The officers and trustees are listed; Thomas G. Cary is the president.)

507 [Appleton Gift to Boston Athenaeum.] *Norton's Literary Gazette and Publishers' Circular*, n.s. 1 (November 1, 1854), p554 (NcU).
The entire article follows.
"The executors of the late Hon. Samuel Appleton have transferred stocks to the par value of $25,000, to the Boston Athenaeum, from the fund of $200,000, belonging to that estate, which they were directed by the deceased to distribute at their discretion, for 'scientific, literary, religious or charitable purposes.' It will be remembered that at the time an effort was made last year to place the Athenaeum on a firm basis, the President of the Corporation announced a donation of $25,000 from a source which he was not at liberty to name. It now appears that the above arrangement was then agreed upon. The interest of the donation is to be applied to the purchase of books. The Athenaeum has received the interest which has accrued since the original subscription was made. The sum is $1,600, which can at once be applied to increasing the library."

508 [Boston Athenaeum.] *National Magazine: Devoted to Literature, Art, and Religion*, 9 (October 1856), p382–83 (InU, NcU).
The entire article follows.
"The *Boston Athenaeum* has a library containing fifty thousand volumes of books. In the upper story of the building is a hall or gallery for paintings and statuary. Last spring, the company, in order to increase its means, issued four hundred shares of new stock, at three hundred dollars per share. Eleven men immediately took each three thousand dollars' worth of this new stock, and the balance has since been all disposed of; thus raising one hundred and twenty thousand dollars to pay off some existing liabilities, and forming the basis of a permanent fund for the benefit of the society. The Perkins family gave to this society sixty-one thousand dollars. Other large and liberal donations were received from different persons, until the society were able to erect a library building, at a cost of one hundred and thirty-six thousand dollars, on a lot of ground that cost fifty-five thousand dollars."

509 [Facsimiles of Scottish Manuscripts in the Boston Athenaeum.] *Nation*, 12 (February 23, 1871), p126, 220 wds (NcU).
The article summarized below refers to a three volume set published from 1867 to 1872, prepared in the General Registry Office of Scotland.
The Boston Athenaeum has just received a valuable work, published by the [British] Ordinance Survey Office, *Facsimiles of National Manuscripts of Scotland*, photozincographed by Sir H. James, similar to the *National Manuscripts of England*. (Two volumes are described.) A third volume is in course of preparation.

510 [The Boston Athenaeum's Reproduction of the Domesday Book.] *Nation*, 12 (March 2, 1871), p143 (NcU).
The entire article follows. The compilers of this bibliography have been unable to locate the article to which it refers.
"We gave last year a list of libraries in this country possessing the photozin-

cographic reproduction of the Domesday Book. The Boston Athenaeum may now be added."

511 [A New Catalogue for the Boston Athenaeum.] *Nation*, 17 (July 10, 1873), p25, 420 wds (NcU).

The article summarized below apparently refers to an article by Charles A. Cutter that appeared in the January 1869 issue of *North American Review* (*see 645*).

An interesting catalog is being published at the Boston Athenaeum, mixing authors, titles, and subjects, similar to the catalog of the Boston Public Library, but with improvements. An extremely valuable feature is listing contributions to collections and proceedings of societies separately as well as under the heading for the main work. (Other details are discussed.) Much of the work was done by the late staff member, Mr. Charles Lowell. We hope that Mr. Cutter will have enough assistants to permit him to contribute to the theory of classification and to literature; his account of the catalog at Harvard, lately published in the *North American*, is admirable. The printing of the sheets for the Athenaeum catalog has advanced from A to Boccaccio.

512 [New Catalogue of the Boston Athenaeum.] *Nation*, 18 (February 12, 1874), p105 (NcU).

The entire article follows.

"Six hundred and forty pages of the new catalogue of the Boston *Athenaeum* have been printed, constituting somewhat more than a fifth of the entire work. The outlay up to this point has, if we are not misinformed, exceeded $30,000. The execution is praised in the highest terms. Mr. Charles A. Cutter has of late years had charge of this responsible enterprise."

513 [New Catalogue of the Boston Athenaeum.] *Publishers' Weekly*, 5 (March 7, 1874), p257 (NcU).

This article is almost identical with the one in *Nation* for February 12, 1874 (*see 512*).

514 [The Catalogue of the Boston Athenaeum.] *Nation*, 18 (April 23, 1874), p265, 300 wds (NcU).

The printing of the great catalog of the Boston Athenaeum has now gotten as far as the letter D. To complete the printing, from $13,000 to $16,000 is needed; friends of the Athenaeum will have to contribute part of this. Mr. Ezra Abbot, in making a liberal donation, says that this catalog has the best features of existing catalogs as well as peculiar excellences of its own. The references under subjects are as helpful as those under authors. The details about the contents of voluminous collections is carried farther than in any other catalog and is of the highest value in research. Contributions may be sent to Mr. George Abbot James at the Athenaeum.

— BOSTON LIBRARY SOCIETY

515 "Boston Library." *American Bibliopolist*, 7 (August 1875), p183, 180 wds (NcD, OC).

Statistical summary of the 1874 report of the Boston Library. The collection has increased by 16,372 volumes to a total of 276,922 in the main library and its six branches. Circulation was 758,417. Since 1867, 90,782 people have applied to use the library. The periodical reading room had 249,870 visitors last year, who used 348,772 magazines. Losses for the year totaled 85, while 4,169 volumes and 15,889 pamphlets were donated.

— BOSTON SOCIETY OF NATURAL HISTORY LIBRARY

516 Gould, Augustus A. "Notice of the Origin, Progress and Present Condition of the Boston Society of Natural History." *Congregational Education Society. Quarterly Journal* [American Quarterly Register], 14 (February 1842), p236–41 (NcU).
The parts of the article about libraries (p236–37, 239–40) are summarized below.
The collection of a library was one of the objectives in the formation of the society. (The officers are listed.) The librarians have been Seth Bass, Charles Amory and Charles K. Dillaway. All members of the society have free access to the library. When the society was founded, one barrier to progress in the study of natural history was the absence of books. Scattered volumes have been collected; there are now 1,000 in the library. Most have been donations; the rest have been bought through private subscription. No money has been drawn from the general fund for purchasing books. (Several of the donors and the important donations are described.) The legacy of the late Ambrose Courtis has also provided for the constant increase of the library; one-third of the interest from his $10,000 legacy is used for the purchase of library books.

— COLUMBIAN CIRCULATING LIBRARY

517 "Columbian Circulating Library." *American Ladies' Magazine; Containing Original Tales, Essays, Literary and Historical Sketches, Poetry, Criticism, Music, and a Great Variety of Matter Connected With Many Subjects of Importance and Interest* [Ladies' Magazine], 2 (October 1829), p488 (NcU).
The entire article follows; it refers to Boston.
"The efforts of Miss Nutting to establish in this city, a reading room for ladies, is well known. Circumstances (to use a modern philosophical word, substituted for *fate*) prevented the success she anticipated; but those who avail themselves of the advantages her library offers, will find there is a benefit resulting from experiments that aim at improvement, even though they are in their first object unsuccessful. The additions of books, prints, drawings, &c. which Miss Nutting made to her collection, partly in consequence of her reading room, has rendered her library much more valuable and attractive. We hope the ladies will not permit her to lose by the exertions which she has made in their service. The library is kept at No. 43, Cornhill."

— CONGREGATIONAL LIBRARY ASSOCIATION

518 "The Congregational Library Association: Its Origin and Objects." *Congregational Quarterly*, 1 (January 1859), p70–73 (InU, IEG).
The original purpose of the Congregational Library Association was to collect records of the church fathers in New England and current records likely to have historical value. First organized in February 1851, the Association was reorganized in May, 1853 when it merged with the Pastoral Association of Massachusetts. The membership was extended, largely to New England, rather than being confined to the Boston area. The Association was first incorporated in

1854. Membership is open to ministers and laymen of the Orthodox Congregationalist denomination at $1.00. There are more than 2,000 members and the collection contains 5,000 bound volumes, 16,000 pamphlets, more than 1,000 manuscripts, and a number of portraits, newspapers and periodicals. The library of the American Statistical Society is held on deposit. The Association's library has developed primarily through donations. A building has been purchased to house the library, to provide income through office space rentals to benevolent societies of Boston, and to serve as a "Congregational Home" in the sense of a central meeting place.

519 Clark, Joseph S. "Congregational Library Association." *Congregational Quarterly*, 1 (July 1859), p327–32 (IEG, InU).
(The sixth annual report.) During the preceding year 680 new members increased the total to about 2,300. The collection increased by 876 bound volumes; 1,980 pamphlets; 125 manuscript documents; and 19 new periodical subscriptions, bringing the totals to 5,627 bound volumes; 16,880 pamphlets; 925 manuscripts; and 43 periodicals. The only cost to the Association for these additions was the postage and freight since they were all donations. The $1.00 membership fee makes one a member for life. Rentals from office space amounted to $1,040. The *Congregational Quarterly* began publication and the American Congregational Union in New York became a co-partner in this enterprise with the second number. (The treasurer's report, a list of individuals and organizations contributing to the building fund, and a list of the society's offices are included, along with a strong appeal for funds to pay for the building.)

520 "Congregational Library Association." *Congregational Quarterly*, 2 (July 1860), p348–49 (IEG, InU).
The Association's seventh annual report is summarized below.
Membership increased to 2,772 with the addition of 472 new members. Donations to the collection amounted to 703 bound volumes, 5,630 pamphlets, 70 manuscripts, and 12 current periodicals which increased the collection to 6,010 bound volumes, 22,510 pamphlets, and 1,023 manuscripts. The library provides a public committee room which is heavily used. The economic troubles which began in 1857 have made it impossible to reach the building fund's goal and efforts to solicit contributions will be temporarily discontinued. Nonetheless, the library and the Committee Room will remain open to the public. The *Congregational Quarterly* has become increasingly popular.

— EAST BOSTON LIBRARY ASSOCIATION

521 [Officers of the East Boston Library Association.] *Norton's Literary Gazette and Publishers' Circular*, n.s. 1 (October 16, 1854), p532 (NcU).
The entire article follows.
"The following gentlemen were recently chosen as officers of the East Boston Library Association, for the ensuing year: President, Benj. Pond; Vice President, John P. Averill; Treasurer, Wm. D. Macy; Recording Secretary, George W. Merritt; Corresponding Secretary, James F. Blackington; Directors, Nelson Curtis, M. B. Leonard, Milford J. Cole, George E. James, Rev. D. A. Wallace, J. B. Spare. The library contains at present about 1000 volumes, and the affairs of the Association are in a very prosperous condition."

U.S. — Massachusetts

— GENERAL THEOLOGICAL LIBRARY

522 [General Theological Library of Boston.] *Publishers' Weekly*, 3 (March 15, 1873), p265 (NcU).
The entire article follows.
"The General Theological Library of Boston though less than eleven years old, numbers about 600 members and annual subscribers. Its increase of books has been on the average 1,000 a year, and they are now circulating in forty-two towns and villages of Massachusetts and New Hampshire. Books are taken to any distance. It was founded for the benefit of all religious denominations, and is managed, supported and used by all."

— LORING'S SELECT LIBRARY

523 [Current Best Sellers.] *Literary World*, Boston, 1 (August 1870), p45, 310 wds (NcU).
The article summarized below refers to the commercial circulating library operated by A. K. Loring.
There is no better criterion of the condition of the Boston literary market than the aspect of affairs at Loring's Library. Just now it tells that the popular appetite for books is dull, the population decimated, and the popular mind lethargic; the demand for books is less than half what it is in other seasons of the year. Many of the readers who remain in town find it too hot to read. However, many books are read, even with the mercury near 100 degrees; the attendants at the library have given us a list of the new books in most demand. Of course, novels take the lead, as they should in this weather which unfits one for struggling with philosophy or the hardest of facts. (Twelve titles are given.) Among the more substantial books, these are most sought for: (Four titles, mainly concerned with travel, are listed.)

— MASSACHUSETTS HISTORICAL SOCIETY LIBRARY

524 "Account of the Books and Manuscripts, Lately Deposited by the Old South Church and Society in the Library of the Massachusetts Historical Society." *Massachusetts Historical Society, Boston: Collections*, 2d ser., 7 (1826), p179–85 (IEN, NcU).
Rev. Thomas Prince of Boston, a collector of books, documents, and other printed materials about New England, began his collection in 1703. After his death in 1758, his collection eventually found its way to the Old South Church and Society. The historical portion of the Prince collection, named "The New England Library," was stored in the steeple of the Old South Church but was little used. In December 1813 the Massachusetts Historical Society petitioned the proprietors of the New England Library to deposit the collection with the society. A year later they voted to accept the petition with the following stipulations: all materials are to be kept in the possession of the Historical Society; the pastors of the Old South Church will have the right to inspect and to borrow materials in the collection; and the Old South Church reserves the right to take back the collection at any time.

525 Jenks, William. "An Account of the Massachusetts Historical Society." *Massachusetts Historical Society, Boston: Collections*, 3d ser., 7 (1838), p1–26 (IEN, NcU).

The parts of the article about libraries are summarized below.

Rev. Prince collected numerous documents for his New England Library, of which only a portion survived the Revolutionary War; his collection now is a part of the Society's library. Many books also were destroyed in the 1764 Harvard Library fire, and therefore it is not surprising that literary men should seek a means of safely preserving books (p7–8). The Society's library is in a room of the Massachusetts Bank and may be used by any person in accordance with the regulations of the Society (p14). The Society's library consists primarily of books on American history. It has subscriptions to several periodicals and newspapers, but the sets of back issues are far from complete. Also, there are state and federal documents as well as maps in the library's collection. Certainly, the library has benefited from donations made by earlier Society members (p18–22).

— MASSACHUSETTS HORTICULTURAL SOCIETY LIBRARY

526 [Library of the Massachusetts Horticultural Society.] *American Agriculturist*, 33 (January 1874), p5 (InU, NcU).
The entire article follows. It refers to E. W. Buswell.
"A Fine Catalogue of a Fine Library is that of the Massachusetts Horticultural Society, recently issued. The library is rich in new and old books relating to horticulture, and its treasures are always accessible to those interested in consulting it. Here is one library at least in the care of those who desire to make it useful, and the Massachusetts Society deserve great credit not only for accumulating such a fine collection of books, but for publishing a complete catalogue which gives not only subjects but authors in a manner for ready reference. Horticulturists visiting Boston should not fail to see this library, and if they do not find the veteran Buswell at the rooms ready to serve them they will find his place filled by his wife or son, either of whom are always ready to make a stranger welcome."

— MASSACHUSETTS SCIENTIFIC LIBRARY ASSOCIATION

527 Brooks, Edward. "Boston Scientific Library." *American Annals of Education* [American Journal of Education], 1 (November 1826), p180–82 (NcU).
Typically, public libraries acquire books on most subjects, but few on scientific subjects. There exists a need for a circulating library with a specialized collection comprised of publications about improvements in science, the arts, and manufacture. The potential advantages of this type of library are numerous and would be enjoyed by men in many different occupations. Accordingly, at a recent meeting of gentlemen, chaired by Prof. Ticknor, it was agreed: 1) to establish the Massachusetts Scientific Library Association; 2) to require a subscription of $100 for membership; 3) to use these funds to purchase a circulating library which would contain only materials on philosophy, commerce, geography, and agriculture; and 4) to form a committee to solicit members.

— MECHANICS' APPRENTICES' LIBRARY

528 J., H. "The 'Poems' Returned." *Lowell Offering*, 3 (July 1843), p234–37 (NcU, OC).
(A dialogue between "Samuel" and "Emma," a brother and sister. For the most part, Emma gives her brother information and he merely comments ap-

provingly.) The Mechanic Apprentice Library Association was founded on February 22, 1820, the first apprentices' library in the world. Until 1828 the Massachusetts Charitable Mechanic Association managed the library at which time an Association of Apprentices was formed and took partial responsibility for the library; in 1832 the Apprentices took full control. Membership is open to all Boston apprentices. The Association provides an elocution class and has current newspapers and periodicals for its members to read. The library and other association activities provide intellectual improvement. (Emma reads four long extracts from a volume of poems read by members on various anniversaries; she gives her brother the name of a bookstore where the volume can be obtained.)

— MERCANTILE LIBRARY

529 "Mercantile Library." *American Annals of Education* [American Journal of Education], n.s. 1 (May 1830), p238 (NcU).
The article which follows presumably refers to the Boston Mercantile library.
The report offered by Mr. Coates, at a late meeting of the proprietors, contains an outline of the institution. The society was the first established on the same plan in this country, and was founded ten years ago. Since then it has at times suffered much discouragement. The library now contains one thousand eight hundred and forty-six volumes, generally well chosen, and its organization insures a permanent increase.

530 "An Address Delivered Before the Mercantile Library Association, at the Odeon in Boston, September 13, 1838. By Edward Everett, Honorary Member of the Association. Boston: William D. Ticknor. 8 vo. pp. 40." *North American Review*, 48 (April 1839), p545, 180 wds (InU).
The article reviews the address.
Mr. Everett's address reveals his great and varied powers. His object was to furnish something instructive for the young merchants, for whom the Association was formed. The discourse contains a series of observations on the accumulation of capital, the system of exchanges, the security of property and the credit system.

531 "Boston Mercantile Library Association." *Literary World*, N.Y., 3 (November 25, 1848), p845–46 (NcU).
The association celebrated its anniversary November 15 with a speech by Daniel Webster and a poem by James T. Fields. The Hall at Tremont Temple was filled with a large enthusiastic audience. A number of prominent persons were seated on the platform including Robert Winthrop, Charles Sumner, Governor Briggs, Mayor Quincy and his father Josiah Quincy, President Everett, Oliver Wendell Holmes and the "merchant princes" of Boston. Mr. Webster spoke on the history of the formation of the Constitution. The speech was a model of synthesis, comprehension and logic, but without Webster's usual impassioned declamations. Mr. Fields' poem was on the subject of the Post of Honor which he approached from an unconventional view with satire, humor and wit. Webster and Fields were each given three cheers by the audience.

532 "Boston Mercantile Library Association." *Norton's Literary Gazette and Publishers' Circular*, 2 (June 15, 1852), p108, 300 wds (ICN, NcU).

We learn from the association's annual report that that institution is flourishing. Until last year the annual addition of books was small, and there were only 9,000 volumes in the collection. Last year, however, over 2,510 books were added to bring the library's collection up to 11,451 volumes, and nearly 70,000 books were circulated among the association's 2,323 members. The association is free of debt and has capital assets of $77,500. Mr. William F. Poole lately was appointed librarian.

533 "The Boston Mercantile Library." *Norton's Literary Gazette and Publishers' Circular*, 2 (October 15, 1852), p188 (ICN, NcU).
The entire article follows.
"The Boston Mercantile Library are desirous of erecting a new building, not, indeed, to rival the beautiful Athenaeum, but to accommodate more conveniently their increasing numbers of books. A small fund for this purpose has already been accumulated, but the subscriptions of merchants and others are needed for the accomplishment of their object. In such a city their claims will not long go begging. Having secured the services of an accomplished librarian, through whose tact and energy the library is likely to be rapidly advanced, they make this public call at a very favorable moment."

534 [Boston Mercantile Library Association.] *National Magazine: Devoted to Literature, Art, and Religion*, 2 (June 1853), p571 (InU, NcU).
The entire article follows.
"The Boston *Mercantile Library Association*, which was formed in 1820, has a library of 14,000 volumes, and was never more prosperous than at present. Plans are being laid to erect a new edifice for the better accomodation of the Association, at a cost, with the land, of some $60,000. The building fund of $20,000, given by merchants some years since, has recently been largely increased by new donations, in which list the names of Abbott Lawrence, Nathan Appleton, Samuel Appleton, William Sturgis, and John P. Cushing appear, with $1,000 against each name."

535 "Boston (Mass.) Mercantile Library Association." *Norton's Literary Gazette and Publishers' Circular*, 3 (July 15, 1853), p115 (ICN, NcU).
The entire article follows.
"The Thirty-Third Annual Report of this Association, for the year ending April 1853, has recently been printed. It shows that the Library, in all its various departments, has never been in a more vigorous condition than it is at the present time. 2175 volumes have been added to its shelves during the past year, so that it now owns 13,626 volumes. Thirty-three magazines and reviews, exclusive of newspapers, are taken at the Reading Room. The society now numbers 2215 members.
"The effort to procure funds for the erection of a permanent building for the Association is constantly making progress, and to that end the energies of its officers will continue to be devoted.
"Mr. W. F. Poole continues to discharge the duties of Librarian."

536 [Boston Mercantile Library Association.] *National Magazine: Devoted to Literature, Art, and Religion*, 3 (August 1853), p187 (InU, NcU).
The entire article follows.
"The *Boston Mercantile Library Association* contains 13,626 volumes, of which nearly 2,000 were added during the past year. The reading room is in

constant receipt of twenty-five daily and ninety-six weekly American and foreign newspapers, besides being supplied with the principal reviews and magazines. The whole amount of receipts during the past year was $7,667.52; the expenditures, including investments, and premiums on them, were $7,609.36. During the winter the society furnished two series of lectures, on Mondays and Wednesdays of each week, yielding to its treasury the net income of $1,584.60."

537 [Lectures at the Boston Mercantile Library Association.] *National Magazine: Devoted to Literature, Art, and Religion*, 4 (May 1854), p478 (InU, NcU).
The entire article follows.
"The *Boston Mercantile Library Association* have been very successful in their course of lectures during the past winter. The amount received from the sale of tickets, as stated in a recent report, was $5,031; expended for hall, lectures, advertising, &c., $3,292.57; leaving a balance of $1,788.43. The net income from this source has exceeded that of any previous year. Lecturing there does not appear to be an obsolete or unprofitable business."

538 [Thirty-fourth Annual Meeting of the Boston Mercantile Library Association.] *Norton's Literary Gazette and Publishers' Circular*, n.s. 1 (May 1, 1854), p226, 180 wds (NcU).
The thirty-fourth annual meeting of the Boston Mercantile Library Association was held April 19. President James A. Woolson's report says that total expenditures for the year were $7,684.74, of which $1,538.77 was for books and $1,250 was for the permanent fund. The catalog now has 15,247 volumes, with 1,621 added last year. Circulation last year was 81,000 volumes. There are 2,078 members. A new building is needed. Towards its creation some prominent Boston merchants have subscribed some $10,000, and the Association has invested $20,400. Newly-elected officers are Seymour Lyman, President; Augustus Hammond, Vice-President; John B. Norris, Corresponding Secretary; Hiram W. H. Blodget, Recording Secretary; Jacob H. Brown, Treasurer; and Fred W. [i.e., William Frederick] Poole, Librarian.

539 [Catalogue of the Boston Mercantile Library Association.] *Norton's Literary Gazette and Publishers' Circular*, n.s. 1 (October 16, 1854), p532 (NcU).
The entire article follows.
"The Directors of the Mercantile Library Association of Boston, will shortly issue a full and complete catalogue of the books, &c., in the library, which will form a work of 300 pages. The books will be classed both by their titles, and the names of the authors. Mr. Wm. F. Poole is engaged in the preparation of this important hand-book, and will undoubtedly exhibit his well-known ability in this department."

540 "Catalogue of the Mercantile Library of Boston. 8 vo. Boston: J. Wilson & Son, 1854; pp. xxiii, 289." *Norton's Literary Gazette and Publishers' Circular*, n.s. 2 (January 15, 1855), p25–26 (MnU).
The excellent historical sketch in this volume tells about the origin of the library in 1820 and its growth to a collection of 16,000 volumes serving about 2,000 members with a circulation in 1853 of 81,000 volumes. Mr. William Frederick Poole, the librarian, prepared the catalog; it is well adapted to the needs of a circulating library in these ways: First, each title is short, not

exceeding a single line. Second, each work is cataloged under author and subject; fiction is cataloged under author and title. Third, when there are two or more volumes of a work, the content of each volume is listed in small print—also, each of two or more editions is listed in small print. The catalog of a library for study and research, such as a college library, should have fuller titles and a complete analytical and alphabetical index.

541 [Autograph Letters by U. S. Presidents Given to the Boston Mercantile Library Association.] *National Magazine: Devoted to Literature, Art, and Religion*, 8 (May 1856), p477 (InU, NcU).
The entire article follows.
"*James T. Fields* has presented to the Boston Mercantile Library Association a series of autograph letters of all the Presidents of the United States, handsomely framed in the order of their seniority in office. Among them is a letter by John Adams, dated Philadelphia, April 8th, 1777, addressed to his son, John Quincy Adams, who was then nine years of age."

— PUBLIC LIBRARY

542 "Boston Free Library." *Norton's Literary Gazette and Publishers' Circular*, 2 (September 15, 1852), p169 (ICN, NcU).
The entire article follows.
"It is known to many of our readers that an effort has for some time past been making in the City of Boston to establish a grand Public Library, free to all classes, and intended not merely for reference, but more particularly for circulation. The subject has of late been referred to a committee, consisting of Hon. Edward Everett, Hon. George Ticknor, Sampson Reed, and Nathaniel B. Shurtleff, Esquires, and they have reported in its favor, recommending, however, no attempt for the complete purchase of such a library at once, but rather advising that a small beginning be immediately made, and that a steady and gradual increase be sought. We shall be disposed to discuss this project more fully hereafter."

543 "Boston Public Library." *Norton's Literary Gazette and Publishers' Circular*, 2 (November 15, 1852), p214, 280 wds (ICN, NcU).
The Public Library recently received a $50,000 donation from Mr. Joshua Bates with the stipulation that a library building with a reading room accommodating 150 readers must be provided by the city. That stipulation of course will be met, and the donation has been accepted. As specified by a city ordinance, seven trustees must be selected to oversee the affairs of the library.

544 "Public Library of Boston." *Norton's Literary Gazette and Publishers' Circular*, 3 (March 15, 1853), p39–40 (NcU).
Librarian Edward Capen reports on the organization of the Boston Public Library. We reprint the Boston ordinance establishing it, as similar libraries are being formed elsewhere. The trustees are Edward Everett, George Ticknor, John P. Bigelow, Nathaniel B. Shurtleff, Thomas G. Appleton, Alderman Sampson Reed and Common Councilman George W. Warren. Their first meeting was Monday, February 14. Everett was elected President. From May 24, 1852 until then, there was a 13-member management board, with the mayor as chairman. Finding a room for the library was difficult, but now a room on Mason Street designed by N. B. Shurtleff is nearly ready for books. The Hall or Reading Room

is not so far advanced. The library will open with about 6,000 volumes. In accordance with Mr. Bate's donation, the city will soon buy land for a large library building, whereupon $50,000 can be drawn from Mr. Bates.

545 [The Boston Public Library.] *Literary World*, N.Y., 12 (March 26, 1853), p253, 230 wds (NcU).
The article summarized below is from the Boston *Advertiser*.
The Boston Public Library is not only to be a circulating library of popular works, but also a reference library for study. The letter accompanying the donation of Mr. Everett and the 1852 report of the Trustees make clear that the library is to serve scientists, statesmen and scholars as well as the general public. A large public reading room and ample room for reading and consulting books are part of the plans. A large donation has been received from Mr. Bates. The city is making arrangements for the library on Somerset Street.

546 [George Ticknor's Gift to the Boston Public Library.] *National Magazine: Devoted to Literature, Art, and Religion*, 3 (August 1853), p188 (InU, NcU).
The entire article follows.
"At a recent meeting of the Trustees of the *Boston Public Library*, the librarian announced a donation of more than six hundred choice volumes given by George Ticknor, Esq. This donation consists of works pertaining to American history, of complete sets of American periodicals, and of more miscellaneous works. Much of the collection is said to be of great rarity and value."

547 [Boston Public Library.] *National Magazine: Devoted to Literature, Art, and Religion*, 3 (December 1853), p565 (InU, NcU).
The entire article follows.
"The committee authorized by the City Council to purchase a site for the Public Library of Boston, have concluded the purchase of the 'Wheeler estate,' and one of the estates adjoining on Boylston, near Tremont-street, the same being a portion of the Apthorp estate. The price paid is about seventy thousand dollars. In size, location, and fitness, in every way, it is believed by the warmest friends of the institution to be a most excellent site."

548 "Public Library of Boston." *Norton's Literary Gazette and Publishers' Circular*, n.s. 1 (March 15, 1854), p143, 430 wds (NcU).
The library is about to be opened to the public. There are 12,000 volumes now on the shelves, and the catalog will go to press immediately. The library will be open daily, except Sundays and holidays, for the delivery of books from 3–8 P.M. and for consultation from 9 A.M. to 9:30 P.M. (Regulations concerning eligibility for borrowing purposes are quoted.) Those persons eligible include city officials; Boston clergymen; teachers in private schools; members of the normal school; medal scholars; selected pupils of the public schools; non-residents who donate at least $100 to the library; anyone who deposits the cost of the book borrowed; and all other inhabitants of Boston over twenty-one who ought to enjoy the privilege, or are certified by some respectable and responsible citizen who undertakes liability for any losses.

549 [Opening of the Boston Public Library.] *Norton's Literary Gazette and Publishers' Circular*, n.s. 1 (May 15, 1854), p253 (NcU).
The entire article follows.

"The new Public Library was opened to the citizens of Boston on the 1st instant. Its reading room is remarkably well supplied with American and foreign journals, and its catalogue numbers about 12,000 carefully-selected volumes. On the first day, about eight hundred accounts were opened with persons desiring to take out books. Among the books most sought for thus far, have been Mrs. Mowatt's 'Autobiography of an Actress;' 'The Lamplighter;' 'Hillard's Six Months in Italy,' and Mrs. Hare's 'Passion Flowers.' "

550 [Boston Public Library.] *Norton's Literary Gazette and Publishers' Circular*, n.s. 1 (October 2, 1854), p493 (NcU).
The entire article follows.
"The Boston Public Library now numbers—including duplicates, but not including pamphlets—over 15,000 volumes; and in one day of Sept., 535 volumes were delivered to as many persons in five hours. The subscribers to the rules, &c., number 6,000; and the numbers that have received permission to take books are over 4,600. The volumes lost or damaged are very few, and the amount received from fines will more than cover the whole."

551 [Boston Public Library.] *National Magazine: Devoted to Literature, Art, and Religion*, 6 (January 1855), p92–93 (NcU).
The article is written by the periodical's Boston correspondent; the part of the article about the Boston Public Library (p93, 170 wds) is summarized below.
After two years of existence, the library has 16,000 volumes. This collection has been increasing at the rate of 6,000 per year; 7,000 individuals have enjoyed library privileges. While 60,000 to 70,000 volumes are borrowed annually, only 15 were missing at year end. A current periodicals reading room is connected with the library, which badly needs a fireproof building. It is hoped that construction on a new building can begin within a year.

552 "The Boston Library." *National Magazine: Devoted to Literature, Art, and Religion*, 6 (March 1855), p286, 230 wds (InU, NcU).
(From the second Annual Report.) The library had expected to add about 3,500 volumes with the income from the Bates and Phillips donations. Actually 6,533 volumes and about 3,000 pamphlets have been acquired, of which over 2,000 volumes and almost all the pamphlets have been donations. The trustees expect the future rate of growth to be about 6,000 volumes per year. This will provide a 100,000 volume library in fourteen years.

553 "Boston Public Library—Books on Music." *Dwight's Journal of Music, a Paper of Art and Literature*, 8 (October 20, 1855), p21–22 (NcU).
The Boston Public Library is as wisely managed as it is well endowed. It bids to become what a public library should be—a collection, freely accessible to all, of all the printed sources of information in every department of human knowledge. The fine arts will not be neglected. We have often spoken of the want of a good musical library in this country. At their request, we have recently furnished that library with a list of some 300 volumes relating to music, as a basis for purchases in that department. The list includes works of a scientific, historical, biographical, aesthetic, practical, or merely amusing character. Some are not in English; a good English translation is to be preferred when available. General readers and scholars are provided with sources. The list for the Boston Public Library is a good beginning, but it is only a beginning. We should go further and include books of music as well as books about music.

554 Hillard, George S. "The Public Library of the City of Boston." *American Journal of Education* (Barnard), 2 (August 1856), p203–09 (NcU).

Establishment of the Boston Public Library was motivated largely by the perception that the opportunity for education should be extended to the city's adult citizens. In 1848, after having obtained legislative approval, the City Council passed a law authorizing the establishment and maintenance of a public library. From 1849 through 1853 the library was the recipient of private donations. Joshua Bates, a London citizen who was a native of Boston, contributed $50,000 with the stipulations that income from the money was to be used for book acquisitions and that the city must properly house the library. A schoolhouse was fitted up for this purpose, and in the spring of 1854 it was first opened to the public. During 1853 a lot was purchased and planning was begun for a new library building; the fire-proof structure is scheduled for completion in the summer of 1857. At present there are 25,000 volumes in the library; circulation averages 350 books per day; and 10,000 borrowing permits are outstanding.

555 "The Public Library of Boston." *American Journal of Education* (Barnard), 7 (September 1859), p253–69 (NcU).

The establishment of the Boston Public Library was indirectly influenced by Alexandre Vattemare's attempts in 1841 to persuade Boston literary and scientific societies to merge their libraries into a public city library. Through his mediation, the city received two shipments of books, the first in 1843 and the second in 1847, from the Municipal Council of Paris in exchange for publications previously sent by Boston. In 1847 Mayor Josiah Quincy, Jr. strongly recommended the establishment of a library as did a committee which had been selected to study the proposed library. In January, 1858 the Boston Public Library's new building was opened to the public. (A description of the building and statistics of the current library operations are given. The article concludes with extracts of addresses delivered by Robert E. Winthrop, Alexander H. Rice, and Edward Everett at the dedication of the new building. Floor plans and exterior and interior views of the library accompany the article.)

556 Ticknor, George. "Joshua Bates." *American Journal of Education* (Barnard), 7 (September 1859), p270–72 (NcU).

This article by George Ticknor originally appeared in *Appleton's New Encyclopedia*; the part about libraries (p271–72) is summarized below.

In 1852 Bates, a London resident who was born near and received his early commercial training in Boston, happened to read the official notice of the plan to start a public library in Boston. He immediately was convinced that such a plan would permanently benefit the city; subsequently he pledged an endowment of $50,000. The income from that fund was to be used for the purchase of books on the condition that the city would provide accommodations for their use. During the construction of the new library building, Bates also donated between 20,000 and 30,000 books to the library. His generosity will benefit present and future Bostonians.

557 "Edward Everett." *American Journal of Education* (Barnard), 7 (December 1859), p325–66 (NcU).

The part of the article about libraries (p342–43) is summarized below. Excerpts from Everett's speech at the dedication of the Boston Public Library, January 1, 1858, are reprinted in the article (p365–66); his portrait is reproduced (p324).

In a letter to the mayor of Boston, Everett proposed in 1848 a plan for a public library which since has been realized. Mayor Bigelow made the first contribution for the library, and Everett sketched out a plan for its development. Subsequently, a board of trustees was appointed; in 1852 the board, in conjunction with the city government, opened the library in temporary quarters. In January 1858 the new library was dedicated; it is a valuable asset to the city of Boston.

558 "Boston Public Library." *Massachusetts Teacher: a Journal of School and Home Education*, 13 (January 1860), p32–33 (NcU).

The article, summarized below, contains extracts from the seventh annual report of the Boston Public Library.

During the past year, 7,192 volumes and 1,317 pamphlets have been added to the collection which now contains 78,043 books and 19,255 pamphlets. Catalogs for the collection in the lower hall have been published. This collection contains popular books, which are always in great demand, while the collection in the upper hall comprises scientific books. The reading room is open daily, except holidays and Sundays, from 9:00 a.m. to 10:00 p.m. The purpose of this library is to provide our citizens with books of practical value which cannot be found in the town's circulating libraries or bookstores. We cannot fully foresee the library's future benefits to the community. Last year library expenditures totaled $27,337. Among donations to the library were two valuable collections: 347 Chinese historical and literary works and 500 works on the history and art of music.

559 [Smith, Charles Card.] "Index to the Catalogue of Books in the Upper Hall of the Public Library of the City of Boston. Boston: George C. Rand and Avery, Printers to the City. 1861. Royal 8vo. pp. viii. and 902." *North American Review*, 93 (October 1861), p567–70 (InU, NcU).

The article reviews the index.

In less than ten years the library has become one of the nation's largest. We give an account of its history and present condition, drawn from the annual reports of trustees and from other documents. The first steps toward formation were made in 1847. In 1852 a board of trustees was organized and a librarian appointed. The reading room opened in 1854; a new building, containing an upper and a lower hall, opened in 1858. Charles C. Jewett aided the trustees in producing this catalog and the 1858 catalog, which are well adapted to public use. The catalog is alphabetical, with titles listed under the names of authors and under appropriate subjects. Summaries are made for the contents of every multi-subject, multi-volume work. Complete lists of Congressional documents and the sessional papers of the British Parliament, cataloged here for the first time, are also given.

560 [Hale, Edward Everett. Card Catalogs.] *Christian Examiner*, o.s. 71, 5th ser. 9 (November 1861), p454–57 (IEG, NcU).

The preparation of a catalog for a large library no longer is a routine task. The card catalog is the best way to show the holdings of a library; however it does not necessarily follow that the printed catalog can be dispensed with. During the past three years the Boston Public Library has arranged and cataloged its 75,000-volume collection. Additionally, Mr. Jewett, the librarian, has supervised the preparation of a printed index to the catalog, and the staff has undertaken an analysis of the library's Congressional and Parliamentary documents. The index should prove to be particularly useful to students outside of Boston. We regret the trustees' decision to give borrowing privileges to almost everyone in Boston, for this means that many of the students who go to the library often will find that the books they need are checked out.

561 Gilman, Daniel C. "Catalogue of the Boston Public Library." *New Englander and Yale Review*, 21 (January 1862), p135-39 (InU).

Review of *Index to the Catalogue of Books in the Upper Hall of the Public Library of the City of Boston*, Boston: 1862.

The trustees of the Boston Public Library, as shown by establishing two departments, one for reference and one for circulation, have tried to gratify both the scholars and the general reading public. The catalog lists 55,000 volumes in the upper or reference collection, and almost 20,000 in the lower half. Only the Astor Library has grown so rapidly. The Boston catalog is arranged alphabetically by author with press-marks indicating the location. Each volume is also listed under one or more additional headings. The catalog lists the contents of each volume in larger sets; each of these volumes is listed under author. Public documents of the United States and Great Britain are included. The catalog was prepared by C. C. Jewett, with the assistance of Messrs. Vinton and Jillson.

562 "A Boston Notion." *Nation*, 4 (January 24, 1867), p73-75 (NcU).

Many an elderly man can remember the days when he had only a few books to read. He can rejoice that his children have dozens of Tennysons, can look at stereoscopic views, and subscribe to magazines. A letter from a member of the Boston Public Library Examining Committee says that people ought to give up the idea of protecting books in favor of the idea of getting as many books as possible worn out by use. If a user of the Boston Public Library wants a book not in the collection, the library buys it unless there is a moral objection. The losses of books in circulation are very low. The reading room has been noisy, but now, with a new system of charging out periodicals, it is quieter. The value of such an institution is so great as to be immeasurable. When will New York have a free library?

563 Boston Public Library. *Bulletin*, 1-2 (October 1867-October 1876) (IEN).

The compilers of the present work have seen 27 out of 35 issues that appeared before 1876 and have seen the index for volumes 1 and 2 that covers these 35 issues. Of the issues examined, the ones through March 1869 were bi-monthly and the ones after that date (with a few exceptions) appeared at three-month intervals. The following note is based on what was learned from examining the 27 issues and the index; individual articles are not listed separately in this bibliography.

In all the issues, these items are present: the names of the members of the Board of Trustees, the names of the principal officers of the library, the days and hours of opening, the rules about eligibility to use the library, and a list of books (in later issues, "The more important books") added to the library since the list in the last *Bulletin*. This list occupies most of the pages in each issue.

The notes that appear only once or a few times are of two kinds: those about the library as a service organization and those that describe its collections. The ones about the library as an organization mainly describe catalogs and finding lists, announce or describe the establishment of branches, or report on progress in constructing additions or alterations to the building. Brief notices appear occasionally to remind readers to report changes of address, to remind them of their privilege of recommending books for the collection, or that "special students" will be notified of arrival of books in their fields of interest if they will tell the Superintendent what their interests are.

In the earlier issues, short notes about collections mainly make appeals for contributions of materials, especially those on the subject of Boston. These references to desiderata continue throughout the period; however, in later years, mainly in the 1870's, longer articles describe the library's holdings in various subjects. Examples of these discussions in volume 1 are: several articles about the Tosti collection of engravings, beginning with one in the March 1869 issue on p146; "To the Medical Profession" (about medical books), in the June 1869 issue, p166; "Our Art Department and Its Literature" in the April 1870 issue, p227; "To Teachers" (books on education and on subjects taught in school), June 1870, p252; "George Ticknor's Bequest" (Spanish and Portuguese books), April 1871, p322–23; and "Works on Military Service" (gifts by General Sylvanus Thayer), July 1871, p348.

In volume 2, some of the notices about the collections are bibliographical essays that evaluate the significance of individual works. Examples are: several articles about the Barton collection with emphasis on its Shakespeariana, beginning with one on p164 in the July 1873 issue; an article, "Cremation as a Mode of Interment and Related Subjects" on p268 in the July 1874 issue; "Works on Costume" on p348–50 in the April 1875 issue and "Centennial Reading" (about Boston and vicinity from 1761 to 1776) on p382–89 of the July 1875 issue.

564 [Popular Books in the Boston Public Library.] *Nation*, 6 (January 16, 1868), p51–52 (NcU).

In the last report of the Boston Public Library, we learn that the institution maintains its high character, that it is growing rapidly (it is second among American libraries), that it is heavily used, and offers well-selected reading. Some interesting tables show the relative popularity of various authors. (Statistics are quoted for leading authors of fiction, poetry, drama, travel, history, and children's books.)

565 [The *Bulletins* of the Boston Public Library.] *Nation*, 8 (February 11, 1869), p110, 330 wds (NcU).

Mr. William A. Wheeler, well known as a lexicographer, has obtained a congenial post as General Assistant in the Boston Public Library. The eighth number of the *Bulletin*, in which his name appears, has a list of books added to the library or newly located during November and December, 1868, and a list of duplicates in American history, offered for exchange. The issue also contains a list of deficiencies in American periodicals and almanacs, a list of embossed books for the blind, and an announcement of the library's willingness to purchase books not in the collection and duplicates of heavily used items. These *Bulletins* are sold at the library for two cents each; hundreds of persons in the U.S. would gladly pay fifty cents or more for a year's subscription.

566 Davis, L. Clarke. "The Public Library of Boston." *McBride's Magazine* [Lippincott's Magazine of Literature, Science, and Education], 3 (March 1869), p278–93 (NcU).

Reference is made to several types of libraries that preceded free public libraries: commercial circulating libraries, social libraries, and apprentices' libraries. Then the history of the Boston Public Library is traced. The idea existed in the 1840's; Joshua Bates' offer of money in 1852 gave impetus to the planning and the library opened in 1854; other gifts are described, as is the handsome new building, opened in 1858. The growth of collections through gift and purchase is described, as are the problems caused by loss and mutilation of books. Clarke believes that, through the generosity of the citizens of Boston, the library has become very beneficial; everyone should pay homage to that city.

567 "Public Libraries." *Massachusetts Teacher: a Journal of School and Home Education*, 22 (April 1869), p137, 170 wds (NcU).

The popularity of the Boston Public Library is attested by the ever increasing circulation and attendance figures. The library continues to fulfill its designated role, providing supplement to the education received in public schools. Presently the library has 145,000 volumes making it the largest collection in the United States except for the Library of Congress. The city cannot but be grateful to those distinguished citizens who oversee the library's administration. At Ipswich the free public library founded by the late Augustine Heard opened last Tuesday; it contains 4,000 volumes.

568 [Tosti Collection of Engravings.] *Nation*, 8 (April 8, 1869), p276, 150 wds (NcU).

The March *Bulletin* of the Boston Public Library mentions the acquisition, through the liberality of Mr. Thomas G. Appleton of an excellent collection of engravings, part of the estate of the late Cardinal Tosti. It is said to contain 10,000 plates, 600 of them framed and the rest in richly bound volumes. They are expected to arrive in the spring, along with an antique bust presented by the Cardinal's heir. Along with the valuable collection of engravings at Harvard, the Tosti collection will provide Bostonians with a rich store of material in this branch of art.

569 [Two Projects of the Boston Public Library.] *Nation*, 9 (July 15, 1869), p50, 250 wds (InU).

The Boston Public Library is collecting all printed material about the recent jubilee. Even the most dastardly of the attacks made upon the festival and the city by foreign detractors will be preserved. A circular, containing thirty questions relative to library economy and experience, was sent to libraries in the U.S. and Europe, but 70 American institutions have not yet answered. All libraries interested in tabulating information for the benefit of all should help in collecting it. The statistics of all libraries, even small ones, are of some value to those managing similar institutions, if to no one else.

570 [Special Collections of the Boston Public Library.] *Nation*, 9 (November 11, 1869), p411, 610 wds (InU).

The Boston Public Library will accept written material illustrating the recent Humboldt anniversary or the Stowe-Byron controversy. Other collections in the library of this type record Lincoln's assassination, Edward Everett's death, the great fire in Portland and other topics. A collection of Frankliniana is planned. The library is rich in religious materials, especially on New England and the Methodist church. Only the Union Theological Library of New York, with its 28,000 volumes, has a larger collection of religious materials than does the Boston Library, with 15,000. A "Class List of Fiction" has recently been issued of the library's fiction collection; it usually gives a full list of each author's works, and the real names of pseudonymous writers. The list sells for 2¢, and is kept current with 2¢ monthly bulletins. Similar catalogs for poetry and other departments are planned.

571 [Boston Public Library Establishing Branches.] *Nation*, 10 (January 20, 1870), p42, 450 wds (NcU).

More people come to the Boston Public Library each year so there is undesirable pressure on the Boylston Street institution. It is planned to establish branches in order to relieve this pressure and to accommodate more citizens. In the city proper about one out of eight and a half of the residents has taken out books. In East Boston, one person in twenty-six has used books; in South Boston, one in fourteen; and in Roxbury, one in sixteen. We must suppose that there is more than one reader for each book taken out. The central library can spare duplicates for the branches and doubtless the city government will not be niggardly.

572 [The Merit of Different Works of Literature.] *Nation*, 10 (February 3, 1870), p75, 410 wds (NcU).

The seventeenth annual report of the Trustees of the Boston Public Library is the most valuable yet, containing statistics of libraries in Massachusetts, the rest of the United States, and elsewhere. The Examining Committee suggests that the library's bulletins and catalogs should show the value of various kinds of novels and of novelists on a scale of merit. This would amount to an *index expurgatorius*. A better mode of enlightening readers is used in the public library of Milan: Public-spirited and learned men give short lectures on "the moral worth of the most important works of the human intellect." Such lectures cannot cover much ground, but they could be solid and of lasting value. These lectures would have greater capacity for good than all the lyceum talks we have heard in the last fifteen years.

573 [The Boston Public Library.] *Nation*, 10 (June 9, 1870), p370, 240 wds (NcU).

Number 13 of the *Bulletin* of the Boston Public Library, as usual, contains information of value to scholars and specialists. It announces the completion of the catalog of the Prince Library, in three parts: books printed in or relating to America; theological works; and a synoptical summary of the manuscripts. The *Bulletin* catalogs 5,100 prints in the Tosti-Appleton collection of prints, leaving about 1,200 to be cataloged; the library is strengthening its collection of art reference books relevant to the prints. The library is making a special collection about Boston history and topography and is preparing a card catalog of books in Bates Hall.

574 [The Boston Public Library.] *Nation*, 11 (July 14, 1870), p27 (NcU).
The entire article follows.

"The managers of the Boston Public Library announce that they are gathering materials — pamphlets, broadsides, prints, newspapers, and so forth — for the purpose of making volumes commemorative of Dickens, and they ask the assistance of all their friends, as they desire to make as full as possible the evidence of the loss sustained by his death. Also, as formerly, the managers desire to make volumes commemorative of the recent 'Memorial Day,' by which term is doubtless meant the day otherwise known as 'Decoration Day' — a designation not so good, perhaps, as that here suggested, but one that it will be found difficult to displace."

575   [The Ticknor Bequest.] *Nation*, 12 (May 25, 1871), p359, 300 wds (NcU).
  The late George Ticknor's bequest of Spanish works to the Boston Public Library consists of 3,760 printed books, 14 manuscript volumes, 598 pamphlets, and several unbound manuscripts. The only collections of equal value are the Spanish books in the British Museum and the private library of Lord Holland. Ticknor also left the city four thousand dollars, the income of which is to be used for additions to the collection. Only books of permanent value are to be added; at the end of twenty-five years the fund may be used for solid acquisitions in languages other than Spanish and Portuguese.

576   [The Boston Public Library compared with Italian Libraries.] *Nation*, 13 (August 10, 1871), p90, 420 wds (NcU).
  The nineteenth *Annual Report* of the Boston Public Library testifies to the prosperity of that institution and furnishes many useful hints and statistics for other libraries. Last year, 18,000 volumes were added while the Astor Library added but 1,500 volumes to its jealously secluded stock. The Superintendent for the Boston Public has found an indication of American interest in the higher forms of literature: Twenty U. S. libraries receive the publications of the Chaucer Society while there are only eight in England and one in Ireland. (Statistics for 1870 of Italian libraries outside Rome are compared with those of the Boston Public Library.) The total gain of the Italian libraries was but 11,706, compared with the Boston Library's 18,000.

577   Plumley, G. S. "George Ticknor's Spanish Collection." *American Bibliopolist*, 3 (November 1871), p432–34 (NcD).
  The article was reprinted fiom *Harper's Magazine* 43 (November 1871) p893–96 *(see 578)*.

578   [Plumley, G. S.] "George Ticknor's Spanish Collection." *Harper's Magazine*, 43 (November 1871), p893–96 (NcU).
  The author's name is supplied in the reprint of this article in *American Bibliopolist* 3 (November 1871), p432–34 *(see 577)*.
  Ticknor, a tireless scholar who traveled and studied all over Europe, began making his excellent collection of Spanish literature in 1817. It is now in the Boston Public Library; the only Spanish collections equal to it are the one in the British Museum and Lord Holland's private collection. Ticknor bequeathed all of his Spanish materials together with $4,000 in cash on condition that the library meet six terms, which are listed. As of last April, the collection contained 3,760 printed volumes, 14 bound manuscripts, 598 pamphlets and many unbound manuscripts. Arrangement and classification is now complete, and a catalog is being prepared. Many books contain annotations, copied extracts, and marginal notes by Ticknor. Included are many defaced books condemned by the Inquisition, and four official publications of accusations and burnings directed by the Inquisition.

579   "The Boston Public Library." *Appletons' Journal: a Magazine of General Literature*, 6 (December 2, 1871), p629–31 (NcU).
  Any resident of Boston may borrow books from the Public Library merely by signing for them; no fees or recommendations are required. The result of this

trust is evidenced in the library's popularity, its high circulation figures and the low number of abuses of the borrowing privilege. The building features two divisions: the Lower Hall, where patrons may borrow popular books, and Bates Hall, where scholars have access to a full reference collection, an extensive scholarly library, and writing desks and materials. A reading room adjacent to the Lower Hall features newspapers and magazines in several languages. The users of the library represent all ages and incomes; the largest numbers come in the evening after school and work are over. The collection grows constantly; in most cases books suggested by a patron are purchased. Hours of service are liberal. (Circulation and collection figures for 1869-70 are included.)

580 [Boston Public Library; A Correction.] *American Bibliopolist*, 4 (March 1872), p124 (ICU, IEN, OC).
The entire article follows.
"We find that we last month [*see 122*] considerably understated the number of books in the Boston Public Library. The superintendent informs us that the Library contains 192,000 volumes, or nearly 40,000 more than we credited it with, in our literary gossip, on page 66."

581 B., [Boston Public Library.] *Publishers' Weekly* [Publishers' and Stationers' Weekly Trade Circular], 2 (August 8, 1872), p132-33, 230 wds (NcU).
Our fine library is conducted on the most liberal principles. The building is now being enlarged and improved because almost from its opening, it has proved inconvenient, poorly lighted, and too small. Contractors, real estate holders and others have clamored for a new building, but the changes now underway will meet all demands for some years to come. The growth of the library has been wonderful and it is free in the broadest sense of the word. The question of opening on Sunday is not yet settled; however, the drift of public opinion is in that direction.

582 [Boston Public Library.] *Publishers' Weekly* [Publishers' and Stationers' Weekly Trade Circular], 2 (September 5, 1872), p233 (NcU).
The entire article follows.
"The frequenters of the Boston Public Library will have in a few days Mr. Winsor's 'Handbook' to guide them in their researches. The enterprising superintendent does not mean to rest on this good work, but is now engaged on a catalogue of history, biography, and travel, which will be ready in October, in which the works are classified by subjects instead of by authors or alphabetically. Under each head is given a list of the works bearing on the topic, with the number of the shelf on which they may be found. Important dates in biography and history are also presented, whereby the catalogue contains much information."

583 [Guides to the Books in the Boston Public Library.] *Nation*, 15 (September 12, 1872), p168, 580 wds (NcU).
Mr. [Justin] Winsor, Superintendent of the Boston Public Library, is able to produce an abundance of guides to his collection; other librarians either cannot make catalogs or cannot print them. To the second edition of the finding list for history, biography, and travel in the Lower Hall, Mr. Winsor has added excellent notes; it is as though a book on what to read had been combined with an ordinary library catalog. For the subjects of biographies he gives dates of birth and death and labels such as "American poetess" or "English physician";

for voyages, he gives dates as well. A person with a strong imagination is carried through a distant country by reading the title of a travel book, and the title of a book of sermons produces for him a gentle shudder. But Mr. Winsor's purpose is utilitarian: to make sure that the reader gets the best book on each subject.

584 Winsor, Justin. "The Boston Public Library." *Publishers' Weekly* [Publishers' and Stationers' Weekly Trade Circular], 2 (October 24, 1872), p413-15 (NcU).

The article summarized below is an extract from Winsor's twentieth annual report.

The library now has 194,000 volumes, giving us second place for size among the libraries of the country; nearly 14,000 volumes and 11,000 pamphlets have been added this past year. Circulation has been nearly a third more than last year; of the books taken from the library, only one out of 9,351 was not recovered. Authorities now agree that it is impractical to print a book catalog for a large, rapidly growing collection such as ours. We are adapting a plan from the University of Leyden for printing on sheets of thin paper, cutting and pasting individual entries on to cards, posting other copies of the sheets as current acquisitions lists, and using other copies for other purposes. We are continuing the publication of printed book lists for the most popular library departments.

585 [Sunday Opening at the Boston Public Library.] *Nation*, 16 (February 20, 1873), p133 (NcU).

The entire article follows.

"The Boston Public Library has at last been opened on Sunday, but only as yet in the afternoon and evening, and with access only to periodicals and books of reference. The attendance has been large, orderly, and respectable, and the selection of reading (as it could hardly fail to be) eminently proper and edifying."

586 [Shakespeareana at the Boston Public Library.] *Nation*, 16 (May 22, 1873), p354 (NcU).

The entire article follows.

"The Boston Public Library has just acquired by purchase about 12,000 volumes of the private library of the late Thomas P. Barton, of this city. It is in all respects a highly valuable collection, but is most to be prized on account of its Shakespereana, amounting to some 2,000 volumes, and including a very perfect copy of the first folio. No other library in the country, it is said, whether public or private, can in this department now compare with the Boston Library."

587 [Tosti Collection of Engravings at the Boston Public Library.] *Nation*, 16 (June 19, 1873), p417 (NcU).

The entire article follows. There is a further reference to this catalog in the *Nation* for August 21, 1873 *(see 588)*.

"The Boston Public Library has just finished, in a supplementary list, its catalogue of the Tosti collection of engravings presented to it by Mr. Thomas G. Appleton. A few copies have been printed on tinted paper."

588 [Catalogue of the Tosti Collection.] *Nation*, 17 (August 21, 1873), p129, 270 wds (NcU).

The article refers to another in the January 13, 1870 issue of the *Nation (see 646)*, and to a second in the *Nation* for June 19, 1873 *(see 587)*.

Boston (Public)

We alluded, several weeks ago, to the completion of the catalog of the Tosti Collection of engravings in the Boston Public Library. The parts have now been issued together as a section in one of the library's *Bulletins*. This is an accurate list of the 6,500 prints given by Mr. Appleton to the library; it is produced in a praiseworthy manner, thanks mainly to the painstaking work of Mr. James L. Whitney. This catalog is superior to the one of the Gray Collection at Harvard, made by Mr. Louis Thies and discussed in our January 13, 1870 issue; the Tosti catalog has an index of painters and designers as well as cross-references under subjects. However, the two collections are weak in nearly the same way; for instance, few English engravers appear in either. We hope that both collections will be placed in the future art museum of Boston.

589 [The Boston Public Library.] *Nation*, 17 (September 4, 1873), p161, 400 wds (NcU).

We mention the Boston Public Library frequently, not from partiality but to provide information about this example of the way such an institution should be operated. The twenty-first *Annual Report* tells that the library now consists of the central building and three ward or district branches with more than 220,000 volumes in all. The Barton Library is the most important acquisition of the year. The hotly contested Sunday opening of the Periodical Reading Room has brought in a kind of reader not reached before; use has been one-half to one-third of the weekday average, and the users have been uniformly decorous. The catalog of the history, biography, and travel books in the Lower Hall has notes to aid further reading on any topic; the notes discriminate among books, but without bias. This catalog should sit beside the regular catalog in every similar library in the country.

590 [Barton Library.] *Literary World*, Boston, 4 (January 1874), p126, 380 wds (NcU).

The article summarized below was condensed in the issue of the *Nation* for January 22, 1874 *(see 592).*

The Barton Library, recently added to the Boston Public Library, is, beyond doubt, the richest Shakespearean collection in America. (The collection is briefly described.) These volumes have been cataloged, for the most part, by Mr. William A. Wheeler, Assistant Superintendent of the library, whose scholarship and judgment have been amply demonstrated in his labors on *Webster's Dictionary* and other works. He plans to prepare a Shakespeare cyclopaedia, with information about the poet's life, his works, and the lives and writings of his editors, translators, commentators and critics. Wheeler will doubtless enlist the help of other scholars. The result will fully vindicate the wise liberality of the government of the library in making the Barton purchase.

591 [Shakespeare Collection in the Boston Public Library.] *Publishers' Weekly*, 5 (January 10, 1874), p34 (NcU).
The entire article follows.

"The Boston Public Library possesses, by the accession of the Barton Library, the richest Shakespearian collection in America, and one of the finest in the world. Every one will be glad to learn that Mr. Wm. A. Wheeler, the Assistant Superintendent, and one of our best bibliographical scholars, is to utilize this material in a Shakespearian Encyclopaedia under the title, 'A Cyclopaedia of Shakespearian Literature; designed to elucidate the Biography of the Poet, the Antiquities, Geography, Topography, Political and Natural History, and

U.S. — Massachusetts

Bibliography of his Works, and the Lives and Writings of his Editors, Translators, Commentators, and Critics.' He will enlist Shakespearian scholars elsewhere in the work, which will be of utmost importance. We shall return to the subject again."

592 [William A. Wheeler's Plans for a Shakespeare Cyclopaedia.] *Nation*, 18 (January 22, 1874), p60 (NcU).
The entire article follows; it is condensed from an article in the January 1874 issue of the *Literary World* of Boston *(see 590)*.
"The *Literary World* states that Mr. Wm. A. Wheeler, Assistant Superintendent of the Boston Public Library, in cataloguing the newly-added Barton Library, has been led to feel the need of and to undertake to prepare a Cyclopaedia of Shakesperian Literature, designed to elucidate the biography of the poet, the antiquities, geography, topography, political and natural history, and bibliography of his works, and the lives and writings of his editors, translators, commentators, and critics. Mr. Wheeler expects the co-operation of eminent Shakesperian scholars."

593 [Boston Public Library.] *Publishers' Weekly*, 5 (March 28, 1874), p337 (NcU).
The entire article follows.
"Bulletin No. 28 of the Boston Public Library, a pamphlet of 44 pages, brings up the list of additions of books and alterations of place to the end of the year 1873. It also gives the information necessary in the annexation of Charlestown and Brighton. There are now *five* branch libraries to be cared for along with the Great Library in Boston."

594 [Scott's Shakespeare in the Boston Public Library.] *Nation*, 18 (April 2, 1874), p220-21 (NcU).
The article refers to *Archibald Constable and His Literary Correspondents*, by Thomas Constable, 1873.
Mr. Justin Winsor of the Boston Public Library comments on a statement in the recent life of Archibald Constable, the Scottish publisher. Sir Walter Scott once began to edit a set of Shakespeare's works. When the firm failed in 1826 only three of twelve volumes were complete; they were sold for waste paper. However, a copy of each of the three volumes, perhaps the only one in existence, is in the Barton Collection of the Boston Public Library. Evidently, Scott was a careless editor. Mr. Winsor, in an account of the Barton Collection in the *Boston Advertiser*, asks if any American owns the four volumes of documents and papers about Shakespeare advertised in Thorpe's London catalog of 1844.

595 [Cataloguing of the Barton Collection in the Boston Public Library.] *Nation*, 18 (April 30, 1874), p283 (NcU).
The entire article follows.
"For the more perfect cataloguing of the Barton collection in the Boston Public Library, the Superintendent would like to ascertain the number of early Shakspere rarities in this country, and to hear of the present owners of any of the following: (1) First folio, 1623; (2) second folio, 1632; (3) third folio, 1663 and 1664; (4) fourth folio, 1685; (5) any separate issues of single plays before 1700; (6) ditto of altered plays before 1700; (7) ditto of the so-called spurious plays; (8) any of 'Venus and Adonis' before 1700; (9) of 'Lucrece' before 1656; (10) of the 'Passionate Pilgrim' before 1613; (11) Sonnets, 1609; (12) Poems, 1640."

596 [Charlestown Branch of the Boston Public Library.] *Literary World*, Boston, 4 (May 1874), p191 (NcU).
The entire article follows.
"The report of the superintendent of the Boston Public Library, for March, contains a table showing the comparative demand for different periodicals at the reading room of the Charlestown Branch. In February and March, *Harper's Weekly* was called for 419 times; *Oliver Optic's Magazine*, 416; *Harper's Monthly*, 225; *Scribner's Monthly*, 97; *Atlantic*, 46; *Old and New*, 45; *Galaxy*, 38; *Lippincott's*, 28; *Overland*, 21; *Every Saturday*, 18; *North American Review*, 13; *International Review*, 5. The same document shows that of the number of volumes of the following authors owned by the Library, the per cent remaining on the shelves, that is, not called was: Scott, 66; Cooper, 47; Irving (Works), 65; Dickens, 53; Thackeray, 68; Southworth, 13."

597 [Boston Public Library.] *Publishers' Weekly*, 5 (May 9, 1874), p458 (NcU).
The entire article follows.
"Mr. Winsor's report of the operations of the Boston Public Library for the month of March shows a use during that time of 73,484 volumes, of 467,855 volumes during the past year, and of 5,130,389 volumes since the establishment of the library in 1853. As in most libraries, Mrs. Southworth leads in popularity, but 13 per cent. of the volumes of her works owned by the library remaining on the shelves, as compared with 53 per cent. of Dickens', 47 of Cooper's, and 66 of Scott's. The librarian notes there are now in the library 251,896 volumes, which will soon be increased 10,000 volumes by the addition of the Barton Library."

598 "Histories of Booksellers." *Publishers' Weekly*, 5 (June 13, 1874), p549, 250 wds (NcU).
The following is one of those admirable notes which make the catalogs of the Boston Public Library so valuable. It is inserted under the title of [Henry] Curwen's much-attacked *History of Booksellers* in Bulletin no. 29, April, 1874. (The note is then quoted. It compares Curwen's work with similar books, and gives their call numbers.)

599 [Cremation Bibliography.] *Nation*, 19 (August 6, 1874), p89 (NcU).
The entire article follows.
"The bibliography of cremation as a mode of interment, and of related subjects, is given in Bulletin No. 30 of the Boston Public Library. When the works mentioned are not to be found in that library, it is so stated; the Astor Library being most frequently referred to."

600 "Boston Public Library." *American Bibliopolist*, 6 (September–October 1874), p119, 170 wds (ICU, NcD).
Mr. Winsor, in his last Superintendent's Report, writes about progress in the construction of the addition to the central building. The new addition will provide more space for staff, several special collections, the card catalogs, and patent reports. Much valuable material will be made safe from fire. Mr. Winsor continues to publish, in his report, the recondite notes on Shakespeare quartos published before 1623.

601 [Boston Public Library.] *Publishers' Weekly*, 6 (September 19, 1874), p313 (NcU).

The entire article follows.

"The Twenty-second Annual Report of the Trustees of the Boston Public Library shows a use, during the past year, of 553,129 volumes, while the consulting hall was visited by some 72,313 visitors, making a total of 625,442 books in circulation during that time. The library now numbers 260,550 volumes, of which 51,094 were added during the year—the largest addition ever yet made in twelve months. This is explained, however; by noting that during the year several smaller libraries were incorporated into the Public Library. As yet, it is thought, the Sunday service has not proved a remarkable success, but there is no intention on the part of the trustees of discontinuing it, sufficient use having been made of it by those who on other days are prevented from doing so, to justify its continuance."

602 "Wheeler." *American Bibliopolist*, 6 (November–December 1874), p150, 240 wds (ICN, OC).

William A. Wheeler, Assistant Superintendent of the Boston Public Library, died on October 28, aged thirty-nine. Wheeler was in charge of the library's catalog department and had been affiliated with the library since 1868. He was well known for his work as a lexicographer. He had assisted Worcester in the preparation of his dictionary and in 1860 made arrangements with the Merriam's to revise Webster's dictionary. James L. Whitney succeeds Wheeler as Assistant Superintendent.

603 [Death of Mr. William A. Wheeler.] *Nation*, 19 (November 5, 1874), p300 (NcU).

The entire article follows.

"We regret to record the death, on October 28, of Mr. William A. Wheeler, Assistant Superintendent of the Boston Public Library, and well-known for his lexicographical labors. He was formerly employed in the preparation and revision of our two rival dictionaries, passing from Worcester to Webster; edited an American edition of Hole's 'Brief Biographical Dictionary,' a 'Dickens Dictionary,' and other works; and was engaged, when attacked by his last illness, upon a 'Dictionary of Shaksperian Reference.' In compiling the catalogues of the library, his services were constant and of great value. He had not completed his thirty-ninth year."

604 [British Patents and Shakespeare Plays in the Boston Public Library.] *Nation*, 19 (November 12, 1874), p318 (NcU).

The entire article follows.

"Bulletin No. 31 of the Boston Public Library states that the number of persons who consult the British patents in that institution has risen to nearly or quite 1,500 per annum. The specifications now number 2,400 large volumes. Monthly bibliographical notes on the early quarto issues of Shakspere's plays before the first folio of 1623 will be sent by the Superintendent of the Library to persons whose studies lie in the same direction. They are printed for the purpose of testing their accuracy, and will finally appear in the catalogue of the Barton Library."

605 [Dawkins's Cave-Hunting.] *Nation*, 20 (February 4, 1875), p77 (NcU).

The article refers to William Boyd Dawkins's book, *Cave Hunting: Researches on the Evidence of Caves Respecting the Early Inhabitants of Europe*, London, 1874. The entire article follows.

"Bulletin No. 32 of the Boston Public Library gives, in a note on Dawkins's

'Cave-Hunting,' a long and useful list of kindred scientific works, among which occur a few titles extracted from the book itself. The Superintendent requests the aid of scientists in perfecting this enumeration for future use in the library's catalogue."

606 "The Prince Library." *Literary World*, Boston, 5 (April 1875), p169, 1650 wds (NcU).

The visitor to the Boston Public Library may, with permission, and accompanied by a guide, see the Prince Library, one of the most notable collections of early American books in existence. At the age of sixteen, Prince began to collect books and manuscripts on the civil and religious history of New England. He bequeathed his collection to Old South Church; in 1866 the officers of the church deposited the remainder of it in the Boston Public Library. Cotton Mather wrote more of the books than did anyone else. (Several titles by him, by members of his family, and by other early religious leaders are listed.) The manuscripts, mostly letters, include seven volumes of Mather papers. The number of books devoted to controversy indicates that the church of those days was distinctly militant.

607 [Shakespeare Collection in the Boston Public Library.] *American Bibliopolist*, 7 (April 1875), p87–88 (NcD).

The Boston Public Library has recently acquired the library of Mr. Barton of New York which contains a fine Shakespeare collection; a catalog was begun shortly after this acquisition. Winsor decided to make the library's Shakespeare collection the distinctive feature of the catalog. In his monthly reports Winsor has begun to publish a list of the folios and quartos in the Barton collection along with notes about other copies known to be in this country and those sold at various times in England. This information will be in the catalog when it is published.

608 [Books in the Boston Public Library.] *Nation*, 20 (April 29, 1875), p293 (NcU). The entire article follows.

"In Bulletin No. 33 of the Boston Public Library, the patrons of that institution are treated to the bibliography of Lexington, Concord, and Bunker Hill, and two pages are occupied with an analytic account of works on costume. As usual, these lists refer to works in the Library, but are serviceable anywhere."

609 [Justin Winsor's Planned Bibliography of Shakespeare Quartos and Folios.] *American Bibliopolist*, 7 (August 1875), p184–85 (ICU, NcD).

The contents of this article are quite similar to the contents in another on the same subject in the *Nation* for August 19, 1875 *(see 611)*.

Winsor, the Superintendent of the Boston Public Library, has been engaged for some time in compiling a bibliography of original folios and quartos of Shakespeare with special reference to copies owned in America. (The article includes a reprint of the prospectus from James R. Osgood & Co.) Mr. Winsor has been printing notes on the volumes in his monthly reports to his trustees; it is proposed to publish these notes, revised and enlarged, with heliotype facsimiles of title pages and other pages. Subscriptions are now being taken; the edition will be limited to 250 signed copies and the price will be $25.00.

610 [Books in the Boston Public Library; Changes in Its Catalogue.] *Nation*, 21 (August 5, 1875), p85 (NcU).
The entire article follows.

U.S. — Massachusetts

"Bulletin No. 34 of the Boston Public Library devotes seven closely-printed pages to a comprehensive survey of the literature of the history of Boston during the Revolutionary period, beginning with the 'writs of assistance' in 1761 and ending with the evacuation of Boston, in March, 1776. Somewhat more than two pages are similarly occupied with a directory to works on ornament and decoration. It is annonced that the cards of the public card-catalogue will hereafter be printed in autograph fac-simile by Osgood's heliotype process."

611 [Justin Winsor's Planned Bibliography of Shakespeare Quartos and Folios.] *Nation*, 21 (August 19, 1875), p119, 320 wds (NcU).

This article, based on the prospectus issued by J. R. Osgood & Co., is in effect an abridgement of the one in the August 1875 *American Bibliopolist (see 609)*.

612 "Public Libraries and Fiction." *Literary World*, Boston, 6 (September 1875), p48–49 (NcU).

From the Twenty-Third Annual Report of the Trustees of the Boston Public Library we learn that during 1874, prose fiction and juveniles constituted 81 percent of the circulation from one branch, 79 percent from another and 78 percent from another. A daily paper, in a recent article, concealed this fact and noted an alleged decrease in the demand for fiction at the Central Library. (The Library's report is quoted; it denounces ephemeral literature that fosters discontent with homely duties and causes mental disease and moral irregularities.) The trustees of the library see what is right but do what is wrong; they take no effective measures to curtail the supply of harmful books. They should remove the books from the shelves and discontinue the heavy outlay for them.

613 [The Boston Public Library and Mr. Winsor.] *Nation*, 21 (November 4, 1875), p293 (NcU).

The entire article follows.

"Bulletin No. 35 of the Boston Public Library, besides the usual list of accessions for the month (October), contains carefully-prepared bibliographical helps to students of the following subjects; Waterloo and the Campaign of 1815; Newspapers; John Wesley; and Architecture. It appears that the Library of Congress has 4,800 volumes of newspapers; the Boston Athenaeum, 4,500; the American Antiquarian Society (Worcester), 4,000; the New York Historical Society, about 3,800; the Boston Public Library, 3,500; the Wisconsin Historical Society, about 2,500. Mr. Justin Winsor is to be the editor of a new quarterly whose interest and importance will be apparent when its title is named—the *Fac-similist*. It will be published by J. R. Osgood & Co., and each number will contain from twelve to sixteen heliotype reproductions of rare engravings, MSS., title-pages, etc., accompanied by twenty pages of letterpress. The size is folio."

614 [Bulletin of the Boston Public Library.] *Publishers' Weekly*, 8 (November 6, 1875), p714 (NcU).

The entire article follows.

"Bulletin No. 35 from Boston Public Library contains an extra quantity of valuable bibliographical matter, including articles on 'Waterloo and the Campaign of 1815;' 'Newspapers,' a very valuable bibliography, including magazine articles on journalism; 'John Wesley,' and 'Architecture.' This number completes the second volume of the Bulletins, and a title-page and index to the bibliographical notes will be issued.

"The series of notes on Centennial reading will be continued for 1776 in the next Bulletin."

— SOCIAL LAW LIBRARY

615 "Social Law Library." *Monthly Anthology and Boston Review*, 1 (June 1804), p384 (NcD, NcU).
The entire article follows.
"On Wednesday, 13th June, the first annual meeting of this new institution was held at Concert Hall. The following gentlemen were chosen officers for the year ensuing — viz.
       Hon. THEOPHILUS PARSONS, Esq. Presid't.
       Hon. Christopher Gore, Esq.
       Hon. Rufus G. Amory, Esq.   } Trustees.
       Hon. Joseph Hall, Esq.
       Ebenezer Gay, Esq. Treasurer.
       Peter Thacker, Esq. Clerk."

— STATE LIBRARY

616 "Massachusetts State Library." *Norton's Literary Gazette and Publishers' Circular*, 3 (May 15, 1853), p84, 220 wds (ICN, NcU).
We have received a copy of the *Annual Report* of this library for last year, presented to the legislature by the librarian, Dr. Barnas Sears. The total number of volumes added by purchase was 180; by domestic exchanges, 351; by international exchange through Mr. Vattemare, 255; by international exchange through the State Department, 4; by donation, 20; and by other means, 18. Among important recent purchases are Hansard's *Parliamentary Debates* and a complete set of the British *Statutes at Large* from Magna Charta to 15 Victoria. The necessity for providing safe and ample space for this library is urged with much force by the librarian. (The trustees are named.)

617 [Massachusetts State Library.] *Norton's Literary Gazette and Publishers' Circular*, n.s. 1 (October 2, 1854), p493, 200 wds (NcU).
The contract for the interior finish of the State Library has been awarded to Messrs. Cushing and Mack, iron workers of Lowell. This room, measuring 88 feet long, 40 feet wide and 40 feet high, is to be constructed entirely of cast iron, including the ceiling, which is to be suspended from the roof. Two stories of galleries are to encircle the sides of the room, which will be open in the center from floor to ceiling, with stained glass in the ceiling. The sashes, shutters and frames of the windows are to be metal, with French plate glass. The main floor rests on arches of masonry. Every part of the building is thus fire-proof. Only the library of the U.S. Capitol, in Washington, which is also of iron, will compare with this library room.

— THEOLOGICAL LIBRARY (FOURTH SOCIAL LIBRARY)

618 "Libraries." *Monthly Anthology and Boston Review*, 4 (August 1807), p428–29 (NcU).
It is a pleasure to notice the development of professional libraries in our community. Law and medical libraries have been in existence here for some time. Recently some ministers have established the Theological Library. They

have been aided in their efforts by a valuable gift of books from the English Society for the propagation of the Gospel, sent to King's Chapel. Many books which belonged to that church were lost during the Revolution. Any person having books with gold imprint on the cover "De Bibliotheca de Boston" may know that they are from the church and is asked to return them to the Chapel Society or to the Theological Library on Devonshire Street.

BROOK FARM

619 Alcott, A. B. "Catalogue of Books." *Dial: A Magazine for Literature, Philosophy, and Religion*, 3 (April 1843), p545–48 (NcU).
The entire introduction to the list of 218 titles follows.
"Mr. Alcott and Mr. Lane have recently brought from England a small but valuable library, amounting to about a thousand volumes, containing undoubtedly a richer collection of mystical writers than any other library in this country. To the select Library of the late J. P. Greaves, 'held by Mr. Lane in trust for universal ends,' they have added many works of a like character by purchase, or received as gifts. In their Catalogue, from which the following list is extracted, they say, 'the titles of these books are now submitted, in the expectation that the Library is the commencement of an institution for the nurture of men in universal freedom of action, thought, and being.' We print this list, not only because our respect is engaged to views so liberal, but because the arrival of this cabinet of mystic and theosophic lore is a remarkable fact in our literary history."

CAMBRIDGE — HARVARD COLLEGE LIBRARY

620 "Bibliographical Notices of Harvard College Library." *Monthly Anthology and Boston Review*, 5 (February 1808), p82–88 (NcU).
This is the first in a series of four articles; for the other three *see 621, 622 and 623*.
The department of Oriental Literature owes its fine collection principally to the generosity of Thomas Hollis, Lincoln's Inn, London, who gave the library more than 3,000 volumes. His aim was to furnish the college with works by the best authors, and with rare books. Hollis wrote remarks in some of the books. (Fifteen titles are listed with extensive annotations, some by Hollis.)

621 "Bibliographical Notices of Harvard College Library." *Monthly Anthology and Boston Review*, 5 (March 1808), p140–43 (NcU).
This is the second in a series of four articles; for the others *see 620, 622, and 623*.
Five of the most curious and valuable books in the library, dating from the 16th to the 18th century, are listed with annotations. Some of the remarks are by the donor, Thomas Hollis.

622 "Bibliographical Notices of Harvard College Library." *Monthly Anthology and Boston Review*, 5 (April 1808), p193–97 (NcU).
This is the third in a series of four articles; for the others *see 620, 621, and 623*.
Ten works are discussed; they date from the 16th to the 18th centuries, and are all gifts of Thomas Hollis.

623 "Bibliographical Notices of Harvard College Library." *Monthly Anthology and Boston Review*, 5 (July 1808), p350–53 (NcU).
The article is last in a series of four articles; for the first three *see 620, 621, and 622*.
The titles annotated cover a variety of topics and are classified in department III (Miscellaneous) according to the arrangement of the catalog of 1790. The six works listed were printed in the 16th, 17th, and 18th centuries.

624 "University Reading Room." *North American Review*, 5 (September 1817), p432, 160 wds (InU, NcU).
A reading room has recently been established at Harvard University. The periodicals, pamphlets, newspapers, etc. received in it will, at the end of each year, be bound and deposited in the library. It is hoped that publishers will be willing to support it by sending periodicals, pamphlets, etc. gratuitously. Contributions may be sent to Andrews Norton, the librarian, or to Cummings & Hilliard, booksellers, in Boston.

625 "Professor Ebeling's Library." *North American Review*, 8 (July 1818), p288 (InU).
The entire article follows.
"Mr. Ebeling, the celebrated Professor in the Academy at Hamburgh, one of the most esteemed and respected of the German literati; the bosom friend of Klopstock, and entrusted with his papers, died the last summer at a great age. He had passed much of his life for the last fifty years in labouring for America — having published many volumes of American Geography and Statisticks. He left a collection of materials relating to America more complete, it is believed, than any extant, consisting of 3200 to 3500 vols. — 18 Port Folios of manuscript collections, and 10,000 maps. We are happy to state, that Hon. Israel Thorndike of Boston, desirous that our country should have the benefit of this great fund of information, has purchased the whole, and presented it to the Library of the University."

626 "Munificent Donation." *Niles' National Register*, 14 (July 4, 1818), p328 (InU, NcU).
The entire article follows. It refers to Christoph Daniel Ebeling.
"It is stated in the *Boston Daily Advertiser*, that a gentleman of Boston has purchased and presented to the University in Cambridge, the very large and valuable library of the late professor Ebeling of Hamburgh. Besides being very full and rich in other departments, it is said to contain the best collection in the world of books and works relating to America."

627 [Walker, James.] "A Sermon, occasioned by the Death of Thomas Hollis, Esq. By Jeremiah Hunt. London. 1731..." *Christian Examiner*, 7 (September 1829), p64–104 (NcU).
The article reviews the book by Hunt, as well as three others on the same subject whose titles are also included in the heading. The part about libraries (p91, 240 wds) is summarized below.
Hollis wrote that a public library should have books pro and con about arguments and reasonings of scripture, so that students may judge for themselves. The books and philosophical apparatus which he sent were destroyed when Harvard Hall burned on January 24, 1764. The fire is supposed to have begun in a beam under the hearth of the library, which had been used the day

before by the General Court. As it was vacation, only a few students were in their rooms, and the fire was not discovered until it was too late. About 6,000 volumes were consumed, including the whole library of Dr. Lightfoot, the library of Dr. Theophilus Gale, some theological works presented by Bishop Sherlock, and Latin and Greek classics presented by Bishop Berkeley.

628 [Parkman, Francis.] "Catalogue of the Library of Harvard University, in Cambridge, Massachusetts. Cambridge. E. W. Metcalf. 1830. 3 vols. 8vo." *Christian Examiner*, o.s. 8, n.s. 3 (July 1830), p321-38 (IEG, NcU).

The article reviews this catalog and two others listed in the title; the parts about libraries (p321-25, 335-38) are summarized below.

The catalog of the Harvard College Library, listing 30,000 volumes, is a handsome, well-arranged publication that was prepared by Mr. Peirce, the librarian. It is a three-volume work: in the first two volumes there is an alphabetical listing of books; the third volume is a subject listing. We are especially proud of the growing number of libraries in this country. Europe has many important libraries, e.g., Cambridge, the Bodleian Library, and the Royal Library in Paris, but we shall refrain from comparing them to ours. Returning to the Harvard Library, although this country's preeminent library, it has a number of deficiencies: it needs money for acquisitions; its collection is weak in certain areas; and it is in need of a new building. Cambridge's libraries and Boston's Athenaeum are public treasures whose continued prosperity is in the best interest of the public.

629 "Harvard University." *American Monthly Review*, 1 (May 1832), p433, 200 wds (InU, NcU).

(An announcement of acquisitions for the Harvard College Library since September 1, 1831.) A total of 1,225 volumes and 212 pamphlets, making up 798 separate works has been added. (Eleven of the more important works are listed.)

630 "Library of Harvard College." *Literary World*, N.Y., 3 (August 5, 1848), p531 (NcU).

The article that follows was taken from the *Cambridge Chronicle*.

"At the recent annual examination by the Committee appointed for that purpose, it appeared that there are now belonging to the various Libraries connected with the University, about 82,000 volumes, besides a large and very valuable collection of unbound Tracts, maps, plans, etc. There are in the Public Library, Gore Hall, 55,000; Law Library, Dane Hall, 12,000; Theological Library, Divinity Hall, 3,000; Medical Library, Medical Hall, 2,000; Society Libraries, 10,000 — in all 82,000. Fifteen hundred and twenty-three bound volumes and 2,520 pamphlets have been added during the past year."

631 [Bowen, Francis. Book Review.] "A Sketch of the History of Harvard College, and of its Present State. By Samuel A. Eliot. Boston: Little & Brown. 1848. 12 mo. pp190." *North American Review*, 68 (January 1849), p99-128 (NcU).

The parts of the article about libraries (p105, 220 wds) are summarized below.

The College Library now contains 53,000 volumes. Gore Hall cost $73,000 initially plus $750 annually for fuel, but a plain fire-proof building large enough to hold 100,000 volumes could have been built for $40,000. A $21,000 subscription was made to buy books when Gore Hall was built. Three-fourths of this fund has been spent. Much money has been squandered on architecture.

The report of the college treasurer for 1835 estimated that the Gore Library would cost $35,000.

632 "Harvard College." *Inquirer* [Christian Inquirer], 4 (August 3, 1850), p2, 830 wds (MB).

A part of the article, with the heading, "The Library," (500 wds) is taken from the *Boston Daily Advertiser.*

A new arrangement of books has been effected after a recent sizable addition to the collection, and the catalog has been brought up to date. The library is open to the public for study purposes. In Gore Hall there are 57,000 volumes in addition to pamphlets, newspapers, and maps. The other libraries are: Law, 13,000 volumes; Divinity School, 3,000 volumes; Medical, 1,200 volumes. There are 10,000 volumes in the society libraries. During the previous year 1,751 volumes and 1,219 pamphlets, exclusive of duplicates, have been added. All purchased books have been for the faculty of the Lawrence Scientific School. The Donation Fund has been exhausted and until another is acquired the library's income will be $450 per year which may only be used for purchases in certain subject areas. The librarian, Dr. Thaddeus William Harris; and his assistant, Rev. John Langdon Sibley, are to be commended for their excellent work.

633 [Recent Acquisitions at Harvard.] *North American Miscellany and Dollar Magazine*, 4 (1852), p55 (NcU).

The entire article follows.

"During the past year, the Library of Harvard University has received the addition of 1616 volumes, and 1539 pamphlets. Nearly one-half of these were donations from individuals. The purchase of Professor Jacobi's Mathematical Library, of Berlin, by Mr. George Bond, for the College, is mentioned as a very important acquisition, as this Library was considered one of the most complete private collections in Europe."

634 "Harvard College." *Norton's Literary Gazette and Publishers' Circular*, 2 (June 15, 1852), p107, 1170 wds (ICN, NcU).

A fire on January 24, 1764 destroyed the Harvard College Library. Today, eighty-eight years later, the library has a collection of 92,000 volumes. In 1841 the library occupied Gore Hall, an inspiring gothic style building that is laid out in the form of a Latin cross. The building's interior forms a beautiful hall with a vaulted, ribbed ceiling. The Theology, Law, Medicine, and Science Libraries are located in other buildings. The books in Gore Hall are arranged according to subject in a classification scheme originated in 1822 by Joseph G. Cogswell, now director of the Astor Library. The library has many valuable books, manuscripts, documents, journals, and maps. Visitors may use the books within the library; full and part-time students who are in residence have borrowing privileges. This valuable library deserves continued liberal support. (An exterior view of Gore Hall accompanies the article.)

635 "Harvard College Library." *Norton's Literary Gazette and Publishers' Circular*, 2 (August 15, 1852), p151 (ICN, NcU).

The entire article follows.

"From an account in the *Cambridge Chronicle* of the recent annual examination of the College Library, it appears that there are now 92,000 volumes belonging to the various departments, including the Theological, Law, Medical and Society Libraries, besides 26,000 unbound books and pamphlets. The

U.S. — Massachusetts

additions during the past year have amounted to 1,529 volumes and 2,453 pamphlets. Notwithstanding the size of the Library and its richness in some departments, it is lamentably deficient in many particulars. The Committee of the Board of Overseers appointed a sub-committee of their number, consisting of the Rev. Dr. Sharp, the Rev. Dr. Jenks, and George Livermore, Esq., to prepare the annual report, and to present to the Legislature and the public a statement of the many deficiencies and urgent wants of the Library."

636 "Harvard College Library." *Norton's Literary Gazette and Publishers' Circular*, 3 (March 15, 1853), p40, 190 wds (NcU).

From the annual report of President Sparks for the last academic year, we learn that 1,529 volumes and 2,443 pamphlets, exclusive of duplicates, newspapers and periodicals, were added. Of these, 676 volumes and 1,945 pamphlets, including a collection of the late Dr. Pierce, were donations. Several people (named) have given gifts of money or particular books. More than $10,000 has been raised to buy books to supply deficiencies in the department of English literature. All of the manuscript papers relating to the history of the College have been chronologically arranged, and bound in a series of volumes, an index to which is now in progress. The Law Library now numbers 14,000 volumes; the "Phillips Astronomical Library," 870 quartos and octavos.

637 [Annual Report of Harvard College Library.] *Norton's Literary Gazette and Publishers' Circular*, n.s. 1 (July 15, 1854), p362, 190 wds (NcU).

The annual examination of the Harvard College Library took place recently; 1,778 volumes and 1,842 pamphlets were added. Of these, 1,327 volumes and 1,767 pamphlets were special gifts. (Several are discussed.) Marble busts of Edward Everett and President Walker have been placed in the library.

638 [Donation of American Sunday School Union to Harvard Library.] *Norton's Literary Gazette and Publishers' Circular*, n.s. 1 (October 2, 1854), p493 (NcU).

The entire article follows.

"The American Sunday School Union have made a liberal donation to the library of Harvard University, of all their publications, amounting to more than nine hundred volumes. This movement on the part of the Board of the S. S. Union, will doubtless be followed by similar donations to kindred institutions, and other societies will adopt the same mode of perpetuating their influence."

639 [Present Holdings and Recent Acquisitions of the Harvard University Libraries.] *Norton's Literary Gazette and Publishers' Circular*, n.s. 1 (November 1, 1854), p554 (NcU).

The entire article follows.

"The Annual Catalogue of HARVARD COLLEGE states that the total number of volumes in the libraries of the University, is as follows:

College Library	about	65,000
Medical Library	"	1,600
Law Library	"	14,000
Theological Library	"	4,500
Society Libraries of Students	"	13,000
Total, about		98,100

Besides these volumes there are probably more than 25,000 pamphlets. The annual income from the permanent fund, for purchasing and repairing books, amounts to about three hundred dollars only. Nearly all the books in the College Library are donations. The 'Massachusetts Sabbath School Society' (Orthodox Congregational), have recently presented to this Library a number of volumes in continuation of the series of about 650 volumes which were given by them last year. The Directors have made great exertions to obtain the names of the anonymous authors, and with much success."

640 [Harvard College Library.] *National Magazine: Devoted to Literature, Art, and Religion*, 9 (October 1856), p382 (InU, NcU).
The entire article follows.
"*Harvard College* now numbers in all its libraries more than one hundred thousand volumes. Seventy thousand books and thirty thousand pamphlets constitute the Public Library in Gore Hall. Mr. Sibley, the librarian, has made an appeal to the public for further donations, as its shelves cannot be greatly enriched by purchase in consequence of the limited fund at the disposal of the library for such purposes. This fund yields now but little more than three hundred dollars per annum."

641 "The Library." *Harvard Advocate*, 2 (October 12, 1866), p24–25 (InU).
The library of the College needs about two dollars where it now has one. It has a fund of about $39,000; it was reported eight years ago that a fund of $80,000 or $100,000 was needed. Mr. Sibley has posted a list of forty-six volumes and three pamphlets that are missing. In view of the small sum available for purchases, Sibley's concern for the return of these materials is understandable. Only $2,398.56 was spent for books and periodicals last year; a large portion of the library's total budget came from charges against students. The library, according to a report by three professors, would need $2,400 just to keep up to date in political economy, history, Latin, Greek, and bibliography. Students must buy for themselves many of the books they require because the library does not have adequate funds.

642 [The Harvard College Library.] *Nation*, 4 (January 31, 1867), p84 (NcU).
The entire article follows.
"At a recent meeting of the Board of Overseers of Harvard College the Committee on the Library recommended that the library should be weeded out and its worthless books disposed of, and that greater facilities should be given the public for its use. They rightly held that the use of a library was to diffuse and not shut up knowledge, and therefore demanded a convenient reading-room and the opening of the library on every day of the year except Sundays and public holidays. The committee also thought that the library should have an annual income of at least $10,000; and that the first and chief necessity was a new library building. The friends of the college will, therefore, be called on to subscribe for two funds of $150,000 each, one to defray the expense of a new building and the other to furnish an income for the purchase of books."

643 [Needs of the Harvard College Library.] *Nation*, 6 (June 25, 1868), p511–12 (NcU).
A single uncomplimentary remark in an article on the Harvard College Library in the *Pall Mall Gazette*, that the "library is sadly deficient in the literature of the last ten years," should attract attention to the crying want of a permanent library fund. The library is now open seven hours a day and a classed

catalog is being prepared. However, many books in the library are out-of-date and a large part of the annual increase consists of clearings of closets and garrets. The library cannot inform users of the latest theories and discoveries; professors have to spend their own money on recent books. Mr. William Gray's gifts of $5,000 per year for five years caused increased use of the library; but recently, except for some restricted funds, the library has had only $400 per year to cover a variety of subjects. Few books now cost less than $5.00.

644 Cutter, Charles A. "Annals of the Bodleian Library, Oxford, A.D. 1598–A.D. 1867; with a Preliminary Notice of the Earlier Library Founded in the Fourteenth Century. By the Reverend William Dunn Macray, M.A., Chaplain of St. Mary Magdalene and St. Mary Winton Colleges; Editor of 'Chronicon Abbatiae Eveshamensis,' etc. London, Oxford, and Cambridge: Rivingtons. 1868." *North American Review*, 107 (October 1868), p568–93 (InU, NcU).

(The article begins with a review of Macray's book. Librarians and users of the Bodleian are described.) The Harvard College Library would make an interesting book. We propose here to cover the main points of the library's history, its present condition and wants. Harvard's library was once the best in America, but no longer. Many of its departments are weak. Built largely by gifts, the collection is uneven and inadequate. Purchases have not been continuous; much material is badly dated. Other Boston libraries can only slightly help the college. A new building is needed to replace Gore Hall, but money for new books and periodicals is needed more. Remodelling has been proposed. Weeding has been suggested, but all books have value. The library has changed in recent years; it is used more, is open longer, has better catalogs, and gives better personal assistance to readers.

645 Cutter, Charles A. "The New Catalogue of the Harvard College Library." *North American Review*, 108 (January 1869), p96–129 (NcU).

In 1861 Ezra Abbot, head cataloger of the Harvard Library, undertook the planning for the library's new catalog. Because book catalogs soon become obsolete and are expensive to produce, Abbot determined that a card catalog, using five by two inch cards, would be more feasible for the library. Books, pamphlets, and periodicals are cataloged according to a set of rules developed by the library staff. Abbot modified existing classification schemes to produce an alphabetical-classed system, i.e., the main subject headings are arranged alphabetically with the subdivisions, also arranged alphabetically, appearing under the main headings. (An extended discussion on p110–29 examines the complexities of cataloging and classification and distinguishes between the various systems for the arrangement of library catalogs.)

646 "Gray Collection of Engravings." *Nation*, 10 (January 13, 1870), p30–31 (NcU).

The collection of engravings bequeathed by the late Francis Calley Gray to Harvard College has been placed in an alcove in Gore Hall, the College Library. Mr. Louis Thies has charge of the collection; he has, with the assistance of Mr. Ezra Abbot, published a handsome catalog listing its contents. If engravings are kept in portfolios, they need to have catalogs that give enough information so a student will know which portfolio to consult; engravings hung on the wall or bound in volumes are easier to use because ordinarily an attendant must handle the portfolio for the student. The engravings in the Gray Collection should be exhibited. (The strengths and weaknesses of the collection and of its catalog are then discussed.)

647 "Harvard College." *Appleton's Journal: a Magazine of General Literature*, 3 (March 5, 1870), p254–60 (NcU).
The part of the article about libraries (p254–55) is summarized below.

John Harvard and the college's other founders placed great emphasis on the school's library, with the result that Harvard College soon boasted the finest library in America, totaling 5,000 volumes in 1764. That year the Harvard Hall, which housed the library, burned along with the entire collection. The legislature soon financed a new building. The book collection, funded by legislative appropriations and private donations, grew to 12,000 by 1790. The library was moved to Gore Hall in 1840 when there were 40,000 books. This building has never been well suited as a library and allows little space for expansion of the collection. Funds have been limited; the collection's rate of growth can no longer compete with that of such libraries as the Library of Congress or the Astor Library. The Library of Congress also surpasses the Harvard College Library in excellence of management and service. An exterior view of Gore Hall accompanies the article.

648 B. [Harvard University Library.] *Publishers' Weekly* [Publishers' and Stationers' Weekly Trade Circular], 2 (August 8, 1872), p132 (NcU).
The entire article follows.

"The Alumni and friends of Harvard University will be glad to learn that the Library building is to be radically improved and enlarged, so that its capacity will be adequate to 25,000 additional volumes. Various improvements will be made in the arrangement of the books, so that they will be easier of access, and more in accordance with the wants of students than is possible with the present accommodations. It is a pity that the proper authorities could not see their way clear to erect a new building, instead of tinkering the present old and inconvenient, dimly lighted and poorly arranged structure; but in lack of it, we are thankful for what is now being done."

649 [Gift of Charles F. Bradford to the Harvard College Library.] *Nation*, 18 (January 29, 1874), p76–77 (NcU).
This article was greatly condensed in the *Publishers' Weekly* for March 14, 1874 *(see 650)*.

Mr. Charles F. Bradford, of Roxbury, has presented to the library of Harvard, his manuscript work, in three thick volumes, entitled *Index to the Notes of D. Diego Clemencin in his Edition of "Don Quijote," Madrid, 1833–39*, with numerous references to difficult passages in the text; there are references in the margin to Mr. Ticknor's *History of Spanish Literature*. Mr. Bradford had already presented the library with a copy of the best edition of Clemencin's *Don Quijote*. Bradford's new index represents a labor of love of more than fifteen years. It is beautifully bound, and is in his own handwriting, so neat and even that it is as clear to the eye as print. This is really a special dictionary, both for language and subject-matter of the greatest work the Spaniards produced.

650 [Gift of Charles F. Bradford to the Harvard College Library.] *Publishers' Weekly*, 5 (March 14, 1874), p273, 130 wds (NcU).
This is a greatly condensed version of the article on the same subject in the *Nation* for January 29, 1874 *(see 649)*.

651 [Harvard College Library.] *Publishers' Weekly*, 5 (March 28, 1874), p337 (NcU).
The entire article follows; it refers to Charles Sumner.
"It is said that Senator Sumner has given the Harvard College Library, within the past few years, upwards of 5,000 pamphlets and 1,000 volumes, many of them of great value. His own collection was small, but very choice."

652 [Gore Hall.] *American Bibliopolist*, 7 (August 1875), p173 (NcD).
The entire article follows.
"GORE HALL, the library building at Harvard, is now very much overcrowded, and the authorities are debating whether to enlarge it or erect a new building. Mr. Sibley, the librarian, fovours [sic] the latter course, and declares Gore Hall a building never entirely exempt from dampness, from which intending donors turn aside because they do not consider it fire-proof, from which the stones began to tumble down within a few years after it was erected, and which was 'unfit for a library from the first, because erected in ignorance of the wants of a library.' Mr. Sibley has worked in Gore Hall ever since it was completed in 1842, and ought to know something about it."

— HARVARD MUSICAL ASSOCIATION LIBRARY

653 [Additions to the Library of the Harvard Musical Association.] *Dwight's Journal of Music, a Paper of Art and Literature*, 12 (March 13, 1858), p399, 180 wds (NcU).
Additions to the library of the Harvard Musical Association during the past year are listed. Twelve titles are given. Biographies, periodicals, annual reports, a library catalog, criticism, and collections of music are among the kinds of works added.

— SPARKS LIBRARY

654 [Sale of the Jared Sparks Library.] *Nation*, 11 (September 22, 1870), p191, 170 wds (NcU).
This library was bought by Cornell University *(see 792 and 793)*.
The library of the late Jared Sparks, biographer of Washington, Franklin, and others, is to be sold during the coming winter. It would be a good nucleus for a new college or city library. We do not see why Americans should go to Germany to buy entire libraries and at the same time allow collections made here, which are much better adapted to our wants, to be dispersed at auction. Mr. Sparks's historical manuscripts were deposited in the Harvard College Library some years ago.

655 [Sparks Library Catalog.] *American Bibliopolist*, 4 (February 1872), p63, 350 wds (NcD).
This library was acquired by Cornell University *(see 792 and 793)*.
We direct the attention of our readers to the sale at auction of the library of the late historian, Jared Sparks. (C. A. Cutter, librarian of the Boston Athenaeum, who wrote the introductory preface to the catalog, is quoted.) He says that although the words scarce and rare have been used very sparingly in describing the collection, an examination of the catalog reveals that many of the books are rare or uncommon, and that nearly all of them have decided historical value. Sparks chose his books carefully, and had the will and opportunity to

procure what he needed. His library has attractions for both bibliomaniacs and scholars. As we go to press, we learn from the auctioneers (Messrs. Leonard), that the entire library has been disposed of by private sale.

CHARLESTOWN — NECK SCHOOL LIBRARY

656 "School Libraries." *American Annals of Education*, 3d ser., 8 (December 1838), p569, 210 wds (NcU).
For a recent examination of the Charlestown, Massachusetts public schools, one student presented an essay about his school. His description of the library, quoted in the article, is summarized below.
I wish to express my gratitude to the town's citizens for their efforts to acquire the library, which now has 370 volumes on history, biography, and other subjects. The library, considered to be the property of the Neck School, is available to all students in the school.

CONCORD — PUBLIC LIBRARY

657 [New Library Building for Concord, Mass.] *Nation*, 17 (October 9, 1873), p241-42 (NcU).
Last week the town of Concord formally received the handsome library building presented by its citizen, Mr. William Munroe. Brief speeches were given by Mr. R. W. Emerson and others. Mr. Frederick Hudson outlined the history of Concord libraries. By January 1 the library will contain eleven thousand books and some original manuscripts, which were given by Mr. James T. Fields, and were written by celebrated authors, including some of the town's own residents. (A summary of Emerson's remarks is given.)

658 [Public Library at Concord, Mass.] *Publishers' Weekly*, 4 (October 25, 1873), p452, 270 wds (NcU).
The most interesting feature of the new library at Concord, Massachusetts, dedicated this month, is the collection of works by natives of Concord. Just two hundred years ago the town founded a library, with rules for its use. Since then Concord has become, in literature, the most famous village in America. The native collection fills a considerable amount of space in the new building. (Individual writers are mentioned.) This example affords an excellent hint to other libraries; the prominent libraries in each town should endeavor to make complete collections of locally written and published books; these collections will be very valuable in the future.

DANVERS *see* PEABODY

GLOUCESTER — SAWYER FREE LIBRARY

659 [Public Library at Gloucester, Massachusetts.] *Norton's Literary Gazette and Publishers' Circular*, n.s. 1 (November 1, 1854), p554 (NcU).
The entire article follows.
"The Public Library at Gloucester is now in successful operation. This

U.S. — Massachusetts

institution is one of the most popular in the community. It comprises a large collection of the most valuable works, and is almost the only public library in Essex County."

GROTON — PUBLIC LIBRARY

660 [Cutter, Charles A. The Groton, Mass., Library Catalogue.] *Nation*, 21 (July 1, 1875), p8, 300 wds (NcU).

Cutter is identified as the author of this article in Daniel C. Haskell's *The Nation, Volumes 1–105, New York, 1865–1917, Indexes of Titles and Contributors*, 1953, v. 2, p116.

The Public Library of Groton, Massachusetts has just published a catalog which is no doubt useful. We wonder, however, why such catalogs which are mainly titles of books include author entries only if the library has more than one book by the same author. Surely some authors such as Boswell, Gibbon, Lamb, Macaulay, and Milton will be represented in many small libraries by only one work. Books must occasionally be asked for by their authors' names. The rule seems to be unreasonable; the addition of author entries in library catalogs would be very useful.

HOLYOKE — PUBLIC LIBRARY

661 [Holyoke, Mass. to Establish a Public Library.] *American Bibliopolist*, 2 (February 1870), p77 (ICN, ICU).
The entire article follows.
"A public library is to be established in Holyoke, Mass. Mr. J. C. Parsons has made the generous offer of $20,000 ($5,000 for himself and $15,000 for the Parsons Paper Company), to purchase land and erect a library building, provided a like sum is raised to furnish it with books, etc. This amount has been pledged. The Holyoke Water-Power Company will probably give the land."

HYDE PARK — PUBLIC LIBRARY

662 [Hyde Park Public Library.] *Literary World*, Boston, 6 (July 1875), p22 (NcU).
The entire article follows.
"Mr. W. E. Foster, Librarian of the Hyde Park Public Library, has sent us a copy of his Annual Report. From this we learn that the total number of volumes in the Library — which has been open a little more than a year — is 4,439. The total number drawn from the Library during the year ending March 8th, was 26,694. The Librarian writes at some length about the selection of books and literary criticism, — which latter, he says, 'it is not safe to trust.'"

LANCASTER — TOWN LIBRARY

663 [Lancaster, Mass., Public Library.] *Literary World*, Boston, 5 (April 1875), p174 (NcU).
The entire article follows.

"The annual report of the Public Library at Lancaster, Mass., exhibits that institution as in a very prosperous condition. The total number of volumes in the Library Feb. 1st, 1875, was 8,525, of which 771 have been added during the last year. The number of books loaned between Feb. 1st, 1874, and Feb. 1st, 1875, was 9,521, — an average monthly circulation of nearly 800. Oliver Optic is the most popular writer of fiction, the demand for his books representing a percentage of five. Jacob Abbott ranks next, and W. D. Howells last. We are glad to notice that of the 548 volumes purchased for the Library last year, only 153 belonged to the department of fiction, these figures including 'juveniles.' "

LAWRENCE — FREE PUBLIC LIBRARY

664 [Lawrence, Mass., Public Library.] *Publishers' Weekly*, 4 (October 25, 1873), p452 (NcU).
The entire article follows.
"The Lawrence (Mass.) Public Library, established one year ago, has an average weekly circulation of 2,500 volumes, which is claimed to be the largest circulation enjoyed by any library in the country in a city less than five times the size of Lawrence. It is one book a week for every twelve inhabitants (population, 30,000), and one book a week for every five volumes in the library. The population is largely made up of mill operatives, and the proportion of standard books drawn is larger than might be expected, being very nearly the same as in the Boston library."

665 [Lawrence, Mass., Public Library.] *Publishers' Weekly*, 5 (March 7, 1874), p257 (NcU).
The entire article follows.
"The second annual report of the Lawrence, Mass., Public Library shows satisfactory results. The accessions to the Library during the past year have been 3,326 volumes, making, in all, 11,411, exclusive of pamphlets. Over one-half of the patrons of the Library are found among the industrial classes, and a large proportion of the remainder are clerks or merchants. School attendants comprise but little over one-tenth of the whole number registered."

— PACIFIC MILLS LIBRARY

666 "Library for Factory Operatives in Lawrence, Mass." *American Journal of Education* (Barnard), 1 (May 1856), p649, 510 wds (NcU).
The article summarized below contains extracts of a letter which describes the library at the Pacific Mills in Lawrence.
One cent is deducted from each employee's weekly wage; the deduction is used to support a library, which now has between 1,600 and 1,800 volumes. The library, established with a $1,000 donation from the company and a gift of books from an individual, is open during the noon hour on three weekdays and for two hours after work on Saturday. The library's annual income is $750. In addition, the company contributes $300 per year for books, library facilities, and a librarian. The existence of this library secures the following objectives: for each employee, his deduction gives him access to a valuable library; suspicions of patronage are discredited because management and labor are working together in a cooperative enterprise; and the weekly deductions, although small, in the aggregate provide a large income.

LYNN

667 "School Libraries." *American Annals of Education*, 3d ser., 4 (May 1834), p214–16 (NcU).

Opponents of school libraries argue that children already read too much and that reading interferes with the more serious studies; on the other hand, proponents counter that facts prove this not to be true. Surprisingly, both of these views may be correct, for if libraries were more wisely selected, then children could read fewer, but better books. To realize this ideal, teaching libraries long have been recommended. An account from the *Lynn Weekly Messenger* describes just such a library in a ward of that town. The school library contains nearly 200 volumes, donated by local citizens, and it is said that the library is deeply appreciated by the students.

MIDDLESEX COUNTY — LYCEUM

668 "Middlesex County Lyceum." *American Annals of Education* [American Journal of Education], n.s. 1 (October–November 1830), p452–63 (NcU).

The article reprints two reports presented at the semi-annual meeting of the Middlesex County Lyceum; the part of the first report about libraries (p454) follows.

"The possession of a library should be a primary object with all lyceums. Its extent must, of course, depend on their pecuniary resources. History, biography, voyages and travels, are well calculated to elicit a taste for reading, and impart useful knowledge. Works on science, scientific periodicals, and an encyclopedia will all prove valuable helps to the young inquirer, whether farmer, mechanic, or manufacturer, and should be procured as soon as circumstances will permit."

NEW BEDFORD — FREE PUBLIC LIBRARY

669 "New Bedford Free Library." *Norton's Literary Gazette and Publishers' Circular*, 2 (October 15, 1852), p188 (ICN, NcU).

The entire article follows.

"An effort similar to that we have spoken of in Boston, is now going on in New Bedford, Mass. A Library is to be established with the same ends in view, to wit, the extension of popular education. Its affairs are to be under the management of six trustees—three elected by the City Council, and three, the Mayor, the President of the Common Council, and the Chairman of the Committee on Public Instruction, who are members of the board, *ex-officio*. The trustees, as now elected, are as follows: —William J. Rotch, Matthew Howland, Henry H. Crapo (Mr. C. being chairman of Committee on Instruction), James B. Congdon, Abner J. Phipps, and Simpson Hart."

670 [The New Bedford Library's Genevan Bible.] *American Bibliopolist*, 2 (February 1870), p77 (ICN, ICU).

The entire article follows.

"In reference to an old Bible in the New Bedford Library, the *Standard* of that city says: 'It was published in 1610—the year before our common version, King James's Bible, was published. This old Bible is what is called the Genevan

Bible, which is based on the translation made by Coverdale in 1535. This Bible contains the Apocrypha, a catechism, and Sternhold and Hopkin's version of the Psalms, with music to many of them, and if it were in a better state of preservation would be a curiosity worth having.'"

— LYCEUM

671 "Library of Useful Knowledge. Published under the Superintendence of the Society for the Diffusion of Useful Knowledge. London. Baldwin and Cradock. 1828. 8vo. 35 No's." *Christian Examiner*, 6 (March 1829), p71–86 (NcU).

The article reviews the set of books, *Library of Useful Knowledge*, and an address by Thomas A. Greene to the members of the New Bedford Lyceum. The parts about libraries (p82–83, 290 wds) are summarized below.

Lyceums could well have been called libraries; their goals are similar. Lyceums have libraries but add regular meetings as well. Some have apparatus and models for illustrating the sciences, and some have buildings with rooms for the library, lectures, etc.

NEWBURYPORT — PUBLIC LIBRARY

672 P., B. K. [Subscription for a Library in Newburyport.] *National Magazine: Devoted to Literature, Art, and Religion*, 5 (September 1854), p284–85 (InU, NcU).

The article refers to preparations for the Newburyport, Mass. Public Library, opened in 1854; the entire article follows.

"Our young cities and towns are rapidly falling into the plan of establishing public libraries. Almost every week some new movement of this character is announced. The 'sons' of Newburyport are now taking measures to endow such an institution in that beautiful city. The subscription paper for this purpose, which is growing into a generous size, is headed by Hon. Josiah Littie, with the munificent sum of $5,000. There is a promise of a large and valuable library for the improvement and pleasure of coming generations. In the old world vast piles of literature are aggregated together in royal libraries for privileged eyes; in the new, our libraries are innumerable and *circulating*."

NORTHAMPTON — PUBLIC LIBRARY

673 L. "Equal Rights in the Public Library." *Index*, 6 (April 15, 1875), p172, 640 wds (NcD).

The article appeared originally in the newspaper, the *Hampshire Gazette*. It is sent to the *Index* by Seth Hunt, who writes that its author is the minister of the First (Orthodox) Church of Northampton, Massachusetts.

The desire to have more Catholic books in the Northampton Public Library was expressed in a recent town meeting. Sectarian differences cannot be taken into account in selecting for libraries. The only questions are these: Is it a good book? Is it likely to be read? Can we afford to buy it? Every citizen has the same privilege of requesting the addition of any book not in the library. If one wants a book that advocates or controverts any religious opinions, the library should buy it if it is a decent book and there is money to buy it. There are no sectarian distinctions in good literature. May Catholics and Protestants never cease to read each others' books. The only real difficulty is in finding the money to buy the books they want to read.

PEABODY — PEABODY INSTITUTE LIBRARY

674 "Danvers, (Mass.)." *Norton's Literary Gazette and Publishers' Circular*, 3 (March 15, 1853), p40 (NcU).
The entire article follows.
"We learn from Peabody's American Chronicle, that the eminent banker, 'George Peabody, Esq., of London, has made an additional donation to his native town of Danvers of ten thousand dollars, making a total of thirty thousand, for the purpose of sustaining an Institution to be established in Danvers, for a public library, and in procuring lecturers. This is another evidence of the noble generosity of MR. PEABODY. It was intimated to him that his first donation was inadequate to fully carry out the object of his gift, and he at once forwarded a sight draft to the trustees of the former fund to relieve them of all embarrassment.'"

675 [Library of the Peabody Institute, Danvers.] *Norton's Literary Gazette and Publishers' Circular*, n.s. 1 (November 1, 1854), p554 (NcU).
The town later changed its name to Peabody. The entire article follows.
"About two thousand volumes of standard works, the donation of Mr. Peabody, have been received by the Trustees and placed in the Library of the Peabody Institute, in Danvers. The Peabody Library is now open daily for the delivery of books, between the hours of 3 and 8 P.M. E. B. Hickley, Esq., is Librarian."

PLYMOUTH — PILGRIM SOCIETY LIBRARY

676 Cogswell, W. "History of the 'Pilgrim Society,' With a Brief Account of the Early Settlement of Plymouth Colony." *Congregational Education Society. Quarterly Journal* [American Quarterly Register], 11 (August 1838), p82–90 (NcU).
The parts of the article about libraries (p86–87, 89) are summarized below.
In the building of the society erected in 1824, there is a room for a library and a cabinet of curiosities; it contains a number of volumes and early manuscripts. Eventually, a copy of each work published by the Pilgrims and their descendents should be deposited there. James Thacher, M.D., is the librarian and cabinet keeper; his biography is given.

QUINCY — PUBLIC LIBRARY

677 [Adams, Charles Francis, Jr.] "The Experience of a Public Library." *Nation*, 14 (May 23, 30, 1872), p334–35, p350–51 (NcU).
Adams is identified as the author of this article in Daniel C. Haskell's *The Nation, Volumes 1–105, New York, 1865–1917, Indexes of Titles and Contributors*, 1953, v. 1, p. 28. "The town of X" in the article is undoubtedly Quincy; Adams was an active trustee of its public library at the time.

The books of Mrs. Southworth and Mrs. Caroline Lee Hentz are in heavy demand in public libraries; the use of better books can be encouraged in these potent engines of popular education. A new library in the town of X is heavily used; eighty percent of the circulation is fiction. The appetite for novels is natural; human beings demand the story teller. Few workingmen are equal to reading economics or physics. In the library of X., travel is second to fiction in popularity; other kinds of books are in little demand. (The relative popularity of many authors is discussed.) A public library needs a catalog that indicates the character of each book; bibliographical learning is out of place in it. Pamphlets containing courses of reading would help. Finally, the career of the librarian must be made a specialty; it is incomparably more attractive than that of a school teacher.

678 [Cutter, Charles A.] "Catalogue of the Public Library of Quincy, Mass." *Nation*, 21 (October 14, 1875), p251-52 (NcU).

Cutter is identified as the author of this article in Daniel C. Haskell's *The Nation, Volumes 1-105, New York, 1865-1917, Indexes of Titles and Contributors*, 1953, v 2, p116. Cutter refers to Charles Francis Adams, Jr.

The common dictionary library is disheartening to the reader as it offers no help in the selection of what to read. The Boston Public Library demonstrated with its class list of History, Biography and Travel (1873) that popular reading can be encouraged, directed and improved by the careful use of notes and references. Mr. Adams has improved on Mr. Winsor's ideas. The Quincy catalog omits imprints but includes notes such as *Illustr., Portraits, Fiction, Juv. Fict.*, and phrases explaining misleading titles. Tables of contents and analytics are listed. Almost four thousand references to magazine articles are included. The most important feature of the catalog is the inclusion of notes on single works, most of which praise the books; a few notes warn or condemn. Various courses of reading are listed in fine type under every important subject. The catalog is more valuable than if its cost were spent on additional books aimlessly used.

679 Adams, Charles F., Jr. "The Quincy Library Catalogue." *Nation*, 21 (November 4, 1875), p291, 150 wds (NcU).

This is a letter from Adams to the editor of the *Nation (see 678)*. The letter is summarized below.

The many very gratifying responses to the notice in your October 14 issue about the catalog of the Quincy Public Library induce me to call attention to an error in it. The writer of the notice attributed the work solely to me; I quote from the preface: "The catalogue, both properly as such and in its cross references to contents, is almost exclusively the work of Miss M. B. Merriam, who also prepared a number of shorter notes." Miss Merriam is a professional and an accomplished cataloger; I am neither.

680 [Public Library, Quincy, Mass.] *Publishers' Weekly*, 8 (November 6, 1875), p715 (NcU).

The entire article follows.

"The 'Catalogue of the Quincy (Mass.) Public Library' patterns closely after that of the Boston Library in style, method, and annotations, but in this latter particular it presents valuable new features. These are the definition of blind titles by an abbreviation, such as 'Fict.,' 'Jun.,' etc., the explanation of obscure titles by parenthetical notes, and like practical guidings. Mr. Charles

Francis Adams, Jr., is understood to have had to do with its preparation. The librarian is Miss. Mary J. Brooks, Quincy, Mass., and copies may be had of her at $1 in paper, or $1.35 in cloth, which is, we presume, cost price."

TAUNTON — OLD COLONY HISTORICAL SOCIETY

681 [Old Colony Historical Society.] *National Magazine: Devoted to Literature, Art, and Religion*, 4 (April 1854), p382 (InU, NcU).
The entire article follows.
"An association has lately been formed, of which Nathaniel Morton, of Taunton, Mass., is the president, to be called the *Old Colony Historical Society*, for the purpose of preserving and perpetuating the history of the old colony in Massachusetts, and of collecting and holding documents, books, and memoirs relating to its history."

— SOCIAL LIBRARY

682 "Taunton (Mass.) Social Library." *Norton's Literary Gazette and Publishers' Circular*, 3 (January 15, 1853), p3 (ICN, NcU).
The entire article follows.
"It gives us pleasure to state, at the suggestion of a correspondent, that one of the most flourishing libraries, for its size, in the State of Massachusetts, is the Taunton Social Library, incorporated in 1825, and ever since in active operation. It numbers about thirty-five hundred volumes, for the most part well selected; and our correspondent informs us that three thousand volumes are annually taken out. Mr. Benjamin R. Dean, a graduate of Brown University in 1826, is the Librarian, and Hon. S. L. Crocker, Hon. H. Williams, Rev. E. Maltby, T. Gordon, Esq., and Rev. C. H. Bingham, are the Directors.
"The 'Bristol Academy,' of the same town is now purchasing a library of from 500 to 1,000 volumes, consisting of encyclopedias, lexicons, editions of the classics, grammars, &c."

WAYLAND — FREE PUBLIC LIBRARY

683 Wight, John B. "Town Libraries. Dr. Wayland." *Inquirer* [Christian Inquirer], 5 (September 27, 1851), p4, 910 wds (MiU).
The article is the text of a speech made by Wight.
I wish that it were possible for me to tell everyone about the public library that recently was opened in Wayland [Massachusetts]. More than two years ago, President Wayland of Brown University offered $500 to the town for a public library on the condition that another $500 be raised by local subscription. The matching sum was collected, and after some legal and planning delays, a room in the town hall was outfitted for the library. A committee of clergymen and learned citizens selected books for the library, which has become a favorite meeting place for all of the town's inhabitants. The library books are in constant demand; it is easy to see that in the future this library will help the town's citizens to become more intelligent, refined, courteous, and enlightened. Similar libraries should be established in other cities and towns.

WEST ROXBURY — PUBLIC LIBRARY

684 "West Roxbury, Mass." *Norton's Literary Gazette and Publishers' Circular*, 3 (February 15, 1853), p18 (ICN, NcU).
The entire article follows.
"An effort is making in West Roxbury to establish a Public Library. One gentleman is said to have contributed a thousand dollars for the purpose, while he is ready to contribute the further sum of five thousand dollars, provided that fifteen thousand dollars is raised by other individuals within the current year."

WILLIAMSTOWN — LYCEUM

685 "Williamstown Mass. Lyceum." *American Annals of Education* [American Journal of Education], n.s. 1 (March 1830), p143–44 (NcU).
The entire article was taken from the *Williamstown Advocate*; the part of the article about the Lyceum's library (p144) follows.
"The society has a library of over one hundred volumes, which it is expected will be doubled in the course of two or three weeks—We have no doubt that the Institution has been and will continue to be useful, and hope the young men of this town will come forward and avail themselves of its benefits."

— WILLIAMS COLLEGE LIBRARY

686 "Williams College Library." *Norton's Literary Gazette and Publishers' Circular*, 3 (March 15, 1853), p37, 1170 wds (ICN, NcU).
Founded in 1793, the Williams College Library was located in Old West College where it remained until 1828 when it was moved to the chapel. In 1847 the library occupied Lawrence Hall, built through the generosity of Mr. Amos Lawrence and planned by Prof. C. C. Jewett. Following is Prof. Jewett's description of the library: The octagonally shaped building was designed to accommodate a library of 30,000 volumes, was to be made of brick, and was to cost no more than $7,000. In the main reading room eight Ionic columns, arranged in a circle, support a dome that is surmounted by a lantern. The shelves along the walls can hold up to 10,000 volumes, and two more levels of shelves can be added when needed. The librarian's desk is located in the center of the room. The periodicals reading room, a meeting room, workrooms, and offices are in the basement. The library now has 7,000 volumes. (An exterior view of Lawrence Hall accompanies the article.)

WORCESTER

687 "John Green and the Free Public Library, Worcester, Mass." *American Journal of Education* (Barnard), o.s. 13, n.s. 3 (September 1863), p606–09 (NcU).
John Green, M.D. (portrait provided in the article) was one of the earliest friends of the Worcester District Medical Library. In 1855 his private library was placed in the Worcester Lyceum and Library Association for the use of the public for a term of not less than five years. In 1859 he announced to the Directors of the Lyceum and to the mayor his intention to give to the city these and other volumes as a basis for a public library. Then, in December, 1859, he deeded

his library of 7,000 volumes to the city on condition that the custody and management of the library be vested in a board of directors and that the city provide a librarian and a suitable library building. Construction of the library building commenced in 1860; it was ready for occupancy in 1862. (Excerpts from the 1862 annual report and the library regulations are reprinted.)

— AMERICAN ANTIQUARIAN SOCIETY LIBRARY

688 "American Antiquarian Society." *Today: A Boston Literary Journal*, 2 (July 3, 1852), p9, 250 wds (MeB, NcD).

The information in the article summarized below is rearranged and presented in another article in *National Magazine*, vol. 1, p179, August 1852 *(see 689)*.

The proceedings of the Society's last three meetings have been published in a beautifully printed pamphlet. The new library building in Worcester, designed for the use of the society, has been approved and construction begun. The funds for the new building, which will cost $15,400, are at hand. The contract calls for completion by October next. The building will be a simple parallelogram, fifty feet wide, eighty feet long and forty two feet high from ground to eaves. It is to be built in a tasteful and pleasing style without sacrificing convenience and economy to architectural beauty. The ornaments will be simple, graceful and appropriate. The Society has recently made numerous and valuable additions to its library.

689 [Library Building for the American Antiquarian Society.] *National Magazine: Devoted to Literature, Art, and Religion*, 1 (August 1852), p179, 220 wds (InU, NcU).

The article contains the same information, somewhat rearranged, as does an article in *Today: A Boston Literary Journal*, vol. 2, p9, July 1852 *(see 688)*.

690 "Worcester Antiquarian Society." *Norton's Literary Gazette and Publishers' Circular*, 2 (November 15, 1852), p211, 1310 wds (ICN, NcU).

The Antiquarian Society was founded in November 1812. It had a small but respectable library which in 1820 was moved into a building that a year later was deeded, along with $24,000, to the Society by Mr. Isaiah Thomas. The Library now has about 20,000 books as well as pamphlets, manuscripts and portraits. Due to dampness and the lack of space in the building now occupied, the decision was made by the Society to construct a new building that will cost approximately $18,000 and will be completed at some time this spring. (An exterior view of the library accompanies the article.)

— YOUNG MEN'S LIBRARY ASSOCIATION

691 "Worcester (Mass.) Young Men's Library Association." *Norton's Literary Gazette and Publishers' Circular*, 3 (July 15, 1853), p115 (ICN, NcU).
The entire article follows.

"This new society, incorporated in Mafch last, has just published, in a pamphlet form, its Charter and By-laws, and a catalogue of its books. Over a thousand well selected volumes are already possessed by the Society, and there is every indication that the Library will be well and permanently established."

692 [Young Men's Library Association of Worcester.] *Norton's Literary Gazette and Publishers' Circular*, n.s. 1 (October 16, 1854), p532 (NcU).
The entire article follows.
"By the first Annual Report of the Young Men's Library Association, of Worcester, we learn that the number of volumes presented during the first year of its existence was 867; volumes purchased, 877. Mr. John Gray, Librarian."

Michigan

ANN ARBOR — UNIVERSITY OF MICHIGAN LIBRARY

693 [University of Michigan Library.] *Norton's Literary Gazette and Publishers' Circular*, n.s. 1 (October 16, 1854), p532 (NcU).
The entire article follows.
"The University of Michigan at Ann Arbor, has a library of 7,000 vols. The last catalogue is an 8 vo. pp 48, published in 1846. Mr. J. H. Vance, Librarian."

694 [Michigan University Library.] *Publishers' Weekly*, 5 (February 7, 1874), p141 (NcU).
The entire article follows.
"The Grand Duke Alexis has given to the library of Michigan University, the History of the Russian Empire, 10 volumes; History of Russia, 22 volumes; Course of Civil Law, 3 volumes; Manual of Criminal Law, 1 volume; Historical Notes of the First Fifty Years of the University of St. Petersburg, 6 volumes; Extracts from the Reports of the Condition and the Acts of the University of Moscow, Notices Published by the University of St. Vladimir for 1871, '72, '73, containing the Yearly Report for 1872, and other information referring to University Life, Notes of the University of New Russia from the time of its foundation, containing, among other matters, the Report of the University for last year, 10 volumes."

LANSING — STATE LIBRARY

695 [Report of the Michigan State Library for 1873 and 1874.] *American Bibliopolist*, 7 (February 1875), p3 (ICN, ICU).
The entire article follows.
"We have received from Harriet A. Tenney, State Librarian, a Report of the State Librarian of the State of Michigan for 1873 and 1874, from which we learn that the 'total number of books, pamphlets and maps in the care of the State Librarian is 45,745, and their value is estimated at $90,000, an average of nearly two dollars per volume.' We are glad to perceive that there is such evidence of progress in the formation of a library, but it is evident that it is yet greatly in need of miscellaneous books, especially in the department of American History. We are glad to see that a lady occupies the post of honor as a librarian. We know no reason except a lack of training why intelligent women should not more frequently occupy a similar position."

Missouri

696 "The School Law." *American Journal of Education,* St. Louis [Journal of Education], 1 (January 1869), p81, 440 wds (MoS).

We learn that at this session of the legislature an amendment to the school law will be proposed, permitting school officials to appropriate small amounts for school libraries. The amendment will be welcomed especially in districts where public school libraries have already been established by subscription, as for example in St. Joseph where a library is flourishing. The small fraction from the school fund, together with income from subscriptions, will provide for periodical subscriptions, additional books, and maintenance costs. Experience elsewhere has shown that any attempt to depend on the school fund alone will be disastrous; thousands of failures in other states should teach us to be cautious.

697 "The School Law. – Libraries." *American Journal of Education,* St. Louis [Journal of Education], 1 (February 1869), p96, 650 wds (MoS).

We hope that the amendment permitting trustees to spend a small amount for library purposes will be proposed in the legislature. The amendment is desirable because it is permissive, not mandatory; local effort will be required. Larger towns will be likely to establish libraries first; they should use subscription funds, as well. Smaller towns would imitate them. We have no faith in free libraries for children as well as adults; we do have faith in the ability of the American people to establish and maintain libraries if they mainly rely upon their own resources, untrammeled by binding legislation.

698 "School Libraries." *American Journal of Education,* St. Louis [Journal of Education], 2 (February 1870), p109, 600 wds (MoS).

In reading, children increase their stores of learning and catch an inspiration which their school books do not contain. Reading relieves the tedious sameness of geography, arithmetic and grammar. Books prevent idleness and crime; they subdue the passions and inspire attention, obedience, and love. A library is a sort of "savings bank" from which users may draw the sustenance of the mind while leaving its stores for future generations to use. A library in each school district of Missouri would be invaluable. The public school libraries of St. Louis and St. Joseph are working wonders; the state should help those in other localities who wish to establish libraries.

699 Calkins, R. R. "Public Libraries." *American Journal of Education,* St. Louis [Journal of Education], 3 (December 1870), p5–6 (MoS).

The article refers to one in the July 1870 issue of the same periodical (vol. 2, p203–04) *(see 210).*

Mr. Ira Divoll, in your journal, referred people to me who were interested in starting a library; several have written and I wish to say a few words to all of your readers who are interested. If the citizens of a town really want a library, the problem of getting one is easily solved. Libraries are as necessary as schoolhouses. Make a beginning and the state will come to your assistance; if each of 100 people gives you $10, you will have $1,000, enough to buy good, interesting, popular books. Then citizens will give you more books and people will become members of your library association by paying for annual or life memberships. If you want a railroad you subscribe stock and you vote appropriations; a library

ST. LOUIS

700 Morgan, H. H. "A Few Words About our Libraries." *Western: A Journal of Literature, Education, and Art.*, n.s. 1 (1875), p764–70 (InU).
The article apparently is referring to St. Louis libraries.
The Mercantile Library estimates that it had 42,013 volumes as of 1874; the Public School Library had 38,758 as of May 1, 1874. Patrons need to know where to find information related to their particular interest; librarians have insufficient time to become knowledgeable enough to advise on this matter. (Books like Moore's *What to Read and How to Read it*, Putnam's *Best Reading*, and the library primer of the Boston Public Library are described and recommended.) Readers need self-help tools. A topical catalog of our libraries would take several years; such a catalog of some departments generally used, such as physical science and literature, should be started. Cooperation between librarians and readers will decrease inconveniences in using libraries. The purchase of new books is not the chief function of libraries; people need to be able to use them. When they are able to do so, libraries will receive better support.

— MERCANTILE LIBRARY

701 "St. Louis Mercantile Library Association." *Norton's Literary Gazette and Publishers' Circular*, 2 (March 15, 1852), p45, 260 wds (ICN, NcU).
According to its annual report, the association has enjoyed a prosperous year. Its plan of organization is similar to that of the New York Mercantile Library Association. Clerks can join after paying a $2.00 initiation fee and a quarterly fee of $.75; merchants also can join but at higher membership fees. The Mercantile Library Hall Company, a separate body like New York's Clinton Hall Association, has been chartered and will provide a new building for the library. Soon, 1,000 volumes from the now defunct St. Louis Lyceum will be transferred to the library. Having started with nothing only six years ago, the library now has a collection of about 7,000 volumes valued at $11,270 and other property worth $14,621.

702 [St. Louis Mercantile Library Association.] *Norton's Literary Gazette and Publishers' Circular*, 2 (September 15, 1852), p169 (ICN, NcU).
The entire article follows.
"Mr. Wm. P. Curtis, the Librarian of the *St. Louis Mercantile Library Association*, has recently been visiting the Eastern Libraries. He informs us that in seven years they have collected eight thousand volumes, purchased not according to what they could buy, but according to what they wanted. They are about to enter a new library building, the whole expense of which is almost $100,000, erected for them by an association of merchants, and ultimately to be owned by the Library Association."

703 [St. Louis Mercantile Library.] *National Magazine: Devoted to Literature, Art, and Religion*, 2 (June 1853), p571 (InU, NcU).
The entire article follows.
"The annual report of the *St. Louis Mercantile Library* for the year 1852

U.S. — Missouri 188

represents its affairs as in a most prosperous condition. The aggregate number of volumes now in the library is 8,777, of which 1,478 have been added during the year at a cost of over $2,000 — nine hundred and one volumes having been secured by purchase, and five hundred and seventy-seven by donation. The whole number of members is 774. A new Library Hall is erecting for the association at a cost of $100,000, subscribed mainly by citizens of St. Louis, a single gentleman, Henry D. Bacon, Esq., contributing the sum of $20,000."

704 "St. Louis Mercantile Library." *Norton's Literary Gazette and Publishers' Circular*, 3 (December 15, 1853), p217-18 (NcU).
The *Journal* mentioned in the article is not identified.
The St. Louis Mercantile Library has received some interesting literary relics of the late (1848-49) French Revolution from Mr. Boernstein, an editor of this city. The *Journal* says he made the collection himself. There is at least one newspaper from each day of that time, including some newspapers which lasted only one day. Nowhere else is such a complete collection to be found. There are five parts to the collection: two volumes of newspapers and posters, a volume of official investigations of the insurrections of May 15 and June 22-26, and two volumes of pamphlets and periodicals.

705 [Mercantile Library Association of St. Louis.] *Norton's Literary Gazette and Publishers' Circular*, n.s. 1 (March 15, 1854), p144 (NcU).
The entire article follows.
"From the Eighth Annual Report of the Mercantile Library Association of St. Louis, it appears that the entire number of volumes now in that library is 10,563, of which 1,788 have been added during the last year. The value of the books is estimated at $17,265, and the whole property belonging to the Association at $22,761. During the year, 9,885 volumes were issued to 684 readers, showing an increase of 70 readers and 480 volumes upon the previous year. The number of members of the Association is 944. The receipts for the year were $7,693. John T. Douglass is President of the Association, Wm. P. Curtis, Librarian."

706 "Mercantile Library Association of St. Louis." *DeBow's Review*, 18 (May 1855), p382-83 (InU, NcU).
There are 11,943 volumes in the library, valued at $19,578.81. During the previous year 781 volumes were purchased and 597 were donated. A fire at a bindery had caused the loss of all the previous year's periodicals and 129 other volumes. In the preceding year, 870 readers have borrowed 10,983 volumes. A record was not kept of the number of books used in the reading room. (The recently elected officers are listed.)

707 [Catalogue of the St. Louis Mercantile Library.] *Nation*, 18 (June 4, 1874), p362 (NcU).
The entire article follows.
"We have been favored with a copy of the 'Classified Catalogue of the St. Louis Mercantile Library,' a handsomely printed volume, imperial 8vo, pp. 762. The first part arranges the works under the three general heads of history, philosophy, and poetry, with numerous subdivisions; the second part consists of a general alphabetical index; and, taken together, they well fulfil the main purpose of the catalogue as a ready finding-list. The number of works embraced in it is 40,440, and the collection, without being marked by special features such as

distinguish the somewhat larger library of the Wisconsin Historical Society, has perhaps a not inferior capacity for usefulness, and is certainly one on the possession of which the people of St. Louis are to be congratulated. The industry and care which produced the catalogue in the short space of twelve months deserve to be emulated by other libraries."

— PUBLIC SCHOOL LIBRARY

708 Hermes. "Mr. Divoll and the Public School Library at St. Louis." *American Journal of Education*, St. Louis [Journal of Education], 1 (September 1868), p1-2 (MoS).

In 1857 [Ira] Divoll began working to establish a library to supply reference and miscellaneous books for teachers, school officials, students and the public. His plan was presented and accepted by the board in January 1860, but was not put into operation until after the war. In 1865, a charter was obtained, and the library began operating with about 2,000 volumes. The library grew to 5,000 volumes after one year, 10,000 after two years, and now has 13,000. Growth has been due to labor by the directors and friends, not public money; measures are now being taken to incorporate the library into the public school system. In the 16 months prior to May 1868, 76,000 volumes were lent. The Board of Public Schools should support the library, as it is a proper means of education. Library membership may be gained for a nominal fee.

709 Harris, W. T. "Book Classification." *Journal of Speculative Philosophy*, 4 (1870), p114-29 (NcU).

A librarian requires a sound classification system. Any classification system depends on a philosophical system as a base. The author has considered the problem in preparing the catalog of the St. Louis Public School Library. For that catalog, he has used a system based on Bacon's classification of human faculties—memory, imagination and reason. (Bacon's system is described in some detail, and twelve of the classification schemes mentioned in Edward Edwards's work, *Memoirs of Libraries*, are more briefly described.) The main divisions of the classification scheme of the St. Louis Public School Library are science, art and history. (An outline of the schedule is given.)

710 [St. Louis Public School Library.] *Publishers' Weekly*, 5 (February 7, 1874), p142 (NcU).

The entire article follows.

"The St. Louis Public School Library has now 35,200 volumes, including the collections of the Academy of Science, and has lately dedicated a new reading room, supplied with 242 periodicals. The circulation of books last year amounted to 96,000 volumes; the total membership was 5,054. Membership costs $12 for life, payable at once, or in installments of from $1 to $4, within a period of four years, or $3 per annum."

UNION — FRANKLIN COUNTY PUBLIC SCHOOL LIBRARY

711 H. "Franklin County." *American Journal of Education*, St. Louis [Journal of Education], 3 (January 1871), p10 (MoS).

The article summarized below refers to item 699 in this bibliography.

I have read your article on public libraries by Prof. Calkins; I think your readers might like to know how we started a library in Franklin County. About a year ago our school held a successful public exhibition; at its close, a citizen suggested that in order to show the children and teachers that the town appreciated their efforts in the entertainment and in the work of the school, generally, the citizens then present should organize an association and appoint a committee to receive subscriptions and purchase books for a public school library. Enough money was subscribed to purchase two hundred volumes; we hope to have five hundred before another year has passed. Others should follow our example.

New Hampshire

CONCORD — METHODIST GENERAL BIBLICAL INSTITUTE LIBRARY

712 "Methodist Biblical Institute." *National Magazine: Devoted to Literature, Art, and Religion*, 1 (August 1852), p181 (InU, NcU).
The part of the article about the library follows.
"The Library has been considerably improved the past year. Some excellent friend, whose name is unknown, has recently paid $50 for its improvement. It has now about two thousand volumes."

— NEW HAMPSHIRE HISTORICAL SOCIETY LIBRARY

713 Bouton, Nathaniel. "An Account of the New Hampshire Historical Society." *Congregational Education Society. Quarterly Journal* [American Quarterly Register], 10 (February 1838), p229–41 (NcU).
References to the library of the society are scattered through the article.
The act of incorporation states that the association was formed to collect and preserve books and papers illustrating New Hampshire history. The association may choose and obtain a building for its books. The constitution provides that a librarian shall be an officer of the society. (Nine subject interests of the society are listed; the types of materials wanted by the society — books, laws, journals, etc. — are also listed.) The society has been engaged in collecting acts and documents relating to New Hampshire. The library contains 1,500 volumes and a considerable collection of pamphlets and newspapers; it also has minerals, manuscripts, old coins and Indian relics. (The chief donors are listed; each librarian is named and his period of service given.)

— PUBLIC LIBRARY

714 [Public Library for Concord, New Hampshire.] *National Magazine: Devoted to Literature, Art, and Religion*, 7 (November 1855), p477 (InU, NcU).
The entire article follows.
"The *City Council of Concord, N.H.*, have passed an ordinance for the establishment and perpetual maintenance of a public library. A pledge made by John L. Emmons, Esq., of Boston, a native of Concord, will give $1,000 to start with; and $300 is promised by Octavius Rogers, Esq., besides many donations of books and money from benevolent and patriotic persons. The Council appro-

priates, in addition to the above, $15,000 for the purchase of library furniture and books."

— STATE LIBRARY

715 [New Hampshire State Library.] *American Bibliopolist*, 3 (September 1871), p324 (NcD, OC).
The entire article follows.
"A gentleman once visited the State Library of New Hampshire, wishing to consult Jefferson's 'Notes on Virginia.' The Librarian, who was elected to his office because he was a Democrat, fumbled about the shelves for awhile, and then said to the applicant, 'I cannot find them, and I presume Mr. Jefferson took them up before he died.'"

GREAT FALLS — MANUFACTURERS AND VILLAGE LIBRARY

716 "Great Falls, (N.H.)." *Norton's Literary Gazette and Publishers' Circular*, 3 (March 15, 1853), p40, 200 wds (NcU).
The public library in this manufacturing village is known as the Manufacturers and Village Library; it was started in 1842, but not completely organized until 1849. It now numbers about 3,000 volumes, and is enjoyed generally by the various residents of the town. The library is owned by shareholders, with each share worth $5.00, subject to an annual tax of $1.00. Each shareholder may draw two books per week. Any female operative in the mills may take out one volume per week by paying 50 cents per year, and any male operative or resident of the town may do the same on the annual payment of $1.00. Mr. H. Y. Hayes is librarian. Great Falls Manufacturing Company has annually subscribed one hundred dollars to the library. The number of volumes has been increasing by 300 to 400 per year.

HANOVER — DARTMOUTH COLLEGE LIBRARY

717 [Gifts to Dartmouth College.] *National Magazine: Devoted to Literature, Art, and Religion*, 1 (October 1852), p378 (InU, NcU).
The entire article follows. It refers to Nathaniel Bradstreet Shurtleff.
"We learn that Dr. George C. Shattuck, of Boston, of the class of 1803, has liberally presented $1,000 to Dartmouth College, to be expended in the purchase of works on the natural sciences; and Dr. Shurtleff, of the same city, has given $1,000, to be expended under the direction of the Professor of Moral and Intellectual Philosophy, for books in that department of study."

718 [Dartmouth College Libraries.] *Publishers' Weekly*, 5 (February 7, 1874), p141 (NcU).
The entire article follows.
"The two open literary societies at Dartmouth College propose to consolidate their libraries, at about 10,000 each, with the college library of 20,000. The idea is good, for the society libraries are apt to be weaklings, since no one has time to manage them, besides duplicating on the college library."

— NORTHERN ACADEMY OF ARTS AND SCIENCES

719 "Literary and Scientific Institutions of the United States." *Congregational Education Society. Quarterly Journal* [American Quarterly Register], 15 (November 1842), p175–81 (NcU).

The article was drawn from the data in the First Annual Report of the Northern Academy of Arts and Sciences, prepared by Professor William Cogswell of Dartmouth College; the parts about libraries are summarized below.

(Following a brief historical introduction, the various institutions are described individually. For most, information is given concerning the number and types of materials in the library.) The Northern Academy of Arts and Sciences has begun establishing a library to promote its objective of encouraging a taste for literature and science. About 300 books, 80 volumes of newspapers, 90 files of unbound newspapers and enough pamphlets to fill one hundred volumes if they were bound are deposited in the library.

NEW HAMPTON — NEW HAMPTON ACADEMICAL AND THEOLOGICAL INSTITUTION LIBRARY

720 Wording, William E. "Historical Sketch of the Academical and Theological Institution at New Hampton, N.H." *Congregational Education Society. Quarterly Journal* [American Quarterly Register], 14 (May 1842), p351–56 (NcU).

The parts of the article about libraries (p354–55) are summarized below.

The Theological Department has a library of 600 well selected volumes, and is constantly increasing. Each of the literary societies also has a well selected library of 600 volumes. Their reading rooms contain the leading political and religious papers of the state, and the reviews and popular periodicals of the union. About 1834, a Library and Missionary Society was formed in the Female Seminary, and most of the young ladies join it. Its character and proceedings are well known through its annual reports.

PORTSMOUTH — ATHENAEUM

721 "Portsmouth Athenaeum." *Norton's Literary Gazette and Publishers' Circular*, 3 (April 15, 1853), p64, 500 wds (ICN, NcU).

The library in Portsmouth, New Hampshire, incorporated in 1817, has more than 8,000 volumes and a well supplied periodicals room. The Athenaeum occupies a three-story brick building that was purchased some years ago for $7,500. The reading room is on the first floor; the library is on the second floor; and a museum occupies the third floor. Since its founding the library has received a number of books and gifts of money from generous donors. Each year about 200 volumes are added to the collection. The library is owned by shareholders; nonshareholders can use the library on the premises upon paying an annual fee of $6.00. The library is open daily from sunrise until 10 P.M.

New Jersey

722 "New Jersey. Annual Report of the Trustees of the School Fund of the State of New Jersey, October 5th, 1839, pp. 32. Ditto. for 1804 pp. 64." *Con-*

necticut Common School Journal and Annals of Education, 3 (June 1, 1841), p168–69 (NcU).
The part about libraries (p169, 830 wds) is summarized below.
In the last report of the Trustees, they recommended that in each school district, a small sum should be set apart each year for a library; they also recommended certain selections from a series published for New York state. Messrs. Harper have now published a series especially for New Jersey, fifty volumes, at a price of $20. District libraries are intended to fill a need that has long been deplored; many sections of this state are deficient in useful books. Of what use is it to teach a child to read unless you supply him with books? The trustees earnestly request the legislature to set aside $10 from the school fund for each district in which the inhabitants contribute an equal amount.

723 "Literature and Art. Educational Notes." *New Outlook* [Christian Union], 3 (April 5, 1871), p215 (ICU).
The part of the article about libraries follows.
"Rutgers College is to receive $30,000 from the estate of the late Mrs. Sophia Kirkpatrick of New Brunswick, N.J.: and Princeton, $150,000. The friends of Princeton have been appealed to for contributions for the erection of a library building for the books of the institution, which now number 28,000 volumes, and for those to be purchased with the annual fund of $6,000 given to the college by Mr. John C. Green of this city."

NEWARK — LIBRARY ASSOCIATION

724 [Newark Library Association.] *Norton's Literary Gazette and Publishers' Circular*, n.s. 1 (February 15, 1854), p80, 190 wds (NcD).
The directors of the Newark Library Association, in their seventh annual report, speak of continued financial prosperity but complain of a lack of public interest in the association. Newark has more than 50,000 inhabitants but the number of individuals borrowing books last year was only 706. (Annual receipts and expenditures are given.) A debt of $8,000 could be cancelled with a little exertion, making possible a doubling of the number of volumes added each year. The Museum of the New Jersey Natural History Society is to be located in the association's library.

New York

725 "School District Libraries." *American Annals of Education*, 3d ser., 5 (June 1835), p281, 220 wds (NcU).
A bill recently passed by the New York State Legislature provides that 1) the inhabitants of each school district may levy a tax, not to exceed $20, to support a library; 2) in any subsequent year the inhabitants of each district may levy a tax, not to exceed $10, to purchase additions to the library; 3) some person in the district may be appointed librarian; and 4) the tax will be collected in the same manner as a tax for building a school.

726 "School District Libraries." *American Annals of Education*, 3d ser., 7 (October 1837), p441–47 (NcU).

About two years ago a law, granting taxing authority to school districts to establish libraries, was enacted in New York. Whether the influence of the district libraries is good or bad ultimately depends upon the character of the books selected. In choosing books for a school library one must consider: 1) whether a particular book will produce more evil than good; 2) the necessity to exclude partisan or sectarian books; and 3) the dangers associated with too much reading. In a pamphlet, William P. Page discusses the quality of education afforded by New York public schools. He recognizes the district library's potential for improving the quality of education; he notes that the common school has been not only "wretchedly defective" but also discouraging to the scholar, leaving him without even the desire to read, the one ability obtained from district school education.

727 "Education." *Jeffersonian*, 1 (February 17, 1838), p1 (InU, NcU).

The entire article follows. It refers to New York state.

"A Memorial is now circulating in several Counties, praying the Legislature to provide more efficiently for the formation of COMMON SCHOOL LIBRARIES in the several Districts throughout the State. We ask the friends of the great and good cause of Universal Education to resolve, one and all, that they shall be presented to every freeman for his signature. On the plan proposed, thousands now miserably restricted in their opportunities of reading, or denied any facilities at all, may be cheaply and advantageously provided. We shall speak further on this head in our next.

"The Memorial above spoken of will probably be given hereafter."

728 "Education." *Jeffersonian*, 1 (February 24, 1838), p9, 750 wds (InU, NcU).

An appeal for greater interest in education in the state of New York. The part of the article which is about libraries follows.

"We want, especially, COMMON SCHOOL LIBRARIES. A small but judicious selection of the best standard authors in History, Geography, Morals, Natural Science, etc., etc. held in each School District as the property of that District, and lent in turn from house to house would be worth ten times its cost expended in Seminole Wars or additions to the Standing Army. It would strengthen every person's interest in the District, the School, and all that concerns them. It would afford profitable and desirable reading for every youth in the State — many thousands of whom are now virtually destitute. It would soon render each District substantially an Association for Intellectual and Moral Improvement. It would advance the Cause of Education in every way, and to an indefinite but signal extent."

729 "Common School Libraries." *Jeffersonian*, 1 (March 3, 1838), p19, 450 wds (NcU).

The article summarizes action in the New York State Senate during the previous week.

The Senate, acting as the Committee of the Whole, took up the bill to appropriate the income of the United States Deposit Fund for purposes of education and the diffusion of knowledge. Various views were expressed about the section of the bill providing for additional appropriations to the district libraries. One member thought that only the booksellers would benefit; another pointed out how inexpensive the books were and felt that no one could calculate the

New York (State)

benefit to be derived from these libraries; another reminded the members that the people in each district could decide for themselves whether to have a library. No vote was taken before the Senate adjourned.

730 Page, W. P. "School District Libraries." *Jeffersonian*, 1 (May 26, 1838), p119–20 (IEN, NcU, TxU).
The statement summarized below was addressed to the State Legislature.
Concerning the proposed law providing for the use of surplus tax revenue to support school district libraries, permit me to offer a brief statement of facts in support of my previously expressed views. A teacher reported to me that there are many benefits afforded by school district libraries. Other teachers testified that these libraries contribute to the students' learning, promote the habit of reading, and keep the boys out of mischief. Opponents of school libraries argue that books will be lost or stolen and fear that immoral or irreligious books will be put in the schools. However, it is difficult to imagine that parents knowingly would select such books for the school libraries; and furthermore, my inspection of the school libraries in Geneseo showed that few books had been lost or damaged. I submit, therefore, that the proposed law should be passed.

731 "Common School Libraries." *Jeffersonian*, 1 (July 7, 1838), p161–62. (NbO, NcU).
We are proud that New York State is a pioneer in providing common school libraries. Each district will be able to draw at least $10 per year and should be able to acquire a useful library. People who cannot afford to buy books will be able to read one book per week if a fifty-volume library is procured, and if people meet when they draw and return books, a lyceum can be formed. No self-respecting family will return soiled or torn books and losses will be small. Harpers have gotten up a set of fifty volumes (listed in the article) for $20. Each district should plan this fall to obtain a library when the money becomes available next winter.

732 "The Common School Library." *Connecticut Common School Journal and Annals of Education*, 1 (December 1838), p43 (NcU).
The entire article follows.
"Offered for sale [i.e., *The Common School Library*] by the American Society for the Diffusion of Useful Knowledge, has begun to obtain much favor in the State of New York. $330,000 must be expended there within three years in school libraries; and it is to be hoped that many good books will be offered for that object."

733 "Extracts from Governor Seward's Message to the New York Legislature, January 1, 1839." *Common School Journal*, 1 (Feb. 1, 1839), p45–48 (NcU).
The parts of the article about libraries (p47–48) follow.
"Provision has been made for the establishment of school district libraries. If I do not greatly err, this cheap and easy mode of bringing into contact with the juvenile powers the discoveries of science and the mysteries of the arts, will be the era of a new impulse to the cause of Education. The Common Schools may resist every other influence, but they cannot withstand that of the general improvement of the community. I cannot too earnestly solicit your cooperation in the beginning of this wise and momentous policy... I submit also whether it would not be well to require, that a popular treatise upon agriculture should be contained in the district school libraries."

734 "New York System of Public Instruction." *Common School Journal*, 1 (March 15, 1839), p81–88 (NcU).
The part of the article about libraries (p86–87) is summarized below.

Three years ago, teachers' departments were created in one academy in each of the eight senatorial districts. Each academy was given $500 to purchase apparatus and a library. New York has provided that $55,000 in state money, plus an equal sum raised in the towns, be applied for a term of three years to purchase libraries for the several district schools. In three years, six or seven hundred thousand volumes will be distributed throughout the state, more than one volume to each child between five and fifteen years of age. The project is one of the noblest enterprises of modern civilization. If the books are to bring good results, they must be carefully selected.

735 "District School Libraries in New York." *Common School Journal*, 2 (March 2, 1840), p72–74 (NcU).

In 1835 the New York Legislature authorized school districts to raise money for libraries through taxation but few did. In 1838 Governor Marcy recommended using the state school fund to match money raised by districts; now almost all districts have libraries. (The passage on this subject in the Governor's inaugural address is quoted in the article and summarized here.) Our citizens look with anxiety and hope to the legislature's proceedings in regard to education. Elementary education is only the first stage; there should be advance beyond it. District libraries are beneficial in this respect but few have been established. I recommend that further measures be taken to cause their introduction. A compulsory assessment in each district would be possible but I recommend, instead, giving each district an amount equal to the amount that the district raises by taxation.

736 "District School Libraries in New York." *Connecticut Common School Journal and Annals of Education*, 2 (May 1, 1840), p195–96 (NcU).
The article summarized below is partially drawn from the Massachusetts *Common School Journal (see 735)*.

The 1835 New York legislature authorized school districts to raise money for libraries. With supplementary funds available since 1838, nearly every district is now procuring a library. (Governor Marcy's 1838 message, proposing matching funds from the federal surplus for districts raising money for libraries, is quoted.) The proposal was referred to the committee on colleges and common schools chaired by D. D. Barnard. (The part of his report on common school education referring to libraries is quoted.) The recommendation of Marcy and the legislative committee became an important instrument of popular education. (The *Journal of Commerce* is quoted; it describes the impact of the law, and draws comparisons among various libraries. Statistics of expenditures and library size are included.) Stupendous results are developing in the New York library system. It is an incalculable moment in the improvement of our country.

737 [School District Libraries.] *Poughkeepsie Casket*, 4 (October 3 1840), p102, 190 wds (NjR, NHi).
The notice summarized below is a reprint from the newspaper, *New Yorker*.

Trustees of common schools who are responsible for procuring school district libraries are advised to immediately submit their orders to booksellers or the publisher' agents so that the books may be shipped before navigation ends. Country journalists would provide a useful service if they would notify their readers of this fact. Two 100-volume series have been published; a fifty volume series will be made available in a few weeks. The titles in these three series were selected with the approval of the Superintendent of Common Schools and are sold at prices lower than those charged for similar publications.

738 "The District School Library." *New World. A Weekly Family Journal of Popular Literature, Science, Art and News*, 1 (November 21, 1840), p399, 400 wds (InU, NcD).

The district school libraries are accomplishing important intellectual achievements. An ample fund wisely administered will help perpetuate our social, civil and religious institutions, and our republican form of government. Soon every school district will have a library. The first and second series of *Harper's District School Library* are excellent, and the *New-York Commercial Advertiser*, in a review here reprinted, praises the forthcoming third series. The third series includes works on history, biography, mechanical science, metaphysics, ethics, agriculture, astronomy, chemistry and belles lettres. Many of the works are original and written expressly for the third series. The authors include Washington Irving and several others (named). The books included in the third series were selected with the assistance of John C. Spencer, the Secretary of State of New York State, who is a principal architect of the district school library plan.

739 "School District Libraries." *New World. A Weekly Family Journal of Popular Literature, Science, Art and News*, 2 (January 2, 1841), p16, 260 (NcD, OC).

The school district library system of New York is considered worthy of national emulation. The Harper publishing firm is to be praised for providing three series of fifty volumes each, specially selected and prepared for the district libraries. A fourth series has been announced.

740 "Note—History and Progress of School District Libraries." *Connecticut Common School Journal and Annals of Education*, 3 (March 1, 1841), p119–20 (NcU).

In his annual report for 1833–34, the New York superintendent of common schools recommended establishing school district libraries. In 1835 each district was authorized to raise $20 by tax for the project. There was little response. In 1838, Governor Marcy recommended using part of the federal surplus for libraries in districts raising an equal amount by taxation. The result was the Library law of 1838, by which $53,000 a year for three years was appropriated. The law was extended to five years, resulting in the expenditure of $530,000 for 2 million volumes by late 1843. On December 31, 1840, there were 422,459 volumes, costing an average of 45 cents each in the libraries ($94,998.56 total). Proper, useful books were chosen, chiefly the three series by Harper and Brothers. Great benefit is and will be gained. New York has influenced other states to undertake similar projects.

741 "*The School District Library*. Third Series. New York, 1840. Harper and Brothers. 50 vols. 18mo." *Methodist Quarterly Review*, 23 (April 1841), p320–22 (InU, NcU).

The latest set of books for school district libraries contains more original works than did previous sets. There are books treating religious subjects but these books are non-sectarian. In 1835 the New York Legislature passed legislation allowing each school district to levy a tax for a district library. Beginning in 1838, $55,000 was appropriated annually for three years for district library book purchases. The money was distributed according to the number of children between the ages of five and sixteen in each district, and had to be matched by the district. The appropriation was later extended to five years. By the spring of 1840 more than 6,000 of the total of 10,000 districts had acquired libraries containing an aggregate of about 250,000 volumes. By now, almost all the districts have taken advantage of the law and have collections totalling about 1,000,000 volumes.

742 "New York. Annual Report of the Superintendent of Common Schools, made January, 1841, pp. 138." *Connecticut Common School Journal and Annals of Education*, 3 (April 1, 1841), p129–40 (NcU).

The part about libraries (p132, 600 wds) is summarized below.

It appears that the number of volumes in the school district libraries on December 31, 1840, was 422,459 and that $94,998.56 had been spent during that year for the purchase of books. Almost all of the selections have been useful and proper books. Mostly, the three series published by Harper have been chosen; however, other collections have been approved or their defects have been pointed out. The results of the establishment of these libraries have been very gratifying; half a million valuable books have been circulated among those who are least able to procure them for themselves. No friend of his country can contemplate the consequence for a population of nearly three million without blessing a kind Providence for casting our lot where the cultivation of the human mind is so eminently the object of legislative care.

743 "District Libraries." *Connecticut Common School Journal and Annals of Education*, 4 (June 1, 1842), p134 (NcU).

The article is a part of the *Annual Report* of the Superintendent of Common Schools of New York. The entire article follows.

"The institution and wide dissemination of district libraries, has been attended with the most favorable results upon the advancement and improvement of the district schools. It is indeed difficult to conceive of a measure more directly and certainly adapted in its effects, present and prospective, to extend the sphere of information, to invigorate the moral influences pervading an intelligent community, and to cement the institutions of our favored land, than the introduction into every school district of a judicious and well selected library, open to the perusal of all, and constantly increasing in extent and value."

744 "Common School Libraries." *Genesee Farmer*, 7 (February 1846), p39 (InU, NcU).

The entire article follows.

"These libraries do not, as a general thing, contain a fair proportion of books on rural affairs. It is true, the agricultural literature of this country can not boast of having achieved much; nevertheless, there are a few very valuable works which ought to be in every Common School Library in the State. The 'American Shepherd,' by L. A. Morrell; and Mr. Downing's 'Fruits and Fruit Trees of America,' and 'Landscape Gardening,' have elicited high commendation, and discuss, in a fitting manner, subjects that should be studied by all. The authors are both New Yorkers, and we know no better way to enlist the best talent in the State in the service of its great agricultural interest, than to take a decent notice of those that really do confer on the farming community a substantial benefit. 'The American Poulterer's Companion,' by C. N. Bement, should not be overlooked in this connection."

745 "The Farmer's Library and Journal of Agriculture." *Genesee Farmer*, 7 (August 1846), p178, 580 wds (InU, NcU).

The first volume of the *Farmer's Library* has just been issued, and the *Journal of Agriculture*, edited by John S. Skinner, has just completed its first volume. There are between nine and ten thousand common school libraries in New York. Among the several millions of volumes in these libraries not even one in a hundred deals with agriculture. The *Farmer's Library* and the *Journal of Agriculture* are worthy of a place in every school and town library.

746 "Prison Libraries." *Inquirer* [Christian Inquirer], 1 (September 25, 1847), p193, 2270 wds (ICM).

A letter from St. Louis says that several gentlemen are taking a subscription to purchase books and organize a library for the jail that serves the city and county there; the advice of the editor of the *Christian Inquirer* is sought. The editor promises that the lists of holdings of two prison libraries in New York State, together with a report from the Prison Association, will be sent to St. Louis. The first of these libraries, at Mount Pleasant Prison, consists of 800 volumes, mainly gifts, and is insufficient to meet the demand. The Legislature has recently made an appropriation that will be of some help. However, many prisoners cannot read; a teacher and texts are needed. The report of the Clinton State Prison says that moral tales help create a taste for reading. Prisoners have some time each day when they can read; more religious books are needed.

747 "Education." *Niles' National Register*, 75 (January 10, 1849), p30, 300 wds (NcU).

The success of public schools is directly connected to the support of public libraries. In 1838 the New York State Legislature passed a law which provided for the establishment of libraries in school districts, and to this end $81,624 was expended last year by the state. Also, nearly 1,300,000 books have been distributed since the law's enactment. John Jacob Astor has bequeathed $400,000 to New York City for the establishment and maintenance of a library for public use. The trustees intend to apply to the Legislature for an act to incorporate the library.

748 "Agricultural Books for School Libraries." *Genesee Farmer*, 11 (March 1850), p76 (InU, NcU).

The entire article follows.

"We have been requested to call the attention of Trustees to the propriety of purchasing Agricultural Books for School Libraries. We think the bare mention of the matter will suffice. We will not insult the intelligence of Trustees who are Farmers, by attempting to show the propriety of this course, or urge upon them the performance of this duty. We have a good assortment of Agricultural Books for sale at our office—the best works published. In our next number we will give a full list, with prices."

749 [Acquisition of Books for New York School District Libraries.] *Literary World*, N.Y., 12 (February 12, 1853), p132, 170 wds (NcU).

A bill reported in the Senate of New York would provide for the circulation of lists of standard works of American authors to school district trustees to be used in selecting books for district school libraries. The Superintendent of Common Schools is to order the books selected by each county and is to pay for them from each county's allotted funds.

750 "Public Libraries in New York City." *Ladies' Repository: A Monthly Periodical, Devoted to Literature, Art, and Religion*, 16 (August 1856), p505, 250 wds (NcU, OC).

A table lists 27 libraries and gives the number of volumes in each; there are 337,290 volumes in all of the libraries. There are 11,748 public school libraries in New York State with no less than 1,505,370 volumes. The number of volumes is also given for each of seven large European libraries: "The Paris National Library is said to contain 824,000 volumes; Munich Royal, 600,000; St. Petersburg Imperial, 446,000; Copenhagen Royal, 412,000; Göttigen University, 360,000; Berlin Royal, 500,000; and the London British Museum, 490,000."

751 "James Wadsworth." *American Journal of Education* (Barnard), 5 (September 1858), p389–406 (NcU).

The part of the article about libraries (p401–04) is summarized below.

James Wadsworth (portrait provided in the article) largely was responsible for the introduction of the New York district school library system. In April, 1835 the New York Legislature laid the legal foundations for school libraries. To induce some districts to raise the tax money needed to establish school libraries, Wadsworth offered to pay part of the initial cost for each library, but often his offer was rejected. Since voluntary compliance was too slow, Wadsworth proposed that a portion of state revenue should be distributed to school districts for the support of libraries; under this plan each district would be legally obligated to raise a matching sum. The district library law of 1838 virtually duplicated his proposal.

752 "American Common School Society." *American Journal of Education* (Barnard) 15 (June 1865), p247–60 (NcU).

The parts of the article about libraries (p248, 255–57, 260) are summarized below.

J. Orville Taylor, editor of the *Common School Assistant*, selected a series of books for district libraries in 1836. The school district library system in New York owes much to James Wadsworth. He suggested distributing Hall's *Lectures on School-Keeping*, which led to the idea of supplying children, teachers and parents with other books. (Five letters are reprinted showing Wadsworth's efforts to secure funding for school libraries.) In 1835, the legislature of New York authorized school districts to impose a tax to purchase school libraries. When little progress ensued, Wadsworth recommended using some of the income from the United States Deposit Fund for libraries, which was done. (Legislator Henry S. Randall is quoted concerning the libraries, as is Speaker G. W. Patterson, who gave Wadsworth full credit for them.) Wadsworth also erected a public library in Geneseo, endowing it with $10,000.

753 "The American Society for the Diffusion of Useful Knowledge." *American Journal of Education* (Barnard), 15 (June 1865), p239–45 (NcU).

The part of the article about libraries (p241–44) is summarized below.

In 1837, the society produced "Prospectus of a Library for Schools and Families," probably the earliest published plan of a systematic, comprehensive library. It was estimated that $15,000 would be needed to execute the plan.

The society set up standing committees to oversee the library's development. Harper and Brothers agreed to publish the books decided upon. The passage of the New York state law about school libraries hastened progress. In 1839, the society presented the U.S. Congress with a document intended to improve public instruction, including a proposal for a national school library. The superintendent of common schools of New York refused to acknowledge the society's instrumentality in preparing and distributing the set of books which he chose for the libraries. With its resources spent and now with no hope of recovering its debts, the society suspended operations in support of school libraries.

754 "Free Libraries." *American Bibliopolist*, 4 (March 1872), p120 (IEN, OC).
The entire article follows; it was printed originally in the *New York Commercial*.
"The bill introduced by Mr. Judd, in the Assembly, to establish Free Libraries in towns, villages and cities, by a small *per capita* appropriation, merits and will receive some discussion. The subject is well worthy of consideration. In villages and cities it might be well to apply to this purpose the moneys collected from police court fines, or from violation of city ordinances, when they are not otherwise appropriated."

755 "Free Public Libraries in New York." *Publishers' Weekly* [Publishers' and Stationers' Weekly Trade Circular], 2 (October 24, 1872), p415–16, 520 wds (NcU).
The article consists of the text of "An Act to Provide for the Formation of Free Public Libraries," chapter 458 of the 1872 acts, passed May 1, 1872 by the legislature of New York State. The act is summarized below.
Any town, city, or village may, by resolution of its town council, board of trustees, and town auditors, establish and maintain a free library. For buildings or rooms and for the foundation of such a library, not more than one dollar for each person voting in the last election may be appropriated; for the maintenance and increase of the library, the appropriation may not be more than fifty cents for each person voting. Such a library may not be established unless a majority of the taxable citizens have signed a petition requesting it.

ALBANY — STATE LIBRARY

756 "Remarks Concerning the Catalog of the New York State Library." *Literary World*, N.Y., 6 (April 20, 1850), p391, 1000 wds (NcU).
The library consists of two departments, the Law Library and the Miscellaneous Library. In May 1844, when the library was put under the administrative control of the regents of the University of the State of New York, it had a collection of 10,000 volumes; in six years 15,000 volumes have been added. Great attention to detail has gone into the preparation and arrangement of the catalog. Also, it is a pleasure to note the attention given by the regents to the department of American history.

757 "New York State Library." *Norton's Literary Gazette and Publishers' Circular*, 2 (October 15, 1852), p188 (ICN, NcU).
The entire article follows.
"The building for the New York State Library, at Albany, is rapidly advancing. It stands directly back of the capitol, and fronts upon two streets.

If finished in style corresponding to its interior it will be an honor to the State. We trust that the Legislature will see the importance of enlarging the valuable collection which this library now possesses, so soon as this fire-proof building shall be ready to accommodate accessions. The influence of the Library is felt all over the State, and will be still more when the projected University is established."

758 "New York State Library." *Norton's Literary Gazette and Publishers' Circular*, 2 (December 15, 1852), p235, 800 wds (ICN, NcU).

In 1818 the New York State Legislature appropriated $3,000 for the establishment of the State Library. By 1845 the library owned more than 10,000 volumes and over the years had acquired some valuable private collections. The library has two departments, Law and Miscellaneous, and in 1850 the library's eight-volume book catalog was published. As of March, 1852, there were 27,789 bound volumes in the collection. The library is located in the Capitol Building but soon will occupy a new building. The library is open to the public from nine to four during sessions of the Legislature and the courts. (An exterior view of the new building accompanies the article.)

759 "New York State Library—International Exchange." *Literary World*, N.Y., 12 (May 7, 1853), p382, 850 wds (NcU).

(A list of about 100 volumes received by the library from French donations through Vattemare's international exchange system.) A catalogue of works received from Belgium and the Netherlands is being prepared.

760 [New York State Library.] *National Magazine: Devoted to Literature, Art, and Religion*, 2 (June 1853), p571 (InU, NcU).
The entire article follows.

"The *New-York State Library*, at Albany, is said to be one of the most interesting in our country. Additions are constantly being made, and those of the past year are especially worthy of note. Several valuable works from the library of the distinguished Dr. Jarvis, of Middletown, Conn., have been purchased. Six hundred volumes were received from the Library of St. Mark's, Venice, as a present to the State, and make an important addition to the Italian literature of the collection. Over one hundred volumes were also sent from the Royal and National Library at Munich, in Bavaria. These embrace the transactions of the Royal Society of Bavaria, and the proceedings of other learned institutions. Presents of books have also been received from the Netherlands, Belgium, France, and Holland [sic]. The miscellaneous library of the Hon. Harmonus Bleecker, amounting to three or four thousand volumes, has been donated, and will hereafter form a part of the State collection."

761 D. [New York State Library.] *Literary World*, N.Y., 12 (August 6, 1853), p29–30 (NcU).
This article was copied almost verbatim in *Norton's Literary Register*, vol. 3, p150, for September 15, 1853 *(see 763)*.

(Several recent valuable acquisitions relating to America are described.) Several fine sets of books have been received from foreign governments and universities in exchange for the *Natural History of New York;* the state's expenditure on this work has been unjustly criticized in the past. Two outstanding acquisitions have been a Koran in Arabic and one in the Kufic script. The legislature has purchased the papers of George Clinton, including the treasonable papers found in Major André's boot when he was captured.

762 [Manuscripts acquired by the New York State Library.] *National Magazine: Devoted to Literature, Art, and Religion*, 3 (September 1853), p284 (NcU).

The following article refers to the George Clinton papers.

"Valuable additions to our Revolutionary History have been obtained recently by Mr. Randall, Secretary of our State, which the Library committees of the Senate and Assembly were invited to examine at Albany. Among the manuscripts is the 'Treasonable Correspondence found concealed in Major André's boot when that officer was searched by his captors, Paulding, Williams, and Van Wart.' The papers consist of an enumeration of the number and disposition of the American troops at West Point, and a description of the fortifications, with suggestions in regard to weak and exposed points. There is also the pass from General Arnold, under which André, as 'Mr. John Smith,' was returning to the British camp."

763 D. "New York State Library." *Norton's Literary Gazette and Publishers' Circular*, 3 (September 15, 1853), p150, 520 wds (NcD).

The article is taken almost verbatim from an article in the *Literary World*, vol. 12, August 6, 1853 *(see 761).*

764 [New York State Library.] *Norton's Literary Gazette and Publishers' Circular*, n.s. 1 (March 15, 1854), p143, 280 wds (NcU).

The New York State Library spent $3,079.01 for books, $1,522.36 for bindings and $723.41 for international and state exchanges in 1853, according to its annual report to the State Legislature. The donations, primarily through the agency of Mr. Vattemare, have been interesting and valuable. Sources include individuals and institutions in the Netherlands, Belgium, France, the German states, and Denmark (some are listed).

765 [New York State Library Catalog.] *National Magazine: Devoted to Literature, Art, and Religion*, 10 (March 1857), p286 (InU, NcU).

The entire article follows.

"The Regents of the University have caused to be prepared, under the authority of the Legislature, a new catalogue of the Books in the New-York State Library. From this publication we learn that there has been an increase of twenty thousand three hundred and sixty volumes in five years. The total number of volumes now in the library is forty-three thousand six hundred and thirty-four, of which thirteen thousand six hundred and twenty-three are law books."

766 [Washington Manuscripts in the New York State Library.] *Nation*, 18 (June 18, 1874), p394, 150 wds (NcU).

The fifty-sixth *Annual Report* of the trustees of the New York State Library has, besides the usual catalog of books received during the year, a supplementary catalog of manuscripts and notes about manuscripts purchased in 1871 and received in 1873 relating to George Washington. In this purchase are included the first draft of the Farewell Address, an autograph manuscript reviewing the qualifications of his generals, and a statement of his household expenses during part of 1789, as well as a dress sword, sent, according to tradition, by Frederick II.

U.S. — New York

— YOUNG MEN'S ASSOCIATION LIBRARY

767 "Young Men's Institute, Albany." *Norton's Literary Gazette and Publishers' Circular*, 2 (October 15, 1852), p188 (ICN, NcU).
The entire article follows.
"The new building now occupied by the Young Men's Institute, at Albany, is one of the most attractive of its kind which we have ever seen. The files of newspapers there displayed are very numerous, and the selection of other periodicals is good. The Lecture Room has a very attractive look, and the Library is constantly increasing in value. The Young Men's Association seems to be flourishing every way since its recent removal from the Exchange to this new edifice in State-street, near Broadway."

768 "Albany (N.Y.) Young Men's Association." *Norton's Literary Gazette and Publishers' Circular*, 3 (March 15, 1853), p40 (NcU).
The entire article follows.
"We have received the annual report of this Association, presented last month at its 20th annual meeting, together with a new edition of the charter, by-laws, &c. From the former pamphlet, an octavo of 60 pages, containing full details from every department of the Association we gather the following facts. 231 vols. have been purchased by the Library, and 79 volumes have been given to it during the year now closed, making the total number of volumes at the present term, 6,952. 82 newspapers and 25 other periodicals are received at the Reading Room. The present number of members is 1,484, of whom 498 have been received during the year. The financial receipts of the year were $6,402, 76, the expenditures $4,502. Mr. A. F. Lansing is Librarian."

ALBANY COUNTY — ALBANY COUNTY AGRICULTURAL SOCIETY

769 Burl, Jesse. "Address [on the Third Anniversary of the Albany County Agricultural Society.] *American Farmer*, 3 (November 23 and 30, 1821), p275–77, 285–86 (InU, NcU).
The part of the article about libraries (p285, 280 wds) is summarized below.
An agricultural library is recommended to help improve agriculture by promoting knowledge. (Several titles are suggested that could form the basis of a library at a cost of less than $50.) Most agricultural works are written by farmers, many of whom have successfully used the discoveries of science. Chemistry, especially, has been helpful in improving agriculture.

NEW YORK — BROOKLYN

see also FLATBUSH

— ATHENAEUM

770 [Athenaeum at South Brooklyn.] *Literary World*, N.Y., 12 (February 5, 1853), p110, 340 wds (NcU).
(A description of the building at the corner of Atlantic and Clinton Streets for the Athenaeum at South Brooklyn, which is nearing completion.) The cost of the building and site will not go much over $50,000. The library room is 21

by 70 feet; the reading room, 25 by 42 feet. The third floor is to be a lecture room with a gallery.

771 "Brooklyn (N.Y.) Athenaeum." *Norton's Literary Gazette and Publishers' Circular*, 3 (February 15, 1853), p19 (ICN, NcU).
The entire article follows.
"The building intended for this association, located on the corner of Atlantic and Clinton streets, is now almost complete. Its cost will be not far from $50,000. In addition to a few rooms which may be rented, it contains a Library room, 21 ft. by 70; a Reading Room, 25 ft. by 42; a Conversation Room, 21 ft. by 36; and a Lecture Room, 90 ft. by 30, which will seat over 1,800 persons. We congratulate our Brooklyn neighbors, and especially those who are inconvenienced by the removal of the N.Y. Mercantile and Society Libraries, that they are to have, on the other side of the waters, such excellent accommodations."

772 [Brooklyn Athenaeum.] *Norton's Literary Gazette and Publishers' Circular*, n.s. 1 (March 15, 1854), p144 (NcU).
The entire article follows.
"We congratulate our friends of the Brooklyn Athenaeum on the gratifying results of their labors, as evinced in the First Annual Report of the Trustees of that institution. Scarcely two years have elapsed since its foundation, and it is now in possession of a commodious building, with a well-stocked newsroom and reading-room, and a library numbering at present about 2,600 volumes. From the Treasurer's report, it appears that $60,000 have been received from subscribers to the capital stock, $2,400 from contributors to the literary fund, and $3,596 from the earnings of the institution. Of this amount, $49,728 have been expended for the land and building, and $2,045 for books. The President is John N. Taylor; Mr. Ethan A. Doty, recently connected with the New York Mercantile Library, has just been appointed Librarian."

— LONG ISLAND HISTORICAL SOCIETY LIBRARY

773 [Fourth Annual Report of the Long Island Historical Society.] *Nation*, 5 (August 1, 1867), p84 (NcU).
The part of the article about the society's library follows.
"The librarian acknowledges the gift of the reports of the Massachusetts Board of Education, complete in thirty-five volumes. The first of the series were written by Horace Mann and being now rather scarce it is well to know where they may be consulted. The same donor, Dr. Samuel A. Green, of Boston, has presented other sets of reports — of the State, and of the Massachusetts Horticultural and Agricultural societies, together with a long line of Harvard College catalogues. A large number of books have been received from the authors themselves — an excellent example for all others. Perhaps the most interesting contribution to the history of the rebellion is the five-folio volumes of *The Index* — the late Anglo-Confederate organ."

774 [Long Island Historical Society Library.] *Publishers' Weekly*, 5 (March 7, 1874), p257 (NcU).
The entire article follows; it refers to George Hannah.
"The Long Island Historical Society's library, lately injured by fire, is now open again. Mr. Hanna [sic] the librarian, is appealing for means to provide for the creation of a new library building at Clinton and Pierrepont streets."

— MERCANTILE LIBRARY

775 "Mercantile Library Building, Brooklyn." *Harper's Weekly*, 13 (February 6, 1869), p84, 350 wds (InU, NcU).

The Brooklyn Mercantile Library building was formally opened on January 18. James Frothingham, Chairman of the building committee, addressed the visitors, reviewing the development of the building since 1862. The first gift was $5,000 from Mr. Chittenden. By December, 1864, $30,000 had been raised; by February, 1865, $80,000. Chittenden doubled his subscription provided that the rest of the sum be raised by June, 1865. In May $125,000 had been subscribed. The cost of the building and ground was $227,600, most of which has been paid. The main building is flanked by office buildings. The location is Montague Street near City Hall. The building is modern gothic in red brick. The first floor has the general reading room, a lecture room, and the ladies' reading room. The library is on the second floor with room for many thousand more books. Presently the shelves contain only the old library.

776 [Brooklyn Mercantile Library.] *American Publisher and Bookseller*, 2 (March 1869), p11 (DLC).

The entire article follows.

"The new building of the Brooklyn Mercantile Library was thrown open to the public lately. The building is on Montague Street, opposite the Academy of Music. On the occasion of the opening, addresses were made by Henry Ward Beecher, A. A. Low, S. B. Chittenden, and numerous other prominent personages; after which a subscription was made to procure money to purchase books, when the following subscriptions were received: A. A. Low, $5,000; S. B. Chittenden, $2,500; A. B. Baylis, $500; A. H. Frothingham, $500; Frank Morgrand, $500; James P. Wallace, $500; W. Newton Adams, $500; Wm. E. Dodge, $500; James R. Taylor, $500; J. P. Robinson, $500; Edwards Pierrepont, $500; Albert Mason, $500; Gen. H. W. Slocum, $100; C. Frothingham, $25. The Officers of the Library are Mr. L. B. Noyes, Librarian, and Willis A. Bradwell, Assistant Librarian."

777 [Brooklyn Mercantile Library.] *Nation*, 9 (December 30, 1869), p586, 270 wds (InU, NcU).

Many of the benefactors of the Brooklyn Mercantile Library also aid the Historical Society. The library best answers the popular need; it has been growing rapidly since being moved to its present quarters. The first *Bulletin* of the librarian, just issued, reports 24,000 volumes in the library with the expectation of doubling the collection in four years. Though not large, the library will more than meet the ordinary demand for it as a circulating library. Books not on the shelves will usually be procured upon request. The reading rooms are well supplied with current periodical literature. The *Bulletin* has a classified catalog of books added recently. After the bridge is built, the Brooklyn Mercantile Library and the Historical Society library might be easier to consult during the day than the Mercantile or Astor Libraries in downtown New York. The *Bulletin*, therefore, might have future reference value.

778 [Brooklyn Mercantile Library.] *Publishers' Weekly*, 7 (January 30, 1875), p113 (NcU).

The article reprinted below refers to Stephen Buttrick Noyes, librarian of the Brooklyn Mercantile Library.

"Mr. Noyes, of the Brooklyn Mercantile Library, proposes to begin printing at once on the general catalogue to which we lately referred. It will be on the one alphabet or 'dictionary' plan, entries of author, title, and subject being given. He estimates it will comprise about a thousand octavo pages, and cost about $6000 to print. The library now contains 50,000 volumes. The upper tier of the main library hall has been lately fitted with shelving, so that there is still vacant space for 20,000 more volumes."

— NAVY YARD LIBRARY

779 "Seamens' Libraries." *Christian Herald and Seaman's Magazine*, 10 (December 6, 1823), p448 (NcU).
The entire article follows.
"On the suggestion of the Chaplain, through the instrumentality of a benevolent gentleman who has been engaged in procuring other libraries, the officers and crew of the United States sloop Erie, provided for the vessel, previous to her sailing, a well chosen library, consisting of about five hundred volumes, of which one hundred were adapted to the use of the crew, containing among them a suitable number of moral and religious books. This library is promised to be conveyed, on the return of the Erie from her cruise, to a General Library, which the Chaplain is actively engaged in establishing at the navy-yard, Brooklyn."

780 "Naval Institute at Brooklyn." *Sailors' Magazine and Seamen's Friend*, 6 (January 1834), p145–46 (MdAN).
The article is taken from the *Journal of Commerce*. A footnote by the editor of the *Seamen's Journal* reports that the Marine Insurance Offices of New York have given $500 to the project described in the article.
An association, called the Naval Lyceum, has recently been formed at the Brooklyn Navy Yard. A public spirited individual is procuring a library for it. The nucleus is 400 volumes, all that remain from the 2000 volume library of the ship, *Franklin*. The gentleman is asking other citizens for donations. (Several fine gift volumes are described.) We trust that many others will encourage this enterprise in the interest of the navy to which the nation is indebted for no small share of its glory.

781 Maury, Matthew F. "Scraps from the Lucky Bag, No. III: Details of the School-Ship." *Southern Literary Messenger*, 6 (December 1840), p786–800 (NcU).
The article was reprinted in *Army and Navy Chronicle*, 11 (Dec. 17, 1840), p385–89 *(see 782)*. The part about libraries (p799–800) is summarized below.
The moral and intellectual condition of the Navy has improved due to the creation of libraries on ships. Credit for these libraries belongs to Mr. Wood, the originator of mercantile library associations in America and England. In 1821, Wood went aboard the *Franklin 74* and addressed the crew about procuring a library. The men agreed, and $800 was immediately subscribed by the men and officers; 1500 volumes were bought. Commodore Stewart designated a room as a library, and appointed a librarian. The books which were returned at the end of the cruise were used to found a library in the Brooklyn Navy Yard, and later formed the nucleus of collections in the Naval Lyceum and the New York Navy Yard. The commodore attested to the library's benefits, and the Navy Department has furnished every ship with a small library. Well-regulated school ships could be useful.

U.S. — New York

782 [Maury, Matthew F.] "Our Navy — No. III. Details of the School-Ship." *Army and Navy Chronicle*, 11 (December 17, 1840), p385–89 (NcU).
The article is reprinted from the December 1840 issue of *The Southern Literary Messenger (see 781)*. The part about libraries (420 wds) is on p389. The article in *The Army and Navy Chronicle* is signed H. B.

BUFFALO — GROSVENOR LIBRARY

783 [Grosvenor Library.] *Publishers' Weekly*, 4 (October 25, 1873), p452 (NcU).
The entire article follows.
"The Grosvenor Library at Buffalo is rapidly increasing and is expecting a large invoice of German books selected by a committee of German *literati* named for that purpose; its French department is also growing and boasts a complete set of the *Revue des deux Mondes* and a hundred and five volumes of *La Mode*. A complete collection of topographical maps of Europe is under way. Among late presentations is a set of the *American Gas Light Journal*, from D. J. Steele, Esq., of the Buffalo Gas Works. This library is spoken of as, for its size, one of the best selected and best managed to be found. A catalogue has been prepared, which will be put to press as soon as means are received."

784 [Resignation of Mr. Sheldon.] *Literary World*, Boston, 4 (January 1874), p128 (NcU).
The entire article follows; it was copied verbatim in the *Publishers' Weekly* for January 10, 1874 *(see 785)*.
"Mr. Alex J. Sheldon, during the last four years Librarian of the Grosvenor Library, Buffalo, N. Y., has been compelled by ill health to resign his office. He desires to obtain literary employment, either as editor of a weekly paper, or as purchaser of books for libraries. Those who desire the services of an intelligent and experienced gentleman will do well to address him at Buffalo."

785 [Grosvenor Library.] *Publishers' Weekly*, 5 (January 10, 1874), p34 (NcU).
This is a verbatim copy of an article that appeared in the January 1874 issue of the *Literary World*, Boston *(see 784)*.

786 [Grosvenor Library.] *Publishers' Weekly*, 5 (February 7, 1874), p142 (NcU).
The entire article follows.
"Alexander J. Sheldon, resigning his position as librarian of the Grosvenor Library, Buffalo, N. Y., has received a resolution of thanks from the board of trustees, together with a letter from the prominent citizens of the place, in recognition of his bibliographical attainments and the zeal and courtesy with which he discharged his important duties. Mr. Sheldon is desirous of making journalistic arrangements; meantime he offers his services as bibliographer to library committees to advise in organizing, or to purchase books. He may be addressed at 93 Folsom street, Buffalo, or care of this office."

787 [Periodical Index.] *Publishers' Weekly*, 7 (January 30, 1875), p114, 160 wds (NcU).
The article summarized below is from the *Buffalo Courier*.
Mr. Alexander J. Sheldon, until recently the librarian of the Grosvenor

Library, has been engaged in a work of great usefulness, an index to American and foreign periodicals. The work will supplement Poole's *Index* but will be more comprehensive and will have a better plan; it will be modeled on Todd's *Index Rerum*. The author has just completed an elaborate historical work about Niagara.

788 [New Librarian for Grosvenor Library, Buffalo, N.Y.] *American Bibliopolist*, 7 (February 1875), p2 (ICU).
The entire article follows.
"The Grosvenor Library of Buffalo, N.Y., has been fortunate in securing for its librarian the services of Mr. James W. Ward, formerly of this city. Mr. Ward is a gentleman of much general culture, and under his care we have no doubt the library will become one of the best of its kind in the United States."

— YOUNG MEN'S ASSOCIATION LIBRARY

789 [Buffalo Young Men's Association.] *National Magazine: Devoted to Literature, Art, and Religion*, 3 (August 1853), p188 (InU, NcU).
The entire article follows.
"From the annual report of the *Buffalo Young Men's Association*, we learn that the number of volumes added during the year is, by purchase, 836, and by donation, 82. Total additions, 918. The whole number of volumes drawn from the library during the year has been 14,440. The receipts of the association, exclusive of the building fund, were $6,405 46; its expenses, $5,421 47."

FLATBUSH — DUTCH REFORMED CHURCH
SUNDAY SCHOOL LIBRARY

790 Prince, John D. "The Sunday-School Library; How One School Manages It." *Sunday-School Times*, 17 (July 3, 1875), p428, 2130 wds (NcD).
This is a paper which had been read before a New York State Sunday-School convention.
The system adopted by the Reformed-Dutch Church Sunday-School of Flatbush, Long Island makes possible a correct report of every class and of circulation of books from the library without interrupting the teaching; it is used everywhere except in the Infant Department, which has its own library. Each seat in the school has a number and, for circulation purposes, this number is used by the person sitting in the seat. A board in the library displays these numbers, each with a place for a book "tag." When a book circulates, its tag is placed on this board with the seat number for the person borrowing. When classes are dismissed, they come to the library one by one, where the librarian hands the class representative books for that class. Each representative turns in the roll and distributes the books to other class members.

HOMER — CORTLAND ACADEMY LIBRARY

791 "School Libraries." *American Annals of Education*, 3d ser., 6 (April 1836), p183 (NcU).
The entire article follows.
"A joint Committee of the Trustees of Cortland Academy, and the citizens

of Homer, N.Y., where the said academy is located, have recommended the establishment of a library for the use of the academy, of the value of at least $1,000. Efforts have also been making to procure a cabinet of minerals. We mention these things for the sake of example, though it is truly surprising that an almost universal want of libraries in academies and schools should render such examples so necessary."

ITHACA — CORNELL UNIVERSITY LIBRARY

792 "New Acquisitions." *Cornell Era*, 4 (February 2, 1872), p248, 350 wds (NIC).

In 1872 the University acquired the library of President Sparks and the collection of paleontological casts made by Professor Ward, of Rochester. The Sparks library of Americana consists of 5,000 volumes and 4,000 pamphlets. Books published in the colonial period and in the years just after the Revolution have become expensive and difficult to acquire. The casts were a gift of Ezra Cornell.

793 "The Sparks Library." *American Bibliopolist*, 4 (March 1872), p122 (ICU, IEN, OC).

The entire article follows; it refers to Jared Sparks and Andrew Dickson White.

"Cornell University is favored in having a president far-seeing and energetic, and a patron able and willing to furnish the 'sinews of war' on demand. This must explain the fact that the valuable library of the late President Sparks has become the property of the university aforesaid. When it was announced that the entire collection was to be offered at public sale, a lively competition was anticipated over the rarer treasures of the library. But President White 'interviewed' Mrs. Sparks with results most satisfactory to himself and the college. Henceforth the new library building at Ithaca will contain, as one of its possessions, the 'Sparks Collection' of books and manuscripts. The price paid is understood to be about $12,000."

794 "The University Library." *Cornell Era*, 5 (November 22, 1872), p85–86 (NIC).

The library has just occupied new quarters, the hall being 100 by 50 feet. The twenty-four alcoves provide space for 500,000 volumes. The collection already numbers about 35,000 volumes and a hundred or more periodicals are received. The collection includes the private libraries, or parts of them, of Goldwin Smith, Charles Anthon, Franz Bopp, Jared Sparks, and President White. The arrangement is adapted from the system devised by Brunet. The cases are numbered and the shelves are lettered, beginning with "A" for the bottom shelf. Each case on the gallery has a number exactly 100 larger than the case immediately below it. Several special subject catalogs are being prepared. The librarian is available to help students, especially in the afternoons. The library is open from 8:00 a.m. until dark every weekday.

795 [Slavery Collection at Cornell University.] *Nation*, 19 (August 13, 1874), p103, 160 wds (NcU).

What is probably the most nearly complete collection accessible to the public on the subject of slavery and its abolition in this country is in the Cornell

University Library. The nucleus of this collection was formed by the late Rev. S. J. May. Prof. Willard Fiske, the librarian, contemplates printing a brief catalog of these books, but no funds are available for the work. Contributions for this purpose would doubtless be very acceptable. Also, books and, particularly, files of anti-slavery periodicals, would be thankfully received; there is an especial lack of the literature of the Pennsylvania abolitionists.

796 [May Collection on Slavery at Cornell University.] *Nation*, 19 (November 5, 1874), p300 (NcU).
The entire article follows.
"A private circular, bearing the signatures of Wm. Lloyd Garrison, Wendell Phillips, Samuel May, and Gerrit Smith, calls attention to the 'May Collection' of books and pamphlets relating to slavery and the anti-slavery movement in this country in the library of Cornell University. Though the original collection has received important accessions, and is already the best and largest of its kind in the United States, it still lacks many of the rarer publications, long since out of print. 'It is especially deficient in the anti-slavery publications which emanated from Philadelphia, and it also lacks a file of the *Liberator* and other anti-slavery journals, the early volumes of which are now very difficult to obtain.'"

797 "Library Privileges." *Cornell Review*, 2 (April 1875), p325-27 (DLC, NNCorM).
We are quite sure that most people who daily use the University Library are unaware that its 40,000 volumes have been carefully selected and include many outstanding works. However, we are pleased to note that this year's senior class probably used the library more than did any previous class. The seniors requested direct access to the books, but their request was denied by the librarian, who explained that even the admission of graduate students and faculty into the stacks caused considerable disorder. Perhaps more students could be given direct access if the librarian were given one or two more assistants. As it is, students often cannot obtain needed books because of professors who have checked them out. We think that no one should be allowed to keep a book longer than ten days.

NEW YORK

see also BROOKLYN *and* FLATBUSH

798 "Libraries." *Philadelphia Album and Ladies' Literary Port Folio* [The Album, and Ladies' Weekly Gazette], 1 (September 20, 1826), p6 (ICN).
The entire article, taken from *N. Y. Advocate*, follows.
"There are about thirty circulating libraries in this city, and three thousand young lady customers who devour the contents of every new novel that appears. Of late, however, novel reading has given place to the theatrical mania."

799 "Literary Reading-Room." *Federal American Monthly* [Knickerbocker], 13 (March 1839), p277, 180 wds (NcU).
The annual fee is $5.00 for membership in the reading room at Number 1, Ann Street, one door from Broadway, next door to the office of the *New Yorker*, and opposite the Astor House. British, American and French periodicals and

newspapers are available, along with new books and pamphlets. The membership fee is half that charged at other reading rooms.

800 "Astor Library." *Norton's Literary Gazette and Publishers' Circular*, n.s. 1 (June 15, 1854), p299–300 (NcU).

We take pride in the opening of the Astor Library, which promises to elevate the literary taste and promote the scientific advancement of our whole country. Numerous places provide popular reading materials, but libraries for writers and scholars are usually poor. In New York, the Historical Society has 25,000 volumes; Columbia College, 16,000; the University and the natural history library, 1,500; and the two theological seminaries, the Geographical Society and the Ethnological Society very little. Until the opening of the Astor Library, scholars in the city have been half-starved. Thus, we are pleased with the nature of the new library. If editors, teachers, ministers and authors are well provided for, all will benefit. We are surprised at the criticism of the Trustees for their course. We hope that other cities founding libraries from donations influenced by Mr. Astor's example will be so well managed.

801 [Buxton's Offer of a Circulating Library.] *Norton's Literary Gazette and Publishers' Circular*, n.s. 1 (November 1, 1854), p554 (NcU).

The entire article follows.

"Mr. Charles Buxton (of the firm of Truman, Hanbery & Co.), has offered to furnish a circulating library, containing $25 worth of books, to any number of shopkeepers who are willing to receive and manage the same. Each volume is to be lent on the payment of one half-penny a week, and the proceeds so obtained are to be given to the shopkeepers. Mr. B. will change the books which have been sufficiently used, and bind those which require it, if reasonable care has been employed to preserve them. Valuable books may thus be changed from one location to another, affording a pleasant variety of reading."

802 "City Young Men," *Nation*, 2 (March 15, 1866), p326–27 (NcU).

The article is about hardship and depravity among the poor young men of New York City. After discussing their heavy consumption of alcohol, the Mercantile Library is mentioned, and then, a little later, the YMCA's plans, involving a library, are described. The two sections of the article (on p327) are quoted below.

"How far even the better class of them are gone in this respect may be guessed by anybody who takes the trouble to watch that, to us, very repulsive performance, an election of officers at the Mercantile Library Association."

"The Young Men's Christian Association is making an effort now to do something towards remedying the evil by procuring a large building in some central position, with branches in outlying districts, to contain a free reading-room, a circulating and reference library, and to furnish lectures and other means of instruction, besides advice to the friendless and assistance to the sick or needy."

803 "The Public Library the Complement of the Public School." *Nation*, 2 (June 26, 1866), p810–11 (NcU).

We seldom have the luxury of praising our city government, so with zest we praise Councilman [William B.] White for his proposition looking toward the establishment of a public library. The library is the natural complement of the common schools, aiding young people in self-cultivation. The expense need not be great, and no better antidote could be provided for the bane of bar-rooms, billiard saloons, and gambling houses. If the public library has any power against the dominion of Satan, this city is a satisfactory place to try out that power. The Astor's purpose is too narrow; a library similar to Boston's is needed, where, in the circulating collection, the object is to have books worn out as soon as possible by use — after which they are replaced. If New York had such a library, benefactors like Mr. Joshua Bates of Boston would be attracted to it.

804 [Cobden Club Publications for Libraries.] *Nation*, 17 (August 28, 1873), p145, 150 wds (NcU).

The [New York] *Times* states that the British consul in this city has been requested to ascertain whether there are any libraries or institutions in this area which wish to receive, free, the publications of the Cobden Club. We do not know whether the club is making the same offer in other parts of the United States. The organization, of course, is interested in enlightenment on politico-economic subjects. Contradictory protectionist propaganda is distributed free by a Pennsylvania society (unnamed).

— LIBRARIANS' CONFERENCE, 1853

805 "Librarians' Convention." *Norton's Literary Gazette and Publishers' Circular*, 2 (July 15, 1852), p128, 810 wds (ICN, NcU).

It has been proposed that a librarians' meeting should be convened immediately after the August meeting of the American Association of Science. To insure its success, the librarians of our larger libraries should issue a statement calling for such a meeting. Library management and book selection, arrangement, and conservation are among the topics that should be on the agenda of the meeting. Such a meeting would particularly benefit those librarians who rarely have the opportunity to exchange information with their colleagues. At the very least we hope that an informal preliminary meeting will be held to make plans for a larger gathering next year.

806 "Librarians' Convention." *Norton's Literary Gazette and Publishers' Circular*, 2 (September 15, 1852), p169 (ICN, NcU).

The entire article follows.

"Of course the suggestions thrown out in our paper two months ago, in regard to the propriety of having a *Librarians' Convention* follow after the Scientific meeting, cannot be carried out this year. We have, however, had assurances from Librarians in various parts of the country, that their cooperation shall be mostly freely given for the advancement of this project, whenever the proper time shall come; and we have reason to hope that before long, some measures will be taken for the definite arrangement of such a Convention. Every month shows us its increased importance, an indication of which may be seen in the multitude of Young Men's Libraries which are springing up all over the land."

807 "Librarians' Convention." *Norton's Literary Gazette and Publishers' Circular*, 3 (February 15, 1853), p18, 1000 wds (ICN, NcU).

The proposal that a librarians' convention be held last August was well received, but the convention was not held because the meeting of the Association for the Advancement of Science was cancelled. It is understood, however, that the Association will meet this June in Cleveland, and therefore it again is proposed that a librarians' convention be held immediately afterwards. We trust that action on this proposal soon will be undertaken by its supporters. This meeting would be useful for a number of reasons: librarians from our newer libraries would profit from information about library management; ideas would be exchanged about the preparation of catalogs, book preservation, building new libraries, and so forth; and there would be useful discussions about bibliography, literature, and other topics too numerous to list. We cannot overemphasize the importance of this meeting.

808 "Librarians' Convention." *Norton's Literary Gazette and Publishers' Circular*, 3 (March 15, 1853), p38 (NcU).
The entire article follows.
"We continue to receive assurances from various quarters of the land, of the interest which is felt in this enterprise. It has been suggested by some that the desire which will be generally felt this summer for visiting the Great Exhibition, and the low rates of travel to this city, will make New York the most fitting place for this meeting. In that case, a later date than formerly thought of would probably be better — namely, about the beginning of September — when the attractions of the Exhibition would be the greatest; the Astor Library in full operation, and the salubrity of the city unquestioned.
"A full expression of opinion on this and other matters connected therewith, is very desirable; and we hope that a definite announcement may soon be made of both the time and the place of meeting."

809 "Librarians' Convention." *Norton's Literary Gazette and Publishers' Circular*, 3 (April 15, 1853), p62 (ICN, NcU).
The entire article follows.
"The desire for a Librarians' Convention is certainly spreading. Among other things pertaining thereunto, which have reached us since our last, is a letter from a prominent Librarian of Philadelphia, urging New York for the place, instead of Cleveland, and recommending the month of October for the time. That month, however, is, we think, more likely to be a busy time with College Librarians than September. Letters from Cincinnati and St. Louis assure us of the cooperation of Librarians at the West. We hope to receive still more of such letters from other Librarians, both far and near."

810 "Topics for Discussion at the Librarians' Convention." *Norton's Literary Gazette and Publishers' Circular*, 3 (June 15, 1853), p98 (NcU).
Each person attending the conference should be prepared to contribute. Every librarian or superintendent, present or not, should provide a succinct account of his library through January 1, 1853. Questions and papers on general subjects should be prepared. Each person coming should be prepared to discuss one of the subjects in the synopsis of library economy which follows. One topic is the library: its character; within this topic, reference, circulating, general and special libraries will be covered. The library building is a second topic; it will concern architectural taste, adaptations for each individual library, general topics, special features peculiar to reference and circulating libraries, reading rooms, and other collections like museums and picture galleries. Library management is the third topic; it will include the librarian, the arrangement of books, catalogues, lending regulations, and other miscellaneous items.

811 [Librarians' Convention.] *National Magazine: Devoted to Literature, Art, and Religion*, 3 (August 1853), p187 (InU, NcU).
The entire article follows.
"A *convention* is to be held in this city in September, composed of librarians and others interested in bibliography. It is proposed to consider the best means of advancing the prosperity and usefulness of public libraries, and for the suggestion and discussion of topics of importance to book collectors and readers. The convention will be attended by the librarians of prominent institutions in this and other cities."

812 [The Librarians' Convention Commences its Sessions Today.] *Norton's Literary Gazette and Publishers' Circular*, 3 (September 15, 1853), p150, 160 wds (N).
The Librarians' Convention, a call for which was made last May, commences its sessions today at the smaller chapel of New York University, fronting on Washington Square. We will report its meetings in full, next month. Librarians and others living in New York City have been promoting the objects of the convention and are providing for the pleasure of those who attend. We are confident of a pleasant and profitable conference, the first, we hope, of a series which will greatly enhance the interests of libraries from one end of our land to the other.

813 "The Libraries of New York City." *Norton's Literary Gazette and Publishers' Circular*, 3 (September 15, 1853), p149-50 (N).
The gathering of librarians at the convention now in session in the city furnishes us with the opportunity to describe the libraries of New York City. (Statements about individual libraries follow, giving, usually, location, size, history, and the name of the librarian. The foremost library, the Astor, is described first, followed by the Society Library, the Mercantile Library, the Apprentices' Library, the library of the Mechanics' Institute, and the Printers' Library. Academic libraries that are described are those at Columbia College, the Union Theological Seminary, the General Theological Seminary, and the Free Academy. Other libraries described are those of the New York Law Institute, the New York Hospital, some seminaries for young ladies, and some libraries of religious organizations. A few private libraries and commercial circulating libraries are briefly mentioned.)

814 Smith, Lloyd, Charles Folsom, and Charles C. Jewett. "Distribution of Public Documents." *Norton's Literary Gazette and Publishers' Circular*, 3 (December 15, 1853), p215, 450 wds (NcU).
The Convention of Librarians of the United States, which assembled in New York City on September 15, 1853, appointed the three authors as a committee to draw up the following petition, which is now ready for signatures. Secretaries of literary institutions and others are urged to send their names to committee members. A summary of the petition follows.
Documents should be accessible to all citizens; Congress is asked to order that they be distributed annually to the principal libraries of the country where they will be accessible, yet preserved for future generations. At least three hundred copies of each document should be printed for distribution. The Smithsonian Institution is the agency most suitable to distribute them; it should retain some copies for libraries that are not yet formed.

815 "Useful Library Furniture." *Norton's Literary Gazette and Publishers' Circular*, n.s. 1 (June 1, 1854), p271–72 (NcU).

At the Librarians' Convention last fall, Mr. Charles Folsom of the Boston Athenaeum displayed some of his inventions which have been useful in libraries. Among them are a table for displaying large works containing prints and a book clasp designed to hold bound newspaper volumes together so that they may be shelved standing up alongside folios.

— AMERICAN AND FOREIGN CHRISTIAN UNION LIBRARY

816 "Our Library." *Christian World* [American and Foreign Christian Union], 6 (November 1855), p541, 350 wds (NcU).

We at the office of the American and Foreign Christian Union have long felt the need of a complete library of the literature of Romanism and the Reformation. Such a collection is needed for reference in our duties and to answer inquiries from elsewhere. There should be a special repository of this kind in New York, accessible to all. We have a small collection already. Through the liberality of a zealous friend, the Board of Directors have made a small appropriation for this purpose. We have purchased over 100 volumes from the library of a priest who has recently thrown off his popish trammels. We solicit donations to replenish this armory of material to prosecute the war against error. We also solicit books in any language relative to the history, doctrines, practices, worship and controversies of Rome — books on either side of the question.

— AMERICAN INSTITUTE LIBRARY

817 "The American Institute." *American Agriculturalist*, 1 (February 1843), p327, 350 wds (InU, NcU).

A reading room is being considered by the American Institute. Periodicals dealing with agriculture, science and art would be provided. Members would pay an annual fee but strangers could use the rooms free of charge. Flooring would be laid from gallery to gallery at the west end of the first floor of the Repository. This would provide 1,600 square feet. The library would adjoin. It is believed that this will be the first reading room in America devoted to agricultural reading. It is expected that of the 400,000 people who annually visit New York, many will be interested in agriculture and will use the reading room.

818 [Library of the American Institute of New York.] *Norton's Literary Gazette and Publishers' Circular*, n.s. 1 (April 15, 1854), p196 (NcU).

The entire article follows.

"The American Institute of the city of New York has just issued a circular soliciting donations of public documents. Its library now comprises about seven thousand volumes, including many rare publications. The rooms of this Association are central and commodious, and the want of such works is seriously felt, not only by the members, but by the public generally, who come there expecting to find complete collections. At the January meeting of this Society, a committee of exchange was appointed to cooperate with kindred institutions for a full interchange of works of merit. Similar committees have recently been appointed by the New York Mercantile Library Association and the Wisconsin Historical Society. We know not but the results of such exchanges may be as valuable in their way as those conducted on a more extended scale by Mr. Vattemare."

— APPRENTICES' LIBRARY

819 [Cutter, Charles A. J. Schwartz' Theory of Library Catalogues.] *Nation*, 20 (March 4, 1875), p151, 760 wds (NcU).

Cutter is identified as the author of this article in Daniel C. Haskell's *The Nation, Volumes 1-105, New York, 1865-1917, Indexes of Titles and Contributors*, 1953, v. 2, p116.

Mr. J. Schwartz, Jr. of the New York Apprentices' Library, has proposed a novel and important plan for a library catalog. Professor Jewett provided rules for an author catalog, but showed little understanding of the principles of subject catalogs. Professor Abbot's main attention was on the subject catalog. Others prepared dictionary catalogs, using title entries. Mr. Schwartz devised a catalog which combines subjects (classes), titles and authors. He also developed a system for arranging books by combining the topical, numerical and alphabetical methods. Although Mr. Schwartz's system is not entirely new he has shown original insight and has brought to the attention of others the possibility of an improved library catalog.

— ASTOR LIBRARY

820 "Public Library." *Jeffersonian*, 1 (August 4, 1838), p195 (IEN, NcU).

The entire article follows.

"The Boston Daily Advertiser a few days since, stated that a distinguished citizen of New York had made a splendid donation to the city, for the purpose of establishing a public library. The statement made in the Advertiser being somewhat indefinite, that paper of Thursday has the following paragraph on the subject;

" 'Mr. John Jacob Astor, with an enlightened and liberal spirit, which does him immortal honor, has made to the corporation of the city of New York, a donation amounting to $350,000, for the establishment of a Public Library, including a lot of land, most eligibly situated, for the erection of a building for the accommodation of the institution. We could state some other particulars, but we deem it proper to wait until they should reach us from another source.' "

821 "Astor Library." *Harbinger, Devoted to Social and Political Progress*, 8 (February 3, 1849), p110, 1300 wds (NcU).

The article summarized below was taken from *Tradesman's Journal*.

The Astor Library will be built; $160,000 is set aside for its future maintenance. Thus, the library will avoid the fate of the 300,000 volume Zaluski Library which was broken up for lack of funds. All of New York's publishers should send free copies of publications to the Astor Library. There are only 182 libraries in the country [sic]; they contain 1,294,000 volumes. (Eleven large European libraries are named; the number of printed volumes for each is given and the number of manuscripts is given for some. Reference is also made to the Alexandrian Library in Egypt, the libraries of ancient Rome, and the library at Constantinople.) Unlike Europe, America has no free libraries.

822 Cogswell, J.G. "The Astor Library." *Literary World*, N.Y., 4 (April 7, 1849), 315-16 (IEN, NcU).

Cogswell's letter to the editors is summarized below.

Messrs. Editors — If you think that it would be of interest to your readers, I would be glad occasionally to provide lists of some of the more important books purchased for the Astor Library. My reasons for doing so are to keep readers informed about the library and to elicit from scholars their suggestions about ways in which the collection could be improved. (A list of forty recently purchased books about the fine arts follows the article.)

823 Cogswell, J. G. "Astor Library—No. II." *Literary World*, N.Y., 4 (April 14, 1849), p337–38 (IEN, NcU).
Cogswell's letter to the editors is summarized below.
Messrs. Editors—As building of the Astor Library soon will begin, it seems appropriate to present the following list of the principal architectural works collected for it. In the next issue of *Literary World* I shall give an account of the library's history. Respectfully yours, J. G. C. (The list of books follows.)

824 Cogswell, J. G. "The Astor Library—No. III." *Literary World*, N.Y., 4 (April 28, 1849), p375–76 (IEN, NcU).
Cogswell's letter to the editors is summarized below.
Messrs. Editors—You kindly permitted me to place a brief essay about the history of the Astor Library in your columns, and in the belief that the public would be interested in the legal foundations of the library I must ask you to publish the codicil to Mr. Astor's will. 'The transcripts of the codicil, dated August 22, 1839, and the act to incorporate the trustees of the library, enacted January 18, 1849, follow this letter.)

825 "The Astor Library in New York." *Literary World*, N.Y., 5 (September 22, 1849), p251, 810 wds (NcU).
The article summarized below is reprinted from the *Journal of Commerce*.
Demolition work has begun in Lafayette Place for the construction of the Astor Library building. Alex Saelizer is the architect. The building is expected to cost $75,000. The library collection will be located on the second floor. The first floor will contain reading and lecture rooms. The distinctive feature of the building is its extensive use of iron to provide light-weight strength. Cogswell has already collected 20,000 volumes which are housed at 32 Bond Street. These books may be used by the public.

826 "Astor Library." *New York Chronicle*, 1 (November 1849), p345, 210 wds (NjR).
Work on the preparations for a building for the Astor Library has begun. The chosen site is on Lafayette Place, and the building will be in the Byzantine style. The building will be 120 feet long, 65 feet wide and will rise 67 feet above the sidewalk. The amount authorized for the building is $75,000, with an additional $8,000 for furnishings. The architect is Alexander Saelizer of Berlin. The appropriation for both the building and the library is $400,000. J. G. Cogswell has already collected about 20,000 volumes in Europe.

827 [The Astor Library.] *Literary World*, N.Y., 8 (March 1, 1851), p172, 300 wds (NcU).
Part of the article summarized here was taken from the *New York Tribune*.
The annual report of the Astor Library notes that the library building should be completed by the summer of 1852. The building will have 65 feet of frontage, extending to 120 feet in depth. The collection already contains 25,027 volumes. Book expenditures were $8,273.42 in the previous year. Cogswell had "an anticipatory catalogue" printed listing 50,000 volumes. He is soon to go on a

New York (Astor)

second buying trip to Europe and this catalog will help in making selections and avoiding duplication. The catalog was prepared at Cogswell's expense.

828 [Astor Library to Open Next September.] *North American Miscellany and Dollar Magazine*, 4 (1852), p107 (NcU).
The entire article follows.
"It is expected that the Astor Library will be opened to the public next September. It now comprises about 60,000 volumes: Dr. Cogswell having added, during his late visit to Europe, some 28,000 volumes, at a cost of about $30,000. The unexpended portion of the fund appropriated for the purchase of books will suffice to increase the number of volumes in the library to 100,000."

829 "The Astor Library—Return of Mr. Cogswell." *Norton's Literary Gazette and Publishers' Circular*, 2 (January 15, 1852), p4 (ICN, NcU).
The entire article follows.
"MR. JOSEPH G. COGSWELL, the distinguished Librarian of the Astor Library, has just returned from Europe, where he made purchases for that Institution to the amount of over twenty thousand volumes. They have been selected for purposes of general reference, and with the intention of having the various departments of literature and science equally well furnished with standard works. It will be remembered that among the earlier purchases for this Library, were many in Bibliography, and the information thus held at command cannot have failed to be of important service in the recent selections. Most of the books lately bought have already arrived in New York. But few cases, however, can at present be opened for the want of room in which to display them.
"We learn that the new Library building in Lafayette Place, will be completed in the spring, but will not be dry enough for receiving the books before the following autumn."

830 "Dr. Cogswell—Astor Library Report—One Hundred Thousand Volumes." *Literary World*, N.Y., 10 (February 28, 1852), p154-55 (NcU).
Cogswell's report on the Astor Library indicates that 60,000 volumes of a 100,000 volume goal for the beginning collection have been acquired. Cogswell notes that the library is purchasing expensive works in many fields in order to provide needed books not available in other libraries in the city. Cogswell asked to be allowed to provide a bibliographical collection at his own expense, and more than 2000 volumes have been acquired in this collection.

831 "Astor Library." *Norton's Literary Gazette and Publishers' Circular*, 2 (March 15, 1852), p45, 640 wds (ICN, NcU).
The article includes a lengthy quotation from the report by Cogswell which it mentions. Both the article and the quotation are summarized below.
The report of the Trustees of the Astor Library recently was submitted to the New York State Legislature. It is only two pages long; appended to it is Dr. Joseph Cogswell's report listing his purchases abroad, donors for 1851, and the financial statement. He stated that last year about $30,000 was spent on over 25,000 books and that the collection now has about 60,000 volumes. Concerning Dr. Cogswell's selections, we quote from his report: "I have attempted to give equal attention to all departments of learning, but the nature of the individual disciplines has resulted in greater expenditures in some areas than in others, especially civil engineering, architecture and the arts. The library has repeatedly invited suggestions for purchases from scholars."

U.S. — New York

832 "Astor Library of New York." *Norton's Literary Gazette and Publishers' Circular*, 2 (March 15, 1852), p43, 3000 wds (ICN, NcU).

The Astor Library, endowed by John Jacob Astor, was incorporated in 1849, one year after his death. The Trustees and Dr. Joseph G. Cogswell, Director, are to be commended for their efficient management of the library and for faithfully carrying out Mr. Astor's wishes. We quote for our readers the part of Astor's will pertaining to the library. Work on the new library building in Lafayette Place soon will be completed. A detailed description of the building, i.e., its architecture, construction, floorplans, and so forth, was published in the *Journal of Commerce*, and that description is reprinted for our readers. (A picture of the exterior of the building accompanies the *Norton's* article.)

833 "The Astor Library." *Norton's Literary Gazette and Publishers' Circular*, 2 (September 15, 1852), p169, 320 wds (ICN, NcU).

The building for the Astor Library will not be finished until next spring. However, this delay could prove to be beneficial, for it is very important that the books in the various departments be properly arranged, a task requiring much time and labor. The public probably will be surprised by the size and the richness of the various subject collections — especially the bibliography collection, selected by Dr. Cogswell.

834 "Astor Library." *Norton's Literary Gazette and Publishers' Circular*, 3 (February 15, 1853), p18, 480 wds (ICN, NcU).

The article, summarized below, is a quotation from the Astor Library's annual report as printed in the *Daily News*.

Work on the building at Lafayette Place was completed during the year, but due to the walls' dampness it was deemed advisable not to move the books into the building until this April. The library should be open by May 1st. To date, $70,000 has been spent on the lot and the building while $75,364 has been spent on books, which now number between 60,000–65,000 volumes. Dr. Cogswell now is in Europe on a buying trip and is authorized to spend $25,000. By opening day the library should have about 80,000 volumes. Mr. Astor's will prescribes that $120,000 is to be spent for books initially. Of the $400,000 bequeathed by Mr. Astor, $333,333 has been received, and the final installment is forthcoming. The library's assets total $452,367.

835 "Astor Library." *Norton's Literary Gazette and Publishers' Circular*, 3 (April 15, 1853), p64, 480 wds (ICN, NcU).

While we are anxious to see the Astor Library open, we are pleased that the Trustees and the Librarian are willing to take the time to make certain that the library will be convenient for its users and to make judicious book selections. The public can rest assured that the library is in competent hands. The report (summarized below) appeared in the *New York Daily Times:*

We have learned that the library will not open until September or October because of construction delays. Dr. Cogswell's recent purchases have not even arrived from Europe, and his earlier purchases still are in their shipping crates. There has been considerable speculation about the library's probable regulations, but our readers can feel confident that no unreasonable regulations will be adopted and that women will have equal access to the library.

836 "Astor Library." *Town and Country*, N.Y. [Home Journal, N.Y.], 8 (April 16, 1853), p2, 800 wds (NN).

The building in Lafayette Place is receiving the decorator's finishing touches; probably it can be opened by the first of September. We looked into the edifice the other day and were struck with its singular elegance and the convenience of its principal hall. The ground floor is divided into small rooms for various purposes; broad marble steps lead up to the center of the hall which occupies the rest of the building. Most of the ceiling is glass, and the prevailing color is white, making the room brilliant. Four graceful winding stairs lead up to a gallery. However the building is not large enough. We estimate that it will hold 100,000 volumes, the size of the intended opening collection; in a few years an enlargement will be needed. The library will benefit the entire country because the knowledge it contains will spread through lectures, books and articles.

837 "The Astor Library." *Town and Country* [Home Journal], N.Y., 8 (August 20, 1853), p2, 300 wds (NN).

We ventured to peep into the magnificent rooms of this institution the other day and were gratified to find that more than half of the work of arranging the books is completed. Dr. Cogswell cannot name a day for opening because he is determined to finish his task before readers are admitted. However, the day is not far off and we are confident that the studious public will be grateful to the librarian for the excellence of the library. In the number of its volumes the Astor stands at the top of the list of American libraries. Unlike libraries that accumulate gradually, it has no dead weight; in this respect it is unequalled.

838 Cogswell, Joseph G. "The Astor Library." *Town and Country* [Home Journal], N.Y., whole no. 413 (January 7, 1854), p1, 6900 wds (NN).

John Jacob Astor generously gave $400,000; it is now seen that this is not enough to provide what is needed. Most of the money allotted to book purchases has now been spent. The building was begun more than four years ago. (Its location is described and its appearance, outside and inside.) Some have mistakenly compared it with first class libraries of Europe; the British Museum is far larger and costs in one year more than the entire cost of the Astor. The Brunet classification system is used in the Astor. (The nature of the collection in each of its main classes is described in some detail.) The library will open on January 9 so anyone may come and see how much truth there is in this description of the library.

839 "The Astor Library." *Norton's Literary Gazette and Publishers' Circular*, n.s. 1 (January 15, 1854), p34, 530 wds (NcU).

The article is based on part of an article that appeared in *The Home Journal* (later, *Town and Country*) on January 7, 1854 *(see 838)*.

The rooms of the Astor Library were opened for visitors on January 9. The library itself will open in February. The building was completed less than six months ago. Since then, the nearly 80,000 volumes have been classified, cataloged and arranged on the shelves. Mr. Joseph G. Cogswell is responsible for accomplishing this undertaking so quickly. The principal portion of the library is contained in a room 100 feet long, 64 feet wide and 50 feet high, with a capacity of 100,000 volumes. There are seven open-ended alcoves such that for every 51 wall shelves, there are 72 in the alcoves. There are two stories, similarly arranged. The alcove sectors are separated from the open area by a light iron railing. This area contains reading tables. Besides the main hall there are two smaller rooms devoted to European and American public documents.

840 Cogswell, Joseph G. "The Astor Library." *Norton's Literary Gazette and Publishers' Circular*, n.s. 1 (February 1, 1854), p58–60 (NcU).

We reprint part of a letter from Dr. Cogswell showing what has been done in the Astor Library. Brunet's system of classification has been used. Each division of the library is described with frequent notes of specific holdings, total numbers of books, and problems encountered in selection. The collections of mathematics, languages, history and bibliography are described as especially strong, with the natural sciences rich, also. An alphabetical catalog is now complete, with every title on a separate slip. A copy will be prepared for the use of readers. Classified catalogs of the department will also be prepared. The library is to be open Monday through Saturday from 10 A.M. to 5 P.M. Books must be requested in writing and used in the building only. No one may enter the alcoves or remove a book from its place without supervision by an officer of the library.

841 "Astor Library." *National Magazine: Devoted to Literature, Art, and Religion*, 4 (March 1854), p286–87 (InU, NcU).

The Astor Library has recently been opened for public use. The building and its site cost $100,000 or one-fourth of the total bequest. About 80,000 volumes are in the library, and the books are arranged into departments. Apparently the library is chiefly intended to serve professional men and students of literature, although provisions have been made to accommodate women. The library's books have been selected with the aim of supplying the deficiencies of other libraries in the city. A fund will provide two or three thousand dollars annually for the increase of the library.

842 "The Astor Library and Its Founder." *Emerson's Magazine and Putnam's Monthly* [United States Magazine], 2 (October 1855), p137–45 (InU, NcU).

John Jacob Astor was born in Waldorf, Baden in 1763 and died in New York in 1848. He acquired a vast fortune, largely in the fur trade. As a service to New York and in order to advance useful knowledge, he left $400,000 for the creation of the library. Eleven trustees were to administer the grant. J. G. Cogswell, the first superintendent, has acquired most of the 80,000 volumes currently available during several trips to Europe. The library is one of reference. The books do not circulate, but may be used by anyone over sixteen. The library building, designed by A. Saelizer, was completed in July 1853, opened for inspection in January 1854, and for use the following month. In the nineteen months of operation 33,000 people have requested more than 100,000 volumes. The only catalog of the library is the catalog of prospective acquisitions, prepared by Cogswell, and printed in 1850. (The article contains illustrations of the exterior and interior of the building and two portraits of Astor.)

843 "The Astor Library." *National Magazine: Devoted to Literature, Art, and Religion*, 7 (December 1855), p568, 210 wds (NcU).

William B. Astor has donated to the Astor Library 85 square feet of land adjacent to the library building. This more than doubles the area of the library's site. Astor has also, on two other occasions, given the library donations; one of a large sum for the building expenses beyond those provided by the original bequest; another of $2,500 for a special department of practical and mechanical science. (Several recently acquired works are listed.)

New York (Astor)

844 "Astor Library, in New York." *American Journal of Education* (Barnard), 1 (May 1856), p648, 250 wds (NcU).

Excerpts from the seventh annual report of the trustees of the Astor Library are reprinted in the article summarized below.

Since the library's founding, $120,331 has been spent for books and binding; approximately 90,000 volumes now are in the collection; and the total cost of the present building, including site, is $120,352. In just two years, due to the high rate of acquisitions, the library has nearly reached its maximum storage capacity. The problem, however, has been alleviated by the generosity of William B. Astor, who donated to the library three lots adjacent to the library building. These lots will be used for future expansion. The worthy example of the father is followed by his son.

845 Boswell, James I. "In the Astor Library." *Ladies' Repository: a Monthly Periodical, Devoted to Literature, Art, and Religion*, 24 (April 1864), p193-95 (InU, NcU).

Few New Yorkers know about the Astor Library because they are more concerned with commerce than with reading. The newspaper is all the businessman has time to read. Scholars rightly prefer old libraries filled with old editions, whereas the Astor is a new library containing newer annotated editions. However, praise is due to Mr. Astor for providing this library.

846 Norton, Frank H. "The Astor Library." *American Publisher and Bookseller*, 2 (April 1869), p5, 320 wds (DLC).

The article summarizes part of an article in *Galaxy*, 7 (April 1869), p527-37 *(see 847)*.

847 Norton, Frank H. "The Astor Library." *Galaxy*, 7 (April 1869), p527-37 (ICN, NcU).

Part of the article summarized below is reprinted in *American Publisher and Bookseller*, 2 (April 1869), p5 *(see 846)*.

As early as 1839 John Jacob Astor intended to found a public library for New York City; he died in 1848 and bequeathed $400,000 for that purpose. The Astor Library opened its doors in January 1854 with a collection of about 80,000 volumes. When the library soon needed more room, Astor's eldest son, William, paid for the construction of a new building on a lot adjacent to the library. The library addition opened in September 1859. Subsequent donations brought the Astor family's total contribution to $700,000. The library now has more than 137,000 volumes. A tour of the alcoves reveals an order based on creation itself, beginning with books on geology and progressing through biology and botany to the records of man's endeavors. Many rare and valuable books are included in the collection. Examination of circulation statistics for 1867 shows that the library's users were two-thirds idlers and one-third workers.

848 Norton, Frank H. "Ten Years in a Public Library." *Galaxy*, 8 (October 1869), p528-37 (ICN, NcU).

When I joined the staff of the Astor Library in 1855, Dr. Cogswell was its director. It seems to me that the library then was visited by more prominent men than now is the case. Washington Irving once requested Mr. Fiske, one of my colleagues, and me to witness his signing of his will. Other famous visitors included George Catlin, Richard Cobden, William Thackeray, Edward Everett, the Prince of Wales, Prince Napoleon, Mr. Barnum, and four ex-Presidents.

Besides the well-known visitors, there were numerous eccentrics who came to the library regularly. Such a library as the Astor is a good place to study human nature. The library's collection is notable for its purity and lack of "facetiae."

849 Hall, A. Oakey. [Hours of Opening of the Astor Library.] *American Bibliopolist*, 1 (December 1869), p358–59 (ICU, OC).
The entire article follows.
"Mayor Hall, in a recent speech, is reported to have said, with more force than flattery: 'I stand here tonight as an *ex-officio* trustee of the Astor Library. I intend to come down upon those trustees some day like a wolf on the fold. I intend to surprise the old fogies of that establishment by the renewal of a resolution to open that library at Christian hours in the evening. I don't hope to succeed at first, but I intend to peg away at it, for the idea that the City of New York should have its greatest library closed at dusk is one that I don't intend to submit to.'"

850 "The Astor Library." *American Bibliopolist*, 4 (January 1872), p17–18 (NcD, ICU).
The article summarized below was reprinted from the *New York Evening Post*.
The Astor Library may be depriving New York of the library it really needs. It is now short of funds, and its 150,000 volumes (as of 1870), are insufficient. (The populations and library holdings of ten European cities are listed for comparison.) The Boston Public Library is also larger. The Astor, maintained solely by the Astor family, has little opportunity to expand, while the British Museum has developed through bequests from several sources (some of which are discussed.) In New York, the Lenox Library occupies a different building instead of being part of the Astor collection. Great libraries elsewhere are not so divided. Only when several specialists collect for one library does it become what it should be. We ought to have a first-rate library, and if Mr. Astor will permit others to share in creating it, we shall some day have one.

851 "A Noble Institution Not Overpraised." *New Outlook* [Christian Union], 8 (October 8, 1873), p290–91 (NcU).
The article is summarized and approved in an article in *Appletons' Journal*, 10 (November 8, 1873), p602–03 *(see 852)*.
The Astor Library has now served New York for nearly twenty years. When John Jacob Astor founded the institution, he knew that other libraries would provide entertaining works and circulate light materials; his purpose was to serve the industrious scholar. The directors of the library have maintained not only the letter but the spirit of this purpose. Critics who complain about the nature of the collection, comparing it unfavorably with less scholarly libraries, are under no compulsion to use the facilities; as for the size, recall that the institution is young and growing. The facilities and services are designed for a specific clientele, and all who enter for purposes of serious research are treated well. Circulation figures for 1872 indicate that more than 26,000 readers were served in that year.

852 [The Astor Library.] *Appletons' Journal: a Magazine of General Literature*, 10 (November 8, 1873), p602–03 (NcU).
The article quotes, summarizes and briefly indicates approval of an article which appeared in *New Outlook* [Christian Union], 8 (October 8, 1873), p290–91 *(see 851)*.

The Astor Library has been criticized unfairly by people who think it should serve a purpose other than that intended by its founder. In a defense recently published in the *Christian Union*, it is noted that John Jacob Astor established the library as a place for serious study rather than a popular reading room. We feel that it fulfills this goal admirably though the library needs the funds to purchase more new books.

853 [Publication of the Letters of Joseph Green Cogswell.] *Publishers' Weekly*, 5 (March 14, 1874), p273 (NcU).
The entire article follows.
"A selection from the letters of the late Joseph Green Cogswell, first librarian of the Astor Library, forming a narrative of his life, has been prepared by a lady to whom a large mass of his correspondence was intrusted for this purpose. It is proposed to print two hundred copies of this, for private circulation, by subscription, in a handsome quarto volume, from the Riverside Press, Cambridge, at the price, and of the full value of $5.00. The number of copies being so restricted and the contents being in the nature of an autobiographic memorial of one so respected and beloved, this volume will have an assured appreciation. Subscriptions may be addressed to George S. Hillard, 62 Pinckney street, Boston."

854 [The Astor Library.] *Nation*, 18 (June 18, 1874), p394 (NcU).
The entire article follows.
"The annual report of the trustees of the Astor Library shows the whole number of books and pamphlets to have been on the 1st of January 147,640. The increase during 1873 was but 3,462 volumes, of which nearly half (1,607) were gifts, and of these again more than half (923) from one donor, Mr. Wm. B. Astor. While the resources of the library are thus manifestly insufficient, it is gratifying to learn from the report that the number of readers increases in a higher ratio than the library itself (ten per cent. in the one case; two and a-half in the other)."

855 "J. G. Cogswell." *American Bibliopolist*, 6 (September–October 1874), p120, 250 wds (NcD).
The article summarized below was reprinted from *The Athenaeum*.
Anna Eliot Ticknor has had privately printed "A Life of Joseph Green Cogswell, as Sketched in His Letters." Cogswell was known to European booksellers and librarians as the first librarian of the Astor Library in New York, which some feel owes its existence to him. Cogswell lived with Astor for many years and persuaded him to provide for the library in his will. Cogswell undertook as many as seven book-buying voyages to Europe where he made many friends. An intimate friend of Washington Irving, Mr. Brevoort and other distinguished Americans, he was well liked in social circles as a kind, benevolent man as well as a scholar. He died in November of 1871 at age 85.

856 [Astor Library.] *American Bibliopolist*, 7 (June 1875), p136, 180 wds (NcD).
The Astor Library in New York now contains 150,000 volumes; it had only 20,000 in 1850. During 1874 2,666 volumes were added, of which about three-fourths were donated. This may seem a small number but no attempt is made to obtain everything published. In no sense is the Astor a circulating library, so light and ephemeral works are not purchased. In 1874, 34,854 readers used

127,579 books. These figures do not include visitors admitted to the alcoves. The privileges granted to these visitors are almost unique to the Astor Library. Almost every responsible person bringing an introduction to the superintendent, or presenting other suitable guarantees, is allowed access to the shelves. Of the 6,838 alcove readers in 1874, two-sevenths were in the department of patents.

857 [The Astor Library.] *Nation,* 21 (July 8, 1875), p27 (NcU).
The entire article follows.
"Whatever improvements one could wish in the administration of the Astor Library, there is no denying its great public usefulness; the increased attendance in its reading-rooms has been very noticeable of late years. The Twenty-sixth Annual Report of the trustees shows an addition of 2,666 books, of which 1,938 were by donation — upwards of 700 volumes coming from the Astor family alone. The total number of volumes is now 150,306, and 127,579 were delivered to readers, who in 1874 numbered 34,854, against 29,438 in 1875. Twenty-five years ago there were only 20,000 volumes in the library. Fifteen years ago, only 59,516 volumes were consulted. More than two-sevenths of the alcove readers frequented the department of patents. The endowment of the library is now $775,336, against the $400,000 of John Jacob Astor's will."

858 "The Astor Librarianship." *American Bibliopolist,* 7 (December 1875), p266–67 (NcD).
The article summarized below is reprinted from the *New York World* of February 18, 1876, p4, column 6. This issue of the *American Bibliopolist* was apparently printed in 1876, but it is included in this bibliography because it is dated before 1876.
The death of Dr. Straznicki leaves the Astor Library in search of a new librarian, upon whose gifts and devotion the prosperity of a great library depends. A great librarian must perceive the relation of books to human thought and to the tendencies and needs of the human society in which he lives. He must combine many different and contrasting qualities. The trustees of the Astor Library would do well to go outside the ranks of professed librarians to select Carson Brevoort, as the new librarian; he is an accomplished scholar who is now a member of their board. If New York is to take its place among world capitals, it will happen only when positions like the direction of its chief public library are recognized as objects worthy of the ambition of its best and ablest citizens.

— BLOOMINGDALE ASYLUM FOR THE INSANE — LIBRARY

859 "Library for the Insane." *Norton's Literary Gazette and Publishers' Circular,* 2 (October 15, 1852), p188 (ICN, NcU).
The entire article follows.
"The Appletons have given two hundred volumes to the Bloomingdale Asylum for the Insane. Dewitt and Davenport, Putnam and Sears are also mentioned in the *Times,* as contributors to the same object."

— COLUMBIA UNIVERSITY LIBRARY

860 "The Library of Columbia College." *University Quarterly: Conducted by an Association of Collegiate and Professional Students, in the United States and Europe,* 3 (January 1861), p41–61 (InU, OO).

New York (City)

The library of Columbia College has more than 13,000 volumes and 2,500 unbound pamphlets; 850 volumes were recently removed to the Law School Library. Columbia's is a scholastic library, and is deficient in modern and current works of entertainment. Selectivity rather than volume makes for a good collection. The Columbia library attempts to serve only the college, not the whole city of New York. (The library building is described. The libraries of the college are discussed, as are prominent donors. Holdings of the library in various subjects are described. Authors, editions, and specific titles are frequently cited.) The collection about Greece and Rome is particularly rich.

861 Hooper, William B. "Columbia College." *Appletons' Journal: a Magazine of General Literature*, 5 (May 20, 1871), p583–86 (NcU).
The parts about the college library (p583 and 586) are summarized below.
At the time of the Revolution most of the books disappeared but many years later some seven hundred volumes were found in a room at St. Paul's Chapel. At the time of the dispersion, the collection included many valuable works because governors of the province had made gifts, as had Dr. Bristowe and the Earl of Bute; a copy of each of the books issued by the Oxford University Press helped to make a fine and extensive library. At present, the library is over the chapel; the collection is not very large but it contains rare and valuable works. Portraits of the college presidents and some of the more distinguished professors hang on the walls.

— COOPER UNION LIBRARY

862 "The Cooper Union." *Nation*, 2 (June 5, 1866), p714–15 (NcU).
The part about the library at the Cooper Union (240 wds) is summarized below.
If a visitor is in no hurry to get to the exhibition rooms, he might stop by the library. The reading-room is not very well lined with books, but the magazine and newspaper stands are exceedingly well supplied. The spacious room is free to all the city and, apparently, to all papers. (The names of a variety of magazines and papers are given.) Papers in foreign languages are available. In its first year, the room was visited by 200,000 people; in its seventh year, the number probably exceeds 250,000. Everyone is welcome who will take off his hat and behave with propriety; the room is meant for poor men's use and pleasure.

863 [Cooper Union, N.Y., Library.] *Publishers' Weekly* [Publishers' and Stationers' Weekly Trade Circular], 2 (October 24, 1872), p416 (NcU).
The entire article follows.
"The Library of the Cooper Union, N.Y., was opened on Sunday, Oct. 13, from two till nine P.M. Over seven hundred people availed themselves of the privilege, and the librarian reports order and decorum among this large number."

864 [Gift to the Cooper Union Library.] *Publishers' Weekly*, 5 (March 14, 1874), p273 (NcU).
The entire article follows; it refers to the Empress Augusta, wife of William I.
"The Empress of Germany has sent to the reading-room of the Cooper Union, through Mr. Bancroft, forty photographs, exhibiting the various instru-

ments, carriages, and apparatus used by the Sanitary Commission of Prussia in the Franco-Prussian war. These are now on exhibition."

— EQUITABLE LIFE ASSURANCE BUILDING

865 [Plan for a law library in the Equitable Building, New York.] *Albany Law Journal*, 11 (January 30, 1875), p84, 160 wds (NcU).

The prominent lawyers who will have offices in the Equitable Building, New York, have suggested to the society the propriety of setting aside a large room to be a library for the exclusive use of the tenants. Each lawyer would be invited to lend the library such books as he wishes; there would be a small annual fee for the purchase of more books. The company would care for the room. With such a library, the Equitable would become a more desirable place for lawyers than the Temple in London. The company is said to be seriously considering the proposition.

866 [Plans for a Law Library in the Equitable Life Assurance Building in New York.] *Albany Law Journal*, 11 (February 6, 1875), p86–87.

The article refers to another one on the same subject in the previous issue *(see 865)*.

As we mentioned in our last issue, the lawyers who have offices in the Equitable Life Assurance building in New York propose to found a library for the use of the legal tenants. They have written to the president of the insurance firm, pointing out that a library containing all law books of value would be convenient; they also propose telegraphing from the courts and having a bulletin containing calendars of local and other courts. The president has made a favorable response. The building, when fully leased, will have offices for more than a hundred lawyers; with a law library it will become truly a temple of law as well as of business.

— LAW INSTITUTE LIBRARY

867 "The Law Library of New-York." *National Magazine: Devoted to Literature, Art, and Religion*, 9 (September 1856), p287, 240 wds (NcU).

The article may refer to the Law Institute Library in New York City; no record has been found of "The Law Library of New-York."

The Law Library of New-York is probably the richest law library in the country in terms of rare and valuable works on legal topics. The library has a very full collection of reports of cases in American, English, Scottish and Irish courts; sets of American and English statutes; and the publications of the English Records Commission. There is an almost complete set of English Reports from 1216 to date. The State Papers of England and America are a feature of this Institution of peculiar value. The library owns the charters of the American colonies, the Congressional Papers from 1791 to date, and the New York State Papers since 1691. The library also owns other early English law documents including the "Monumenta Ecclesiastica" which covers the seventh to the tenth centuries.

868 "The New York Law Institute Library." *Albany Law Journal*, 10 (April 4, 1874), p219–20 (NcU).

Making the catalog of a public library is very laborious and the work is soon out-of-date. About twenty-five years ago Mr. S. Hastings Grant of the

New York Mercantile Library prepared a classified catalog which has been a model for others. Now another advance has been made: the catalog of the New York Law Institute, a volume of more than 600 pages. The alphabetical catalog occupies less than 250 pages; the distinctive features follow it. The classified subject index occupies about 200 pages; names of authors of books that have been printed or reprinted since 1869 are in italics. There is a 27-page list of American reports, statutes, and digests. Other sections include lists of British reports, collections of cases, accounts of trials, legal periodicals and abbreviations. The association has a membership of more than 600 and the library contains 17,000 volumes. We understand that Mr. William H. Winter is mainly responsible for this excellent catalog.

— LENOX LIBRARY

869 [Gifts of Collections to Public Libraries; Proposed Gift by James Lenox.] *Nation*, 10 (January 20, 1870), p42, 280 wds (NcU).

Through an error, discovered after most of this bibliography had been indexed, this article appears in two places. Because it discusses benefactions other than the proposed gift by James Lenox, it is also entered as item 118. To remove either item would, properly, have meant the renumbering of several hundred items and index terms. The compilers hope that they will be forgiven for leaving both items in the bibliography.

Mr. Spofford, the Librarian of Congress, in his recent address before the [American] Social Science Association, said that there are more volumes in private libraries in this country than in public libraries and that there are many rare and costly books in private hands of which no copies are to be found in public libraries. The destiny of the private libraries is to be bequeathed to public libraries—for example, the Bowditch, Parker, and Ticknor collections in the Boston Public Library. The first instance in New York City was announced last week: Mr. James Lenox, whose private library is probably the finest in America, will give it to the city, together with a building to be erected for it. We hope that Mr. Lenox's rival collectors will make gifts, and that the practices of the Astor Library will be avoided in the new institution.

870 [James Lenox to Give His Library to New York.] *American Bibliopolist*, 2 (February 1870), p76, 180 wds (ICN, ICU).

This is a somewhat abridged version of an article that appeared in the *Nation* for January 20, 1870 *(see 869)*.

871 "The Lenox Library." *American Bibliopolist*, 2 (February 1870), p52–53 (ICU, NcD).

The article summarized below is a reprint of an article from the *Evening Post*, and two from the *Tribune* of January 29th. The articles are not entirely in agreement.

A new library is to be given New York by James Lenox. It will be opposite the Park, and will contain Lenox's entire collection of statuary, paintings and books. His library is perhaps the most valuable in America; he may make further endowments for its extension. As a permanent literary repository, it will attract materials from private libraries and galleries which would otherwise be dispersed. Scholars have long known about the collection, which contains many valuable items (some are described), but few people have been able to use it. Lenox will donate land, erect a building costing at least $300,000, give his own library, and provide other funds if they are needed. One article from the *Tribune* implies that the funds, not less than $500,000, and the land will be given to the town of Hempstead. The people of the town propose to give $100,000 of the money derived from the sale of some land to purchase library books.

872 Lenox, James. "The Lenox Collection of Shakespeare Folios." *American Bibliopolist*, 2 (June–July 1870), p181–87 (ICN, NcD).

The article summarized below appeared a few months after the Lenox Library had been incorporated.

I have in my possession a very remarkable set of the different editions of Shakespeare's plays in folio. I propose to describe them, mentioning in what ways they vary from Lowndes' *Bibliographer's Manual*. My copies are in fine condition; every leaf is genuine. The body of the article consists of detailed descriptions of folios in the four editions published through 1685. At the end is a list of quartos, briefly described.

873 [Lenox Library Building.] *American Bibliopolist*, 3 (April 1871), p104 (NcD, OC).

The entire article follows; it was reprinted from the *New York Sun*.

"The building of the new Lenox Library is to be on Fifth Avenue, between Seventy-first and Seventy-second streets. It will be one hundred and ninety-two feet front and a hundred and fourteen feet deep, three stories high, and fireproof throughout, costing, with the site, a million of dollars. How much the library fund will be is not known, but it will doubtless be ample. The library will render to people up town the same service as the Astor to people down town. But the Astor ought to pull out in view of such rivalry. It is sadly behind hand in new publications. The new works of the day are not to be found there. Reason — poverty."

874 [Lenox Library.] *Appletons' Journal: a Magazine of General Literature*, 6 (October 7, 1871), p414, 710 wds (NcU).

Mr. James Lenox, as modest as he is generous, is building a magnificent library and museum which will be free to the public. It is located on the finest site on Manhattan Island, across from Central Park. The building, which will be completed next summer, will also house Mr. Lenox's extensive collection of rare literary and historical artifacts as well as many old and modern masterpieces of art. The benefit to scholars and students is inestimable. The donation will fill a lamentable gap in present American collections in the areas of early American history, Biblical bibliography, and Elizabethan literature.

875 [Lenox Library.] *Appletons' Journal: a Magazine of General Literature*, 7 (June 8, 1872), p638–39 (NcU).

The slowly rising walls of the Lenox Library present an impressive sight to visitors to Central Park. When completed the building will comprise two stories and an attic. The main entrance, on Fifth Avenue, will open onto a courtyard flanked on one side by the reading room and library wing and on the other by the museum wing; the attic will house the art collection donated by James Lenox. The structure is being built of limestone, and will cost nearly $500,000; the public will have free access to it. Lenox is also giving the institution his collection of rare books and manuscripts. This generous gift from Mr. Lenox will result in an institution of scholarly research which will rival those in Europe.

876 [Mr. George Henry Moore, L.L.D.] *American Bibliopolist*, 5 (January 1873), p2 (NcD).
The entire article follows.
"Mr. George Henry Moore, L.L.D. — Idoneus homo — for upwards of thirty-three years connected with, and for the last twenty-five years, librarian of the New York Historical Society, has just been appointed, by the trustees, superintendent of the Lenox Library."

877 [Lenox Library.] *Publishers' Weekly*, 5 (February 7, 1874), p141 (NcU).
The entire article follows.
"The Lenox Library Building, Fifth avenue and Seventy-second street, approaches completion, and presents a superb appearance from the park. Its main building has ninety-five feet front, the two projecting wings adding each forty-eight feet frontage, in Greek architecture. It will cost $500,000."

— LYCEUM OF NATURAL HISTORY LIBRARY

878 "Lyceum of Natural History in the City of New York." *American Repertory of Arts, Sciences, and Manufactures*, 1 (February 1840), p43–46 (TU).
The parts of the article about the library are summarized below.
The Lyceum instituted a library and museum while located in a city building at the rear of City Hall. The library and museum were enriched by donations from foreign societies, naturalists, and their own members. The Lyceum was moved to the City Dispensary in 1828, and remained there eight years. Students at New York University had the benefit of the library and museum during the latter part of this period. The library moved to the new building, constructed for the Lyceum, when it was opened in 1836. The library and museum are open to all citizens without charge, subject to some necessary regulations. Donations of books and of specimens for the museum are respectfully solicited.

— MEDICO-LEGAL SOCIETY

879 [Medico-Legal Society Library.] *Publishers' Weekly*, 5 (February 7, 1874), p141 (NcU).
The entire article follows.
"In his last Presidential address to the Medico-Legal Society, Mr. Clark Bell reiterated the desirability of founding a complete library of medico-jurisprudence, which department is very inadequately represented in existing libraries. Exclusive of pamphlets there are from 1,000 to 1,500 volumes published in this country and in Europe, and the sum of $2,500 would probably establish the library upon a permanent basis. Under the resolutions making it the duty of each member to contribute one volume annually, 100 volumes were donated last year, besides $327.50 in cash. Immediate steps are to be taken to complete the work, and it is proposed to allow non-members contributing the free use of the library."

880 [The Library of the Medico-Legal Society of New York.] *Nation*, 21 (October 28, 1875), p277 (NcU).
The entire article follows.
"The Medico-Legal Society of New York solicits contributions to its library either in money or in books; the proceedings of medical societies, and official reports of or concerning insane asylums throughout the country, are especially

desired. Donors not members will be allowed liberal access to the library, which at present is kept by Mr. R. S. Guernsey, at 150 Broadway, and is likely to have a place beside the general law library of the Equitable Assurance Building."

— MERCANTILE LIBRARY

881 "New York Mercantile Library." *American Annals of Education* [American Journal of Education], 2 (August 1827), p508–09 (NcU).

The article is composed of extracts from the 1827 report of the Board of Directors of the Association.

The members should be proud that the Association has overcome the adversities of its early years. Last year 471 new subscribers joined the Association while in 1822 there were only 204 members; even as recently as January 1825 there was only a total of 438 members. At the last annual meeting the library held 2,200 volumes; during the past year more than 1,000 books were added to the collection. Books on the subjects of history, biography, voyages, and travel were purchased. Also, books of poetry, romance, or imagination were acquired even though these subjects are of secondary importance to an individual's intellectual development.

882 "Mercantile Library Association." *New York Mirror, a Weekly Gazette of Literature and the Fine Arts* [New York Mirror, and Ladies Literary Gazette], 5 (January 26, 1828), p231, 1030 wds (InU, NcU).

The seventh anniversary meeting was held at the Masonic Hall on Broadway. The principal speaker was Mr. Maxwell, editor of the *Journal of Commerce*. He urges the young clerks to read and educate themselves because the successful merchant is often called upon to serve the community or nation. Advantages will follow the young man who follows the moral precepts found in the scriptures. Avoid frivolous reading in favor of geography, travel, history and maritime law. At the meeting it was reported that there are more than 1500 subscribers, although only about 950 take books from the library. The library has about 4400 volumes. Annual dues are $2.00; life membership is $25.00.

883 "Clinton Hall Association, and Mercantile Library Association." *Magazine of Useful and Entertaining Knowledge*, 2 (March 1831), p199–201 (IEN, InU).

The Clinton Hall Association was formed to provide the Mercantile Library Association with a lecture hall, quarters for its library and reading room, and the foundation for a large library to serve the business community. The Clinton Hall Association has a capital stock of $50,000 divided into 500 shares valued at $100 each; 321 shares already have been subscribed. The Mercantile Library Association and the Academy of Design at present occupy the Clinton Hall Association's new building. The Mercantile Library Association was formed in 1820 when it was recognized that New York City's 6,000 clerks needed an organization that could provide them with useful instruction and could help safeguard their morals. In 1821 the Association had 130 members and 1,000 volumes in the library; its membership now has increased to 1,000 and its library to approximately 6,000 volumes.

884 Metcalf, Samuel L. "The Interest and Importance of Scientific Geology as a Subject for Study." *Federal American Monthly* [Knickerbocker], 3 (April 1834), p225–35 (InU, NcU).

New York (Mercantile)

The introductory lecture for a course in geology given before the Mercantile Library Association of New York. Geology is the fashionable science of the day and one can now learn in a few lectures what formerly took a lifetime. The last twenty or thirty years have seen the development of a body of demonstratable geological knowledge to replace the speculations of the past. (The principles and purposes of geologic study are given; then oxidation and the force of water are discussed as two of the most powerful geological forces.) Geology provides support for the concepts of natural theology and, therefore, is not in conflict with religion.

885 "Mercantile Library Association." *New York Literary Gazette*, 1 (February 9, 1839), p14 (NcU).
The entire article follows.
"The Board of Directors of this useful and honorable Institution, having effected the preliminary measures necessary to carry into operation the Elementary Course of Instruction alluded to in the 18th Annual Report, await the action of the members of the Association. All those who are in favor of the adoption of the plan, and are willing to support it, are requested to send in their names, with address and folio, under cover to the secretary, on or before the 14th inst."

886 "Mercantile Library Association." *New York Literary Gazette*, 1 (February 16, 1839), p22 (NcU).
The entire article follows.
"We have received the well written *Annual Report of the Board of Directors* of the Mercantile Library Association, and cannot too strongly express our gratification in the continued success of this valuable institution, as evinced by the report. The association is out of debt, and the gross receipts for the last year were something more than eight thousand dollars. The support given by this institution to periodical literature, is very great; the reading room 'now furnishes the reader,' says the report, 'with ninety periodicals, in every department of knowledge, general, literary, and scientific; and, probably, presents a greater variety and extent of periodical literature and science, than any other similar establishment in the country.' We do not hesitate to say, that the Mercantile Library is destined, at no distant time, to become the largest and most useful library in America."

887 "Mercantile Library Association [New York City]." *Federal American Monthly* [Knickerbocker], 13 (March 1839), p276–77 (InU, NcU).
At an estimated cost of $8,000 the association proposes to offer a series of four courses of thirty to thirty-five lectures each, as well as incidental lectures one or two evenings each week. Tickets for the whole series will cost $3.00. The association has more than 4,000 members and expects to increase to about 5,000. Mr. Edward Coffin is the association's president. (The course proposal is quoted from his report to the board of directors at the eighteenth annual meeting.)

888 "New York Mercantile Library Association." *New World. A Weekly Family Journal of Popular Literature, Science, Art, and News*, 2 (February 20, 1841), p128 (NcD, OC).
The entire article follows.
"This Institution has now 3,586 members. Its Library consists of 32,296 volumes, besides 115 periodicals and journals, both foreign and domestic."

U.S. — New York

889 "Major Tochman." *New World. A Weekly Family Journal of Popular Literature, Science, Art, and News*, 3 (December 4, 1841), p365 (InU).
The entire article follows. It refers to Gaspard Tochman.
"This accomplished gentleman has, in the course of the present week, delivered two lectures on Poland, before the Mercantile Library Association and other intelligent citizens, to the eminent gratification of large audiences. He writes and speaks with fluency and correctness. He is to pronounce a third lecture, in continuation of his course, though separate from that of the Association, next Monday evening. He will treat of the Government and Policies of Russia."

890 "Mercantile Library Association." *New World. A Weekly Family Journal of Popular Literature, Science, Art, and News*, 4 (March 12, 1842), p177, 500 wds (InU, NcD).
The New York Mercantile Library Association's twenty-first annual report indicates that the institution's prosperity is undiminished. The Association directs and restrains the tastes and desires of its members, causes them to work together in the quest for knowledge and literary objectives, and helps to enhance the dignity of mercantile pursuits. Through the Association a love of literature is fostered and the mind acquires knowledge; leisure is used wisely. Every merchant should support its activities and programs. These include a library; a reading room supplied with American and foreign periodicals; a museum; an art gallery; classes in foreign languages and the various aspects of mercantile education; and a register for merchants and clerks, including a list of those seeking employment.

891 [The Mercantile Library Association of New York.] *New World. A Weekly Family Journal of Popular Literature, Science, Art, and News*, 5 (November 12, 1842), p320, 240 wds (NcD).
Last Wednesday the Mercantile Library Association celebrated its twenty-second anniversary. Charles Eames delivered an excellent address, and a poem was read. After the program many members of the audience went to Nibblo's Gardens for dinner; the food was very bad. Speeches were made by the mayor and Messrs. Evarts, Keese, and Sargent. The program also included several musical selections.

892 "Mercantile Library Association." *New World. A Weekly Family Journal of Popular Literature, Science, Art, and News*, 6 (February 18, 1843), p219, 900 wds (InU, NcD).
The annual report indicates that the New York Mercantile Library Association is rapidly becoming an important literary institution. The books are suffering damage by users; greater efforts need to be made to detect and punish the offenders. Music classes are available as part of the system of study supported by the Association. The classes, which are given on any subject that a sufficient number will voluntarily study, receive part of the necessary financial support from the Association. A circulating library, with separate cataloging and a changeable stock of books might be desirable. The sale or exchange of books in the circulating collection that have short-lived attractiveness to readers would greatly reduce their cost to the Association. Currently the Association is out of debt. The number of members has declined because of the general depression in business. However, about $3,000 has been applied to the increase and preservation of the library. Receipts in 1842 were $6,139.90; expenditures, $5,784.37.

893 "New York Mercantile Library Association." *New York Chronicle*, 1 (April 1849), p124 (ICN, NjR).
The entire article follows.
"At the 28th Annual Meeting of this Society, Jan. 9th, 1849, it was stated that the members now numbered 3004, being a net gain during the year of 243. The books added in the same time, were 2276 volumes, at a cost of $3,392, making the total number of the Library 25,881."

894 [Professor Filopanti's Lectures.] *Literary World*, N.Y., 7 (November 2, 1850), p355, 290 wds (NcU).
Professor [Quirico] Filopanti has commenced his lecture series before the Mercantile Library Association [New York City] with a lecture entitled "Influence of Secret Societies upon the Ancient and Modern Revolutions of Rome." The *Tribune*'s [presumably the *New York Daily Tribune*] report of the lecture is reprinted.

895 "The Annual Report of the Mercantile Library Association." *Literary World*, N.Y., 10 (January 24, 1852), p71 (NcU).
The entire article follows.
"The Annual report of the MERCANTILE LIBRARY ASSOCIATION of this city exhibits a healthy state of prosperity. The library, which is abundantly supplied with the best new foreign publications, particularly of England, numbers now more than thirty-three thousand volumes, of which about three thousand have been added during the past year. The number of persons entitled to the use of the library is some four thousand. The income for the year was $8,612, mainly derived from the payments of clerks entitled to membership on the most favorable terms of two dollars each. These facts are an honor to the mercantile class of this city. For the character of the library and its intelligent resources we may add that no collection in this city is more resorted to by authors, and nowhere do members of the press and others receive more courteous attention."

896 [Mercantile Library Association Course of Lectures.] *Literary World*, N.Y., 10 (January 24, 1852), p71 (NcU).
The entire article follows.
"The course of Lectures of the Institution for the new year opened with an animated and resolute address by Mr. H. J. Raymond, on the Uses of Literature, which was followed by a well stated, hopeful argument by Prof. G. W. Greene, of Brown University, of 'the grounds for confidence in the triumph of the liberal cause in Europe,' in the course of which he reminded his audience of the assumed position of Louis Philippe even in January, 1848 – 'For nearly eighteen years he was designated as the Napoleon of France. Only three weeks before his fall he had heard a celebrated lecturer proclaim him to be the wisest prince of Europe.' Such is the fallacy of fact opposed to a great principle!"

897 "New York Mercantile Library Association." *Norton's Literary Gazette and Publishers' Circular*, 2 (March 15, 1852), p45, 560 wds (ICN, NcU).
According to the association's annual report, the library added 2,832 volumes in 1851 to bring its collection up to 33,140 volumes. The reading room received 176 periodicals – 100 American, 57 English, 11 French, and 8 German. More than 1,000 new members joined last year; the total number of members is 3,797. For the year over 100,000 books were circulated. The association deserves the support and encouragement of everyone who is a friend of education.

U.S. — New York

898 [Qualifications of a Librarian.] *Norton's Literary Gazette and Publishers' Circular*, 2 (March 15, 1852), p45–46 (ICN, NcU).
We quote the recommendations presented in the New York Mercantile Library Association's annual report; if adopted, these recommendations would do much to improve any library. The librarian should be appointed for life — dependent of course upon his continued good conduct. He should have an education that familiarized him with all aspects of his profession, and he should be a person who, by his personal worth and merit, will command respect. Harris, Cogswell, Jewett, and Folsom have given the public confidence in the libraries that they head. The appointment of a well qualified librarian would place this library upon a firm foundation.

899 "New York Mercantile Library." *Norton's Literary Gazette and Publishers' Circular*, 2 (September 15, 1852), p169 (ICN, NcU).
The entire article follows.
"Over two thousand volumes have been added to this Library between January and July of the current year; and the receipts for the whole year will probably equal $9,000. There are now more than 4,000 paying members, besides some four or five hundred life and honorary members, stockholders, &c. When the attractive nature of the reading-room is considered, containing, as it does, one hundred and twenty periodicals, besides newspapers and works of reference, it will be easily believed that its rooms are constantly crowded. It seems to us that there is need of immediate action for the provision of more ample accommodations, both for books and for readers."

900 "The New York Mercantile Library." *Norton's Literary Gazette and Publishers' Circular*, 2 (December 15, 1852), p236 (ICN, NcU).
The entire article follows.
"The New York Mercantile Library have now in their collection thirty-seven thousand volumes, to which they are making constant additions.
"A meeting of the Members has been recently held to consider the project of removing from their present location. A very decided opinion was expressed in favor of moving up-town. It was made very clear that something must speedily be done, either the enlargement of the rooms now occupied, or the removal to other quarters.
"A geographical room, free to the public as well as to members, has been recently thrown open, and stocked with a variety of valuable and interesting charts, maps, atlases, globes, etc."

901 "Thackeray's Lectures." *Norton's Literary Gazette and Publishers' Circular*, 2 (December 15, 1852), p237, 300 wds (ICN, NcU).
Mr. Thackeray's lectures have been well received in New York by large, fashionable, and intelligent audiences. His lectures about wits of earlier times have added greatly to his popularity; his criticism is discriminating and his humor subtle. The Mercantile Library is to be congratulated for sponsoring this lecture series; are there not other speakers from abroad whom the library could invite?

902 "New York Mercantile Library Association." *Norton's Literary Gazette and Publishers' Circular*, 3 (January 15, 1853), p3–4 (ICN, NcU).
The reports of the Treasurer and the Board of Directors were presented at the association's annual meeting. Total income last year was $10,127 while

expenditures totaled $10,034. The number of members who joined last year is 1,293, of whom 140 are subscribers paying $5.00 per year; there now are 4,194 paying members. Last year 4,346 volumes were acquired, of these 4,156 were purchased and 190 were donated. The library now has 37,486 volumes. The lectures have proved popular. Some remarks were made about the crowded conditions in the library and the institution's relationship with the Clinton Hall Association. We were pleased to learn that the Clinton Hall Association's Trustees have arranged to purchase the Astor Place Opera House for the Mercantile Library, which is the fifth largest library in the country and the second largest one in New York City.

903 "New York Mercantile Library." *Norton's Literary Gazette and Publishers' Circular*, 3 (February 15, 1853), p18–19 (ICU, NcU).

The announcement that the Clinton Hall Association had purchased the Astor Place Opera House for the Mercantile Library was received with mixed feelings by the members of the Mercantile Library Association. Those members who live in Brooklyn of course were opposed to a change in the library's location while the other members decidedly were in favor of the change. The Board of Directors wisely voted to accept the offer of the Clinton Hall Association's Trustees. A report on this matter is forthcoming.

904 [New York Mercantile Library Association.] *National Magazine: Devoted to Literature, Art, and Religion*, 2 (April 1853), p381 (InU, NcU).
The entire article follows.
"The thirty-second annual report of the *New-York Mercantile Library Association* shows a large increase both in members and volumes in the library. It is now the fifth in the United States, and is surpassed in this city only by the Astor Library. The amount expended for books during the past year is nearly $5,000. The number of volumes added to the library is 4,346. The whole number of volumes is 37,486. Of the number added during the past year, 1,063 are in History and Geography, 138 in Theology, 814 in Mental and Moral Science, and 1,656 in fiction. The profits derived from the lectures during the past year, amounting to $1,500, have been permanently invested for the benefit of the Institution."

905 [New York Mercantile Library.] *National Magazine: Devoted to Literature, Art, and Religion*, 2 (June 1853), p571 (InU, NcU).
The entire article follows.
"The Directors of the New-York *Mercantile Library* and the Clinton Hall Association, have agreed that the library shall be removed to Astor-place. It is proposed to demolish the Astor-place Opera House and erect a suitable library building on its site. The removal will not probably be effected until January, 1854."

906 "New York Mercantile Library Association." *Literary World*, N.Y., 13 (September 17, 1853), p126–27 (NcU).

The association was founded in 1820, and its library opened in 1821 with 700 volumes. In 1830 the library possessed 6,000 volumes and presently has nearly 40,000 volumes. The Association recently purchased the Astor Place Opera House, and alterations to its interior, to cost approximately $100,000, are underway. The reading room and the library, with a planned capacity of 120,000 volumes, will occupy a spacious domed area in the building.

907 [New York Mercantile Library Association.] *National Magazine: Devoted to Literature, Art, and Religion*, 3 (November 1853), p476 (InU, NcU).
The entire article follows.
"*The New-York Mercantile Library Association* was founded in 1820. Its library of seven hundred volumes was opened in 1821. Since then it has steadily increased, until it now numbers forty thousand volumes. The Astor-place Opera-House has been purchased by the Association, and is to be disemboweled and fitted up for the reception of its handsome library. On the first floor will be the reading-room, sixty-two feet by eighty-five, with all the accommodations of tables and desks, where from three hundred to four hundred persons may read without inconvenience."

908 [New York Mercantile Library Association.] *Norton's Literary Gazette and Publishers' Circular*, n.s. 1 (March 15, 1854), p143, 630 wds (NcU).
The thirty-third Annual Report of the Board of Directors shows the library to be flourishing. Receipts for 1853 were $9,165.18; of which $3,264.45 was spent for books; $791.09 for periodicals, and $467.46 for binding. The number of volumes, as of January 1, 1853, was 37,846. Since then, 107 were donated and 2,793 were purchased, making the present total 40,746. There were 4,483 paying members and 4,877 total members on January 1, 1854. Annual circulation is estimated at 130,000. The reading room has been re-carpeted. In all, 195 periodicals are being constantly received. An historical, geographical and statistical reference library is proposed. A description of the new building in Astor Place is given, which the Association expects to occupy about May 1. D. R. Budd is President; S. H. Grant is Librarian.

909 [New York Mercantile Library Association Building Completed.] *Norton's Literary Gazette and Publishers' Circular*, n.s. 1 (June 1, 1854), p281, 230 wds (NcU).
The New York Mercantile Library Association's new building has been completed. Horatio Seymour, Governor of New York, will give an address at the opening ceremonies to be held June eighth. The merchants of New York have contributed $60,000 to the building fund. A downtown office has been opened on Nassau Street where books may be received within two or three hours after they have been requested. Four or five deliveries a day have been made during the two weeks this office has been open. Establishment of a reading room and a reference library have been proposed if the branch office continues to be as much used as it has in the last two weeks.

910 [New York Mercantile Library Association.] *Norton's Literary Gazette and Publishers' Circular*, n.s. 1 (June 15, 1854), p308–09 (NcU).
The library was begun in 1820. After seven years it had 4400 volumes; annual receipts were $1750. Life membership subscriptions were then initiated, first costing $25 each and soon $100 each. Thousands of dollars were raised. By the spring of 1828 the success of the institution was thus established. Lectures and classes were arranged, purchases of books made, and the institution become useful to merchants' clerks and to the whole community. The library now has over 41,000 volumes and 5400 members. The reading room has 214 periodicals and newspapers, and can accommodate 500 readers. The institution's location in the heart of the city has extended its usefulness. It contains a variety of works (some are listed). Since 1820, there have been 20,200 members, and 49,800 volumes have been cataloged. (Statistics of total and average expenditures are

given.) The new building, just furnished, cost $246,000, leaving an indebtedness of $86,000.

911 [New York Mercantile Library Association.] *National Magazine: Devoted to Literature, Art, and Religion*, 6 (April 1855), p382 (InU, NcU).
The entire article follows.
"The last Annual Report of the *New-York Mercantile Library Association* shows that the present number of members is 4,603; the total accessions for the year 1854 being 1,216, only 411 having withdrawn during the same period. The expenditures for 1854 amounted to $10,214 09; of which $2,074 17 was spent for books, $944 90 for periodicals, and $381 22 for binding, besides $212 from the Demilt legacy. The number of volumes added by donation 142, and by purchase 2,267; of which 90 are folios and quartos, 767 octavos, and 1,552 duodecimos. No institution of the country has more spirit or more success."

912 H., I. F. "The Classified Index to the Catalogue of the N. Y. Mercantile Library." *Norton's Literary Gazette and Publishers' Circular*, n.s. 2 (May 15, 1855), p196, 620 wds (MnU).
A classification is a thing of utility and the most convenient system is the best. An alphabetical catalog is of no help when you do not know the subject matter of the books. A classification that is best for one person may not be the best for another; it must be designed for the mass of people who use it. From looking at the class for New England I can guess about the nature of individual books there; I may guess wrong but it is humanly impossible to place each book between the two that resemble it the most. Nothing would be gained by arranging books within a class alphabetically or by date of publication. A separately bound alphabetical list could be made for those who simply want to know whether a particular book is in the library.

913 [New York Mercantile Library Receives Portrait of President Grant.] *American Bibliopolist*, 2 (February 1870), p77 (ICN, ICU).
The entire article follows.
"Mr. Wilson G. Hunt has presented to the Mercantile Library Association of this city a half-length portrait of President Grant. Mr. N. B. Kittle, the artist, was favored with several sittings, and the portrait is considered an excellent likeness."

914 Hassard, J. R. G. "The New York Mercantile Library." *Century, a Popular Quarterly* [Scribner's Monthly], 1 (February 1871), p353–67 (NcU).
The New York Mercantile Library is now the fourth largest library and the largest lending library in the country. William Wood deserves much credit for its creation. Its history is summarized. The Clinton Hall Association served almost as a board of trustees. The library has had three locations, and may be moved again. The reading room is well-stocked with periodicals, newspapers and reference works. The library is used by patrons from all walks of life. (The arrangement of the building and the books is described, as are the delivery and check-out systems.) As of April 30, 1870, 12,867 persons were entitled to use the institution. There are 120,000 volumes. Circulation for last year was 234,120. Of these, 169,646 were works of fiction. (The reading interests of patrons are discussed.) Multiple copies are often bought. (The administration of the library and the annual elections are described. The article is illustrated with interior and exterior views and a drawing of a book ticket.)

U.S. — New York

915 [Sunday Opening of the Mercantile Library.] *Nation*, 14 (April 4, 1872), p217, 560 wds (NcU).

Mr. Charles Collins, a director of the Mercantile Library [in New York City] recently addressed a letter to the Rev. Dr. [Edward Abiel] Washburn, Rector of Calvary Church, in which he tells why the directors wished to open the library on Sunday. He reports that the Clinton Hall Association, which owns the library's building, has refused permission and asks Dr. Washburn which of the laws of God would be violated if the library were opened. Dr. Washburn replies, in a paper which Mr. Collins has had printed, that it would be eminently in the spirit of Christ's teaching to give poor clerks and apprentices a means for improving their minds and morals; the opening of libraries is a Christian duty. (A discussion by the editor follows, comparing the New England Sunday with the Roman Catholic one.) Perhaps the churches would have more recruits from reading-rooms than reading-rooms would have from churches.

916 [Sunday Opening of the New York Mercantile Library Reading Room.] *American Bibliopolist*, 4 (June 1872), p295 (IEN, OC).

The entire article follows.

"The New York Mercantile Library Reading-room will be open for the use of members on Sundays, from one to nine P.M. The vote of the members was so overwhelmingly (1,200 out of 1,400) in the affirmative on the Sunday question that the Clinton Hall Association cheerfully granted consent to the opening of the building."

917 [Lecture course at the New York Mercantile Library Association.] *American Bibliopolist*, 4 (November 1872), p578 (ICU, NcD, OC).

From the New York *Evening Mail*. The entire article as given in the *American Bibliopolist*:

"The Mercantile Library Association continues its good service to the reading and thinking public, by providing an excellent course of lectures this season. It is necessary only to mention the names of the speakers to direct attention to the excellence of the course, which begins on Monday evening, at Steinway Hall. They are as follows: 1. George McDonald, subject 'Thomas Hood;' 2. Edmund Yates, 'The English Parliament;' 3. Miss Lillian Edgerton, 'Gossip, its Cause and Cure;' 4. Wendell Phillips, 'Daniel O'Connell;' 5. Bret Harte, 'The Argonauts of '49;' 6. Prof. J. F. Petter, 'Snow, Ice, and Glaciers;' 7. Henry Ward Beecher, subject to be announced; 8. Mrs. Scott-Siddons, 'Readings in Costume;' 9. Col. John Hay, 'Heroic Life in Washington;' 10. John B. Gough, 'Now and Then;' (new). The subscription for these ten lectures is but $5, and this includes a reserved seat."

— NATIONAL TEMPERANCE SOCIETY

918 "Temperance Saloons, Coffee-Houses, Etc., Etc." *National Advocate* [National Temperance Advocate], 1 (August 1866), p121 (OO, TxU).

The article is about temperance coffee-houses. The part about reading rooms in those coffee-houses follows.

"The proposed reading room attachment, in addition to its temperance character, would be a vast source of usefulness, as well as relaxation and enjoyment. Here the temperance and Christian young men would become acquainted and attached to each other, and informed on all subjects of reform and Christian enterprise. In this manner they would strengthen and confirm each other's principles and good habits, and organize their influences for active duties."

919 "How to Spend Winter Evenings." *National Advocate* [National Temperance Advocate], 3 (January 1868), p6–7 (TxU).

The article is, for the most part, a portion of a manuscript sent by George S. Blackie, M.D., editor of the *Southern Son*, a paper in Nashville, Tennessee. He recommends reading as a winter evening diversion. He apparently refers to Divisions of the National Temperance Society. The part of the article about libraries follows.

"I also recommend the formation of Division Libraries. There are many of us able to buy one or two books a winter, if not far more. Say we spend five dollars only in little trifles—tobacco, pipes, odd magazines, or anything. That five dollars from each member would soon make a good library fund, and instead of only two good books a winter, we could have at our command forty or fifty, and all our own. Books, improving books, are easily had. So long as A. Strahan of New-York, and Ticknor & Fields of Boston, and The National Temperance Association are publishing as they now do, the young men are safe in ordering a library at random from any of them."

920 Judson, E. Z. C. "Pawned and Redeemed; or, Tempted, Wrecked, and Rescued. A Temperance Story." *National Advocate* [National Temperance Advocate], 3 (June 1868), p81–82 (TxU).

This is chapter XI of a serialized story. The part about libraries follows.

"....Now that I have determined to stop drinking, I must keep away from my club and the saloons where I have hitherto spent my evenings. I know not how to pass my time. I am lonesome at home. You temperance men have reading-rooms, I suppose, where you can meet and enjoy temperance literature, get the news of the day, and all that?

"*I am ashamed to say that we have not!** We have Lodges and Divisions to meet in and pass our evenings; but few of these have any libraries, though all should have them. It would be a noble work were we to have a temperance reading and news-room, where strangers could come to enjoy an idle hour and learn the places of our various meetings. Had I the wealth of some of our leaders, the city should soon boast of such a place!"

*How long shall it be so? — E. Z. C. J.

921 C., N. E. "Fight Them with Books." *National Advocate* [National Temperance Advocate], 6 (February 1871), p20 (TxU).

This article is about the publication and distribution of books and tracts promoting temperance. The part about libraries (200 wds) is summarized below.

The reform purposes of a temperance organization can be aided by the establishment of a library of temperance books and tracts. Such a collection would be especially beneficial to children and young people. Every temperance organization should have such a library; the members of the organization should devise ways to encourage reading of the books. Once there were few books on the subject of temperance; now there are many.

NEW-YORK HISTORICAL SOCIETY LIBRARY

922 [New-York Historical Society.] *National Magazine: Devoted to Literature, Art, and Religion*, 3 (August 1853), p188 (InU, NcU).

U.S. — New York

The entire article follows.
"At a recent meeting of the *New-York Historical Society*, among the donations received were the original deed of the Knickerbocker Insurance Company, the first institution of the kind in this city — organized in 1797, and a specimen of the timbers of the *Royal George* man-of-war, sunk off Spithead upwards of seventy years since. The society resolved that a sufficient sum has been obtained to warrant the commencement of the new fire-proof building for the library and valuable collections of the society. A paper on the 'Title of the United States to the Northwest Territory,' was read by Mr. Joseph Blunt, of this city. The society then adjourned, to meet again on the first Tuesday in October next."

923 "New Library Building." *National Magazine: Devoted to Literature, Art, and Religion*, 7 (December 1855), p568–69 (NcU).
The cornerstone for the library of the New-York Historical Society was laid on October 17, at the corner of Second Avenue and Eleventh Street. The location has many historic associations: it was once part of Peter Stuyvesant's farm. Nearby are the tombs of the colonial and early New York state governors.

924 [The Collections of Peter Force.] *Nation*, 1 (November 2, 1865), p564, 500 wds (NcU).
This collection did not go to New York; it was acquired by the Library of Congress.
A movement is on foot in New York, under the auspices of the N. Y. Historical Society, for securing to this city the library and historical collections of Peter Force of Washington. His countrymen owe him gratitude for the great fifteen volume "American Archives" series which is a documentary history of the American Revolution and the formation of the Constitution. His magnificent library, containing travel accounts, laws, reports, maps, periodicals and newspapers, should be kept intact as part of a public library; $100,000 in gold has already been offered for it as a speculation. Its integrity should be assured by the cooperation of all who understand the importance of historic truth.

925 [General De Peyster's Gift of Dutch Books to the N. Y. Historical Society.] *Nation*, 1 (November 16, 1865), p623, 180 wds (NcU).
The New-York Historical Society has recently received a valuable and appropriate gift from General John Watts De Peyster, author of *History of Carausius* and other valuable monographs connected with the land of his ancestors. He has just presented his entire collection of Dutch books which consists of several hundred volumes brought together in Europe at a large expenditure of time and money. This gift undoubtedly makes the Historical Society the richest collection in the United States that relates to the native country of the colonists of "Nieuw Amsterdam."

— NEW YORK HOSPITAL LIBRARY

926 "Sailors Inclined to Read." *Sailors' Magazine and Seamen's Friend*, 1 (September 1828), p27 (MdAN).
The entire article follows.
"A physician in New-York, who frequently visits the hospital of the city, has just informed us, that about *one fourth* of the inmates of that institution are seamen — that all have access to a library, and he is satisfied from personal observation, that the seamen read more than all the other occupants of the

house. He adds, that he has seen them have two or three volumes of Scott's Family Bible at the same time, and that, separate from the library, the sailors, themselves, take several daily papers. We leave these facts to speak for themselves on the importance of providing Libraries and Reading Rooms for seamen."

— NEW YORK SOCIETY LIBRARY

927 M. [Hamilton's Copy of the *Federalist* deposited in the New-York Publick Library.] *Monthly Anthology and Boston Review*, 4 (November 1807), p601 (NcU).

The article is reprinted from *The Port Folio* by Oliver Oldschool, n.s. 4 (November 14, 1807), p318 *(see 928)*.

928 M. [Hamilton's Copy of the *Federalist* deposited in the New-York Publick Library.] *Port Folio* by Oliver Oldschool, n.s. 4 (November 14, 1807), p318 (NcU).

The entire article follows; it refers to a copy of the *Federalist* deposited in the New York Society Library. This article set off a controversy about the authorship of some of the parts of the work; Hamilton's copy apparently disappeared long ago. See Jacob E. Cooke's introduction, pxxiii–xxiv, in the edition of *The Federalist* published by the Wesleyan University Press in 1961.

"Mr. Oldschool, The Executors of the last will of General Hamilton have deposited in the Publick Library of New-York a copy of 'The Federalist,' which belonged to the General in his lifetime, in which he has designated, in his own hand-writing, the parts of that celebrated work written by himself, as well as those contributed by Mr. Jay and Mr. Madison. As it may not be uninteresting to many of your readers, I shall subjoin a copy of the General's *memorandum* for publication in *The Port Folio*. —M.

"Nos. 2, 3, 4, 5, 54, Mr. Jay.
"Nos. 10, 14, 37 to 48 inclusive, Mr. Madison.
"Nos. 18, 19, 20, Mr. Hamilton, and Mr. Madison jointly—all the rest by Mr. Hamilton."

929 "Mr. Poe's Lecture." *Literary World*, N.Y., 3 (February 12, 1848), p30 (NcU).

The lecture was given by Edgar Allan Poe.

The subject of this gentleman's discourse at the Society Library was the Cosmogony of the Universe. He began by reading a letter found in a bottle drifting upon the sea and dated 2848. The letter was an original and brilliant affair, showing the folly of philosophers of the 19th century in depending on the Baconian method for acquiring knowledge. Mr. Poe proposed his own theory of the origin of the universe, involving the combination of various kinds of atoms to form larger masses. The telescope at Cincinnati and the instrument of Lord Ross have not explored the nebular theory but have, instead, confirmed it. The lecture lasted two hours and a half. Although parts of it were too abstruse, the boldness of the speculations and the vivacity of the reading made the whole performance entertaining; publication of the lecture will be eagerly anticipated by the author's many admirers.

930 "The New York Society Library." *Literary World*, N.Y., 3 (February 12, 1848), p30, 400 wds (NcU).

The library is among the four oldest institutions in the city. It has been a kind of higher university for young men and residents of the city for generations. If located in Boston or New Haven the library would be venerated and well supported by public and private grants. In New York the library is comparatively neglected, although it is inferior to none in the country save Yale and Harvard. A catalog newly received from the librarian, P. S. Forbes, reveals a discriminating use of funds from which nearly 1,000 volumes were added in the past year.

931 [The New York Society Library.] *Norton's Literary Gazette and Publishers' Circular*, 3 (January 15, 1853), p4 (ICN, NcU).
The entire article follows.
"*The New York Society Library* have sold their building, at the corner of Broadway and Leonard streets, to D. D. HOWARD, ESQ., of Irving House celebrity, and are to move up town, perhaps as high as Union Park. The price received for their present structure is understood to have been $110,000 cash. For the present they will occupy temporary quarters, the prices of good building sites being so extravagant."

932 [Advertisement for the New York Society Library.] *Literary World*, N.Y., 12 (February 5, 1853), p119 (NcU).
The advertisement is reproduced below.
"New York Society Library,/ 346 and 348 Broadway,/ Corner of Leonard street./ The Collection of Books,/ both for reference and circulation, is one of the largest and best in this country./ The Reading Room/ is liberally and punctually supplied with American and Foreign Newspapers and Periodicals./ The Alphabetical and Analytical/ Catalogue,/ A large octavo, of nearly Seven Hundred pages, for Sale at the Library Rooms."

933 "Society Library, N.Y." *Norton's Literary Gazette and Publishers' Circular*, 3 (February 15, 1853), p19 (ICU, NcU).
The entire article follows.
"It is reported that this association will occupy, for a time, Rooms in the new Bible House, in Fourth Avenue, near Eighth street. The vicinity of Astor Place is rapidly becoming the centre of literary attractions; but the objects of the various associations which are to be located in that neighborhood are so entirely distinct, and yet so kindred in their character, that contiguity is, in our opinion, a decided advantage. Within a few rods of one another may soon be seen the Astor Library, the Society Library, the Mercantile Library, the Cooper Union, and the great establishment of the Bible Society, to say nothing of the University Building, with the rooms of the Historical and Geographical Societies. On the whole, it would be hard to find in the city a better location for these various institutions than the one around which they have almost by accident clustered."

934 [Annual Election of Officers for the New York Society Library.] *Norton's Literary Gazette and Publishers' Circular*, n.s. 1 (May 1, 1854), p226 (NcU).
The entire article follows.
"At the annual election for officers of the New York Society Library, held on the 25th ult., the following gentlemen were appointed Trustees, most of them having filled that office during previous years: — Gulian C. Verplanck, William

Inglis, Alexander R. Rodgers, Dayton Hobart, Frederic De Peyster, James De Peyster Ogden, Joshua Coit, Joshua Delafield, James H. Titus, Charles M. Leupp, John H. Gourlie, James W. Beekman, Henry J. Anderson, Stephen C. Williams, and John Bigelow."

935 [New York Society Library.] *Publishers' Weekly*, 5 (May 9, 1874), p458 (NcU).
The entire article follows.
"At a meeting of the shareholders of the New York Society Library, held Tuesday evening, 28th ult., at the Library Building, University Place, the following Trustees were elected for the ensuing year: Frederic De Peyster, Otis D. Swan, William J. Hoppin, William Adams, Charles R. Swords, Evert A. Duyckinck, Henry C. Dorr, Charles E. Strong, Stephen P. Nash, Robert Lenox Kennedy, Edward Schell, Frederick Sheldon, John L. Cadwalader, Henry Drisler, and Richard E. Mount."

— PHOENIX SOCIETY LIBRARY

936 "Improvement of Our Colored Population." *American Annals of Education*, 3d ser., 3 (December 1833), p596–97 (NcU).
The part of the article that is about a library is quoted below.
"A Library and Reading Rooms have recently been opened under favorable auspices by the Phoenix Society of colored people in New York; and a single individual, has made them a present of more than three hundred and thirty volumes of new and valuable books. The objects of the institution are general improvement, and the training of their youth to habits of reading and reflection. They hope by attracting their attention and occupying their leisure hours, to save many from the haunts of vice and wickedness, and turn their feet from the path of ruin to that of virtue and usefulness. They ask of all who sympathize with them in their condition and efforts, to make their donations of maps, books and journals, through Mr. Samuel E. Cornish, their agent."

— PRINTERS' FREE LIBRARY

937 [Printers' Free Library, New York City.] *Norton's Literary Gazette and Publishers' Circular*, n.s. 1 (April 15, 1854), p196, 550 wds (NcU).
The directors of the Printers' Free Library were elected recently. The receipts of the library were $458.38, of which $378.47 was donated. The total amount of the fund, excluding books, fixtures, etc., is $890.42. Publishers have donated 174 volumes to the library; 146 are bound. Of the 123 subscriptions at one dollar a year, 106 are new, including 64 in the past six months. The librarian reports that 102 members used the library last year, and estimates that 5,000 volumes were read. The condition of the library has improved, but the fund is still too small. George Bruce has agreed to give $100 for every $1000 raised from other sources. Someone has been engaged to solicit donations. If $10,000 should be subscribed by the end of the year, the library would have a secure foundation. The library is open to all on weekday evenings.

938 [Printers' Free Library of New York.] *National Magazine: Devoted to Literature, Art, and Religion*, 4 (June 1854), p572 (InU, NcU).
The entire article follows.
"*Mr. George Bruce*, the veteran type-founder, has offered $1,000 to endow

U.S. — New York

and extend the Printers' Free Library of our city, under the direction of the New-York Typographical Society, if others will add $9,000 within the current year. Though nominally for the use of the disciples of Faust, it is practically open to all who choose to avail themselves of the contents of its well-filled shelves, or its well-supplied reading room."

— PRISON ASSOCIATION

939 [Prison Association of New York.] *Nation*, 19 (September 24, 1874), p203 (NcU).
The following article may refer to the Richmond County Jail; Mr. Larry E. Sullivan, Librarian of the New-York Historical Society writes that he can identify only one prison on Staten Island in 1874, the county jail, located in the courthouse. The entire article follows.
"The Prison Association of New York will gladly receive at their rooms, No. 19 Centre Street, contributions of books, magazines, etc., for the newly-provided library for the penitentiary on Staten Island. Money for the purchase of books for the same destination may be sent to Wm. C. Gilman, Treasurer, 46 Pine Street."

— TEMPLE EMANUEL LIBRARY

940 [Temple Emanuel Library.] *Nation*, 14 (January 11, 1872), p24, 470 wds (NcU).
The article refers to earlier ones *(see 50 and 51).*
We find pleasure in remembering that the first recommendation for the purchase of the *Hebraica* and *Judaica* belonging to the bookseller Frederick Muller was made by Dr. Felsenthal of Chicago in the *Nation*. The library, today opened to the public of New York City as the Temple Emanuel Library comprises little more than three thousand volumes and, in some divisions contains few books. (The divisions are listed.) In this, as in most other Hebrew libraries, books printed in Venice and Amsterdam are most frequently found; other Italian towns are conspicuous, as well. (Many places of publication, mainly in Europe, are listed, and prominent printers are named.)

941 [Books and Manuscripts Acquired by the Library of Temple Emanuel in New York.] *American Bibliopolist*, 4 (September 1872), p451 (ICU, OC).
From the *New York World*. The entire article as given in the *American Bibliopolist:*
"A valuable addition to the literary treasures of New York has been made by the purchase of the collection of printed books and manuscripts of Hebrew and Jewish literature lately submitted for sale *en bloc* by Mr. Frederick Muller, of Amsterdam. The whole collection, comprising 1,600 printed books and forty manuscripts in Hebrew, and 1,200 printed books and twenty manuscripts of Jewish literature, are now deposited in the library of the Temple Emanuel in this city. In this marvellous collection are the rarest editions of the fifteenth and sixteenth centuries, and one of the Hebrew manuscripts is a vellum of the thirteenth century. Nearly all the manuscripts are inedited. The price fixed by Mr. Muller for the whole collection was $4,000 in gold, and much credit is due to the Temple Emanuel for its enterprise in securing so great a treasure."

942 "A Jewish Library." *Appletons' Journal: a Magazine of General Literature,* 8 (October 12, 1872), p417, 700 wds (NcU).

One of the rarest and most valuable collections in the country is located at the Hebrew Temple Emanuel in New York City. It was collected by an Amsterdam bookseller and willed to the congregation. The books and manuscripts encompass the many languages necessary to represent the extent of Jewish literature. Books printed before the 16th century are as well preserved and readable as any printed since. The first fifty years following Gutenberg's invention saw a flourishing of Jewish writing; many fine examples from this period are included in the collection. The majority of editions were printed in Venice and Amsterdam; after Italy and the Netherlands the most frequently represented country is Germany. The manuscripts include medieval and modern specimens.

— UNION THEOLOGICAL SEMINARY LIBRARY

943 "Library of the New York Theological Seminary." *Biblical Repository and Classical Review* [American Biblical Repository], 12 (July 1838), p253, 230 wds (NcU).

The directors of the New York Theological Seminary have recently purchased the library of the Rev. Dr. Leander Van Ess of Bavaria in Germany, who was well known as the agent of the British and Foreign Bible Society among the Roman Catholics there. This library contains over 13,000 volumes; some examples are listed. The library is quite full in the department of church history. Dr. Van Ess spent 40 years collecting the library, and has generously sold it to an American seminary for about one-fifth of its original cost to himself. The purchase is already made; the books are probably on their way to New York. They will be housed in a new building, being erected now for the library and other purposes, which will be ready in early autumn. The accession of the library is highly auspicious and creditable.

944 "The Van Ess Library." *Biblical Repository and Classical Review* [American Biblical Repository], 13 (October 1838), p508–09 (NcU).

The article summarized below refers to an article in *Biblical Repository and Classical Review*, 12 (July 1831), p253 *(see 943).*

We have already reported that the New York Theological Library has purchased the library of the Rev. Dr. Leander Van Ess of Bavaria in Germany. The purchasing agent, Mr. Wolf of Erlangen, wrote to the Rev. Dr. McAuley, of New York, that the library contains 14,000 volumes, including many rare and precious books. (Part of Wolf's letter is quoted.) It says that the library contains a rare collection of all the pamphlets of the Reformation, which came from the Monastery of St. Mary in Westphalia. The young Dr. Van Ess was there when the King of Prussia suppressed all monasteries. Each monk secured something for himself just before the edict of suppression, and Dr. Van Ess took many of the works of the library. Being the only one to have a key to a closet marked "Libri Prohibiti," Van Ess procured the pamphlets, which had been gathered by the monastery during the Reformation.

— UNIVERSITY OF THE CITY OF NEW YORK LIBRARY

945 [Additions to the Library of the University of the City of New York.] *National Magazine: Devoted to Literature, Art, and Religion,* 8 (January 1856), p95 (InU, NcU).

The entire article follows.

"The University of the city of New-York has recently received the following very valuable additions to its library: From the Royal Observatory at Greenwich, England—the Greenwich Astronomical Observations, in quarto volumes, from 1836 to 1850; Reductions of Lunar and Planetary Observations; Magnetic and Meteorological Observations, in seven volumes, with various pamphlets on astronomical science. From the Radcliffe Observatory at Oxford—their Observations from 1840 to 1853."

— YOUNG MEN'S CHRISTIAN ASSOCIATION LIBRARY

946 McC. "Officers and Their Duties. The Librarian." *Young Men's Christian Journal*, 5 (December 1859), p160–161 (Natl. Council of YMCA's of the U.S.A., New York City).

In most American YMCA's the librarian is the only officer in daily attendance; therefore he is seen as the main representative of the association. He should have a thorough knowledge of books and authors, and a readiness to aid users in their researches; he should take a deep personal interest in their spiritual well-being. Mr. A. C. A. Taylor, librarian of the Boston Association, who recently died, was an example of a good librarian; he was devoted to his duties, concerned for young men, and self-sacrificing in spirit. Four hundred young men walked in his funeral procession; a subscription was taken to purchase the cemetery lot where he is buried. The librarian needs to be careful about small things: promptly opening the room, recording circulation, etc. He should prepare a monthly report which he should make interesting. If he has to collect dues he should be patient and good humored.

947 "Young Men's Christian Association Building, New York." *Harper's Weekly*, 13 (October 23, 1869), p686, 465 wds (InU, NcU).

The new building, located at Fourth Avenue and Twenty-third Street, is in Renaissance style. Part of the basement and first floor will contain the gymnasium. The second floor will house the reception room, reading room, the secretary's room, three parlors, dressing room and washroom. The lecture room extends through the second and third floors and will seat 1640 people. The third floor contains a small lecture room, three classrooms, and the library which extends up through the fourth floor. The fifth floor will include a picture gallery. The library has a capacity of 60,000 volumes. During the winter there will be a course of twelve lectures. The total cost of the structure is $500,000, of which $100,000 remains to be paid. (There is a picture of the exterior of the building on page 685.)

948 "The New York Young Men's Christian Association." *Harper's Weekly*, 13 (December 11, 1869), p785–86 (InU, NcU).

The Association has a membership of about 3000, and has opened several branches in the city. Space at headquarters is inadequate so an appeal has been made for money for a new building. Some of the wealthy citizens of New York have responded generously; almost $300,000 has been raised without a public appeal. The proposed building and its site will cost nearly $500,000. The first, fourth and fifth floors will be rented out; income will retire the debt and provide operating expenses. The Association's quarters on the second and third floors will consist of a lecture room seating 1500, a library, reading room, prayer-meeting room, gymnasium, bowling alley, and parlors. The writer hopes that girls and women will be admitted to the new facilities. (The article includes sketches of the proposed lecture hall, reading room, and library.)

949 "The Library of the Young Men's Christian Association of New York." *Appletons' Journal: a Magazine of General Literature*, 4 (November 19, 1870), p613, 470 wds (NcU).

A library has recently been opened in the new building of the Young Men's Christian Association. The spacious room is lit by a skylight and gas jets and has room to accommodate 50,000 volumes and about 200 readers. A reading room on the first floor supplies foreign and domestic newspapers and magazines. The Association intends to provide a reading and reference collection comprising the best of English literature and has already collected about 3000 works; the library will also include foreign classics. These are classified and cataloged in a way which will allow any number of future additions. The reader may borrow a book by signing a request slip which is held by the librarian until the book is returned. The number of readers is increasing, but because of lack of funds, the size of the collection has not kept pace. (A view of the interior is shown.)

950 "Library of the N. Y. Association." *Association Monthly*, 1 (December 1870), p331, 300 wds (OO, Natl. Council of the YMCA's of the U.S.A., New York City).

The cover of the December issue (p321) shows an interior view of the library.

The library room of the New York City YMCA is 30 by 72 feet with a 30 foot ceiling which contains a skylight. Founded in 1852, the library contains almost 4,000 volumes. It is open from 8:30 a.m. to 10:00 p.m. and is free to anyone over sixteen years of age, whether a member or not.

951 [Plans for the New York City YMCA Library.] *Nation*, 12 (March 9, 1871), p158, 190 wds (NcU).

The New York City Young Men's Christian Association will contribute $10,000 toward the purchase of the library of the late Thomas P. Barton if it can obtain $40,000 more, with the understanding that the 16,000 volumes in this library will be added to the 3,600 now in the YMCA Library and that the library will be open freely to the public, both day and evening. There will still be room for 20,000 volumes, with ample accommodation for readers. The directors hope in this way to found a public library comparable to those in Boston and Philadelphia. The Barton library is strong in natural history, belles-lettres and bibliography; in Shakespeariana it is unsurpassed in this country. A gift to the association of $500 will entitle the giver to a life membership; $1000 will entitle the giver to a membership in perpetuity.

ROCHESTER — ATHENAEUM AND MECHANICS' ASSOCIATION LIBRARY

952 "Rochester (N.Y.) Athenaeum and Mechanics' Association." *Norton's Literary Gazette and Publishers' Circular*, 3 (February 15, 1853), p19, 200 wds (ICN, NcU).

We have received a copy of the annual report of the Association, presented January 4, 1853 and we abstract it: The number of members is 1509; the receipts,

$2,306; and the expenditures, $1,923; 585 volumes have been added, bringing the total to 7,005 volumes. In buying books, special attention has been paid to biographies of mechanics and the history of their arts. The institution shares in the general prosperity of young men's libraries. The reading room is spacious and Corinthian Hall, its lecture hall, is large and well lighted. It should be examined by those about to erect similar edifices.

— THEOLOGICAL SEMINARY LIBRARY

953 Freeman, Z. "Library of Rochester Theological Seminary." *Norton's Literary Gazette and Publishers' Circular*, 2 (March 15, 1852), p45, 950 wds (ICN, NcU).

The library purchased many valuable books at the sale of Dr. Jarvis' library. (A few of those books are listed in this article.) The last shipment of books from Germany consisted mostly of standard works in sacred literature, translations of the Scriptures, and Biblical exegeses. The library recently purchased the 4,600 volume collection of the late Dr. Neander, who drew upon his collection for his studies in church history. The Neander collection, purchased for $2,300 is a valuable addition to the library and should arrive from Germany in late spring.

954 "Rochester University." *Norton's Literary Gazette and Publishers' Circular*, 3 (January 15, 1853), p3 (ICN, NcU).

The entire article follows.

"The library of the celebrated Dr. Neander, about which there was at one time so much discussion in the newspapers, has been, at length, received at the Rochester Theological Seminary. It numbers 4,600 volumes, the larger part of which are the original sources which were consulted in the preparation of his works.

"We understand that this institution has lately been presented with a valuable set of the Historical Collections of this country by a gentleman of New Jersey, and that this is intended as a nucleus for a valuable Library of American History.

"Choice modern works have been added to this nucleus, so that the Seminary and University libraries now number 10,000 volumes."

955 "A Day in the Neander Library." *Norton's Literary Gazette and Publishers' Circular*, 3 (March 15, 1853), p37-38 (NcU).

Neander's library was purchased by the Rochester Theological Seminary.

Standing in Neander's collection gives one the feeling of his presence. The library lacks the amusing and entertaining. Whatever illustrated the character of man as a moral and religious being was interesting to the late historian. There is little mere literature, and few works of physical science. The collection numbers not quite 5,000 volumes. Many are rare and very expensive. Its four hundred gigantic folios, and numerous large and solid quartos are very valuable. Moreover, the core of the library consists of original sources from which he wrote his church history and kindred works. The collection includes a complete collection of the Church Fathers; the works of the scholars and schoolmen of the Middle Ages; 1200 writings of the reformers; later sources of church history; modern works of church history; a department of ancient and modern philosophy; and a division of New Testament philosophy and exegesis.

SCHENECTADY — UNION COLLEGE LIBRARY

956 "Union College Library." *Norton's Literary Gazette and Publishers' Circular*, 3 (January 15, 1853), p3 (ICN, NcU).
The entire article follows.
"At the recent sale of Major Douglas's Library in this city, many of the most important works in Civil Engineering were purchased for the library of Union College, which makes their collection of such works (in connection with the private library of Professor Gillespie), one of the best in the country."

957 "The Endowment Fund." *Union College Magazine*, 11 (June 1873), p261-64 (NSchU).
The part of the article about libraries (p263) follows.
"Many of the donors have designated the manner in which they desire their gifts to be used; others have left them to be expended at the discretion of the President. Most of the undesignated gifts have been assigned to the library fund, and it is earnestly desired that this fund may be so enlarged that a handsome income will be provided for the increase of the library and its necessary expenses. This object will be prominently presented to the friends of the College, and it is hoped will meet with a willing and liberal response."

958 Potter, Horatio. "Union University. The Library." *Union College Magazine*, 11 (June 1873), p264-69 (NSchU).
The article refers to another article which precedes it in the same issue of the *Union College Magazine (see* 957).
The preceding article refers to the goal of enlarging the library. Fundraising for a new fire-proof building will begin soon; the building will contain all of the libraries of the college. The collection itself must be improved first. Large purchases will be made to keep it current. The present science collection will be expanded. General literature will not be overlooked. Books will be provided, and measures taken to show students the necessity of becoming acquainted with them. (The President of the Alumni Association is quoted concerning the importance of more general literary culture among college students.) Some students come from well-educated families with good reading habits and liberal culture. Others have had no such training, and have never learned to love good reading. A good library can inspire a love of good letters and stimulate students to higher achievement.

SYRACUSE — FRANKLIN INSTITUTE LIBRARY

959 "Franklin Institute, Syracuse, N. Y." *Norton's Literary Gazette and Publishers' Circular*, 3 (February 15, 1853), p19 (ICN, NcU).
The entire article follows.
"We learn from a correspondent at Syracuse, that about three hundred volumes were added to this Young Men's Library during last year, so that its entire number of volumes is now about two thousand. Between two and three hundred dollars are appropriated to its annual increase. A catalogue was published in 1851, to which is prefixed a brief history of the Institution."

TROY — YOUNG MEN'S ASSOCIATION LIBRARY

960 [Nineteenth Annual Report of the Troy Young Men's Association.] *Norton's Literary Gazette and Publishers' Circular*, n.s. 1 (January 1, 1854), p9 (NcU).
The entire article follows.
"The nineteenth annual report of the Troy Young Men's Association shows the affairs of that institution to be in a flourishing state. 2,750 volumes have been added to the library during the last year, most of them books of a solid character."

YATES COUNTY — FARMER'S CLUB

961 Bigelow, Artemas and Daniel Lee. [List of Books for an Agricultural Library; Letter to Daniel Lee, Editor and Reply.] *Genesee Farmer*, 7 (February 1846), p36, 600 wds (InU, NcU).
(Bigelow, Secretary of the Farmer's Club of Yates County, New York, writes asking for a list of books for an agricultural library to serve the needs of fifty to one hundred farmers. Lee's reply notes that several similar requests have been received, and contains a list of about fifteen titles.) To these add the volume, nature itself, which is available to all yet cannot be bought at any price. Books deserve respect but one must always be keenly aware of nature's process.

North Carolina

CHAPEL HILL — UNIVERSITY OF NORTH CAROLINA

962 [Needs of the University of North Carolina Library.] *Nation*, 12 (March 9, 1871), p158, 300 wds (NcU).
The present building up of libraries in this country is one of the healthiest symptoms of the times. It occurs almost entirely in the North, and we may forget in what a slough of ignorance the South still lies; our sympathy and aid should be prompt. We have read a very forlorn account of the condition of the library of the University of North Carolina, probably the largest library in the state, with 7,000 volumes. Two thousand of these were purchased in 1859; perhaps 2,000 more are state and federal documents, and there are some disused college textbooks. This is a disgrace, not only to North Carolina but to the nation; we hope that benevolent persons will remember the library, which is at Chapel Hill.

NEW BERN — NEW BERN LIBRARY SOCIETY

963 "Literature of North Carolina." *Monthly Anthology and Boston Review*, 3 (July 1806), p355–57 (NcU).
The article is an extract from a letter to the editors from a gentleman in Raleigh, N. C. The part about libraries (p357) follows.
"A public library has been founded in Newbern by a donation of $500 from Thomas Tomlinson. It is divided into eighty shares of $20 each; all the shares are

filled, and books purchased. It is contemplated to extend the number of shares to 120. I know of no other public libraries in the state, except one in Iredell county, established by a society called the Centre Benevolent Society, which has subsisted nearly twenty years."

Ohio

964 "Common Schools of Ohio." *Common School Journal*, 1 (March 1, 1839), p68-72 (NcU).

The part of the article about libraries, "Common School Libraries" (p71), follows.

"The subject commends itself to the judgment of all, and is of too much importance to be any longer neglected. It is spoken of with deep interest throughout the state, and the public appear to expect some action on the part of the legislature. New York has appropriated a sum of money to each of the districts, on condition, that they will raise in the district an equal amount for the purchase of district libraries. That state, though much larger than our own, has but very few more districts than Ohio."

965 "Ohio. Second Annual Report of the State Commissioner (H. H. Barney,) of Common Schools, to the General Assembly of Ohio, for 1855. 128 pages." *American Journal of Education* (Barnard), 2 (September 1856), p531-40 (NcU).

Extracts from the report are reprinted; the part about libraries (p536-38) is summarized below.

During 1854 and 1855, 258,926 books were distributed to Ohio's district school libraries at a cost of $150,787. The district school library has become an essential part of the education system. Men of experience will attest that a child who is provided with a sound, basic education and who has acquired a reading habit is well prepared to cope with the conflicts of life. The most effective means to advance our prosperity is to develop our intellectual skills and moral values; district libraries provide the books which serve to develop these capacities. Furthermore, these libraries instill the reading habit in our children and serve to uplift the educational and moral standards of our citizenry.

CINCINNATI

966 "Cincinnati Sabbath Schools" *Ladies' Repository: a Monthly Periodical, Devoted to Literature, Art, and Religion*, 16 (August 1856), p505 (NcU, OC).

The entire article follows.

"From the fifth annual report of the Society of Religious Inquiry, in regard to the Sabbath schools of Cincinnati, we gather the following as the statistics for the year 1856 [there followed a table that is here reformatted to text]: *Methodist* — 32 schools, 733 teachers, 4,530 scholars, 13,931 library books; *Presbyterian* — 19 schools, 376 teachers, 2,329 scholars, 6,634 library books; *Baptist* — 10 schools, 145 teachers, 1,156 scholars, 2,383 library books; *Society of Relig. Inquiry* — 9 schools, 136 teachers, 790 scholars, 840 library books; *Union* —

6 schools, 83 teachers, 700 scholars, 1,350 library books; *Episcopal*—4 schools, 93 teachers, 615 scholars, 2,181 library books; *Congregational*—3 schools, 63 teachers, 295 scholars, 1,120 library books; and *Miscellaneous*—19 schools, 326 teachers, 2,182 scholars, 5,485 library books. Totals—102 schools, 1,955 teachers, 12,597 scholars, 33,924 library books. There has been an increase over the year 1855 as follows: Of schools, 6; of teachers, 106; of scholars, 241; and of volumes in libraries, 1,460. The sum of $6,000 was contributed during the year ending in April, 1856, for general mission purposes."

— CINCINNATI LAW LIBRARY

967 [Cincinnati Law Library.] *Literary World*, Boston, 6 (August 1875), p36–37 (NcU).
The entire article follows.
"Messrs. Robert Clarke & Co., have published 'The Cincinnati Law Library Association,' an address delivered by W. S. Scarborough in June last. It gives an interesting history of the Library, which dates back to 1846, and contains valuable information and suggestions for the guidance of those who are organizing libraries. The institution is now in a very flourishing condition, having 9,151 volumes, and adding new books annually."

— CINCINNATI LIBRARY

968 [Early Library in Cincinnati.] *American Bibliopolist*, 2 (January 1870), p21 (ICU, NcD, OC).
The entire article follows.
"At the last meeting of the Historical and Philosophical Society of Ohio, Mr. Robert Clarke read an interesting paper on the first library formed in the Northwestern Territory. Mr. Clarke produced evidence to show that a library was begun in Cincinnati in 1802."

— HISTORICAL AND PHILOSOPHICAL SOCIETY OF OHIO LIBRARY

969 [Treatment of Pamphlets in the Historical and Philosophical Society of Ohio.] *Publishers' Weekly*, 7 (January 30, 1875), p114, 310 wds (NcU).
This article is identical with part of an article in the *Nation* for January 21, 1875 *(see 366)*, that is on this library.
In a recent report, Mr. Julius Dexter, Librarian of the Historical and Philosophical Society of Ohio, in Cincinnati, gives an interesting statement about his method of treating pamphlets. Cards, numbered in black, are used to record bound volumes and cards numbered in red are used for pamphlets. Each pamphlet is numbered to correspond to its card and the pamphlets are placed in boxes; when a box is filled, the numbers for its first and last pamphlets are written on the outside. Boxes are laid on their sides on the shelves, in piles four boxes high. The card catalog, arranged by author and subject, shows the number for each pamphlet. This treatment keeps the pamphlets clean and uncreased, and is economical of space. A series of reports may be scattered through a dozen boxes, but the cards are together in the catalog drawer and readily show the location of the pamphlets.

— PUBLIC LIBRARY

970 [Reading in the Cincinnati Public Library.] *Nation*, 15 (October 10, 1872), p234, 420 wds (NcU).

Mr. William F. Poole's fifth *Annual Report* on the Cincinnati Public Library furnishes additional evidence of what may now be called a general law: about three-fourths of the adult and juvenile books taken out of our public libraries are fiction. (Statistics of three libraries are given.) Mr. Poole does not particularly regret the demand for fiction but would be glad to see Mrs. [E. D. E. N.] Southworth, Mrs. [Ann Sophia] Stephens, and Mrs. [Caroline Lee] Hentz suppressed. The Cincinnati library has been open on Sunday for more than a year and a half. (Statistics are given.) Those who fear that the Sunday library will draw off attendance from church will be encouraged to learn that afternoon attendance is much greater. Many young men now spend a portion of the day in reading; in general, the books called for have been instructive. The same word comes from England in response to Mr. Poole's report.

971 "The Cincinnati Public Library." *Publishers' Weekly* [Publishers' and Stationers' Weekly Trade Circular], 2 (October 24, 1872), p416, 500 wds (NcU).

Mr. William F. Poole's fifth annual report of the library gives many interesting facts. The collection has increased from less than 25,000 volumes in January, 1871 to nearly 50,000 volumes. The circulation has nearly doubled and the use of the reading rooms has more than trebled. A collection of 214 English tracts covering the years from 1640 to 1658 has been purchased at a very low cost. (The percentage of books in the main subject classes and the names of the most popular authors are given.) The library has been opened on Sunday for more than a year and a half; it is heavily used on that day, particularly in the afternoon and evening. Mr. Poole reports that it has attracted many of the class of young men who would ordinarily spend Sunday in a less profitable manner.

972 [Sunday Opening at the Public Library of Cincinnati.] *American Bibliopolist*, 5 (May–June 1873), p77, 270 wds (ICU, NcD).

The Cincinnati Public Library was the first in this country to open on Sundays when it began doing so two years ago. The annual report of librarian William F. Poole is quoted, describing the lack of opposition by religious leaders to the Sunday opening. Support is widespread and use of the library has increased. The ratio of books to periodicals in circulation has risen recently — 9,820 books and 12,915 periodicals this last year, as against 6,475 books and 13,442 periodicals last year. The daily average of Sunday circulation has increased from 383 to 437.

973 [The Cincinnati Public Library.] *Nation*, 17 (August 14, 1873), p113, 280 wds (NcU).

Mr. William F. Poole's report on the Cincinnati Public Library for the year ending June 30 is very encouraging. The number of volumes is nearly 60,000. The percentage of books circulated from the different classes is about the same as last year. It remains true that the utility of any popular library is to gratify the taste of novel readers. The experiment of Sunday opening is so successful that officers of the Young Men's Christian Association report that they know of no opposition to it among the clergymen and laymen who are members of their organization.

974 [Cincinnati Public Library.] *Publishers' Weekly*, 5 (March 14, 1874), p273 (NcU).
The entire article follows.
"The fine new building of the Cincinnati Public Library, containing by far the handsomest library hall in the country, is now open to the public. It was dedicated the 25th of February with an address by Hon. Geo. M. Pendleton. Mr. Vickars is Mr. Poole's successor as librarian, and has a staff of twenty-five."

— YOUNG MEN'S MERCANTILE LIBRARY ASSOCIATION

975 "Cincinnati Mercantile Library." *DeBow's Review* [The Commercial Review], 7 (September 1849), p278 (NcU).
The entire article follows.
"We have received the Report for 1849. The regular and honorary members reach 1,517 in number. The library consists of 8,195 volumes—2,098 volumes, at a cost of $1,955.61, having been added in one year. Numerous lectures, within the past year, have been delivered before the association. We congratulate the society upon its eminent and flattering success. The officers for 1849, are George T. Stedman, President; Joseph C. Butler, Vice President; James Lupton, Corresponding Secretary; Robert L. Fabian, Recording Secretary; George S. Dodd, Treasurer: H. D. Huntington, Charles Reakirt, Charles J. Adams, W. H. Davis, Samuel Richardson, Directors."

976 "Cincinnati Mercantile Library, 1852." *DeBow's Review* [DeBow's Southern and Western Review], 12 (April 1852), p459 (NcU).
The entire article follows; it refers to H. D. Huntington.
"James Lupton has been elected President; E. B. Hinman, Vice; H. D. Huntingdon [sic] and L. A. Ostrom, Secretaries; Charles R. Fosdick, Treasurer. The Directors are Mess. Chenowith, Woods, Merriam, Thompson and Caldwell. Mr. Fabian, the late Secretary, has removed to New Orleans, and is mentioned in high terms by the Board. The receipts of this association are $7,779.01 for 1851, and the expenditures for books, lectures, and refitting rooms, $5,330.22. The library now contains 11,769 volumes. All praise is due to this worthy and estimable association."

977 "Cincinnati (Ohio) Young Men's Mercantile Library." *Norton's Literary Gazette and Publishers' Circular*, 3 (March 15, 1853), p40 (NcU).
The entire article follows.
"The 18th annual report of this Association was presented in January, from which it appears that the number of volumes now owned by the Library, is a little less than thirteen thousand. During the past year 484 volumes have been added by purchase, 219 by donation, and 168 by the binding of periodicals, making an aggregate of 872. One hundred newspapers and sixty other periodicals are received at the Reading Room. The present number of members is 2,300, of whom $77 have been received during the past year. The aggregate receipts were $15,740, and the expenditures $15,570. Mr. R. H. Stephenson has been appointed Librarian in the place of Mr. C. E. Cist, resigned. A new and elegant suite of rooms has been fitted up with great liberality for the use of the Library and Reading Room."

978 [Young Men's Mercantile Library Association of Cincinnati.] *Norton's Literary Gazette and Publishers' Circular*, n.s. 1 (March 15, 1854), p143-44 (NcU).
The entire article follows.
"The Young Men's Mercantile Library Association of Cincinnati have published their Nineteenth Annual Report for the year 1853. From it we learn that the present number of members is about 2,400; the receipts for the year were $9,243; the number of books on the catalogue is 13,839, of which 1,198 were added during the last year. Within this period, 23,892 volumes have been drawn from the library, making an average monthly circulation of nearly 2,000. Henry D. Huntington is President sf [sic] the Board of Directors, and R. H. Stephenson, Librarian."

COLUMBUS — STATE LIBRARY

979 [Ohio State Library.] *Publishers' Weekly*, 5 (April 4, 1874), p360 (NcU).
The entire article follows.
"Mr. Walter C. Hood, of Marietta, Ohio, has been appointed by Governor Allen as State Librarian to fill the position of S. G. Harbaugh, whose term expired on March 23. Mr. Harbaugh has served as Librarian twelve years from March, 1862, receiving consecutive appointments of two years each from six Governors. His daughter, Miss Mary C. Harbaugh, is retained as assistant."

DELAWARE — OHIO WESLEYAN UNIVERSITY LIBRARY

980 [Library of Ohio Wesleyan University.] *Norton's Literary Gazette and Publishers' Circular*, n.s. 1 (July 15, 1854), p362 (NcU).
The entire article follows.
"The library of the Ohio Wesleyan University, located at Delaware, Ohio, will be largely increased during the ensuing year. The donation of ten thousand dollars by William Sturges, of the firm of Sturges & Ellis, N.Y., will be expended by the President mainly in Europe. A large edifice, to cost over $15,000, is now in process of erection, and will be finished for the reception of the library next year."

GREENFIELD — SOCIAL LIBRARY

981 Simmons, Charles B. "Memoirs of Townships. — Greenfield." *Firelands Pioneer*, 1 (November 1858), p13-18 (NcD, OCl).
The part about a library, on p17, is reproduced below:
"'The Social Library of Greenfield' was established in the year 1818. Through the energy of Eli Halladay, Samuel Spencer, Erastus Smith, E. B. Simmons, Bildad Adams and others, the library continued in existence for many years."

WESTERVILLE — OTTERBEIN UNIVERSITY LIBRARY

982 [Facsimile of *Codex Sinaiticus* Probably Lost in Library Fire at Otterbein University.] *American Bibliopolist*, 2 (February 1870), p77 (ICN, ICU).

The entire article follows.
"The burning of the library of Otterbein University, at Westerville, Ohio, renders it probable that one of the very valuable facsimile copies of Tischendorf's *Codex Sinaiticus* was consumed. It will be recollected that soon after Tischendorf's discovery of the very old manuscript of the New Testament bearing the above name, the Russian government issued some facsimilies at great expense. These were sparingly distributed among the great libraries and institutions of learning, only a very few coming to this country. On hearing of the work, some of the Otterbein faculty sent a letter to St. Petersburg asking the gift of a copy. The imperial government was obliging enough to return a favorable answer, and the shelves of Otterbein were graced by the treasure. As before said, it is to be feared it has now perished, leaving the admonition that such rarities should be kept in none but fire-proof buildings."

Pennsylvania

983 Tyson, J. R. "Annual Discourse Delivered Before the Pennsylvania Historical Society." *Hazard's Register of Pennsylvania*, 8 (November 1831), p309-18 (NcU).
The parts of the article about libraries (p314, 317) are summarized below.
Libraries for the public are perhaps to be found in every county in Pennsylvania. The Philadelphia library has national prominence. The library is now the largest on this side of the Atlantic. In 1785, it had 5,487 volumes; by 1806 it had 14,218; and now it has more than 37,000 volumes. A glance at its catalog shows its merits. The first directors, appointed in 1731, are listed. In 1777, James Logan gave 3944 volumes. An act of the legislature in 1791 annexed the Loganian to the Philadelphia Library; the books were placed in the same building in May, 1794.

984 Shunk, F. R. "7th Annual Report on the Common Schools, Colleges and Academies of Pennsylvania." *Connecticut Common School Journal and Annals of Education*, 3 (June 1, 1841), p161-65 (NcU).
The part of the article about libraries, "Establishment of School Libraries," (p161, 170 wds) is summarized below.
The next subject of the Legislature is the establishment of district school libraries. A small annual appropriation, to be paid to districts raising an equal or greater sum, the whole to be used to buy useful books on subjects of general interest, would be a means of creating libraries of useful knowledge in the districts within a few years. Such libraries are the legitimate result and support of a well regulated system of common school education. They bring knowledge to every man's door, and are calculated to improve the taste, and to strengthen the moral and intellectual faculties of the people. Improvements in printing, and the consequent reduction in the price of books, make it an easy matter for each school district to accomplish this purpose.

985 Kieffer, D. S. "School Libraries." *Pennsylvania School Journal*, 1 (May 1853), p428-29 (IU).
The article is a letter from Kieffer in response to an earlier article by Thomas H. Burrowes.

There is little reason to plan for library rooms when there is first no plan for forming a school library. One method I have used is to have each student who desires use of a library contribute at least two books. The collection of volumes thus accumulated is circulated among the contributors. This plan is self-perpetuating as more new students provide more new books. By applying this plan, every school house in the state can have a beginning library by the end of the school year in 1854. (A list of some of the books from Kieffer's school library follows.)

986 R., J. S. "School Libraries." *Pennsylvania School Journal*, 1 (June 1853), p458–59 (IU).

It can not be disputed that every school ought to have a library and that every school may achieve this goal. The availability of a school library has incalculable good influence on the reading habits and moral development of school children and their families. Although many books may be obtained for the library through donations, this method is unsatisfactory; frequently, donated books are of a doubtful quality. It is better to purchase selected volumes, having solicited the funds from the community. The school children themselves can do the fund-raising. A library for the Male and Female Grammar Schools of the N. W. Ward, Reading, Pennsylvania, was established in this manner a year ago. The children made two collections and raised enough money for two hundred books which now are in constant demand.

987 "School Libraries." *Pennsylvania School Journal*, 1 (June 1853), p451–52 (IU).

The article refers to another by D. S. Kieffer in the May 1853 issue of the same periodical *(see 985)* and one signed J. S. R. in the June 1853 issue *(see 986)*.

The plan proposed by Mr. D. S. Kieffer of establishing a school library by contribution of books is opposed by J. S. R. who contends that donations of money are more useful for starting a library. There are arguments for and against each view. The contribution of books is favored because people are more likely to give books than money; J. S. R. favors the donation of money in order to have more control over the selection of the books, avoiding unwholesome or duplicate volumes and making certain there are no important works missing. These arguments actually apply equally to each viewpoint: unwholesome donations should be rejected and duplicates are often desirable. A happy combination of the plans would allow for initial contributions of good books and then of either specific volumes or of sums of money in order to complete the collections.

988 "Minutes of the Second Annual Meeting of the Pennsylvania State Teachers' Association, [Dec. 27, 1854] Afternoon Session." *Pennsylvania School Journal*, 3 (January 1855), p194 (IU).

The part of the minutes about district school libraries (520 wds) is summarized below. It apparently refers to the report of James C. Challens *(see 220)*.

James R. Challen [*sic*], Jr. of Somerset read a report on district school libraries; a resolution and amendment were appended to the report. One member of the assembly asserted that such libraries are the legislature's responsibility; another thought the matter should be left to the teachers and county superintendents. Several commented on the value of libraries to education although one member thought they might distract the student from his school studies. The amended resolution, which commends the establishment of school libraries to directors, teachers, superintendents and legislators, was passed unanimously.

989 "Libraries." *Pennsylvania School Journal,* 4 (May 1856), p323–26 (DeU, IU, TxU).

Libraries have two objectives: first, to collect and preserve books for posterity and, second, to make these books available to the public. The former objective remains meaningful, but with the increasing number of published books and the decrease in book prices the latter objective probably soon will come to an end. The demise of town circulating libraries and the decline in the number of books recently reported by New York district school libraries obviously indicate that the second objective of libraries has become less important as more and more people choose to purchase their own books rather than to borrow books from libraries. For this reason, the establishment of state-supported district libraries would be a waste of our tax dollars; also, for the same reason, it is fortunate that the Legislature rejected the proposal to provide each one of our school libraries with dictionaries.

990 Zercher, J. J.; McCaskey, J. P.; and Geist, I. S. "District and County Institutes." *Pennsylvania School Journal,* 11 (June 1863), p377–82 (CoGrS).

The parts of the article about libraries, "District Institute Library" and "Librarian" (p381, 210 wds) are summarized below.

A committee of the School Board of Lancaster recommended the formation of a teachers' library, and the appropriation of money for that purpose, to be followed by annual appropriations thereafter. The sum of money need not be over $25–30, enough to purchase Barnard's educational works, which will serve as a nucleus for the library. Fines for non-attendance at district sessions collected from delinquent teachers might also be used to purchase works. The teachers would thus have access to reading material which they need but cannot afford. A teacher in some central location where the District Institute meets might be placed in charge of the library. That person would then keep a register of books taken out and returned, indicating when and by whom.

991 "Acts Relating to Common Schools Passed During the Session of 1864." *Pennsylvania School Journal,* 12 (June 1864), p360–62 (CoGrS).

The part of the article about libraries, "District and School Libraries," p360–61, is summarized below; it is a copy of the act passed by the Pennsylvania Senate and House of Representatives to promote the establishment of district and school libraries.

When a district school library is formed, the Board of Directors of the school district shall select its location and provide bookcases. The Board, or a committee of the Board, shall receive monies, and select and purchase books. No district funds may be used to purchase library books in district or school libraries except for the professional reading of teachers. Legal ownership of the district library and its materials shall remain with the Board of Directors. Any resident of the district over age twelve may use books free of charge. Rules and regulations are made by the Board of Directors. The Secretary of the Board or designee will be the district librarian. Only pupils may take books from the school library. The school library legally belongs to the proper board of directors. Common school directors may receive gifts to increase or support either district or school libraries.

992 "School Libraries." *Pennsylvania School Journal*, 13 (April 1865), p218–19 (IU).
The article refers to item 991 in this bibliography.
The Pennsylvania library act of 1864 tried to do as much for the promotion of libraries as is right and requisite for the state to do. Our object is to suggest some modes of procuring funds for the purchase of school libraries in addition to those named in the article on page 360 of the June 1864 issue of the *Journal*. There are three, which should be tried in this order: 1) the contribution of money or of proper books by the pupils; 2) the procuring of money, for the purchase of books, by means of an exhibition; and 3) the collection of money, for the same purpose, by subscription. Donation of books by the community is not suggested, because improper or unsuitable works would probably thereby be introduced.

993 "School Libraries." *Pennsylvania School Journal*, 14 (October 1865), p68, 790 wds (IU).
The reference in this article to the June 1864 issue of *Pennsylvania School Journal* is to item 991 in this bibliography. The article from the January 1864 issue is item 207 and the article from the August 1864 issue is item 223.
An act passed by the Legislature in 1864 encourages the establishment of district and school libraries. The text of the act is given in the June 1864 issue of the *Pennsylvania School Journal*; its main features are summarized in the present article. The teacher can direct the progress of the district library by starting and guiding the project; he can establish the school library himself with the help of the pupils. Ideas to aid in the establishment of school libraries are to be found in the January and August issues for 1864 of the *Pennsylvania School Journal*. Not only is the fall of the year the best time to broach new subjects such as this one, but the times demand the effort because young people need the right kind of reading. The state should not select and buy books for the people, nor should it tax the public for such a purpose; after the teacher demonstrates the desire for books and shows that they will be read, the people can and will buy them.

994 H. "Self-Improvement—A Library." *Pennsylvania School Journal*, 14 (March 1866), p214, 380 wds (CoGrS).
The article summarized below was reprinted from the *Hazleton Sentinel*.
Lyceums and libraries are effective means of self-improvement; both are neglected in Hazleton, although a literary society has just been organized. A public library would involve considerable expense, but if young men engaged energetically in the work, a liberal public would doubtless assist them. A library might be connected with the proposed town hall. A library and reading room would attract young and old persons and would aid in diffusing much useful information. Young men usually seek some company in the evenings after work, and the only places here are the bar-room and the saloon. The library would counteract such evils, and the young would be furnished with entertainment and good counsel.

995 Moore, Mrs. John G. "School Libraries." *Pennsylvania School Journal*, 22 (December 1873), p199, 290 wds (CoGrS).
The state makes ample provision for the education of children, but few have access to libraries. Higher schools are well supplied with them, but not many children attending public schools ever extend their education to the higher schools. In many public schools, the literary culture of pupils is neglected. If each school had a library, teachers and pupils would be aided. The duties of a

librarian are comparatively light and would not interfere with a teacher's other duties. In many studies, certain books are valuable auxiliaries. A school library would meet the children's need for books and encourage them to read.

HARRISBURG — STATE LIBRARY

996 "State Library." *Pennsylvania School Journal*, 4 (August 1855), p34, 460 wds (IU).

The circular from Dr. William R. Dewitt, the state librarian, to editors deserves the attention of those who desire to see written a full and accurate history of Pennsylvania. No historian has yet been able to write such a work; the materials must be accumulated now before they are lost. If these treasures are deposited in the State Library the work will be more easily effected and will be better as well. (A copy of Dewitt's circular, dated June 27, 1855, is reprinted. The circular asks the readers to deposit old manuscript letters, papers, public documents, printed pamphlets and books with the Pennsylvania State Library. Authors and publishers are also invited to deposit copies of their works in the State Library.)

997 Dewitt, William R. "Report of the [Pennsylvania] State Librarian for 1855." *Pennsylvania School Journal*, 4 (May 1856), p347-49 (DeU, IU, TxU).

Dewitt's entire report (summarized below) was reprinted in the periodical.

The $1,000 appropriated by the last Legislature for law books has been expended for that purpose. The $500 appropriated for other books also has been spent; $200 was expended for binding. The completion of additional bookcases has been delayed. The library each year has been receiving law reports from other states, yet for the past several years none has been sent by this state in return. This situation is being corrected and it is proposed that the Legislature provide the money needed to purchase the State's reports for future exchange. The library now has approximately 200,000 volumes; it is hoped that in the future the collection of the law department can be made complete; furthermore, the library's collection of periodical literature is fragmentary and deserves to be expanded. The state library should be regarded as a depository of books that will be used by future generations.

998 "The State Library." *Pennsylvania School Journal*, 17 (August 1868), p34-35 (IU).

The annual report for 1867 of the State Librarian, Wein Forney, has been received. Presently containing 28,323 books, maps, etc., the library is located on the second floor of the new extension to the Capitol. The room is 102 feet long, 54 feet wide and 24½ feet high, with a wide gallery on all sides. Books have been placed on the shelves, but the shelves provided are already crowded. Alcoves will need to be built to provide for the approximately 60,000 volumes which will be added in the next twenty years. The annual increase of the library is now about 800 volumes. The expense during 1867 was $3,226.37 plus the librarian's salary. Miscellaneous expenses amounted to $998 and $1,384 was spent for law books. More light and better ventilation are needed. The librarian has done a good job in obtaining full information on newspapers and periodicals in the state.

LEWISBURG — UNIVERSITY LIBRARY

999 "The Library at Lewisburg." *Christian Chronicle*, 4 (April 11, 1849), p138, 660 wds (NRAB).

One of the most important problems of American higher education is the need for large libraries which serve as repositories of man's intellectual records. All too frequently, colleges are equipped with imposing buildings for classrooms and observatories, and endowed with professorships while their libraries are neglected. Thus far, $100,000 has been subscribed to establish the University at Lewisburg. Given the importance of the library to its University, it is hoped that individuals will again come forward to contribute to the special library fund.

1000 Bates, Samuel P. "Report on the University at Lewisburg." *Pennsylvania School Journal*, 11 (May 1863), p347-52 (CoGrS).

The part of the article about libraries, "Library," (p351, 590 wds) is summarized below.

The library has about 3000 volumes; these are mostly standard works. The library is open regularly, but is not heated in the winter, so maximum use is not made of it. In the past, when colleges were places of quiet resort and meditation, the library was one of their chief agencies. Now, the habit of deep reading has been supplanted by vigorous training in colleges. A student must learn, however, that it is not what a professor puts into his head, but the thoughts which come out of it which measure his learning. Libraries encourage patient research, careful investigation, reflection and judgment. During his stay in college, the student should have the fields of knowledge opened up to him, and should begin his labors in scholarship.

MEADVILLE — ALLEGHANY COLLEGE LIBRARY

1001 Bates, S. P. "Allegheny College." *Pennsylvania School Journal*, 11 (March 1863), p285-88 (CoGrS).

The part of the article about libraries, "Library," (p286-87) is summarized below.

The library contains about 8000 volumes, including many rare and costly books and many valuable works of art. Dr. Alden, the first president of the college, says there is an extensive range of Greek and Roman classics and of the ancient fathers of the Christian church; there are books in thirty ancient and modern languages, and a fine collection in history, belles lettres and other branches of literature and science. Few library collections have a better foundation, but books of more recent publication are needed. To make a library accessible and to preserve books, the library should be kept warm, well-ventilated and opened daily. In order that a library be used well, students should be required to write about subjects necessitating library research. Such assignments would make research indispensable, awaken the spirit of inquiry and establish a good habit.

NORRISTOWN — MONTGOMERY COUNTY AGRICULTURAL SOCIETY LIBRARY

1002 "Agricultural Library." *American Agriculturist*, 19 (July 1860), p219 (InU, NcU).

The entire article follows.

"We are glad to learn from Mr. Chas. J. Elliott, that the Montgomery County (Pa.) Agr. Society have just established a library for the use of the Society, and voted an annual appropriation of $100 to keep it supplied with agricultural and horticultural literature. Such a library would be valuable in connection with every town and county association. If kept at a central point, the members could draw out and exchange over books several times during a year, and a few books would be used by a considerable number of persons, who might not perhaps purchase them for their own individual libraries. The Library of the Montgomery Society is to be kept in the new and spacious village Library Buildings at Morristown. [Norristown?] Mr. E. gives especial credit to Col. Thomas P. Knox, Pres. of the Society, for active and efficient efforts in getting up the Library."

NORTHERN LIBERTIES — LIBRARY AND READING ROOM COMPANY

1003 "Library and Reading Room Company of the Northern Liberties. Annual Report." *Hazard's Register of Pennsylvania*, 10 (November 24, 1832), p332, 490 wds (InU, NcU).

The directors report that receipts for the past year totalled $1460.02; this figure is broken down into eight categories. Sixty-five shares of stock were sold at $5 per share, and 150 stockholders paid $3 each for the year. Expenditures totalled $1460.72, with $484.70 being spent to purchase 747 volumes, and $266.20 being spent for a librarian and for the rent of rooms. Nine categories of expenditures are listed in all. The company owns 1653 volumes, and there are 386 deposited there by members. Thirty daily newspapers and periodicals are received from America, Britain and Europe. The board unsuccessfully sought to procure foreign manifests arriving at the port. A copy of the latest United States census was received. Thirty-two members lent the company $10 each, without interest, for five years, to purchase books; this expenditure has now been made.

1004 "Library and Reading Room of the N. L." *Hazard's Register of Pennsylvania*, (January 4, 1834), p6–7 (InU, NcU).

The article summarized below is reprinted from the *Philadelphia Gazette*.

The fourth annual meeting of the Library and Reading Room Company of the Northern Liberties was held. Receipts for last year were $700; $254 were expended in books, papers and periodicals, and the remainder for incidental expenses. About three hundred volumes have been added since the last annual report. There are now 200 stockholders, besides the annual subscribers. Greater public encouragement is needed for the library. A series of public lectures will be given during the present winter in the room immediately over the hall. The library contains about 2500 volumes, newspapers from the principal cities of the union, periodicals, minerals, and geological specimens. A lecture room has been joined with the library room. Directors were elected. (They are listed.) Two resolutions were adopted concerning the library's relation to general education, and the efforts of the membership to extend the benefits of the society to more people.

Philadelphia

PHILADELPHIA (see also PENNSYLVANIA — NORTHERN LIBERTIES)

1005 Coxe, Alexander S. et al. "Project of a Reading Room." *Port Folio* by Oliver Oldschool, 3rd ser. 3 (February 1814), p155–58 (InU, NcU).

Philadelphia has fallen behind New York and Boston in the effort to provide reading rooms. Such rooms are valuable agencies for social intercourse, an activity essential to general improvement. A number of subscribers have begun to plan for two or three reading rooms in suitable areas of the city. The project is being called to the attention of the general public so that they might appreciate its value. In each of the proposed establishments there will be a room for reading only, and another room for conversation and other activities. Each reading room will be supplied with newspapers and periodicals, as well as maps, gazetteers, and works on politics and economics. Each institution will be under the control of the subscribers.

1006 Wharton, Thomas I. "Provincial Literature of Pennsylvania." *Hazard's Register of Pennsylvania*, 6 (August 28, 1830), p134–140 (InU).

The article is concluded in the September 4, 1830 issue (p145–49) *(see 1017)*. The parts of the article about libraries (p139, 340 wds) are summarized below.

In 1730, Franklin proposed the formation of the first joint library in Philadelphia. The next year he set on foot proposals for a public library, procuring 50 subscribers, for an initial membership fee of 40 shillings plus 10 shillings a year for 50 years. — James Logan died in 1751, leaving to Pennsylvanians the Loganian Library, which he had spent fifty years collecting. His will states that he left more than 100 folio volumes, in Greek, for the advancement of classical learning. The collection included all the Greek mathematicians, the most valuable Latin authors, and many modern mathematicians.

1007 "Hon. John Sergeant's Address to the Apprentices' Library Company." *Hazard's Register of Pennsylvania*, 10 (December 1832), p373–81 (ICN, NcU).

The part of the address about libraries (p380–81) is summarized below.

The Library Company of Philadelphia is one of this city's many republican institutions. It serves the entire populace of the city — not just its students and scholars. The library now has nearly 800 shareholders. The annual cost to each shareholder is only $6.40, and for that small sum a man and his family can select books from a 40,000-volume collection. According to Benjamin Franklin, we are indebted to the city's young mechanics for the founding of the library. Let us demonstrate our gratitude by doing something for our apprentices. That primarily is what the Apprentices' Library is intended to do as it was established over twelve years ago for their benefit. The library has over 8,000 volumes and an average of 900 users per month. The Apprentices' library has done much good, but it needs to be expanded and it needs financial support.

1008 "Libraries in Philadelphia." *Hazard's Register of Pennsylvania*, 12 (August 10, 1833), p87, 400 wds (InU, NcU).

The article summarized below is reprinted from the *Commercial Herald*. It refers to a notice in the *Boston Mercantile Journal* which is also discussed in "Public Libraries," *Hazard's Register of Pennsylvania*, 12 (August 10, 1833), p86–87 *(see 72)*.

The *Boston Mercantile Journal* says that public libraries there contained 45,000 volumes, and that it was believed that Philadelphia contained one good library of 25,000 volumes. We have inquired about public libraries in Philadelphia, and present the following table as a result. (Twenty-six Philadelphia libraries are listed, together with the number of volumes each contains.) The total number of volumes is 111,550; many are scarce. Included are gifts from Louis XVI and Napoleon, the best works on medicine, surgery and science, and what may be the only complete copy of the "Fathers" in this country.

1009 "Libraries in Philadelphia." *Niles' National Register*, 45 (September 7, 1833), p22-23 (NcU).

This article is almost the same as the one summarized in item 1008. The *Niles National Register* article omits one library in the list and there are a few other changes.

1010 "Library of Friends, Philadelphia." *Norton's Literary Gazette and Publishers' Circular*, 3 (February 15, 1853), p19, 280 wds (ICN, NcU).

Among the many libraries of Philadelphia is one belonging to the Friends, which numbers 5,300 volumes and is constantly increasing. One of its most able supporters informs us that it has a very fine collection of tracts especially relating to religious controversies and the history of the Friends. A collection of standard literature, history, travels, etc. has been selected with a view to exclude everything prejudicial to the mind and morals of youth. The Biblical Library, belonging to the Bible Association and Friends in America, contains more than two hundred Bibles in various languages. (A vulgate Bible, written about 900 A.D., and a Bible printed in Venice in 1478 are described.)

1011 [Rush Bequest and Colwell Gift.] *Nation*, 8 (June 3, 1869), p435, 440 wds (NcU).

A Philadelphia correspondent writes about the bequest of the late Dr. James Rush to the Philadelphia Library Company and Mr. Stephen Colwell's gift of a professorship and library to the University of Pennsylvania. Dr. Rush has left the bulk of his estate and a square of ground for a reading library (not a circulating one). Rush was a learned and eccentric person and his will is full of odd provisions; however, the bequest is likely to be very useful. Mr. Colwell, a wealthy iron-master and diligent student of political economy, is giving his large library—about ten thousand volumes—to the University together with a sum of money to establish a chair of political economy and social science, with Dr. [Joshua Hall] McIlvaine as the occupant. Other merchants and manufacturers are contributing to this fund.

1012 [American Manners.] *Appleton's Journal: a Magazine of General Literature*, 13 (January 30, 1875), p149-50 (NcU).

The part of the article about libraries (240 wds) is an anecdote, attributed to Mrs. Lucy Hooper, which also appeared in an article by Mrs. Hooper in *Lippincott's Magazine* for February 1875 *(see 1013)*.

1013 Hooper, Lucy H. "The Stranger Within the Gates of Paris." *McBride's Magazine* [Lippincott's Magazine of Popular Literature], 15 (February 1875), p248-53.

The part about a library (p252-53) is summarized below.

When I visited a public library in Philadelphia, I found an American gentleman engrossed in a volume. His chair was tipped back and his feet rested on a table; I was appalled by his rude posture. When I found the book I sought, it proved too large and too high on the shelf for me to lift down. Seeing my dilemma, the reader leaped to my assistance and courteously removed the volume from the shelf, dusted it with his handkerchief and laid it on the table. As I thanked him I was struck by the difference in his manners and those of the French. No gentleman of that nationality would be found in such an unseemly posture, but neither would he have ever considered lifting a finger to help an unknown woman.

— APPRENTICES' LIBRARY COMPANY

1014 "Apprentices' Library." *Hazard's Register of Pennsylvania*, 1 (April 19, 1828), p256 (NcU).
The entire article follows.
"The average number of boys using the Library [Apprentices' Library of Philadelphia] during the past year exceeded 600, being considerably greater than at any former time. The new applicants during the same period amounted to 612, and those now using the library 778. New members elected since last report 19. Receipts $550.25, expenditures $561.02."

1015 "To the Apprentices Library Company of Philadelphia." *Hazard's Register of Pennsylvania*, 3 (March 21, 1829), p186–87 (NcU).
The article reprints the annual report in its entirety; a summary follows.
Having outgrown its present quarters, the library has been moved to rooms in a building on Carpenter Street, which have been leased for five years at $125 per year. With the new shelving the library will be able to accommodate 15,000 volumes. In the past year the library has added 450 books to its collection, which now numbers 5,000 volumes. Expenses incurred last year totaled $905.89. Since its opening in 1820, 4,000 boys have used the library. In the past the library's continued existence occasionally has been problematic because of insufficient income. Indeed, only $500 has been donated to the library during the nine years of its existence; nevertheless it is hoped that because of its demonstrated value to the community the library will not be allowed to wither away.

1016 Garrett, Philip. "Annual Report of the Apprentices' Library Company, of Philadelphia — Read March 8, 1830." *Hazard's Register of Pennsylvania*, 5 (March 20, 1830), p190, 800 wds (NcU).
Committees were appointed to purchase and preserve books, to care for the room and the furniture, and to audit the accounts. Since the last report, more than 1450 volumes were added; 1130 were purchased, 320 were donated and 489 were rebound. There are now 6,000 volumes in the library. About 682 boys use the library in an average month; 584 of these are new applicants. Last year, 65 new members were added, and $1001.66 was expended for books, salaries and incidental expenses. Over $1500 was added through donations and bequests. A monthly report has been commenced. This institution was founded ten years ago; it has not received the favor it deserves, but its benefits may yet be extended more widely. Receipts and expenditures each amounted to $3,390.63. (Tables describing receipts and expenditures are given.)

1017 Wharton, Thomas I. "Provincial Literature of Pennsylvania." *Hazard's Register of Pennsylvania*, 6 (September 4, 1830), p145–49 (InU).
The article is the sequel to one in the August 28, 1830 issue (p134–40) *(see 1006)*. The parts about libraries are summarized below. The "city library" may mean the Apprentices' Library.

U.S. — Pennsylvania

In his *Observations on a Variety of Subjects, Literary, Moral and Religious, Written By a Gentleman of Foreign Extraction, Who Resided Some Time in Philadelphia*, Rev. Mr. [Jacob] Duché bears testimony to the love of letters in Philadelphia. He says the librarian of the city library assured him that for one person of distinction and fortune, twenty tradesmen frequented the library. The city library has 459 works printed in Philadelphia before the Revolution. Of these, 425 are original books and pamphlets, and 34 are reprints of foreign works. Thomas Penn endowed a public library in Lancaster called the Juliana library after his wife.

1018 Garrett, Philip and Mason, Samuel. "[Report of] Apprentices' Library Company [Philadelphia]." *Hazard's Register of Pennsylvania*, 7 (May 21, 1831), p331–32 (NcU).

During the past year 1,300 volumes were added, 1,110 by purchase and 190 by gifts. There are now 6,500 volumes in all. Eighty-seven new members have been added. The average number of applicants for books is 768, comprised of boys between 7 and 21. Their behavior is good. A catalog was made in early autumn. We propose opening the library four nights a week instead of two, as we do now. Though lacking in funds and suffering other discouragements, the library gives great benefit to the young. All of the work selected must either inform the understanding or benefit the heart. Except from a few people, the library has received little public support.

1019 Garrett, Philip. "Apprentices' Library Company." *Hazard's Register of Pennsylvania*, 9 (March 31, 1832), p207–08 (IEN, NcU).

Following is a summary of the company's annual report.

Because of the increased circulation of books, the library will be open four nights a week instead of two as now is the practice. The library has 1,031 members; 17 new members joined during the past year. The collection has about 7,000 volumes; of these, 623 were added last year. The treasurer's report, which is appended, shows expenditures of $289.93 for acquisitions and binding and $571.18 for salaries, rent, and incidental expenses. The Board has guarded carefully against the introduction of demoralizing or frivolous books. The efforts of the company to improve the habits of our apprentices and to make them better informed citizens have proven to be successful.

1020 Troth, Henry. "Apprentices' Library Company." *Hazard's Register of Pennsylvania*, 10 (May 1835), p282–83 (ICN, NcU).

Following is a summary of the company's annual report.

That this institution has continued to meet the expectations of its founders is confirmed by the addition of 625 new members. Last year the library added 166 volumes to bring the collection up to 9,000 volumes. Our contributors are invited to examine the appended treasurer's report. The company did not receive part of its anticipated income due to the financial difficulties of the Chesapeake and Delaware Canal Company in which we hold stock. This loss of income either will have to be made up out of our capital or by outside contributions. Due to our fifteen years of service to the community, the Board has the fullest confidence that generous support will be forthcoming from the public. The library was founded to give the city's apprentices access to the literary treasures of the past and present and to provide them with the benefits of an elementary education.

— ATHENAEUM

1021 "Athenaeum." *Hazard's Register of Pennsylvania*, 1 (April 19, 1828), p255, 375 wds (ICU).

The article summarized below is an extract from the report of the directors of the Philadelphia Athenaeum.

About eighty-nine newspapers and forty-one journals are available in two reading rooms. These include British and French publications. There is also a collection of more than 4000 volumes. The library is open fifteen hours daily except Sunday. The collection includes more than sixty maps, as well as encyclopedias, gazetteers and other reference works ("works of reference and authority"). The library may be used by visitors when introduced by members. More than 1000 visitors used the library last year. Receipts amounted to $3186.51; expenditures $2,742.74. The expenditures included $695.43 for books and $335.60 for newspapers. The librarian received $600.00. (The names of fifteen directors are listed.)

1022 Biddle, Nicholas, Norris, Samuel and Vaux, Roberts. "Athenaeum." *Hazard's Register of Pennsylvania*, 3 (February 7, 1829), p91–92 (InU, NcU).

The annual meeting of the stockholders of the Athenaeum of Philadelphia was held February 2, 1829. Nicholas Biddle was appointed chairman. The fourteenth annual report notes that the Athenaeum's receipts amounted to $3,001.41, including $1,544.00 as annual payments from 362 stockholders, $150.00 from six new stockholders, and $638.00 from 94 subscribers. Expenses for the year were $2,315.01, including $333.57 for books, journals and binding; $283.88 for newspapers; $104.60 for postage; $600.00 for the librarian's salary; and $484.72 for rent. The invested funds as of January 24, 1829 totaled $8,995.45. During the last year 200 volumes have been added to the collection, and over 1,000 visitors have used the Athenaeum's rooms.

1023 "Athenaeum." *Hazard's Register of Pennsylvania*, 5 (March 6, 1830), p153–54 (NcU).

The article summarized below includes a reprint of the annual report.

At the annual stockholders' meeting of the Philadelphia Athenaeum, officers were elected for the ensuing year; also, the Directors' and the Treasurer's reports were read. Last year the Athenaeum received an income of $2,940.32 and after expenses enjoyed a surplus of $79.93. There are now 436 stockholders. The library contains 5,300 volumes, receives 75 American newspapers as well as 4 newspapers from England and 2 from France, and subscribes to 32 periodicals. The Directors acknowledge the generosity of two donors, Samuel Breck for his gift of 863 books and the late William Lehman for his gift of $10,000. The latter gift will be invested, and it is hoped it ultimately will be used to finance a building suitable for the Athenaeum.

1024 "Athenaeum." *Hazard's Register of Pennsylvania*, 7 (February 26, 1831), p135–36 (InU, NcU).

The article reprints the seventeenth annual report of the Philadelphia Athenaeum as presented at the annual meeting; a summary follows.

Officers and the board of directors were elected. (Their names are listed.) The expenditures of the Athenaeum for the preceding year were: for books, magazines and foreign journals, $688.01; for newspapers, $311.05; for maps,

$70.00; for binding, $143.87; and $600.00 for the librarian's salary. Total income was $2,631.00 while expenditures were $3,057.92. The excess of expenditures resulted from binding of worn books, the acquisition of some needed furniture, and a frame for the maps. A legacy of $10,000 was received during the last year from the estate of William Lehman. The permanent fund is $18,909.87, almost all of it invested in the funded debt of Pennsylvania. The collection contains 6,000 volumes; about 82 periodicals are received as well as the local papers. There were more than 1,100 nonmember visitors in the preceding year.

1025 Evans, Cadwalader, Vaux, Roberts, Smith, William, and Wharton, Thomas I. [Philadelphia] "Athenaeum." *Hazard's Register of Pennsylvania*, 11 (February 23, 1833), p127, 680 wds (InU, NcU).

(The report of the 1833 annual meeting and the 18th annual report are given.) The treasurer received $2910.25 during the past year, with $1584 coming from stockholders, $627 from interest on stock exclusive of the Lehman Fund, $457 from 68 visitors, and $125 from the sale of 5 shares. (Other sources are outlined.) Disbursements amounted to $2992.46; $697.05 was spent for books, maps, magazines, foreign periodicals, and English newspapers; $377.57 was spent for American newspapers, $475 for rent, and $600 for the librarian's salary. (Other lesser expenditures are also listed.) The capital was increased by $2558; annual income increased $232. (The amount of investments is listed.) There are 422 stockholders. The library has about 6500 volumes valued at $10,000 and insured for $3000. We propose raising the price of shares, which now cost $25. Annual visitors are charged $8. More patrons might be attracted if the benefits were better known.

1026 "Athenaeum—Nineteenth Annual Report." *Hazard's Register of Pennsylvania*, 13 (February 15, 1834), p103, 490 wds (InU, NcU).

The directors submit a statement of the finances and general condition of the institution for the last year. The amount received last year was $3,078.50, of which $1,652.00 came from 413 stockholders; there were 78 subscribers for a year and portions of a year. Disbursements totalled $3,025.57; this amount is broken down into 11 categories. The amount of capital invested in stocks and mortgages is $22,528.21, including income from the William Lehman Fund for the construction of a suitable building. The present accommodations are not large enough, and are not fireproof. The idea of constructing a fireproof building has been received with approbation, but it has not yet been adopted. John L. Harris of Burlington, N.J., bequeathed 500 volumes last year. More than 1,100 visitors were introduced to the Athenaeum last year. This establishment has economically and substantially indulged the cultivation of literary taste in Philadelphia.

1027 "Athenaeum of Philadelphia. Twentieth Annual Report." *Hazard's Register of Pennsylvania*, 15 (February 21, 1835), p128, 600 wds (InU, NcU).

The directors of the Athenaeum submit a statement of the finances and general condition of the institution for the past year. The receipts of the institution were $2945.31, which was obtained from six sources. Of that amount, $1600 was derived from the 415 stockholders. Disbursements were $2964.50; this amount is broken down into ten categories. The amount of capital invested in stocks and mortgages is $23,117.10. Finances are thus in good condition; soon the Athenaeum may afford a building of its own. A member of the institution,

John Savage, died last year and bequeathed $1000 for the institution. More than 900 visitors toured the rooms of the Athenaeum last year. The number of stockholders is gradually increasing; public estimation remains high.

— CHRISTIAN HALL LIBRARY

1028 [Two Addresses by Judge Thayer.] *Nation*, 12 (March 16, 1871), p181 (NcU).

The article reports the publication of an address by Judge M. R. Thayer of the District Court of Philadelphia, *The Law, Considered as a Progressive Science*, and of another about libraries. The part of the article about the second address is given, verbatim, below.

"Judge Thayer has also printed his 'Address delivered at the opening of the Library of Christian Hall,' at Chestnut Hill, one of the suburbs of Philadelphia. Besides giving a modest mention of the liberality of Mr. Henry J. Williams, for many years one of the leading lawyers of Philadelphia, in thus founding a library for the use of his neighbors, Judge Thayer sketches for their benefit the history of libraries, showing how, from similar and even smaller benefactions, some of the greatest storehouses of learning have taken their start, and in time become the workshops for the most acute and the most active and useful intellects of their respective localities — at times, indeed, of the world. The scholarly tone of this brief address shows that its author has made effective use of the larger field opened to him in his varied career as lawyer and judge."

— FEMALE LITERARY ASSOCIATION

1029 "Female Literary Association of Philadelphia." *Genius of Universal Emancipation*, 3d ser., 3 (December 1832), p29–30 (InU).

(The association's constitution is reprinted.) The association's membership consists of black women who believe that they must overcome the general prejudice against their race through self-education. They are agreed to develop their individual talents. Among the officers specifically designated in the constitution are a president, vice-president, secretary, treasurer, agent, and librarian. The librarian is to have charge of the association's books, seeing that they are placed in the library after each meeting. The agent is authorized to subscribe for periodicals as directed by the association, and to care for them. The annual subscription from each member shall be $1.50.

— FRANKLIN INSTITUTE LIBRARY

1030 "Franklin Institute. The Twenty-first Quarterly Meeting of the Institute was Held at Their Hall, on the 16th of April, 1829." *Franklin Institute, Philadelphia: Journal*, 7 (April 1829), p290–93 (NcD).

The part of the article about libraries (p291) follows.

"The Library has received several additions since the date of the last quarterly report, by purchase, donation and exchange, comprising some valuable works. The library is kept in the managers' room, which is warmed and lighted every evening, and is open to the members of the Institute. Several of the daily journals are also received."

U.S. — Pennsylvania

— FRIENDS' FREE LIBRARY

1031 [Friends' Library at Germantown, Pennsylvania.] *Nation*, 18 (April 9, 1874), p236, 390 wds (NcU).

The entire article is a quotation from a letter written by a resident of Germantown (already a part of Philadelphia). The article is summarized below.

We have a small library, established by the Friends but open to the public. It contains four thousand volumes, including few works of the imagination; novels are strictly excluded. The recent annual report of the librarian, William Kite, contains the following suggestive passage (summarized in this abstract): I have been interested in the influence of the library in weaning young people from a desire for fiction. Most of them, after first asking for novels, settle down to good reading. Purveyors to the reading classes are responsible for this appetite for the wholesome or poisonous food; if the directors of public libraries could but see this evil and aid in checking it, they would confer a great benefit on young people.

— GERMAN SOCIETY LIBRARY

1032 A. "The German Society's Library." *Hazard's Register of Pennsylvania*, 7 (April 23, 1831), p267, 400 wds (InU, NcU).

The library belonging to the German Society of Philadelphia contains almost 3000 volumes in German and English. The *Leipziger Literatur Zeitung* and the *Zeitung für die Elegante Welt* are regularly received and a collection of several hundred volumes recently collected in Germany by an agent is expected to arrive soon from Hamburg. Only society members may use the library. Applicants must be of German birth or ancestry, and elected by a majority of the members. New members pay a fee of $8.00. The annual dues are $1.25. The library is open three hours each Saturday afternoon.

— LIBRARY COMPANY OF COLORED PERSONS

1033 "Library of the People of Color." *Hazard's Register of Pennsylvania*, 11 (March 16, 1833), p176, 260 wds (NcU).

In the periodical the page is misnumbered 186.

We the people of color of Philadelphia have organized an institution called the Philadelphia Library Company of Colored Persons to promote among our youth a proper cultivation for literary pursuits and mental improvement. The effort is neither fractional nor sectarian, being designed by and for the entire population of Philadelphia. We appeal to friends of science and of the people of color for such books or other donations as will facilitate the objective of the institution. (The names and addresses of ten men authorized to solicit and receive donations for the company are given.)

1034 "To the Public." *Genius of Universal Emancipation*, 3d ser., 3 (May 1833), p103, 250 wds (InU).

The article is reprinted from the *U.S. Gazette*.

The Philadelphia Library Company of Colored Persons is now organized. Its purpose is to improve the minds of the young. The organization is not sectarian, nor is it a factional effort; it is intended to serve the entire city and county of Philadelphia. Books and other donations are solicited and may be given to any of the following: Robert C. Gordon, Jr., Frederick A. Hinton, Daniel B. Brownhill, James Needham, Thomas Butler, Wm. G. Gordon, Robert Purvis, Daniel Colly, Junius C. Morel, and Morris Brown, Jr.

— LIBRARY COMPANY OF PHILADELPHIA

1035 Saunter, Samuel. "The American Lounger, No. XXVI." *Port Folio*, by Oliver Oldschool, 2 (July 10, 1802), p209–10 (NcU).

In a memorial to the Directors of the Library Company of Philadelphia, which a lady has signed "Literary Leisure," the library is criticized because it is open only in the late afternoon. This is a poor time for serious study because of the drowsiness brought on by dinner; the library should be opened at an earlier hour. Saunter has been asked to pass the memorial along to the directors, but has little influence with them and has chosen to publish it. It has been suggested that the library's current hours of opening result from a shortage of funds; Saunter is doubtful about this.

1036 "Library" [Company of Philadelphia]. *Saturday Magazine: Being in Great Part a Compilation from the British Reviews, Magazines, and Scientific Journals* [National Recorder], 2 (December 4, 1819), p353–54 (ICU).

As the manner in which shares in the Library Company of Philadelphia are sold seems not to be generally known, we wish to state that there are now about 780 stockholders. The number of shares is not limited; the price is $40 plus an annual payment of two dollars. The real value of a share was recently calculated at $78. There are about 24,000 volumes in the building. All of the money from new shares and annual payments is laid out for books except for a small amount used for other expenses. Directors are appointed by stockholders at annual meetings. Those wishing to purchase shares should apply to James M. Parke, treasurer.

1037 [Longer Hours at the Philadelphia Library Company.] *Saturday Magazine: Being in Great Part a Compilation from the British Reviews, Magazines, and Scientific Journals* [National Recorder], 2 (December 4, 1819), p360, 210 wds (ICU).

The stockholders of the Philadelphia Library met last Saturday to discuss keeping the library open the whole day instead of just in the afternoon, as at present. Everyone seemed convinced that it would be advantageous, were it not that book purchases would have to be reduced. It was then proposed to raise the annual payment one dollar per share. This proposal was opposed on the grounds that additional hours would aid only men of leisure, but raising the payment would reduce its use by the mass of society. We agree that inducing everyone to read is more important, but also would like to see the library open all day. Sales of new shares may make it prudent to incur the additional expense. Forty-one people voted in favor of opening the library all day; 357 voted against it.

1038 "William MacKenzie." *Hazard's Register of Pennsylvania*, 3 (May 16, 1829), p319–20 (InU, NcU).

William MacKenzie was born in 1758 and died in 1828. He was a member of Philadelphia's mercantile community and a collector of books. At his death he bequeathed to the Library Company of Philadelphia five hundred volumes of his English books printed after 1700 to be chosen by the directors. He also willed the Library Company, for the increase of the Loganian Library, all of his books which were printed before 1700 as well as 800 of his French and

Latin books to be selected by the directors. Most of MacKenzie's other books have been purchased from his executors for the Library Company and the Loganian Library.

1039 "Library Company of Philadelphia." *Hazard's Register of Pennsylvania*, 9 (March 10, 1832), p160, 160 wds (InU, NcU).
Part or all of the article was taken from the *National Gazette*.
The Philadelphia Library Company is about to receive approximately 5,500 rare, curious, and expensive books from the library of Mr. James Cox, long a popular drawing master of this city. The books are on the fine arts and various kinds of literature. Mr. Cox will receive an annuity in payment for them. At a special meeting of the stockholders, held on Saturday, it was unanimously resolved to petition the Legislature to vest in the stockholders the power to fix the amounts of the annual payments.

1040 [Smith, John Jay.] "Notes for a History of the Library Company of Philadelphia." *Hazard's Register of Pennsylvania*, 16 (September 26, 1835), p201–08 (InU).
Several of the early records of the Library Company are quoted. The organization and financing of the company, James Logan's recommendations of books, and the acquisition of books in England are the subjects of chapter one. The rest of the article includes information about processing books, the rules of the library, the good relations with Thomas Penn, and year to year accounts of gifts, increases in membership and books, the directors, the now-discontinued museum, librarians, security, and mergers with the Union Library Company and others. Additional topics are the move to Carpenters' Hall in 1773, the use of books by the Continental Congress, Revolutionary War activity, post-war renewal, aborted plans for a building to be shared with the Philosophical Society, the role of Franklin, the building occupied in 1790, and the acquisition of the Loganian Library. There are 44,000 books in the collection now; 836 members pay $4 annually.

1041 S[mith, John Jay]. "Notes for a History of the Library Company of Philadelphia." *Portfolio, and Companion to the Select Circulating Library*, Part 1, no. 7 (September 26, 1835), p100–03 (NcD).
This article is the same as the one in item 1040. Its author was also the editor of *Portfolio*; he gave the editor of *Hazard's Register* permission to publish the article simultaneously.

1042 "The Philadelphia Library." *Niles National Register*, 49 (October 24, 1835), p125–26 (NcU).
The article summarized below was reprinted from the *Philadelphia Gazette (see 1041)*.
For a complete history of the library see Smith's article in *Waldie's Port Folio*, September 26, 1835; a summary of the article is provided for our readers who may not have previously seen it. The Library Company was formed in 1731 with the price per share of forty shillings; there were fifty subscribers. James Logan was appointed to draw up a list of books to be acquired for the library, and the first shipment of books arrived in 1732 from London. The library then was open one hour on Wednesday and six hours on Saturday to "any civil gentleman." Presently, the library has 44,000 volumes and 836 members.

1043 "Public Library in Philadelphia." *American Magazine of Useful and Entertaining Knowledge*, 2 (November 1835), p91, 250 wds (NcU, OC).

Founded by Franklin in 1731, the library is today one of the nation's largest. The first books were purchased in 1732 from a list drawn up by James Logan. Franklin printed the library's notices, J. Brientnal served as secretary, and P. Sing engraved a seal; for these services they were given the free use of the library. Franklin became the librarian. In 1740 the library was in a room of the State House and was moved to Carpenters' Hall in 1771. Two other library companies merged with the library in 1769 and 1771. The library was incorporated in 1742. Today the volumes number 42,000.

1044 "The Library Company of Philadelphia, and the Loganian Library." *Norton's Literary Gazette and Publishers' Circular*, 2 (July 15, 1852), p127, 1550 wds (ICN, NcU).

Founded in 1731, the Library Company counted among its early benefactors Benjamin Franklin, who subscribed £100, and James Logan, who drew up the list of books initially to be acquired. The library at first was kept in Robert Grace's chambers; it was moved in 1740 and again in 1773 to different locations; and in 1790 it occupied its present quarters in a building on Fifth Street. The library has 51,000 volumes as well as a valuable collection of old newspapers. It is open daily except Sunday from ten until sunset. James Logan intended to construct a building for his 10,000 volume collection; however that intention was not realized, and his collection was transferred after his death to the Library Company. The Loganian collection has many valuable books and manuscripts, all of which may be consulted by the public. (An exterior view of the library accompanies the article.)

1045 "Catalogue of the Philadelphia Library." *Norton's Literary Gazette and Publishers' Circular*, 3 (December 15, 1853), p217, 170 wds (NcU).

A third volume of the catalog of the Philadelphia Library will be published in 1854; it will include all books added since the two-volume catalog of 1835. It will include the supplements of 1844 and 1849. The catalog will be classified and subdivided like the large catalog, and will contain an index to all three volumes. The index will contain authors', translators', and annotators' names, all subjects treated, and the most important words on the title page of each book.

1046 "Franklin's Club for Mutual Improvement." *American Journal of Education* (Barnard), 8 (March 1860), p251-52 (NcU).

The journal reprints an extract from Benjamin Franklin's *Autobiography;* the part of the extract about libraries is summarized below.

I proposed that a public subscription library be founded and I drew up the necessary plans and regulations. Because of the low rate of literacy at that time, only fifty persons were willing to subscribe money for this venture. The books were imported, and the library was open one day per week. Its success was soon manifested: reading became fashionable: donations of books were forthcoming; and libraries in imitation of Philadelphia's were established in other towns. The library afforded me the means of self-improvement; reading was the only amusement in which I indulged.

1047 Read, J. M., Jr. "The Old Philadelphia Library." *Atlantic*, 21 (March 1868), p299-312 (InU, NcU).

U.S. — Pennsylvania 276

The origins of the Library Company of Philadelphia are traced back to Franklin's Junto. Several of the shares of the stock in the library are traced through their various owners. The provisions of James Logan's will which required the librarian and some of the trustees to be his descendants are explained. The merger of the Loganian Library with the Library Company (in 1792) is described. The article provides the names of many shareholders, trustees and librarians and enumerates some of the particularly valuable holdings. A few incidents in the history of the library are provided, for example, the story of the acquisition and later return to Britain of five volumes of the Irish State Papers.

1048 [Rush Bequest to Philadelphia Library Company.] *Nation*, 9 (July 22, 1869), p70, 470 wds (InU).

The Philadelphia Library Company has not yet acted upon the late Dr. Rush's bequest of a lot and a fund sufficient to build a new library on it. Hesitation stems from the location of the site, and the smallness of the fund after the building is completed. We regard both reasons as insufficient. The location would be as convenient as the Astor Library is in New York, and the Philadelphia library lacks the resources to refuse even a small fund after the building is completed. The Philadelphia library should be in a fire-proof building; the management is somewhat slipshod; and the foreign purchaser has few qualifications for his job. The Rush bequest should be accepted and used to revive, redirect and improve the library. Eventually, the library should be free to the public, and in any event it would likely receive the private libraries of Philadelphia as their owners die.

1049 [Rush Legacy to Philadelphia Library.] *American Bibliopolist*, 2 (January 1870), p21 (NcD, OC).

The entire article follows.

"The legacy of the late Dr. James Rush to the Philadelphia Library was hampered by various conditions. No newspapers were to be admitted into the Library, but, what was worse, it was to be removed to a point so distant from the centre of the town that it would be of little practical value to the citizens. The executors insisted upon a rigid compliance with the terms of Dr. Rush's testament; but after a good deal of severe thinking, the embarrassed gentleman have [sic] hit upon the expedient of keeping their old library where it is, and of building a new library upon the site designated by the eccentric testator."

1050 [The Rush Bequest to the Philadelphia Library.] *Nation*, 16 (May 29, 1873), p368 (NcU).

The entire article follows.

"The Supreme Court of Pennsylvania has sustained the executors of the late Dr. Rush in their litigation with the Philadelphia Library, and the result will be the erection of an uncommonly fine fire-proof library building on the corner of Broad and Christian Streets — a part of the town considered not very respectable, and certainly now at some distance from the centre of the best population. As soon as completed, it will be offered to the Philadelphia Library, when the question of accepting the legacy under its peculiar conditions will recur, and perhaps reasons be found for not declining it."

— LOGANIAN LIBRARY (see also PENNSYLVANIA — PHILADELPHIA — LIBRARY COMPANY OF PHILADELPHIA)

1051 "Loganian Library." *Hazard's Register of Pennsylvania*, 1 (March 1, 1828), p133–35 (NcU).
The will of the late James Logan, dated November 1749, contained provisions for the establishment and maintenance of a public library that would bear his name. The rental income from specified properties was to be used to support the library. Logan bequeathed approximately 2,500 volumes to the library, and later a son, William, added 1,000 volumes to its collection. In accordance with the will's stipulations, the library, during the intervening years, has been under the administration of directors assisted by representatives of the Logan family. One son, James, was particularly active in the affairs of the library, which in 1828 possessed a collection of 5,000 books. Currently, the Pennsylvania Legislature is considering a bill (reprinted in the article) which will grant the library relief from taxation on the premise that it is a public institution.

1052 Rawle, William, Jr. "Philadelphia Library." *Hazard's Register of Pennsylvania*, 7 (January 15, 1831), p47, 200 wds (InU).
The Loganian Library fire of the 6th of this month was not as destructive as had been feared. However, a portrait of James Logan and a bust of William Penn have been lost. The Pennsylvania and Fame Fire and Hose Companies are particularly responsible for the quick action that saved the library. The fire began in the chimney.

1053 "Loganian Library." *Hazard's Register of Pennsylvania*, 10 (September 29, 1832), p200–01 (IEN, NcU).
The article summarized below was reprinted from the *National Gazette*.
The trustees of the Loganian Library have purchased the 2,000-volume collection of the late Zaccheus Collins. One of the collection's oldest books is *Hortus Sanitatis* (1492). The collection has many works by recognized authorities in natural history, a number of valuable editions of the *Bible*, pamphlets, belle-lettres, periodicals, select novels, and editions of all of the classical authors. We commend the trustees for their decision to purchase this fine collection.

1054 [Loganian Library.] *National Magazine: Devoted to Literature, Art, and Religion*, 1 (November 1852), p476 (InU, NcU).
The entire article follows.
"Among the manuscript curiosities in the Loganian Library, Philadelphia, is a copy of the Bible on parchment, attributed to the eleventh century; also an illuminated *Psalter* of exquisite beauty, on vellum, without date, but supposed to be a specimen of Italian art, and executed about the beginning of the fifteenth century. The library also possesses a copy of the 'Golden Legend,' printed by Caxton, 1483, of which early specimens of English printing, only five perfect copies are known to our bibliographers."

— MERCANTILE LIBRARY

1055 "Mercantile Library." *Hazard's Register of Pennsylvania*, 3 (February 14, 1829), p110–11 (NcU).
At the seventh annual meeting of the Mercantile Library Company of

Philadelphia, the reports of the Directors and the Treasurer were submitted; the election of officers was held; and several resolutions were passed, one of which authorized that 200 additional shares of stock be issued for sale. The reports, reprinted in the article, are summarized below.

Last year seventy-five shares of stock were put up for sale; of these thirteen shares remain unsold. An act of incorporation has been obtained for the Company. The Directors noted that 400 volumes were added to the library collection during the past year. Due to the good attendance for the last year's lecture series on mercantile law, a second series is being planned. The Treasurer reported that the Company has 287 stockholders and 60 subscribers. He announced that the Company experienced a deficit in last year's budget; previously deficits have been covered by the sale of stock in the Company.

1056 Hopkinson, Joseph. "Introductory Discourse, to the Mercantile Library of Philadelphia." *Hazard's Register of Pennsylvania*, 4 (November 14, 1829), p310–13 (NcU).

The speech was the introductory lecture to his course on mercantile law. It was delivered to a large and respectable audience on Thursday evening, November 5, 1829. We reprint the text of the speech (summarized here): The spirit of education is everywhere awake in America. The Mercantile Library of Philadelphia is a distinguished example of an association formed to provide the means to acquire knowledge. In it, there is mutual encouragement and aid in procuring knowledge, and a common stock furnished at a common expense. A member of such a society must feel a sensibility for the honor of the country.

1057 "Mercantile Library Company." *Hazard's Register of Pennsylvania*, 5 (January 30, 1830), p73–74 (NcU).

At the annual meeting of the Mercantile Library Company of Philadelphia, the Directors and the Treasurer presented their reports; several resolutions were passed; and the election of officers was held. The Directors' report is reprinted in the article; a summary follows.

It was reported that out of the 200 shares of stock issued for sale last year, 120 shares remain outstanding; 90 were sold to new members; and 3 were purchased by old members. The Board revealed that the Company experienced a small deficit in the preceding year. The officers have arranged for a lecture series on mercantile law and various general subjects to be presented before the membership. Since the publication of the catalog, the library has added 700 volumes to its collection. It lent 8,000 volumes last year, and on each evening an average of 100 individuals visited the library.

1058 "Mercantile Library Company." *Hazard's Register of Pennsylvania*, 7 (March 12, 1831), p164–65 (NcU).

At the ninth annual meeting of the Mercantile Library Company of Philadelphia, the Treasurer reported that at the end of the year the Company had a surplus of $42.91. It was resolved that each subscriber's fee be set at $3.00 per year and that not more than 500 shares of stock should be authorized for sale. The article reproduces in full the Directors' report which is summarized below.

The Directors have made arrangements for a series of lectures to be presented before the Company. During the past year 402 volumes were added to the library, thereby increasing its size to 3,320 volumes. The library subscribes to five weekly and three semi-weekly newspapers and to seven periodicals. A committee has been appointed to investigate the need for larger accommodations.

1059 Bevan, Matthew L., and Cope, Thomas P. "Mercantile Library." *Hazard's Register of Pennsylvania*, 11 (February 2, 1833), p74–75 (InU, NcU).

The eleventh annual meeting of the Mercantile Library Company was held January 10, 1833. (The annual report of the Board of Directors is given.) A search was made for a new, permanent location for the library. It was decided to purchase a suitable lot and to erect a building for the library, but no land was found which was both desirable and moderately priced. An estimate of the cost of the building and plans for its construction are ready. A schedule of lectures was planned last year, but other engagements by the speakers prevented its being carried out. Last year 9585 volumes were lent. There are 550 members, 82 of whom are subscribers and 467 stockholders. There are more than 4,000 volumes in the library. Thirty-three shares of stock remain to be sold. Receipts last year were $1,509.37; expenditures were $1,436.56. (The directors for next year are listed.)

1060 Cope, Thomas P. "Thirteenth Annual Report, to the Mercantile Library Company." *Hazard's Register of Pennsylvania*, 15 (March 1835), p174–75 (IEN, NcU).

In accordance with the company's recommendation, the Board of Directors has attempted to locate larger accommodation for the library, thus far without success. Several locations were inspected but for various reasons were found to be unacceptable. Although the Board agrees that a change of location is advisable, it holds the opinion that the move should not be made to a place that is less than satisfactory. Several names were deleted from the list of subscribers because of the nonpayment of dues; the Board notes that the company would be better served if its subscribers were more punctual with their dues. The company now has 475 stockholders and 95 subscribers; the library has 4,489 volumes, subscribes to 11 periodicals, and made 12,311 loans last year. It is estimated that the library will have a $300 surplus this year which will be applied to the purchase of books.

1061 "Philadelphia Mercantile Library Company." *American Magazine of Useful and Entertaining Knowledge*, 1 (April 1835), p361, 170 wds (NcU).

In 1834 the library increased by 326 volumes; at the end of the year there were about 4500 volumes. The company receives seven daily papers and eleven monthlies and lent 12,300 volumes during 1834. The object of the library is to provide standard works in the literature of the day, and records of passing events, at a moderate expense.

1062 Hopkinson, Joseph. "Concluding Lecture, Delivered Before the Athenian Institute and Mercantile Library, Tuesday, April 17, 1838." *Select Circulating Library* [Waldie's Select Circulating Library], 11, Part 1 (1838) p294–98 (NcD).

Common sense, that is, seeing things as they really are, is man's most useful faculty; it does not deal in abstractions or theories. Men of genius often lack it; they live in a region above the business of life. Walter Scott was a rare instance of the combination of genius and good sense; he never let his imagination run wild. Oliver Goldsmith lacked common sense but he was so simple and good that humanity must not condemn him. Byron's imagery, on the other hand, is overwrought, his poetry discordant, and his work and life licentious. The most

U.S. — Pennsylvania

valuable discoveries have not been the fruits of great learning, but of good sense. Bacon was a man of good common sense; Newton, Franklin, and William Penn were, also. Common sense dictates that we value domestic bliss; bachelors are to be pitied.

1063 Reed, Henry. "A Lecture on the Literary Opportunities of Men of Business, Delivered before the Athenian Institute and Mercantile Library of Philadelphia, April 3, 1848." *Select Circulating Library* [Waldie's Circulating Library], 11, Part 1 (1838), p289–94 (NcD).

I use the term "men of business" to include people in a variety of occupations. Anyone who can read a newspaper can enjoy reading literature. Obstacles are the lack of time, the lack of taste for reading, the idea that reading can cause a person to dislike or neglect his work. But reading can create harmony among men. Reading matter is easily available; a person can detect bad books by considering their effect on him. The reading of drama is advocated; it is wrong to use literature in vainly trying to converse like a book.

1064 Bethune, G. W. "Lecture Delivered before the Athenian Institute and Mercantile Library, in Philadelphia, on the Life and Opinions of Socrates." *Select Circulating Library* [Waldie's Circulating Library], 12 (July 3, 1838), p102–05 (NcD).

Socrates deserves the highest place among the examples of moral dignity afforded by the history of heathen nations. His life is traced and the events leading to his death are described. He believed in a single supreme God; a number of possible reasons are given for his apparent worship of minor gods. His moral opinions were defective, as can be seen from the way he treated women and from his own admission that the Divine Original had veiled many things in mystery. If Socrates had lived today, he surely would have been a Christian. Several pagan beliefs and myths are cited that could easily have come from Old Testament teachings and events. Socrates deserves credit for his virtue and wisdom but we need a better wisdom than man can teach.

1065 "Mercantile Library Company." *Select Circulating Library* [Waldie's Select Circulating Library], Part 2, no. 20 (November 12, 1839) p2–3 (OC).

Most of the article summarized below is quoted from the Philadelphia *National Gazette*.

We wish to express our highest admiration for the lecture of John Sergeant before this company. We quote from an editorial in the *National Gazette*: The main topic of the lecture was commercial character at the present time. An unforgettable part of the lecture described the agony of the failing merchant. The lecture taught that the merchant's most precious capital is his integrity. The Mercantile Library Company would do well to extend the lecture's influence in a more permanent form.

1066 [Mercantile Library Company of Philadelphia.] *Norton's Literary Gazette and Publishers' Circular*, 3 (March 15, 1853), p40 (NcU).

The entire article follows.

"The Mercantile Library Company of Philadelphia have made their thirtieth annual report, by which we learn that the number of volumes purchased during the year, was 744, at a cost of $719.60; and the number drawn from the library was upwards of 35,000. The incumbrances against their building are likely to be entirely removed within a few years—when their Institution will be in a very flourishing condition. A. McElroy, Librarian."

1067 [Philadelphia Mercantile Library Company.] *National Magazine: Devoted to Literature, Art, and Religion*, 2 (May 1853), p476 (InU, NcU).
The entire article follows.
"We learn from the Thirtieth Annual Report of the *Philadelphia Mercantile Library Company*, that seven hundred and forty-four new volumes have been purchased during the year, at a cost of $719.60; and the number drawn from the library was upward of thirty-five thousand. The incumbrances on the building are likely to be entirely removed in a short time."

1068 Barnwell, James G. "An Error We Are Glad to Correct." *Publishers' Weekly*, 6 (August 15, 1874), p171, 160 wds (NcU).
The article is a letter from Barnwell, Chairman of the Library Committee of the Mercantile Library of Philadelphia, to the Editor of the *Weekly (see 136)*.
In your issue of July 11th you state that not one of the libraries of the United States has subscribed to Edward Arber's transcript of the Stationers' Company registers. This statement is grossly incorrect as far as the Mercantile Library of Philadelphia is concerned, as any one may learn from the printed list of subscribers. For several years this library has been increasing at a more rapid rate than any other in the country. We may be called strong in the departments of bibliography and literary history; in ninety-nine cases out of one hundred it would be quite safe to assume that we have any work of merit on those subjects.

1069 [Mercantile Library of Philadelphia.] *Publishers' Weekly*, 6 (November 14, 1874), p551 (NcU).
The entire article follows; it refers to James G. Barnwell, long a member of the board of the Mercantile Library and apparently refers to the *Bookseller*, London.
" 'A gentleman in this city, Mr. J. G. Barnwell,' writes Mr. J. V. Whittaker, from Philadelphia, to the *Bookseller*, 'who holds an honorary position in the Mercantile Library, has spent many years in gathering materials for a work on anonyms and pseudonyms. He has some 8,000 items in his collection, but I fear there is no chance of its being printed, as, while the cost of production is known, the profits to the producer must, to quote the words of Herbert Spencer, "be relegated to the regions of the unknowable." ' "

— METHODIST EPISCOPAL UNION CHURCH LIBRARY

1070 "Library." *Hazard's Register of Pennsylvania*, 7 (April 9, 1831), p240 (InU).
The entire article follows. Apparently, it was taken from *Poulson's Daily Advertiser*, Philadelphia.
"About one year since a library company was formed, attached to the Methodist Episcopal Union Church, in North Fourth street, which has had a continued accession of choice works; and will continue to be supplied (as the funds will admit) with such works as will be approved of by all favorable to mental improvement. The terms are moderate, requiring one dollar in advance, and one dollar annually, accessible to all persons who may be recommended by a member.
"At the first annual meeting recently held, a resolution was adopted,

dividing the stock into two hundred equal shares, at five dollars each share, transferable at any time, subject to an annual fee of fifty cents, and permitting such as have paid their first year's dues to have one share by the payment of three dollars."

— PENNSYLVANIA LIBRARY OF FOREIGN LITERATURE AND SCIENCE

1071 "Library of Foreign Literature & Science." *Hazard's Register of Pennsylvania*, 8 (December 10, 1831), p375–77 (InU, NcU).

The article summarized below was reprinted from the newspaper, the *National Gazette*.

At a meeting of the subscribers to the proposals for the formation of a public library of foreign literature and science held on November 21, 1831 a committee reported on the need for such a library. The committee's report included a proposed constitution containing ten articles. The committee recommends that the library be formed, and that officers be appointed who will then seek an act of incorporation. There are no libraries in Philadelphia that presently receive the wealth of available French literature. Spanish poetry and drama are not available, nor the many useful government reports for the Spanish American republics. The committee is uncertain about the demand for German literature but believes there is a sizable interest in the German language. The proposed constitution suggests that the price of shares in the Pennsylvania Library of Foreign Literature and Science be $30, with annual contributions of $3.00.

1072 Sergeant, John. "Annual Report of the Executive Board of the Pennsylvania Library of Foreign Literature and Science." *Hazard's Register of Pennsylvania*, 10 (December 1, 1832), p341–42 (InU, NcU).

Previous plans for a library of foreign literature and science were abandoned, despite the great need for such a collection. Over a year ago, a company was successfully organized for the purpose. Subscriptions were circulated; a meeting of subscribers was held November 21, 1831. An executive board was organized, and a charter was obtained in March of 1832. Agents were appointed to purchase books abroad. The board appropriated $1836 in all, with $600 for French literature, $400 for German, $286 for Italian, $250 for Spanish, and $250 for works of science. After a delay, the books have arrived; there are more than 2,000. Catalogs will be prepared and the books arranged in two or three weeks. The board calls for more support for the library, which is the only one of its kind in this country. A valuable library has been begun; it should be augmented.

1073 Du Ponceau, P. S., and Sergeant, John. "Library of Foreign Literature." *Hazard's Register of Pennsylvania*, 12 (November 30, 1833), p345–46 (InU, NcU).

The stockholders of the Pennsylvania Library of Foreign Literature and Science met November 11, 1833. Officers were elected and the annual report of the directors read. The difficulties of the library now seem lessened. The library is the only institution in the city, perhaps in the country, to offer facilities to students of foreign literature. The acquisition of foreign languages is a useful as well as scholarly endeavor. The departments of German, Spanish, Italian and some French books are the best in this or any neighboring city. There are 2000 to 3000 volumes in the libraries. The directors appeal to the public for assistance.

Mr. Du Ponceau will give a public discourse in January. The library has been moved to one of the large rooms in the basement of the Athenaeum. A librarian will distribute books from 2 P.M. until sunset on Wednesdays and Saturdays. Catalogs will soon be ready.

1074 "Mr. Du Ponceau's Discourse on Foreign Literature and Science." *Hazard's Register of Pennsylvania*, 14 (August 9, 1834), p81–88 (InU, NcU).

This discourse on the necessity and means of making American literature independent of that of Britain was delivered to the Pennsylvania Library of Foreign Literature and Science on February 15, 1834.

The library is a unique institution. Exposure to European literature will enlarge American ideas and raise our intellectual reputation. British writers have disparaged American taste and culture. Literature has not flourished here for several reasons, but recent writers have made progress. American libraries are small but well-chosen. The size of libraries does not show a nation's intellect. America has long followed British thinking, but there is growing contact with Germany and France. Imitating the literature of a foreign language has always been respectable; this library aids in doing that. We need not fear impairing the purity of the English language; England does this much more than we do. All desiring to promote American honor should support our library.

— PHILADELPHIA LAW ASSOCIATION LIBRARY

1075 Mitchell, James T. "Library of the Philadelphia Law Association." *Albany Law Journal*, 2 (November 12, 1870), p383, 400 wds (NcU).

The author was the librarian of the Philadelphia Law Association; he refers to an article abstracted in this bibliography *(see 164)*.

In your last number, Mr. Hackett does a great injustice to this library. He says that the books are badly arranged, being kept in two rooms separated by a hall and that both are crowded. This is true but the rooms are only six feet apart; one contains reports and the other, texts. When he says that the library is not up-to-date his information must be from someone who has not been in it for fifteen years. We think it is the most nearly perfect working law library in America. Our sets of English and Irish reports are complete, our set of American reports lacks only three volumes, and we have reports from other countries. We have all the textbooks of any importance. The library of Benjamin H. Brewster, late attorney-general of Pennsylvania, is nearly as complete but the lawyers of Philadelphia do not need to depend on it.

— UNIVERSITY OF PENNSYLVANIA LIBRARY

1076 Bates, Samuel P. "Report on the University of Pennsylvania." *Pennsylvania School Journal*, 11 (June 1863), p371–77 (CoGrS).

The part of the article about the library, "Library and Apparatus," (p375, 730 wds) is summarized below. It refers to a report about the University at Lewisburg, which appeared in the May issue of the *Pennsylvania School Journal; (see 1000)*.

The library of the University of Pennsylvania was founded in 1750. A catalog was printed in 1829; the preface to that catalog notes that the collection was begun by donations, and that Louis XVI of France gave books to the library. There are now about 4000 volumes in the library; it is rarely opened, as city libraries and private collections are used instead. When we visited it, the library room was dusty, damp and cheerless. We believe that the authorities have been wrong in allowing their library to be neglected. Libraries are essential in teaching students habits of investigation and of searching materials about given subjects. It is doubtful whether other Philadelphia libraries meet the needs of the students adequately; a great library attracts literary men and distinguished scholarship. A good library would add to the honor and prestige of the university.

PITTSBURGH — YOUNG MEN'S MERCANTILE LIBRARY

1077 "Pittsburg, (Penn.) Young Men's Mercantile Library." *Norton's Literary Gazette and Publishers' Circular*, 3 (March 15, 1853), p40 (NcU).
The entire article follows.
"The annual report of this Library, presented at the end of 1852, states the number of volumes now in its possession to be 1,940. Mr. F. S. McNamara is Librarian."

SCHUYLKILL COUNTY — SCHOOL DISTRICT

1078 "Schuylkill [County Teachers' Institute Resolution on School Libraries.]" *Pennsylvania School Journal*, 21 (February 1873), p263 (IU).
The entire article follows.
"At the recent teachers' institute of Schuylkill county the following resolution was, after a full discussion, passed unanimously:
"*Resolved*, That this convention recommend the passage of an act for Schuylkill county, empowering school boards to appropriate annually a sum not exceeding one-half mill of the assessed valuation, toward the establishment and maintenance of a public school library in every borough and district."

1079 "Public School Libraries." *Pennsylvania School Journal*, 21 (March 1873), p296, 670 wds (IU).
The article refers to another article in the February 1873 issue of the *Pennsylvania School Journal (see 1078)*.
In the papers of Schuylkill County, County Superintendent Newlin argues in favor of public libraries established by a tax voluntarily levied by school boards. We reprint his argument: Public school libraries are the complement of public schools. Our public schools are excellent, but not one in twenty persons can get books for self-improvement after leaving school. These libraries can be used by adults desiring to become well-informed as well as by children. The library would be an antidote to allurements to vice and immorality. The expense of starting it would not be a burden, and an annual tax of half a mill would be sufficient. Establishing the library would not be compulsory, but merely optional, and towns already having libraries would be able to have better ones.

UPLAND — CROZER THEOLOGICAL SEMINARY LIBRARY

1080 [Crozer Theological Seminary Library.] *Publishers' Weekly*, 5 (March 28, 1874), p337 (NcU).
The entire article follows.

"In writing of the Bucknell Library, Crozer Theological Seminary, Rev. Prof. Krauth says truly: 'Next to what it has, a library is rich in what it omits. Useless books are worse than useless in a library; they are pernicious. They hide and supplant the good books. They make haystacks to hide needles. A library should separate the sheep from the goats.'"

WESTCHESTER

1081 [Cabinet of Natural Science and Chester County Athenaeum in Westchester, Pa.] *Norton's Literary Gazette and Publishers' Circular*, 3 (September 15, 1853), p150 (N).
The entire article follows.
"A correspondent from Westchester, Pa., under date of Sept. 12, 1853, writes us:
" 'We have in this place a Cabinet of Natural Science, which contains a collection of specimens in all departments of Natural History, and a Library of about 460 volumes of good and well-selected scientific works. There is no Librarian, the books and specimens being under the care of curators. It has no printed catalogue. We also have a Library (circulating), called "The Chester County Athenaeum," containing 1,750 volumes, embracing, in a small way, works in the various departments of English literature. The Librarian is Miss Emma Hunter. A catalogue has been published.' "

— CHESTER COUNTY ATHENAEUM

1082 Babb, Samson, and Darlington, William. "Chester County Athenaeum."
Hazard's Register of Pennsylvania, 11 (March 16, 1833), p167, 178-79 (InU, NcU).
(The minutes of the annual meeting and the annual report of the directors are given.) After six years, the institution continues to flourish. The library has been nearly doubled since the last annual report. Congressman David Potts and others have furnished many works. A collection from the papers of General Anthony Wayne of autograph letters and signatures of Revolutionary war figures was donated by Isaac Wayne and will serve as the nucleus of a combined museum and library on the Revolutionary period. (These autograph documents and letters are listed.) There are 103 autograph signatures. A portrait of Dr. Jacob Ehrenzeller was acquired. The treasurer's balance is $87.47.

1083 Thomas, Isaac, and Darlington, William. "Chester County Athenaeum."
Hazard's Register of Pennsylvania, 15 (March 14, 1835), p191-92 (InU, NcU).
The annual meeting was held February 20, 1835. Officers were elected. (They are listed.) The report of the directors regarding finances was read and adopted. The annual report of the directors was ordered published; it follows. The Athenaeum is prospering, gradually gaining in strength and value. Interest remains steady; there has been no material variation in total membership in the past year. Funds are sufficient, but it would be desirable to have more money for more newspapers and journals, and for binding. (Various donations to the library are acknowledged.) All of the editors of the borough now use the Athenaeum free of charge, in return for copies of their own newspapers and others which they can easily spare. This is an advantageous arrangement.

WILLIAMSPORT — WILLIAMSPORT DICKINSON SEMINARY LIBRARY

1084 Bates, S. P. "Report on Dickinson Seminary, Williamsport." *Pennsylvania School Journal*, 11 (April 1863), p319–20 (CoGrS).

The part about libraries, "Library and Apparatus," (p320) follows.

"The institution is not as yet supplied with any library. There are, however, three literary societies which have each a library comprising in the aggregate some 1700 volumes, well selected, which in a measure supply the place of a regular college library. The amount and quality of chemical and philosophical apparatus is quite limited. It is not well provided with cases and is in considerable disorder. By the addition of some leading articles and a careful repair of that possessed, its practical value would be greatly improved."

YORK — LYCEUM

1085 "Constitution of the York County Lyceum." *Hazard's Register of Pennsylvania*, 16 (August 15, 1835), p136 (InU, NcU).

The article is reprinted from the *York Republican;* the part about the library follows.

"Art. 9. It shall be the duty of the Librarian carefully to keep all books belonging to the Society, arrange them in alphabetical order, number, and label each with the name of the society; to receive all contributions of books, and such other articles as may be presented to the Society, and to keep a record of all books drawn out of the library from time to time."

Rhode Island

1086 "Libraries." *Rhode Island Institute of Instruction Journal*, 2 (October 1–15, 1847), p163–211 (NcU).

The positive value of reading, books, and accessible public libraries is attested to by men whose intellects have been enriched by reading and by the availability of books. (A list of major European libraries with the sizes of their respective collections is provided in a footnote on p166.) In view of the advantages derived from libraries, it is of interest to briefly recount the history of the district school library system in New York from 1827 when Governor DeWitt Clinton first advocated establishment of such a system. In 1835 the New York legislature finally enacted the law which provided the legal foundation for the district library system. Then, in 1839, Massachusetts followed New York's lead. The Rhode Island act relating to public schools also provides for the establishment of district libraries. (Excerpts from the law are provided in the article.) Catalogs to aid in the selection of books for school libraries are herein reprinted (p177–204), as is a specimen list of rules to regulate the use of the library.

1087 "Act to Provide for the Voluntary Incorporation of Library, Academy, and School Associations." *Rhode Island Institute of Instruction Journal* [Reports and Documents Relating to the Public Schools of Rhode Island for 1848], (1849), p436, 450 wds (NcU).

The act, passed by the Rhode Island General Assembly in June of 1847, is reprinted. There are five sections, covering the establishment of associations to procure and maintain libraries, requirements for legal recognition, rules for selling shares, election of officers, and the recording of documents in the town books of land evidence where the library, academy or school-house is situated.

1088 Barnard, Henry. "Library." *Rhode Island Institute of Instruction Journal* [Reports and Documents Relating to the Public Schools of Rhode Island for 1848], (1849), p379–90 (NcU).

The article summarized below refers to page 45 of the same issue of the *Rhode Island Institute of Instruction Journal*; this reference was probably intended to be page 457, which does contain a list of reference books; the article containing this list is summarized in this bibliography as item 1107. The article also refers to the catalog of the Pawcatuck Library on pages 429–548 of the same issue. The articles containing this catalog and explanatory remarks about it are summarized in this bibliography as items 1107 through 1112.

Every school should have a library; it should include books on education for school officers, parents and teachers; books of reference for teachers; books to circulate among pupils; and books to circulate among parents and other adults. Provision for the library should be made in the arrangement and furniture of a school house. (A catalog of books on education suggested for libraries follows; for each book, bibliographic information is given. For many, the table of contents or an annotation is provided.) Readers wanting a list of books of reference are referred to page 45 [*sic*] of this issue; those wanting books for juvenile and adult reading are advised to consult the catalog of the Pawcatuck Library on pages 429–548 of this issue.

1089 "Public Libraries in Rhode Island." *Rhode Island Institute of Instruction Journal* [Reports and Documents Relating to the Public Schools of Rhode Island for 1848], (1849), p425–28 (NcU).

In proportion to population, Rhode Island has the most public libraries with over 500 volumes of any state or nation. (Those in Providence are listed in a table with the number of volumes each contains. The Brown University Library and the Athenaeum are discussed; their history is sketched, their progress shown, and some donors listed. The libraries of Newport, Portsmouth, Smithfield, Burrillville, Gloucester, Foster, Warwick, Coventry, Barrington, South Kingstown, Charleston and Westerly are described. Statistics are given for most of these. A tabular view of libraries in Rhode Island is given; it is arranged by county and then city, and gives information about the number of libraries and number of volumes in each town.) Most are open to all residents who will obey the rules and pay 1¢ per week for the use of a volume.

1090 "The Rhode Island Institute of Instruction." *American Journal of Education* (Barnard), 14 (September 1864), p559–80 (NcU).

The part of the article about libraries (p575) follows below. It refers to Henry Barnard.

"Before Mr. Barnard left the State, a library of at least five hundred volumes had been secured for at least twenty-nine out of the thirty-two towns; and, there were good reasons to believe that the work, so auspiciously begun, would not be suspended until every town and every large village should be supplied with a library of good books, to carry the blessings and advantages of knowledge to every workshop and every fireside."

NEWPORT — REDWOOD LIBRARY

1091 "Redwood Library, Newport, R. I." *Norton's Literary Gazette and Publishers' Circular*, 2 (December 15, 1852), p235–36 (ICN, NcU).

The origin of the Redwood Library can be traced to a literary and philosophical society that was formed in 1730. The society later organized a library as a way to promote knowledge and virtue. Eventually, the society would devote all of its energies and resources to book collecting. In 1747 Abraham Redwood gave the library £500 for the purchase of books, and he subsequently persuaded members of the society that a new library building was needed. Newport citizens raised £5,000 for a new library that was completed in 1750. The library's collection is particularly strong in the classics and theology and has 6,000 volumes. The library survived the Revolutionary War intact, but since then public interest in the library has waned from time to time. (An exterior view of the library accompanies the article.)

PROVIDENCE

1092 "The Public Libraries of Providence, R. I." *Norton's Literary Gazette and Publishers' Circular*, 3 (November 15, 1853), p194, 1940 wds (NcU).

The article refers to another about the libraries of New York City in *Norton's Literary Gazette and Publishers' Circular* 3 (September 15, 1853), p149–50; *(see 813).*

The following libraries are discussed: those of Brown University, the Athenaeum, the Historical Society, the Franklin Lyceum, the Mechanics' Association, the Friends' Yearly Meeting School, the Bar Library, the Franklin Society and some school and circulating libraries. Some or all of the following information is given for each library: number of volumes; the location; year founded; strengths of the collection; a description of the building; the financial support for the library; catalogs; the hours the library is open; and the names of the library staff. A table of the number of volumes in each library is given; there are 69,300 volumes in Providence altogether.

1093 Gimmell, William. "Nicholas Brown." *American Journal of Education* (Barnard), 3 (August 1857), p291–312 (NcU).

The parts of the article about libraries (p299–300, 308–09) are summarized below.

In 1832 members of the Brown University Corporation decided to raise $25,000 for use as a permanent fund to support the library. Nicholas Brown (portrait printed in the article) subscribed $10,000 to the fund. In time the amount was raised, and for many years the income from this fund has been used to purchase books. In 1834 Brown provided the money needed to construct Manning Hall, which houses the library and the college chapel; it was dedicated in February 1835 (p299–300). Brown in 1836 offered a lot and $6,000 to build a library for the Providence Athenaeum as well as $4,000 for the purchase of books on the condition that the Athenaeum would provide $10,000 for the building and $4,000 for books. The terms of the offer eventually were met, and the new building opened in July 1838. At present, the library has 21,000 volumes and 572 shareholders (p308–09).

— ATHENAEUM

1094 "Providence Athenaeum." *Norton's Literary Gazette and Publishers' Circular*, 3 (January 15, 1853), p3 (ICN, NcU).
The entire article follows.
"The Seventeenth Annual Report of this Institution has recently appeared, from which we learn that its library now numbers 17,377 volumes, of which 775 volumes have been received during the last year.
"The Athenaeum building has been recently repaired and enlarged, and a catalogue of the books is almost ready for publication."

1095 [Report of the Directors of the Providence Athenaeum—1854.] *Norton's Literary Gazette and Publishers' Circular*, n.s. 1 (November 1, 1854), p554, 190 wds (NcU).
The 19th report of the directors of the Providence Athenaeum was submitted on Monday, September 25, 1854. Mr. John Pitman is the president; Mr. William S. Patten is vice-president. J. Dunham Hedge has been appointed librarian. During the past year, 780 volumes were added to the library, giving it a total of 18,800. Donations numbered 104. The board is concerned that too frequent introduction of ephemeral literature into the library will make its character too much like that of a circulating library, to the manifest detriment of its true function and best interests. Friends of the institution have purchased a water-color painting done by Edward G. Malbone of Newport in 1801.

— BROWN UNIVERSITY LIBRARY

1096 "Library Catalogue of Brown University." *Christian Review*, 8 (December 1843), p499–514 (IEG, NcU).
The article summarized below is a review of the catalog of the Brown University Library.
Selecting the most satisfactory cataloging and arrangement of books for a library destined to grow is difficult. Mr. Jewett, the librarian of Brown University, has prepared a two-part catalog, consisting of author and subject indices, that ranks favorably among other examples of American bibliography. The work's preface traces the history of the institution's library, including information about the many benefactors and the recent erection of a new building. The library, indeed the university, has grown entirely due to private contribution; it is the only university in the state. The importance of higher education, and of the library within the university, should be better appreciated by the general public.

1097 Bowen, Francis. "Catalog of the Brown University Library." *North American Review*, 58 (January 1844), p227–36 (NcU).
An increasing interest in reading coupled with lower book prices has encouraged the establishment of public libraries in the United States, yet these collections cannot be compared to Europe's great collections. Unfortunately, this also is true of American college libraries where the relationship between scholarship and the library collection ought to be understood. The unwarranted multiplication of academic institutions has contributed to this situation. Neither the Harvard Library nor the Yale Library is adequate to support the needs of higher education. Though smaller than these two institutions, the Library of Brown University is providing for the enlargement of its collection, now num-

bering 10,000 volumes. Charles C. Jewett, the librarian, has compiled a two-part catalog of the collection: an author-title listing and a subject classified listing, both arranged alphabetically. His work is to be commended. Brown University was incorporated in 1764, and its library has acquired a valuable collection of books.

1098 G. "Mr. Guild's Purchases for the Library of Brown University." *Literary World*, N.Y., 10 (January 3, 1852), p7–8 (NcU).

The article summarized below was taken from the *Providence Journal* for December 18, 1851.

Mr. Guild, librarian at Brown University, made extensive purchases from the library of the late Dr. Jarvis. Jarvis was a book lover with good taste who had enjoyed unusual opportunities to build his collection. Mr. Guild has made judicious and intelligent choices. He demonstrated that he was an apt pupil of Professor Jewett. Among the books purchased are Folard's *Polybius*, Brotier's *Tacitus*, Breguigny's *Tables Chronologiques*, five folios of Duchesne's *Historie Francorum Scriptores*, and Gibbon's own copy of *Spanheim*.

1099 [Brown University Library.] *National Magazine: Devoted to Literature, Art, and Religion*, 1 (August 1852), p179 (InU, NcU).

The entire article follows; it probably refers to Dr. George Washington Bethune and Edward Norris Kirk.

"Commencement at *Brown University* took place the 14th ult.; there were sixteen graduates. The Phi Beta Oration was delivered by Rev. Dr. Bethune. The discourse before the Society of Missionary Inquiry was delivered by Rev. Mr. Kirk. The additions to the library during the year have been one thousand one hundred and thirty-two volumes, nine hundred and thirty-two by purchase, and two hundred by donation; folios two hundred and eight, quartos one hundred and forty-two, octavos two hundred and sixty-eight, the other 12 mos. and 16 mos., making the whole number upward of twenty-four thousand volumes. The fund for the increase of the Library and Philosophical Apparatus is $25,000, and that 'for the purpose of Education' is $181,000. Commencement next year will be on the first Wednesday in September."

1100 "Brown University." *Norton's Literary Gazette and Publishers' Circular*, 2 (August 15, 1852), p149 (ICN, NcU).

The part of the article about the library (500 wds) is summarized below.

The Library Committee's report commends Mr. Guild, the librarian, for his preparation of the supplemental catalog. During the past year the library added 1,132 volumes; a valuable group of these was acquired with the purchase of the late Rev. Jarvis' private library. The collection now totals 24,350 volumes and has 9,000 pamphlets. The supplemental catalog is ready to go to press. The report strongly recommends the construction of a new library building.

1101 "Library of Brown University, Providence, R. I." *Norton's Literary Gazette and Publishers' Circular*, 2 (August 15, 1852), p147, 1800 wds (NcU).

In 1768 the first books for the library were procured in England; these formed the nucleus of a collection which now numbers 24,350 volumes, exclusive of pamphlets and duplicates. In 1831 a subscription drive, having a goal of $25,000, was initiated. Book selection was to be the responsibility of a committee chosen from the University governance. Only $19,437 was raised; this sum was invested, and its interest was reapplied to the principal until $25,000 had accumulated. Money first became available for books and equipment in 1839. Manning Hall houses the library and a chapel; it was erected in 1835 at the expense of Nicholas Brown. In 1843 a catalog of the library collection prepared by the librarian, Professor C. C. Jewett, was published. Various plans, involving the purchase of books, were undertaken in the 1840s to correct deficiencies of the collection. (Regulations of the library are given. An exterior view of Manning Hall accompanies the article.)

1102 [Brown University.] *Norton's Literary Gazette and Publishers' Circular*, 3 (April 15, 1853), p65 (ICN, NcU).
The entire article follows.
"The Librarian of *Brown University* has issued a circular requesting that any publications relating to that Institution prior to 1840, particularly annual and triennial catalogues, programmes of commencements and exhibitions, discourses before Literary Societies, and the pamphlet publications of college officers, may be forwarded to him for the formation and completion of the Library files."

1103 [Donation of Paris Newspaper to Library of Brown University.] *Norton's Literary Gazette and Publishers' Circular*, n.s. 1 (May 1, 1854), p226 (NcU).
The entire article follows.
"A complete set, of 142 folio volumes, of the *Moniteur Universal*, the far-famed Paris newspaper, has been presented to the Library of Brown University, by a munificent citizen of Providence. This journal dates back to 1789, and has been the official organ of the ruling factions and changing governments of France from that time to the present. Of course, its historical value is inestimable."

1104 [Tallmadge Bequest to Brown University.] *Norton's Literary Gazette and Publishers' Circular*, n.s. 1 (October 2, 1854), p493 (NcU).
The entire article follows.
"The executors of the will of the late Hon. James Tallmadge, of New York, have recently forwarded to Brown University a legacy of one thousand dollars left by him to the library of that institution. Mr. Tallmadge was a graduate of Brown University of the class of 1798."

1105 Guild, Reuben A. "The Library of Brown University." *University Quarterly: Conducted by an Association of Collegiate and Professional Students, in the U.S. and Europe*, 3 (April 1, 1861), p253-72 (InU).
Rhode Island College, now Brown University, had almost no library in 1770. Many donations have since been made to it. In 1831, subscribers raised $19,437.50; the interest is being used to purchase books. Erected by Nicholas Brown at his own expense, the library, Manning Hall, was dedicated in 1835. A full catalog of the library's 10,235 bound volumes was made by C. C. Jewett in 1843. In 1845, after special purchases of German, French and Italian books and standard English works, the library had nearly 19,000 volumes. Though not large, the library of Brown University is unusually valuable. Many books have been selected with reference to the wants of students and gentlemen engaged in literary and scientific research. The library and the societies currently have 36,000 volumes combined. (College tutors serving as librarians prior to 1824 are listed, as are regulations governing the library.)

— RHODE ISLAND HISTORICAL SOCIETY LIBRARY

1106 Staples, William R. "An Account of the Rhode Island Historical Society."
Congregational Education Society. Quarterly Journal [American Quarterly Register], 11 (May 1839), p362–68 (NcU).

References to the library of the society are scattered through the article, and are summarized below.

The charter of the society requires that two cabinets be established containing documents and records relating to the history of the state. One shall be in Newport, and one in Providence. The constitution provides for a librarian as an officer of the society; the duties of the librarian and cabinet keepers include preserving and keeping a catalog of materials, announcing donations, and making an annual written report of new acquisitions. (The subjects of interest to the society are listed. The collection of materials has received special emphasis. Several groups of papers are described.) The cabinets were placed in the Providence Library Company and the Redwood Library in Newport. The cabinet in Providence is now in the Arcade there; a new building is planned. (Each cabinet keeper in the two districts is named, and his period of service given.)

WESTERLY — PAWCATUCK LIBRARY ASSOCIATION

1107 "Catalogue of Books in Pawcatuck Library, Arranged According to Subjects." *Rhode Island Institute of Instruction Journal* [Reports and Documents Relating to the Public Schools of Rhode Island for 1848], (1849), p457–521 (NcU).

The entire catalog is copied verbatim.

"It is arranged by subject classes, and gives the title, author and library number for each work. There are 27 classes: dictionaries and books of reference; religion; law and government; education; agriculture; commerce; manufacture and trades; architecture and landscape gardening; fine arts; mental philosophy; moral philosophy; logic; rhetoric and composition; elocution; political economy; physical sciences and mathematics; geography; history (large); biography (large); voyages; travels; poetry and drama (large); critical essays, reviews, speeches; general literature; tales, etc.; juvenile reading; and collectanea."

1108 "Catalogue of Pawcatuck Library, Arranged According to Authors."
Rhode Island Institute of Instruction Journal [Reports and Documents Relating to the Public Schools of Rhode Island for 1848], (1849), p523–48 (NcU).

The entire catalog is copied verbatim. It is arranged by the author's last name and gives the title and the library number for each work.

1109 "Constitution and By-Laws of the Pawcatuck Library Association."
Rhode Island Institute of Instruction Journal [Reports and Documents Relating to the Public Schools of Rhode Island for 1848], (1849), p433–35 (NcU).

The two documents were prepared by collating and revising the constitution and by-laws of several similar associations, chiefly those of the Providence Athenaeum. The constitution is reprinted; there are eleven articles which govern the name of the association, the selection and duties of officers and the Board of Directors, annual meetings, the sale of shares, and provisions for amendments. The by-laws are then reprinted; the thirteen articles cover the hours the library is open, circulation rules, requirements for an individual to use the library, fines, and the duties of the librarian.

1110 "Explanatory Remarks on the Catalogues" [of the Pawcatuck Library Association]. *Rhode Island Institute of Instruction Journal* [Reports and Documents Relating to the Public Schools of Rhode Island for 1848], (1849), p437–40 (NcU).
 The first catalog is one of subjects. No one should have to see the book in order to learn of its contents or subject. Selection may be made from the catalog alone. The works in each subject are arranged alphabetically by author or by the leading word in the title if no author is given. Edited works are entered by editor and biographies by subject. A second catalog, of authors, is also available. The books are arranged on the shelves by size and type of binding. Sets and series of works are listed also in the subject catalog. The subject catalog also has a section on dictionaries and books of reference. These are especially valuable, particularly the *American Encyclopedia* and the *Penny Cyclopedia*.

1111 "Index to the Catalogue of the Pawcatuck Library." *Rhode Island Institute of Instruction Journal* [Reports and Documents Relating to the Public Schools of Rhode Island for 1848], (1849), p455–56 (NcU).
 This is a list of the headings in the subject catalog of the library, followed by a reference to the author catalog. The subject catalog itself is reprinted in the Institute's *Journal (see 1107)* and so is the author catalog *(see 1108)*.

1112 "Sketch of the Organization and Regulations of the Pawcatuck Library Association." *Rhode Island Institute of Instruction Journal* [Reports and Documents Relating to the Public Schools of Rhode Island for 1848],)1849), p429–32 (NcU).
 A public library was created at a meeting in Westerly on December 7, 1847. (The resolutions adopting it are quoted.) A subscription paper announces that shares are $2 each; none shall be valid unless there are 250 by January 1, 1848. By December 27, 300 shares were subscribed for; a committee was appointed to draft a constitution and by-laws, that were reported and adopted on January 17. Officers were elected January 24. The constitution was recorded in the Book of Land Evidence of Westerly on January 31. A book selection committee, appointed December 27, asked the state school commissioner to select books; $1100 was spent, plus $200 for other library expenses. There are more than 2050 volumes and even more distinct works. (The books are described; some sets are listed.) Regular annual expenses will not exceed $100. Additional income will be used to replace and add books.

South Carolina

CHARLESTON — BETHEL UNION

1113 [Plan for Libraries in Boarding Houses.] *Christian Herald and Seaman's Magazine*, 11 (February 21, 1824), p125, 200 wds (NcU).

U.S. — South Carolina

The material summarized below appeared as part of the second annual report of the Charleston Bethel Union.

The board of the Charleston Bethel Union reported that it had passed a resolution to establish libraries in boarding houses. Notice of the resolution and a request for donations of books for these libraries has been published in several newspapers. The establishment of such libraries is of vital importance. Seamen cannot be induced to be quiet and sober at a boarding house without some entertainment. Providing books, current periodicals, and interesting tracts is, we believe, the only effective means of competing with the haunts of vice.

— MERCANTILE LIBRARY ASSOCIATION

1114 "Mercantile Library of Charleston [South Carolina]." *DeBow's Review*, 18, n.s. 1 (May 1855), p654, 420 wds (InU, NcU).

The president of the Mercantile Library Association has visited several cities to examine the newspaper reading desks of their libraries. The Young Men's Mercantile Library Association of Cincinnati being thought to have the best desks, copies of them have been ordered for the Charleston library. Several banks and insurance companies in Charleston have either paid $200 for five year memberships for their employees, or have made donations to help defray the costs. Subscriptions are being placed for American and foreign newspapers.

COLUMBIA — AFRICAN METHODIST EPISCOPAL CHURCH LIBRARY

1115 Pickett, David. "Our Freedmen's Libraries." *American Unitarian Association Monthly Journal*, 10 (November 1869), p447, 240 wds (NcD).

A resolution of thanks from the Quarterly Conference of the African Methodist Episcopal Church in Columbia, S. C., dated Sept. 18, 1869, and signed by David Pickett. A 48 volume library has been sent by the American Unitarian Association to be kept in the parsonage or church for the use of the members. Pickett is the presiding elder of the quarterly conference.

— UNIVERSITY OF SOUTH CAROLINA LIBRARY

1116 "South Carolina College Library." *Norton's Literary Gazette and Publishers' Circular*, 3 (December 15, 1853), p213, 940 wds (NcU).

The library was established with the college in 1805. Early records are deficient with regard to accounts, but a librarian was hired, and $18,000 was appropriated before 1805, though how much was spent remains uncertain. Records show that $5,757 was spent on the library between 1813 and 1836, but its excellent reputation indicates that that figure is probably too low. From 1836 to 1853, the legislature appropriated $43,000 to increase the library, and $19,374 was spent from the surplus in the tuition fund. Though small, with over 20,000 volumes, the library is well-selected and handsome. Several titles are described. The library is open every weekday from 9 A.M. to 10 P.M. during the term, and on Wednesdays during vacations. Trustees, professors, students, and all who have donated $100 to the library can use it, as can others given approval. F. W. McMaster is the present librarian.

Vermont

BURLINGTON — LYCEUM

1117 "Burlington (Vt.) Lyceum." *Norton's Literary Gazette and Publishers' Circular*, 2 (December 15, 1852), p236 (ICN, NcU).
The entire article follows.
"A correspondent of the *N.Y. Times* states that the Burlington (Vt.) Lyceum, which was organized last year, for the purpose of establishing a Library and Reading Room, as well as for other purposes, is in a flourishing condition. Its library, already respectable in size and value, is receiving constant additions by an annual appropriation from the funds of the Lyceum, and by liberal individual donations."

— UNIVERSITY OF VERMONT LIBRARY

1118 Winslow, William C. "The Library of Vermont University." *University Quarterly: Conducted by an Association of Collegiate and Professional Students, in the U.S. and Europe*, 4 (July 1861), p30–48 (InU).
The original university library was destroyed by fire in 1824. In 1836 the Corporation appropriated $10,000 for a new library. The Faculty of the University drew up lists of needed books and Joseph Torrey went to Europe to make the purchases. Torrey served as librarian until 1841. Prof. N. G. Clark has been the librarian since 1853. The library's budget is about $380 per year, provided by the Wheeler Library Fund, the Strong Fund, and student fees. Most of the library's increases are the result of private donations. Presently the library contains about 10,000 volumes, not counting about 4,000 volumes available in three student society libraries. A 164 page catalog has been published providing both an alphabetical list by author and a classified list of the collection. (Reference is made to the most significant titles owned by the library in the broad subject areas of "theology," "jurisprudence," "sciences and arts," "belles lettres," and "history.")

1119 [An Art Gallery for the University of Vermont.] *Nation*, 17 (October 30, 1873), p290 (NcU).
The entire article follows.
"A circular which has been sent us from the University of Vermont, calls attention to the fact that as long ago as 1830 this institution introduced into its course systematic instruction, by lectures, on the theory and principle of the fine arts. Provision has now been made by Mr. Trenor W. Park, of Bennington, for an art-gallery, by the addition of a third story to the library building. The trustees solicit works of art of unquestionable merit, or funds with which to procure them, from all who are disposed to take an interest in this enterprise."

PITTSFORD — MACLURE LIBRARY

1120 W., P. H. [William Maclure's Gifts for a Free Library in Pittsford, Vermont.] *Norton's Literary Gazette and Publishers' Circular*, n.s. 2 (June 15, 1855), p255, 550 wds (MWiW).

The page in the periodical is incorrectly numbered as 265; the library was named the Maclure Library.

In Pittsford, Vermont, there is a library of about 2000 volumes which had its origin in a gift from William Maclure, made nearly twenty years ago. A resident heard of Maclure's generosity and wrote to him in Mexico, telling him that recent improvement in the schools had caused young people to want more books and asking him for a gift of $400 to be matched in Pittsford; Maclure made the gift. When the librarian thanked him, Maclure said he would give $100 apiece to any four towns that would provide $100 for a free library. But the librarian was then planning a free normal school, and asked Maclure for $25,000 to be matched in Vermont. The philanthropist was interested but died before he could help.

RUTLAND — AGRICULTURAL LIBRARY SOCIETY

1121 Joslin, J. J. "Ag'l. Library Association — A Good Move." *American Agriculturist*, 22 (February 1863), p38 (InU, NcU).
The entire article follows.
"J. J. Joslin, Rutland Co., Vt., writes that an Agricultural Library Association has just been formed in the town where he resides, and agricultural works amounting to $250 are already purchased. A 'Farmers' Social Club' for discussing appropriate subjects, is connected with the association."

ST. JOHNSBURY — ST. JOHNSBURY ATHENAEUM

1122 [New Library Building in St. Johnsbury, Vt.] *American Bibliopolist*, 2 (February 1870), p77 (ICN, ICU).
The entire article follows; it refers to the St. Johnsbury Athenaeum.
"The new library at St. Johnsbury, Vt., is the most costly public building in the State, with the exception of the Capitol. Together with the library, it is the gift of the Messrs. Fairbanks, of that village."

Virginia

ALEXANDRIA — ALEXANDRIA LIBRARY

1123 [Alexandria, Virginia, Public Library.] *Norton's Literary Gazette and Publishers' Circular*, 2 (September 15, 1852), p169 (ICN, NcU).
The entire article follows.
"An effort is also making to invigorate and enlarge the Public Library at *Alexandria, Va*. About 4,000 volumes are already collected there; but as we learn from a private source, the present plan is to add such modern publications as will make the whole collection more attractive and available."

NOTTAWAY COUNTY — AGRICULTURAL SOCIETY LIBRARY

1124 Jones, James. "An Address, Delivered before the Agricultural Society of Nottaway." *American Farmer*, 4 (January 24, 1823), p363-65 (InU, NcU).

In the course of the address the following recommendation is made (p364): "I most seriously recommend to this society the formation of a library for the exclusive use of its own members, to be made up of such publications, as relate to every branch of rural economy: of these there are abundance, of modern production and of intrinsic excellence and worth; well calculated to instruct, to improve, and amply to repay the expense of procuring, as well as the trouble of reading. — The establishment of such institutions have [sic] been sanctioned, and their utility fairly tested, by the examples and practice of nations, communities, and societies, in all times and in all countries, since the invention of the art of printing. Like the circulating system of the blood, which carries life and vigour and health to every part of the animal, these great arteries of science diffuse knowledge and improvement and civilization throughout the remotest extremities of the social body."

PETERSBURG — PETERSBURG LIBRARY ASSOCIATION

1125 "Petersburg (Virg.) Library Association." *Norton's Literary Gazette and Publishers' Circular*, 3 (July 15, 1853), p115, 350 wds (ICN, NcU).

An enterprising society has just been organized under this name and obtained an act of incorporation from the legislature of the state. A correspondent writes: We have leased a hall and two rooms. The books will be placed in the galleries of the hall; the lower part of the hall will be the lecture room. One of the two rooms will be a reading room and the other, a conversation room. We have subscribed to $200 worth of papers, reviews, etc., we plan a series of lectures next winter and a committee is selecting books; we plan to purchase about 4,000 books by next October. They will be works of reference and standard works, not trash. This is not a reading community; we hope to cultivate a taste for reading. We have a good librarian, Thomas S. Pleasants; we hope to increase our stock and eventually have our own building.

1126 [Petersburg (Va.) Library Association.] *Norton's Literary Gazette and Publishers' Circular*, n.s. 1 (May 1, 1854), p226 (NcU).

The entire article follows.

"The Petersburg (Va.) Library Association has now been in operation one year, and is already in possession of 3,600 well-selected volumes. Of these, 3,260 were purchased at an average cost of $1.10 per volume, the remainder being donations. An alphabetical catalogue has been prepared, and will be soon published. Thos. S. Pleasants, Librarian."

1127 "Petersburg Library Association." *Southern Quarterly Review*, 26 (July 1854), p271 (NcU).

The entire article follows.

"The annual report of the Directors of this Association, closing with March last, shows the Institution to be in a very flourishing condition. We can speak of the Library from personal observation, and bear grateful testimony to the courtesy, intelligence, enterprise and honorable ambition of the officers and members of the Institution. A large, growing and well selected library, constantly in use by eager citizens desiring knowledge and curious in study; — crowded lecture-rooms, silently watchful of all that falls from the lips of the speaker; — the old and young, male and female, all zealously uniting in the common cause; — all seeking to combine the elegant and the useful in knowledge; — the truthful and the beautiful; — these are the proofs which the people of Petersburg daily give of the utility of their Library Association, and of the wise use which they are making of it."

RICHMOND

1128 "Wynne." *American Bibliopolist*, 7 (April 1875), p80–81 (NcD).
The article summarized below was abridged from the Richmond *Evening News*.
T. H. Wynne, former librarian and Virginia State Senator, died February 24, 1875. He was the first librarian of the Mercantile Library Association of Richmond. His friends included many important Virginians. Wynne came to the Virginia Senate in 1872. He served well, securing appropriations to publish archival records, to enlarge the State Library and to restore material taken from the State Capitol just after the Civil War. The library now has a better room, more volumes, numerous portraits and busts of Virginians, and many rare historical documents. Wynne was author and editor of various publications. (His series of privately printed works is listed.) He collected books and objects of vertu and of antiquarian and historic interest, even replacing much of his valuable library destroyed by fire on April 3, 1865. Wynne's death is a serious loss to the student of American history.

— STATE LIBRARY

1129 Barksdale, G. A. "The State Library of Virginia. A Glance at Its Paintings and Statues." *American Bibliopolist*, 7 (April 1875), p99–100 (NcD).
The article summarized below was reprinted from the *New York Evening Post*.
About thirty-five portraits and a dozen pieces of statuary are briefly described; for each, the name of the artist is given and the subject and general appearance are noted. The locations of the pieces in the library are often given, and occasionally, the cost. Appended to the article is a note about the death of Senator Wynne, the Corresponding Secretary and Librarian of the Virginia Historical Society. The letter by R. A. Brock, accepting appointment as Senator Wynne's replacement, is reproduced.

Washington Territory

OLYMPIA — TERRITORIAL LIBRARY

1130 "Washington Territorial Library." *Norton's Literary Gazette and Publishers' Circular*, 3 (May 15, 1853), p84 (ICN, NcU).
The entire article follows.

"At the last session of Congress an appropriation of $4,000 was made for the establishment of a Library in this newly organized Territory. This amount has been recently expended by his excellency Gov. Stevens, who has been aided in his selection of books in different departments of learning by prominent scientific gentlemen. From personal knowledge upon the subject, we feel confident that the Library will be of great service to the people for whom it is designed, and who cannot fail to appreciate the care which has been exercised in its purchase."

Wisconsin

MADISON — FREE LIBRARY

1131 Butler, J. D. "Libraries as Leaven." *American Bibliopolist*, 7 (August and October 1875), p189–92 and 237–40 (NcD).

An address given May 31, 1875 at the inauguration of the Free Public Library of Madison, Wisconsin. On page 237, at the beginning of the second part, a note incorrectly states "Concluded from page 196."

My subject is the relation of libraries to the increased diffusion of knowledge. Knowledge is sometimes divided into forty departments; these departments should be represented in a library, each in proper proportion to make a harmonious whole. Madison, in opening a free library, has out-stripped other Wisconsin towns; the small tax and gifts from individuals will cause the collection to grow. Many will use it for amusement; good fiction is true to the principles of life, if not the facts. People will come for instruction; professional men and others will find answers to questions. Travel books will be popular and some persons will use the books telling what to read; a few will be inspired and some will make up for the lack of a liberal education. A library reminds me of Raphael's painting, "The School of Athens" in which the Greek philosophers and men of learning are represented as teachers.

— STATE HISTORICAL SOCIETY LIBRARY

1132 [Tank Collection in the Wisconsin Historical Society.] *Nation*, 5 (October 24, 1867), p328 (NcU).

The entire article follows.

"The Wisconsin Historical Society, of Madison, has received a highly valuable donation of some five thousand volumes, the library of Mr. Van der Meulen, a Dutch clergyman near Rotterdam, from his daughter, Mrs. Otto Tank, of Green Bay, the State paying the cost of transportation, etc. This collection is chiefly theological, and chiefly in the Dutch language, but it is also rich in Dutch history, and contains works on general history, philology, and natural history. About half the books are unbound, and many are bound in old vellum. The society's library previously amounted to ten thousand volumes."

1133 [Historical Societies in the West.] *Nation*, 10 (March 17, 1870), p175 (NcU).

In discussing the Wisconsin Historical Society, the article includes the following statements about its library, copied verbatim.

"It has a library of nearly 50,000 volumes and pamphlets, including a collection of 1,545 bound volumes of newspapers, of which 152 belong to the last century—a department in which we should doubt if it were excelled by the largest libraries in the country. It also possesses 1,600 pamphlets and documents relating to the rebellion, the British Patent Office reports, etc., etc."

1134 [The State Historical Society of Wisconsin and the Connecticut Historical Society.] *Nation*, 11 (October 20, 1870), p260 (NcU).
The part of the article about a library is copied below.
"The State Historical Society of Wisconsin, one of the most vigorous the country can show, added last year to its library the entire set of English Patent Office Reports—some twenty-five hundred in number—which will be continued at the rate of one hundred yearly. This year it has received from the Master of the Rolls his complete set of Chronicles and Calendars of State Papers, numbering about one hundred and sixty volumes. The library now contains fully forty-six thousand volumes, about half of which are bound. It is very rich in newspapers."

1135 [The Wisconsin Historical Society Library.] *Nation*, 12 (February 16, 1871), p107 (NcU).
The entire article follows.
"It is pleasant to witness the yearly growth of the Wisconsin Historical Society, whose seventeenth annual report is before us. We have more than once referred to its valuable library, which now contains 45,530 volumes, documents, and pamphlets, including the unusual and (west of the Alleghenies) unequalled number of 1,601 volumes of bound newspapers. Three of these last were printed in the seventeenth century, 153 in the eighteenth, and the remainder during the present century. The principle that unto him that hath shall be given, is the best guide for would-be donors to libraries as to universities, and *a fortiori* to would-be founders of either. If it is duly heeded in this instance, the Wisconsin Society is likely to establish the strongest claim on the liberality of the West, at least."

1136 [Wisconsin State Historical Society.] *Nation*, 16 (February 13, 1873), p113–14 (NcU).
The part of the article (p113–14) about the library of the society is copied verbatim, below.
"It is stated in the 18th Annual Report that 'the average increase of the Massachusetts Historical Society, the pioneer institution of the kind in the country, has been 625 volumes, while ours, since its reorganization, has averaged 2,800, and during the past six years, but little short of 5,000 annually.' The 19th Annual Report just issued shows an increase for 1872 of 2,166 volumes and 1,528 documents and pamphlets. Of the former, 404 were newspaper files, making a total number of 2,044, distributed in the three centuries as follows: 54 in the seventeenth, 146 in the eighteenth, and the remainder in the present century. The library is also strong in containing 360 volumes on genealogy alone; 865 local histories of towns and counties; and 175 local histories of churches."

1137 [Catalogue of the Wisconsin State Historical Library.] *Nation*, 18 (January 15, 1874), p40, 160 wds (NcU).
Most of this article was published verbatim in *Publishers' Weekly* for February 7, 1874 *(see 1138).*

We have received the catalog of the Wisconsin State Historical Library in two volumes, prepared by the librarian, Mr. Daniel S. Durrie, and his daughter. It is a plain, unpretentious finding list, giving all the essential facts about each book, with numerous cross-references. We often have had occasion to note the richness of this collection; newspapers occupy nine pages of this catalog, and genealogical works, seven; there are more than 240 volumes of pamphlets on religious subjects. Prof. [William Francis] Allen's selected catalog of the Tank collection is appended.

1138 [Wisconsin State Historical Library.] *Publishers' Weekly*, 5 (February 7, 1874), p141, 160 wds (NcU).

The article quotes most of an article in the *Nation* for January 15, 1874 *(see 1137)*.

1139 Sabin, J[oseph]. "Wisconsin Literature." *American Bibliopolist*, 6 (November–December 1874), p158–60 (ICU, OC).

A review of: Wisconsin State Historical Society, *Report and Collections*, ed. by Lyman C. Draper. Madison, 1855–72, 6 vols.; Durrie, Daniel S. *A History of Madison, the Capital of Wisconsin; Including the Four Lake Country, to July, 1874, with an Appendix of Notes on Dane County and Its Towns*. Madison, 1874, 420 p.; Wisconsin State Historical Society Library. *Catalogue*, comp. by Daniel S. Durrie and Isabel Durrie. Madison, 1873, 2 vols.

The State Historical Society of Wisconsin has the second largest state-supported library. The catalog lists almost 60,000 volumes and pamphlets. Unlike most state libraries which are mainly collections of public documents and law books, the Wisconsin library contains the works that relate to the state and the Northwest. There is a large newspaper collection; town histories and American genealogical works are collected. Daniel S. Durrie is the librarian and is assisted by his daughter, Isabel. The catalog has several typographical errors and some errors of fact. Lyman C. Draper owns an important private collection relating to the Northwest.

1140 [Catalogue of the Wisconsin State Historical Society Library.] *Nation*, 21 (November 4, 1875), p293 (NcU).

The entire article follows.

"The valuable catalogue, in two volumes, of the Wisconsin State Historical Society's library, which was published in 1873, has now been enlarged by a supplementary catalogue. It embraces the additions from July 1 of that year to August 1 of the present. The number of registered titles is about 65,000, an increase of upwards of 8,000 in the above-mentioned interval. Among the notable accessions are works relating to the American Revolution, the Rebellion, and the American Indians — the last being derived from Mr. T. W. Field's sale."

1141 Sigma. "Lyman C. Draper." *American Bibliopolist*, 7 (December 1875), p249–50 (NcD).

The article is copied from the New York *Daily Graphic* of October 16, 1875. Most of it is about Draper's personal collection of historical manuscripts; the first part of the article (p149), concerning the Wisconsin Historical Society Library, is reproduced below.

"MADISON, Wis., September 30. — 'How came you to have such a superb library out in this neck of woods?' I asked of a prominent Madisonian to-day as

I strolled through the great historical collection in the most unique State House in America.

" 'Draper did it,' he answered briefly.

" 'Who is Draper?'

'Lyman C. Draper came here when there was only a handful of books, and by the aid of men whom he inspired has increased the library to more than 65,000 volumes of books, besides many tons of pamphlets and periodicals.' "

— UNIVERSITY OF WISCONSIN LIBRARY

1142 [Norwegian Books in the University of Wisconsin Library.] *Nation*, 15 (December 5, 1872), p365 (NcU).

The entire article follows.

"The library of the University of Wisconsin at Madison has just received about four hundred volumes from Norway, the result of a concert given for the purpose last May by Ole Bull. It already had upwards of two hundred Norwegian books, and the collection is now a fine one, probably unique in this country."

Europe

1143 "Modern Libraries." *Saturday Magazine: Being in Great Part a Compilation from the British Reviews, Magazines, and Scientific Journals* [National Recorder], 2 (July 24, 1819), p62–63 (ICU, NcU).
The article summarized below is taken from *English Magazine*.
About 150 German cities possess libraries open to the public. We present them from the *Ephemerides of Weimar*, with an estimate of the works contained in the principal ones. Thirty German cities possess over 3 million works or printed volumes in their principal libraries, excluding academic dissertations, detached memoirs, pamphlets or manuscripts. A similar sketch of the state of public libraries in France is contained in M. Petit-Radel's *Recherches sur les Bibliothèques Anciennes et Modernes*. There are 273 public libraries in France; nothing is known of the size of 80, but there are 3,345,287 volumes in those whose size is known. Several of the libraries are not open to the public; others are open only for a short time. Soon every chief town will have a library that is really public.

1144 "Account of Public Libraries." *American Annals of Education* [American Journal of Education], 1 (November 1826), p667–72 (NcU).
Education would be better served if men of wealth would give to libraries funds for book collections on certain subjects, e.g., American history, rather than endow professorships. Such collections would furnish both students and teachers with the means of instruction. (In light of this observation, the article reports statistics, e.g., founding dates and the size and the composition of collections, for the major libraries in the following European countries: England, Scotland, Ireland, Russia, Sweden, Germany, Poland, France, Denmark, Switzerland, Spain, and Italy.)

1145 "A Comparative and Chronological Table of the Largest Libraries in the World." *American Journal of Science*, 31 (January 1837), p178 (InU, NcU).
The entire table, slightly altered typographically, follows.

	Contains vols.	Manuscripts
Paris: Royal Library (founded 1595)	626,000	80,000
Munich: Royal Lib. (1595)	540,000	16,000
St. Petersburg: Imperial Lib. (1728)	432,000	15,000?
Copenhagen: Royal Lib. (1648)	410,000	16,000?
Vienna: Imperial Lib. (1440)	284,000	16,000
Berlin: Royal Lib. (1661)	280,000	5,000
Pekin: Imperial Lib. [no date]	280,000	[?]
Dresden: Royal Lib. (1556)	260,000	2,700

	Contains vols.	Manuscripts
Gottingen: University Lib. (1736)	250,000	5,000
London: Lib. of the Brit. Museum (1759)	220,000	22,000
Oxford: Bodleian Lib. (1480)	200,000	25,000
Wolfenbuttel: Ducal Lib. (1604)	200,000?	4,500
Madrid: Royal Lib. (1712)	200,000	2,500?
Paris: Lib. at the Arsenal [no date]	186,000	5,000
Stuttgart: Royal Lib. (1765)	174,000	1,800
Milan: Brera Lib. (1763)	169,000	1,000
Naples: Lib. of Bourbon Museum [no date]	165,000	3,000
Florence: Magliabecchian Lib. (1714)	150,000	12,000
Breslau: University Lib. [no date]	150,000	2,300
Munich: University Lib. (1595)	150,000	2,000?
Edinburgh: (1682)	150,000	6,000
Jedo: Lib. of the Sjogoun [no date]	150,000?	[?]
Miako: Lib. of Mikado [no date]	150,000?	[?]

Bib. Univ. Geneva, Oct. 1835

1146 "Public Libraries in London and Paris." *Eclectic Magazine of Foreign Literature*, 12 (November 1847) p289–305 (IEN, NcU).

The article summarized below is a reprint of a portion of an article in the *British Quarterly Review*, August, 1847.

Our purpose in this article is to summarize the history of libraries in London, particularly the British Museum, and to compare them to those of Paris. A library was founded in London as early as 1684. In 1753 Parliament authorized the purchase of Sir Hans Sloane's private collection, which together with the Cottonian collection of MSS became the British Museum. (Other private collections which have been added to the British Museum since it opened in 1757 are described.) The four public libraries in London now have a combined collection of 397,000 volumes in comparison to the 1,300,000 volumes held by Paris' five public libraries. Thus, it would seem that the student is better served in Paris than in London. This situation, however, can be remedied if Parliament provides for the enlargement of the British Museum and the establishment of two other libraries.

1147 "Public Libraries in Europe." *Eclectic Magazine of Foreign Literature*, 14 (July 1848), p429, 180 wds (IEN, NcU).

There are 383 public libraries in Europe. By country, this total breaks down as follows: France 107; Lombardy and Venice 41; Prussia 30; Great Britain and Ireland 28; Spain 17; the Papal States 15; Belgium 14; Switzerland 13; Russia 12; Bavaria 11; Tuscany 9; Sardinia 9; Sweden 8; Naples 7; Portugal 7; 5 each in Holland, Denmark, and Saxony; Baden 4; Hesse 4; and 3 each in Württemberg and Hanover. Of the major European capital cities, Weimar has 803 volumes for every 100 citizens; Munich 750; Copenhagen 465; Dresden 432; Florence 313; Rome 306; Berlin 162; Paris 143; and London 20. London, therefore, compares quite unfavorably with these cities.

1148 "Public Libraries." *Bankers Magazine*, 3 (December 1848), p372–78 (NcU).

The article first appeared in *Chambers's Edinburgh Journal*, 9 (January 1, 1848), p9.

The libraries of the Vatican and at St. Mark's in Venice contain many rare books and original manuscripts. Cosimo de' Medici founded a library in Florence in 1560; his main pursuit thereafter was enlarging the collection. In France the libraries of 195 towns contain 3,000,000 volumes and are open for the inspection of any visitor. The five great Paris libraries comprise 1,378,000 volumes. These have free access but employ secret police to guard against mutilation or theft of books. The Imperial Library in Russia, the third largest in Europe, is little used; access to the books is difficult. The Göttingen Library might be called the "most useful library in the world"; open daily, it lends to anyone and has a complete catalog. (An essay from *Haydn's Dictionary of Dates*, chronologically outlining the history of European libraries from antiquity to the present, is reprinted in the article.)

1149 "Library Statistics." *Daguerreotype: a Magazine of Foreign Literature and Science*, 3 (December 23, 1848), p212-14 (NcU, OOxM).

The article, summarized below, was reprinted from "Library Statistics," *Chambers's Edinburgh Journal*, n.s. 10 (October 14, 1849), p252-53 which in turn was extracted from an article in the *Journal of the Statistical Society of London*, August 1848.

Unlike the national libraries on the continent which are often circulating libraries, English libraries receiving public funds are generally unavailable to the public. The size of these European libraries is not in proportion to the cities that contain them. London, for example, has only 20 books per 100 inhabitants, while Paris has 143 books per 100 people and Munich has 750 books per 100 residents. France with 107 has a greater number of public libraries than any other European country. There are 383 European public libraries with more than 10,000 volumes, comprising a total of 20,012,735 volumes. (A list of 23 libraries of over 100,000 volumes, and the volume holdings of 16 English libraries are provided.) In the United States there are 81 public libraries containing 955,000 volumes. The British Museum's collection has increased much more slowly than that of other libraries due to a reliance on donations.

1150 "Public Libraries." *Bibliotheca Sacra [and Theological Review]*, 6 (February 1849), p202 (NcU).
The entire article follows.
"The number of public libraries in Europe is stated at 383; of these, 107 are in France, 41 in Austria, 30 in Prussia, 28 in Great Britain, 17 in Spain, 15 in the Papal States, 14 in Belgium, 13 in Switzerland, 12 in Russia, 11 in Bavaria, 9 in Tuscany, 9 in Sardinia, 8 in Sweden, 7 in Naples, 7 in Portugal, and the others in the remaining States. The number of volumes in the libraries of the chief European cities, compared with each 100 of the respective population, is as follows.

"Weimar	800	Parma	278	Edinburgh	116
Munich	750	Prague	168	Petersburgh	108
Darmstadt	652	Berlin	162	Brussels	100
Copenhagen	465	Madrid	152	Stockholm	98
Stuttgart	452	Paris	143	Naples	69
Dresden	432	Venice	142	Dublin	49
Hanover	335	Milan	135	Lisbon	39
Florence	313	Vienna	119	London	20"
Rome	306				

1151 "The Public Libraries of Europe." *Literary World*, N.Y., 5 (December 15, 1849), p510–12 (NcU).

In Scotland the four university libraries receive grants from the government. The Library of the Faculty of Advocates in Edinburgh, a public library supported by fees collected from those men who are admitted to the bar, is one of the five libraries in Great Britain that is entitled to receive a copy of every book published in the country. Itinerating libraries were first started in Scotland by Samuel Brown; these libraries are very popular and have been introduced on the Continent. Among the six public libraries in Ireland are the Trinity College Library, Archbishop Marsh's Library, and the Dublin Society Library. In Belgium there are fourteen public libraries; of these the three largest are the Royal Library in Brussels and two university libraries, one at Ghent and the other at Liége. Parochial libraries are found in the larger Belgian cities; many societies also have their own small libraries. It is part of the Belgian government's policy to support and encourage that country's public libraries.

1152 "The Public Libraries of Europe." *Literary World*, N.Y., 6 (January 12, 1850), p26–28 (NcU).

The three largest libraries of Rome are the Casanate Library, 120,000 volumes; the Vatican Library, 100,000 volumes, and the Angelica Library, 85,000 volumes. The national and university libraries of Italy are accessible to the public and contain many valuable manuscripts and incunabula. Municipal and monastic libraries exist throughout Italy; however there are no libraries available to the working classes, which to date have exhibited little interest in reading. In France there are 107 strictly public libraries holding approximately 4,000,000 volumes. M. Guizot claims that public libraries benefit the literature and the character of the French people. Public libraries as well as book publishers receive financial support from local and national governments. The town library of Boulogne, founded in 1798, has a history and a collection typical of many other provincial libraries.

1153 "The Public Libraries of Europe." *Literary World*, N.Y., 6 (January 19, 1850), p60–61 (NcU).

The public libraries of Germany are so numerous that this article will consider in detail only those libraries having more than 50,000 volumes. There are 169 libraries, each having a collection of 10,000 volumes or more, in the German States, Prussia, and Austria; the total number of books held by these libraries is approximately 3,700,000 volumes. In Germany there are two main kinds of libraries: the university libraries and the town libraries. Recent statistics reveal that the libraries of Denmark contain more books in proportion to population than do the libraries of any other European country. (Lists of the principal libraries of Sweden, Norway, Russia, Spain, and Portugal are provided.)

1154 "British and Continental Libraries." *Eclectic Magazine of Foreign Literature*, 21 (October 1850), p222–31 (IEN, NcU).

The article summarized below was printed originally in the *Eclectic Review*, for July 1850.

The report from the Select Committee on Public Libraries, lately released, reveals that there are only a few public libraries in Great Britain but that the demand for them is growing. The paucity of public libraries forces many of our British scholars and writers to travel either to London or the Continent in order to find the books that they need. The above mentioned document provides ample evidence that foreign libraries are much better than ours. For example, while there are 458 libraries on the continent of Europe there are only 34 in Great Britain and Ireland. These statistics and others given in the article indicate that the British public ought to support the establishment of more public libraries.

1155 [Fétis, François Joseph.] "Hints for the Formation of a Musical Library; from the French of M. Fétis." *Dwight's Journal of Music, a Paper of Art and Literature*, 9 (July 26, 1856), p131-33 (NcU).

A collection should meet the owner's needs; no one can possess everything valuable. The most complete musical library ever collected was that of Padre Martini. (Other European collections are mentioned). A fine music collection would be formed by uniting the works of the Ecole Royale de Musique and the Bibliothèque du Roi. A great public library of music should have two great divisions — musical literature and practical music. Musical literature should contain the general literature of music, the history of music by periods, and all that relates to the theory and practice of music. The division of practical music should contain vocal and instrumental music. Subdivisions of both musical literature and practical music are offered. The collections of individuals would comprise only sections of such a great music library. There are several sources from which to obtain titles for such a library, including the author's *Historical Dictionary of Musicians*.

1156 "Libraries in Europe." *American Journal of Education* (Barnard), 2 (August 1856), p212-14 (NcU).

The article reprints extracts of S. H. Grant's letter from Europe which originally was printed in the thirty-fifth annual report of the New York Mercantile Library. At the end of the article is a table (p214) reproduced from Burritt's *Year Book of the Nations*, which provides statistics of the principal European public and university libraries.

The Liverpool Free Library comprises three buildings: the two Lending Libraries located in the North and South Districts of the city and the Reference Library which is centrally located. Damaged bindings were noticed in the Portico Library; Mr. Panizzi of the British Museum agreed that the damage may have been caused by the presence of burning gas. The circulating libraries of London differ from those of the United States, being almost entirely operated by booksellers who rent portions of their stock. The Bibliothèque St. Genevieve in Paris is so convenient and comfortable to use that restrictions are made to prevent students from spending their evenings there reading novels. The Royal Library in Berlin provides the best example of the organization and management of a large library. The superintendent, [G. H.] Pertz, was particularly helpful.

1157 Simeon, Sir John, bart. "Books and Libraries," *Pennsylvania School Journal*, 12 (January 1864), p208-14 (IU).

The article, taken from the *Upper Canada Journal of Education*, was originally a lecture. The part about libraries (p211-14) is summarized below.

Famous ancient libraries, such as those of Athens, Rome and Constantinople, were established and embellished by rulers and their successors and were often relocated or destroyed as the consequence of wars. In the Middle Ages in Europe several great libraries were developed from the collections of wealthy men and rulers. Englishmen also collected books and manuscripts, frequently donating them to the universities. Book collecting flourished in France and became very fashionable before the Revolution there. The National

Library of England, housed in the British Museum, originated in the Royal Collection donated to the public in 1757 by George II, a collection of books and manuscripts begun in the time of Henry VII. There have been several valuable additions to the British Museum through purchase and gift; it now numbers 600,000 volumes. The building is designed to contain 1,500,000 volumes but is expected to be filled within the next forty years.

1158 [Statistics of European Libraries.] *Nation*, 4 (May 23, 1867), p409–10 (NcU).

Apparently, the article is based on another article in *Pall Mall Gazette*.

According to the Italian statistical bureau, among European countries the relation of public library holdings to population is highest in Bavaria, with 26.4 volumes per 100 persons; Italy is next with 19.5; France next with 11.7; Prussia follows with 11; Belgium 10.4; Austria 6.9; Great Britain 6; and Russia has only 1.6. The Bureau has no precise rule as to what constitutes a volume; furthermore, a comparison of the number of books in the hands of the people would no doubt give Britain a higher place. The selection of reading matter made by the Italians affords a fresh demonstration that the tendency of the age is more toward the positive sciences and away from scholastic studies. (Statistics are given, showing more reading in science, in history, and in several general subjects than in theology.)

1159 "The Libraries of the Middle Ages and Their Contents." *Catholic World*, 5 (June 1867), p397–413 (NcU).

The article appeared originally in the *Dublin University Magazine*; the part about libraries (p397–404) is summarized below.

During the fourteenth century, libraries were filled with copies of the Scriptures, theological works, and the classics. Libraries and books were greatly appreciated by the various Roman Catholic orders, especially the Dominicans. The manuscript collection of the Sorbonne deserves special attention. Unfortunately, many of the abbey libraries experienced losses of books because of unscrupulous borrowers and destructive fires. As a rule, the university libraries that were under the patronage of the nobility were not so carefully guarded as were the abbey libraries. The collection of the Bibliothèque Royale has its origin in the collection in the Sainte Chapelle of Saint Louis' palace.

1160 [Free Libraries in Europe.] *Nation*, 9 (September 16, 1869), p231, 270 wds (InU, NcU).

We should like information showing the success of the 10,000 free or nearly free school libraries created throughout France, which contain more than a million books. French parents complained twenty years ago that there were no books they dared give their daughters. Since then, some writers have tried to fill this need. One would like to know the character of the books in these libraries, and whether they are both moral and interesting. Germany, always well-provided with libraries, has established Volksbibliotheken in recent years for popular use. Italian libraries are not free, but require a small fee from borrowers. Perhaps our own libraries should do likewise, as people value what they pay for. Two libraries otherwise similarly situated should try the two systems. A small payment may keep many away; perhaps only those would pay who do not need any obstruction to make them appreciate the privilege.

1161 "A Valuable Library." *Appletons' Journal: a Magazine of General Literature*, 5 (February 18, 1871), p207, 330 wds (NcU).
Prior to the siege in Paris, a library including rare books was removed. Recently these volumes were sold in London for a sum which indicates the war has not affected book and manuscript prices in that city. A list of some of the books and the amounts they brought is included; the total sum was £1,984, 19^s.

1162 [Books from the Abbey of St. Blasien.] *Nation*, 21 (September 23, 1875), p199, 160 wds (NcU).
The Benedictine Abbey of St. Blasien, in the Black Forest, was rich in manuscripts until the French began to harry the country in the early part of this century. At that time, most of the manuscripts were taken by the monks to the Monastery of St. Paul, near Klagenfurt, in Carinthia. Dr. Alfred Holder is now searching in the library of St. Paul for St. Blasien manuscripts and catalogs of manuscripts. His skill in palaeography makes it certain that if anything is to be found, he will get hold of it.

Middle Ages

1163 Nordhoff, Charles. "Concerning Books." *Ladies' Repository: a Monthly Periodical Devoted to Literature, Art, and Religion*, 16 (August 1856), p492–95 (NcU).
In England there were no libraries except in the monasteries. The library at Oxford in the thirteenth century contained only a few tracts, kept in chests. A few signed receipts exist for books borrowed by King John. The royal library of Jean le Bon of France, a contemporary of John of England, contained no more than ten volumes. In 1373 Charles le Sage had a library of 900 volumes; a catalog of this library still exists. Some catalogs of monastic libraries also have been preserved. Most of them mention only a few books in the vernacular; Glastonbury Abbey in 1248 owned only four books in English. Sometimes monasteries put verses on their windows, along with authors' portraits to indicate the libraries' holdings. The history of writing surfaces, the development of printing, and the introduction of modern punctuation are briefly discussed.

1164 Dexter, Henry M. "A Few Notes of Old Libraries." *Congregational Quarterly*, 2 (January 1860), p14–20 (IEG, OC).
It may be of interest to our readers to learn about early monastic libraries—but few of these were deserving of the name library because their collections had so few books. Due to the scarcity of books prior to the invention of the printing press, booksellers would lend books as do our circulating libraries. In 1342 Parisian booksellers were required by law to reserve copies of books for loan and to display catalogs which listed these books along with loan charges — one such catalog is reproduced. English monastic libraries did not have large collections as is evidenced by the 1350 catalog, also reproduced, of the Depying Priory. With the invention of the printing press, books became more accessible, and public and private libraries flourished. Oliver Heywood, an English Puritan Divine, in 1664 prepared a catalog of his library, which is reprinted for our readers' examination.

Individual Countries

Austria

1165 [Letters Found in the Clam-Gallas Library.] *Nation*, 4 (March 21, 1867), p229 (NcU).

Clam-Gallas was the name of a prominent Austrian family; however, the compilers of this bibliography have been unable to determine the exact location of the library and whether the library was open to anyone other than members of the family. The entire article follows.

"There was lately discovered in a corner of the Clam-Gallas library a quantity of letters forming part of the original correspondence of Count Matthias Gallas, during the Thirty Years' War. Among them were three hundred and twenty-one dated documents from the years 1633 to 1636, with a number of others belonging to the same period, but without dates. The most important are those of 1634, which refer directly to Wallenstein. Between the 20th of January and the 1st of April, 1634, there are sixty-three letters from imperial generals, Medici, Suys, Piccolomini, Manadas, Colloredo, and others, to Gallas; and a letter from Gallas to the Emperor dated Frauenberg, Feb. 24. This discovery can hardly fail to clear up some disputed points with regard to Wallenstein's conspiracy."

VIENNA — HOFBIBLIOTEK

1166 [Imperial Library of Vienna.] *National Magazine: Devoted to Literature, Art, and Religion*, 8 (January 1856), p95 (InU, NcU).

The entire article follows.

"The imperial library of the court of Vienna contains more than *sixteen thousand manuscripts* in the Greek, Hebrew, Chinese, Arabic, &c., languages on parchment, and nearly twelve thousand in the European languages upon paper, twelve thousand incunabula, nearly two hundred and eighty thousand modern books, more than six thousand volumes of music, and eight thousand eight hundred autographs of distinguished persons. There are besides in Vienna seventeen libraries, among which the private imperial library and that of the university are the most considerable."

Bavaria *see* Germany

Belgium

1167 "A Bibliographic Hoax." *Daguerreotype: a Magazine of Foreign Literature and Science*, 2 (May 20, 1848), p330–31 (NcU, OOxM).

Chalons, President of the Society of Bibliographers at Mons, prepared a catalog of the library of a non-existent Count de Fortsas. The library was supposed to contain only unique items. Many famous bibliographers were deceived and went to Binche, near Mons, in Belgium, to participate in the auction. Baron de Reiffenberg, Librarian of the Royal Library at Brussels, had requested and received a special allowance from the Minister of the Home Department in order to make needed purchases at the sale.

1168 "The Libraries of Belgium." *Norton's Literary Gazette and Publishers' Circular*, n.s. 1 (January 15, 1854), p34–35 (NcU).

The most extensive library in Belgium is the Royal Library in Brussels, with 180,000 volumes of printed books, 20,000 manuscripts, many maps and plans, 30,000 engravings and drawings, and over 14,000 medals and coins. Its annual appropriation is 60,000 francs; annual increase is about 3,000 volumes. The public library at Ghent has 59,650 volumes of printed books and 597 manuscripts; the annual increase is 650 volumes. The public library at Liège has 58,000 volumes of printed books, 430 manuscripts, 26,000 pamphlets, and an annual increase of 700 volumes. The oldest library in Belgium is at the University of Liège; it now has over 60,000 volumes and 302 manuscripts. There are seventeen other public libraries in Belgium (listed by location), the oldest of which is the library at Antwerp, founded in 1476; it now contains 20,000 volumes. (The libraries at Tournay, Bruges, Mons and Namur are also discussed.)

BRUSSELS — BIBLIOTHEQUE ROYALE

1169 "A Visit to the Burgundian Library at Brussels." *Norton's Literary Gazette and Publishers' Circular*, 3 (May 15, 1853), p81–82 (NcU).

The article summarized below was reprinted from *Fraser's Magazine*, 47 (January 1853), p83–87.

The collection has more than 20,000 ancient manuscripts; it probably began in the fifteenth century under the patronage of Philippe le Bon. Much was probably lost during the three centuries of warfare in the Netherlands. The collection was in Paris from the time Belgium was annexed by France until 1815. Some manuscripts were destroyed by fire in 1831. Several manuscripts of different types were added at various times. (Several manuscripts in the collection are described, including a Bible owned by Philippe le Bel, King of France; *History of Rome and Mythology*, written for Charles le Téméraire; Marguerite of Austria's music album; a Bible written for Charles the Bold; *Education des Demoyselles* by the Cheyvalier de Latour; and the book of the *Toison d'Or*.) Few could visit the library only once. Printing can serve both good and evil.

1170 "Belgian Libraries." *National Magazine: Devoted to Literature, Art, and Religion*, 4 (April 1854), p382 (InU, NcU).

The entire article follows.

"The number of public libraries in Belgium is twenty-one. The principal of them is, of course, the Bibliothèque Royale at Brussels. It contains 180,000 volumes, 19,688 manuscripts, 30,000 engravings, and 14,000 medals and coins. It increases its collection by, on an average, 3,000 volumes a year. The libraries next in importance are those of the University of Louvain, which has 60,000 volumes; the University of Ghent, 59,650 volumes; Tournay, 26,230 volumes; Antwerp, 19,148 volumes; Namur, 17,000 volumes; Mons, 15,000 volumes; Bruges, 10,500 volumes; and Ypres, 9,500 volumes."

— BOLLANDISTS

1171 "The Bollandists and Their Library." *American Bibliopolist,* 7 (June 1875), p158–59 (NcD).

A correspondent visiting Brussels writes of the workshop of the Bollandists, a literary corporation begun in the early seventeenth century to collect and publish authentic records of early and medieval church history through lives of all the saints. For every day of the year the lives and legends of the saints commemorated on that day are collected and recorded. The work now comes down to late October; the task is so vast that it may never be finished. The library contains various printed lives of saints and many old manuscripts. Other works in the library cover various related fields. The work has been continuous, systematic and orderly, as if done by one mind. The achievement seems remarkable, considering that Belgium is not a reading nation, having only two or three good booksellers, little native literature, and few libraries.

Bohemia

PRAGUE — UNIVERSITY OF PRAGUE LIBRARY

1172 [Acquisition of Prof. Hermann's Library by the University of Prague.] *National Magazine: Devoted to Literature, Art, and Religion,* 9 (July 1856), p94 (InU, NcU).

The entire article follows; it refers to Carl Friedrich Hermann. An even shorter version of the same article (not included in this bibliography) appeared in the August, 1856 issue of this periodical on p9.

"The library of the late *Professor Hermann,* of Göttingen, the renowned philologist, has been purchased by the University of Prague. It consists of eleven thousand volumes, of which four thousand are pamphlets."

Czechoslovakia *see* Bohemia

Denmark

COPENHAGEN

1173 [Royal Library at Copenhagen.] *Biblical Repository and Classical Review* [Biblical Repository and Quarterly Observer], 5 (January 1835), p255 (NcU).

The entire article follows.

"The royal library at Copenhagen contains about 400,000 volumes, and is one of the largest in the world. It was founded by Frederick II, and the building was completed in 1669. It has five divisions; 1. Northern library, contains every thing relating to Danish literature, and much of that of Sweden and Norway.

2. Many typographical curiosities relating to this literature. 3. Very valuable collections of MSS. many of them oriental. 4. Ten or twelve thousand early printed MSS. and books. 5. More than 81,000 engravings. The University Library has more than 100,000 volumes, and many valuable MSS. Its oriental books are of great worth. The Clas[s]en library has 30,000 volumes, and is very rich in physics, mathematics, &c."

1174 [Libraries of Copenhagen.] *Norton's Literary Gazette and Publishers' Circular*, n.s. 1 (July 15, 1854), p362 (NcU).
The entire article follows.
"Copenhagen, a city of about 130,000 inhabitants, has only four public libraries. Of these, the principal is the Royal Public Library, founded by King Frederic III, in 1650, with about 400,000 vols. of printed books, and 15,000 manuscripts. The library is still in the building erected by its founder, and which has been open for public use since the year 1794. Prof. Werlauff, librarian. The others are the University Library, with about 120,000 vols., and Prof. P. Godt Thorsen as librarian; the Royal Private Library, Prof. J. M. Thiele, and Classensche Library, L. H. Olufsen, librarian."

— KONGELIGE BIBLIOTEK

1175 "Royal library of Copenhagen." *Eclectic Magazine of Foreign Literature*, 23 (June 1851), p288 (NcU).
The entire article follows.
"The Royal Library of Copenhagen is about to receive an accession to its treasures, consisting of about 40,000 printed books, and 400 manuscripts, devised to it by M. Engelstoft, national historiographer, who is lately deceased. With these additions the printed volumes of the library exceed, it is said, 500,000 and the manuscripts 11,000."

England

1176 "Circulating Libraries." *American Journal of Science*, 5 (1822), p175 (InU).
The entire article follows.
"According to a published account there are in England about 600 reading companies or associations, (consisting of from 10 to 25 or more members) which procure for their special use such publications as they may wish to peruse, and at certain periods those books which have been the round among the members, are at a general meeting of the company sold to the highest bidder. The funds are thus replenished, and knowledge and entertainment of the best kind agreeably, and cheaply provided."

1177 "Itinerating Libraries." *American Annals of Education*, 3d ser., 1 (July 1831), p333, 320 wds (NcU).
With the itinerating library system, the collection of books is divided into parcels, each one containing forty to fifty volumes, which are circulated among the parishes. This plan was adopted thirteen years ago for East Lothian, England. At that time 250 books were divided into five divisions; now 2,000 volumes

are divided into fifty divisions. It is calculated that yearly each book circulates five times. These libraries are popular in England; one has been sent to Jamaica; and they seem suitable for use in our country.

1178 "Library for the Poor." *American Annals of Education*, 3d ser., 4 (August 1834), p359–61 (NcU).

One evening in a remote part of England, a gentleman inquired if there was a library nearby. He was told that there were two libraries in town and that they charged fees for their use. He responded that these libraries certainly could not be afforded by the poor. Therefore, with the aid of the parish minister, he raised a donation to found a library for the poor, charging only a penny each month to its users. The benefits of the library are confirmed by one member who related that since the library's opening he has ceased spending money each evening at the pub; moreover his household has become more orderly and has been entertained by the books.

1179 [Palfrey, John Gorham.] "*The Compact, with the Charter and Laws of the Colony of New Plymouth; together with the Charter of the Council at Plymouth, and an Appendix, containing the Articles of Confederation of the United Colonies of New England, and other valuable Documents. Published ... April 5, 1836.* Under the Supervision of William Brigham, Councellor at Law. pp357, 8 vo. Boston; Dutton & Wentworth, Printers to the State. 1836." *North American Review*, 44 (April 1837), p537–41 (InU, NcU).

A summary of the part of the review about libraries (p540) follows.

The rarity of the Acts of the Commissioners of the United Colonies is reportedly due to the fact that at one time the papers were purchased at an auction and were eventually used for wrapping paper. This fact is analogous to the story, related by John Bale, about the monastery libraries during the reign of Henry VIII. Many of the libraries' books were purchased by individuals who used the paper to scour candlesticks and to rub their boots. Some of the books were sold to grocers and soap-sellers, and many books were shipped to bookbinders on the Continent. One merchant bought the contents of two libraries for only forty shillings. According to Gale, "This stuff hath he [the merchant] occupied in the stead of gray paper by the space of more than these ten years, and yet he hath store enough for as many years to come."

1180 R[eed], C[aleb]. "Secular and Religious Education." *New Jerusalem Magazine*, 13 (November 1839), p105–08 (NIC).

The parts of the article about libraries (p105, 107) are summarized below.

Libraries and other institutions have arisen recently to promote and extend learning among the common people. Like schools, they have neglected the truths of religion. In cities and towns, where education is most prevalent, crime has increased rather than decreased. (Statistics are given for ten small circulating libraries in the parishes of St. George, St. James, St. Anne, and Soho, London.) The works in those libraries are divided into twelve classes, some indicating particularly good or bad books. (The number of books in each class is then given, and its percentage of the total circulation.) The poorer classes of literature are often more popular. Reading is not necessarily a good thing.

1181 "British Learned Societies." *Dwight's American Magazine, and Family Newspaper ... for the Diffusion of Useful and Moral and Religious Principles*, 3 (June 26, 1847), p404–06 (NcD).

The information is taken from a report issued by the American Society for the Diffusion of Useful Knowledge. The scattered references to libraries are quoted below.

Referring to the Royal Society: "The library and museum are worthy of the institution." Among the objects of the London Institution are "the acquisition of an extensive library of the most valuable books in all languages, ancient and modern...." Referring to the London Institution's building: "A library, 97 feet by 42, is in the second story." Surrey Institution members have access "1. To the newsroom, furnished with papers, gazettes, &c. 2. To the reading room, containing the literary journals, new books, pamphlets, &c. 3. To the lectures. 4. To the laboratory. 5. To the library of reference. 6. To the library of circulation."

1182 "Tastes of the Guardsmen in Literature." *Daguerreotype: a Magazine of Foreign Literature and Science*, 2 (February 26, 1848), p91, 870 wds (NcU, OOxM).

The article, summarized below, originally appeared in *Chambers's Edinburgh Journal*, n.s. 8 (December 4, 1847), p62.

A manuscript list of books in a library for the use of privates in a household regiment has been marked to indicate the most popular books. Novels form the bulk of the library, and the more popular authors include Scott, Bulwer-Lytton, and Dickens. Other popular reading includes Wellington's dispatches, the English histories of Hume and Smollett, Scott's biography of Napoleon, *The London Journal*, and *The Pilgrim's Progress*. It is well that some effort is being made to improve the intellectual and moral condition of the soldiers. However, greater judgment ought to be exercised in selecting the books. Several of the works listed in the catalog might have been left out, while many instructive books should have been included.

1183 "The Public Libraries of Europe." *Literary World*, N.Y., 5 (December 1, 1849), p461–63 (NcU).

In March 1849 a Select Committee was appointed by the House of Commons to investigate extending public library service in England, and we shall provide for our readers a series of abstracts of the Committee's report. The testimony of distinguished witnesses from the Continent, the United States, and England was heard. The final result shows that England, when compared to other countries, has inadequate library services for the public. Tables are reproduced which show the total number of public libraries in selected European countries and which separately list the principal European public and university libraries. The public libraries of England are not strictly free, for various restrictions are imposed upon patrons. Among the various types of English libraries investigated by the Committee were religious, parochial, and mechanics' libraries. In London the working classes have been well served by the coffee houses and tea rooms which provide newspapers and other periodicals.

1184 [Free Public Libraries.] *Norton's Literary Gazette and Publishers' Circular*, 2 (December 15, 1852), p236 (ICN, NcU).

The entire article follows. The allusion to the Oxford library refers to an article in the *Gazette* for November 15, 1852, too short for this bibliography; the reference to Marylebone is to item 1261 in this bibliography and the reference to the Manchester library is to item 1275. The "particulars" include articles on the Liverpool Free library *(see 1208)* and the Bolton Free library *(see 1197)*.

"Free Public Libraries are certainly getting fashionable. Both in our own country and in England, efforts are making, with more or less energy, to supply the various cities and large towns with the means of popular reading and study.

"We have already alluded to the projects for public Libraries on foot in Oxford, England, and in Marylebone Parish, London, and we have also announced the opening of the Manchester Free library. From our recent files of English papers we learn still more about such efforts, and presuming they will interest our readers, we subjoin a few particulars, derived almost wholly from that most excellent journal, the London Athenaeum."

1185 "Library Architecture." *Norton's Literary Gazette and Publishers' Circular*, 3 (March 15, 1853), p40 (ICN, NcU).
The entire article follows.
"Messrs. Papworth, Architects of London, have prepared a work, published by Chapman & Hall, on 'Museums, Libraries, and Picture Galleries, Public and Private, their establishment, formation, arrangement, architectural construction, &c.' The work is imperial octavo, illustrated with ten plates."

1186 "Papworths' Treatise on Museums, Libraries and Picture Galleries." *Norton's Literary Gazette and Publishers' Circular*, 3 (June 15, 1853), p97–98 (NcU).
The article summarized below refers to the book, *Museums, Libraries and Picture Galleries, Public and Private*, by John Woody Papworth and Wyatt Papworth (London: Chapman and Hall, 1853).
The treatise was written because of the act of Parliament pertaining to the establishment of libraries in every town, and was intended to aid in carrying out the act. The treatise may be interesting to those preparing for the Librarians' Convention. There are differences of opinion on several points. Extracts from the treatise follow. Seven principles are discussed concerning library buildings. The purchase of books is discussed; a separate reading room for periodicals is not recommended. General suggestions for the reading room are made. The needs of the population should be considered. Voting on proposed acquisitions may be useful. Reading interests and the place of fiction are discussed. Rules for the care of reference books are described. Lending libraries are discussed; several are mentioned. The librarian's duties and qualifications are discussed. Catalogs are very important; types of catalogs, and processing, are explained.

1187 [Circulating Libraries.] *Norton's Literary Gazette and Publishers' Circular*, n.s. 1 (May 15, 1854), p254, 400 wds (NcU).
The article summarized below was written by the London correspondent of one of the New York papers.
The circulating library system has gradually advanced during my own recollection. Once, the chief staple was fiction, but now all good works in all subjects except religion are circulated. This, for example, has made Dickens more popular, but has cost him money. When he published "Pickwick" and "Nickleby," sales were immense. The shilling monthly payment for the serial was convenient and attractive. Advertisers thronged to the publications because of the large number of sales. Circulating libraries then began hiring out the serials at just one penny for "a read." The number of readers has subsequently increased, but the number of purchasers has decreased. Thus, while *Bleak House* had a higher readership, it sold fewer copies. Advertisers, not thinking about the many people who read it under the penny-reading system, saw the lower sales figures and did not patronize it. Thackeray has received similar treatment.

England

1188 "The Circulating Library." *Norton's Literary Gazette and Publishers' Circular*, n.s. 2 (June 15, 1855), p252–53 (MWiW).

The article is an extract from Charles Knight's *The Old Printer and the Modern Press*, London, Murray, 1854.

The circulating library, by the beginning of this century, was to be found in most market towns. It gave authors, printers, and booksellers a new kind of popular fiction to produce and distribute. Later, the novel, *Waverly*, and others by the same author changed the library's nature. Authors began to experiment with new types of fiction; some travel books and memoirs came into the libraries, as well. The circulating library is now, in many instances, an instrument of popular enlightenment but the older type, with light romantic fiction, still exists in smaller towns and some watering places. Circulating libraries have not hurt the sale of books but have, instead, greatly promoted it. One of the first book clubs was established by Robert Burns; Lord Brougham advocated them. In Scotland, lending libraries and itinerating libraries have been successful but few exist in England except in connection with schools or under the direction of dissenting ministers; in these libraries users do not get to choose the books, so are prevented from reading the best books of amusement.

1189 [Discoveries of Manuscripts in English Libraries.] *Nation*, 2 (March 29, 1866), p403, 400 wds (NcU).

The lack of full and accurate catalogs of England's great libraries, particularly of their manuscripts, has long been a complaint among scholars; the libraries of individual colleges and societies have fared somewhat better. Private collectors, as a group, are not unduly familiar with their treasures; a few years ago, the Rev. Mr. Groome discovered among the manuscripts of Mr. John Tollemache, M. P., an English romance of about 1430–50, "Sir Generides," previously unknown. It has been edited and will be a Roxburghe Club publication. Mr. Henry Bradshaw, of King's College, Cambridge, has recently discovered two leaves of this romance. Still more recently, Mr. W. Aldis Wright, the librarian of Trinity College [Cambridge], has found a single leaf and the complete poem in the Trinity Library; he will undoubtedly publish the poem soon.

1190 [Bequests of W. F. Fairholt.] *Nation*, 2 (May 8, 1866), p580 (NcU).

The entire article follows. It apparently refers to the Society of Antiquaries in London and the museum that was operated by the Shakespeare Birthplace Trust.

"The late W. F. Fairholt, whose death we announced last week, has bequeathed his large collection of books of pageants, which contains many rare volumes, to the Society of Antiquaries, and with it the manuscript of an unfinished work from his pen on the pageants of the Middle Ages. His Shakespeariana, which includes a large volume of Shakespeare drawings, he has left to the Museum at Stratford-on-Avon, and a number of volumes, which he names, to the British Museum. The remainder of his library will be sold for the benefit of the Literary Fund."

1191 "The King's Library." *American Bibliopolist*, 1 (October 1869), p302 (ICU).

The entire article follows. It was taken, for the most part verbatim, from *The Book Rarities in the University of Cambridge*, 1829, by C. H. Hartshorne.

"When George the First sent the Bishop of Ely's books to the University of Cambridge, he sent at the same time a troop of horse to Oxford, which gave rise

Europe

to the following well-known epigram from Dr. Trapp, smart in its way, but not so clever as the answer from Sir William Browne.

> The King observing with judicious eyes,
> The state of both his universities,
> To one he sent a regiment: for why?
> That learned body wanted loyalty.
> To th' other he sent books, as well discerning
> How much that body wanted learning.
>   THE ANSWER.
> The King to Oxford sent his troop of horse,
> For Tories own no argument but force;
> With equal care to Cambridge books he sent,
> For Whigs allow no force but argument.

The books were received Nov. 19, 20, &c. 1715. The King purchased them for six thousand guineas, and munificently presented them to the public library. — Hartshorne."

1192 "Free Reading-Rooms." *Putnam's Magazine*, n.s. 5 (May 1870), p612, 300 wds (InU, NcU).

Free reading rooms and libraries are already established in several English cities. They are for the benefit of the poorer classes and those to whom the suffrage has recently been extended. Some are supported by the city governments, others by contributions. They are providing clean, pleasant places for workingmen to go, where they can improve themselves by reading. America also needs free news rooms and libraries.

1193 "Ruskin on Bibliomania." *American Bibliopolist*, 4 (November 1872), p585, 160 wds (ICU, NcD).

The article summarized below is a quotation from *Sesame and Lilies*.

How much do you think we spend on our libraries, public or private, compared with what we spend on our horses? A man who spends lavishly on his library is called a bibliomaniac but men who ruin themselves because of their horses are not called horse-maniacs. How much do you think the contents of private and public libraries in the United Kingdom would fetch in comparison with its wine cellars? If public libraries were half as costly as public dinners, even foolish men and women might suspect that there was good in reading; the cheapness of literature makes people forget that if a book is worth reading it is worth buying.

BIRMINGHAM — PUBLIC LIBRARY

1194 "The Birmingham Shakespeare Memorial Library." *Publishers' Weekly* [Publishers' and Stationers' Weekly Trade Circular], 1 (May 23, 1872), p466–67, 400 wds (NcU).

We have just received the first part of the catalog of this library, issued to show what editions have been secured and how many are still needed. The collection is weak in American and colonial editions; it is hoped that possessors of Shakespeareana will be willing to give or sell to the library. The catalog, compiled by J. D. Mullins, is an admirable piece of bibliography; titles are given in full and old or rare editions are clearly described. The library, founded in 1864, the tercentenary of Shakespeare's birth, now numbers 4,012 volumes.

1195 [Birmingham, England, Shakespeare Library.] *American Bibliopolist*, 4 (June 1872), p299 (IEN, OC).

The entire article follows.

"A Shakespeare Library was founded at Birmingham, eight years ago; it now numbers more than four thousand volumes of Shakespeariana, including nearly four hundred different editions of the Poet's works. An excellent catalogue of the latter, compiled by Mr. J. D. Mullins, has just been issued. Among the few rarities, may be mentioned a copy of the play 'Henry the Fifth,' 1608."

1196 "Shakespeare Memorial Library." *American Bibliopolist*, 7 (February 1875), p27, 470 wds (NcD).

The Shakespeare Memorial Library, founded in 1864 at Birmingham, England, has already become the largest collection of Shakespeare's works and the literature about them. Several famous Shakespearian scholars have contributed to enrich its shelves. Local annual subscriptions acquire all ordinary and accessible works, while more valuable and rare volumes have been given or bequeathed. The library is open to visitors and students of the Birmingham Free Library, though no books can be taken from the reading room. The library is a unique memorial to the bard's genius. American authors and publishers are asked to contribute any Shakespearian works to the library through Mr. Joseph Crosby in the Western States and Mr. J. Parker Norris in the rest of the country. It is requested that a notice of the book's title, place of publication, etc., be sent if no copy is donated, so that it can be purchased.

BOLTON — PUBLIC LIBRARY

1197 "Bolton Free Library." *Norton's Literary Gazette and Publishers' Circular*, 2 (December 15, 1852), p237 (ICN, NcU).

The entire article follows. The Bolton Public Library opened in 1853.

"From the source above mentioned [*London Athenaeum*] we learn that the movement in favor of a Free Library and Town Museum at *Bolton*, is progressing in such a way as to leave little doubt of its ultimate success. The subscriptions, we are told, already amount to about £1,000. The donations of books and specimens for the museums are considerable; and the appeal made to the rate-payers on the question of a *public* adoption of the scheme, with its responsibilities, pecuniary and other, has been answered by an overwhelming majority in the affirmative."

BORDESLEY — ABBEY LIBRARY

1198 Dexter, Henry M. "A Private Library of the Fourteenth Century." *Congregational Quarterly*, 2 (July 1860), p268, 550 wds (NcD, OC).

About 1359 Guy Beauchamp, Earl of Warwick, bequeathed his library to Bordesley Abbey. (The list of about 40 titles is reproduced in French; it includes several romances. Entries are by title.)

BURSLEM — WEDGEWOOD INSTITUTE

1199 "Thomas Carlyle on Books." *American Bibliopolist*, 2 (January 1870), p24 (ICU, OC).

Europe

The entire article follows.

"The secretary to the Wedgewood Institute, Burslem, has received the following letter from Mr. Thomas Carlyle: 'Messrs. Chapman & Hall are directed to send you five volumes, viz., Sartor and Heroes, one volume; Schiller and Sterling, one volume; Cromwell, three volumes. The utility of your enterprise will depend mainly on your judgment in selecting books—on your earnestly and sedulously choosing books that are nourishment to the mind of a man, and rigorously rejecting what are poison (by far the most numerous class at present.) —T. Carlyle, Chelsea, November 5.' "

CAMBRIDGE — CAMBRIDGE UNIVERSITY LIBRARY

1200 [Discovery of Missing Documents in the Cambridge University Library.] *Nation*, 1 (August 10, 1865), p180, 250 wds (NcU).

The part of the article summarized in the last sentence of this abstract is inaccurate and misleading. The manuscripts do have a bearing on Waldensian history; however "The Noble Lesson" was not a Biblical version, but a poem in the old Vaudois dialect; the dates are only approximations. Henry Bradshaw discussed the whole matter in detail in his article, "On Recovery of the Long Lost Waldensian Manuscripts," p1-15 in *Collected Papers of Henry Bradshaw*, Cambridge University Press, 1889.

In this country we have experienced the evils arising from incompetent librarians and the want of intelligence among those where we most look for it — the custodians of books. However, matters here have hardly reached the point that they have in the Cambridge University Library. We learn from a book by Dr. [James Henthorn] Todd that the librarians there, ever since 1659, have failed to make themselves acquainted with the manuscripts under their charge. A series of important documents about the Waldenses has been reported missing for two hundred years. Mr. Henry Bradshaw of King's College has discovered them. They have bearing on ecclesiastical history; they show that the famous Biblical version in the Romance language, "The Noble Lesson" was produced in A.D. 1400, not A.D. 1100.

1201 [Printed Books Containing Mss. Notes in the Cambridge University Library.] *Nation*, 2 (February 1, 1866), p146, 300 wds (NcU).
The article refers to Francis Douce.

A novel catalog has just been published, of "Printed Books Containing Mss. Notes and Adversaria Preserved in the University Library, Cambridge," by H. R. Luard and Churchill Babington. The idea of preserving traces of the studies and tastes of eminent owners of books is praiseworthy. One of the most careful annotators of his books was the famous antiquary, Francis Druce [sic]. His library was bequeathed to the Bodleian at Oxford; almost every book in his collection has his notes, few of which have been published. The proposed publication of selections from his manuscripts would make one of the most curious books of "ana" ever published.

1202 [Mr. Bradshaw's Discoveries in the Cambridge University Library.] *Nation*, 4 (February 7, 1867), p104 (NcU).
The entire article follows.

"Mr. Henry Bradshaw, of the Cambridge University Library, has made two noteworthy discoveries in that library. He has found some fragments of a Troy

Book, written by John Barbour, the Scottish poet, intermixed with Lydgate's poem, in all about 2,200 lines. The evidence leaves not the slightest doubt of the authorship. Subsequently, in a MS. at Oxford, Mr. Bradshaw found 1,200 lines more of the same poem. The other finding is 40,000 lines of 'Lives of the Saints,' also by John Barbour. Were all librarians of English libraries as industrious as Mr. Bradshaw, many more valuable relics would doubtless be brought to light."

— CAMBRIDGE UNIVERSITY — TRINITY COLLEGE LIBRARY

1203 [Bohemian Manuscript at Trinity College, Cambridge.] *American Bibliopolist*, 7 (April 1875), p64–65 (NcD).

Rev. A. H. Wratislaw has written to the *Athenaeum* concerning a manuscript which was noticed in the Gale collection in the Trinity College Library, Cambridge, last autumn. The manuscript contains two-thirds of Dalemil's *Bohemian Chronicle*, tracing Czech history in verse from the Tower of Babel to 1314. It has the same date as the earliest hitherto known complete manuscript of the chronicle, which was recently found in Vienna. Pan Jireczek was preparing an edition of that manuscript in Prague, and now awaits a transcript of the new discovery before publishing. Other Bohemian manuscripts besides the one in the British Museum may exist in Great Britain. Anyone who possesses or knows of such manuscripts should contact Wratislaw immediately.

CHELTENHAM — SIR THOMAS PHILLIPPS'S LIBRARY

1204 [Library of Sir Thomas Phillipps.] *Nation*, 18 (May 14, 1874), p315 (NcU).

The entire article follows.

"The library of the late Sir Thomas Phillipps, at Thirlstane House, Cheltenham, England, which is said to have cost the learned baronet about a million dollars, and which is nearly as well known as any of the great public libraries of Europe, will continue accessible to the public. It has been settled on Mrs. Katherine S. Fenwick, the youngest daughter of the late baronet, and on her sons after her. A new catalogue is now in preparation. The sum left for its maintenance being inadequate for that purpose, the trustees have determined to make a charge for a copy of any manuscript for which application may be made."

EXETER — EXCHEQUER CHAMBER LIBRARY

1205 [Saxon Manuscript in Exeter Exchequer Chamber.] *American Bibliopolist*, 1 (November 1869), p345 (ICU).

The entire article follows.

"The Priceless Saxon MS., the gift of Leofric, the first Bishop of Exeter, which was said to have disappeared from the Chapter Library, never was there. It is safe among other MSS. in the Exeter Exchequer Chamber."

LEEDS — MECHANICS' LIBRARY

1206 "Leed's [sic] (Eng.) Mechanics' Institution." *Norton's Literary Gazette and Publishers' Circular*, 3 (January 15, 1853), p3 (ICN, NcU).

The entire article follows.

"The annual soirée of this Association, was held at Leeds on the eighth of last month, LORD JOHN RUSSELL presiding, and delivering a long address upon the general state of knowledge at the present time.

"The annual report of the Institution stated that its number of members was 2,142; its library contained 8,714 volumes; its reading-room contained 43 newspapers and 56 reviews and magazines. Plans are making for providing at a cost of £8,800, a building which should have a reading-room for 200 persons, a lecture-room for 1,400, a library for 25,000 volumes, and large rooms for classes."

LIVERPOOL

1207 "Literary Institutions in Liverpool." *Monthly Anthology and Boston Review*, 4 (November 1807), p597–98 (NcU).

Liverpool is now wealthy enough to turn its attention to learning and fine arts. Public institutions of a literary character have increased rapidly here in the last ten years. The public reading rooms yield to none, and the six-year old botanic garden is among the best in England. The first reading room is the Athenaeum, with the most select collection of books I have ever known. There is no library in America with so general a collection of standard works in every branch of knowledge. The Lyceum has a more elegant and convenient reading room, but its library is nothing better than that of a common circulating library such as the Boston Social Library; the annual subscription is only half a guinea.

— FREE LIBRARY

1208 "Liverpool Free Library." *Norton's Literary Gazette and Publishers' Circular*, 2 (December 15, 1852), p236–37 (ICN, NcU).

The Liverpool Free Library and Museum for the People first opened its doors to the public on October 18th. Its establishment was motivated by the late Earl of Derby's bequest of 18,700 different specimens to the city. The library's collection now totals 10,000 volumes. Despite the library's small rooms and the limited selection of books, library attendance has remained steady since opening day. Often, twenty to thirty men can be observed sitting on the floor of the reading room with books resting upon their knees. Supporters of the library are determined to secure a larger and better reading room.

1209 "Liverpool Free Library." *Norton's Literary Gazette and Publishers' Circular*, 3 (December 15, 1853), p217, 1100 wds (NcU).

According to the first annual report of this library, it opened in October of 1852. Since then, 128,083 works have been used. Demand is great. As only 140–160 persons can get into the present rooms at one time, the rooms are quite crowded. At the beginning of the year there were about 10,000 books. Added during the year were 3,960 volumes, including 700 volumes and 40 pamphlets by donation, and a collection of maps and charts. There are now 13,456 volumes in the collection. A table lists the number of volumes in each of fifteen subject classes. Total expenditures for books for the reference library were £1,060 9^s 7^d. Another table shows the proportion of the demand for the various subject classes; novels were most popular. Use of the library is not limited to a single class of society.

1210 [Library Circulation in Liverpool, England.] *National Magazine: Devoted to Literature, Art, and Religion*, 5 (July 1854), p94, 240 wds (NcU).

A recently issued report on the reading and readers of Liverpool's free libraries for the first quarter of an unspecified year indicated that biography and history combined is the most popular subject area with 8,576 volumes issued. The other reading categories and the number of volumes issued are: novels, 4,203; miscellaneous literature, 868; geography and travel, 579; poetry and drama, 254; theology, morality and metaphysics, 218; natural history, 181; commerce and political economy, 18; and science and art 215. Marryatt is more often read than Scott.

1211 "Liverpool Free Library." *National Magazine: Devoted to Literature, Art, and Religion*, 6 (January 1855), p86 (NcU).

The entire article follows.

"The London Athenaeum gives some minute and very striking statistics respecting the Liverpool Free Library, which show an unexpected interest among the poorer classes of England for good literature. It says—'It is a noticable fact that the larger proportion of solid reading is among the really working classes, the lighter literature more among young men in offices and shops.'"

1212 [Liverpool Public Library.] *Publishers' Weekly*, 4 (October 25, 1873), p452 (NcU).

The entire article follows.

"The catalogue of the reference department of the Liverpool Public Library, which consists of 61,600 volumes, has just been published. The work has occupied five years in compilation, at a cost of over £1,000, exclusive of printing."

— LYCAEUM

1213 "Liverpool Lycaeum." *Pcrt Folio* by Oliver Oldschool, 2 (November 6, 1802), p348, 900 wds (InU, NcU).

The Liverpool Lycaeum has just acquired a new building of simple but beautiful design. The building is only one story, with a basement, and houses a coffee room and a library. The library is a rotunda forty-five feet across and forty feet high. Lighting comes from a central skylight in the dome. There are twelve recesses for books which in turn support a gallery six feet wide. The gallery will house shelving nine feet high. There is also a reading room, thirty-three by twenty-one feet. The exterior of the building uses columns as part of the architectural ornamentation.

LONDON

1214 [Chinese Libraries in England.] *Biblical Repository and Classical Review* [Biblical Repository and Quarterly Observer], 6 (July 1835), p257 (NcU).

The entire article follows.

"The principal Chinese libraries in England are the following: 1. The late

Dr. Morrison's, now deposited at the Mission-house, Austin Friars, London. 2. The one at the British Museum, 600 vols. 3. That of the East India Company. 4. The one belonging to the London University, presented by Dr. Gregory and Mr. Bentley. 5. That of the Royal Asiatic Society, amounting to 2610 volumes, presented by Sir G. Staunton. There are in a library at Paris, 4000 Chinese volumes."

1215 "Public Libraries in England." *Norton's Literary Gazette and Publishers' Circular*, 3 (April 15, 1853), p64, 320 wds (ICN, NcU).
The article summarized below was reprinted from the *Athenaeum* (March 12, 1853).
The free public library movement has at last come to London. The Court of Common Council recently adopted a resolution that supports the establishment of public libraries and instructs the Library Committee to study and report upon this matter. A proposal to open the library of the London Institution to a larger circle of readers was made but subsequently was not accepted by a majority of the Institution's members. The Battersea Literary and Scientific Institution, which opened only six months ago, has shown much progress; it now has 227 members, and about 1,100 volumes, and circulated 660 books each quarter.

1216 "Our London Letter." *Norton's Literary Gazette and Publishers' Circular*, 3 (December 15, 1853), p215, 200 wds (NcU).
The part of the article about libraries is summarized below.
The libraries at Marylebone and Finsbury are still in a state of stagnation. We are to have some new free libraries; in Bolton one with about 1,450 volumes was opened a few weeks ago and the members of the Tamworth Library, founded under the auspices of the late Sir Robert Peel, have just held their annual meeting. The Bury Athenaeum, replacing a predecessor, has just been opened, with Lord Stanley presiding at the ceremony. Mr. Sims, of the British Museum, has just published a handbook about that library that also gives information on other libraries of London.

1217 [John Payne Collier's Elizabethan Reprints.] *Nation*, 2 (January 25, 1866), p113 (NcU).
The part of the article about libraries is copied below. It is part of a letter from Collier to the London *Athenaeum* complaining about the British reception of his series of reprints.
"The British Museum has not one of the originals (so far as I can ascertain from the multifarious and overgrown catalogues), and yet it has never given the slightest support to my undertaking. In London and its neighborhood there is no library, either public or private, that seems to wish to possess even such a book as a faithful reproduction of the first edition of the works of Lord Surrey and Sir Thomas Wyatt whose poems almost alone fill the long dreary interval between the reigns of Richard II. or Henry IV. and that of Elizabeth."

1218 [Public Libraries in London.] *Publishers' Weekly*, 7 (January 30, 1875), p114 (NcU).
The entire article follows.
"One of the interesting features of the London *Athenaeum*, since September, has been the series of papers on the public and quasi-public libraries of London, among which have been or will be described, Sion College Library, the Library at Lambeth Palace, the Library of Dr. Williams, the Guildhall Library,

the Library at Westminster Abbey, and the Cathedral Library at St. Paul's; the Library of the Patent Office, the Libraries of Lincoln's Inn, Gray's Inn, and the Inner and Middle Temple; the Library of the College of Physicians, also of the College of Surgeons; also the Libraries of the Royal Society, of the Society of Antiquaries, and of the British and Foreign Bible Society."

— BRITISH MUSEUM

1219 [Rules for the British Museum's Reading Room.] *Museum of Foreign Literature, Science, and Art,* 4 ([April], 1824), p384, 300 wds (InU, NcU).

This is a copy of the "Directions Respecting the Reading Room of the British Museum."

"The room is open from 10:00 until 4:00 on week days, and is closed for a week at Christmas, Easter, and Whitsuntide. Application to use the room must be made in writing to the principal librarian. The applicant may be admitted immediately, or his application may be laid before either the next general meeting or the Committee of trustees. An applicant should furnish a satisfactory recommendation as it is unwise to admit complete strangers. Permission to use the reading room is generally given for six months; thereafter a new application must be made. Readers must allow a reasonable time for the staff to locate materials, especially printed books. Readers may make one or two extracts from manuscripts, but may not copy the whole without permission. While taking notes the copier may not lay the paper on which he is writing on any part of the manuscript or book; tracings cannot be made without permission."

1220 "British Museum." *Museum of Foreign Literature, Science, and Art,* 26 (June 1835), p712 (InU, NcD).

The entire article follows; it was reprinted from the *Times* of London.

"The number of persons who visited the British Museum in 1829, was 68,101; in 1830, 71,336; in 1831, 99,912; in 1832, 147,896; in 1833, 210,495; in 1834, 237,366. The number of visitors to the reading-rooms, for the purposes of study and research, was, in 1810, 1950; in 1815, 4300; in 1820, 8820; in 1825, 22,800; in 1830, 31,300; in 1831, 38,200; in 1832, 46,680; in 1833, 58,000; and in 1834, 70,266. The number of visits made to the galleries of sculpture, by artists and students for the purposes of study, was, in 1831, 4938; in 1832, 4740; in 1833, 4490; and in 1834, 5645."

1221 [Recent British Publications.] *Biblical Repository and Classical Review,* [Biblical Repository and Quarterly Observer], 6 (October 1835), p503 (NcU).

The part of the article about libraries follows, altered typographically.

"In the British Museum in 1832, compared with 1821, were the following literary treasures. In 1821: 115,925 printed books, 17,937 manuscripts, and 16,923 charters. In 1832: 218,950 printed books, 21,604 manuscripts, and 19,093 charters. The great increase of books was owing to the accession of a library of George III. An elaborate catalogue is nearly ready."

1222 [Visitors to the British Museum.] *Daguerreotype: a Magazine of Foreign Literature and Science,* 1 (October 2, 1847), p239 (InU, NcU).

The entire article follows.

"A parliamentary return, just issued, shows that 825,901 persons visited the British Museum during the year 1846. Of these 750,601 inspected the general collections, 66,784 studied in the library, 4,126 visited the sculpture gallery, and 4,390 the print room; 52,287 went over the Tower. The number of visitors to the National Gallery during the year 1846 was 608,140."

1223 "British Museum." *Bibliotheca Sacra* [and Theological Review], 5 (May 1848), p388–89 (NcU).

The article summarized below draws from an article in *British Quarterly Review*, 6 (August 1847), p72–114.

The library is not far from the center of London. It includes manuscripts, printed books, ancient sculpture, museums of natural history, prints, medals, maps, charts, and the nucleus of an ethnographic museum. The buildings are vast but as yet incomplete. Parliament devoted £2,061,895, or $10,309,475 to the British Museum in 1847–48. The real estate cost one half of this sum. The collections of Sir Hans Sloane, the first two earls of Oxford, the Cottonian manuscript collection and the library of Arthur Edwards became the British Museum. There were not more than 40,000 printed books when the museum opened in 1757. (Several of the major additions are described.) The museum has 130,000 pamphlets. (Recent additions are listed.) The library added 45,000 volumes in 1846; 20,000 were from the Grenville bequest and 3,000 by the copyright act. There are 350,000 volumes now, containing 550,000 works.

1224 "British Museum." *Norton's Literary Gazette and Publishers' Circular*, 2 (October 15, 1852), p188–89 (ICN, NcU).

The entire article follows.

"A recent report of Mr. Panizzi, Librarian of the British Museum, announces the fact that there are at the present time in that library 465,000 volumes, which number will be increased the present year to 470,000 volumes. This is 240,000 more than it contained in 1836.

"Two important inquiries now arise: first, how to provide for the anticipated increase of the next thirty years; and, second, how to provide for the immediate increase of the next five years, while more ample accommodations are preparing. It is expected that in five years 80,000 volumes will be added, and that in thirty years the size of the present library will be doubled."

1225 "British Museum." *Norton's Literary Gazette and Publishers' Circular*, 2 (November 15, 1852), p214, 210 wds (ICN, NcU).

Newspaper accounts report that complaints continually are being made about the British Museum. As far as we can tell, these complaints are engendered by the Museum's need for more shelves, seating, and a catalog. Mr. Panizzi is attempting to solve these problems, but circumstances seem to have impeded his efforts to do so.

1226 [British Museum.] *National Magazine: Devoted to Literature, Art, and Religion*, 1 (December 1852), p568 (InU, NcU).

The entire article follows.

"A report from Mr. Panizzi gives an account of the present condition of the department of printed books in the British Museum. At the end of the year 1846, the library of printed works consisted of 230,000 volumes; at this moment it consists of 465,000, and by the end of the present year it will amount to 470,000 volumes. During the last fifteen years the library has therefore increased at the rate of sixteen thousand volumes a year on the average."

1227 [British Museum.] *National Magazine: Devoted to Literature, Art, and Religion*, 2 (January 1853), p91 (InU, NcU).
The entire article follows.
"The report of Mr. Panizzi states that the *Library of the British Museum*, at the close of 1836, contained two hundred and thirty thousand volumes of printed books, and has since increased to four hundred and sixty-five thousand, showing an annual increase of sixteen thousand volumes. The amount of shelving at present provided is fifty-five thousand four hundred feet; and the trustees have now to provide room for the eighty thousand volumes which will be added to the library during the coming five years."

1228 "British Museum Catalogue." *Norton's Literary Gazette and Publishers' Circular*, 3 (March 15, 1853), p39, 420 wds (NcU).
The article summarized below is taken from part of an article on the British Museum in *Quarterly Review*, 92 (December 1852), p157–82.
We presume no more will be said about forcing the Trustees to attempt the physical impossibility of creating a general printed catalog of the Museum for current use. This suggestion was used by some to censure covertly the library department, and by some deluded by the catalog's usefulness. No power of men or money, however, could ever complete one. The only practical idea in the Report for a printed catalog would be for some completed and closed class or period, such as books in the museum printed before 1501, which would be of less general use and quickly out-dated. A better way would be for all the libraries of Europe to contribute to a general catalog of all books known to have been printed before 1501, with initials to indicate which library has them. The catalogs could be updated with a hand-stamp.

1229 "British Museum Catalogue." *Norton's Literary Gazette and Publishers' Circular*, 3 (May 15, 1853), p83 (ICN, NcU).
The entire article follows.
"A London correspondent, who has every means of information upon the subject, writes us as follows:
" 'In one of your late numbers of the Literary Gazette, you alluded to the British Museum Catalogue as if there were none, or a very poor one. The fact is that the Museum Catalogue is by far the best of any public library in the world. All of the books, pamphlets, maps, and even hand sheets, that are in the library, are well catalogued, and the Catalogues are easy of reference to every reader.'
"We are happy to correct any false impression which we may have conveyed, but yet we hardly know to what our correspondent alludes; for, in common with most of our countrymen who are conversant with such matters, we have long been aware of the skill and efficiency which is exercised in the management of this world-renowned library."

1230 "British Museum." *Norton's Literary Gazette and Publishers' Circular*, 3 (July 15, 1853), p115, 760 wds (ICN, NcU).
The article summarized below was taken from the London *Literary Gazette*.
Among the additions to the manuscript department during the last year were "The Bedford Missal" written and illuminated in France between the years 1423 and 1430, "The Breviary of Isabella of Castile," 1496 and 97, and "The Book of Hours of Juana, daughter of Ferdinand and Isabella, wife of Philip the Fair," 1496. (Several significant acquisitions of 17th and 18th century British documents and letters are described.) In the Department of Antiquities,

sculptures from Mesopotamia have been arranged and coins and other objects have been received. In the Natural History Department, numerous fossils have been received and in the Department of Prints and Drawings, Sir William Gell's drawings made during his travels around the Mediterranean have been acquired, as well as drawings by Rubens, Jordaens, and other masters.

1231 [British Museum Catalog.] *National Magazine: Devoted to Literature, Art, and Religion*, 3 (November 1853), p475 (InU, NcU).
The entire article follows.
"During a late debate in the House of Commons, it was stated that the *Catalogue of the Library of the British Museum*, now in process of compilation, has already cost a hundred thousand pounds, and is so far from being complete that it cannot be finished in less than forty years. This catalogue already fills twelve thousand folio volumes. When completed it will form a 'neat and portable work of thirteen thousand volumes.'"

1232 [British Museum.] *National Magazine: Devoted to Literature, Art, and Religion*, 3 (December 1853), p565 (InU, NcU).
The entire article follows.
"The estimated total number of volumes now in the library of the *British Museum* is five hundred and ten thousand one hundred and ten. The additions since 1848 have been at the rate of fifteen thousand volumes a year."

1233 [British Museum Reading Room.] *National Magazine: Devoted to Literature, Art, and Religion*, 8 (January 1856), p94 (InU, NcU).
The entire article follows.
"The largest reading-room in the world is now nearly completed in the British Museum. It is circular, one hundred and forty feet in diameter, and one hundred in height. The tables will accommodate nearly four hundred readers. The wrought iron book-cases will contain one hundred and two thousand volumes. The cost of the room will be about $500,000."

1234 "The British Museum." *American Journal of Education* (Barnard), 8 (March 1860), p314, 220 wds (NcU).
A century passed between the purchase of Montagu House for the library and the completion of the new buildings. In his will, Sir Hans Sloane suggested the establishment of the Museum and offered his collection to Parliament for £20,000. The offer was accepted by an act that also authorized £10,000 to purchase the manuscripts of the Harleian Library to which were added the Cottonian Library and the library of Major Arthur Edwards. By the same act a lottery was held; the proceeds, £100,000, were used to pay for the Sloane and Harleian collections and for the purchase and repair of Montagu House, to which the Harleian collection was moved in 1755. The Museum opened to the public in January, 1759.

1235 [Retirement of Panizzi.] *Nation*, 1 (August 3, 1865), p147, 200 wds (NcU).
The approaching retirement of Mr. Antonio Panizzi from the post of principal librarian of the British Museum is announced. There is perhaps no other public servant to whom men of letters throughout the world owe so much. When Panizzi was a political refugee from Italy, Lord Brougham was influential in obtaining a position in the British Museum for him. His untiring energy over-

came the dead weight of trustees and others; for some years he has had almost uncontrolled sway in his department. Many Americans can testify to the liberality of the provisions for users of the magnificent Reading Room. The library now approaches 800,000 volumes, trebled in extent since Panizzi's accession to office.

1236 [The British Museum.] *Nation*, 2 (May 15, 1866), p611 (NcU).
The entire article follows.
"The expenditures of the British Museum during the past year amounted to over half a million of dollars, viz., £101,808 14^s. 4^d., and the sum required for the present year is estimated at a larger figure. The number of persons, exclusive of readers, who visited its general collections during the twelve months was 369,967, and the number of readers 100,721 — a daily average of 349, each reader consulting twelve books daily. Valuable acquisitions have been made to the department of Oriental, British, and mediaeval antiquities and ethnography, and the Greek and Roman departments have been enriched by a number of antiquities from the Pourtalis sale. Prof. Owen reports 16,700 additions to zoology, 10,079 to geology, and 3,623 to mineralogy."

1237 [Hebrew Books in the British Museum.] *Nation*, 4 (March 21, 1867), p228, 240 wds (NcU).
The article is based on one in *The Spectator*.
The *Catalogue of the Hebrew Books in the Library of the British Museum* has recently been published. In 1759 there was only one Hebrew volume in the library; now there are 10,000, which form the largest existing collection of these books. The places of publication of the volumes show the sad history of the dispersion and persecution of the race. Many of the books are written in Spanish or German or Arabic, but in Hebrew characters. Most of the books are about the Bible or related topics, but five hundred are on science, history or geography, and 750 relate to poetry or criticism.

1238 [Hebrew Books in the British Museum.] *Nation*, 5 (August 1, 1867), p84, 230 wds (NcU).
A *Catalogue of the Hebrew Books in the Library of the British Museum* has just been printed. This is the largest collection in the world, comprising 10,000 volumes. The catalog is arranged under authors' names and under such headings as "Bible," "Mishna," and "Talmud." (The numbers of books in various categories is given.)

1239 "Obituary." *American Bibliopolist*, 1 (October 1869), p305 (ICU).
The entire article follows.
"We are sorry to record the death of Mr. [Thomas] Watts, of the British Museum. He died suddenly, on the 9th of September. He was Keeper or Superintendent of the Library of the British Museum, and had been connected with it for some thirty years, rising from assistant to keeper.
"His knowledge of books was most extensive. He was thoroughly capable and very courteous in the performance of his duties in placing the stores in his care at the disposal of the public. He was not only a librarian but an author, and an able philologist and linguist. It is expected that at some future time a volume of his collected writings will be published. We understand that these, had he lived, would have been published under his own supervision."

1240 [The British Museum's 1869 Acquisitions.] *American Bibliopolist*, 2 (January 1870), p26 (ICU, NcD, OC).

The entire article follows.

"The annual increase of books in the library of the British Museum is very great. In the year of 1869 there were added to this collection 42,331 volumes and pamphlets (volumes of newspapers and books of music included), of which 992 were presented, 6099 were received in pursuance of the English copyright laws, 346 came in under international copyright treaties and 34,394 were purchased. There also were 33,403 parts of volumes—a separate number of periodical publications and of works in progress. Of newspapers published in the British Islands, 1145 sets were received. There were received 2121 pieces of music, and 779 portions of musical works in progress."

1241 [Criticism of a British Museum purchase at Auction.] *American Bibliopolist*, 2 (January 1870), p24 (OC).

The entire article follows.

"At a recent auction sale of a library in Dublin, much surprise was expressed that an old book sold for thirteen pounds and odd shillings. A well-known dealer who was present exclaimed, in a perfectly audible voice: 'There is an example of a purchase for the B. M. (British Museum); if I had offered that volume to them last week for fifty shillings, they would not have taken it; but, as the sale is a public one, their agent buys it for five times the money.'"

1242 "*Lives of the Founders of the British Museum; with Notices of Its Augmentors and Other Benefactors, 1570–1870*, by Edward Edwards. New York: J. W. Bouton, 1870. 8 vo." *Nation*, 11 (September 8, 1870), p158–59 (NcU).

In writing biography nowadays one tendency is to string together sketches of men who are similar in character or profession. Mr. Edwards's book is a somewhat weak example of this tendency, but not the worst. He gives accounts of the lives of men all of whom were collectors, and he relates their lives to the history of the museum. His stories are long-winded and his style formal; also, he inserts his opinions on irrelevant matters. However, the early lives contain some new and important matter. (Sir Robert Cotton's career is traced.) The generosity of benefactors has been important because the government has not supported the institution well until the last thirty years. Edwards includes information about librarians Planta, Ellis, and Panizzi; framing the famous cataloging rules; and present plans for finding more collection space.

1243 [The British Museum.] *Nation*, 11 (September 22, 1870), p192, 180 wds (NcU).

These figures about the British Museum will interest some of our readers. We doubt if there are many ways in which a man who writes can be of more service in our day and country than he can by calling attention to the existence, elsewhere, of the great libraries, those makers and furnishers of scholars, which we yet lack. Last year, nearly 68,000 books, pamphlets, pieces of music, files of newspapers, etc. were added to the Museum's library. The total number of readers was 103,884 and the number of visitors, 460,635.

1244 "British Museum." *American Bibliopolist*, 4 (January 1872), p8 (ICN, ICU, NcD).

The entire article follows. It refers to Robert Cowtan, whose book appeared in 1872.

"Can you inform me where I can get the latest information as to the British Museum Library—its extent, number of books, accretions by gift or purchase, and generally the annual rate of increase? Is there any new publication on the subject? — NEW YORK

"[The only recent works on the present state of the British Museum are, *Hand-Book to the Library*, by Richard Sims, 1854; *A Handy-Book*, by T[homas] Nichols, 1870; *Lives of the Founders of the British Museum*, by Edward Edwards, two Parts, 1870, and the Annual Parliamentary Returns. Mr. R. Cowton [sic], who is connected with the institution, has announced a volume of *Memories of the Library of the British Museum.* — Ed.]"

1245 [The British Museum.] *Publishers' Weekly* [Publishers' and Stationers' Weekly Trade Circular], 2 (October 24, 1872), p416–17, 230 wds (NcU).

The British Musuem is now said to have one million books in its library; the idea of printing its catalog has been abandoned because the hundreds of thousands of ephemeral publications would make it so large that it would, for practical purposes, be useless. The number of American books is said to be greater than in any American library; a catalogue of them has been prepared by Henry Stevens, who had the largest share in procuring them. (The number of editions of several British classics in the library is given.)

1246 [Catalog of British Museum Manuscripts.] *American Bibliopolist*, 5 (February–March 1873), p26 (IEN, OC).

The entire article follows.

"We hear that the keeper of the MSS. in the British Museum intends to issue a catalogue of the oldest manuscripts in the national collection, with autotype fac-similes of the choicest early illuminations and texts. The copies are wonderfully successful, and give the effect of the involved Anglo-Saxon patterns and colors with great softness and delicacy, while the often faded texts are even clearer in the autotypes than in the originals."

1247 [Branches for the British Museum.] *Nation*, 16 (June 12, 1873), p402, 270 wds (NcU).

Statistics in the article summarized below were corrected in a note too short for this bibliography, in the June 19 issue of the *Nation* on p417. The proportion of the readers to the population should have been "per 1000," not "per 100."

Mr. Leone Levi writes in the London *Athenaeum* that the number of readers in the British Museum has decreased in ten years; it was 46 per 100 [sic] inhabitants of London in 1861 and 32 per 100 [sic] inhabitants in 1871. He says that the museum is less centrally located now, and that the catalog requires too much time to consult. He recommends using the library's duplicates to establish branch libraries. He also recommends specialized reading rooms [in the main building], one for history, one for science, etc. In the Boston Public Library, branches have been very successful; perhaps some day books will be sent by pneumatic tubes to readers in the branches.

1248 [French Revolutionary Posters in the British Museum.] *American Bibliopolist*, 6 (May–June 1874), p70 (NcD).

The part of the article about libraries follows.

"During the great French Revolution a daring collector, Dufourny, used to get up in the darkness of the night and take down from the walls the bills posted there in day-time, which it was forbidden to touch under penalty of death. The collection which he thus formed at the imminent peril of his life is now in the British Museum, as well as a very curious collection of the posters of 1848."

1249 "Late Additions to the British Museum." *Appletons' Journal: a Magazine of General Literature*, 12 (September 12, 1874), p341-42 (NcU).

The parts of the article which deal with the Departments of Printed Books and of Manuscripts (610 wds) are summarized below.

During the year 1873, the Department of Printed Books received 105,697 articles including books, pamphlets, newspapers and pieces of music. These items came to the museum in part through purchase and donation, but mainly as a result of British copyright laws which make available to the museum a copy of every book published. Among the acquisitions is a rare, perhaps unique, copy of Tyndale's "Exposition of the fyrste Epistle of seynt Jhon," printed in 1531. The museum also purchased a set of Chinese historical works and is currently cataloging them. Acquisitions in the Manuscripts Department include an illuminated French calendar, "Hours of the Virgin," and sixty-three oriental manuscripts in fourteen different languages.

1250 "British Museum Prints." *American Bibliopolist*, 6 (September-October 1874), p119-20 (ICU, NcD).

The third volume of the *Catalogue of Satirical Prints and Drawings in the British Museum*, being compiled by Mr. F. G. Stephens, is nearing completion. The present plan is to close this volume at the death of George the Second, in 1760. It will, therefore contain Hogarth's most important work. The article contains a long list of events and persons satirized in the prints in the volume.

1251 [Reresby Manuscript at British Museum.] *American Bibliopolist*, 6 (November-December 1874), p145, 170 wds (NcD).

The original manuscript of the memoirs of Sir John Reresby, last governor of York and "Parliament Man" during the reigns of Charles II and James II, was added to the British Museum last year. The printed version of the memoirs seems to have been a paraphrase of this original, with much material not printed at all. The original includes new historical points, an account of the Reresby family and details of Sir John's early life, education and relations with the great families of the day. J. J. Cartwright of the Public Record Office in London will bring out a literal and complete edition of these memoirs next year.

1252 [British Museum Manuscript Acquisitions.] *American Bibliopolist*, 7 (February 1875), p10 (ICU).

The entire article follows.

"The library of the British Museum purchased no less than 3,415 manuscripts last year. Among them was a curious treatise in French on the Holy Sacrament, composed by King Edward VI, of England, in 1549, and written in his own hand."

1253 "Warren." *American Bibliopolist*, 7 (February 1875), p27, 300 wds (ICU, NcD).

An obituary of Edward Alfred Warren, dead at age thirty-eight, who for nearly twenty years was engaged in supervising the transcription and arrangement of thousands of titles for the Catalogue of the Printed Book Department in the British Museum. A passage quoted from the *Pall Mall Gazette* notes that Mr.

Warren died of a disease aggravated by the unwholesomeness of his working quarters. Warren's doctor had examined the room and found it unfit, but instead of being assigned a new work area Warren had merely been reprimanded by the chief authority of the museum for bringing in the doctor without authorization.

1254 "Simons." *American Bibliopolist*, 7 (June 1875), p136, 200 wds (NcD).

Nathaniel Wells Simons, a retired assistant in the library of the British Museum, has died at 78. A good Welsh scholar and an authority on the Junius controversy, Simons served thirty-two years with the library, mostly in the compilation of the Catalogue, before retiring in 1870. (Simons' part in the Junius controversy is described.)

1255 [British Museum Anecdote.] *American Bibliopolist*, 7 (October 1875), p215 (NcD).

The entire article follows.

"An Englishman was boasting to a Yankee that they had a book in the British Museum which was once owned by Cicero. 'Oh, that ain't nothin',' retorted the Yankee; 'in the museum in Bosting they've got the lead-pencil that Noah used to check off the animals that went into the ark.'"

— HOUSE OF COMMONS LIBRARY

1256 "House of Commons' Library." *Museum of Foreign Literature, Science, and Art*, 26 (January 1835), p115 (InU, NcU).

The entire article follows. It refers to a fire that occurred in 1834.

"It is feared that the losses at the house of commons' library will turn out to be more extensive than was at first expected. It was thought that all the books on the lower floor, where members used to sit to read and to consult the works, were saved, although it was known that all those on the upper story were destroyed: it is now apprehended that between 4000 and 5000 volumes are lost. It may be remembered that an interchange of parliamentary works recently took place between the chambers of France and those of England. Out of upwards of 1500 of these volumes, very few are preserved. Those sent to the house of lords are safe. The chief girders, &c., for the roofs of the old house of lords and the painted chamber, are now on the walls, and iron girders are being placed in the stone building of the commons."

— LONDON AND NORTHWESTERN RAILWAY STATION LIBRARY

1257 "At the London and North Western Railway Station." *Norton's Literary Gazette and Publishers' Circular*, 3 (January 15, 1853), p3 (ICN, NcU).

The entire article follows.

"A book society and reading-room have been commenced for those employed upon the railway. The rate of subscription is very low, and the right of using books is forfeited by those dismissed from service. The railway directors furnish the room."

— LONDON INSTITUTION

1258 "An Account of the London Institution." *Monthly Anthology and Boston Review*, 4 (July 1807), p348–55 (NcU).

The article is taken from the *London Monthly Magazine*, May 1807; the parts about the library are summarized below.

One of the purposes of the London Institution is the acquisition of a library of books in all ancient and modern languages, and a reading room containing foreign and domestic periodicals, pamphlets and new publications. (The by-laws are summarized, including the rules for the library.) No book may be removed; a catalog is kept in manuscript. (The house of the institution is described.) The newspaper room is behind the entrance hall; it contains London newspapers, gazeteers, directories, books of reference, and records of the House of Commons. On each end are other smaller rooms — the one on the left contains reviews, magazines, periodicals, pamphlets and modern books; the one on the right, foreign papers and journals. The library, occupying five rooms on the first floor, has nearly 10,000 volumes; about half are in quarto and folio. The library cost nearly £9000. Professor Porson is the principal librarian.

— LONDON SOCIETY OF BIBLICAL ARCHAEOLOGY LIBRARY

1259 [Library of the London Society of Biblical Archaeology.] *American Bibliopolist*, 4 (July–August 1872), p375 (ICN, NcD).

The entire article follows.

"The London Society of Biblical Archaeology has lately received a rich present for its library, in the shape of an ancient Sepher-Torah, dating from the tenth century. This manuscript is the only copy of the Pentateuch as used by the Aden Jews, descendants of the pre-Mohametan inhabitants, which has reached England, and the Society is indebted to the liberality of Captain F. Pirdeaux, of Aden, for the gift."

— LONDON UNIVERSITY LIBRARY

1260 "University of London. Notice of the Courses of Lectures During the Session 1829-30." *American Annals of Education* [American Journal of Education], 4 (September–October 1829), p464–71 (NcU).

The part of the article about libraries ("Library," p471) follows.

"A collection has already been made of more than eight thousand volumes, and it is daily increasing. It consists chiefly of such works as the Students must consult in the prosecution of their studies at the University. The Library is open every day from ten in the morning to four in the afternoon, and the books may be consulted by all the students of the University. Separate Libraries have been formed for the use of the Law and of the Medical Students, to which they will have access in the evening."

— MARYLEBONE PARISH PUBLIC LIBRARY

1261 "Marylebone Free Library." *Norton's Literary Gazette and Publishers' Circular*, 2 (November 15, 1852), p214 (NcU).

The entire article follows.

"The Parish of Marylebone, one of the largest in London, is making an effort to secure for itself a large Free Public Library. Many influential citizens are engaged upon the undertaking, and it has every prospect of success."

1262 [Kinds of Books and Periodicals Being Read in the Marylebone Free Library.] *Norton's Literary Gazette and Publishers' Circular*, n.s. 1 (October 2, 1854), p492–93 (NcU).

The Marylebone Free Library, located at 27 Gloucester Place, New Road, opened January 30, 1854 as a free library. During the last six months, 17,397 readers there have read over 18,000 volumes, averaging 122 volumes daily. The classes of books delivered are: literature, poetry, drama and serials 9,785; history, biography, voyages and travels 6,592; sciences and arts 979; theology 283; philosophy 268; law, politics and commerce 256. The 9 works of Dickens have had 1,467 readers, the most of any writer. (A long list is given of books issued at least 30 times to readers at the Marylebone Library, together with the number of times each was requested. The *London Journal* was first, followed by the *Illustrated London News, Arabian Nights, Chambers's Journal, Robinson Crusoe, Bleak House, Oliver Twist, Valentine Vox, Nicholas Nickleby* and *Wild Sports of the West*.)

— MECHANICS' INSTITUTION LIBRARY

1263 "London Mechanics' Institution." *Museum of Foreign Literature, Science, and Art*, 4 (February 1824), p191, 230 wds (InU, NcU).

Last month a meeting was held to provide a home for the Institution and to consider a sub-committee's draft of laws for the organization. It was recommended that the Institution receive donations of money, books, and other items; that there should be established a reference library, a circulating library, and a reading room; that a museum be created; that a series of lectures be provided; that elementary schools be established; and that an experimental workshop and laboratory be provided for the instruction of mechanics. The trustees for 1824 are Dr. Birbeck, H. Brougham, J. Walker, and Mr. Alderman Key.

— MUDIE'S CIRCULATING LIBRARY

1264 [Acquisitions by Mudie's Circulating Library, London.] *Norton's Literary Gazette and Publishers' Circular*, 2 (December 15, 1852), p237 (ICN, NcU).

The entire article follows.

"Mudie's Circulating Library, of London, announces the purchase, for the use of its patrons, of 300 copies of Thackeray's new story, 'Esmond,' and from seventy to three hundred copies of such books as 'Palissey the Potter,' just reprinted in this country by Messrs. Ticknor, Reed & Fields, 'Village Life in Egypt,' Lives of Niebuhr, Chalmers, Jeffrey, and S. M. Fuller, 'Uncle Tom's Cabin,' 'Queechy,' 'Blithedale Romance,' 'Roughing it in the Bush,' &c."

1265 [Mudie's Library.] *Literary World*, Boston, 4 (March 1874), p160, 260 wds (NcU).

The famous Mudie's Library, in London, was established in 1840; it now occupies an area equal to that of eight houses. In 1864 it became a stock company, its value being estimated at £100,000. It now contains about 16,000 volumes of current literature. As soon as a book is re-published in a cheap edition, it is not requested much, unless it is by Charles Dickens. In one of the library's clearance catalogs, slightly more than half are written by women. Scientific books are vastly increasing in popularity; the fairy tales of science, told by a Huxley or a Darwin are beginning to be as eagerly demanded as the works of popular novelists. The first circulating library was founded in London by Wright, a bookseller, around the year 1730.

— PUBLIC AMERICAN LIBRARY

1266 [Public American Library in London.] *Museum of Foreign Literature, Science, and Art*, 4 (June 1824), p570 (InU, NcU).
The entire article follows.
"We congratulate the public on the convenience and luxury of the Institution of a *Public American Library* in London. Mr. Miller, of New Bridge-street, who has long been known as the commercial medium of literary intercourse between America and Great Britain, has engrafted on his trade a *Subscription Library* for American books and newspapers; and in these elegant rooms may be seen the newspapers of that vast continent, and the various current productions of the press. American residents in London are of course its eager patrons; but it is little less interesting to persons connected with America, and to speculators in translantic literature, which is every month becoming a subject of increased interest, by the originality of many works, and by the talents and genius of the writers."

— ROYAL SOCIETY OF ARTS LIBRARY

1267 "Economic Library." *American Journal of Education* (Barnard), 3 (August 1857), p271–72 (NcU).
The announcement summarized below was reprinted from the *Journal of the Society of Arts*, January 22, 1857.
The Society of Arts desires to form a library; the collection will consist of English and foreign language publications relating to the subject of the condition of the working classes. The library will collect the annual reports and other publications of charitable institutions. Persons who receive these publications are urged to forward them to the society so that its plans can be successfully carried out. A detailed, but by no means exhaustive, list of various published items suitable for acquisition is provided in the announcement.

— STUDENT'S LIBRARY

1268 C., F. [Student's Library, London.] *Publishers' Weekly*, 5 (January 10, 1874), p34 (NcU).
The entire article follows.
"A Student's Library, for art students, divinity students, examination students, law students, medical students, professional students of all kinds, science students, and general students of every description, was opened in London on the 1st of January. The library is established for the convenience of all students in town or country who desire to carry on their studies at times and places chosen by themselves. Subscription, for one volume at a time, one guinea a year. A reading room will be opened for subscribers at one guinea a year, or 2^s. a month extra. Prospectuses and other information are supplied by Librarian, care of Messrs. Harwar, Furnival's Inn, London."

1269 [Student's Library, London.] *Publishers' Weekly*, 5 (February 7, 1874), p142 (NcU).
The entire article follows.
"London has a new library enterprise in 'The Student's Library,' for the purpose of supplying science and professional students, and general students of every description, with books for their particular study. Every book in print is

supplied to subscribers, according to their class of subscription; and every book of the same nature out of print will be acquired by the library as soon as possible. A special subscription has been arranged for all expensively illustrated works of art, architecture, civil engineering, geography, or science. A reading-room has also been opened, which contains files of daily and weekly journals, special, professional, technical, and scientific journals, and a well-selected library of reference."

— WESTMINSTER PARISH FREE LIBRARY

1270 "Free Library for Westminster." *Norton's Literary Gazette and Publishers' Circular*, 3 (January 15, 1853), p3 (ICN, NcU).
The entire article follows.
"Mr. Charles Knight proposed, at the meeting in favor of Repealing the Taxes on Knowledge, that a memorial should be raised to Caxton, the early English printer, in the form of a library at Westminster, free to all classes. 'Everywhere in the metropolis,' remarks the Athenaeum, in noticing this suggestion, 'a feeling in behalf of this order of popular institutions is growing up and spreading. Not only in Marylebone, but in Lambeth, Southwark, Finsbury, and other parishes of London, the sentiment is growing into a motive power.'"

MANCHESTER

1271 "Public Libraries in Manchester, Eng." *Norton's Literary Gazette and Publishers' Circular*, 3 (May 15, 1853), p83, 290 wds (ICN, NcU).
The London *Athenaeum*, which has always manifested much interest in public libraries, gives the following information about libraries in Manchester: In a communication to the *Journal of the Society of Arts*, it is stated that of all the English provincial towns, Manchester has the largest number of public and semi-public libraries. (The total number of libraries in several English towns is given.) Manchester's 61 libraries are in three groups: special libraries, containing 13,000 volumes; 42 circulating libraries, containing 35,000 volumes; and 14 public and institutional libraries containing 178,200 volumes. (The total number of volumes in each of several of the free and subscription libraries in this last group is given.)

— CHETHAM'S LIBRARY

1272 "The Library of Humphrey Chetham, at Manchester." *Norton's Literary Gazette and Publishers' Circular*, n.s. 1 (July 15, 1854), p359-61 (NcU).
The article summarized below is continued in the issues of September 1, 1854, p438-40, and September 15, 1854, p463-66 *(see 1273 and 1274)*.
The Chetham Library is not well known, even in Manchester. Chetham was a Manchester warehouseman who died in 1653. In his will, he left £1000 and the residue from his personal estate for a library in Manchester; £200 to buy "godly English books" for churches; £100 to buy a building called "the college" to house the library; and provisions for selecting a board of trustees. The building was purchased in 1654, the first purchases of books were made in 1655 and the board of trustees set up in 1665. By June of 1663, globes, maps and 1,423 volumes had been purchased at a total cost of £959 18^s. 10^d., excluding conveying and other costs. These purchases were mostly works of theology or history. What was done with the other money from the estate is not clear.

1273 "The Library of Humphrey Chetham, at Manchester." *Norton's Literary Gazette and Publishers' Circular*, n.s. 1 (September 1, 1854), p438–40 (NcU).

The article summarized below is a continuation of that in the issue of July 15, 1854, p359–61 *(see 1272)*, and is concluded in the issue of September 15, 1854, p463–66 *(see 1274)*.

Part of the money from the estate was misappropriated to the "hospital" for the maintenance and education of poor boys, also set up in the will. By 1693, there were 3,543 volumes that had cost £2,469 15^s. By 1743, total expenditures for books had been £5,127 19^s 9^d, an average of £50 per year. Early in the 18th century, several eminent men visited the library; their comments about it are quoted. A catalogue was compiled in 1791 and supplemented in 1826, dividing the 14,276 volumes into five classes; totals are given for each class. The old books should be supplemented by new ones; only 1250 volumes were added from 1825 to 1845. The library compares unfavorably with the "hospital" in endowment (3/5 that of the hospital), and income (1/5 that of the hospital), although both pay equally on the fixed costs of the combined operation.

1274 "The Library of Humphrey Chetham, at Manchester." *Norton's Literary Gazette and Publishers' Circular*, n.s. 1 (September 15, 1854), p463–66 (NcU).

The article summarized below is a continuation of that in the issue of July 15, 1854, p359–61, and that in the issue of September 1, 1854, p438–40 *(see 1272 and 1273)*.

The Chetham hospital has prospered and grown, but not the library. (A number of printed books in the collection are listed and two collections of tracts are described.) A valuable portion of the library are the 137 volumes of manuscripts, 31 of which are Oriental and 106 European. (The classes of the European manuscripts and the Chetham papers, which are kept in the Archives, are listed and described.) There is a printed catalog of the extensive collection of ballads, proclamations and other broadsides; the collection contains 1309 poetical broadsides and 1,791 in prose. This collection is divided into poetry and prose parts (total holdings are shown). The Chetham Library should be separated from the hospital.

— FREE LIBRARY

1275 "The Manchester (Eng.) Free Library." *Norton's Literary Gazette and Publishers' Circular*, 2 (October 15, 1852), p188 (ICN, NcU).

The entire article follows.

"The Manchester (Eng.) Free Library, formed by subscriptions to the amount of £12,000, collected in that town alone, has just been opened to the public. The books, although in one building, are really in two libraries, one of 16,000 vols. for reference, and one of 5,000 vols. for circulation. Rich and poor united in the subscriptions. As an indication of the general interest taken in this matter by men of small means, it is asserted that £800 was raised in small sums from 20,000 different persons."

1276 "Manchester Free Library." *Norton's Literary Gazette and Publishers' Circular*, 3 (December 15, 1853), p217, 360 wds (NcU).

The detailed report of the Manchester Free Library helps us judge the reading class and the comparative popularity of authors there. Shakespeare is most in demand, followed by *The Arabian Nights, Ivanhoe,* and *Robinson Crusoe.* Biography is much read, and much history is begun though comparatively little is completed. Books of travel, shipwreck and adventure are frequently called for. These details are interesting, and we hope future reports will show the progress of popular taste. A series of such reports would have historical interest in the future.

1277 "The Manchester Free Library." *Norton's Literary Gazette and Publishers' Circular,* n.s. 1 (February 15, 1854), p80, 560 wds (NcD).

In our December 1853 issue, we gave our readers some particulars from the first annual report of the Manchester Free Library. There are other details of equal interest: The report is prepared by the principal librarian, Edward Edwards and begins with a history of the free library movement in Great Britain. The Manchester library contains 25,299 volumes, 22,939 of which are now available to users; 15,744 in the reference department (non-circulating) and 7,195 in the lending department. A table gives the number of volumes in the reference and lending departments in six major subject fields, the total circulation in each field and the average circulation per volume. Edwards complains about several defects in the Public Libraries Act.

1278 [Books Read at the Manchester Public Free Library.] *Norton's Literary Gazette and Publishers' Circular,* n.s. 1 (October 2, 1854), p493, 250 wds (NcU).

The total number of qualified borrowers of books at the Manchester Public Free Library is now nearly 7,000. The annual report tells us about the reading preferences of those borrowers. Of all the books in the library, the one most in demand was Shakespeare, taken out 352 times during the year. *The Arabian Nights* was second, followed by Scott's *Ivanhoe* and *Robinson Crusoe.* All of Defoe's novels were in great demand, the average circulation being nearly 130. *Gulliver* was issued 123 times. Also in demand were Cumming's *South Africa,* Dana's *Two Years Before the Mast,* and Layard's *Nineveh.* Books of travel and biography were much called for; works on Napoleon were popular. History was not neglected; Macaulay was the most popular, having been read 124 times. Lingard and Hume were also called for, but only two people finished either one. Many began Alison, but only one finished his work.

1279 [Manchester Libraries.] *American Bibliopolist,* 4 (December 1872), p631 (ICU, OC).
The entire article follows.
"The *Manchester Courier* says that the Manchester free libraries have proved highly successful. The number of times that persons have availed themselves of the libraries during the year 1871–2 was 2,264,688, against 2,112,900 the previous year. The accessions amount to 14,387 volumes."

1280 [Manchester Free Public Libraries.] *Publishers' Weekly,* 5 (March 14, 1874), p273 (NcU).
The entire article follows.
"The Manchester Public Free Libraries report that 2,501,564 persons have availed themselves of their use during the library year 1872–3. In the Reference Library there are now 50,508 volumes, and in the Lending Department 76,584 making a total of 127,092 volumes. The principal Librarian is Dr. Crestadoro, and the Sub-Librarian Mr. W. E. A. Axon, F.R.S.L."

NORWICH — FREE PUBLIC LIBRARY

1281 [Free Public Library in Norwich.] *Norton's Literary Gazette and Publishers' Circular*, n.s. 1 (October 16, 1854), p533 (NcU).
The entire article follows.
"The first stone of a free public library was laid in Norwich, on the 13th of September. The building will adjoin the Norfolk and Norwich Literary Institution, and the cost of its erection will be £3,098."

OXFORD — OXFORD UNIVERSITY LIBRARIES

1282 "University of Oxford." *Bibliotheca Sacra* [and Theological Review], 4 (November 1847), p773–88 (NcU).
The parts of the article about libraries (p775, 777–78) are summarized below.
In the Peckwater quadrangle of Christ Church is the library, 161 feet in length, containing 12 busts, 295 paintings and collections of books, coins, prints, manuscripts, etc. The library at All Souls is a room 200 feet long, 39½ broad and 40 in height, with 2 ranges of book cases containing over 40,000 volumes. Completed in 1749, the Radcliffe library has books principally in natural history and medicine. The Bodleian library, founded in 1602, has the right to a copy of every work printed in the Kingdom, an annual acquisitions income of £2000, several special collections, and between 200,000 and 500,000 volumes. A part of the Bodleian library is in the building called the Schools.

— OXFORD UNIVERSITY BODLEIAN LIBRARY

1283 "Royal Society of Literature. Third Ordinary Meeting, Dec. 21." *Museum of Foreign Literature, Science and Art*, 8 (April 1826), p379–80 (ICN, OCl).
Mr. Tyler presented a paper about the study of Greek literature in England. Among its earliest English students was Humphrey, Duke of Gloucester, who gave Oxford University more than 600 volumes of the ancient authors. Unfortunately, only a folio of Valerius Maximus has survived; the other volumes were destroyed during the reign of Edward VI because of the suspicion that they contained popish teachings. John Tiptoft, Earl of Worcester, collected manuscripts both for his own use and to enrich Oxford's Humphrey Library. After Tiptoft's execution, George Neville, Archbishop of York, managed to save the manuscripts for Oxford; however they too were destroyed during Edward's reign.

1284 "History of the University of Oxford." *Congregational Education Society Quarterly Journal* [American Quarterly Register], 11 (February 1839), p241–47 (NcU).
The article is a sequel to an article in the same periodical, 10 (November 1837), p178–181, which contained nothing about libraries. The part of the February 1839 article about libraries, "Libraries, Museums, etc." (p244–45) is summarized below.
Sir Thomas Bodley founded the Bodleian Library, giving his books and money for staff salaries and repairs to the building. The library receives copies of every work printed in the country. It is also supported by matriculation fees

and an annual tax. The officers are a Board of Curators, a librarian, two under librarians, and two assistants. Estimates of the number of volumes contained in the Bodleian library range from 200,000 to 500,000. John Radcliffe founded Radcliffe's Library, appropriating in his will £40,000 for the building and the ground, £100 per annum to purchase books, and £150 per annum for the librarian. The collection receives books in medicine and natural history. John Kidd, M. D., is now librarian.

1285 [Catalog of Manuscripts in Oxford University Libraries.] *Norton's Literary Gazette and Publishers' Circular*, 1 (June 1851), p5 (DLC, ICN).
The entire article follows.
"The Oxford University comprises 20 Colleges and 5 Halls, most of which possess their own quite valuable Libraries. As only the University Library proper (the celebrated Bodleian) issued Catalogues of all its manuscripts, Mr. Coxe, the assistant Librarian, has taken on himself the tedious labor of registering the manuscripts in the different College Libraries, and has already finished a large quarto volume, in which 3,000 titles are recorded, and to which the index only is wanting."

1286 [Macray's *Annals of the Bodleian Library*.] *Nation* 7 (October 29, 1868), p352, 890 wds (NcU).
Very pleasant reading is to be found in Rev. William Dunn Macray's *Annals of the Bodleian Library, Oxford, A.D. 1598–1867*; it is beautifully printed and shows great care, industry and research. It is delightfully indifferent to all the rules of bibliography and talks with almost equal praise about the great prizes of the library and of collections of useless treasures. Apart from the charming tidbits of bibliographical and personal histories, the book shows how a library is a standing invitation to all collectors to make it the final receptacle of their lifelong labors. (Anecdotes from the book are given.)

1287 "The Bodleian Library." *American Bibliopolist*, 1 (December 1869), p354–56 (ICU).
The article was "to be continued" but its continuation has not been located by the compilers of this bibliography.
Bodley was born in Exeter on March 2, 1544. During the reign of Mary the family fled to the continent and returned when Elizabeth became queen. Bodley received instruction at Geneva and, after returning to England, Oxford. In 1566 he earned the Master of Arts degree and in 1569 he and Bearblock were elected to the proctorship at Oxford. In 1585 he entered the ambassadorial service of Elizabeth. Bodley aspired to higher office but the struggle for position between Essex and Burleigh ruined his hopes. He then resolved to leave government service, and turned his attention to the development of the Oxford library. In this he had four aids: scholarly knowledge, money, friends, and leisure. In 1609 he wrote his autobiography and died in 1612.

1288 "The Bodleian Library." *American Bibliopolist*, 2 (January 1870), p25 (ICU, OC).
The entire article follows.
"Professor Stubbs has been elected to the curatorship of the Bodleian Library at Oxford, vacant by the death of Professor Conington, by seventy-eight votes. His opponent, Professor Rolleston, obtained thirty-six votes."

1289 [Gift for the Bodleian.] *American Bibliopolist*, 4 (June 1872), p296 (IEN, OC).
The entire article follows; it apparently refers to one of Cicero's orations.
"We understand that a most interesting relic of the early Oxford Press has been lately discovered at Bramshill Park, used as 'waste' to make up a binding. It is a portion of the 'Oratio pro T. A. Milone,' thus furnishing another issue from Rood's press to add to those few already known. Sir William Cope, Bart, although a devoted lover of books himself, and the owner of a very fine library, has, with a liberality that does him infinite credit, presented these leaves to the Bodleian, believing that Oxford should be the 'fittest resting place.'"

— PUBLIC LIBRARY

1290 [Oxford Public Library.] *Norton's Literary Gazette and Publishers' Circular*, n.s. 1 (October 2, 1854), p493 (NcU).
The entire article follows.
"On the first of June the Oxford Public Library and Reading Room was opened, and, according to the official returns, made up to the 31st of August, it appears that during the period the number of visitors was 36,639; the number of books delivered to persons for reading, 6,942; and the number of books presented, 2,665. Among the recent contributors to the library are — Mr. Justice Erle, Sir W. P. Wood, the Rev. D. Barnes, Dr. Macbride, and Mr. J. H. Parker, bookseller."

PENZANCE — PUBLIC LIBRARY

1291 [Public Library of Penzance, England.] *American Bibliopolist*, 3 (October 1871), p368 (NcD, OC).
The entire article follows; it was reprinted from the London *Athenaeum*.
"The Public Library at Penzance possesses a gift from Mr. J. O. Halliwell, of which the British Museum might be proud, — namely, a noble collection of volumes illustrative of the ancient English stage, its acted drama, its literature, and its history. Penzance is worthy of this donation. The spirited little town is the intellectual capital of Cornwall. The unanimity with which every effort is made there for local and for general good, is pleasantly attributed, by some of the inhabitants, to the fact that Penzance is exempt from the affliction of having to return a member to Parliament."

PLYMOUTH — COTTONIAN LIBRARY

1292 [Cottonian Library of Plymouth, England.] *National Magazine: Devoted to Literature, Art, and Religion*, 3 (October 1853), p380 (InU, NcU).
The entire article follows.
"*William Cotton, Esq.*, of Highland House, Ivybridge, has presented to the inhabitants of Plymouth, England, his fine collection of illustrated books and valuable old prints, accumulated at a very considerable expense in the course of a series of years. It was first opened to the public on the first of June, and is called the 'Cottonian Library.'"

ROCHDALE — CORPORATION FREE LIBRARY

1293 P., J. "The Value and Use of Books." *American Bibliopolist*, 5 (January 1873), p11, 220 wds (ICU, NcD).

The Bishop of Manchester used a beautiful description of the value and use of books, taken from a recent publication, in his speech at the opening of the Rochdale Corporation Free Library. (In the article the passage is quoted in full; it is summarized here:) Thank God for books, especially good books. They are the spirits of the noble and mighty in all ages, and speak to all men. They unearth ancient records, reveal the heavens, and show us the earth and the sea. They take us into their confidence, tell us of joy and sorrow, introduce us to the choicest friends and sing sweet songs. We can consult them whenever we like, and they never tire us even while they instruct us.

WINDSOR

1294 [Knight Library.] *American Bibliopolist*, 5 (April 1873), p53 (NcD).
The entire article follows.
"At a meeting of friends and admirers of the late Mr. Knight, held at Mr. Routledge's house, a committee was formed to collect subscriptions for a memorial to the deceased. The form which the memorial shall take has not yet been decided on. There is a talk of founding a free library at Windsor, to be called the Knight Library."

— WINDSOR CASTLE

1295 [Publication of Drawings and Writings of Da Vinci in Windsor Castle.] *Nation*, 1 (November 23, 1865), p657, 240 wds (NcU).

The designs, drawings, and writings of Leonardo da Vinci are among the choicest treasures of the Royal Library at Windsor Castle. This collection comprises about two hundred detached sheets; a further portion of Leonardo's manuscripts is in the Imperial Library [Bibliothèque Nationale] at Paris. It is now planned to publish the ones at Windsor in facsimile, with a translation and notes by Mr. [Antonio] Panizzi and Dr. [William] Sharpey, Secretary of the Royal Society. There will be twenty parts at one guinea each, the publication to commence early in 1866.

YORK — ARCHBISHOP EGBERT'S LIBRARY

1296 K., W. T. "The First English Catalogue." *American Bibliopolist*, 2 (January 1870), p19 (ICU, NcD).
The entire article follows.
"The state of learning in the eighth century may be conjectured from the poetic catalogue of books in the celebrated library of Egbert, Archbishop of York, which, as Mr. Sharon Turner says, is the oldest catalogue of books, perhaps, existing in all the regions of literature, certainly the oldest existing in England. This curious document, which is in Latin, has been imitated; it opens thus:
>Here duly placed on consecrated ground,
>The studied works of many an age are found,

Europe 344

> The ancient fathers' reverend remains,
> The Roman laws which freed a world from chains.
> Whate'er of lore passed from immortal Greece,
> To Latium lands, and gained a rich increase;
> All that blest Israel drank in showers from heaven,
> Or Afric sheds, soft as the dew of even;
> Jerom, the father 'mong a thousand sons,
> And Hilary, whose sense profusely runs.
> "Where can I find a more complete description of this catalogue?"
>   W. T. K.

YORKSHIRE

1297 "Yorkshire Mechanics' Institute." *Norton's Literary Gazette and Publishers' Circular*, 2 (December 15, 1852), p237, 230 wds (ICN, NcU).

We have learned from a report of the Yorkshire Union of Mechanics' Institutes that 1852 was a good year for its members. In 1852 there were 123 member institutes compared to 117 in 1851; 113 institutes reported that 388,202 books were circulated during the year; and 73 institutes received 6,667 periodicals and 416 newspapers in 1852. If encouraged, these institutes one day could play an important role in public education.

France

1298 "Public Libraries in France." *American Annals of Education*, 3d ser., 1 (August 1831), p396 (NcU).

The entire article follows.

"In Paris the Royal Library has above 700,000 printed volumes, and 70,000 MSS. The library of Monsieur, 150,000 printed volumes, and 5000 MSS. The library of St. Genevieve, 110,000 printed volumes, and 2000 MSS. The Mazarine library, 92,000 printed volumes, and 3000 MSS. The library of the city of Paris, 20,000 volumes. All these are daily open to the public. In the departments, there are 25 public libraries, with above 1,700,000 volumes; of which Aix has 72,670, Marseilles 31,500, Toulouse 30,000, Bordeaux 105,000, Tours 30,000, Lyons, 106,000, Versailles 40,000, and Amiens 40,000. In the royal library of Paris there are several uncollated MSS. of the Scriptures. A noble scheme is now on foot to place a public library in *every one* of the 40,000 *communes of France* by individual subscription."

1299 "Literary Institutions in France. Libraries." *Congregational Education Society. Quarterly Journal* [American Quarterly Register], 9 (February 1837), p238–63 (NcU).

The part of the article about libraries ("Libraries," p249–50) is summarized below.

(For each library mentioned, the staff is listed, the location given and the hours of operation cited.) The Royal Library, with over 700,000 volumes, is the largest in France. The royal and special school of oriental languages, established near the Royal Library, was founded in 1795. A course on antiquities is offered at the King's Library. The Mazarin library was founded in 1648 and now has 100,000 volumes. The Library of St. Genevieve has 260,000 volumes; the Library of the Arsenal has 180,000 printed volumes and 5000 manuscripts; and the Library of the city of Paris has 45,000 volumes.

1300 [Public Libraries of France.] *National Magazine: Devoted to Literature, Art, and Religion*, 6 (February 1855), p190–91 (InU, NcU).
The entire article follows.
"From an official return, recently published in Paris, it appears that the number of public libraries in France, excluding those of Paris, and those of certain semi-public institutions, is 338, and that they possess 3,689,369 volumes and 44,070 manuscripts. It appears, moreover, that they are frequented on an average by 3,649 readers daily, (a very small number for so large a population as that of France,) and that they cost annually, for employes and new purchases, not more than £16,000. Forty-one of these are, it is added, open to the public every evening."

1301 [French Public Libraries.] *National Magazine: Devoted to Literature, Art, and Religion*, 6 (May 1855), p479 (InU, NcU).
A shortened version of this article appeared on p6 in the June 1855 issue of the same periodical. The entire article follows.
"The French Minister of Public Instruction has issued a work on the Public Libraries of France and Algiers, from which it appears that, *excluding Paris*, there are in all the libraries 8,733,439 printed works, and 44,070 manuscripts. Bordeaux has 123,000; Lyons, 130,000; Rouen, 110,000; Strasbourg, 180,000; Troyes, 100,000; Avignon, 60,000; Dijon, 80,000; Versailles, 56,000; Tours, 57,500; Grenoble, 80,000; Nantes, 45,000; Marseilles, 51,000; Amiens, 53,000; Toulouse, 50,000. In 1853–4 there were expended for all these libraries 407,781 francs, of which sum only 184,227 francs were for the purchase of books and binding. There are 338 public libraries."

1302 [School Libraries in France.] *Nation*, 7 (October 8, 1868), p293 (NcU).
Among some "interesting scraps of foreign literary news" is the following, quoted in its entirety.
"Another item of some interest — as showing that it is not only American publishers who practise at the same time an enlightened self-interest and a beneficent generosity — is to the effect that H. M. Hachette & Co., in imitation of Messrs. A. S. Barnes & Co. and Messrs. Appleton & Co., have recently placed at the disposal of the Minister of Instruction more than 10,000 volumes, which are to be placed in the school libraries of the people. They consist of light reading and instructive works, and have, of course, been accepted."

1303 [School Libraries in France.] *Nation*, 10 (April 7, 1870), p225, 180 wds (NcU).
We find, in the latest [French Government] *Exposé de la Situation de l'Empire*, that during 1868 the number of school libraries in France increased by 1,296; the number of volumes lent was 206,161, only 7,186 more than were lent by the Boston Public Library in 1869. (Other statistics are given.) One would like to know what kind of books are purchased, what are read most, and what classes of people read them. The government of France appears well satisfied with the results.

1304 [Scholastic Libraries in France.] *Publishers' Weekly*, 6 (September 19, 1874), p313 (NcU).
The entire article follows.
"The Committee of Public Instruction to make a list of the 'Scholastic Libraries' in France has just completed its task. The report shows that, in 1865, the number was 4833, containing 180,854 volumes, while at present, not including the department of the Seine, the country possesses 15,623 such establishments, disposing of 1,474,637 works."

1305 [The Bonnange System for a Catalogue.] *Nation*, 19 (October 29, 1874), p286 (NcU).
Part of a review of the contents of the September 1874 issue of *Polybiblion* (Paris) is reproduced below. The men mentioned are Ferdinand Bonnange and, apparently, the lexicographer, Maximilien Paul Émile Littré *(see 1306 and 1307)*.
"M. Bonnange's 'Projet d'un Catalogue universel des productions intellectuelles' has been put in practice in several of the Government offices in France, and has won a warm eulogium from Littré. We judge it to be the system of card catalogues now and for many years past adopted in all our great libraries."

1306 [More about the Bonnange System for a Catalogue.] *Nation*, 19 (November 5, 1874), p301, 210 wds (NcU).
The article summarized below refers to item 1305 in this bibliography; item 1307 is a comment on 1305 and 1306. The article below does not clearly explain how the device works.
Our conjecture was correct, last week, that M. Bonnange's proposal is for a card catalog, already adopted by many excellent libraries. However, his invention is distinctive. His cards are in two parts: the upper part is hinged to the lower part. There is a hole in the foot of the lower card so that an endless screw can pass from the front of the compartment to the end of the file where it is connected to a large nut. By turning the screw, the file can be compressed or loosened. When the cards are loose, they can be read like a book. They may be kept in a drawer or on top of a counter. M. Littré praises card catalogs in general and calls M. Bonnange's invention ingenious.

1307 [Weaknesses of the Bonnange System of Cataloging.] *Nation*, 19 (November 19, 1874), p331-32 (NcU).
The entire article summarized below is a quotation from a letter received from "a valued correspondent, whose experience in the matter of which he writes entitles his opinion to great weight." It refers to items 1305 and 1306 in this bibliography and cannot easily be understood by itself.
A catalog made according to the Bonnange system, described in nos. 487 and 488 of the *Nation*, must be much more bulky than those now in use in American libraries. He gives a picture of a stand holding 16,000 cards; a stand of similar size in the Harvard College Library will hold 225,000 cards. The catalog of the Bibliothèque Nationale, if made with equal thoroughness, would cover 46,000 square feet and the union catalog of French books and manuscripts in French libraries, which the author urges, would require a small village. The cost of cards is nearly five times that of the Harvard cards. However, the *Système Bonnange* has some great advantages: its cards would be easier to read; some method of fastening the cards, in book form, is necessary in our town and city libraries.

AMIENS — BIBLIOTHEQUE MUNICIPALE

1308 [Manuscript in the Library at Amiens.] *Daguerreotype: a Magazine of Foreign Literature and Science*, 3 (December 9, 1848), p189, 175 wds (OOxM).
From *Journal des Savants*.
A manuscript by Roger Bacon which had been hidden away in the Abbey of Corbey for several centuries has been placed in the library at Amiens. The title on the first sheet is *Rogerius Bacon, ordinis minorum, de rebus physicis, monasterii sancti Petri Corbeiensis*. There are 193 folio sheets of vellum. The writing is of the fourteenth century. The work is primarily an examination of the physical philosophy and metaphysics of Aristotle.

BORDEAUX — BIBLIOTHEQUE MUNICIPALE

1309 [Municipal Library of Bordeaux.] *Nation*, 14 (June 6, 1872), p375 (NcU).
The entire article follows.
"The guardians of the municipal library of Bordeaux, which has long had a collection of twenty-one volumes bearing the signature of Montaigne, have lately discovered another on its shelves, a copy of the 'Historia Regni Hungarici' of Bonfinius, a large folio, in fine preservation. Apropos to this discovery, *La Gironde* recalls the sale of a copy of Caesar's 'Commentaries,' with autograph annotations by Montaigne, to the Duc d'Aumale for 5,650 francs. It had cost its previous possessor 1 franc. Perhaps no book ever yielded a greater percentage of profit."

CORSICA

1310 [Libraries of the Island of Corsica.] *Norton's Literary Gazette and Publishers' Circular*, n.s. 1 (July 15, 1854), p362 (NcU).
The entire article follows.
"Among the libraries of the Island of Corsica, the City Library of Ajaccio and the Library of Bastia are the most extensive. The first one consists of about 21,000 volumes, and has been founded by Lucien Bonaparte; the other one, founded by Giov. Carlo Gregori, one of the most distinguished Corsicans, numbers about 16,000 volumes."

METZ

1311 [Military Library of Metz.] *Publishers' Weekly* [Publishers' and Stationers' Weekly Trade Circular], 2 (September 5, 1872), p233 (NcU).
The entire article, which follows, was reprinted from the London *Athenaeum*.
"The celebrated Military Library of Metz has been transferred to Berlin for the use of the Prussian staff. It consists of about 40,000 printed volumes, some of which are of extreme rarity, also of precious MSS. and drawings. Whether

the library is much needed at Berlin is a matter open to question. If it is, there is, unfortunately, no building at present fit for its reception, so that the books are likely to remain for a long while stowed away in their packing-cases."

PARIS

1312 "State of Public Libraries in Paris." *Museum of Foreign Literature, Science, and Art*, 12 (April 1828), p704, 150 wds (InU, NcU).
(A statistical table. The number of volumes in each of thirty-four Parisian libraries is given; the table lists two other Parisian libraries but does not indicate the size of their collections.) Permission is required to visit thirty-one of the thirty-six libraries listed.

1313 "Public Libraries in Paris." *American Annals of Education*, 3d ser., 9 (January 1839), p46 (NcU).
The entire article follows.
"By the latest reports which have just been published in France, it appears that the Royal Libraries and the other public repositories in Paris, contain 1,823,500 volumes of works in every department of literature, 180,000 manuscripts, 100,000 coins and medals, 1,600,000 engravings and prints. The Royal Library alone is said to contain 900,000 volumes; 300,000 plans and maps, and a very extensive collection of rare prints and coins."

1314 Barry, P. "P. Barry's Letters from Europe and the World's Fair." *Genesee Farmer*, 12 (September 1851), p202–08 (InU, NcU).
After descriptions of the public gardens, the menagerie, and the botanical and mineral specimens in Paris, a library is mentioned without being identified (p204): "But I have said nothing of the library, it is worthy of all the rest. It contains the most interesting works upon natural history and travels to upwards of 30,000 volumes, besides upwards of 100 magnificent folio volumes of drawings of plants and animals." Later the Bibliothèque Nationale is mentioned (p205): "The National Library, founded nearly 500 years ago occupies a great building. It contains about 1,500,000 volumes, 100,000 volumes of manuscripts, 400,000 medals, 1,000,000 engravings, 300,000 maps, &c. To the library is attached a school for the living oriental languages. There are more than 20 other extensive libraries."

1315 "Literature and the War." *American Bibliopolist*, 2 (October 1870), p279–80 (NcD).
The part of the article referring to libraries (p279, 250 wds) is summarized here. The article is taken from *Trübner's Record*.
It is reported that five classes of the Institute of France have decided to protest the possible bombardment of monuments, libraries and museums in Paris. We assure the members of the Institute that the national monuments, libraries and museums will be held "sacred" by the German armies. The German army has been recruited from all ranks of society and is teeming with scholars, savants, and students, classes hardly found in the French army. The appeal to scholars in the German army seems uncalled for. They are fully aware of what Europe owes to French culture, science and art.

1316 [Laugel, Auguste.] "The Libraries of Paris." *Nation*, 20 (February 25, 1875), p131-32 (NcU).

Laugel is identified as the author of this article in Daniel C. Haskell's *The Nation, Volumes 1-105, New York, 1865-1917, Indexes of Titles and Contributors*, 1953, v. 1, p45.

No capital of Europe except London has libraries so magnificent as those of Paris; the Bibliothèque Nationale is in some respects superior to the British Museum. The Bibliothèque Nationale consists of many departments. (Several are described. Then follow short descriptions of the Mazarine, the Arsenal, the Sainte-Geneviève, and the new library of the City of Paris.) One of the peculiar institutions of Paris is the large group of small libraries which are combined reading rooms and circulating libraries. Men and women come to read, for a trifling sum, the newest books and periodicals. The books are unbound, often tattered and torn, but some of them have become valuable because they are first editions of the romantic school of the nineteenth century. The persons in charge now want high prices for any book they sell. Private clubs are now building libraries; in fifty years the circulating libraries may disappear.

1317 [Reply to M. Laboulaye.] *American Bibliopolist*, 7 (April 1875), p64, 180 wds (NcD).

M. Laboulaye said the other day in the French national assembly that the great schools of Paris are almost destitute of libraries. The *Bibliographie de la France* gives the following information: Ecole de Droit—11,000 volumes (but a poor room); Ecole de Médecine—32,000 volumes, with the anatomical collection known as Musée Orfila in an adjoining six-room suite; Collége de France—no library; Ecole des Mines—7,000 volumes; Ecole Normale Supérieure—30,000 volumes in general literature and 10,500 in science. From these figures it would appear that M. Laboulaye's picture is exaggerated.

— ACADEMIE DES SCIENCES MORALES ET PUBLIQUES

1318 "M. Guizot on American Literature and International Exchanges." *Norton's Literary Gazette and Publishers' Circular*, n.s. 2 (May 15, 1855), p207, 650 wds (MnU).

At a recent meeting of the French Academy of Moral and Political Sciences, M. Guizot, the distinguished historian and statesman, presented a large number of books collected through M. Vattemare's international exchanges, many of them from the United States. (Some of Guizot's remarks are translated verbatim and some are summarized.) The United States is erroneously believed to be exclusively devoted to material things; for some years there has been a great intellectual movement there. Mr. Norton's *Literary Gazette* shows the extent of Americans' literary activity. The great number of public libraries in the United States also indicates the scientific and literary activity there. (Statistics are given for major cities; none of these libraries is government supported. Vattemare's work is praised; Guizot had originally distrusted his plans.)

— BIBLIOTHEQUE DE L'ARSENAL

1319 [Library of the Paris Arsenal.] *American Bibliopolist*, 7 (December 1875), p247 (ICN, NcD).

The entire article follows.

"The library of the Paris Arsenal is now opened. It is one of the richest in

Paris, as it contains 20,000 volumes and 80,000 manuscripts, and is especially rich in theatrical documents."

— BIBLIOTHEQUE HISTORIQUE DE LA VILLE DE PARIS

1320 [Bibliothèque Historique de la Ville de Paris.] *Publishers' Weekly*, 5 (February 21, 1874), p189 (NcU).
The entire article follows; it is from the *Athenaeum*, London.
"The new library of the city of Paris, intended to replace that which was unfortunately destroyed at the burning of the Hôtel de Ville by the Communists, was opened to the public Jan. 3d. The new library occupies a portion of the Hôtel Carnavalet, in the Rue Sévigné, near Musée Historique, now in process of formation. Although, alas! but a poor substitute for the splendid collection of 125,000 volumes which perished, the new library, even in point of numbers, has made a fair commencement. It contains as many as 23,000 volumes or pamphlets, and 15,000 engravings. About 8,000 of the books and 12,000 of the engravings have been presented to the library; the rest have been purchased. Only about 100 volumes from the old library were saved for it."

— BIBLIOTHEQUE NATIONALE

1321 "Bibliothèque Royale, de Paris." *American Journal of Science*, 8 (1824), p376 (DLC, IEN, InU).
The entire article follows; apparently it was taken from the *Revue Encyclopédique*.
"This library contained in 1791, only 150,000 volumes; at present it includes more than 450,000. In 1783, it numbered only 2,700 port-folios of engravings, and now there are 5,700. Its annual increase is 6,000 French works, and 3,000 foreign, which permits us to hope that in fifty years, this magnificent establishment will have doubled its literary and scientific treasures."

1322 Aldrich, [Mr.] "Letters from Mr. Aldrich." [The Bibliothèque Royale, Paris.] *New World. A Weekly Family Journal of Popular Literature, Science, Art and News*, 6 (February 18,1843), p211–13 (NcD).
The part of the letter about libraries (p212, 550 wds) is summarized below.
The Bibliothèque Royale is pre-eminent among the libraries of Paris, and perhaps of the world. The author spent two days there but two years would not have been enough for a thorough examination; there are more than a million volumes. Books are kept in cases with wire gratings. All classes of people use the library; anyone may obtain a book immediately by writing the author and title on a slip of paper and handing it to a librarian. One superb gallery existed in the time of Mazarin. Early manuscripts and letters of famous men are exhibited. The cabinet of medals and the cabinet of engravings are described.

1323 "Bibliothèque Royale, Now National Library at Paris." *Bibliotheca Sacra* [and Theological Review], 5 (May 1848), p383–85 (NcU).
This library has the largest collection in the world. The length of the building is 540 feet, the breadth 130. (The history of the library is outlined briefly; Louis XIII and Louis XIV augmented its holdings greatly.) The government has made an annual grant for many years. The library has five distinct sections: printed works; manuscripts, genealogies, etc.; medals, antique gems, etc.; engravings; the zodiac and antique marbles. There are nearly 400 readers each

day. The works are kept in wire enclosed book-cases. There are 100,000 medals and coins; 80,000 volumes of manuscripts; 1,400,000 plates of engravings in 9000 volumes or portfolios; 60,000 portraits; 300,000 maps, charts, etc. Paris has five public libraries, with 1,300,000 volumes of printed books. (A table of the holdings of each is given.) The effect of the recent revolution on the libraries is not yet known.

1324 [The Imperial Library of Paris.] *National Magazine: Devoted to Literature, Art, and Religion*, 7 (July 1855), p95 (InU, NcU).
The entire article follows.
"The *Imperial Library of Paris* is stated to have received five hundred donations of books, manuscripts, medals, antiquities, &c., in the course of the past year. Among them were several Russian and Armenian books and manuscripts of considerable value; some old Greek medals; a number of the coins put into circulation by the Crusaders; and several stones containing inscriptions and mosaics from the ruins of Carthage. The library also exchanged surplus copies of books for other works, with the British Museum, the Royal Asiatic Society, the Smithsonian Institute, the Academies of Munich, Stuttgardt, Christiana, &c."

1325 [Anglo-Saxon Psalter in Bibliothèque Impériale.] *National Magazine: Devoted to Literature, Art, and Religion*, 9 (August 1856), p189, 260 wds (NcU).
An Anglo-Saxon psalter, formerly preserved in the library of La Sainte Chapelle at Bourges, is now in the Bibliothèque Impériale. The manuscript is a folio volume of 196 pages. The Latin and Anglo-Saxon versions are on opposite pages. Several canticles, the symbol of St. Athanasius, and the Litanies of the Saints follow the psalter. Leopold Delisle thinks the manuscript dates from the eleventh century; it appears to have been made for a lady. Some paleologists have dated this manuscript as seventh century. Delisle believes that the litanies belong to the Gallic liturgy.

1326 [Forgery of French Manuscripts.] *Nation*, 2 (May 8, 1866), p579–80 (NcU).
The forgery of manuscripts is a distinct and remunerative profession on the continent. A collection of letters of Marie Antoinette has recently occasioned a controversy; the experts who consider them forgeries are generally thought to be correct. M. [Félix Sébastian] Feuillet de Conches, Sub-Director of the Foreign Office, their former owner, has had permission to take documents from the Imperial Library [Bibliothèque Nationale] home with him. He has always returned them, but blank pages have seemed to be missing. In conversation with M. [Jules Antoine] Taschereau, the director of the library, he once claimed that forgery was easy; M. Taschereau listened carefully and became suspicious. A collection of letters from Racine, that had been owned by Feuillet, were auctioned and the purchaser was asked to bring them to the library, where they were found to be copies of some there. It now looks bad for M. Feuillet.

1327 [M. Reclus and the Bibliothèque Nationale.] *Nation*, 14 (June 20, 1872), p405–06 (NcU).
This refers to a series of Alfred Darcel articles, "Les Arts et Les Musées sous la Commune," then appearing in the *Gazette des Beaux-Arts*. Michel-Elie Reclus was director of the Bibliothèque Nationale under the Commune.

In regard to the Bibliothèque Nationale under the Commune, M. Darcel has contempt for M. Reclus, but does not charge him with anything more serious than being over-zealous in carrying out what he and others saw as needed reforms in that library. Reclus lacked discretion; this lack prevented his doing all the good for France which his unselfish nature, elevated spirit, and cultivated mind might have done. No man loved his native country better than he did.

1328 [Montaigne Collection in the Bibliothèque Nationale.] *American Bibliopolist*, 5 (May–June 1873), p77, 170 wds (ICU, NcD).

The National Library of Paris has bought the late Dr. Payen's collection of books, manuscripts, engravings, etc. relating to Montaigne. Payen had planned to write a book about the life and works of Montaigne. The collection includes all known editions of the "Essais" and two copies of the first edition (1580), which brought £82 8^s. at the Radzivill [Radziwill?] sale. J. C. Brunet, in this *Manuel* of 1814, says that edition was then worth just 5 to 7 francs. The second edition of the "Essais" (1588), is nearly as scarce as the first and is more nearly complete. A copy in the Public Library of Bordeaux is full of autograph notes, corrections, suppressions, and additions which until now have never been properly investigated.

1329 [Taschereau and a Stolen Manuscript.] *American Bibliopolist*, 6 (March–April 1874), p37, 380 wds (NcD).

Jules Antoine Taschereau, chief of the Bibliothèque Nationale, has claimed for the library a manuscript among the books of M. Dancoisne to be sold at auction. Entitled "Gratiani collectio ss. Canonum et Decretorum, cum veteribus glossis..." the work is a valuable fifteenth century manuscript. Taschereau claims it was stolen while en route to the Bibliothèque Nationale from the library at Troyes in 1804, but there is some evidence indicating that this manuscript is not the same one stolen. Many manuscripts of the period were duplicated and triplicated, with all of the copies corresponding closely. Thus, we think M. Taschereau will have a difficult job establishing the right of ownership for the Bibliothèque Nationale.

1330 "Bibliothèque Nationale." *American Bibliopolist*, 6 (September–October 1874), p118–19 (NcD).

A curious statistical report has just been published concerning the Bibliothèque Nationale. During the last five months it received 31,101 copies of books, pamphlets, papers, periodicals, etc., published in Paris alone; only 1200 have been retained, the rest being sent to the paper mill, perhaps eventually to record more rubbish. The Library now contains 2,075,871 volumes and about 200,000 manuscripts, 8000 maps and 120,000 pamphlets. The reading room serves 4,300 readers each month; the inner alcove, devoted to use by men of letters and distinction, serves 1150 each month. Full of odd misprints, the catalogs of the institution have been the subject of many jokes, and some queer stories are told about the frequenters of this library. Perfect order and politeness are exercised in this establishment, and it is conducted in a spirit of utmost liberality.

1331 "Vayssard." *American Bibliopolist*, 6 (September–October 1874), p134 (ICN, ICU).

The entire article follows.

"M. Vayssard, a librarian in the National Library of Paris, recently died at the age of eighty. He was remarkable for his wonderful memory of books and his knowledge of the contents of the library, which included more than two million volumes. It is related that a visitor once asked for a novel, of which he did not know the title nor the author's name. He repeated a line or two of the first chapter, and Vayssard brought the book, though it was by an obscure author of the eighteenth century."

1332 "Taschereau." *American Bibliopolist*, 6 (November–December 1874), p158 (ICN, OC).
The entire article follows. It refers to Jules Antoine Taschereau.
"The death is announced from Paris of M. Taschereau, late Director of the National Library. He was specially entrusted with the preparation of the catalogues, and was known in literature by his editions of Molière, Boufflers, and the correspondence of Grimm and Diderot, and by his histories of the life and writings of Molière and Corneille."

1333 [Bibliothèque Nationale Acquisitions through Gift.] *American Bibliopolist*, 7 (April 1875), p65, 150 wds (NcD).
The Bibliothèque Nationale at Paris received more than 1,200 volumes as gifts in the past year, principally presents from foreign governments and scientific societies. (Several special gifts, along with the names of the persons donating them are listed.)

1334 [French National Library.] *American Bibliopolist*, 7 (December 1875), p248 (ICN, NcD).
The entire article follows.
"The French National Library has just acquired the books which formerly belonged to Montaigne. They include many volumes of Notes from the hand of the famous moralist, and were purchased for 34,000 fr."

— BIBLIOTHEQUE STE. GENEVIEVE

1335 "The Library of Saint Genevieve, Paris." *Norton's Literary Gazette and Publishers' Circular*, 3 (October 15, 1853), p169–70 (NcU).
The Library of Saint Genevieve is the largest and most valuable in Paris after the Bibliothèque Nationale. It was founded in 1624 and now has more than 200,000 books and 3000 manuscripts. The library moved into a new building in 1851; its exterior is not at all striking. (The design and furnishings of the library are described.) The catalogs are still in manuscript form, and are accessible only to librarians. A reader must know which books he wants to consult, as there is no subject catalog. The library is used mostly by scholars, and by students living in the classical quarter where it is located. The library is open evenings in the winter. Warm and well-lit, it became such a popular place for students to read light literature that the directors were forced to adopt a rule against the continuous reading of such books. (An interior view of the library accompanies the article.)

1336 [Bust of Ulrich Gering.] *American Bibliopolist*, 6 (March–April 1874), p38, 210 wds (NcD).
A bust of Ulrich Gering, the first Parisian printer, was inaugurated at the library of Sainte Geneviève last March by M. de Fourtou, minister of public instruction, M. Ferdinand Denis, keeper of the library and publishing representatives. About 1470, the first book printed in Paris, "Gasparini Pergamensis

Epistolae," was printed by Gering, Michael Friburger and Martin Crantz. Gering was not a Frenchman but a foreigner born in the Diocese of Constance. The first English printer, William Caxton, was an Englishman from the Weald of Kent. When may we expect, says *The Athenaeum*, to see a statue or a bust of him in the British Museum?

— LOUVRE

1337 "Largest Museum and Library Known." *Eclectic Magazine of Foreign Literature*, 14 (July 1848), p431 (NcU).
The entire article follows.
"It has been decided that the palace of the Louvre shall be connected by additional buildings with that of the Tuileries, and that the royal library shall be deposited there. The entire pile will thus form the largest museum and library in the world."

— SAINT-ETIENNE

1338 [Books in the Saint-Étienne Public Library.] *Nation*, 5 (July 25, 1867), p65 (NcU).
The entire article follows.
"Two hundred inhabitants of Saint-Étienne complained lately by petition to the French Senate that the city council, in stocking the public library of that place, furnished the works of Voltaire, Rousseau, Proudhon, Michelet, Eugene Sue, George Sand, Balzac, and other more or less famous writers. A special report, condemning this selection, was approved by a large majority of the Senate, but eloquently opposed by Sainte-Beuve, albeit he was in feeble health. His attitude on this occasion procured him a complimentary address from the pupils of the Normal School; and the principal, [Desiré] Nisard, having expelled the supposed author, and refused to allow him to return, a general withdrawal ensued, but has since doubtless yielded to a compromise, as such 'strikes' are apt to yield."

1339 "Janin's Library." *American Bibliopolist*, 6 (September–October 1874), p124, 210 wds (NcD).
The library described in this article was never received by the town of Saint-Étienne. Mme. Janin decided against the gift; at the time of her death she was planning to give it to the Arsenal Library in Paris. However, it was apparently broken up and sold at auction. The story is told in the introduction to *La Bibliothèque de Jules Janin*, by Paul Lacroix, Paris, Librairie des Bibliophiles, 1877, p1–17.
The celebrated book critic Jules Janin bequeathed his library to his native town, Saint-Étienne, his wife retaining use of it during her life. The library was the work of a half-century and contains six to seven thousand volumes, including all of the important works of the last forty years and admirable editions of older works as well. Many are complimentary copies printed just for Janin, with dedications in prose or verse. He then had them richly bound by celebrated binders. Some of the dedications are, in effect, manuscript prefaces, and most volumes have letters from the authors inside their covers.

France

STRASBOURG — BIBLIOTHEQUE MUNICIPALE (TO AUGUST, 1870).
see also GERMANY — STRASSBURG — KAISERLICHE UNIVERSITATS UND LANDES BIBLIOTHEK (AFTER AUGUST, 1870).

1340 "The Strasbourg Library." *American Bibliopolist*, 2 (October 1870), p277-78 (NcD).

The article summarized below was based on an article in the *Pall Mall Gazette*.

The library at Strasbourg has been laid in ruins by German bombardment. Printing was probably invented in Strasbourg, and the library was one of the oldest in France, but uneasiness about the library is lessened because it contained few valuable books except for a small folio volume, in a contemporary hand, of the depositions in the lawsuit between Fust and Gutenberg. This volume is an important source for prevalent opinions as to the origin of printing. Other printed works in the library included a copy of the first German Bible, printed by Mentelin; three early Latin Bibles; a rare copy of Vergil and a commentary of Servius upon that poet; a copy of Jerome's epistles; and about 4,000 other books printed before 1500. There were only two or three illuminated manuscripts of great value. We trust that the valuable volumes were placed in safety before the bombardment and were preserved.

1341 Macray, John. "The Library of Strasburg." *American Bibliopolist*, 2 (November-December 1870), p323-24 (NcD).

Part of the article summarized below is taken from the (London) *Times* of October 8 and 12, 1870.

The library of Strasbourg is reported totally destroyed. Not a leaf appears to remain. The collection, which originated in 1765, contained 180,000 printed volumes and 12,000 manuscripts. Among the treasures lost were books printed by Fust, Schoeffer, and Mentelin, a twelfth century manuscript *Hortus Deliciarum*, and the records of the lawsuit between Gutenberg and the heirs of Dreisehn over claims to the invention of typography. The city is blamed for not moving these treasures to safer quarters.

1342 "The Strasbourg Library." *Appletons' Journal: a Magazine of General Literature*, 5 (February 18, 1871), p194-95 (NcU).

The Public or Town Library of Strasbourg, recently destroyed by the Germans, probably grew from a collection bequeathed to the town by John Geiler von Kayserberg who died in 1510. Since this date was only fifty years after the birth of printing, his original collection had more manuscripts than books. At the time of its destruction the library held 180,000 printed books and 1,589 manuscripts and was rich in examples of works pre-dating 1520. This collection included many fine examples of illumination, manuscript documents of the lawsuit between Gutenberg and his partner, and some of the earliest books from the presses of Fust, Mentelin and Eggestein. Despite these treasures and a good collection of modern works, the average daily attendance was only fifty readers.

TOURS — BIBLIOTHEQUE MUNICIPALE

1343 [Tours Municipal Library.] *American Bibliopolist*, 5 (July-August 1873), p109, 300 wds (ICU, NcD).

The article summarized below is reprinted from the *Athenaeum*.

Fears were entertained for the safety of the Tours Municipal Library during the German invasion of France. Dr. Arndt, of the Berlin Royal Library, inspected the Tours library a few months before the war, and remarked that one treasure, a copy of the Mentz Bible of 1462, had been carried away from Germany in one of the first wars of the French Revolution. Taking this hint, the Tours librarian, M. Dorange, packed his books and manuscripts as soon as the Germans reached France, and took them to Biarritz so that they could be shipped if necessary. One such treasure was a fifteenth century manuscript of Livy begun by employees of Balue. When Balue's books were seized by the king in 1469, the manuscript was not finished, so Louis XI had it completed at his own expense. A catalog of the Tours Library is in press.

1344 F., J. W. "Catalogue of Manuscripts in Tours Library." *American Bibliopolist*, 7 (December 1875), p248–49 (NcD).

The librarian of the library at Tours, M. A. Dorange, has compiled a catalog of the manuscripts preserved there. A beautifully printed limited edition has been made; copies will be given as presents to various libraries and foreign governments. The manuscripts at Tours are valuable and interesting, especially the manuscripts of the Evangelists of the eighth century. The catalog lists and describes 2,000 manuscripts, including treasures from the old libraries of the Cathedral, of the Abbey of St. Martin and of the Abbey of Marmontier. Many manuscripts have rare bindings; some of these bear arms of notable houses. (A list of about fifteen of the most precious of the manuscripts is given.) M. Dorange needed more than ten years to complete the catalog, as he had to decipher and read all the manuscripts in order to describe them fully.

1345 F., J. W. [Catalogue of Manuscripts in Tours Library.] *Nation*, 21 (December 23, 1875), p404, 760 wds (NcU).

This article is identical with the one on the same subject in the *American Bibliopolist* for December 1875 *(see 1344)*.

TROYES

1346 "Ancient Manuscripts." *Eclectic Museum of Foreign Literature, Science and Art*, 1 (January 1843), p137, 310 wds (InU, NcU).

The information in the article summarized below was taken from the *Literary Gazette*, London.

In the library of Troyes is a manuscript of the Venerable Bede, carried, probably, from the Abbey of Clairvaux, containing his *Commentary on St. Augustine and the Epistles of St. Paul*. It dates from the eighth or ninth century. The Troyes library also contains many manuscripts that were formerly at the Convent of Port Royal. These include 300 volumes of the writings and autograph correspondence of famous literary persons connected with the convent; one volume contains significant manuscript materials relating to Pascal.

VERSAILLES — BIBLIOTHEQUE MUNICIPALE

1347 [Comtesse du Barry's Library.] *American Bibliopolist*, 7 (February 1875), p7 (ICU, NcD).

The entire article follows.

"The Comtesse du Barry, in imitation of Madame de Pompadour, had formed a library of books, neatly bound in morocco, with her arms gilt on the sides. At her death, by the guillotine, her books were confiscated, and about 400 of them are still in the Municipal Library of Versailles. The rest were lost or stolen. A complete list of them has been found in duplicate in the Arsenal Library, and is now printed, with Introduction and Notes, by M. Paul Lacroix."

Germany

1348 "Libraries in Germany." *Museum of Foreign Literature, Science, and Art*, 8 (April 1826), p381 (MWelC).
The entire article follows.
"The German libraries surpass in number and richness those of any other country of Europe. The library of Vienna contains 30,000 volumes; that of Dresden, 220,000; that of Munich, 400,000; that of Breslau, 160,000; that of Gottingen, 300,000. It is calculated that 150 public libraries contain 3,133,080 printed volumes, besides manuscripts and pamphlets."

1349 "German Libraries." *United States Literary Gazette*, 4 (June 1, 1826), p196 (InU, NcU).
This article is almost exactly the same as one that appeared in the April 1826 issue of *Museum of Foreign Literature, Science, and Art (see 1348).*

1350 [Statistics of German Libraries.] *Escritoir or, Masonic and Miscellaneous Album*, 1 (August 12, 1826), p231 (InU, NcU).
This article is almost exactly the same as one that appeared in the April 1826 issue of *Museum of Foreign Literature, Science, and Art (see 1348).*

1351 "Literary Intelligence." *Philadelphia Album and Ladies' Literary Port Folio*, 1 (August 23, 1826), p6 (InU).
The part of the article about libraries follows.
"LIBRARIES. — It would hardly be supposed by most persons that the German libraries are superior in number and richness to any in Europe. The library of Vienna contains 300,000 volumes; Dresden 220,000; Munich 400,000; Breslau 160,000; Gottingen 300,000. 150 of the libraries are calculated to contain 3,133,080 printed vols. besides MSS. and pamphlets. Of the growing libraries and institutions of this country, we cannot omit mentioning the New York Mercantile Library Association, a most flourishing and growing institution, founded and continued by the Merchants clerks in that city. We propose offering a more particular notice of it in a future number."

1352 [Wallenstein, Jules de.] "Dwight's Travels in Germany; *Travels in the North of Germany, in the Years 1825 and 1826.* By Henry E. Dwight, A. M. New York: G. & C. & H. Carvill. 1829. 8 vo. pp. 450." *North American Review*, 29 (October 1829), p389–417 (InU, NcU).
The part of the review concerning Dwight's observations on libraries (p406–08) is summarized below.
Dwight considered the public and the university libraries to be one of the finer aspects of Germany; he particularly was impressed with the German

university libraries. He lamented that there were no similar collections available in America. The reviewer feels that such libraries may not yet be needed in this country. Importing thousands of books will not create a desire in the people to read them. The study of foreign languages and literatures will be popular with Americans only when their neighboring countries develop social and economic institutions strong enough to make their language important to Americans. In Europe this event has already occurred. Thus it is important to Europeans to be familiar with the language and literature of their neighboring countries. The circumstances of the settlement and political development of the United States has caused Americans to develop an independence of mind that has no need of foreign literature. Dwight's book included several pages of numerical lists of libraries.

1353 "Readers of the Middle Class in Germany." *New World. A Weekly Family Journal of Popular Literature, Science, Art, and News*, 6 (April 8, 1843), p414, 520 wds (InU, NcD).

Extracted from: William Howitt's *The Rural and Domestic Life of Germany, with Characteristic Sketches of Its Cities and Its Scenery,* ... Philadelphia: Carey & Hart, 2v, 1843.

In Germany large libraries are found in the principal cities and the university towns. In other German towns there are subscription libraries, but they are generally inferior to English subscription libraries. The Englishmen who use subscription libraries, even those for artisans, read more of travel, history, and better fiction. In recent years the English have bought cheap reprints of standard authors. In both England and Germany the subscription libraries contain trash, but the libraries in England also furnish more serious information. In Germany the subscription libraries contain a scattering of good works while abounding in trash such as *The Enchanted Dagger, The Ghostly Mother of the Rock of Gutenstein,* and *The Bandit from Honor and Misanthrope.*

1354 [The Munich Library.] *American Publisher and Bookseller*, 2 (March 1869), p5 (DLC).

The entire article follows.

"The Munich Library, the largest in Germany, numbers 900,000 volumes. That of Berlin contains 700,000; Stuttgart 450,000; Vienna 400,000; Darmstadt 300,000. The University libraries are also very large. That of Gottingen numbers 400,000 volumes; Jena 300,000; Breslau 350,000. Heidelberg 220,000; and there are thirteen other University libraries, having upwards of 100,000 volumes. In addition to these there are numerous city, school and private libraries, containing from 50,000 volumes to 200,000 each."

BERLIN

1355 [Public Libraries in Berlin.] *Norton's Literary Gazette and Publishers' Circular*, n.s. 1 (January 1, 1854), p9 (NcU).

The entire article follows.

"The booksellers and other citizens of Berlin have established four public libraries in different parts of the city, designed particularly for the working classes. These Libraries already contain 10,000 volumes; of which 2,389 are upon history; 576, biography; 581 technology; 2,580 works of German literature. Connected with each library is a reading-room, spacious and well-warmed, which is open from 7 to 11 every evening. The number of workmen who frequent these establishments is continually increasing."

1356 [Libraries Established in Berlin.] *National Magazine: Devoted to Literature, Art, and Religion,* 4 (March 1854), p287 (InU, NcU).

This is a slightly abridged version of the article on the same subject that appeared in *Norton's Literary Gazette* for January 1, 1854 *(see 1355)*. A still shorter version (not included in this bibliography) appeared in the May 1854 issue of the *National Magazine.*

1357 "Free Popular Libraries in Berlin." *Norton's Literary Gazette and Publishers' Circular,* n.s. 2 (February 1, 1855), p49, 1250 wds (MWiW).

We have emphasized the need both for endowed reference libraries and for less complete popular libraries where those educated in our public schools may easily continue their intellectual culture. Our readers know how larger cities in England are taking advantage of the Free Libraries Act. In Berlin, four free circulating libraries were established in 1850, each in a different part of the city. They are not tax supported but are sponsored by the Scientific Union (Wissenschaftliche Verein) and receive occasional gifts from the city. (Statistics of volumes held and of use are given.) The Royal Library of Berlin is free but circulation is restricted. (A list of the principal libraries of the city is given, showing the number of volumes in each; it is taken from the latest edition of Petzholdt's handbook of German libraries.)

— ROYAL LIBRARY (KONIGLICHEN BIBLIOTHEK)

1358 [New Building for Royal Library in Berlin.] *Biblical Repository and Classical Review* [Biblical Repository and Quarterly Observer], 6 (October 1835), p503 (NcU).

The entire article follows.

"Berlin is to have a new building for the royal library. That library now contains 250,000 volumes, exclusive of duplicates."

1359 "The Royal Library of Berlin." *Norton's Literary Gazette and Publishers' Circular,* 2 (April 15, 1852), p63, 700 wds (ICN, NcU).

The article summarized below was written by a correspondent for the *Springfield Republican.*

The Royal Library has more than 600,000 volumes and a two-part book catalog: one part, the scientific catalog (250 volumes) lists books by their locations and the second part (650 volumes) lists books alphabetically. Work on a new scientific catalog began in 1844. A user can obtain a book by depositing a note in a special box; within a few hours the book is brought to him for use in the reading room, which is open from nine to four every day except Sunday. Physicians, ministers, lawyers, and university students can borrow books on six-week loans. Other individuals also can borrow books upon obtaining a statement signed by one of the librarians or by one of the above users that guarantees the return of the books. These rules are very simple in contrast to those enforced by American libraries. Also, individuals who have the proper credentials and do not live in Berlin can have books mailed to them anywhere in Germany.

1360 [Royal Library of Berlin.] *National Magazine: Devoted to Literature, Art, and Religion,* 1 (December 1852), p568, 200 wds (InU, NcU).

Europe 360

The Royal Library has recently acquired four private collections: a collection of 404 works on chess; Count Mejan's library of 14,170 volumes, rich in classical, French, and Italian subjects; a library of 921 works on theology and Spanish literature; and a collection of German literature from the fifteenth to the nineteenth centuries containing 21,000 works in 36,000 volumes. The subject catalog of the Royal Library fills 250 volumes; the alphabetical register of books in the library, 650 volumes.

1361 [Prussian Royal Library, Berlin.] *National Magazine: Devoted to Literature, Art, and Religion*, 2 (March 1853), p283 (InU, NcU).
The entire article follows.
"Among the curiosities of the *Berlin Library* is the Bible of Charles I., which he bore with him to the scaffold. It is a small volume, bound in black leather, and bears evident signs of having been much used. By the side of this interesting relic lies Luther's original manuscript translation of the Holy Scriptures. Some of the chapters present a tangled mass of additions, erasures, and amendments. Another interesting MS. is *Goethe's Faust*, which is very clear and legible."

1362 "Royal Library at Berlin." *Norton's Literary Gazette and Publishers' Circular*, 3 (November 15, 1853), p193, 450 wds (NcU).
The Royal Library at Berlin was founded in 1661; a new building was erected in 1780. The library probably contains at least 500,000 printed books and 10,000 manuscripts. Recent liberal appropriations have added 9,000 volumes annually in recent years. The annual amount spent for books is 10,000 thalers; other expenses have been 15,000 thalers. The library is open weekdays and Sundays; thirty to forty thousand books are lent annually. The library owns many incunabula, curious manuscripts, and books interesting because of their associations, including a copy of Gutenberg's Bible of 1450. There is no printed catalog, but there are alphabetical and classified manuscript catalogs. The University at Berlin has 30,000–40,000 volumes, and four public libraries for popular reading are planned. (An exterior view of the library accompanies the article.)

1363 "The Royal Library of Berlin." *Norton's Literary Gazette and Publishers' Circular*, n.s. 1 (October 2, 1854), p492, 520 wds (NcU).
The librarian, Dr. Pertz, has published a report on the library from 1851 to 1853. For the purchase of books, periodicals, maps, and binding 27,000 Prussian dollars were allowed, plus $4,500 for prior expenses, $3,000 to purchase Meusebach's library, and $3,300 to purchase Wetzstein's collection of manuscripts. From this money and donations, 496 manuscripts, 13,870 volumes of printed books, 1,262 volumes of scientific periodicals, 47 maps, 32 pictures, portraits and engravings, and 722 pieces of music were added. Communications by subterranean telegraph have been made between the library and the librarian's residence and the firemen's watch-houses. The new catalog is rapidly advancing; 43 volumes are now written. A series of printed catalogs of manuscripts is in progress. Residents of Berlin borrowed 25,000, 27,000 and 33,500 works, successively, during the years 1851, 1852 and 1853. Learned men not living in Berlin also borrowed books.

1364 T., A. W. "From Berlin, Nov. 4. Music and Missions—Great Collection in the Royal Library—Importance of Musical Libraries." *Dwight's Journal of Music, A Paper of Art and Literature*, 6 (December 2, 1854), p66–67 (NcU).

S. W. Dehn is the librarian of the music department at the Royal Library in Berlin. The collection includes operas, theoretical works, history and biography, and manuscript books. There are 50,000 volumes in the music department alone. Many are those which men do not have in their own libraries, but want to consult at times. An examination of antiquarian catalogs of book sellers in West Germany showed how few works there are on musical topics other then the theoretical, and how difficult it is to collect complete sets of periodicals from second-hand dealers. There are collections available privately, however. If the music societies of Boston gave the proceeds of a few concerts, a fine library could be gathered. Such a collection, available for consultation and copying only, would be most useful. Our colleges collect few books of music; a distinct collection must be made.

1365 "Auction Sales." *Norton's Literary Gazette and Publishers' Circular*, n.s. 2 (January 15, 1855), p33–34 (MnU).
The part of the article about a library (p34) follows.
"We are also informed that there will soon be a large sale of some of the duplicate volumes in the Royal Library at Berlin. Those which will now be offered to the public for the most part relate to German literature, and many rare and curious works will be included in the collection. The catalogue is now in press, and will be issued at an early day. We shall then allude more particularly to its contents."

1366 "The Royal Library at Berlin." *National Magazine: Devoted to Literature, Art, and Religion*, 7 (October 1855), p380, 480 wds (NcU).
The Royal Library at Berlin contains about 600,000 volumes housed in a suite of rooms. All the works on a subject are housed together without regard to language. Each book case is labelled as to the subject covered by the books shelved there. The library's manuscript collection contains autograph materials by Goethe, Frederick the Great, Humboldt, Lessing, and Klopstock. Among the library's other treasures are the Bible and prayer-book of Charles I, Luther's Hebrew Bible and his German translation, a letter from Ignatius Loyola, and Zwingli's Bible.

1367 [Berlin Royal Library Acquires Part of the Otto Jahn Music Collection.] *American Bibliopolist*, 3 (October 1871), p371 (ICU, IEN).
The entire article follows.
"In April last, after the death of Professor Otto Jahn at Bonn, his library of Musical Works, unique of its kind, was sold by auction. The Prussian Government, assisted by Herr Killmann, of Bonn, has recently secured for the Royal Library, at Berlin, the Mozart collection, the most important numbers of the Haydn collection, a good many from the Beethoven, and several from the Gluck. These are inestimable additions to a library now the only one in Europe possessing all the works of Mozart, and which, with some little cost and trouble, may equally secure for itself an entire collection of Haydn, Bach (J.S.), Handel, and Beethoven."

1368 [Retirement of Dr. Pertz of the Royal Library of Berlin.] *Nation*, 16 (May 22, 1873), p355, 160 wds (NcU).
Dr. G. Pertz, Librarian of the Royal Library in Berlin, has just retired at the age of 78. Under his long administration the library has greatly increased in size, and the system of cataloging has been carried to a high degree of perfection.

Dr. Pertz has always been accommodating to strangers. He has taken a prominent place in the advancement of literature and science; his learning and industry are evident in his *Monumenta Historica*. No successor has been appointed. A new library building is needed, the present quarters in the king's palace being inadequate; however the high price of building sites in Berlin may cause a long delay.

1369 [Exhibition at the Berlin Royal Library.] *Publishers' Weekly*, 4 (November 22, 1873), p583 (NcU).

The entire article follows.

"A most remarkable exhibition is just opened at Berlin, in the middle room of the Royal Library, containing one copy of all printed publications, books, pamphlets, pictures, etc., relating to the German-French war. The collection is not only rich, but probably complete, for immediately after the declaration of war King William ordered committees to be appointed in almost every important place, and any publication of this kind, irrespective of cost, to be bought by them. The arrangement of the exhibition has been arranged by the Emperor's private librarian, Louis Schneider."

1370 [The Berlin Royal Library.] *Nation*, 18 (February 26, 1874), p140, 250 wds (NcU).

Perhaps a melancholy satisfaction may be obtained from the knowledge that one product of German civilization is not absolutely perfect. Professor [Theodor] Mommsen, in a recent speech, says that the Royal Library in Berlin is in bad condition. It is much smaller than the principal libraries outside Germany and is barely half the size of the one in Munich. The catalogs are not accessible to readers, and it is difficult to get the books; one out of every six books requested is missing. The library spends only 20,000 thalers annually for books; 100,000 are needed. The building is unsuitable for library purposes.

1371 [The Royal Library at Berlin.] *Nation*, 18 (June 4, 1874), p363, 350 wds (NcU).

The project for a new building for the Royal Library at Berlin is likely to be realized. The present quarters are crowded and poorly arranged; besides, the space is needed for the enlargement of the King's palace. Professor [Theodor] Mommsen's earnest complaint to parliament has had results, and Professor [Karl Richard] Lepsius, who has been librarian since Dr. [Georg Heinrich] Pertz resigned, has shown in his annual report how the library has lagged behind other great libraries. The king is said to favor the plan and is willing to use space now occupied by the barracks of his body guards; however, his military officers oppose. Dr. Lepsius has gone with the royal architect to inspect several large library buildings. If Prussia will stay out of war for a few years, Berlin may obtain a new library and a new cathedral.

— REICHSTAG LIBRARY

1372 [The Library of the German Reichstag.] *Nation*, 21 (September 16, 1875), p181, 180 wds (NcU).

The Library of the German Reichstag, a scientifically-formed Library of Congress, is reported to be making fine progress under the skilful direction of Dr. [August] Potthast. With 40,000 volumes, it is already among the foremost libraries of Berlin. Dr. Potthast has divided it into twenty-three sections. That allotted to the civil process contains complete statutes of the German states; the section for political science includes documents and proceedings of German and foreign deliberative bodies. The library's internal appointments satisfy every requirement for the comfort and convenience of the deputies who use it.

DRESDEN — ROYAL LIBRARY

1373 "Curious Botanical Library." *American Farmer*, 3 (December 21, 1821), p308, 210 wds (InU, NcU).
From *Blackwood's Magazine*.
Louis Bonaparte has given the library at Dresden a set of 135 wooden volumes. Each volume was made of the wood of a particular tree and opens to reveal the bud, fruit, flower, leaves, and other parts of the tree. In the case of plants, such as the rose, that were too small to produce binding material, the binding is made of some other wood and then barred with rose of juniper wood [*sic*].

HANOVER — ROYAL LIBRARY

1374 [Leibnitz Treatise in the Hanoverian Library.] *National Magazine: Devoted to Literature, Art, and Religion*, 4 (June 1854), p572 (InU, NcU).
The entire article follows; it apparently refers to what was then the Royal Library.
"A curious discovery has recently been brought before the world, in the shape of an unpublished treatise by Leibnitz in refutation of Spinoza. The discoverer, M. Foucher de Careil, during his researches in the Hanoverian Library, alighted upon a Latin manuscript entirely written in the hand of Leibnitz; and from this Latin version he has published one in French, under the title 'Réfutation inédité de Spinoza par Leibnitz.'"

MUNICH — BAVARIAN STATE LIBRARY

1375 "Bavarian State Library." *Niles' National Register*, 66 (June 15, 1844), p242 (NcU).
The entire article follows, reprinted from the *London Foreign Quarterly Review*.
"State Library. The king of Bavaria has augmented the funds for the support of the royal state library of Munich from 18 to 23,000 florins, and the exclusive allowance for the purchase of books, is raised from 12,000 to 17,000 florins. It may be remembered that about a year and a half ago, his majesty, by an extraordinary contribution of 8000 florins to the library, furnished the means of completing the previously imperfect collection of Spanish and Portuguese literature. The recent act of royal munificence will place the Munich library on a footing of completeness with which few collections in Europe will bear comparison."

1376 "Munich — The City and University." *Bibliotheca Sacra* [and Theological Review], 5 (May 1848), p378–83 (NcU).
The part of the article about libraries (p381–83) is summarized below.
Begun in 1832 and finished in 1843, the public library and archives can be

entered from Ludwigstrasse where there are eight feet high statues of Aristotle, Thucydides, Hippocrates and Homer. The printed books are arranged in 12 main classes with 180 subdivisions; there are also 12 special collections. The books are arranged by size, folio, quarto and octavo, in each department. Alphabetical and subject catalogs are being prepared; two to three thousand printed volumes are added yearly, and 16,000 florins are spent. The library receives one copy of every book published in the Kingdom. There are over 22,000 manuscripts, arranged by languages. (Several of the more valuable objects are discussed, including incunabula.) There are 400,000 printed works. Philip Von Lichtenthaler is the chief librarian and J. A. Schmeller is assistant librarian; there are 19 subordinate officers.

1377 "Royal Library at Munich." *Norton's Literary Gazette and Publishers' Circular*, 3 (November 15, 1853), p193–94 (NcU).

The building containing the Royal Library at Munich was completed in 1842. Four statues are placed upon the steps before the entrance. A magnificent staircase leads to the library. One hall is the place where books are lent, another is a reading and study room, and still another is reserved for members of the academy and university professors. The library contains more than 400,000 printed works, 22,000 manuscripts and 1500 volumes of incunabula. Visitors cannot go to the shelves unless accompanied by a librarian. The library has no collections of coins, medals, statues, paintings or engravings. The printed books and manuscripts are divided into twelve principal classes, which are subdivided into 180 classes. (The twelve main divisions are listed, and the number of manuscripts in each language is given.) There is an exhibit of the different materials used in book-making. (Several manuscripts and books are described. An exterior view of the library accompanies the article.)

1378 "The Library at Munich." *Appletons' Journal: a Magazine of General Literature*, 5 (January 28, 1871), p118–19 (NcU).

The *Hof-und Staats-Bibliothek* is in a beautiful building and the collection is second in size only to that of the library in Paris. The building is wrought in the Byzanto-Florentine style with imposing façade and elegant interior. Its most notable feature is the lack of restrictions on use; the 800,000 volumes which fill 77 large rooms are free to men of all faiths and nations. The collection includes rare and valuable books and manuscripts in almost all known languages. It is characteristic of German libraries that the collection includes examples which illustrate the history of printing.

STRASSBURG — KAISERLICHE UNIVERSITATS UND LANDES BIBLIOTHEK (AFTER AUGUST, 1870); *see also* FRANCE — STRASBOURG — BIBLIOTHEQUE MUNICIPALE (TO AUGUST, 1870).

1379 [Strasbourg Library to Receive the Landfermann Library.] *American Bibliopolist*, 2 (November–December 1870), p326 (ICU, NcD).

The entire article follows; it was reprinted from the *Pall Mall Gazette*.

"The *reconstruction* of the Strasburg Library is making rapid progress. Besides the united action of the academies and booksellers of all Germany, there are single gifts pouring in of no small value, prompted occasionally by sad enough motives. Thus the well-known scholiarch Landfermann, of Coblentz, has offered his own entire library, the result of many years' careful collection, chiefly rich in philology and history, and containing not a few rare works no longer to be had in trade, to the civil commissary Von Kuhlwetter, as a contribution towards the new Strasburg Library. He had hoped, he adds, to leave these books some day to his son (Johannes Landfermann, a most promising young historian), that he might use them after him. But he had gone down in the trenches before Metz, and the professor did not know what better purpose these books could serve now than the one he has under the circumstances destined them for."

1380 [Re-establishment of the Strassburg Library.] *Nation*, 11 (December 29, 1870), p438, 200 wds (NcU).

The reality of the acquisition of Alsace by Germany appears from the concurrent appeal of fifty German towns and cities for money and books to reestablish the Strassburg Library. Mr. Trübner, 60 Paternoster Row, London, will receive offerings and furnish information. The United States is capable mainly of sending money, yet a respectable collection of books could be made by our publishers and from duplicates in our great libraries. We have a special interest in the establishment of a European library that will not have the enormous advantage of antiquity and with which we may, therefore, properly compare our own libraries.

1381 "Strasburgh Library." *American Bibliopolist*, 3 (August 1871), p279, 210 wds (NcD).

Some manuscripts were lost in the fire at Strassburg. Haenet printed a catalog of them. According to the *National Zeitung*, subscriptions for the Strassburg Library promise to give it a large and valuable collection. Efforts made toward this object in England are highly appreciated abroad. Moreover, contributors and subscribers listed include the Grand Duke of Baden, several universities, several national governments and institutions, and some private men. The collections of Professor Bocking and Professor Van Vangerow, in Heidelberg, both rich in valuable law books and manuscripts, will be added.

1382 [Acquisitions for the New Strassburg Library.] *Nation*, 13 (November 16, 1871), p323 (NcU).

The entire article follows.

"The new Strassburg Library has been enriched by the purchase, for 24,000 francs, of the Heitz library, remarkable for being the fullest collection of works published in or relating to Alsace. This was not accomplished without great opposition on the part of the irreconcilables, though ten years ago, when the city was offered the library, it refused to buy it. Another valuable addition, also by purchase, is the Böcking library, said to be one of the richest in respect of the literature of the Reformation, and unique in its collection of the works of and concerning Hutten and the Obscurants of the 'Epistolae Obscurorum Virorum.' Donations from all parts of the world, and of every degree of value, are flowing in with a gratifying rapidity."

1383 "Restoration of the Strasbourg Library." *Publishers' Weekly* [Publishers' and Stationers' Weekly Trade Circular], 1 (January 18, 1872), p3, 280 wds (NcU).

A movement has been set on foot for the restoration of the Strassburg Library. An honorary committee, under the authority of Count Bismarck-Bohlen, the German governor of Alsace, is to collect American offerings towards the restoration of what is one of the oldest libraries in Europe and one of the most ancient cradles of literature. (The sixteen members of the committee are named; they were mostly publishers of books, periodicals, or newspapers.) Authors are invited to present copies of their works; publishers are invited to donate selections from their lists. Reports of learned societies and duplicates from libraries will be welcome. (Addresses are given of persons to whom gifts may be sent.)

1384 "Collections for the Strasbourg Library." *American Bibliopolist*, 4 (March 1872), p122 (ICU, IEN, OC).
The entire article follows.
"Colonel M. Richards Mucklé, of Philadelphia, is now fully engaged in the work of Strasbourg restoration, and has already been very successful in collecting a large number of works. Mr. E. Steiger, of New York, has accepted the position of recipient of works for the Strasbourg Library which may be contributed north of Philadelphia."

1385 [Heitz Collection in Strasbourg Library.] *American Bibliopolist*, 4 (March 1872), p123 (IEN, OC).
The entire article follows.
"We learn from the *Revue Critique*, that, by the purchase of the fine Heitz Collection, the Strasbourg Library is again the richest in the world in 'Alsatiana,' and that the general library will soon number 200,000 volumes. A rare MS. Strasbourg Chronicle, that of J. J. Meyer, is to be printed in the next volume of the 'Bulletins des Monuments Historiques d'Alsace.'"

1386 [Municipal Library of Strassburg.] *American Bibliopolist*, 4 (May 1872), p250, 430 wds (NcD).
The library was destroyed on the night of August 24, 1870 during the siege of the city. The German government has recently founded a University in Strassburg. The ancient academical library escaped destruction and has been adding additional materials. The Conseil has now decided to create a new municipal library and a commission has been established to assist in the effort. The commission is appealing generally for contributions to be sent to the mayor of Strassburg.

1387 [University Library, Strassburg.] *Publishers' Weekly*, 5 (April 4, 1874), p360 (NcU).
The entire article follows.
"The University Library at Strasburg [sic] has increased 80,000 volumes during the past year, and now numbers about 300,000 volumes in all. Half of these additions have been procured by purchase, the rest through public and private donations."

WARSENSTEIN

1388 "A Library Not a Library." *American Bibliopolist*, 3 (August 1871), p284 (NcD).
The entire article follows.
"A singular description of [a] Library exists at Warsenstein, near Cassel; the books composing it, or rather the substitutes for them, are made of wood,

and every one of them is a specimen of some different tree. The back is formed of its bark, and the sides are constructed of polished pieces of the same stock. When put together the whole forms a box, and inside of it are stored the fruit, seed, and leaves, together with the moss which grows on the trunk, and the insects which feed upon the tree; every volume corresponds in size, and the collection altogether has an excellent effect."

Great Britain

(see also England, Scotland)

1389 [Number of British Libraries.] *North American Review*, 2 (January 1816), p169 (InU, NcU).
The entire article follows.
"There are in England ninety-four publick libraries, eight in Scotland, and ten in Ireland, making one hundred and twelve. These include those of the Colleges, Cathedrals and publick offices."

1390 "Public Libraries and Museums in Great Britain." *Norton's Literary Gazette and Publishers' Circular*, 3 (July 15, 1853), p114–15 (ICN, NcU).
A comment by the editor of the Gazette precedes the article summarized below: "The following article from the *London Athenaeum* presents, in a brief form, the results of the late movements in England relating to Public Libraries. It is interesting in this country, where, without any legislative acts, so much is doing in the way of similar enterprises."
Following is the gist of a report that has appeared at the instance of Mr. Ewart about the results of the two acts for the establishment of public libraries and museums in England and Wales. (Then follow references to seventeen towns in which attempts, usually successful, have been made to establish museums or libraries. The results in each town are given in a brief paragraph.)

1391 [Sunday Libraries.] *Publishers' Weekly* [Publishers' and Stationers' Weekly Trade Circular], 2 (August 22, 1872), p175 (NcU).
The entire article follows; it was taken from the London *Athenaeum*.
"We hear of Sunday libraries in Cincinnati as a novelty. There was a library open on Sundays in Liverpool, from twenty to five and twenty years ago. The readers are said to have been so numerous that they sat on the floor, each man between the legs of the man behind him, like slaves in the old slave ships. The 'unco' guid' people succeeded in shutting up the Sunday Library as profane; but the gin palace was left open. Mrs. Crawshay, of Cyfarthfa, near Merthyr Tydvil, has had five free cottage libraries open during the seven days, in full activity, in a radius of a mile round Cyfarthfa. When the news first got into local papers, opposition was suggested, but the lady said, 'It is too late, they have been in existence a year and a half!'"

Iceland

1392 "Libraries in Iceland." *Norton's Literary Gazette and Publishers' Circular*, 3 (May 15, 1853), p83 (ICN, NcU).
The entire article follows.
"We have been favored by a correspondent with the following interesting particulars in regard to the larger book-collections of that isolated land. In a note which accompanies the list, our friend, who possesses unusual information in regard to the literature of Northern Europe, remarks that he 'collected the following items from Icelandic Journals, and showed them to an Icelander in Copenhagen, who pronounced them to be correct. The list was made last summer, and may be of interest to some of your readers.'"

Name	Location	No. of Vols.	When founded	Catal. published
National, or Diocesan Library,	Reykjavik,	11,000	1821	{ 1828 { 1842
Library of the Northern and Eastern Provinces,	Akureyra,	1,200		1851
Library of the Western Province,	Stykkisholm	1,000	1845	1847
Library of the Reading Circle of Barthastrand District,	Flatey,	1,000	1842	1845
Flatey Foundation for the Advancement of Knowl'ge,	Flatey,	600		{ 1842 { 1844
		14,800		

REYKJAVIK — STIFTISBOKASAFN

1393 Fiske, Willard. "Books for Iceland." *Cornell Era*, 6 (April 10, 1874), p181, 210 wds (NIC).
On August 2, the people of Iceland will celebrate the thousandth anniversary of the birth of their nation. It is proposed that Americans shall take part in the festivities by sending gifts of books to the National Library at Reykjavik. Cases will be forwarded from several (named) American libraries and institutions. In a fortnight or so I shall send a box from Cornell; therefore I shall be glad to receive volumes from professors, students and residents of Ithaca. Maps, engravings, and photographs will also be acceptable.

1394 [Gift of books for the National Library of Iceland.] *Nation*, 18 (April 16, 1874), p250, 110 wds (NcU).
This article is an abridgement of the one in the *Cornell Era* for April 10, 1874 *(see 1393)*.

1395 [Public Library of Iceland.] *Publishers' Weekly*, 5 (May 9, 1874), p458 (NcU).
The entire article follows; it refers to the Stiftísbokasafn.
"In connection with the festivities attending the millenial anniversary of Iceland's colonization—the 1st of August next—when the new constitution granted by the King of Denmark, giving the control of the island into the hands of an elective legislature, goes into effect—it is proposed by some of our men of letters, among them Mr. Longfellow and Mr. Curtis, to present the public library of Iceland a small collection of American books. This library is located at Reykjavik, the capital, and at present numbers some 10,000 vols.; it is called the Stiftisbokasafu [sic]. The matter is in charge of the American Geographical Society, and all desiring to share in this enterprise can do so by sending any contributions to the rooms of the Society at Cooper Institute."

Ireland

DUBLIN — TRINITY COLLEGE LIBRARY

1396 [Theft of Book from Trinity College Library.] *American Bibliopolist*, 6 (November–December 1874), p147 (ICN, NcD).
The entire article follows.
"The disappearance is reported from Trinity College library, Dublin, of St. Columbkill's 'Book of Kells.' The book is valued at £12,000, and a great excitement is said to have been caused by the discovery that it is missing. It is said to have been sent some time ago to the British Museum to be bound, and a demand for its 'immediate delivery' has been forwarded by a special legal messenger to the Museum trustees."

Italy

1397 "History of Education in Italy." *American Journal of Education* (Barnard), 7 (December 1859), p413–60 (NcU).
The article was translated from a work (unnamed) by Georg Karl von Raumer; the part of the article about libraries (p439, 180 wds) is summarized below. Thomas Sarzano is also known as Tommaso Parentucelli.
Cosimo de Medici spent 76,000 ducats for the building of a library in which in 1444 he deposited manuscripts acquired through his mercantile contacts; this was the origin of the Medicean Library. Thomas Sarzano, later Pope Nicholas V, helped Cosimo with the arrangement of the library. During Nicholas V's papacy, the Turks captured Constantinople; consequently Greek manuscripts began to pour into Italy. Nicholas collected approximately 5,000 of these manuscripts which later formed the nucleus of the Vatican Library. At this time, Cardinal Bessarion sent a number of manuscripts to Venice to commence the establishment of the library of St. Mark.

1398 [Statistics of Italian Libraries.] *Nation*, 2 (June 15, 1866), p755 (NcU).
The entire article follows.
"There are in Italy 210 public libraries, containing in the aggregate 4,149,281 volumes. Besides these there are the libraries of the two Chambers, of the Council of State, and many easily accessible large private collections. There are also 110 provincial libraries and those of 71 scientific societies. In 1863, which is the last year for which we have statistics, 988,510 volumes were called for by readers, of which 183,528 related to mathematics and the natural sciences; 122,496 to literature, history, and philology; 54,491 to theology; 70,537 to philosophy and morals; 193,792 to jurisprudence; 261,869 to the fine arts; and 101,797 to other subjects."

1399 M[ario, Jessie] W[hite.] "Italian Libraries." *Nation*, 6 (April 9, 1868), p287–88 (NcU).
Mario is identified as the author of this article in Daniel C. Haskell's *The Nation, Volumes 1–105, New York, 1865-1917, Indexes of Titles and Contributors*, 1953, v. 1, p13.
Florentine libraries in grand-ducal times were well supported; the Palatina alone cost 40,000 francs. Now, the entire National Library is allotted 16,000 francs, of which 8000 go for wages and upkeep, 7000 for subscriptions and just 1000 for books. The libraries are regulated by municipal authorities. Natoli's volume on Italian libraries shows that Italy has more works than any other nation. Early libraries are traced; there are now 210 libraries, of which 164 are public. In all, 4,149,281 volumes are contained in them. Most are old Italian works on theological and religious subjects. Since 1860, Italian libraries have been poorly supported; only $153,264 was spent annually for 164 public libraries. (Statistics of use are given; comparisons are made between libraries. Manuscripts and incunabula are frequently owned; several are mentioned.) The National Library united the Magliabecchiana and the Palatina in 1862. (Other libraries are described.)

1400 "The Libraries of Italy." *American Bibliopolist*, 4 (July–August 1872), p378 (ICN, OC).
The entire article follows.
"There are in Italy, exclusive of the Roman and Venetian States, 210 public libraries, containing 4,149,281 volumes; which gives an average of 19 volumes for every hundred inhabitants. Of these 210 libraries, 28 belong to Sicily, and possess 335,872 volumes. In the Venetian States alone there are 46 libraries, containing 905,895 volumes."

CASSINO — MONTE CASSINO MONASTERY LIBRARY

1401 [Monte Cassino To Be a National Monument.] *Nation*, 3 (October 18, 1866), p304 (NcU).
The entire article follows.
"The Italian Government have resolved to spare the celebrated monastery of Monte Cassino, founded by Saint Benedict himself, and which has passed through so many vicissitudes. It has for many years been the abode of learning rather than piety, and possesses a library filled with valuable manuscripts. It is to be maintained in its present state as a national monument. The archives, library, and monuments of the monastery are intact, and Tosti, its most

celebrated monk, is made the keeper. The convent of San Marco at Florence, famous for the frescoes of Fra Angelico and Fra Bartolomeo, and for its associations with Savonarola, is likewise spared. The rest of the Italian monasteries are broken up, their property confiscated, and their buildings either sold or converted to the uses of the Government."

1402 "Bibliotheca Casinensis." *American Bibliopolist*, 6 (September–October 1874), p138–39 (ICU, NcD).

The Benedictine Abbey of Monte Cassino, near Naples, has long been noted for its fine library of ancient manuscripts. The first volume of a catalog of the manuscripts has just been published. The catalog is perhaps one of the most thorough ever issued; 800 pages are devoted to the description of only 44 manuscripts. Each description is preceded by a chromo-lithograph showing specimens of the writing, initials, rubrication, and ornamentation found in the manuscript. About one-third of the catalog is devoted to a "florilegium" which contains extracts of texts, including important ones that have never been published. Several of the manuscripts are listed. The set will be useful in the better private libraries and will be necessary in repositories of manuscripts.

FLORENCE — NATIONAL CENTRAL LIBRARY

1403 [Commission on Italian Libraries.] *Nation*, 9 (October 7, 1869), p296, 480 wds (InU, NcU).

The article refers to a letter in the *Nation*, vol. 6, p287–88 *(see 1399)*.

An earlier letter on Italian libraries told of the collections there, noting that their resources had fallen off since the grand-ducal supremacy. A commission on libraries headed by Count Cibrario has released its report to the government, concluding that no grand universal library should be formed yet, but that existing libraries should increase their stock. The National Library, in Florence, should be sent the third copy of every publication in the kingdom and copies of all official documents. The commission would unite the Riccardiana and Laurenziana in Florence, and would develop the Marucelliana for students. Alphabetical, subject, and current acquisition catalogs must be made by each library. Rules are given for book circulation and the selection, promotion and pay of librarians. If the government adopts the scheme, it will assume support for libraries now resting with municipal authorities, which may or may not be desirable.

MILAN — AMBROSIAN LIBRARY

1404 [Manuscripts from Ambrosian Library Published.] *Museum of Foreign Literature, Science, and Art*, 4 (February 1824), p191 (InU, NcU).

The entire article follows. It refers to Marcus Cornelius Fronto.

"M. Angelo Mai, prefect of the Vatican Library at Rome, has just published a second edition of the Fragments of the Works of Frontonus [*sic*]. These he had discovered originally in the Ambrosian Library of Milan, but he has now considerably augmented them, by fresh discoveries made in the treasures of the Vatican. The literary public will be gratified to learn that among these augmentations are more than a hundred letters of Marcus Aurelius, Frontonius [*sic*], and others. This edition, styled the *Palimpsest*, is dedicated to the Pope."

1405 Dalton, J. "Cardinal Angelo Mai, and The Ambrosian Library, Milan." *American Bibliopolist*, 2 (February 1870), p84–85 (ICU, NcD).

The article summarized below is reprinted from *Notes and Queries*, 4th Ser. 4 (December 4, 1869), p472–73.

This library owes its existence to Cardinal Federigo Borromeo, nephew of St. Charles. Borromeo founded the Ambrosian College and joined the Ambrosian Library to it, opening it to the public as "Biblioteca Ambrosiana." It is said to contain more than 40,000 volumes and 15,000 manuscripts. Several of the most valuable manuscripts are discussed. Mai was named a doctor of the Ambrosian Library a while after coming to Milan and there he made several discoveries of ancient authors among the manuscripts. Cardinal Wiseman has written of Mai in *Recollections of the Last Four Popes, and of Rome in Their Times*, describing Mai's talent for reading manuscripts twice written, on palimpsests, and listing some of the works he produced between 1813 and 1819. Unfortunately, no life of Mai has yet appeared in English, although abundant materials are available. He died September 8, 1854 at Albano, leaving his manuscripts to the Vatican.

1406 [Ambrosian Library's Syriac Manuscripts.] *American Bibliopolist*, 6 (November–December 1874), p148 (ICN, OC).

The entire article follows.

"Among the very ancient Syriac MSS. in the Ambrosian Library at Milan, is a copy of the Peshito version of the Old Testement, which may be assigned to a period as remote as the sixth century. It is proposed to reproduce this ancient MS. in fac-simile by means of photo-lithography, under the direction of the Rev. Dr. A. Ceriani, the chief librarian of the Ambrosian. The edition will be in two volumes folio, and will consist of 660 photographed pages and about 60 pages of letter-press. The entire cost is estimated at £1,200, and the subscription price for a single copy is £10."

MODENA — DUCAL LIBRARY

1407 Fernow, M. "Account of the Present State of Literature and the Arts in Italy." *Monthly Anthology and Boston Review*, 3 (May 1806), p228–35 (NcD).

The article was taken from the *Monthly Magazine*. The part about libraries (p229) follows; it apparently refers to the Ducal Library at Modena.

"At the library, which is admirably arranged, and is particularly copious in historical works, I spoke with the Padres Pozzetti and Scotti, who jointly perform the office of librarian, which was before held by Tiraboschi, and his predecessor, Muratori, alone. The manuscripts occupy a spacious apartment. Among other curiosities I saw a beautiful copy of Provençal Poems, containing pieces by 143 different poets."

RIMINI — BIBLIOTECA CIVICA GAMBALUNGA

1408 [Public Library at Rimini.] *American Bibliopolist*, 5 (July–August 1873), p114–15 (NcD).

Many volumes held by the public library at Rimini, named the Gambalunga after the person who bequeathed it to the town, have attained additional value in the last two years, as the only other known copies were destroyed by the Paris communists. One example is the book "Les Fantasies de Mère Sote, avec privilège de François Ier," published in 1516. The book was printed on vellum and richly illuminated. The library also contains a small museum dealing with the question as to whether the Etruscans inhabited these regions before the Umbrians, and dealing with Gauls, who occupied the country for only about a hundred years, but who left enough Gallic blood behind to have had an impact, especially in regard to language and manners.

ROME

1409 [Plans for a Library on the History of Rome.] *Nation*, 15 (August 8, 1872), p92, 200 wds (NcU).

The Vatican Library being lacking in modern books and very difficult of access, it has been proposed to establish in Rome a library of works on the history of that city. The foundation of special libraries has been common of late (examples are given), and there is no lack of books on the history of modern Rome. Therefore, if funds can be obtained, a library can be formed quickly which will attract archival material from Italian families. Few Italians are now writing on this subject; foreigners have been doing more. It is to be hoped that native diligence and learning will rival that of the foreigners.

— VATICAN LIBRARY

1410 "Original Letters; from an American Traveller in Europe, to His Friends in This Country. Letter Seventeenth." *Monthly Anthology and Boston Review*, 5 (April 1808), p190–93 (NcU).

The part of the article about libraries (p191, 440 wds) is summarized below.

The most extraordinary object in the Vatican is the library, considered to be the largest in the known world. The Bodleian Library may rival it in numbers but in nothing else; the Vatican Library is fifteen times greater than the library at our university [Harvard]. The building is in the form of a T, about 200 by 900 feet. The books are enclosed for protection. Each alcove contains books on a particular subject or class of literature; the alcoves are marked with the names of their subjects. Each alcove has a painting relating to its subjects. Paintings show inventors and practitioners of arts and sciences from various periods of history. Those in one area depict the development of paper and writing.

1411 "Vatican Library." *Bibliotheca Sacra* [and Theological Review], 4 (May 1847), p409–10 (NcU).

Pope Nicholas V founded this library when he transferred the Lateran collection of early manuscripts to his new Vatican palace in 1447. Sixtus V erected the present building in 1588. There have been frequent purchases, bequests and donations. Most manuscripts are in an immense hall; the books are enclosed in painted cabinets. The halls lack the literary air of a library. (Several manuscripts are discussed.) The printed books, many bound in white vellum, are in glass cases in 8 to 10 rooms. The library lacks many works found in Protestant libraries. There are many engravings. There are 100,000 printed books and 35,000 manuscripts in the library, according to the custodian, but these figures seem excessive. The manuscript treasures are priceless. Complaints are made concerning the policy of the librarian, Cardinal Mai.

SAN LAZZARO

1412 [Island of St. Lazzaro.] *Bibliotheca Sacra* [and Theological Review], 4 (May 1847), p412 (NcU).
The part of the article about a library follows; the library is not identified.
"The library is worthy of a king's palace, most exact in its proportions and tasteful in its ornaments. The beautiful book-cases, made of the pear-tree, contain 15,000 volumes, handsomely bound. Among them are Elzevir and Aldi editions. In another room are 1000 Armenian Mss. mostly inedited and a copy of each of the works which have been printed at the establishment. Among these are translations of Young's *Night Thoughts* and of the *Paradise Lost.*"

SARDINIA

1413 [Libraries of the Island of Sardinia.] *Norton's Literary Gazette and Publishers' Circular*, n.s. 1 (July 15, 1854), p362 (NcU).
The entire article follows.
"The Island of Sardinia has two libraries, belonging to the Universities of Cagliari and of Sassari, and several cloister-libraries. All these libraries contain a number of costly manuscripts, on vellum and paper, rare old Italian and Spanish books, Bibles, Aldines, &c. The library of Cagliari has [sic] already been founded in 1626, but does not contain more than 20,000 volumes — the greatest part of these of value. It has a printed catalogue since 1812; Pietro Martini is the present librarian. The library of Sassari, with Antonio Maria Marras as librarian, numbers only about 1,000 volumes. Of the cloister-libraries, the two most valuable are at Cagliari."

— ROYAL LIBRARY

1414 Botta, Vincenzo. "Public Instruction in Sardinia." *American Journal of Education* (Barnard), 4 (December 1857), p479–504 (NcU).
The part of the article about libraries (p483, 210 wds) is summarized below.
The King's Library contains 30,000 volumes of ancient and modern works on history, travel, the arts, and so forth. There is a good collection of books on military science; also there is an excellent collection of manuscripts. The library has letters of Frederick the Great and Prince Eugene of Savoy as well as autographs of Napoleon. There are 2,000 drawings in the collection, twenty by da Vinci and some by Raphael, Correggio, and Titian. The library also has a fine collection of Chinese miniatures, painted on silk paper, of insects, birds, flowers, plants and dresses.

TRIESTE — TOWN LIBRARY

1415 [Town Library of Trieste.] *National Magazine: Devoted to Literature, Art, and Religion*, 7 (September 1855), p286 (InU, NcU).
The entire article follows.
"The Town Library of Trieste is said to possess seven hundred and seventy-two different editions of Petrarch's Poems, and one hundred and twenty-three

of the works of Pope Pius the Second, (Aeneas Sylvius Piccolomini, Bishop of Trieste.) The Library contains at present twenty-four thousand volumes, mostly works on commerce, navigation, geography, &c. Last year twenty-two very rare editions were added to the collection of the works of Petrarch and Aeneas Sylvius."

1416 [Town Library of Trieste.] *National Magazine: Devoted to Literature, Art, and Religion*, 8 (February 1856), p191 (InU, NcU).
The entire article follows.
"In the *Town Library of Trieste* there are seven hundred and seventy-two editions of 'Petrarch's Poems,' and one hundred and twenty-three of the works of Pope Pius the Second, (Aeneas Sylvius Piccolomini;) and it would need a separate building to hold all the editions of Shakespeare or Bunyan, along with the various literature which their works have called into existence. Within the last ten or twelve months a copy of Matthews's [*sic*] Bible, 1537, has sold for £150; Cranmer's, 1539, for £121; Coverdale's, 1535, for £365. First editions of Shakespeare have repeatedly sold for sums varying from £160 to £250."

TURIN — UNIVERSITY OF TURIN LIBRARY

1417 Botta, Vincenzo. "Public Instruction in Sardinia." *American Journal of Education* (Barnard), 4 (September 1857), p37–64 (NcU).
The part of the article that is about libraries (p58, 180 wds) is summarized below.
The library at the University of Turin was founded by Emanuel Philibert, Duke of Savoy, and has been endowed by successive rulers; it contains more than 110,000 volumes. The collection is strong on the subjects of theology, jurisprudence, politics, medicine, and surgery. The library has Arabic, Greek, Latin, Italian, and French manuscripts; also there is an incunabula collection as well as more than 100 ancient parchment manuscripts and a good collection of books in the fine arts.

VENICE — ST. MARK'S LIBRARY

1418 "Petrarch's Library." *American Bibliopolist*, 3 (November 1871), p440, 400 wds (NcD).
From Edward Smedley's *Sketches from Venetian History*. In the edition that was published by Harper in 1843, the information is found in volume 1, p202–04.
On September 4, 1362 Petrarch wrote to the Venetian Senate offering his books to St. Mark. "I wish, with the good-will of our Savior, and of the Evangelist himself, to make St. Mark heir of my library." The conditions of the gift were that the books never be sold or dispersed and that a building be provided for them. The collection included a manuscript of Homer, the Iliad and part of the Odyssey in Boccaccio's handwriting, and most of Cicero's work as translated by Petrarch. In the seventeenth century Tomasini asked to use the books and found many of them destroyed through neglect. He made a catalog of those that could be salvaged.

The Netherlands

1419 [Bibliography in the Netherlands.] *Publishers' Weekly*, 7 (January 30, 1875), p113, 160 wds (NcU).
The article summarized below is from the *Athenaeum*, London.
Bibliography has been enriched in Holland, we learn from the *Athenaeum*, by a Latin catalog of the Arab codices in the Library of the Royal Society, composed by Mr. B. Friederich, a "Bibliotheca Juridica"; a "Bibliotheca Ichthyologica et Piscatoria," by Mulder Bosgoed; a "Dutch Pacicrisy; or, Index to Law Cases," a voluminous work in four tomes, by Eug. and L. van Oppen. Mr. Campbell, the learned keeper of the Royal Library at the Hague, has continued that splendid work, "Annales de la Typographic Nèerlandaise au Quinzième Siècle." Mr. Spin has described "The MSS. of the Ducal Library at Wolfenbättel, with Paleographic Notes." Inventories of the archives of Zeeland and Middleburg have been published respectively by Mr. Visvlict and Mr. de Stoppelaar. Mr. Hooykaas's "Repertorium of the Literature relating to the Dutch Colonies: a Systematic Catalogue of all the Articles written in Miscellaneous Works and Periodicals published in the Netherlands between 1595-1865," should also be noted.

THE HAGUE — MUSEUM MEERMANNO-WESTREENIANUM

1420 [Museum Wertrenianum.] *National Magazine: Devoted to Literature, Art, and Religion*, 2 (February 1853), p188 (InU, NcU).
The entire article follows.
"The Dutch government has just taken possession of the valuable collections bequeathed to the State by the celebrated bibliopolist, Baron Wertreenen [sic] Van Tiellandt, and is about to form them into a separate museum, to be called the Museum Wertrenianum [sic]. They consist of a library of ten thousand rare and curious volumes, on the history of typography, bibliography, archaelogy, and numismatics; a gallery of pictures by the oldest masters, such as Cimabue, Giotto, etc.; ancient Greek and Roman sculptures, many of which are from Herculaneum and Pompeii; and a collection of ancient Greek, Roman, and oriental coins. Of the books, twelve hundred and thirty-three, it is said, bear date in the fifteenth century. There is, further, a collection of three hundred and eighty-five manuscripts, all anterior to the fourteenth century."

Poland

WARSAW — IMPERIAL UNIVERSITY LIBRARY

1421 [Imperial University Library, Warsaw.] *Publishers' Weekly*, 7 (January 30, 1875), p113 (NcU).
The entire article follows.
"M. C. F. Walther, principal librarian of the Imperial Library of St. Petersburg, published, at the expense of Prince Tossoupoff, in 1864, a 'Cata-

logue Bibliographique et Raisonné' of 'Les Elzevir de la Bibliothèque Impériale Publique de St. Petersbourg' (Dufour). Now M. S. J. Siennicki has followed suit by publishing *Les Elzevir de la Bibliothèque de l'Université Impériale de Varsovie* (Imprimerie du Journal *Wieck*). The volume is well got up, in oldfaced type, and illustrated with twenty-three plates on India paper, showing the various printers' marks of the Elzevirs, and the bookmarks, with autographs, of the libraries from which the finest copies were collected."

Portugal

LISBON — ACADEMY OF SCIENCES LIBRARY

1422 "The Missal of the Abbot Goncalves." *American Bibliopolist*, 6 (July–August 1874), p105, 350 wds (NcD).
The library of the Lisbon Academy of Sciences contains the beautiful missal of Estêvão Gonçalves Neto, which was formerly in the Convent of Jesus. Critics have praised the Pontifical Missal, which was created between 1610 and 1622. Folio size, it is ornamented with eleven pictures, drawn with pen and beautifully colored. Besides the large plates, there are numerous vignettes which show a fertile fancy and the hand of a miniature painter. The large plates are listed. Three years ago the government allowed the Parisian firm of Macia and Company to copy the missal by the chromo-lithographic process. A subscription list has been opened, which includes nearly all the crowned heads and art academies in Europe.

Prussia *see* Germany

Russia

1423 [Russian Bibliographic Work.] *Publishers' Weekly*, 7 (January 30, 1875), p113 (NcU).
The entire article, which follows, was reprinted from the *Athenaeum*, London.
"Russian bibliography has been enriched in 1874 by the indexes of A. Neustroef to various early Russian journals, the catalogue of Russian anonymous books by Gennad, Bertrand's Catalogue to the French Manuscripts in the Imperial Public Library, very many of which, of the highest value, were brought from France during the First Revolution, and by Dr. Harkavi's 'Description of the Samaritan Pentateuch Manuscripts.' This great and unique collection of Samaritan manuscripts was purchased from the Karaite antiquary and traveler, Firkovitch, in 1870."

ECHMIADZIN

1424 [Library of Armenian Manuscripts.] *Nation*, 2 (May 29, 1866), p675 (NcU).
The entire article follows. The town is now in the U.S.S.R.
"At the city of Etchmiadzin, near Mr. Ararat, the seat of the Armenian Patriarch, there exists a splendid library of about 3,000 Armenian manuscripts, which has hitherto been inaccessible to scholars. A catalogue of the library has been prepared, the MSS. are thrown open to scholars, and notice has been given that extracts will be sent to the learned in all parts of the world who will pay the expense of copying them out. Among the works in the library are unpublished books of the Fathers, and unpublished fragments of Aristotle and Diodorus Siculus."

ST. PETERSBURG

1425 "Libraries of St. Petersburgh." *American Journal of Science*, 5 (1822), p177–78 (InU).
The Imperial Library, housed in the Hermitage, contains 300,000 volumes. The Zaluski Library, formerly in Poland, has been housed in a beautiful building, and contains 300,000 volumes. The Zaluski is open to the public. The Library of the Grand Duke Constantine contains about 30,000 volumes in the fields of diplomacy, history and military art. The Academy of Sciences library contains 60,000 volumes, including 3000 in Chinese and other Asiatic languages. The Russian works, 3000 volumes, are kept separately. The Library of the Convent of Newski is made up of Slavonic manuscripts, acts of council, the writings of the German philosopher Wolf and theological writings. The Library of the Corps of Imperial Cadets has over 12,000 volumes. The University Library contains 11,000 volumes. Other libraries in St. Petersburg are those of the College of Medicine and the Economical Society. Additionally there are more than twenty noteworthy private libraries in the city.

— IMPERIAL PUBLIC LIBRARY

1426 [Zalusky Library.] *American Register; or Summary Review of History, Politics, and Literature*, 1 (1817), p368 (InU, NcU).
The entire article follows.
"The library of Zalusky, which belonged formerly to the Republic of Poland, has been, at length, placed in one of the finest edifices of Petersburg, with the inscription 'Imperial Library.' It is one of the richest of Europe; contains 300,000 volumes, and a multitude of precious manuscripts and rare editions."

1427 "The Imperial Public Library at St. Petersburg." *Norton's Literary Gazette and Publishers' Circular*, n.s. 1 (October 2, 1854), p490–92 (NcU).
The article summarized below draws from five sources which are listed at the beginning of the article.
The Imperial Public Library owes much to Russian military power. Begun by the Zaluski family in Poland, the library came to St. Petersburg after the fall of Poland in 1794. The plans of Empress Catherine and Emperor Paul for the library were not executed. The library was moved to its present building in 1801; responsibility for it has shifted several times. The fine Oriental manuscript

collection was drawn from several sources. The library is now first in Europe in terms of numbers; there were 262,000 volumes in 1810, 272,776 books and 13,000 manuscripts in 1831. Arranged in 19 departments are now about 600,000 printed volumes; 21,000 manuscripts; 30,000 autographs; 40,000 engravings; and 50,000 pamphlets. There is a complete manuscript catalog, and printed catalogs of parts of the collection, but no complete printed catalog. Visitors are welcome to examine or use the library.

1428 [Report (1868) of the Imperial Public Library, St. Petersburg.] *American Bibliopolist*, 2 (February 1870), p77 (ICN, ICU).
The entire article follows.
"The imperial public library at St. Petersburg has recently published its report for 1868 in a volume of 250 pages, chiefly devoted to the description of the rare and important collection of manuscripts it acquired, the most remarkable being the well-known 'Sinaitic Codex.' The printed book department was increased by 13,684 volumes. The reading room was used by 73,202 readers, and 240,811 books were consulted."

Scotland

EAST LOTHIAN COUNTY

1429 "Itinerating Libraries." *Museum of Foreign Literature, Science, and Art*, 9 (July 1826), p95, 500 wds (NcU).
From the fourth report of the East Lothian Itinerating Libraries, just published, we learn that founder Samuel Brown has formed five new divisions in the last two years, making a total of 24 fifty-volume divisions. A division is stationed in a village for two years and is cared for gratuitously by a person of character. After two years it is moved and replaced by another division with different books. Donations of books or money are received; no fee is charged unless books are damaged. Brown thinks a fee would be an obstacle to the plan's success. For 1000 volumes forming twenty divisions, there were 921 readers in 1824 and 616 in 1825. Circulation totalled 4554 and 3057 in those years. After the 1826 change, more readers are expected. Brown thinks 65 divisions could supply all of East Lothian County. These would cost £600 to establish, £30 annually to maintain.

1430 "Itinerating Libraries." *United States Literary Gazette*, 4 (July 1826), p313 (InU, NcU).
The entire article follows.
"These valuable institutions for supplying the poor with the means of reading, are increasing in Great Britain. In the county of East Lothian, Scotland, the books are divided into twenty-four divisions, of fifty volumes each. One of these is stationed in a village for two years, and put under the care of any person of good character, who will gratuitously do the duty of librarian. At the end of this period, it is removed to another village, and its place supplied by another division, containing a set of books entirely or almost entirely different. The removes take place at the same time through all the divisions, which revolve, as it

were, in a circle, and thus, by a very simple and cheap process, each of the twenty-four villages has a lot of books every two years."

EDINBURGH

1431 "Literary and Theological Institutions in Edinburgh." *Bibliotheca Sacra* [and Theological Review], 5 (May 1848), p385–88 (NcU).
The parts of the article about libraries (p386–87) are summarized below.
The library of the University of Edinburgh occupies the south side of the building. The Advocates' Library is north-west of the university; it contains the most valuable collection of books in Scotland, 150,000 printed volumes and 1700 manuscripts; the collection of Scottish poetry is very rich. The library receives a copy of every new work published in Great Britain and Ireland. Anyone may use it; members may draw 25 volumes at one time. Thomas Ruddiman, David Hume, Adam Ferguson have been librarians; David Irving now holds the office.

— ADVOCATES' LIBRARY

1432 "Astorga Library." *United States Literary Gazette*, 4 (June 1826), p235 (NcU).
The entire article follows.
"The Astorga library, recently purchased for the Faculty of Advocates at Edinburgh, is supposed to be the most curious collection of Spanish books existing out of Spain. It consists of about eight thousand volumes, and was sold for three thousand pounds. The collection is unrivalled (in so far as England is concerned) as to Romance, Chronicles, and Law. There is also a great deal of the Old Poetry, and a contemporary prose History of the Crusades, which is considered unique. The same body purchased only last year, a very fine Danish library entire at Copenhagen."

1433 "Scottish Manuscripts." *American Bibliopolist*, 3 (December 1871), p486, 190 wds (NcD).
The information is taken from the London *Globe*.
The late Dr. Robert Chambers has bequeathed to the Advocates' Library in Edinburgh a manuscript in ten volumes, "The Lyon in Mourning," written by the Right Rev. Robert Forbes, a bishop in the Scottish Episcopal Church who was under suspicion as a Jacobite at the time of the Stuart uprising of 1745. He was confined in Edinburgh Castle for a while; upon his release, he wrote an account of that rebellion, fixing in the bindings of the volumes some pieces of the Prince's [Charles Edward Stuart, the Young Pretender's] clothing.

— PHILOSOPHICAL INSTITUTION LIBRARY

1434 [Donation by Macaulay to Edinburgh Philosophical Institution Library.] *National Magazine: Devoted to Literature, Art, and Religion*, 7 (November 1855), p477 (InU, NcU).
The entire article follows.
"*Macaulay*, the historian, has presented an extensive and valuable donation of books to the library of the Edinburgh Philosophical Institution, of which he is president. The collection, which is elegantly bound, embraces some of the most important works in English history and literature."

— UNIVERSITY OF EDINBURGH SHAKESPEARE LIBRARY

1435 [Shakespeare Library for the University of Edinburgh.] *American Bibliopolist*, 4 (April 1872), p195 (ICN, OC).
The entire article follows.
"It is a singular circumstance that hitherto there has not been one Shakspearean collection in all Scotland. This will now no longer be the case. Mr. J. O. Halliwell has presented his choice and valuable Shakspearean library to the University of Edinburgh. We understand that in this remarkable collection, besides many rarities of nearly equal value, there are now fewer than thirty-eight of the original early quarto editions of the plays."

GLASGOW — GAS-LIGHT COMPANY LIBRARY

1436 "Mechanics' Institutions." *American Annals of Education* [American Journal of Education], 1 (March 1826), p134–44 (NcU).
The part of the article which describes the mechanics' library sponsored by the gas-light company of Glasgow (p137–39) appeared originally in the *London Mechanic's Magazine*; it is summarized below.
Three years ago the manager of the gas works proposed that the employees contribute a small monthly sum for the purchase of books. The Company agreed to contribute five guineas and to provide a room for the library. Fourteen men joined the first year, and presently all but fifteen employees are members. Not long ago the members decided to present lectures in rotation. Each individual is given two weeks to prepare his lecture before the membership. The library has 300 volumes mainly consisting of books on science, history, and voyages; however no works on religion are admitted since these books would cause disputes among the members.

PERTH — LITERARY AND ANTIQUARIAN SOCIETY

1437 "Perth Literary Society." *Museum of Foreign Literature, Science, and Art*, 10 (May 1827), p478, 470 wds (InU, NcD).
The Literary and Antiquarian Society of Perth is about to publish by subscription a volume of transactions that include some manuscripts owned by the Society. These include a Scottish chronicle covering the years from 1560 to 1654. Several other manuscripts dealing with Scotland are to be included. One of these is the manuscript of a volume printed at Antwerp in 1563 dealing with eighty-three questions of theology and addressed to John Knox.

Spain

1438 "Manuscripts Relating to South America." *United States Literary Gazette*, 4 (May 1, 1826), p117 (InU, NcU).
The entire article follows.
"It is supposed that there are several valuable manuscripts in libraries in Spain, relating to Mexico and South America, never yet published. They would

probably afford useful information respecting the condition of Mexico when first visited by the Spaniards in 1520."

1439 [Spanish Libraries.] *Norton's Literary Gazette and Publishers' Circular*, n.s. 1 (April 1, 1854), p168, 260 wds (NcU).
   The present libraries of Spain are listed. The list comes from Petzholdt's *Anzieger für Bibliographie*. Twenty-one libraries in ten cities are named, along with the date on which each was founded, and the name of the librarian. Eleven of the libraries are in Madrid.

ESCORIAL LIBRARY

1440 [Arabic Manuscripts in the Escorial.] *National Magazine: Devoted to Literature, Art, and Religion*, 9 (August 1856), p190 (InU, NcU).
   The entire article follows.
   "*Professor Joseph Müller*, one of the best Oriental scholars of the day, has been instructed by the King of Bavaria to repair to Spain, there to examine the Arabic MSS. in the Escurial library in Madrid [sic]. They consist of a collection made by Philip II., and which, in spite of the destruction of many of them by fire in 1671, is considered the richest in the world. The Escurial catalogue, by Kasiri, enumerates many, the careful examination of which will doubtless throw new light on Arabic history."

Sweden

STOCKHOLM — ROYAL ACADEMY OF MUSIC LIBRARY

1441 [Library of the Royal Academy of Music in Stockholm.] *National Magazine: Devoted to Literature, Art, and Religion*, 4 (April 1854), p382 (InU, NcU).
   The entire article follows.
   "There has recently been discovered in the library of the Royal Academy of Music at Stockholm the autograph manuscript of a mass composed by Michael Haydn, brother of the illustrious composer. The author presented it to the Academy in 1800, and it was executed for the first time on Christmas day last in the Catholic chapel, in presence of the queen and the queen-dowager."

UPPSALA — UNIVERSITY LIBRARY

1442 [Catalog of Manuscripts at Uppsala University, Sweden.] *Monthly Anthology and Boston Review*, 8 (April 1810), p285 (NcU).
   The entire article follows; Upsal refers to Uppsala.
   "Sweden — M. Aurivilius has printed a concise account of the Greek and Latin manuscripts, in the Library of Upsal. The former are sixteen in number, among which are nine of the New Testament, and of the Alexandrian translation of the old. Among the Latin manuscripts, the author mentions the ten first books of Livy, and a complete Horace. The first appears to be of the tenth, or eleventh

century. Several catalogues of the Library of Upsal have already been published; such as that of the books and manuscripts, given by the high Chancellor Lagardie, to the academy: (folio, Stockholm, 1672;) that of the Arabick, Persian, and Turkish manuscripts, given in 1705, by J. G. Sparrenfeld, (quarto, Upsal, 1806;) and that of ninety-three Greek, Hebrew, Chaldee, and Arabick manuscripts, sent to the Library by J. J. Bioernstael, (8vo. Stockholm, 1785)."

1443 [Codex Argenteus.] *Literary World*, Boston, 6 (November 1875), p88 (NcU).
This article, copied verbatim below, contains several errors. It refers to the "Codex Argenteus," which is a manuscript, not a printed book, at the University of Uppsala.
"A Swedish lady writes that the academical library in Upsala is very large, with 200,000 volumes and 7,000 MSS. The most valuable is the 'Codex Argentems,' or the Silver Book, containing the four Gospels in Moeso Gothic, by Bishop Ulfila; printed; it is said, 1,000 years before Guttenberg was born, with moveable type and 188 leaves."

Switzerland

1444 "Literary Institutions in Switzerland." *Bibliotheca Sacra* [and Theological Review], 5 (November 1848), p791–93 (NcU).
References to libraries are scattered through the article.
The town library at Berne contains 40,000 volumes and many manuscripts; more than 1000 are Helvetic manuscripts. The distinguished Albrecht von Haller, a native of Berne, was once librarian. The library of the University of Zürich has many original manuscripts of early reformers. The town library of Zürich has 45,000 printed volumes and manuscripts, and several literary treasures. The public or city library of Basel contains 50,000 volumes. The Council of Public Instruction controls the public library of Geneva, which is in the basement of the college. That library was founded by Bonivard in 1551, and contains about 40,000 volumes and 500 manuscripts; it is rich in works of ancient theology, and has several letters, books and manuscripts of particular interest.

1445 "Libraries in Switzerland." *American Bibliopolist*, 3 (December 1871), p488 (NcD, OC).
The entire article follows; it was taken from the London *Athenaeum*. It is printed again, with only slight changes in wording, in the July–August 1872 issue of the *American Bibliopolist (see 1446)*.
"It appears from a report presented to the Swiss Statistical Society at the Congress recently held at Basle, that Switzerland can boast of twenty-five public libraries, containing altogether 920,520 volumes; and not fewer than 1,629 other libraries, containing 687,939 volumes. The most extensive libraries are those of Zurich, which contains 100,000 volumes, of Basle, which has 94,000, and of Lucerne with 80,000."

1446 [Swiss Libraries.] *American Bibliopolist*, 4 (July–August 1872), p375 (NcD, OC).
The article is reprinted, with only slight changes in wording, from the

article, "Libraries in Switzerland," in the *American Bibliopolist* for December 1871, vol. 3, p488 *(see 1445)*.

Turkey

CONSTANTINOPLE

1447 [Libraries in Constantinople.] *Norton's Literary Gazette and Publishers' Circular*, 3 (December 15, 1853), p218 (NcU).
The entire article follows.
"There are numerous libraries in Constantinople. The number of volumes which they contain may be estimated at 80,000, reckoning both manuscripts and printed books. The literature of Arabia, Persia, and Turkey is represented in them; and the collection includes philosophical and theological works, poetry, history, books of science, and an immense number of those treatises on conduct and morals, to which the Turks attach great importance."

1448 "Libraries in Constantinople." *National Magazine: Devoted to Literature, Art, and Religion*, 4 (April 1854), p382 (InU, NcU).
The entire article follows; it varies only slightly from item 1447.
"There are numerous libraries at Constantinople: the number of volumes which they contain may be estimated at eighty thousand, reckoning both MSS. and printed books. The literature of Arabia, Persia, and Turkey, is represented in them; and the collection includes philosophical and theological works, poetry, history, books of science, and an immense number of those treatises on conduct and manners to which the Turks attach almost as much importance as the Chinese themselves."

Other Countries

(Outside the United States and Europe)

Australia

ADELAIDE — SOUTH AUSTRALIA PARLIAMENT — LIBRARY

1449 [Parliamentary Library of South Australia.] *American Bibliopolist*, 4 (February 1872), p67 (ICN, OC).
The entire article follows.
"A Catalogue of the Parliamentary Library of South Australia has been compiled by the librarian, Mr. F. Halcomb. The library is not an overwhelming one, seeing that 'the number of books at present in possession of the Houses is reckoned at 6,340.'"

SYDNEY — FREE PUBLIC LIBRARY

1450 "The Free Public Library, Sydney, N.S.W." *Publishers' Weekly* [Publishers' and Stationers' Weekly Trade Circular], 2 (October 24, 1872), p416, 250 wds (NcU).
The article summarized below was taken from *Trübners American and Oriental Literary Record*, London.
Sydney can now boast of having set an example to the citizens of London in the establishment of a really free public library. From the first report of the Trustees we find that though it was opened only in September, 1869, the books have been consulted by 136,957 visitors up to the end of 1871. The library contains about 22,000 volumes, and the number in daily use exceeds 300. Everyone is free to enter and use any volume he likes. The catalog is a model of simplicity and does infinite credit to its compiler, Mr. R. C. Walker, the Librarian. By not allowing visitors to replace volumes, the Librarian and his assistants can determine the kinds of books most in demand. We have little doubt that this library will soon rival in usefulness some of the larger but inaccessible treasures of the mother country.

1451 [Free Public Library, Sydney, N.S.W.] *Publishers' Weekly*, 5 (March 28, 1874), p337 (NcU).
The entire article follows.
"Sydney, New South Wales, is building a Free Public Library. So the good work goes on."

Babylonia and Assyria *see* Mesopotamia

Brazil

RIO DE JANEIRO — BIBLIOTECA NACIONAL

1452 "The Public Library at Rio de Janeiro." *Niles' National Register*, 49 (October 17, 1835), p99 (NcU).
The entire article follows.
"The public library at Rio Janeiro [*sic*] is an edifice connected to the emperor's palace, and contains about 70,000 volumes, most of which are very ancient. It contains a copy of the *first* printed edition of the Bible, on parchment, impressed in 1471, by the wonderful mechanism of *John Faust* [Johann Fust], the inventor of printing."

1453 [Dürer Woodcuts in the Rio de Janeiro Library.] *American Bibliopolist*, 6 (November–December 1874), p147 (ICN, OC).
The entire article follows.
"It is reported that, in the 'Biblioteca' at Rio Janeiro, a discovery has been made of thirty-seven woodcuts by Albert Dürer, in fine condition, the subject the 'Passion of Our Lord,' and dated 1524. No complete set, it is said, can be found elsewhere. In addition, there has also 'turned up' a copy of the celebrated Adam and Eve of 1504."

Canada

HAMILTON — LANCEFIELD'S LENDING LIBRARY

1454 [Lancefield's Lending Library.] *Publishers' Weekly*, 6 (September 19, 1874), p313 (NcU).
The entire article follows.
"At the close of its first year's work Lancefield's Lending Library, of Hamilton, Ontario, makes good returns. The catalogue has increased from the 295 volumes to 1495; its membership now numbers 335, and it has had a circulation through the year of 14,501 volumes. With so successful a start, and with the speedy additions promised by the librarian, the library can expect much from the future."

MONTREAL — MERCANTILE LIBRARY

1455 "Montreal Mercantile Library." *Norton's Literary Gazette and Publishers' Circular*, 3 (February 15, 1853), p19 (ICN, NcU).

The entire article follows.

"The twelfth Annual Report of this Association was presented November 22, and has since been printed. It appears that the whole number of members, life, honorary, and annual, is five hundred and five. It is stated, however, that of 400 clerks employed in retail stores, only 49 belong to this Association. The Library has 3,000 volumes. An unusual feature is well sustained in the reading room, to wit: the register of telegraphic intelligence. Merchants, it appears, depend upon this means for the prompt receipt of news."

ONTARIO

1456 "Public School Libraries in Upper Canada." *Norton's Literary Gazette and Publishers' Circular*, n.s. 1 (January 1, 1854), p9, 350 wds (NcU).

During the last year the legislature of Upper Canada has authorized establishing libraries in each public school municipality in the province. Appropriations were made for 75% of the amount raised locally. Returns were to have been made to the Superintendent of Schools by October 20, but the deadline was extended to July 1, 1854. Still, nearly 200 municipalities sent notice of appropriations before October 20. Thus, it is estimated that 50,000 to 75,000 volumes have already been put in circulation. The selection of books has often been assigned by local authorities to the Chief Superintendent of Schools; sometimes local authorities have made their own selections; and sometimes local authorities have selected to the amount of their appropriation and requested that the Chief Superintendent select the rest. The Superintendent, Mr. Ryerson, prefers the last method. Ryerson has also prepared and distributed annotated lists of books suitable for such libraries.

QUEBEC — PARLIAMENT LIBRARY

1457 "Canadian Parliamentary Library." *National Magazine: Devoted to Literature, Art, and Religion*, 1 (September 1852), p283, 190 wds (InU, NcU).

About 10,000 books have been purchased in England and France, and $20,000 has been used to refit the library. The French government has donated some books. The library has been destroyed and is being replaced. Except for the lost American collection the new library will surpass the old because the books have been more carefully selected. The library will contain more than 40,000 volumes.

1458 [Canada's Library of Parliament.] *National Magazine: Devoted to Literature, Art, and Religion*, 8 (March 1856), p287 (InU, NcU).

The entire article follows.

"The Canadian government has made a very large appropriation for the purpose of replacing the books in the Library of Parliament, destroyed by the great fire at Quebec, a year or two since. During the past fall very large purchases have been made on account of it both in London and Paris."

China

CANTON

1459 "Walks about Canton, in China. Libraries." *Parley's Magazine*, 4 (1836), p146 (InU).
The entire article follows.
"I have often heard of Circulating Libraries; but before I reached this country, I never saw them carried through the streets, so as to accommodate every person at his own door. The librarian, with an assortment of books in two boxes, suspended from a bamboo laid across his shoulder, and with a little rattle is his hand to let people know of his approach, sets off on his circuit, going from street to street, and from door to door. In this way he passes his whole time and gains a livelihood.
"The librarian whom I met at the door of the *hong* this afternoon, loaning books to the servants and coolies of the factories, said that his whole stock amounted to more than 2000 volumes. He loans his books, usually, for a very short time, and for a very small compensation."

HONG KONG

1460 Shuck, J. Lewis. "Cheering Letter from China." *Baptist Record*, 9 (February 28, 1844), p34, 520 wds (KyLoS).
The article is a letter written by Shuck from Hong Kong, September 5, 1843, giving details of missionary work. The part about libraries follows.
"I have reason to believe that I could find a sale for at least a dozen of your Society's Christian Libraries of 45 volumes. If you will let me have one dozen in neat, strong *cases with lock and key*, (at $20) the money shall be forthcoming, Providence favouring. Please kindly send by first ship."

Egypt

ALEXANDRIA — ALEXANDRIAN LIBRARY

1461 Sampsiceramus. [Ancient Library of Alexandria.] *Monthly Anthology and Boston Review*, 3 (January 1806), p5–9 (NcD, NcU).
The article summarized below is concluded in *Monthly Anthology*, 3 (February 1806), p58–61 *(see 1462)*.
Scholars must deplore the loss of the great library at Serapis; it is unlikely, however, that the parchments reputedly burnt by the Saracens still contained any of the collection of the Ptolemies, Lagus and his successor Philadelphus, who founded the Brucheion and the Serapeum libraries, respectively. During Caesar's war on Egypt, part, perhaps all of the Brucheion was destroyed. Any surviving manuscripts were probably removed to the Serapeum. Accounts of various historians establish that ancient manuscripts resided in the Serapeum until 640 A.D., but the contents of that collection are unknown. At that time

Alexandria was taken by the Saracens. The fate of the Serapeum was not known in Europe until 1660 when a collector of Arabian manuscripts produced evidence that the parchments, which were not in accordance with the Koran, had been used as fuel to heat the baths, and were all consumed in six months.

1462 "Account of the Ancient Library of Alexandria." *Monthly Anthology and Boston Review*. 3 (February 1806), p57-61 (NcD, NcU).

The article summarized below is a continuation of the article in *Monthly Anthology*, 3 (January 1806), p5-9 *(see 1461)*.

The evidence that the manuscripts were burned as fuel does not withstand critical examination, and appears to be false. Several historians disprove it, and several more do not mention so important an event. The library of the Ptolemies no longer existed in 640 when the Saracens took Alexandria. With the frequent warfare, it is likely that the library was destroyed or allowed to decay through neglect. Moreover, neither papyrus nor parchment would have served well to heat water. The Brucheion was destroyed under Aurelian, and the Serapeum under Theodosius the Great, at the urging of the bishop of Theophilus, in 391. Thus, the library was probably destroyed by the blind zeal of the Christians. Whatever books remained were probably gathered by the second Theodosius, and later transferred to monasteries, to Constantinople and elsewhere. By the ninth century, many were dispersed throughout Egypt.

1463 "Who Destroyed the Alexandrian Library?" *Iconoclast*, 1 (June 1870), p1, 550 wds (DLC).

The article summarized below was reprinted in *The Index*, vol. 1 (September 17, 1870), p2-3 *(see 116)*.

The story of the burning of the Alexandrian Library by the Saracens is a familiar one, long used as a weapon against the Mohammedan religion. We quote from the *Encyclopaedia Britannica* concerning the library and the story. The Alexandrian Library contained 700,000 volumes, 400,000 in the Brucheion, and 300,000 in the Serapeion. The library in the Brucheion was destroyed in the war with Julius Caesar. The Serapeion library remained and grew larger, but was destroyed when the Temple of Serapis was demolished under the archiepiscopate of Theophilus in A.D. 389. Abulpharagius, a Christian writer living six centuries later, first charged that Amru destroyed the library on the orders of Omar. Few of the 700,000 volumes collected by the Ptolemies remained by then. *Chambers' Encyclopaedia* says that a mob of fanatic Christians led by Theophilus destroyed the temple and probably its literary treasures.

1464 "Who Destroyed the Alexandrian Library?" *Index*, 1 (September 17, 1870), p2-3 (PSC).

The article was reprinted from an article in *The Iconoclast*, vol. 1 (June 1870), p1 *(see 1463)*.

CAIRO — CALIPHATE LIBRARY

1465 "Mahometan Libraries." *American Magazine of Useful and Entertaining Knowledge*, 2 (August 1836), p492, 225 wds (NcU, Oc).

About 1000 years ago the Caliphate library in Cairo filled forty halls with 1,500,000 manuscript volumes, in jeweled leather bindings. In about the year 1080 the library was pillaged by Turkish soldiers at which time many of the bindings were stripped off to be used as shoe-leather. Other volumes were destroyed and many were heaped up in piles that were eventually covered over by wind-blown sand. The hills thus formed near Cairo were called the "Hills of Books."

— KHEDIVAL LIBRARY

1466 [Khedival Library, Cairo, Egypt.] *Publishers' Weekly*, 5 (May 9, 1874), p458 (NcU).
The entire article follows.
"A library has been founded by the Khedive of Egypt at Cairo, for which he is collecting Arabic manuscripts preserved in mosques and monasteries throughout his dominions. He has already obtained thirty copies of the Koran, one of which is said to be 1150 years old."

India

1467 "The King of India's Library." *Ariel*, 2 (July 26, 1828), p51, 330 wds (InU, NcU).
Dabshilim, a king of India, had a library so vast that a thousand dromedaries were required to transport it from place to place. Realizing that he could never read all the books, the king ordered his scholars to make extracts of the most useful of the works' contents. After twenty years' labor, the extracts were compiled into a 12,000 volume encyclopedia, requiring only thirty camels to transport. Still this was more than the king could read so further condensation was ordered. After many years the contents were reduced to such size that a single mule could carry the load. By now, however, the king had grown old and not enough time remained for him to read the extracts. Finally a sage reduced the whole library to a few words. Most of the sciences comprise the single word "perhaps." The whole history of mankind contains only the words "born," "suffer," and "die." The remainder consists of the advice to love only what is good, think and speak only the truth, tame the passions, and realize that there is no happiness without virtue.

1468 "An Eastern Story." *Merry's Museum and Parley's Magazine*, 12 (December 1846), p175, 170 wds (ICN, InU).
An eastern prince who owned a large library ordered his librarians to abstract the contents of its books because he never could expect to read all of them. After twenty years the library was compressed into as many books as could be carried by a camel, but the prince was not satisfied, and so he ordered the library be further condensed. The result was a single volume, but the prince, who by then had become old and infirm, commanded the librarians to try again. The final result was a single sentence: "Man is born—breathes for a while—dies and is seen no more."

Israel

1469 "Further Notices of Ancient Libraries." *Norton's Literary Gazette and Publishers' Circular*, n.s. 2 (July 16, 1855), p295, 370 wds (MWiW).
The article is taken from *Notes and Queries*, vol. 11, for June 23, 1855, p493. It refers to an earlier article in *Norton's Literary Gazette*, n.s.2, for June 15, 1855, p253–55, also from *Notes and Queries (see 13)*.

Your learned correspondent may be able to look before the period of the Ark for the formation of libraries. The sin and discomfiture of Amalek were to be written in a book before the Children of Israel reached Sinai; and Job, who undoubtedly pre-dated Moses, speaks familiarly of books. The Canaanites may have had libraries before the Israelites came because of references to Kirjath-sepher, "the city of books," which was later known as Debir, "an oracle." The use of these names implies a seat of learning. If the Israelites did not destroy the books, they might have continued to use the name, Debir.

Mesopotamia

1470 "Assyrian Libraries." *American Bibliopolist*, 7 (June 1875), p156–58 (NcD, OC).
Every large city in ancient Mesopotamia had a library; the preserved documents frequently indicate that the libraries were for the use of the people. These libraries' collections were almost entirely clay tablets written in cuneiform. Most of the excavated tablets from the libraries of Sennacherib and Assurbanipal were taken to the British Museum. These tablets provide the basis for what is known about Babylonian and Assyrian literature, and include evidence of an early system of marking the tablets in which every work had a unique press-mark. The collection now at the British Museum includes works on agriculture, law, prayers, proverbs, and fables, and documents pertaining to history and government.

Mexico

1471 "Museums and Libraries in Mexico." *Poughkeepsie Casket*, 2 (August 25, 1838), p78 (DLC, NjR).
The part of the article about libraries follows. The first two sentences refer to Mexico City.

"The Public Library contains about 11,000 volumes. There are four convents, all of which have libraries—the total amount of volumes being more than 32,000. It is intended to establish a library and museum at Potosi. In many of the provinces libraries exist, varying from 1000 to 3000 volumes."

Turkey in Asia

MARDIN

1472 "Discovery of an Ancient Book." *American Bibliopolist*, 4 (September 1872), p459–60 (NcD).

The "Panchatantra," a work treating political questions in the guise of fables of animals, grew out of a longer Indian series existing in the sixth century. Though now lost, a translation into Pehlewi done in Persia around 531–579 served as the basis for an eighth century translation into Arabic. According to a thirteenth century Nestorian writer, a certain Periodentes made a Syriac translation of the book from the Indian original around 570. This Syriac version, long sought by oriental scholars, has now been found at Mardin in the library of the Jacobite Monastery there. The successful search for the book is described in some detail. As the owners of the library were unwilling to part with the volume, "Qualilag-v-Damnag," the discoverers had a copy made of its contents, which will soon be published with a translation and an introduction by three German professors.

Venezuela

CARACAS

1473 [Libraries in Caracas, Venezuela.] *Nation*, 3 (November 29, 1866), p424, 170 wds (NcU).

A writer in Trübner's *American and Oriental Library Record* gives a very unfavorable account of three public libraries in Caracas. The National Library, with about 5,000 volumes, is in the Franciscan monastery; its books are in a bad state. The present librarian has a monthly salary of $50 but has received no pay for two years; he may have to do what previous librarians have done, sell some of the books to support himself. The University Library has a valuable collection of a little over 4,000 volumes on natural history and medicine, but has no catalog. The Seminary Library contains theological works of the sixteenth, seventeenth, and eighteenth centuries, some being of bibliographical interest. It has no catalog and no librarian.

Illustrations Accompanying the Articles

The date (in parentheses) is the year of publication of the article; the date of the original drawing or painting is seldom given in the article. The entry number in this volume is in boldface.

Library Buildings or Rooms

American Antiquarian Society, Worcester, Mass. (1852), exterior, **690**.
Astor Library, New York: (1852) exterior, **832**; (1855) exterior and interior, **842**.
Boston Athenaeum (1852) exterior, **502**.
Boston Public Library: (1859) exterior, interior, and plans, **555**; (1871) exterior and interior, **177**.
Brown University Library (Manning Hall) (1852) exterior, **1101**.
Harvard College Library (Gore Hall): (1852) exterior, **634**; (1870) exterior, **647**.
Library Company of Philadelphia (1852) exterior, **1044**.
Mercantile Library, New York (1871) exterior and interior, **914**.
New York State Library, Albany (1852) exterior, **758**.
Redwood Library, Newport, R. I. (1852) exterior, **1091**.
Royal Library, Berlin (1853) exterior, **1362**.
Royal Library, Munich (1853) exterior, **1377**.
Ste Geneviève Library, Paris: (1853) plan, **36**; (1853) interior, **1335**.
Smithsonian Institution, Washington, D.C. (1852) exterior, **371**.
What Cheer House (Hotel), San Francisco (1861) interior, **287**.
Williams College (Lawrence Hall) (1853) exterior, **686**.
Yale College Library: (1843) exterior and plan, **245**; (1847) exterior; **314**; (1852) exterior, **315**.
Young Men's Christian Association, New York: (1869) exterior, **947**; (1869) interior, **948**; (1870) interior, **949**; (1870) interior, **950**.
Young Men's Christian Association, San Francisco: (1869) exterior, **289**; (1869) exterior, **290**.

Plans for a suggested library (1853), **36**.

Portraits

Astor, John Jacob, 1796 and 1816 (1855), **842**.
Bates, Joshua (bust) (1870), **177**.

Brown, Nicholas (1857), **1093**.
Everett, Edward (1859), **557**.
Green, John (1863), **687**.
Ticknor, George (1871), **177**.
Wadsworth, James (1858), **751**.
Wood, William (1857), **109**.

Other Illustrations

Justice John Marshall falling down in the stacks of the Library of Congress (1872), **358**.
Portable bookcase (1838), **214**.
New hinge for doors on bookcases (1828), **71**.

Index

Numbers in this index refer to individual items in the bibliography, not to pages. The index includes not only the *names of all authors* of articles if the names accompany the articles or have been learned from other sources but, as well, the names of all persons mentioned prominently in the articles. It includes, also, the *names of individual libraries* unless they are merely mentioned in lists in the articles. However, libraries lacking distinctive names are included only under the names of the cities or towns where they are located; for example, references to the Boston Athenaeum are under "Boston Athenaeum" and references to the Bibliothèque Municipale in Tours, France, are under "Tours, Bibliothèque Municipale." Under the *name of a city or town* are gathered all references to individual libraries located there, arranged alphabetically by name of library. Under the *name of an American state or foreign country* are listed only the numbers for items that are about libraries in more than one city within the state or country and items about libraries that begin with the name of the state or country. For example, the entry "Massachusetts" is followed by numbers for items, each of which is about libraries in two or more towns in the state; the subdivision "Historical Society" under "Massachusetts" lists all items about the Massachusetts Historical Society. Every reference to an individual library or group of *libraries of a particular type* is listed under the name of the type; if there are more than about half a dozen references to libraries of that type, they are arranged by state or foreign country. For example, all references to the Boston Athenaeum will be included with other references to athenaeums in Massachusetts under the heading "Athenaeums — Massachusetts." If there are more than half a dozen references to any library process or attribute, the heading is subdivided, although in these cases it has seemed more useful to divide according to type of library. Examples of such headings are "Collection building," "Library buildings" and "Library catalogs." Attention should be called to a few headings that the reader might not have chosen: for example, "Series of books for school libraries" and several that begin "Libraries...," "Library...," or "Reading...." Finally, two headings are not really about the subject matter of the articles and a third is partly about the subject matter and partly about the form. The heading "Book reviews" is used for articles that review books of any kind except printed library catalogs; the heading "Lectures sponsored by libraries" is used for articles that summarize the texts of these lectures, no matter what the subjects, and the heading "Library literature" is used for any references to books about libraries other than library catalogs.

Index 396

A

A. 1032
Abbot, Ezra 514, 645–46
Abbott, G. D. 214
Abstracting 1467–68
Academical and Theological Institution, New Hampton, N.H. 720
Académie des Sciences Morales et Publiques, Paris 1318
Academies (schools) 243, 682, 791
Academy of Sciences, Lisbon, Portugal 1422
Acquisitions (*see also* Book selection; Collection building; Gifts) in: athenaeums 493; college and university libraries 323–24, 411, 422, 464, 629, 633, 945, 1098, 1385; commercial circulating libraries 1264; mercantile libraries, 704, 881, 893; music libraries 653; national libraries 355, 1146, 1240, 1252, 1367; public libraries 552; scientific libraries 370, 373; social libraries 1039; state libraries 760–61; theological libraries 943, 954
Adams, C. F., Jr. 677–80
Adams, J. Q. 496, 541
Adams, John 141, 541
Adams & Co., express firm 270
Addresses before members of library associations *see* Lectures sponsored by libraries
Adelaide, South Australia, Parliament Library 1449
Advertisements for: books 91, 95; libraries 932
Advocates' Library, Edinburgh, Scotland 1431–33
Agricultural libraries: in general 141–46, 435, 463, 769, 1124; Maine 435; Massachusetts 463, 526; New York (state) 147–53, 769, 817, 961; Pennsylvania 1002; United States 147–53; Vermont 1121; Virginia 1124
Agricultural library associations 146, 1121
Agricultural Library Society, Rutland, Vt. 1121
Agricultural literature 79, 145, 744–45, 748, 817
Agricultural society libraries: Massachusetts 526; New York (state) 769, 817, 961; Pennsylvania 1002; United States 147–53; Virginia 1124
Agricultural Society of Maine 435
Ajaccio, Corsica, Bibliothèque Municipale 1310
Albany, N.Y.: State Legislature 729, 747, 758; State Library 756–66; Young Men's Association Library 767–68
Albany County, N.Y., Albany County Agricultural Society 769
Albrecht, H. 171, 413, 465
Alcott, A. B. 619
Aldrich, Mr. 1322
Alexandria, Va., Alexandria Library 1123
Alexandrian Library, Egypt 12, 14, 1461–64
Alexis Alexandrovich, Grand Duke of Russia 694
Allegheny College Library, Meadville, Pa. 1001
Allen, W. F. 1137
Alsace 1382, 1385
Alvarado, Calif., Odd Fellows Library 252
Ambrosian Library, Milan, Italy 1404–06
American Academy of Arts and Sciences, Boston 475, 504, 506
American and Foreign Christian Union Library, NYC 193–94, 816
American Antiquarian Society Library, Worcester, Mass. 74, 688–90
American Association for the Advancement of Science, Philadelphia 342
American Bible Society, NYC 77
American Congregational Union, NYC 100
American history *see* Americana
American Institute, NYC 217, 817–18
American Institute of Education 460
American Institute of Instruction, Boston 213
American Library Association (proposed) 130

American Oriental Society, Boston 504, 506
American Revolution 762, 1082
American Seamen's Friend Society, NYC 64–66
American Social Science Association, Boston 54, 117/8, 176, 869
American Society for the Diffusion of Useful Knowledge 214–15, 732, 753
American Statistical Society Library, Boston 518
American Sunday School Union, Philadelphia 218, 638
American Unitarian Association (church): 485, 1115; its Committee on Juvenile Literature 232; its Ladies' Commission on Sunday-school Books 233–35
Americana in: college and university libraries 792–93, 795–96; historical society libraries 442, 524–25, 713, 773, 922, 924, 1106, 1133, 1135–40; Library of Congress 349–51, 354; private libraries 263; public libraries 563, 606, 610; social libraries 928; state libraries 417, 756, 761–63, 766, 996, 1128
Ames, Rev. Mr. 275
Amherst, Mass.: Amherst College Library 470–71; Public Library 472–73
Amiens, France, Bibliothèque Municipale 1308
Amsterdam, Netherlands, private libraries 53
Andover, Mass., Andover Theological Seminary 74–77, 245, 462, 474
Andrade Library 47
Anglo-American Association, London 395, 397
Ann Arbor, Mich., University of Michigan Library 693–94
Annals of the Bodleian Library, Oxford, A.D. 1598–A.D. 1867 (by W. D. Macray) 644, 1286
Anonymous works 128, 1069
Anthology Club, Boston, Mass. 502
Anthon, Charles 794
Anti-slavery movement 795–96
Antoninus, Marcus Aurelius 1404
Appleton, Samuel 466, 507
Appleton, T. G. 568, 587–88

Apprentices' libraries *see* Mechanics' libraries; *see also* names of cities and towns
Arber, Edward 136, 1068
Archaelogical materials in libraries 317
Architectural literature 823, 1185
Architecture of libraries *see* Library buildings
Aristotle 1308
Armenia 1424
Arndt, Dr. 1343
Arsenal Library, Paris 1299, 1319, 1347
Art, collections *see* Engravings
Art, literature about 563
Art exhibitions 492–94
Assyria 1470
Astor, J. J. 747, 800, 820, 824, 832, 842, 845, 847, 851–52
Astor, W. B. 843–44, 847, 850, 854
Astor Library, NYC 17–18, 110, 115, 117/8, 121, 176–77, 561, 747, 800, 820–58, 869, 873
Astorga Library, Edinburgh, Scotland 1432
Asylum libraries 859
Athenaeum, London, Eng. (periodical) 1218
Athenaeums: Connecticut 305; England 1207, 1218; Massachusetts 110, 475, 481–82, 485–514; New Hampshire 721; New York (state) 770–72, 952; Pennsylvania 1021–27, 1081–83; Rhode Island 1089, 1093–95; Vermont 1122
Athenian Institute, Philadelphia 28, 76, 1063–64
Athens, Ga., University of Georgia Library 384
Auctions of books *see* Book auctions
Augusta, Empress of Germany 864
Australia 1449–51
Austria 1165–66, 1354

B

B. 581, 648
B., J. K. 65
B., M. 134, 139

B., W. 463
Babb, Samson 1082
Babbington, Churchill 1201
Babylonia 1470
Bacon, Francis 709
Bacon, H.D. 703
Bacon, Roger 1308
Bailey, H. M. 308
Bailey, J. J. 19
Bailly, M. 2
Baine, Judge 297
Balbi, Adriano 1, 26
Baltimore, Md.: 69, 441; Baltimore Library Company 441–42; Maryland Historical Society Library 441–42; Mercantile Library 443–44; Peabody Institute Library 445
Bancroft, Hubert 263–65
Bancroft Pacific Library, San Francisco, Calif. 263–65
Bangor, Me.: Bangor Theological Seminary 437; Mercantile Library Association 129, 249, 438
Baptists, archives 423
Bar association libraries 389, 867–68, 1075
Barker, John 222
Barksdale, G. A. 1129
Barnard, Henry 197, 302, 1088, 1090
Barney, H. H. 965
Barnwell, J. G. 1068–69
Barry, P. 1314
Bartlet, William 245
Bartlett, J. R. 42
Bartlett, Richard 73
Barton Library, Boston Public Library 563, 586, 590–92, 594–95, 604, 607, 951
Basel, Switzerland 1444–45
Bastia, Corsica, Bibliothèque Municipale 1310
Bates, Joshua 177, 543–44, 554, 556
Bates, S. P. 1000–01, 1076, 1084
Batho[e], William 15
Battersea Literary and Scientific Institution, London 1215
Bavaria see Germany
Bavarian State Library, Munich 760, 1354, 1375–78
Beach, H. P. 319
Beane, S. C. 232
Bede 1346

Beecher, H. W. 123
Belgium 1151, 1167–70
Bell, John 15
Bement, C. N. 744
Benjamin, S. G. W. 41
Berkeley, George 313, 315, 627
Berks County (Pa.) Institute 205
Berlin, Ger.: 38, 1156, 1354–57; Military Library 1311; Reichstag Library 1372; Royal Library (Königlichen Bibliothek) 38, 1156, 1358–71
Bessarion, Johannes, Cardinal 1397
Bethel Union, Charleston, S.C. 1113
Bethel Union, NYC 56
Bethune, G. W. 1064, 1099
Bevan, M. L. 1059
The Bible 670, 1053, 1259, 1361, 1416, 1452, 1469
Bibliography 5, 8–9, 374, 1419, 1423
Biblioteca National, Rio de Janeiro, Brazil 1452–53
Bibliotheca Bibliographica, by Julius Petzholt 8
Bibliothèque Municipale *see* the name of the city or town where the library is located
Bibliothèque *see* the other main word in the name of the library except for the following libraries:
Bibliothèque Historique de la Ville de Paris 1320
Bibliothèque Nationale, Paris 3, 28, 42–43, 1155, 1159, 1299, 1314, 1316, 1321–34, 1337
Bibliothèque Publique et Universitaire de Genève, Geneva, Switzerland 1444
Bibliothèque Royale, Brussels 1168–70
Biddle, Nicholas 1022
Bigelow, Artemas 961
Bigelow, J. P. 557
Binding of books 178–79
Bingham, Caleb 327
Bingham Library for Youth, Salisbury, Conn. 208, 327
Birmingham, Eng., Public Library 1194–96
Bismarck-Bohlen, F. T. A., Graf von 1383
Blackie, G. S. 919

Blacks, libraries for 476, 936, 1033–34, 1115
Blacks, literary associations for 1029
Bloomingdale Asylum for the Insane 859
Blunt, Joseph 922
Boardinghouse libraries 1113
Bodleian Library, Oxford University 644, 1282–89
Bodley, Sir Thomas 1284, 1287
Böcking Collection 1382
Bohemia 1172
Bohemian Chronicle by Dalemil 1203
Bollandists 1171
Bolton, Eng., Public Library 1197
Bonaparte, Louis 1373
Bonaparte, Lucien 1310
Bonaparte, Napoleon 1008
Bond, George 633
Bonivard, François 1444
Bonnange, Ferdinand 1305–07
Book advertisements 91, 95, 124
Book auctions 17, 89, 830, 1161, 1241, 1365, 1367
Book catalogs *see* Library catalogs
Book discounts to libraries 139
Book of Kells 1396
Book reviews 4, 7–8, 18, 26, 48–49, 77, 98, 138, 176, 231, 447, 456, 459, 490–93, 499, 501, 509, 530, 559, 627–28, 631, 644–45, 671, 1139, 1179, 1186, 1201, 1242, 1286, 1352. Reviews are also entered under titles, under names of authors of books, and, when known, under reviewers' names. *See also* Library catalogs; Library literature
Book selection: in general 84, 138, 176, 1199; for agricultural libraries 961; children's libraries 234; college and university libraries 68, 427–28, 1101; military libraries 1182; national libraries 339; public libraries 181, 190, 673, 831, 841; school district libraries 196, 198, 448, 453, 455, 460, 726, 737, 739, 749, 1456; school libraries 215–17, 222–23; Sunday School libraries 232, 234; theological seminary libraries 1080; *see also* Collection building
Bookbinding 178–79

Books: individual books are listed in this index under their titles; entries under authors' names do not include the titles of books.
Books about libraries *see* Library literature
Books, exchange of *see* Exchange of books and periodicals
Boone, Daniel 422
Bopp, Franz 794
Bordeaux, France, Bibliothèque Municipale 1309, 1328
Bordesley Abbey, Eng. 1198
Boston: 69, 72, 475–84, 1364; (literature about Boston) 610; American Academy of Arts and Sciences 475, 504, 506; American Institute of Instruction 213; American Oriental Society 504, 506; American Social Science Association 54, 117–18, 176, 869; American Statistical Society 518; American Unitarian Association Library 485, 1115; Anthology Club 502; Athenaeum 110, 117, 462, 468, 475, 477, 481–82, 486–514, 628; Boston Library 327, 515; Boston Medical Library 489, 490; Boston Society of Natural History 516; Columbian Circulating Library 517; Congregational Library Association 100, 518–20; East Boston Library Association 521; General Theological Library 129, 522; King's Chapel Library 618; Loring's Select Library 523; Massachusetts Historical Society 475, 524–25; Massachusetts Horticultural Society, 526; Massachusetts Scientific Association 490, 527; Mechanics' Apprentices' Library 528; Mercantile Library 167–68, 464, 481, 483, 529–41; Old South Church and Society 524; Public Library 45, 52, 110, 116, 173–74, 177, 182, 187, 191, 465, 469, 481–83, 542–614, 803, 850; Public Library *Bulletin* 565; Social Law Library 615; State Library 616–17; Theological Library (Fourth Social Library) 618
Boswell, J. I. 845
Botta, Vincenzo 1414, 1417

Bouton, Nathaniel 713
Boutourlin, Count 26
Bowdoin College and Medical School Library, Brunswick, Me. 439
Bowen, Francis 631, 1097
Bradford, C.F. 649
Bradford, Gamaliel 88
Bradshaw, Henry 1200, 1202
Brandywine (frigate) 57
Breck, Samuel 1023
Brevoort, Carson 858
Brevoort, J. R. 855
Brigham, William 1179
Bristol Academy Library, Taunton, Mass. 682
British Museum, London: 7, 18, 42–43, 45, 52, 850, 1146, 1149, 1157, 1190, 1214, 1216, 1219–55, 1396, 1470; *General Catalogue of Printed Books* 52, 1231
Brock, R. A. 1129
Brook farm 619
Brooklyn, N.Y.: Athenaeum 770–72; Long Island Historical Society Library 773–74; Mercantile Library 444, 775–78; Naval Lyceum 780; Navy Yard Library 779–82; *see also* Flatbush; New York City
Brooks, Edward 527
Brooks, M. J. 680
Brothers in Unity, Yale College 319
Brown, James 482
Brown, Nicholas 1093, 1101, 1105
Brown, Samuel 1151, 1429
Brown University Library, Providence, R.I. 1089, 1093, 1096–1105
Browne, Sir William 1191
Brownson, O. A. 455
Bruce, George 937–38
Brunet, J. C. 26
Brunswick, Me., Bowdoin College and Medical School Library 439
Brussels, Belgium: Bibliothèque Royale 1168–70; Bollandists 1171
Buckminster, J. S. 499
Buckminster, Joseph 499
Bucknell Library, Crozer Theological Seminary, Upland, Pa. 129, 1080
Bucknell University (The University at Lewisburg), Pa. 999–1000
Buffalo, N.Y.: Grosvenor Library 783–88; Young Men's Association Library 94, 789
Buildings, library *see* Library buildings
Bulletin of the Boston Public Library 563, 565
Bunker Hill, Mass. 608
Bunyan, John 1416
Burgess, A. H. 397
Burl, Jesse 769
Burlington, Vt.: Lyceum 1117; University of Vermont Library 77, 118–19
Burrowes, T. H. 985
Burslem, Eng., Wedgewood Institute 1199
Business literature 427–28
Buswell, E. W. 526
Butler, J. D. 1131
Buxton, Charles 801

C

C., F. 1268
C., N. E. 921
Cabinet of Natural Science, Westchester, Pa. 1081
Cagliari, Sardinia, University Library 1413
Cairo, Egypt: Caliphate Library 1465; Khedival Library 1466
California: 250–51; California Academy of Natural Sciences 250
Caliphate Library, Cairo, Egypt 1465
Calkins, R. R. 699, 711
Cambridge, Mass.: Harvard College Law School, Dane Library 162–63; Harvard College Library 38, 67–68, 74, 110, 157, 462, 464, 468, 477, 588, 620–52; Harvard Musical Association Library 171, 413, 465, 653; Sparks Library 654–55
Cambridge University Library, Cambridge, Eng.: 38, 1191, 1200–03; Trinity College Library 1203
Canada, Parliament Library, Quebec 1457–58
Canton, China 1459

Capen, Edward 544
Caracas, Venezuela 1473
Carlyle, Thomas 395, 1199
Cassino, Italy, Bibliotheca Casinensis 1401–02
Catalogs, library *see* Library catalogs
Catalogue of editions of the Holy Scriptures in Various Languages and Other Biblical Works in the Library of the American Bible Society 77
Catalogue de la Bibliothèque de son Excellence, M. le Comte Boutourlin. Florence, 1831 26
Catalogue of Prints and Drawings in the British Museum: Division I. Political and Personal Satires (by F. G. Stephens) 1250
Catalogue of the Books Belonging to the Library of the University of Vermont 77
Catalogue of the Books in the Boston Athenaeum, 1827 491
Catalogue of the Hebrew Books in the Library of the British Museum 1237–38
Catalogue of the Library of Harvard University, in Cambridge, Massachusetts 628
Catalogue of the Library of the Theological Seminary in Andover 77
Catalogue of the Mercantile Library of Boston, 1854 540
Catalogue of the Pictures Exhibited at the Fourth Exhibition ... Boston Athenaeum, 1830 493
Catalogue of the Pictures in the Athenaeum Gallery, Boston, 1829 492
Cave Hunting (by W. B. Dawkins) 605
Caves 605
Caxton, William 1054, 1336
Censorship 1338
Centennial Exposition, Philadelphia 1876 140
Centre Benevolent Society, Iredell County, N.C. 963
Ceriani, A. M. 1406
Cervantes Saavedra, Miguel de 649

Challens, J.C. 220, 988
Chalons (of Mons, Belgium) 1167
Chambers, Robert 1433
Chapel Hill, N.C., University of North Carolina 962
Charles I, King of England 1361
Charleston, S.C.: Bethel Union 1113; Mercantile Library Association 1114
Charlestowne, Mass., Neck School Library 656
Cheltenham, Eng., Sir Thomas Phillipps Library 1204
Chester, Pa., Crozer Theological Seminary 129, 1080
Chester County Athenaeum, Westchester, Pa. 1081–83
Chestnut Hill, Pa. 1028
Chetham, Humphrey 1272
Chetham's Library, Manchester, Eng. 1272–74
Chicago, Ill.: 387–90; Chicago fire (1871) 387–88, 392; Chicago Historical Society 387; Chicago Library Association 391; Franklin Society Library 392; Free Theological Library 390, 393; Hengstenberg Theological Library 390, 393; Law Institute Library 389–90; Michigan Avenue Free Library and Reading Room 394; Public Library 191, 394–409; Young Men's Association 387; Young Men's Christian Association Library 389–90; Young Men's Christian Union Library 389–90, 410
Children, reading of *see* Reading of children
Children's literature 233
Chinese language and literature, libraries 1214, 1459
Chittenden, S. B. 775
Christian Hall Library, Philadelphia 1028
Christian Library (series) 203
Church, Alonzo 384
Church and synagogue libraries (*see also* Sunday school libraries): California 291; England 1205; Italy 1410–11, 1418; Massachusetts 618; New York (state) 46, 50–51, 940–

Index 402

42; Pennsylvania 1070; South Carolina 1115
Cibrario, Luigi, Count 1403
Cincinnati: 966; Cincinnati Law Library 967; The Cincinnati Library 968; Historical and Philosophical Society of Ohio 366, 968–69; Public Library 184, 970–74; Young Men's Mercantile Library Association 168, 975–78, 1114
Circulating libraries *see* Commercial circulating libraries; Social libraries
Circulation rules *see* Regulations for library use
Cist, C. E. 977
Clam-Gallas Library, Austria 1165
Clapp, Otis 78
Clark, J. S. 519
Clark, N. G. 1118
Clarke, Robert 968
Clarke, Robert, & Co. 967
Classen Library, Copenhagen 1173
Classical libraries 2–3, 12–14, 35
Classification *see* Library catalogs
The Classified Index to the Catalogue of the New York Mercantile Library 912
Cleveland, Ohio 94
Clinton, George 762
Clinton Hall Association, NYC 883, 902–03, 905, 915
Clinton State Prison Library, N.Y. 746
Coates, Mr. 529
Cobden Club 804
Codex Argenteus 1443
Codex Sinaiticus 982, 1428
Coffin, Edward 887
Cogswell, J. G. 17, 86, 177, 634, 822–35, 837–40, 842, 848, 853, 855
Cogswell, W. 676
Cogswell, William 719
Coin collections 1170
Cold Springs, Calif. 253–54
Collection building (*see also* Acquisitions; Book selection; Gifts; Weeding of collections): in general 29, 115, 332; in: college and university libraries 418, 643, 793; music libraries 1155; national libraries 1249; public libraries 177; religious society libraries 485

College and university libraries: in general 39, 1097; in Bohemia 1172; Connecticut 245, 311–25; Denmark 1173; England 1191, 1200–03, 1260, 1282–89; France 1159, 1317; Georgia 384; Germany 1354, 1379–87; Illinois 411–12; Ireland 1396; Italy 1413, 1417; Kentucky 418–23; Louisiana 427–28; Maine 439; Massachusetts 68, 110, 462, 464, 470–71, 588, 620–52, 686; Michigan 693–94; New Hampshire 717–18; New Jersey 723; New York (state) 51, 792–97, 860–61, 945, 956–58, 1393; North Carolina 962; Ohio 980, 982; Pennsylvania 999–1001, 1011, 1076, 1084; Poland 1421; Rhode Island 1089, 1093, 1096–1105; Scotland 1151, 1431, 1435; South Carolina 1116; Sweden 1442–43; United States 67, 74, 78, 82, 135, 154–59, 246; Venezuela 1473; Vermont 77, 1118–19; Wisconsin 1142
College literary society libraries 319, 718
College of New Jersey, Princeton 723
Collier, J. P. 1217
Collier, Payne 52
Collins, Charles 915
Collins, Zaccheus 1053
Columbia, Calif., Presbyterian Church Sabbath School Library 255
Columbia, S.C.: African Methodist Episcopal Church Library 1115; University of South Carolina Library 1116
Columbia University Library, NYC 860–61
Columbian Circulating Library, Boston 517
Columbus, Ohio, State Library 979
Colwell, Stephen 1011
Commerce, literature of 427–28
Commercial circulating libraries: 15; California 256; Canada 1454; China 1459; England 1187–88, 1264–66, 1268–69; France 1316; Massachusetts 517, 523, 528; New York (state) 798–99, 801; United States 160

Committee on Juvenile Literature, American Unitarian Association (church) 232
Common school libraries *see* School district libraries; School libraries
Common School Library (series), Massachusetts Board of Education 196, 198, 448, 453, 732
Common sense 1062
Concord, Mass.: 608; Public Library 657-58
Concord, N.H.: Methodist General Biblical Institute Library 712; New Hampshire Historical Society Library 713; Public Library 714; State Library 715
Congregational Library Association, Boston 100, 518-20
Congress of the United States 30
Conington, John 1288
Connecticut: 180, 195, 202, 208, 299-302; State Library 306-07
Constantinople 1447-48
Convent libraries *see* Monastic libraries
Cooper Union Library, NYC 862-64
Cope, T. P. 1059-60
Cope, Sir William 1289
Copenhagen, Denmark: 1173-74; Classen Library 1173; Copenhagen University Library 1173; Royal Library (Kongelige Bibliotek) 1173-75
Copperopolis, Calif. 256
Copyright law 348, 352, 357, 359, 363, 1249
Corbie Monastery, France 1308
Cornell, Ezra 792
Cornell University Library, Ithaca, N.Y. 51, 792-97, 1393
Corsica 1310
Cortland Academy, Homer, N.Y. 791
Cosimo de' Medici 45, 1148, 1397
Costume, literature about 563, 608
Cotton, William 1292
Cottonian Library, Plymouth, Eng. 1292
Courtis, Ambrose 516
Cowtan, Robert 1244
Cox, James 1039
Coxe, A. S. 1005
Crane, J. T. 236

Crawford County (Pa.) Teachers' Institute 222
Crawshay, Mrs. 1391
Cremation, literature about 563, 599
Crozer Theological Seminary, Upland, Pa. 129, 1080
Curtis, W. P. 702
Curwen, Henry 598
Cutter, C. A. 48, 468, 511-13, 644-45, 655, 660, 678, 819
Cyfarthfa, Wales 1391
Czechoslovakia 1172

D

D. 761, 763
Dabshilim, King of India 1467-68
Dall, C. H. 232
Dalton, J. 1405
Dana, J. D. 325
Dane Library, Harvard College Law School 162-63
Danvers (Peabody), Mass., Peabody Institute Library 383, 674-75
Darlington, William 1082-83
Dartmouth College Library, Hanover, N.H. 717-18
Davis, John 435
Davis, L. C. 566
Dawkins, W. B. 605
Days and hours of opening *see* Hours of opening; Sunday opening
Dean, B. R. 682
DeBow, J. D. B. 426-27
Decoration, literature about 610
Dehn, S. W. 38, 1364
Dejalma 423
DeKay, J. E. 490
Delaware, Ohio, Ohio Wesleyan University Library 980
Denmark 1173-75
De Peyster, J.W. 925
Derby, Earl of (E. S. Stanley) 1208
DeWitt, W. R. 996-97
Dexter, H. M. 1164, 1198
Dexter, Julius 366, 969
Dickens, Charles 574, 1187
Dickinson Seminary Library, Williamsport, Pa. 1084
Discounts on books for libraries 139

Index

District Medical Society, Worcester, Mass. 687
District of Columbia *see* Washington, D.C.
District school libraries *see* School district libraries
Divoll, Ira 210-11, 708
Domesday Book 510
Don Quixote (by Miguel de Cervantes Saavedra) 649
Dorange, A. 1343-44
Doty, E. A. 772
Douce, Francis 1201
Douglas, Major 956
Dowd, C. F. 303-04
Downing, A. J. 744
Drake, S. G. 175
Draper, L. C. 1141
Dresden, Ger., Royal Library (Königlichen Bibliothek) 1373
Drexel, Joseph 116
Droz, Henry 431-32
Du Barry, Jeanne Bécu, Countess 1347
Dublin, Ire., Trinity College Library 1396
Ducal libraries 1407
Duché, Jacob 1017
Dürer, Albrecht 1453
Dufourny, French collector 1248
Du Ponceau, P. S. 1073-74
Durrie, D. S. 1137, 1139
Dutch Reformed Church Sunday School Library, Flatbush, N.Y. 790
Dwight, H. E. 1352

E

East Berlin, Conn., School District Library 303-04
East Boston Library Association, Boston, Mass. 521
East India Company, London 1214
East Lothian County, Scotland, itinerating libraries 1429-30
Ebeling, C. D. 625-26
Echmiadzin, Russia 1424
École Normale, Paris 1338
École Royale de Musique, Paris 1155
Economics literature 323, 427-28

Edinburgh, Scotland: 1431; Advocates' Library 1431-33; Edinburgh University Library 1431; Edinburgh University Shakespeare Library 1435; Philosophical Institution Library 1434
Education, literature about 563
Education of librarians 126-27
Educational value of libraries 20, 158, 209, 220-21, 478, 572, 958, 963, 1000, 1131
Edward VI, King of England 1252, 1283
Edwards, Arthur 1223, 1234
Edwards, B. B. 16
Edwards, Edward 6-7, 11, 40, 48-49, 709, 1242, 1244, 1277
Egbert, Archbishop of York 1296
Ehrenzeller, Jacob 1082
Eigenbrodt, C. G. 252
Eliot, S. A. 492, 631
Elizabethan literature 1217
Ellis, G. E. 498, 501
Elzevir, firm, publishers 1421
Emancipation Proclamation 387
Emanuel, Temple, Library, NYC 46, 50-51, 940-42
Emerson, R. W. 657
Emmanuel Philibert, Duke of Savoy 1417
Emmons, J. L. 714
Encyclopaedia Britannica 126-27
Engelstoft, M. 1175
England: 4, 7, 32, 35, 45, 48, 1149, 1156, 1176-93, 1389-90; and the United States 15-22
Engravings 563, 568, 573, 587-88, 646, 1170
Equitable Life Assurance Building, NYC 865-66
Erie (sloop) 779
Escorial Library, Spain 493, 1440
Ess, Leander Van 943-44
Essai Statistique Sur les Bibliothèques de Vienne (by Adriano Balbi) 1, 26
Essays (by Montaigne) 1328
Europe: 13, 1143-64; and the United States 23-54, 76; in the Middle Ages 13, 1163-64 *see also* Monastic libraries and names of countries, cities, types of libraries, and individual libraries

Evans, Cadwalader 1025
Evans, Charles 416
Evanston, Ill., Northwestern University Library 411
Evening Schools and District Libraries. An Appeal to Philadelphians ... 4
Everett, A. H. 493
Everett, Edward 478, 530, 542, 555, 557
Ewart, William 1390
Exchange of books and periodicals: international (mostly initiated by Alexandre Vattemare) 30-31, 37, 375, 555, 616, 759, 764, 818, 1318; within the United States 616, 818, 892
Exeter, Eng., Exchequer Chamber Library 1205

F

F. 180
F., J. W. 1344-45
Facsimiles of National Manuscripts of Scotland 509
Fac-similist 613
Factory libraries 103, 666, 716
Fairbanks family, St. Johnsbury, Vt. 1122
Fairholt, W. F. 1190
Farmer's Club, Yates County, N.Y. 961
Farmers' libraries *see* entries beginning Agricultural ...
Faust (by Goethe) 1361
The Federalist 928
Felsenthal, B. 46, 940
Female Literary Association, Philadelphia 1029
Fentress, G. W. 126
Fenwick, K. S. 1204
Ferguson, Adam 1431
Fernow, M. 1407
Fétis, F. J. 1155
Feuillet de Conches, F. S. 1326
Fiction 129-30, 174, 180-81, 183-85, 187, 249, 438, 469, 572, 597, 612, 663, 677, 798, 970, 1031
Fields, J. T. 531, 541

Filopanti, Quirico 894
Fires in Libraries: 73, 99, 387-88; college and university libraries 384, 412, 525, 627, 634, 982, 1118; House of Commons 1256; Library of Congress 337, 344; public libraries 1340-42; social libraries 1052; special libraries 392
Firth, Abraham 21
Fisk, Alvarez 428-30
Fisk Free Library, New Orleans, La. 428-30
Fiske, Willard 795, 1393
Flatbush, N.Y., Dutch Reformed Church Sunday School Library 790
Fletcher, W. I. 130, 180, 184
Florence, Italy: Medicea Laurenziana, Biblioteca 1931; National Central Library 1399, 1403; San Marco Convent 1401
Folsom, Charles 86, 462, 502, 814-15
Forbes, P. S. 930
Forbes, Robert 1433
Force, Peter 263, 332, 349-51, 924
Foreign literature libraries 1071-74; *see also* particular foreign languages
Forensic medicine 879
Forgery of manuscripts 1326
Forney, Wein 998
Foster, W. E. 132, 138, 662
Foucher de Careil, L.A., Count 1374
Fowle, William B. 327
France 3, 32, 1143, 1152, 1155, 1159-60, 1298-1307
France, Sénat 1338
Franco-Prussian War 1315, 1340-43, 1386
Frankfort, Ky., Public (i.e. State) Library of Kentucky 417
Franklin, Benjamin 43, 174, 220, 1006-07, 1043-44, 1046-47
Franklin (ship) 55, 780-81
Franklin County Public School Library, Union, Mo. 711
Franklin Institute Library, Philadelphia 1030
Franklin Institute Library, Syracuse, N.Y. 959
Franklin Library Association, Spanish Flat, Calif. 294
Franklin Society Library, Chicago 392

Index

Fraternal libraries 252, 257, 260, 283–85, 292
Free Public Libraries; Suggestions on their Foundation and Administration (by the American Social Science Association) 176
Free Reading Room Association of Spring Garden, Philadelphia 4
Free Reading Room of Spring Garden, for Young Men and Apprentices (1850) 4
Free Theological Library, Chicago 390, 393
Free Town Libraries (by Edward Edwards) 48–49
Freeman, Z. 953
French, B. F. 425–26, 430
French Revolution (1789–1799) 1248
French Revolution (1848) 704
Friends, Society of, libraries 1010, 1031
Friends Free Library, Germantown (Philadelphia), Pa. 1031
Fronto, Marcus Cornelius 1404
Fust, Johann 1452

G

G. 293, 1098
Gale, Theophilus 627
Gallas, Matthias, Count 1165
Gambalunga, Biblioteca Civica, Rimini, Italy 1408
Garrett, Philip 1016, 1018–19
Gas-Light Company Library, Glasgow, Scotland 1436
Geist, I. S. 990
General Theological Library, Boston 129, 522
Genesee Farmer (periodical) 145, 147, 149–53
Genevan Bible 670
Geographical libraries 342
George I of England 1191
George II of England 1157
Georgetown College Library, Georgetown, Ky. 418–23
Georgia: Georgia Historical Society Library 385; University of Georgia Library 384

Gering, Ulrich 1336
German language libraries in the United States 1032
German Society Library, Philadelphia 1032
Germania Musical Society 171
Germantown (Philadelphia), Pa., Friends Free Library 1031
Germany 1143, 1160, 1348–54
Gibbons, Henry 250
Gifts: 75, 114–15, 466, 804, 1190; to: asylum libraries 859; athenaeums 482, 488, 490, 503, 507, 514, 1027, 1093; college and university libraries 78, 156, 311, 315–16, 321–22, 419–20, 620–22, 625–26, 638–39, 642–43, 646, 649, 651, 694, 717, 723, 795, 957, 980, 1011, 1093, 1103–04, 1119, 1201, 1289, 1379–84, 1386, 1435; fraternal libraries 252; historical society libraries 773, 922, 925, 1132; juvenile social libraries 327; learned society libraries 1190, 1434; medical libraries 880; mercantile libraries 270, 534, 775–76, 913; military libraries 169; monastic libraries 1198; national libraries 1175, 1242, 1324, 1333, 1373, 1393–95, 1433, 1457; prison libraries 939; public libraries 177, 395, 397–400, 402, 428–30, 445, 543, 545–46, 554, 556, 563, 568, 574–75, 657, 661, 674, 687, 832, 843, 850, 864, 869, 871, 874–75, 1120, 1272, 1291–92, 1339; religious society libraries 519–20, 1259; school district libraries 198; school libraries 667, 986–87, 992, 1302; social libraries 244, 247, 327, 937, 983, 1011, 1048–51, 1091; special libraries 1214; state libraries 417, 764, 996; theological seminary libraries 259
Gilman, D. C. 316, 318, 561
Gimmell, William 1093
Glasgow, Scotland, Gas-Light Company Library 1436
Gloucester, Mass., Sawyer Free Library 659
Goethe 1361
Göttingen University Library, Germany 1148
Gonçalves Estêvão, Neto 1422

Goodnow Library, Sudbury, Mass. 467
Gould, A. A. 516
Government aid to libraries 29
Grace, Robert 1044
Grant, S. H. 908
Grant, U. S., President 913
Gray, F. C. 503–04, 646
Gray, John 692
Gray Collection, Harvard College Library 588
Great Britain (*see also* England, Ireland, Scotland): in general 1389–91; Parliament 4, 18, 35, 40, 85, 156, 477, 1183, 1256; House of Commons Library 1256; House of Commons, Select Committee on Public Libraries 4, 18, 35, 40, 85, 477, 1183; its *Report* 4, 40
Great Falls, N.H., Manufacturers and Village Library 716
Greaves, J. P. 619
Greece (in classical times) 2, 12–14
Greek literature 1283
Green, J. C. 723
Green, John 687
Greene, G. W. 1, 26, 896
Greene, T. A. 671
Greenfield, Ohio, Social Library 981
Greenleaf Library, Northwestern University, Evanston, Ill. 411
Greenough, W. W. 190
Greenwich, Eng., Royal Observatory 945
Gregori, G. C. 1310
Gregory, D. S. 103
Grimké, T. S. 83
Grimscom, R. D. 205
Grosvenor Library, Buffalo, N.Y. 783–88
Groton, Mass., Public Library 660
Guild, R. A. 90–92, 95, 1098, 1100, 1105
Guizot, F. P. G. 1152, 1318
Gutenberg, Johann 1340, 1342

H

H. 711, 994
H., I. F. 912

Hachette, H. M. & Co. 1302
Hackett, F. W. 162–63
The Hague, Netherlands, Meermanno-Westreenianum Museum 1420
Halcomb, F. 1449
Hale, Charles 377
Hale, E. E. 560
Hale, Nathan 491
Hall, A. O. 849
Hall, S. R. 752
Halliwell, J. O. 1291, 1435
Hamilton, Alexander 928
Hamilton, Can., Lancefield's Lending Library 1454
Hammond, Charles 221
Hannah, George 774
Hanover, Ger., Royal Library (Königlichen Bibliothek) 1374
Hanover, N.H.: Dartmouth College Library 717–18; Northern Academy of Arts and Sciences 719
Harbaugh, M. C. 979
Harbaugh, S. G. 979
Harper's District School Library (series) 738
Harris, J. L. 1026
Harris, John 59
Harris, T. W. 632
Harris, W. T. 709
Harrisburg, Pa., State Library 996–98
Hartford, Conn.: State Library 306–07; Wadsworth Athenaeum 305; Young Men's Institute Library 308–09
Hartshorne, C. H. 1191
Harvard College, Cambridge, Mass.: College Library 38, 67–68, 74, 110, 157, 462, 464, 468, 477, 588, 620–52; Law School, Dane Library 162–63; Musical Association Library 171, 413, 465, 653
Hassard, J. R. G. 914
Hayden, Michael 1441
Hayes, H. Y. 716
Heard, Augustine 567
Hebraica 46, 50–51, 53, 940–42, 1237–38
Hebrews 1469
Heitz Collection, Strassburg, Ger. 1382, 1385
Hengstenberg Theological Library, Chicago 390, 393

Henry VII of England 1157
Henry VIII of England 1179
Henry, Joseph 369
Hermann, C. F. 1172
Hermes 708
Herrick, E. C. 318
Heywood, Oliver 1164
Hickley, E. B. 675
Hildreth, Richard 45
Hillard, G. S. 554
Historical and Philosophical Society of Ohio 366, 968–69
Historical libraries 1320, 1409; private 263, 265
Historical societies 231, 524, 681, 968, 983
Historical society libraries: England 1190; Georgia 385; Illinois 387; Maryland 441–42; Massachusetts 475, 524–25, 676, 688–90; New Hampshire 713; New York (state) 80, 73–74, 922–25; Ohio 366, 969; Rhode Island 1106; United States 161; Wisconsin 129, 1132–41
History, U.S. (literature) *see* Americana
The History of the Boston Athenaeum, 1851 (by Josiah Quincy, Jr.) 501
Hoadly, C. J. 307
Hoaxes 1167
Hoefer, J. C. F. 369
Hofbibliothek, Vienna, Austria 1166
Holder, Alfred 1162
Holland 925, 1132, 1419
Hollis, Thomas 620–22, 627
Holyoke (Mass.) Public Library 661
Homans, I. S. 124
Homer, N.Y., Cortland Academy Library 791
Hong Kong, China 1460
Hood, W. C. 979
Hooper, L. H. 1013
Hooper, W. B. 861
Hopkinson, Joseph 1056, 1062
Horton, R. G. 107
Hospital libraries 926
Hotel libraries 286–88
Hours of opening: 123; in: mercantile libraries 167; public libraries 548, 563, 849, 1355–56; social libraries 1035, 1037, 1109; *see also* Sunday opening

House of Commons, London: Library 1256; Select Committee on Public Libraries 4, 18, 35, 40, 85, 477, 1183; its *Report* 4, 40
Howe, T. O. 363
Howitt, William 1353
Howland, Edward 52
Hoyne, Thomas 402
Hughes, Thomas 395
Hull, Isaac 56
Hume, David 1431
Humphrey, Duke of Gloucester 1283
Hunt, E. B. 342
Hunt, Jeremiah 627
Hunt, T. D. 62
Hyde Park, Mass., Public Library 132, 662

I

Icarian Community Library, Nauvoo, Ill. 171, 413, 465
Iceland 1392
Illinois 386
Illinois College Library, Jacksonville, Ill. 99, 412
Imperial Library, Paris *see* Bibliothèque Nationale, Paris
Imperial Library, Vienna 1166
Imperial Public Library, St. Petersburg, Russia 1148, 1423, 1426–28
Imperial University Library, Warsaw, Poland 1421
Incunabula 1166, 1340, 1342, 1452
Independent Order of Odd Fellows, libraries *see* Odd Fellows libraries
Index to the Catalogue of books in the Upper Hall of the Public Library of the City of Boston (1861) 559, 561
Index to the Notes of D. Diego Clemencin... (by C. F. Bradford) 649
India 1467–68
Indiana 415
Indianapolis, Ind., Public Library 416
International exchange of books and periodicals *see* Exchange of books and periodicals

Ipswich, Mass., Free Public Library 567
Iredell County, N.C., Centre Benevolent Society 963
Ireland 1151, 1389
Irving, David 1431
Irving, Washington 28, 738, 855
Israel 1469
Italy 45, 576, 1148, 1152, 1158, 1160, 1397-1400
Ithaca, N.Y., Cornell University Library 51, 792-97, 1393
Itinerating libraries 229, 1151, 1177, 1429-30

J

J., H. 528
Jackson, Calif., Odd Fellows Library 257
Jacksonville, Ill., Illinois College Library 99, 412
Jacobi, K. G. J. 633
Jahn, Otto 1367
Jamaica 1177
James, Sir H. 509
Janin, J. G. 1339
Jarvis, S. F., sale of his books (1851) 89, 953, 1098, 1100
Jefferson, Thomas 141, 231, 353, 358, 715
Jeffreys, G. W. 141-42
Jenkins, Edward 397
Jenks, William 525
Jersey City, N.J., Young Men's Christian Association 103
Jesus Christ 123
Jewett, C. C. 84, 86, 96, 105, 112, 369, 371, 373-74, 559-61, 686, 814, 1096-97, 1101, 1105
Johnston, H. P. 263, 265
Jones, James 1124
Joslin, J. J. 1121
Judaica 46, 50-51, 53, 940-42
Judd, Mr. (of N.Y. General Assembly) 754
Judson, E. Z. C. 920
Juliana Library, Lancaster, Pa. 1017
Juvenile social libraries 208, 327, 331

K

K., W. T. 353, 1296
Kaiserliche Universitäts und Landesbibliothek, Strassburg, Ger. (after August, 1870) 1379-87; *see also* Strasbourg, France, Bibliothèque Municipale (to August, 1870)
Kentucky, Public (i.e. State) Library 417
Khedival Library, Cairo, Egypt 1466
Kieffer, D. S. 985, 987
King, Horatio 370
King's Chapel Library, Boston, Mass. 618
Kingsborough, E. K. 503-04
Kingsley 312-13
Kirk, E. N. 1099
Kirkland, J. T. 68
Kirkpatrick, Sophia 723
Knight, Mr. 1294
Knight, Charles 1188, 1270
Knox, John 1439
Königlichen Bibliothek, Berlin, Ger. 38, 1156, 1358-71
Königlichen Bibliothek, Dresden, Ger. 1373
Königlichen Bibliothek, Hanover, Ger. 1374
Kongelige Bibliotek, Copenhagen 1173-75

L

L., F. W. 79
La Bédoyère, Henri-Noël-François Huchet, Count 42
Lacroix, Paul 1347
Ladies' Commission on Sunday-school Books, American Unitarian Association (church) 233-35
Lancaster, Mass., Public Library 663
Lancaster, Pa., Juliana Library 1017
Lancefield's Lending Library, Hamilton, Can. 1454
Landfermann, D. W. 1379
Landfermann, Johannes 1379
Lane, Charles 619
Lansing, A. F. 768

Lansing, Mich., Michigan State Library 695
Lauguel, Auguste 1316
Law Institute Library, Chicago 389–90
Law Institute Library, NYC 867–68
Law libraries *see* Bar association libraries; Law library associations; Law school libraries
Law library associations 967
Law school libraries 162–63, 310
Lawrence, Amos 686
Lawrence, Mass.: Free Public Library 129, 184, 249, 664–65; Pacific Mills Library 103, 666
Learned society libraries 506, 1215, 1258, 1267, 1434
Lectures on School-Keeping (by S. R. Hall) 752
Lectures sponsored by libraries: historical society libraries 80; literary association libraries 108; mechanics' libraries 1007; mercantile libraries 28, 76, 274–75, 464, 483, 530–31, 536–37, 884, 887, 889, 894, 896, 901, 904, 917, 1056, 1065; public libraries 20, 1131; social libraries 929, 1074; young men's association libraries 297
Lee, Daniel 961
Lee, E. B. 499
Leeds, Eng., Mechanics' Library 1206
Legislation for libraries *see* Public library legislation; School district library legislation; Social library legislation
Lehman, William 1023–24, 1026
Leibnitz, Baron Gottfried von 1374
Leicester, Eng., Literary and Philosophical Society 21
Leicester, Mass., Public Library 21
Lenox, James 263, 869, 871–72, 874–75
Lenox Library, NYC 850, 869–77
Leofric, Bishop of Exeter 1205
Leonardo da Vinci 1295
Lepsius, K. R. 1371
Lewis, W. L. 491
Lewisburg, Pa., University at Lewisburg Library 999–1000
Lexington, Mass. 608

Lexington Medical Society Library (proposed), Lexington, Ky. 424
Librarians *see* Librarianship; names of individual librarians
Librarians' Conference, NYC (1853) 101, 805–15
The Librarian's Manual (by R. A. Guild) 90–92, 95
Librarianship 19, 41, 86, 101, 131, 677, 810, 858, 890, 898; *see also* Library organization and management
Libraries, advertisements for 932
Libraries, educational value of 20, 158, 209, 220–21, 478, 572, 958, 1000, 1131
Libraries, working conditions in 1253
Library Association, Stamford, Conn. 328
Library Association, Vallejo, Calif. 298
Library buildings: 36, 441, 1185–86; for: athenaeums 497–98, 770–71; college and university libraries 245, 314, 471, 631, 634, 648, 652, 686; historical society libraries 688, 690, 1139; lyceums 1213; mercantile libraries 533, 702, 775, 906; national libraries 335–36, 338, 340–41, 343, 348, 356, 362, 364, 1368, 1371, 1378; public libraries 175, 182, 401, 581, 657, 826, 832, 836, 839, 873, 875, 877, 974, 1281; social libraries 931, 1050; state libraries 617, 757; young men's association libraries 767; young men's Christian association libraries 947–50
Library catalogs: 9, 43, 96, 112–13, 369, 374, 477, 1305–07, 1419; for: agricultural society libraries 526; athenaeums 491, 511–14; college and university libraries 316, 318, 320, 422, 439, 588, 628, 639, 645–46, 1096–97, 1100, 1285, 1421, 1442; historical society libraries 969, 1137, 1140; law libraries 868; mechanics' libraries 819; medical libraries 381–82; mercantile libraries 273, 279, 281, 444, 539–40, 707, 778, 868, 912; monastic libraries 1164, 1296, 1402; national libraries

7, 353, 367, 1228–29, 1231, 1237–38, 1245–46, 1250, 1253, 1359–60, 1362, 1423; private libraries 619, 655, 1198; public libraries 132, 402, 416, 440, 473, 559–61, 563, 582–84, 587–89, 598, 607, 609–10, 660, 677–80, 827, 1194–95, 1212, 1274, 1344; religious society libraries 77; school district libraries 709; school libraries 1088; scientific libraries 372; social libraries 434, 930, 932, 1045, 1107–08, 1110–11; special libraries 1195; state libraries 756, 758, 765, 1449; theological seminary libraries 474; young men's association libraries 440

Library Company of Colored Persons, Philadelphia 1033–34

Library Company of Philadelphia 28, 43, 67, 115, 983, 1007, 1011, 1035–50; *see also* Loganian Library

Library education 126–27

Library equipment 391, 815, 1114; *see also* Shelving

Library legislation, public libraries *see* Public library legislation

Library legislation, school district libraries *see* School district library legislation

Library legislation, social libraries *see* Social library legislation

Library literature: books about libraries or books for the use of librarians. (This list does not include catalogs of individual libraries or books about individual libraries; for them, see the heading "Library catalogs" and the names of the libraries.)

Essai Statistique Sur les Bibliothèques de Vienne (by Adriano Balbi) 1, 26

Evening Schools and District Libraries. An Appeal to Philadelphians... 4

Free Public Libraries; Suggestions on their Foundation and Administration (by the American Social Science Association) 176

Free Town Libraries (by Edward Edwards) 48–49

The History of the Boston Athenaeum (by Josiah Quincy, Jr.) 501

The Librarian's Manual (by R. A. Guild) 90–92, 95

Memoirs of Libraries (by Edward Edwards) 6–7, 40, 709

Museums, Libraries, and Picture Galleries, Public and Private (by J. W. and Wyatt Papworth) 1185–86

Plea for Libraries (by Noah Porter) 82

Poole's Index to Periodical Literature 91, 93, 97–98, 464, 468

Public Libraries in the United States of America, 1876 (U.S. Bureau of Education) 140

Report from the Select Committee on Public Libraries (Parliament) 1849, 4, 40

Library of Congress, Washington, D.C. 30, 47, 73, 99, 102, 115, 121, 135, 231, 332–67, 567

Library of Useful Knowledge (series) 671

Library organization and management 49, 175–76, 424, 699, 991, 1036, 1087, 1109; *see also* Librarianship

Library statistics. Each of the following articles contains statistics on several libraries: Libraries in general 10, 26, 32–34, 39–40, 54, 70, 72, 74, 81, 87, 94, 104–07, 122, 140, 388, 446, 484, 750, 1008, 1092, 1144–45, 1147, 1149–53, 1158, 1168, 1170, 1180, 1298–1301, 1312, 1348, 1354, 1392, 1398–1400, 1425, 1439, 1444–45, 1471; college and university libraries 154–55, 246, 1317; public libraries 183–85; school libraries 1303; Sunday School libraries 261, 966

Library users 500, 562, 571, 665, 700, 848, 1013–14; *see also* Reading habits

Lichtenthaler, Philip von 1376

Lightfoot, Dr. 627

Lincoln, F. W., Jr. 109

Linonian Society, Yale College 319

Lisbon, Portugal, Academy of Sciences Library 1422

A List of the Books of Reference in the

Index

Reading Room of the British Museum (by Edward Edwards) 7
Literary and Antiquarian Society, Perth, Scotland 1437
Literary and Philosophical Society Library, Leicester, Eng. 21
Literary association libraries 21, 108 295, 719, 1029, 1437
Literary Association Library, Stockton, Calif. 295
Literary societies in colleges, libraries 718
Little, Josiah 103, 672
Littré, M. P. E. 1305–06
Livermore, George 18
Liverpool, Eng., 1207: Free Library 1156, 1208–12, 1391; Lycaeum 1213
Lives of the Founders of the British Museum (by Edward Edwards) 1242
Logan, James 983, 1006, 1040, 1042, 1044, 1047, 1051–52
Logan, James, Jr. 1051
Logan, William 1051
Loganian Library, Philadelphia 983, 1006, 1038, 1040, 1044, 1047, 1051–54
London: 4, 17, 1146, 1149, 1161, 1183–84, 1214–18; British Museum 7, 18, 42–43, 45, 52, 850, 1146, 1149, 1157, 1190, 1214, 1216, 1219–55, 1396, 1470; its *General Catalogue of Printed Books* 52, 1231; London and Northwestern Railway Station 1257; London Institution 1215, 1258; London Society of Biblical Archaeology Library 1259; London University 1214, 1260; Marylebone Parish Public Library 1184, 1261–62; Mechanics' Institution Library 1263; Mudie's Circulating Library 1264–65; National Gallery 1222; Parliament 4, 18, 35, 40, 85, 156, 477, 559, 1183, 1256; House of Commons Library 1256; House of Commons, Select Committee on Public Libraries 4, 18, 35, 40, 85, 477, 1183; its *Report* 4, 40; Public American Library 1266; Royal Society of Arts Library 1267; Stowe Library 17; Stationers' Company 136, 1068; Students' Library 1268–69; Westminster Parish Free Library 1270

Long Island Historical Society, Brooklyn, N.Y. 773–74
Loring's Select Library, Boston 523
Louis XVI of France 1008
Louisiana State Library, New Orleans 431–32
Louvre, Paris 1337
Lowell, Charles 511
Luard, H. R. 1201
Ludewig, Hermann 33, 80–81
Lunt, H. E. 232
Luther, Martin 1361
Lyceum of Natural History Library, NYC 878
Lyceums: California 253; England 1207, 1213; Massachusetts 463, 668, 671, 685, 687; Missouri 701; New York (state) 780, 878; Pennsylvania 1085; United States 164–65, 243; Vermont 1117
Lynn, Mass. 667

M

M. 67, 928
M., T. S. 421
M., W. 1399
McC. 946
McCaskey, J. P. 990
Macaulay, T. B. 1434
McElroy, A. 1066
McIlvaine, J. H. 1011
MacKenzie, William 1016, 1038
Maclure, William 166, 1120
Maclure Library, Pittsford, Vt. 1120
McMaster, F. W. 1116
McNamara, F. S. 1077
Macray, W. D. 644, 1286
Madison, Wis.: Free Library 1131; State Historical Society Library 129, 818, 1132–41; University of Wisconsin Library 1142
Mai, Angelo, Cardinal 1404–05, 1411
Maine 435–36
Malcom, Howard 418, 420, 422
Management of libraries *see* Library organization and management
Manchester, Eng.: 1184, 1271; Chet-

ham's Library 1272-74; Free Library 45, 1184, 1271, 1275-80
Manchester, Eng., Bishop of 1293
Mann, Horace 449, 452, 457
Manuel du Libraire et de l'Amateur de Livres (by J. C. Brunet) *3d ed., 1820* 26
Manufacturers and Village Library, Great Falls, N.H. 716
Manuscripts: 509, 1412, 1438; in church and synagogue libraries 1205, 1404, 1411, 1418; college and university libraries 1189, 1200, 1202-03, 1285, 1385, 1396, 1442; ducal libraries 1407; national libraries 1166, 1170, 1230, 1246, 1251-52, 1295, 1319, 1324-26, 1329, 1334, 1361, 1374, 1397, 1428, 1433, 1465; private libraries 1165, 1189; public libraries 578, 821, 1308, 1342, 1344-46, 1405-06, 1444; religious libraries 1424; religious society libraries 1259; scientific association libraries 1422; social libraries 1054; special libraries 1420; state libraries 762, 766
Map libraries 342
Marcus Aurelius Antoninus 1404
Marcy, W. L. 735-36, 740
Mardin, Turkey 1472
Marine Insurance Offices, NYC 780
Mario, J. W. 1399
Marshall, John 358
Martini, Padre 1155
Maryland 69; Historical Society 441-42
Marylebone Parish, London, Public Library 1184, 1261-62
Mason, Lowell 171, 413, 465
Mason, Samuel 1018
Massachusetts: 21, 64, 72, 74, 103, 110, 117, 129, 132, 171, 184, 208, 244, 249, 446-69; Board of Education 447, 456-57, 459-60; General Court 479, 488; Historical Society 475, 524-25; History (literature) 563; Horticultural Society 526; Sabbath School Society 639; Scientific Association 490, 527; State Library 616-17
Mather, Cotton 606
Maury, M. F. 781

Maximilian, Emperor of Mexico 47
May, S. J. 795-96
Mazarine Library, Paris 1299
Meacham, James 377
Meadville, Pa., Allegheny College Library 1001
Means, W. G. 259
Mechanics' libraries: California 268; England 1206, 1263, 1297; Great Britain 4; Massachusetts 528; N.Y. (state) 103, 819, 952; Pennsylvania 120, 1007, 1014-20; Scotland 1436; United States 4, 166
Medical libraries 381-82, 424, 489-90, 687, 879-80
Medical literature 563
Mediceo-Laurenziana, Biblioteca, Florence 1148, 1403
Medicine, forensic 879
Medico-Legal Society Library, NYC 879-80
Medieval libraries 13, 1163-64; see also Monastic libraries
Medill, Joseph 402
Meehan, J. S. 339
Meermanno-Westreenianum Museum, The Hague, Netherlands 1420
Mejan, Count 1360
Memoirs of Libraries (by Edward Edwards) 6-7, 40, 709
Memoirs of Rev. Joseph Buckminster, D.D. and his Son, Rev. Joseph Stevens Buckminster (by Eliza Buckminster Lee) 499
Memorial Day 574
Mental hospital libraries 859
Mercantile libraries: California 132, 269-81; Canada 1455; Illinois 414; Louisiana 433; Maine 129, 249, 438; Maryland 442-44; Massachusetts 464, 481, 483, 529-41; Missouri 111, 173, 700-07; N.Y.(state) 444, 775-78, 802, 881-917, 1351; Ohio 975-78, 1114; Pennsylvania 28, 76, 1055-69, 1077; South Carolina 1114; United States 167-68
Mercantile libraries, branches 909
Merriam, M. B. 679
Mesopotamia 1470
Metcalf, S. L. 884
Methodist Biblical Institute Library,

Index   414

Concord, N.H. 712
Methodist Episcopal Union Church Library, Philadelphia 1070
Metz, France, Military Library 1311
Mexico 1471
Michigan: State Library 695; University of 693–94
Michigan Avenue Free Library and Reading Room, Chicago 394
Middlesex County Lyceum, Mass. 668
Milan, Italy: Ambrosian Library 1404–06; Public Library 572
Military libraries 73, 169–70, 282, 332, 1182, 1311
Military literature 563
Military post libraries *see* Military libraries
Mill libraries 103, 666, 716
Miller, book seller, London 1266
Mills, Caleb 415
Milwaukee, Wis., Young Men's Association 111, 113, 440
Missouri 210, 696–99
Mitchell, J. T. 1075
Modena, Italy, Ducal Library 1407
Mohl, Robert von 324
Mommsen, Theodor 1370–71
Monastic libraries: 1159, 1163–64, 1472; Austria 1162; England 1179, 1198, 1296; Germany 944, 1162; Italy 1401–02, 1413; Mexico 1471; Turkey 1472
Montaigne, M. E. 1309, 1328, 1334
Monte Cassino 1401–02
Montgomery County Agricultural Society Library, Norristown, Pa. 1002
Montreal, Can., Mercantile Library 1455
Moore, G. H. 876
Moore, Mrs. J. G. 995
Moral values in reading *see* Educational value of reading; Fiction; Reading habits
Morgan, H. H. 700
Morrell, L. A. 744
Morton, Nathaniel 681
Mount Pleasant Prison Library, N.Y. 746
Mucklé, M. R. 1384
Mudie's Circulating Library, London 1264–65

Muller, Joseph 1440
Muller, Frederick 50–51, 240–41
Mullins, J. D. 1194–95
Munich, Ger., Bavarian State Library 760, 1354, 1375–78
Munroe, William 657
Museums 878, 1119, 1208, 1222, 1390, 1408, 1420
Museums, Libraries, and Picture Galleries, Public and Private (by J. W. and Wyatt Papworth) 1185–86
Music classes 892
Music libraries: 38; in Europe 1155; Germany 1364, 1367; Illinois 413; Massachusetts 465, 553, 653; Pennsylvania 116; Sweden 1441; United States 171–72
Mysticism 619

N

National Central Library, Florence, Italy 1399, 1403
National Gallery, London 1222
National libraries (*see also* Bibliothèque Nationale, Paris; British Museum; and Library of Congress): Austria 1166; Belgium 1168–70; Branches (proposed) 1247; Brazil 1452–53; Canada 1457–58; Denmark 1173–75; Egypt 1465–66; Europe 750; France 1299, 1319, 1335–37, 1347; Germany 760, 1156, 1358–78; Iceland 1393–95; India 1467–68; Italy 1399, 1403, 1414; Russia 1426–28; Scotland 1431–33; Spain 1440; United States 102; Venezuela 1473
National Temperance Society, NYC 918–21
Nauvoo, Ill., Icarian Community Library 171, 413, 465
Naval Lyceum, Brooklyn, N.Y. 780
Navy Yard Library, Brooklyn, N.Y. 779–82
Neander, J. A. W. 953–55
Neck School, Charlestown, Mass. 656
Negroes, libraries for 476, 936, 1033–34, 1115
Negroes, literary associations for 1029

Netherlands 925, 1132, 1419
Nevada City, Calif., Young Men's Christian Association 258
Neville, George 1283
New Bedford, Mass.: Free Public Library 669–70; Lyceum 671
New Bern Library Society, New Bern, N.C. 963
New Brunswick, N.J. 723
New England: 16, 243–49; (literature about) 524–25; *see also* names of states, cities, towns, and libraries
New England Library, Boston 524–25
New Hampshire: Historical Society 713; State Library 715
New Hampton, N.H., Academical and Theological Institution 720
New Haven, Conn.: Yale College Law School Library 310; Yale College Library 221, 245, 311–25; Young Men's Institute Library 326
New Jersey 103, 722–24
New Jerusalem, Church of the 75, 78, 244
New Orleans: 425–28; Fisk Free Library 429–30; Louisiana State Library 431–32; Mercantile Library Association 433; Public School Lyceum and Library Society (Second Municipality) 425–26, 434
New York (state): 94, 204, 208, 725–55; General Assembly 729, 747, 758; State Library 756–66
New York City (*see also* Brooklyn; Flatbush): 44, 69, 798–804; American and Foreign Christian Union Library 193–94, 816; American Bible Society 77; American Congregational Union 100; American Institute 217, 817–18; American Seamen's Friend Society 64–66; Apprentices' Library 819; Astor Library 17–18, 110, 115, 121, 176–77, 561, 747, 800, 820–58, 869, 873; Bloomingdale Asylum for the Insane 859; Clinton Hall Association 883, 902–03, 905, 915; Columbia University Library 860–61; Cooper Union Library 862–64; Equitable Life Assurance Building 865–66; Law Institute Library 867–68; Lenox Library 850, 869–77; Librarian's Conference (1853) 101, 805–15; Lyceum of Natural History Library 878; Medico-Legal Society Library 879–80; Mercantile Library 167–68, 802, 881–917, 1351; National Temperance Society 918–21; New York City Dispensary 878; New-York Historical Society Library 876, 922–25; New York Hospital Library 926; New York Society Library 927–35; New York Theological Seminary 943–44; New York Typographical Society Library 938; Phoenix Society Library 936; Printer's Free Library 103, 937–38; Prison Association 939; Public Library (proposed) 803; Temple Emanuel Library 50–51, 940–42; Union Theological Seminary 570, 943–44; University of the City of New York 878, 945; Young Men's Christian Association 802, 946–51
Newark, N.J., Library Association 103, 724
Newburyport, Mass., Public Library 103, 672
Newport, R.I.: 120; People's Library 120; Redwood Library and Athenaeum 247, 1091
Newspaper files 345–46, 417, 536, 613, 767, 1103
Newton, Mass., Free Public Library 20
Nicholas V, Pope 1397, 1411
Nichols, Thomas 1244
Nisard, Désiré 1338
"The Noble Lesson" (La Nobla Leyson) (poem) 1200
Nordhoff, Charles 1163
Norris, Samuel 1022
Norristown, Pa., Montgomery County Agricultural Society Library 1002
North Carolina: State Library 231; University of 962
Northampton, Mass., Public Library 673
Northern Academy of Arts and Sciences, Hanover, N.H. 719

Index 416

Northern Liberties, Pa. (*see also* Philadelphia), Northern Liberties Library and Reading Room Company 1003-04
Northwestern University Library, Evanston, Ill. 411
Norton, C. B. 91, 95
Norton, F. H. 847-48
Norwegian books 1142
Norwich, Conn., Second School Society 301
Norwich, Eng., Free Public Library 1281
Nottaway County Agricultural Society, Va. 1124
Noyes, S. B. 778
Nutting, Miss 517

O

Oakland, Calif., Pacific Theological Seminary Library 259
Observations on a Variety of Subjects, Literary, Moral and Religious, written by a Gentleman of Foreign Extraction, Who Resided Some Time in Philadelphia (by Rev. Mr. Duché) 1017
Odd Fellows libraries: Alvarado, Calif. 252; Jackson, Calif. 257; Petaluma, Calif. 260; San Francisco, Calif. 283-85; Shasta, Calif. 292
Ohio: 94, 964-65; State Library, Columbus 979
Ohio Historical and Philosophical Society, Cincinnati 968-69
Ohio Wesleyan University, Delaware, Ohio 980
Old Colony Historical Society, Taunton, Mass. 681
Old South Church and Society, Boston 524
Olds, W. B. 267
Olympia, Wash., Territorial Library 1130
Ontario, Can. 1456
Osgood, Samuel 101
Otterbein University Library, Westerville, Ohio 982
Oxford, Eng.: Oxford University Libraries 644, 1191, 1202, 1282; Bodleian Library 644, 1282-89; Public Library 1184, 1290; Radcliffe Observatory 945

P

P., B. K. 464, 483, 672
P., J. 1293
P., W. F. 481
Pacific Mills Library, Lawrence, Mass. 103, 666
Pacific Theological Seminary Library, Oakland, Calif. 259
Paddock, S. B. 301
Page, W. P. 730
Pageants, literature about 1190
Palfrey, J. G. 1179
Palimpsest (by Angelo Mai) 1404
Palimpsests 1404-05
Pamphlets 366, 969
Panchatantra 1472
Panizzi, Sir Anthony 43, 52, 1156, 1224-27, 1235, 1295
Paper 380
Papworth, J. W. 1185-86
Papworth, Wyatt 1185-86
Paris, France: 32, 45, 1146, 1148, 1155, 1159, 1161, 1299, 1312-17; Académie des Sciences Morales et Publiques 1318; Bibliothèque de l'Arsenal 1299, 1319, 1347; Bibliothèque Historique de la Ville de Paris 1320; Bibliothèque Mazarine 1299; Bibliothèque Nationale 3, 28, 42-43, 1155, 1159, 1299, 1314, 1316, 1321-34, 1337; Bibliothèque Ste Geneviève 36, 1156, 1299, 1335-36; École Normale 1338; École Royale de Musique 1155; Louvre 1337
Parris Commune 1327
Park, T. W. 1119
Parkman, Francis 628
Parliament, House of Commons, Library, London 1256
Parliamentary Report on Public Libraries (House of Commons Select Committee) *1849* 4, 40
Parochial libraries 1151
Parsons, J.C. 661

Index

Patents 604
Patrons of libraries *see* Library users
Patton, R. B. 27
Pawcatuck Library Association, Westerly, R.I. 1088, 1107–12
Payen, Dr. 1328
Peabody, A. P. 456
Peabody, Ephraim 192
Peabody, George 114, 445, 674
Peabody Institute Library, Baltimore, Md. 445
Peabody (Danvers), Mass., Peabody Institute Library 383, 674–75
Pearce, J. A. 377
Penn, Juliana 1017
Penn, Thomas 1017, 1040
Penn, William 231, 1052
Pennsylvania: 983–95; State Library 996–98; State Teachers' Association 988
Pennsylvania Library of Foreign Literature and Science 1071–74
Pennsylvania, University of, Library, Philadelphia 1011, 1076
Penzance, Eng., Public Library 1291
People's Library, Newport, R.I. 120
Peoria, Ill., Mercantile Library 414
Pergamum 14
Periodical indexes 91, 93, 97–98, 133–34, 464, 468, 787
Periodicals 124–27, 134, 402, 563, 565, 596, 1218
Perkins, F. A. 301
Perkins, F. B. 112–13
Perkins, James 490
Perkins, T.H. 490
Perth, Scotland, Literary and Antiquarian Society 1437
Pertz, G. H. 1156, 1368, 1371
Petaluma, Calif., Odd Fellows Library 260
Peters, Richard 142
Petersburg, Va., Library Association 1125–27
Petrarch 1415–16, 1418
Petzholdt, Julius 8
Phelps, W. W. 324
Philadelphia (*see also* Northern Liberties): 69, 72, 1005–13; American Association for the Advancement of Science 342; American Sunday School Union 218, 638; Apprentices' Library Company 120, 1007, 1014–20; Athenaeum 1021–27, 1073; Athenian Institute 28, 76, 1062–64; Centennial Exposition 1876 140; Christian Hall Library 1028; Female Literary Association 1029; Franklin Institute Library 1030; Free Reading Room Association of Spring Garden 4; Friends Free Library 1031; German Society Library 1032; Library Company of Colored Persons 1033–34; Library Company of Philadelphia 28, 43, 67, 115, 983, 1007, 1011, 1035–50; Loganian Library 983, 1006, 1038, 1040, 1044, 1047, 1051–54; Mercantile Library 28, 76, 123, 167, 1055–69; Methodist Episcopal Union Church Library 1070; Pennsylvania Library of Foreign Literature and Science 1071–74; Philadelphia Law Association Library 1075; University of Pennsylvania Library 1011, 1076
Philip II of Spain 1440
Phillipps, Sir Thomas 1204
Philosophical Institution, Edinburgh, Scotland 1434
Phoenix Society Library, NYC 936
Photobibliography 9
Pickett, David 1115
Pilgrim Society Library, Plymouth, Mass. 676
Pirdeaux, F. 1259
Pittsburgh, Pa., Young Men's Mercantile Library 1077
Pittsford, Vt., Maclure Library 1120
Pius II, Pope 1415–16
Plea for Libraries (by Noah Porter) 82
Pleasants, T. S. 1125–26
Plumley, G. S. 578
Plymouth, Eng., Cottonian Library 1292
Plymouth, Mass., Pilgrim Society Library 676
Poe, E. A. 929
Political science literature 324
Pompadour, Madame de 1347
Pond, Enoch 437
Poole, W. F. 91, 93, 97–98, 133–34, 180, 407, 416, 464, 468, 532, 535, 538–40, 970–73

Poole's Index to Periodical literature 91, 93, 97–98, 133–34, 464, 468
Poore, B. P. 358
Porter, N., Jr. 158
Porter, Noah 82
Portico Library, Manchester, Eng. 1156
Portland, Me., Institute and Public Library 440
Portland, Ore., Library Association 111
Portraits 1129
Portsmouth, N.H., Athenaeum 721
Portugal 1422
Portuguese literature 563
Posters 1248
Potter, Horatio 958
Potthast, August 1372
Potts, David 1082
Poverty 480, 1178, 1192
Pradt, J. B. 204
Prague University Library 1172
Presbyterian Church Library, San Jose, Calif. 291
Presbyterian Church Sabbath School Library, Columbia, Calif. 255
Prince, J. D. 790
Prince, Thomas 524–25, 606
Princeton, N.J., College of New Jersey 723
Printed Books Containing MSS. Notes and Adversaria Preserved in the University Library, Cambridge (by H. R. Luard and Churchill Babington) 1201
Printers' Free Library, NYC 103, 937–38
Printing society libraries 392
Prison Association, NYC 939
Prison libraries 746, 939
Private libraries: Austria 1165; California 263–65; Connecticut 89, 315; Denmark 1175; England 17, 619, 1198, 1204, 1289, 1291–92; France 1339; Germany 1379, 1381; Kentucky 420; Louisiana 429–30; Massachusetts 546, 556, 619–20, 625–26, 654–55, 687; Netherlands 53; New York (state) 793, 859, 869, 874–75, 953; Poland 1426–27; Rhode Island 1098, 1100, 1103; Scotland 1435; United States 177

Providence, R.I.: 1089, 1092–93; Athenaeum 1089, 1093–95, 1109; Brown University Library 1089, 1092–93, 1096–1105; Rhode Island Historical Society Library 1106
Prussia *see* Germany
Prussian Royal Library, Berlin 38, 1156, 1358–71
Pseudonymous works 128, 1069
Public American Library, London, Eng. 1266
Public libraries: in general 11, 20, 32, 39, 48–49; in these places: Australia 1450–51; Connecticut 180; England 1184, 1192, 1194–97, 1208–12, 1215, 1261–62, 1270–81, 1290–94; Europe 35, 44; France 3, 1152, 1298, 1300–01, 1308–10, 1328, 1338, 1340–47; Germany 1355–57; Great Britain 4, 18, 1274, 1390; Illinois 386, 394–409; Indiana 416; Italy 572, 1400, 1405–06, 1408, 1415–16; Louisiana 429–30; Maine 436, 440; Maryland 445; Massachusetts 103, 110, 129, 132, 174, 182, 184, 187, 249, 383, 438, 466–67, 469, 472–73, 478–83, 542–614, 657–65, 669–70, 672–75, 677–80, 683–84, 687, 803; New England 248; New Hampshire 714; New York (state) 17, 44, 110, 176, 747, 754–55, 783–88, 800, 803, 820–58, 862–64, 869–77; Ohio 180, 184, 970–74; Pennsylvania 1031; Rhode Island 120; Switzerland 1445; United States 4, 18, 87, 135, 173–91, 994; Wisconsin 1131
Public libraries, branches 182, 571, 596
Public Libraries in the United States of America, 1876 (U.S. Bureau of Education) 140
Public library legislation 386, 396, 754–55, 1215
Public school libraries *see* School district libraries; School libraries
Public School Lyceum and Library Society (Second Municipality), New Orelans, La. 425–26, 434
Publishers' Trade List Annual 137
Publishers' Weekly 124–27, 134
Publishing 119, 139, 178–79

Q

Quebec, Can., Canadian Parliament Library 1457–58
Quincy, J. P. 181
Quincy, Josiah 475
Quincy, Josiah, Jr. 501, 555
Quincy, Mass., Public Library 249, 438, 677–80

R

R., C. 1180
R., J. S. 986–87
Radcliffe, John 1284
Radcliffe Observatory, Oxford, Eng. 945
Railway libraries 1257
Raleigh, N.C., State Library 231
Randolph, A. D. F. 255
Rantoul, Robert, Jr. 447
Rau Collection 323–24
Rawle, William, Jr. 1052
Raymond, H. J. 896
Read, J. M., Jr. 1047
Reading associations 1176
Reading habits (mainly of adults) 83, 129, 160, 174, 183, 249, 276, 300, 469, 523, 549, 564, 596, 970, 1063, 1158, 1180, 1182, 1193, 1209–11, 1262, 1265, 1276, 1278, 1293, 1353; see also Library users
Reading of children 206, 213, 224–25, 232, 300, 331, 667, 698, 726, 730, 964
Reading of seamen 63, 926
Reclus, Michel-Elie 1327
Recollections of the Last Four Popes, and of Rome in Their Times (by Cardinal N. P. S. Wiseman) 1405
Red Cross Library, Cripplegate, Eng. 16
Redwood, Abraham 247, 1091
Redwood Library and Athenaeum, Newport, R. I. 247, 1091
Reed, Caleb 1180
Reed, Henry 1063
Reed, Sampson 542
The Reformation 1382
Regimental libraries 1182
Register of the Stationers Company of London, 1554–1640 (ed. by Edward Arber) 136
Regulations for library use in: college and university libraries 316, 642, 797, 1105; national libraries 1219, 1359; public libraries 548, 562, 579; school district libraries 329, 1086; social libraries 1109, 1258; Sunday school libraries 790
Reichstag Library, Berlin, Ger. 1372
Reiffenberg, F.A.F.T. de, Baron 1167
Religious libraries 16, 1460; see also Church and synagogue libraries; Religious society libraries; Seamen's libraries; Sunday school libraries; Theological seminary libraries
Religious literature 75, 673
Religious society libraries in: Belgium 1171; England 1259; Illinois 389–90; Massachusetts 485, 518–20, 618; New York (state) 816; Pennsylvania 1010; United States 100, 192–94
Rental libraries see Commercial circulating libraries
Report from Select Committee on Public Libraries (Parliament), *1849* 4, 40
Report of Hon. James Meacham... on the Distribution of the Income of the Smithsonian Fund, 1854 377
Report of the Special Committee... on the Distribution of the Income of the Smithsonian Fund, 1854 377
Reresby, John 1251
Revolutionary War (American) 762, 1082
Reykjavik, Iceland, Stiftísbokasafn 1393–95
Rhode Island: 244, 1086–90; Historical Society 1106
Rhode Island College Library see Brown University Library
Rice, A. H. 555
Rich, O. 311
Richardson, A. D. 354
Richmond County, N.Y., Jail Library 939
Richmond, Va.: Mercantile Library Association 1128; State Library 1128–29

Rimini, Italy, Biblioteca Civica Gambalunga 1408
Rio de Janeiro, Brazil, Biblioteca Nacional 1452–53
Roberts, William 78
Robinson, Mr. (Andover Theological Seminary) 474
Robinson, E. 29
Robson, John 391
Rochdale, Eng., Corporation Free Library 1293
Rochester, N.Y.: 94; Athenaeum and Mechanics' Association 103, 952; Rochester Theological Seminary 953–55
Roest, M. 46
Rogers, Octavius 714
Rolleston, George 1288
Rome (in classical times) 2, 13–14
Rome: Historical Library (proposed) 1409; Vatican Library 45, 1148, 1397, 1404, 1410–11
Rosenthal, G. 53
Rosenthal, L. 53
Royal Academy of Music Library, Stockholm, Sweden 1441
Royal Asiatic Society, London 1214
Royal Library, Berlin 38, 1156, 1358–71
Royal Library, Copenhagen 1173–74
Royal Library, Dresden, Ger. 1373
Royal Library, Hanover, Ger. 1374
Royal Library, Sardinia 1414
Royal Library, Windsor Castle, Eng. 1295
Royal Observatory, Greenwich, Eng. 945
Royal Society of Arts Library, London, Eng. 1267
Ruddiman, Thomas 1431
Rules for library use *see* Regulations for library use
The Rural and Domestic Life of Germany, With Characteristic Sketches of its Cities and its Scenery (by William Howitt) 1353
Rush, Benjamin 1050
Rush, James 115, 1011, 1048–50
Ruskin, John 1193
Russell, Lord John 1206
Russia 1148, 1423–28
Rutgers College, New Brunswick, N.J. 723
Rutland, Vt., Agricultural Library Society 1121

S

S. 1041
S., D. C. 224–25
Sabin, Joseph 47, 1139
Saelizer, Alexander 825–26, 842
Sailor's Library (series) 61
St. Blasien Abbey, Breisgau, Ger. 1162
St. Columba 1396
St. Étienne, France 1338–39
St. Johnsbury, Vt., Athenaeum 1122
St. Joseph, Mo., Public School Library 210
St. Louis, Mo.: 700; Lyceum 701; Mercantile Library 111, 168, 173, 700–07; Public School Library 210–11, 226, 700, 708–10
St. Mark's Library, Venice, Italy 760, 1148, 1397, 1418
St. Petersburg, Russia: 1425; Imperial Public Library 1148, 1423, 1426–28
Ste Geneviève Library, Paris 36, 1156, 1299, 1335–36
Sainte-Beuve, C. A. 1338
Salisbury, Conn., Bingham Library for Youth 208, 327
Sampsiceramus 1461
San Francisco, Calif.: 261–62; Bancroft Pacific Library 263–65; Law Library 266–67; Mechanics' Institute Library 268; Mercantile Library 132, 269–81; Military Library 282; Odd Fellows Library 283–85; Sunday School Union 261–62; What Cheer House Library 286–88; Young Men's Christian Association Library 289–90
San Jose, Calif., Presbyterian Church Library 291
San Lazzaro, Italy 1412
San Marco, Convent, Florence, Italy 1401
Sardinia: 1413; Royal Library 1414
Sassari, Sardinia, University Library 1413

Saunter, Samuel 1035
Savage, John 1027
Savannah, Ga., Georgia Historical Society Library 385
Sawtell, R. W. 145
Sawyer Free Library, Gloucester, Mass. 659
Saxon manuscript 1205
Schenectady, N.Y., Union College Library 956-58
Schmeller, A. J. 1376
School district libraries: Canada 1456; Connecticut 195, 202, 299-304, 329-30; Maine 436; Massachusetts 198-200, 208, 436, 447-56, 459-61; Missouri 211, 226, 696-700, 708-11; New Jersey 722; New York (state) 195, 197-98, 200, 204, 208, 725-31, 733-43, 747, 749, 751-53, 964, 989, 1086; Ohio 964-65; Pennsylvania 984, 988-89, 991, 993, 1078-79; Rhode Island 1086-88, 1090; United States 79, 195-212, 218, 220, 302; *see also* School district library legislation; School libraries
School District Library, East Berlin, Conn. 303-04
School District Library, Windsor, Conn. 302, 329
The School District Library (series) 216, 741
School district library legislation in: Connecticut 195; Maine 436; Massachusetts 198-200, 436, 447, 450, 452, 460; New Jersey 722; New York 197-98, 200, 204, 208, 725, 727, 729-30, 735-36, 740-41, 747, 749, 751-52; Ohio 964; Pennsylvania 984, 988-89, 991, 993, 1078-79; Rhode Island 1086-87; United States 207, 211-12, 220
School equipment 452
School libraries (not limited to school district libraries) in: Canada 1456; Connecticut 195; France 1302-04; Massachusetts 208, 461, 656; New York (state) 195, 204, 732, 744-45, 748, 752-53; Pennsylvania 985-87, 989, 991-93, 995; United States 87, 197, 199, 201, 213-26, 667, 989; *see also* Academies (schools); School district libraries; Series of books for school libraries
The School Library (series) 201, 217, 455-56
School Library of the American Sunday School Union (series) 218
Schulze, Johann 411
Schuylkill County (Pa.) School District 1078-79
Schwartz, J. 819
Scientific association libraries 250, 490, 516, 527, 878, 1030, 1081, 1422
Scientific libraries 320; *see also* Smithsonian Institution, Washington, D.C.
Scotland 229, 1151, 1389
Scott, W. A. 274
Scott, Sir Walter 594
Scudder, H. E. 186, 188
Seamen's libraries 55-66, 779-81, 926, 1113
Sears, Barnas 616
Second Municipality (Public School Lyceum and Library Society), New Orleans, La. 425-26, 434
Sergeant, John 1007, 1065, 1072-73
Series of books for school libraries 196, 198, 201, 203, 214, 216-18, 238, 448, 453, 455-56, 732, 741
A Sermon, Occasioned by the Death of Thomas Hollis, Esq. (by Jermiah Hunt) 627
Sesame and Lilies (by John Ruskin) 1193
Seward, W. H. 733
Seymour, Horatio 909
Shakespeare, William 563, 586, 590-92, 594-95, 604, 607, 609, 872, 951, 1190, 1194-96, 1416
Shakespeare Library, University of Edinburgh, Scotland 1435
Shakespeare Memorial Library, Birmingham, Eng. 1194-96
Sharpey, William 1295
Shasta, Calif.: Odd Fellows Library 292; Shasta Library Association 293
Shattuck, G. C. 717
Shaw, W. S. 491
Sheldon, A. J. 784-787
Shelving 71, 182; *see also* Library equipment

Sherlock, Bishop 627
Shipboard libraries *see* Seamen's libraries
Shuck, J. L. 1460
Shunk, F. R. 201, 984
Shurtleff, N. B. 542, 717
Sibley, J. L. 632, 640–41, 652
Siennick, S. J. 1421
Sigma 1141
Simeon, Sir John 1157
Simmons, C. B. 981
Simons, N. W. 1254
Sims, Richard 1244
Sixtus V, Pope 1411
A Sketch of the History of Harvard College, and of its Present State (by Samuel A. Eliot) 631
Skinner, Richard 318
Skowhegan, Me., Library Association 111
Slavery 795–96
Sloane, Sir Hans 1146, 1223, 1234
Smalley, G. W. 397
Smedley, Edgar 1418
Smith, C. C. 559
Smith, Goldwin 794
Smith, J. J. 1040–41
Smith, J. L. 78
Smith, Lloyd 814
Smith, R. L. 78
Smith, William 1025
Smithsonian Institution, Washington, D.C. 18, 102, 105, 332, 344, 347, 351, 355, 358, 368–80
Social law libraries 266–67, 615
Social Law Library, Boston 615
Social libraries: in general 39; in: California 253–54, 294, 298; Connecticut 328, 331; District of Columbia 383; England 1178, 1215, 1258; Illinois 391; Louisiana 425–26, 434; Maine 111; Maryland 441; Massachusetts 489, 515, 521, 682; New England 248; New Hampshire 716; New Jersey 103, 724; New York (state) 103, 817–18, 927–35, 937–38, 959; North Carolina 963; Ohio 968, 981; Oregon 111; Pennsylvania 43, 983, 1003–07, 1011, 1028, 1033–54, 1071–74; Rhode Island 247, 1087, 1091, 1107–12; United States 67, 101, 165, 227–30, 243–44, 435; Virginia 1123, 1125–27; *see also* names of specialized types, e.g., Juvenile social libraries; Social law libraries
Social library legislation 1087
Social Science Association *see* American Social Science Association, Boston
Societé Française de Statistique Universelle, Paris 2
Society for the Promotion of Collegiate and Theological Education at the West 82
Society of Antiquaries 1190
Socrates 1064
Sorbonne, Paris 1159
South Australia Parliament Library 1449
South Carolina University Library, Columbia 1116
Southbridge, Mass., Public Library 132, 469
Southworth, Mrs. E. D. E. N. 187
Spain 1438–39
Spanish Flat, Calif., Franklin Library Association 294
Spanish literature 563, 575, 578, 1432
Sparks, Jared 216, 231, 636, 654–55, 792–93
Sparks Library, Cambridge, Mass. 654–55
Special libraries 103, 1420; *see also* names of particular types, e.g., Historical society libraries; Music libraries
Speleology 605
Spencer, J. C. 738
Spinoza, Baruch 1374
Spofford, A. R. 115, 117/8, 348–52, 354–66, 869
Stamford, Conn., Library Association 328
Stanley, E. S. (13th Earl of Derby) 1208
Staples, W. R. 1106
State libraries, in general 39; in these places: Australia 1449; Connecticut 306–07; Kentucky 417; Louisiana 431–32; Massachusetts 616–17; Michigan 695; New Hampshire 715; New York 756–66; Ohio 979; Pennsylvania 996–98; United

States 231; Virginia 1128-29
Staten Island, N.Y., Richmond County Jail 939
Stationers' Company, London 136, 1068
Statistics of libraries *see* Library statistics
Steiger, E. 1384
Stephens, F. G. 1250
Stephenson, R. H. 977-78
Stevens, Henry 9, 85
Stevens, W. B. 385
Stevenson, Rev. Dr. 297
Stiftísbokasafn, Reykjavik, Iceland 1393-95
Stockholm, Sweden, Royal Academy of Music Library 1441
Stockton, Calif.: Literary Association Library 295; Young Men's Christian Association Library 296; Young Men's Library Association 297
Stowe, C. E. 74
Stowe Library, London 17
Strasbourg, France, Bibliothèque Municipale (to August, 1870) 1340-42; *see also* Strassburg, Germany, Kaiserliche Universitäts und Landesbibliothek (after August 1870)
Strassburg, Germany, Kaiserliche Universitäts und Landesbibliothek (after August, 1870) 1379-87; *see also* Strasbourg, France, Bibliothèque Municipale (to August, 1870)
Stratford upon Avon, Eng. 1190
Straznicki, Dr. 858
Stuart, C. E. (The Young Pretender) 1433
Stubbs, William 1288
Student literary societies (in colleges) 718
Student's Library, London 1268-69
Sturges, William 980
Stuttgart, Ger. 1354
Subscription libraries *see* Social libraries
Sudbury, Mass., Goodnow Library 467
Sumner, Charles 651
Sumner, W. G. 159
Sunday opening (*see also* Hours of opening) 123, 268, 581, 585, 589, 601, 863, 915-16, 970-73, 1391
Sunday school libraries 218, 232-37, 255, 261-62, 790, 966
Surgeon-General's Library, Washington, D.C. 381-82
Swedenborgianism 78, 244
Swiss Statistical Society 1445
Switzerland 1444-46
Sydney, Australia, Free Public Library 1450-51
Syracuse, N.Y., Franklin Institute Library 959

T

T., A. W. 38, 1364
Tallmadge, James 1104
Tank Collection, Wisconsin State Historical Society 1132, 1137
Taschereau, J. A. 1326, 1329, 1332
Tauchnitz edition of English authors 402
Taunton Mass.: Old Colony Historical Society 681; Social Library 682
Taylor, Edward 259
Taylor, John 141
Taylor, O. A. 74, 77, 474
Taylor, T. E. 63
Teachers' libraries 238, 329, 990, 1088
Teachers' Library (series) 238
Temperance libraries 239-40, 918-21
Temperance societies 239-40, 918-21
Temple Emanuel, NYC 46, 50-51, 940-42
Tenney, H. A. 695
Territorial libraries 1130
Territorial Library, Olympia, Washington 1130
Thacher, James 676
Thackeray, W. M. 901
Thayer, M. R. 1028
Thayer, Sylvanus 563
Theological libraries 46, 129, 522, 1132; *see also* Church and synagogue libraries; Religious libraries; Theological seminary libraries

Theological Library (Fourth Social Library), Boston 618
Theological seminary libraries: California 259; Illinois 390, 393; Maine 437; Massachusetts 77, 462, 474; New Hampshire 712, 720; New York (state) 943-44, 953-55; Pennsylvania 129, 1080; United States 241-42; Venezuela 1473; *see also* Religious libraries; Theological libraries
Theological Seminary Library... *see* other part of the name of an individual seminary library
Thies, Louis 588, 646
Thomas, Isaac 1083
Thomas, Isaiah 690
Thomason, bookseller 42
Thomson, Edward 108
Thorndike, Israel 625
Ticknor, A. E. 855
Ticknor, George 177, 499, 542, 546, 556, 563, 575, 578
Tochman, Gaspard 889
Todd, J. H. 1200
Tomlinson, Thomas 963
Torrey, Joseph 1118
Tosti Collection, Boston Public Library 563, 568, 573, 587-88
Tours, France, Bibliothèque Municipale 1343-45
Townsend, Christopher 120
Township libraries 415
Tracts 330
Transcript of the Register of the Company of Stationers of London, 1554-1640 (ed. by Edward Arber) 136, 1068
Trieste, Italy, Town Library 1415-16
Trinity College Library, Cambridge University 1203
Trinity College Library, Dublin, Ire. 1396
Troth, Henry 1020
Troy, N.Y., Young Men's Association Library 960
Troyes, France 1346
Truman, Hanberry & Co., NYC 801
Turin, Italy, University Library 1417
Turner, Sharon 1296
Typographical Society, NYC 938
Tyson, J.R. 28, 76, 983

U

U. 25
Uniform Trade List Annual 137
Union, Mo., Franklin County Public School Library 711
Union catalogs 477
Union College Library, Schenectady, N.Y. 956-58
Union Theological Seminary, NYC 570, 943-44
Unitarian Association (church) *see* American Unitarian Association
United States: 32, 48, 67-140, 1352; and England 15-22; and Europe 23-54, 76; *see also* New England and names of states, cities, towns, types of libraries, and individual libraries
United States (naval vessel) 56
U.S. Army, Office of the Surgeon-General, Library, Washington, D.C. 381-82
U.S. Bureau of Education 140
U.S. Constitution 531
U.S. Geological surveys 320
U.S. Military Post Library Association 169-70
U.S. War Department Library 73, 332
Universe 929
University libraries *see* College and university libraries
University of... *see* other part of the name of an individual university
Upland, Pa., Crozer Theological Seminary Library 129, 1080
Upper Canada 1456
Uppsala, Sweden, University Library 1442-43
Upton, G. P. 388
Users of libraries *see* Library users

V

V., S. 254
Vallejo, Calif., Library Association 298
Van der Meulen (Rev.) 1132

Van Rhyn, G. A. F. 138
Vatican Library, Rome 45, 1148, 1397, 1404, 1410–11
Vattemare, Alexandre 30–31, 37, 555, 616, 759, 764, 818, 1318
Vaux, Roberts 1022, 1025
Vayssard, M. 1331
Venice, Italy, St. Mark's Library 760, 1148, 1397, 1418
Vermont, University of, Library 77, 1118–19
Versailles, France, Bibliothèque Municipale 1347
Vienna, Austria, Hofbibliothek 1166, 1354
Virginia, State Library 1128–29
Von Raumer, G. K. 1397

W

W., P. H. 1120
Wadsworth, James 198, 751–52
Wadsworth Athenaeum, Hartford, Conn. 305
Wakefield, Mass., Town Library 184
Waldensians 1200
Walker, James 627
Wallenstein, Jules de 1352
Ward, J. W. 788
Warren, E. A. 1253
Warsaw, Poland, Imperial University Library 1421
Warsenstein, Ger. 1388
Warwick, Guy de Beauchamp, Earl of 1198
Washburn, E. A. 915
Washington, George, President 422, 502, 766
Washington, D.C.: 332; Library of Congress 30, 47, 73, 99, 102, 115, 121, 135, 231, 332–67, 567; Smithsonian Institution 18, 102, 105, 332, 344, 347, 351, 355, 358, 368–80; Surgeon General's Library 381–82; War Department Library 73, 332; Washington Library Company 383
Washington Territory, Territorial Library 1130
Watterston, George 333–34
Watts, Thomas 1239

Wayland, Francis 683
Wayland, Mass., Free Public Library 683
Wayne, Anthony 1082
Wayne, Isaac 1082
Webster, Daniel 20, 88, 531
Wedgewood Institute, Burslem, Eng. 1199
Weeding of collections 642
Wellman, J. W. 20
West Roxbury, Mass., Public Library 684
Westchester, Pa.: 1081; Chester County Athenaeum 1081–83
Westerly, R.I., Pawcatuck Library Association 1088, 1107–12
Westerville, Ohio, Otterbein University Library 982
Westley & Williams (firm), Copperopolis, Calif. 256
Westminster Parish, London, Free Library (proposed) 1270
Westreenen van Tiellandt, W. H. J., Baron von 1420
Wharton, T. I. 1006, 1017, 1025
What and How to Read (by G. A. F. Van Rhyn) 138
What Cheer House (Hotel) Library, San Francisco 286–88
Wheeler, W. A. 565, 590–92, 602–03
Whitaker, A. E. 280
White, A. D. 793–94
White, W. B. 803
Whitney, Eli 313
Whitney, J. L. 588, 602
Whittaker, J. V. 1069
Wigglesworth, Edward 494
Wight, J. B. 479, 683
Wilcox, E. S. 414
Wilder, David 282
Willard, Sidney 24
Williams, Daniel 16
Williams, H. J. 1028
Williams College Library, Williamstown, Mass. 686
Williamsport, Pa., Williamsport Dickinson Seminary Library 1084
Williams's Library, Cripplegate, Eng. 16
Williamstown, Mass.: Lyceum 685; Williams College Library 686
Wilson, John 60

Winchester, Va., *Gazette* 417
Windsor, Conn., School District Library 302, 329
Windsor, Eng.: 1294; Windsor Castle Library 1295
Winser, F. 177
Winslow, W. C. 1118
Winsor, Justin 469, 582–84, 594, 597, 607, 609, 613
Winthrop, R. E. 555
Wisconsin: State Historical Society Library 129, 1132–41; University of 1142
Wiseman, N. P. S., Cardinal 1405
Wolcott, Conn. 330–31
Women as librarians 695
Women as library users 835
Women, literary associations for 1029
Wood, William 109, 781, 914
Woodcuts 1453
Woodward, R.B. 286
Worcester, John Tiptoft, Earl of 1283
Worcester, Mass.: 687; American Antiquarian Society Library 74, 688–90; District Medical Society 687; Free Public Library 687; Lyceum and Library Association 687; Young Men's Library Association 691–92
Wording, W. E. 720
Working class, libraries for 1355–56; *see also* Mechanics' libraries
Working conditions in libraries 1253
World (i.e., more than one continent) 1–66
Wratislaw, A. H. 1203
Wright, bookseller, London 15
Wynne, T. H. 1128–29

Y

Yale College, New Haven, Conn.: College Library 221, 245, 311–25; Law School Library 310
Yates County, N.Y., Farmer's Club 961
Yeaman, Harvey 417
York County (Pa.) Lyceum 1085
York, Eng., Archbishop Egbert's Library 1296
Yorkshire (Eng.) Union of Mechanics' Institutes 1297
Young men's association libraries: California 293, 297; Connecticut 308–09, 326; Illinois 387, 410; Louisiana 425–26; Massachusetts 691–92; New York (state) 767–68, 789, 960; United States 806; Wisconsin 111, 113, 440
Young men's Christian association libraries: California 258, 289–90, 296; Illinois 389–90; New Jersey 103; New York (state) 802, 946–51; United States 239
Young Men's Christian Union Library Chicago 389–90, 410
Young Men's Institute Library, Hartford, Conn. 308–09
Young Men's Institute Library, New Haven, Conn. 326
Young Men's Library Association, Stockton, Calif. 297
Young Men's Library Association, Worcester, Mass. 691–92
Young Men's Mercantile Library Association, Cincinnati, Ohio 168, 975–78, 1114
Young Men's Mercantile Library, Pittsburgh, Pa. 1077

Z

Z., X. Y. 206
Zaluski Library, Poland 1426–27
Zercher, J. J. 990
Zürich, Switzerland 1444